FOOD & WINE
ANNUAL COOKBOOK 2013

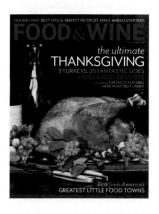

FOOD & WINE
ANNUAL COOKBOOK 2013

EXECUTIVE EDITOR **Kate Heddings**
DESIGNER **Michelle Leong**
FEATURES EDITOR **Michael Endelman**
EDITOR **Susan Choung**
COPY EDITOR **Lisa Leventer**
EDITORIAL ASSISTANT **Elyse Inamine**
SENIOR WINE EDITOR **Megan Krigbaum**
PRODUCTION MANAGER **Matt Carson**
DEPUTY PHOTO EDITOR **Anthony LaSala**

FRONT COVER

PHOTOGRAPHER **Christina Holmes**
FOOD STYLIST **Vivian Lui**
STYLIST **Suzie Myers**

BACK COVER

PHOTOGRAPHER (BEANS) **Con Poulos**
PHOTOGRAPHER (HAM) **John Kernick**
PHOTOGRAPHER (CAKE) **Paul Costello**

ISBN 978-1-932624-54-0

ISSN 1097-1564

Published by
American Express Publishing Corporation
1120 Avenue of the Americas
New York, New York 10036

Manufactured in
the United States of America

FOOD & WINE MAGAZINE

SVP / EDITOR IN CHIEF **Dana Cowin**
CREATIVE DIRECTOR **Stephen Scoble**
EXECUTIVE MANAGING EDITOR **Mary Ellen Ward**
EXECUTIVE EDITOR **Pamela Kaufman**
EXECUTIVE FOOD EDITOR **Tina Ujlaki**
EXECUTIVE WINE EDITOR **Ray Isle**
EXECUTIVE DIGITAL EDITOR **Rebecca Bauer**
DEPUTY EDITOR **Christine Quinlan**

FEATURES

FEATURES EDITOR **Michael Endelman**
RESTAURANT EDITOR **Kate Krader**
TRAVEL EDITOR **Gina Hamadey**
SENIOR WINE EDITOR **Megan Krigbaum**
MARKET EDITOR **Suzie Myers**
EDITORIAL ASSISTANTS **Maren Ellingboe,
Chelsea Morse, M. Elizabeth Sheldon**

FOOD

DEPUTY EDITOR **Kate Heddings**
TEST KITCHEN SENIOR EDITORS **Grace Parisi,
Kay Chun**
SENIOR EDITOR **Kristin Donnelly**
ASSOCIATE EDITOR **Daniel Gritzer**
TEST KITCHEN ASSOCIATE EDITOR **Justin Chapple**
EDITORIAL ASSISTANT **Maggie Mariolis**
TEST KITCHEN ASSISTANT **Gina Mungiovi**

ART

DESIGN DIRECTOR **Patricia Sanchez**
ASSOCIATE ART DIRECTOR **James Maikowski**
DESIGNER **Kevin Sullivan**

PHOTO

DIRECTOR OF PHOTOGRAPHY **Fredrika Stjärne**
DEPUTY PHOTO EDITOR **Anthony LaSala**
ASSOCIATE PHOTO EDITOR **Sara Parks**
PHOTO ASSISTANT **Tomi Omololu-Lange**

COPY & RESEARCH

COPY DIRECTOR **Michele Berkover Petry**
SENIOR COPY EDITOR **Ann Lien**
ASSISTANT RESEARCH EDITORS **Joe Harper,
Erin Laverty**

PRODUCTION

PRODUCTION MANAGERS **Matt Carson,
Amelia Grohman**
PRODUCTION ASSISTANT **Chelsea Schiff**

BOOKS

EDITOR **Susan Choung**
DESIGNER **Michelle Leong**

DIGITAL MEDIA

FEATURES EDITOR **Alex Vallis**
SENIOR EDITOR **Lawrence Marcus**
ASSOCIATE ART DIRECTOR **Jooyoung Hsu**
ASSOCIATE EDITOR **Alessandra Bulow**
ASSISTANT EDITOR **Justine Sterling**
EDITORIAL ASSISTANT **Jasmin Sun**

EDITORIAL CONTENT MANAGER **Kerianne Hansen**

ASSISTANT TO THE EDITOR IN CHIEF
Jacqueline Westbrook

AMERICAN EXPRESS PUBLISHING
CORPORATION

PRESIDENT / CHIEF EXECUTIVE OFFICER
Ed Kelly
CHIEF MARKETING OFFICER /
PRESIDENT, DIGITAL MEDIA
Mark V. Stanich
SVP / CHIEF FINANCIAL OFFICER
Paul B. Francis
VPS / GENERAL MANAGERS
Frank Bland, Keith Strohmeier

VP, BOOKS & PRODUCTS / PUBLISHER
Marshall Corey
DIRECTOR, BOOK PROGRAMS
Bruce Spanier
SENIOR MARKETING MANAGER, BRANDED BOOKS
Eric Lucie
ASSOCIATE MARKETING MANAGER
Stacy Mallis
DIRECTOR OF FULFILLMENT & PREMIUM VALUE
Philip Black
MANAGER OF CUSTOMER EXPERIENCE
& PRODUCT DEVELOPMENT
Betsy Wilson
DIRECTOR OF FINANCE
Thomas Noonan
ASSOCIATE BUSINESS MANAGER
Uma Mahabir
VP, OPERATIONS
Tracy Kelliher
OPERATIONS DIRECTOR (MANUFACTURING)
Anthony White
SENIOR MANAGER, CONTRACTS & RIGHTS
Jeniqua Moore

FOOD&WINE

ANNUAL COOKBOOK 2013

AN ENTIRE YEAR OF RECIPES

FOOD&WINE
BOOKS

American Express Publishing Corporation, New York

roasted beets with pistachios, herbs and orange, PAGE 249

CONTENTS

asian fried and glazed baby back ribs, PAGE 184

FOREWORD

There has never been a better time to eat in America. Small farms are growing magnificent produce, artisans are elevating everyday ingredients and spectacular restaurants are opening everywhere, from giant cities to tiny towns. F&W's *Annual Cookbook 2013* draws on this national food boom, with over 600 recipes from the country's most exciting chefs, farmers, bakers, butchers and home cooks.

This book reflects the American food zeitgeist. For instance, healthy whole grains are bigger than ever; to learn why, try the crisp, fluffy quinoa cakes with spinach (page 272) or earthy kamut spaghetti, delicious with briny clams (page 80). A more adventurous choice is goat—the most popular meat in the world, and more sustainable than beef and lamb. It's incredible in chef Johnny Monis's Thai stir-fry with fresh basil (page 222).

This year's volume also includes recipes from the magazine's new Handbook column, which delivers practical, easy and seasonal dishes. Some of the most memorable include cheesy stuffed shells with fennel and radicchio (our cover recipe), lemony brussels sprout slaw and flash-roasted broccoli with spicy bread crumbs. Dishes like these—all requiring 45 minutes or less of hands-on prep—have made F&W's *Annual Cookbook 2013* the most user-friendly yet, with over 250 fast options. Whether you are attempting to get supper on the table quickly or trying to create an impressive dinner party, this cookbook has something for you. We hope it inspires a mini food boom in your kitchen.

Dana Cowin
Editor in Chief
FOOD & WINE Magazine

Kate Heddings
Executive Editor
FOOD & WINE Cookbooks

Lee Hudson (in red vest) hosts a Thanksgiving dinner at his Napa Valley ranch. The meal features ingredients grown on his property, like the radishes, carrots and cucumbers in the Mexican-inspired crudité platter, OPPOSITE; recipe, page 10.

STARTERS

Green Goddess Dip with Crudités

⟳ **TOTAL: 20 MIN • MAKES 2½ CUPS** ● ●
Loaded with parsley, tarragon and chives, this creamy dip would also be delicious with poached chicken or seafood.

- 1 cup crème fraîche or sour cream
- 1 cup mayonnaise
- ½ cup packed flat-leaf parsley leaves
- 2 tablespoons snipped chives
- 1 tablespoon tarragon leaves
- 1 tablespoon fresh lemon juice
- 1 tablespoon fresh lime juice
- 3 oil-packed anchovies

Salt and freshly ground pepper
Assorted vegetables for dipping, such as sliced black radishes, celery, cucumbers and steamed asparagus

In a blender, combine the crème fraîche and mayonnaise with the parsley, chives, tarragon, lemon juice, lime juice and anchovies and puree until smooth. Season the dip with salt and pepper; serve with the vegetables.
—*David Burtka*

Crudités à la Mexicaine

📷 PAGE 9
⟳ **TOTAL: 25 MIN • 10 TO 12 SERVINGS** ● ● ●
Guajillo chile powder, fresh lime juice and salt punch up this raw vegetable platter. It's fantastic year-round with whatever vegetables are in season.

- 6 small Kirby or Japanese cucumbers, quartered lengthwise
- 4 medium carrots, halved crosswise and sliced into ¼-inch sticks
- 3 medium fennel bulbs— halved lengthwise, cored and sliced crosswise ¼ inch thick
- 1 large bunch of radishes, halved or quartered if large
- 1½ cups green olives, rinsed
- 2 tablespoons kosher salt
- 2 teaspoons pure chile powder, such as guajillo or Colorado

Key limes, halved (see Note)

1. Arrange all of the vegetables and olives on a large serving platter.
2. In a small bowl, combine the salt with the chile powder. Dip a lime half in the chile salt and dab the vegetables with it; squeeze the juice over the vegetables.
3. Serve the crudités with the remaining key lime halves and with the remaining chile salt in a small bowl for dipping.
—*David Tanis*

NOTE If using Persian limes, cut one in half and the other in wedges.
MAKE AHEAD The vegetables can be covered and refrigerated for several hours. Season just before serving.

Pepper-Glazed Goat Cheese Gratin

⟳ **TOTAL: 20 MIN • 8 SERVINGS** ● ○
This warm, sweet-spicy goat cheese dip is a great, easy alternative to a cheese plate.

- 1 pound creamy fresh goat cheese, softened
- 6 tablespoons apricot preserves
- 4 Peppadew peppers, finely chopped
- 1 pickled jalapeño, seeded and finely chopped
- 2 tablespoons minced cocktail onions
- 2 teaspoons Dijon mustard
- 1½ teaspoons dry sherry

Pita chips and toasted baguette slices, for serving

1. Preheat the oven to 400°. Spread the softened goat cheese in a 5-by-8-inch gratin dish in an even layer.
2. In a small bowl, whisk the preserves with the Peppadews, jalapeño, onions, mustard and sherry. Spread the mixture over the goat cheese and bake on the top rack of the oven for about 5 minutes, until warm. Turn on the broiler and broil for about 2 minutes, until the topping is bubbling and lightly browned at the edges.
3. Serve the goat cheese gratin hot, with pita chips and toasted baguette slices.
—*Grace Parisi*

WINE Tart apple–scented sparkling wine: NV Roederer Estate Anderson Valley Brut.

Miso-Infused Cream Cheese Spread

ACTIVE: 15 MIN; TOTAL: 4 DAYS
8 SERVINGS ● ○
Cooks in Japan cure all kinds of food in miso, from fish to tofu. Inspired, chef David Myers of Sola in Tokyo and Comme Ça in Los Angeles uses the fermented soybean paste to flavor cream cheese.

One 8-ounce block cold cream cheese
- 1 cup white miso (8 ounces)

Assorted crudités, rice crackers and *shichimi togarashi* (a Japanese chilespice blend), for serving

1. Tightly wrap the cream cheese in a 12-by-8-inch piece of cheesecloth.
2. Lay a 12-inch piece of plastic wrap on a work surface. With slightly wet hands, spread ¼ cup of the white miso into a rectangle that's roughly the size of the cream cheese. Set the cheesecloth-wrapped cream cheese on top of the miso; spread the remaining ¾ cup of miso all over the top and sides. Wrap in the plastic and refrigerate for 4 days.
3. Unwrap the cream cheese; discard the plastic wrap and cheesecloth. The spread can be served sliced or whipped, with crudités, rice crackers and *shichimi togarashi*.
—*David Myers*

Miso-and-Nut Dip

⟳ **TOTAL: 15 MIN • MAKES ABOUT ⅔ CUP** ● ● ●
Deliciously nutty, this vegan Japanese dip is a healthy change from mayo-based dips.

- 3 tablespoons blanched almonds
- 3 tablespoons walnuts
- ½ cup barley miso

1. Preheat the oven to 350°. Spread all of the nuts in a pie plate and toast for 8 minutes; let them cool, then grind in a mini food processor to a paste.
2. In a medium bowl, stir the miso and nut paste with 3 tablespoons of water and serve.
—*Sylvan Mishima Brackett*

SERVE WITH Crunchy vegetables.

● HEALTHY ● MAKE AHEAD ● VEGETARIAN ● STAFF FAVORITE

pepper-glazed goat cheese gratin

Hummus with Smoked Paprika Butter and Za'atar

ACTIVE: 30 MIN; TOTAL: 2 HR PLUS
OVERNIGHT SOAKING • MAKES 5 CUPS
● ● ●

Minneapolis chef Sameh Wadi offers this hummus—embellished with pools of melted paprika butter and the Middle Eastern spice blend za'atar—at his modern Mediterranean restaurant, Saffron. When you serve it, make sure the hummus is room temperature so the warm butter doesn't harden.

1½ cups dried chickpeas (12 ounces),
    soaked overnight and drained
Salt
  2 large garlic cloves, minced
  2 tablespoons fresh lemon juice
  ½ cup extra-virgin olive oil
  1 cup tahini (8 ounces)
  1 stick unsalted butter
  ½ teaspoon sweet smoked paprika
  ¼ teaspoon hot smoked paprika
  1 teaspoon za'atar (see Note)

1. In a saucepan, cover the chickpeas with 4 inches of water and bring to a boil. Simmer over moderate heat, skimming, until they begin to break down, about 1 hour and 15 minutes. Season with salt and let cool in the water; drain, reserving 1 cup of the liquid.
2. Transfer the chickpeas and reserved cooking liquid to a food processor. Add the garlic and lemon juice and puree until smooth. Add the olive oil and tahini; process until creamy. Season the hummus with salt and mound on a platter, making deep canyons with the back of a spoon.
3. In a medium saucepan, melt the butter over moderate heat until the milk solids just begin to brown, 5 minutes. Stir in both paprikas; cook for 1 minute. Pour the mixture into a heatproof cup; let the solids settle to the bottom. Pour off the clear butter, discarding the solids. Drizzle the butter on the hummus and sprinkle with the za'atar. —Sameh Wadi
SERVE WITH Pita chips, warm pita bread or a crudité platter.
NOTE Za'atar is available at specialty food stores and Middle Eastern markets.

Smoked-Almond Butter with Crispy Rosemary
◌ TOTAL: 15 MIN • MAKES 1¼ CUPS
● ● ●

A food processor quickly transforms smoked and roasted almonds into a fantastic spread. Serve the butter with slices of apples, pears, fennel and celery.

  1 cup salted roasted almonds
    (5½ ounces)
  1 cup smoked almonds (5½ ounces)
  6 tablespoons canola oil
  2 tablespoons rosemary leaves
Salt
Sliced pear, apple, Asian pear, celery
    and fennel, for serving

1. In a food processor, process the roasted and smoked almonds until the nuts are just starting to become pasty. Add 3 tablespoons of the canola oil and process until smooth. Transfer the almond butter to a bowl.
2. In a small skillet, heat the remaining 3 tablespoons of oil. Add the rosemary leaves and cook over moderate heat, stirring, until crisp, about 2 minutes. Using a slotted spoon, transfer the rosemary to a plate and sprinkle lightly with salt.
3. Crumble and stir half of the rosemary into the almond butter and sprinkle the rest on top. Serve the butter with sliced pear, apple, Asian pear, celery and fennel. —Grace Parisi
MAKE AHEAD The butter can be prepared through Step 1 and refrigerated for 1 month.

Baked Camembert with Pears
◌ TOTAL: 20 MIN • 6 SERVINGS ● ●
Pear brandy, maple syrup and buttery Spanish almonds put a modern spin on baked Brie.

One 8-ounce round of ripe Camembert
  1 tablespoon pear brandy
  1 tablespoon pure maple syrup
Pinch of salt
  ¼ cup chopped marcona almonds
  2 Bosc pears, cut into thin wedges
  2 teaspoons freshly squeezed
    lemon juice

Preheat the oven to 400°. Put the Camembert in a small baking dish. In a bowl, combine the brandy, maple syrup and salt; pour over the cheese. Bake for about 7 minutes, until the cheese is very soft. Spoon any liquid over the cheese; sprinkle with the almonds. Toss the pear wedges with the lemon juice and serve alongside the cheese.
—Grace Parisi
WINE Fruity, minerally sparkling wine: NV Domaine de Vodanis Vouvray Brut.

Za'atar-Spiced Beet Dip with Goat Cheese and Hazelnuts

ACTIVE: 20 MIN; TOTAL: 1 HR 30 MIN
MAKES 3 CUPS ● ● ● ●
London chef Yotam Ottolenghi purees beets with Greek yogurt to create this silky, vivid spread. It's delicious on its own or served alongside other meze.

  6 medium beets (1½ pounds), trimmed
  2 small garlic cloves, minced
  1 small red chile, seeded and minced
  1 cup plain Greek yogurt
  3 tablespoons extra-virgin olive oil
1½ tablespoons pure maple syrup
  1 tablespoon za'atar
    (see Note below left)
Salt
  ¼ cup roasted skinned hazelnuts,
    chopped
  2 tablespoons goat cheese, crumbled
  2 scallions, thinly sliced
Warm bread, for serving

1. Preheat the oven to 350°. Put the beets in a small roasting pan and add ¼ cup of water. Cover with foil and bake for about 1 hour, until tender. Let cool slightly,
2. Peel the beets, cut into wedges and transfer to a food processor. Add the garlic, chile and yogurt and pulse until blended. Add the olive oil, maple syrup and za'atar and puree. Season with salt. Scrape into a wide, shallow bowl. Scatter the hazelnuts, goat cheese and scallions on top and serve with warm bread.
—Yotam Ottolenghi and Sami Tamimi
WINE Earthy, dry French rosé: 2011 Domaine Thomas & Fils.

● HEALTHY ● MAKE AHEAD ● VEGETARIAN ● STAFF FAVORITE

za'atar-spiced beet dip with goat cheese and hazelnuts

Hearts of Palm Dip

⏱ **TOTAL: 10 MIN**

MAKES 2 CUPS (8 SERVINGS) ● ● ● ●

Garlic, lime and olive oil transform canned hearts of palm into a luxurious, low-fat dip.

1 large garlic clove, minced
Salt
Two 14-ounce cans hearts of palm, drained and rinsed
¼ cup extra-virgin olive oil
¼ teaspoon finely grated lime zest
Freshly ground white pepper
Plantain chips, pita chips or flatbreads, for serving

Using the side of a chef's knife, mash the garlic to a paste with a generous pinch of salt. Scrape the paste into a food processor. Add the hearts of palm and oil and process to a medium-fine paste. Add the lime zest, season with salt and white pepper and pulse just to blend. Transfer the dip to a bowl and serve with plantain chips, pita chips or flatbreads. —*Grace Parisi*

MAKE AHEAD The dip can be refrigerated for up to 2 days.

Hazelnut Dukka

⏱ **TOTAL: 30 MIN**

MAKES ABOUT 2 CUPS ● ● ● ●

Dukka (which comes from the Arabic for "to pound") refers to crushed nuts and seeds traditionally eaten on bread dipped in olive oil; the blend varies from cook to cook. Eric Monkaba, founder of a cooking school in Cairo, especially likes this garlic-free version.

½ cup hazelnuts
6 tablespoons coriander seeds
3 tablespoons whole cumin seeds
¼ cup sesame seeds
1 tablespoon dried thyme
½ cup salted roasted pistachios
¼ teaspoon cayenne pepper
Salt and freshly ground black pepper

1. Preheat the oven to 350°. Spread the hazelnuts in a pie plate and toast for 12 minutes, until fragrant and the skins blister. Transfer the hazelnuts to a kitchen towel and let cool. Rub the nuts together to remove the skins and transfer to a food processor.

2. In a medium skillet, toast the coriander and cumin seeds over moderate heat, shaking the pan, until golden and fragrant, about 3 minutes. Spread the spices out on a plate and let cool completely, then finely grind in a spice grinder. In the same skillet, toast the sesame seeds over moderate heat until golden, 2 to 3 minutes. Transfer the sesame seeds to the plate to cool. Add the coriander, cumin, sesame seeds and thyme to the food processor along with the pistachios, cayenne pepper and 1 teaspoon each of salt and black pepper and pulse until finely ground. Transfer the *dukka* to a bowl and serve. —*Eric Monkaba*

SERVE WITH Olive oil and crusty bread.

MAKE AHEAD The *dukka* can be kept in an airtight container for up to 4 days or refrigerated for up to 1 month.

Oyster Tartare Sauce with Potato Chips

⏱ **TOTAL: 25 MIN • 4 TO 6 SERVINGS** ●

This ingenious, briny sauce from chef René Redzepi of Noma in Copenhagen couldn't be simpler: Redzepi purees raw oysters with a little of their liquor, plus rice vinegar and grapeseed oil, until creamy. He adds diced blanched vegetables for texture, then serves the dip with potato chips (the sauce is also great with fish). When asked how he makes potato chips, Redzepi says, "You don't need a recipe. It's like making a cup of tea. Just fry the potatoes until crisp." Or simply use good-quality store-bought chips.

½ medium carrot, cut into ¼-inch dice
1 medium red or white turnip, peeled and cut into ¼-inch dice
5 freshly shucked oysters, plus 2 tablespoons oyster liquor
⅓ cup grapeseed oil
2 teaspoons rice vinegar
2 tablespoons chopped parsley
Salt and freshly ground pepper
Potato chips, for serving

1. Bring a medium saucepan of salted water to a boil. Add the carrot and turnip and simmer over moderately high heat until just tender, 2 minutes. Drain well and let cool.

2. In a blender, puree the oysters with their liquor. With the machine on, slowly pour in the oil and puree, then blend in the vinegar. Scrape the sauce into a bowl. Fold in the carrot, turnip and parsley and season with salt and pepper. Set the bowl over crushed ice and serve the dip with potato chips.
—*René Redzepi*

WINE Crisp, salty white: 2010 Domaine Les Hautes Noëlles Muscadet Côtes de Grandlieu.

Broccoli-Cheese Dunk

⏱ **TOTAL: 30 MIN • 6 SERVINGS** ●

This gooey starter is like a deconstructed broccoli quesadilla: Scoop a bit of the cheesy filling onto a corn or flour tortilla and roll it up, folding in the edges.

3 tablespoons extra-virgin olive oil
1½ pounds broccoli, cut into 1-inch florets, stems peeled and diced
1 large garlic clove, minced
1 teaspoon ground coriander
1 teaspoon chile powder
1 teaspoon cumin
½ teaspoon dried oregano
Salt
1 pound sliced provolone cheese
Warm tortillas, for serving

1. Preheat the broiler and position a rack 8 inches from the heat. In a large skillet, heat the olive oil. Add the broccoli and garlic and cook over moderate heat, stirring occasionally, until the broccoli is browned in spots and crisp-tender, about 5 minutes. Stir in the spices. Season with salt and cook for 1 minute. Add ½ cup of water and cook until the broccoli is tender and the liquid has evaporated, about 3 minutes.

2. Arrange half of the cheese in 6 individual gratin dishes. Top with the broccoli and the remaining cheese. Broil until the cheese is melted and browned, about 5 minutes. Serve right away, with warm tortillas.
—*Grace Parisi*

● HEALTHY ● MAKE AHEAD ● VEGETARIAN ● STAFF FAVORITE

broccoli-cheese dunk

Pastrami Toasts with Tangy Toppings

TOTAL: 1 HR 15 MIN
MAKES 2 DOZEN HORS D'OEUVRES ●

RED CABBAGE TOPPING

- 2 tablespoons unsalted butter
- 4 cups finely shredded red cabbage (12 ounces)
- ¼ cup white wine vinegar
- 1 tablespoon sugar

Salt and freshly ground pepper

YELLOW LENTIL TOPPING

- ½ cup yellow split lentils
- 2 garlic cloves, smashed

Salt

- 2 tablespoons unsalted butter
- 3 large scallions, white and tender green parts only, minced
- 1 tablespoon white wine vinegar
- ¼ cup extra-virgin olive oil

Freshly ground pepper

GREEN CABBAGE TOPPING

- ¼ cup mayonnaise
- ¼ cup sour cream
- 1 teaspoon white wine vinegar
- 1¼ cups finely shredded green cabbage (4 ounces)

Salt and freshly ground pepper

Eight ½-inch-thick slices of rye bread, lightly toasted

Whole-grain mustard, for spreading

- ¾ pound sliced pastrami, warmed

1. MAKE THE RED CABBAGE TOPPING In a large skillet, melt the butter. Add the red cabbage and cook over moderately high heat, tossing, until slightly wilted, 5 minutes. Add the vinegar and sugar. Season with salt and pepper. Add 1 cup of water, cover and cook over moderately low heat, stirring, until tender, 20 minutes. Uncover and cook until the liquid has evaporated, 5 minutes.

2. MAKE THE YELLOW LENTIL TOPPING In a medium saucepan, combine the lentils and garlic with 3 cups of water and season with salt. Simmer over moderately low heat until the lentils are just tender, about 15 minutes. Drain, reserving ¼ cup of the cooking liquid; discard the garlic. Wipe out the saucepan.

3. Melt the butter in the saucepan. Add the scallions and cook over moderate heat until softened, about 2 minutes. Add the lentils, vinegar and the reserved ¼ cup of cooking liquid and cook until thickened slightly, about 1 minute longer. Stir in the olive oil and season with salt and pepper.

4. MAKE THE GREEN CABBAGE TOPPING In a bowl, whisk the mayonnaise with the sour cream and vinegar. Stir in the green cabbage and season with salt and pepper.

5. Arrange the rye on a work surface and cut each slice into thirds. Spread with mustard and top with the pastrami. Spoon each topping onto 8 pastrami toasts and serve.
—*Siegfried Danler*

Glazed-Beet-and-Burrata Toasts

TOTAL: 1 HR 15 MIN • 4 SERVINGS ● ●

- 3 beets (about ¾ pound total)
- 4 thyme sprigs
- 1 teaspoon black peppercorns
- 1 tablespoon red wine vinegar
- ½ cup sherry vinegar
- 2 tablespoons sugar
- 1 rosemary sprig

Salt

Twelve 4-by-2-inch slices of dense whole-grain bread, brushed with olive oil and toasted

- ½ pound burrata cheese, cut into 12 pieces
- 12 small watercress sprigs

Extra-virgin olive oil, for drizzling

Flaky salt, such as Maldon, for garnish

1. In a medium saucepan, cover the beets with cold water. Add the thyme sprigs, black peppercorns and red wine vinegar and bring to a boil. Simmer, partially covered, until the beets are tender, about 45 minutes, replenishing the water if necessary. Drain the beets, then peel and cut them into ¼-inch dice.

2. Return the diced beets to the saucepan. Add the sherry vinegar, sugar, rosemary sprig and ¼ cup of water and bring to a boil. Cook over moderately high heat until a syrupy glaze forms, about 12 minutes. Discard the rosemary sprig and season the beets with salt.

3. Top each slice of whole-grain toast with a spoonful of the glazed beets, a piece of burrata cheese and a sprig of watercress. Drizzle with extra-virgin olive oil, garnish with the flaky salt and serve right away.
—*David Hawksworth*

MAKE AHEAD The glazed diced beets can be refrigerated overnight; reheat gently before garnishing and serving.

WINE Rich rosé Champagne: NV Fleury Brut.

Avocado Crostini Two Ways

:( ) **TOTAL: 30 MIN • 8 SERVINGS** ●

Katie Workman tells how to win over children and adults alike in her *Mom 100 Cookbook*. For example, she adds salty, briny anchovies to her parsley pesto for adult guests. For kids, she leaves the avocado crostini plain.

- 1 large baguette, cut into ½-inch diagonal slices (32 slices total)
- ¾ cup extra-virgin olive oil, plus more for brushing
- 1½ cups (packed) flat-leaf parsley leaves
- 2 garlic cloves, sliced
- 3 oil-packed anchovies, drained

Salt and freshly ground pepper

- 2 Hass avocados—halved, pitted and thinly sliced

1. Preheat the oven to 350°. Brush all of the baguette slices with olive oil and arrange them on 2 baking sheets. Bake the baguette slices for about 8 minutes, until they are lightly browned and just crisp.

2. Meanwhile, combine the parsley leaves, garlic, anchovies and the ¾ cup of olive oil in a blender and puree until smooth. Season the pesto with salt and pepper.

3. Top the baguette toasts with the avocado slices and arrange on 2 platters.

4. FOR KIDS Sprinkle salt on the crostini on one platter. Serve.

FOR ADULTS Drizzle the parsley pesto over the crostini on the other platter. Serve.
—*Katie Workman*

MAKE AHEAD The parsley pesto can be covered and refrigerated overnight.

WINE Lively, unoaked Chardonnay: 2010 Toad Hollow Francine's Selection.

● HEALTHY ● MAKE AHEAD ● VEGETARIAN ● STAFF FAVORITE

Salmon Rillettes
TOTAL: 1 HR 45 MIN • MAKES 2 CUPS ●

- ½ pound center-cut skinless salmon fillet
- 1 tablespoon Pernod

Salt and freshly ground white pepper

- 1 celery rib
- 1 leek, halved lengthwise
- 1 small onion, quartered lengthwise
- 1 bay leaf
- 1 teaspoon black peppercorns
- 1 cup dry white wine
- 5 tablespoons unsalted butter, softened
- 1 large shallot, minced (¼ cup)
- ½ tablespoon sour cream
- ¼ pound skinless hot-smoked salmon, flaked
- 2 tablespoons snipped chives
- 1½ tablespoons fresh lemon juice
- 1 tablespoon extra-virgin olive oil
- ¼ teaspoon smoked sweet paprika

Toasted baguette slices, for serving

1. On a plate, sprinkle the salmon with the Pernod and season with salt and white pepper. Cover with plastic wrap and let stand at room temperature for 30 minutes.

2. In a large saucepan, bring the celery, leek, onion, bay leaf, peppercorns, wine and 4 cups of water to a boil. Simmer for 25 minutes.

3. Add the salmon to the pan, cover and remove from the heat; let stand for 10 minutes. Remove the salmon, picking off any peppercorns, and refrigerate until chilled, about 45 minutes. Flake the salmon.

4. In a skillet, melt 1 tablespoon of the butter. Add the shallot and cook over moderate heat until softened. Let cool.

5. In a medium bowl, whisk the remaining 4 tablespoons of butter until smooth. Whisk in the sour cream. Add the cooled shallot along with the poached and smoked salmon, chives, lemon juice, olive oil and paprika and stir until combined. Season the rillettes with salt and white pepper. Serve with toasted baguette slices. —Anna Zepaltas

WINE Smooth, apple-rich Napa Valley Chardonnay: 2011 Franciscan Estate.

Grilled Mackerel with Lardo, Avocado and Jalapeño on Toasts
TOTAL: 30 MIN • 4 SERVINGS

F&W Best New Chefs 2012 Erik Anderson and Josh Habiger of the Catbird Seat in Nashville top these toasts with buttery avocado, making the mackerel even more luscious.

- 1 Hass avocado, thinly sliced
- 1 jalapeño—halved, seeded and very thinly sliced
- 1 teaspoon marjoram leaves, plus more for garnish

Coarse sea salt and freshly ground black pepper

- 1 tablespoon freshly squeezed lemon juice
- 2 tablespoons extra-virgin olive oil, plus more for brushing

Four ½-inch-thick slices of peasant bread

- 1 garlic clove, halved

Two 8-ounce Spanish mackerel fillets, halved crosswise at an angle

- 8 very thin slices of *lardo* (see Note)

1. In a medium bowl, combine the avocado slices with the jalapeño and the 1 teaspoon of marjoram; season with salt and pepper. Add the lemon juice and the 2 tablespoons of olive oil and toss gently.

2. Light a grill and brush the grates with oil or preheat a grill pan. Brush the bread slices with olive oil and grill them over high heat, turning once, until they are lightly charred in spots. Rub the toasts with the cut sides of the garlic clove.

3. Brush the mackerel fillets with olive oil and season them with salt and pepper. Grill the fish skin side down until the skin is lightly charred, about 3 minutes. Carefully flip the fillets and grill until they are cooked through, about 2 minutes longer. Arrange the fish on the toasts, skin side up. Top with the *lardo* slices and avocado salad, garnish with marjoram leaves and serve right away.
—*Erik Anderson and Josh Habiger*

NOTE *Lardo* (cured pork fatback) is available at specialty food shops and Italian markets.
WINE Citrusy New Zealand Sauvignon Blanc: 2011 The Seeker.

Smoked-Salmon Toasts with Mustard Butter
TOTAL: 25 MIN • 10 TO 12 SERVINGS ●

- 1 stick unsalted butter, softened
- 1 tablespoon Dijon mustard
- 1 tablespoon grainy mustard
- ½ teaspoon finely grated lemon zest
- 2 tablespoons chopped dill

Salt and freshly ground pepper

- 1 baguette, sliced ¼ inch thick
- 1 pound thinly sliced smoked salmon

1. Preheat the broiler and position a rack 6 inches from the heat. In a bowl, beat the butter with the Dijon and grainy mustards, lemon zest and 1 tablespoon of the dill and season with salt and pepper.

2. Spread the baguette slices on a large rimmed baking sheet and broil until golden and crisp, 1½ minutes per side. Let cool.

3. Spread the toasts with the mustard butter, top with the smoked salmon and arrange on a platter. Sprinkle with the remaining 1 tablespoon of dill and serve. —*David Tanis*

MAKE AHEAD The mustard butter can be covered and kept in the refrigerator overnight. Let soften before using.

WINE Ripe, full-bodied Chardonnay: 2010 Etude Estate.

Smoked-Salmon Deviled Eggs
TOTAL: 30 MIN • MAKES 8 DEVILED EGGS (16 HALVES) ● ●

- 8 large eggs
- ½ cup finely chopped smoked salmon (2 ounces)
- ⅓ cup mayonnaise
- 2 cornichons, cut into ¼-inch dice, plus 2 teaspoons pickling liquid from the jar
- 2 teaspoons Dijon mustard

Salt

Old Bay seasoning, for sprinkling

1. In a large saucepan, cover the eggs with water and bring to a vigorous boil. Cover the saucepan, remove from the heat and let stand for 10 minutes.

2. Drain off the water and shake the pan gently to crack the eggs. Cool the eggs slightly under cold running water, then peel them under running water. Pat dry.

3. Cut the eggs in half lengthwise and carefully remove the yolks. Transfer the yolks to a bowl and mash well with a fork. Stir in the salmon, mayonnaise, cornichons, cornichon liquid and Dijon mustard. Season with salt. Mound the filling in the egg-white halves and sprinkle with Old Bay. Serve lightly chilled.
—Michael Mina

Herbed Scrambled-Egg Toasts with Bottarga
TOTAL: 35 MIN • 20 SERVINGS ●

16 large eggs
½ cup extra-virgin olive oil
1 teaspoon salt
4 tablespoons unsalted butter, sliced
1½ tablespoons chopped flat-leaf parsley
1½ tablespoons chopped chives
40 thin baguette slices, rubbed with olive oil and toasted
¼ cup finely shaved bottarga (see Note)
Freshly ground pepper
Lemon wedges, for serving

1. In a large bowl, beat the eggs with ¼ cup of the oil and the salt. In a large nonstick skillet, heat the remaining ¼ cup of oil with 1 tablespoon of the butter over very low heat. Add the eggs and cook, stirring with a rubber spatula and gradually adding the remaining 3 tablespoons of butter, until soft, creamy and just beginning to form curds, about 12 minutes. Fold in the parsley and chives.

2. Spoon the eggs onto the toasts and top with the shaved bottarga. Season with pepper and serve warm, with lemon wedges.
—Tamar Adler

NOTE Bottarga (salted, pressed and dried mullet roe) has a deep sea flavor and firm texture. It is available at specialty food stores, Italian markets and online at gustiamo.com.
WINE Lively sparkling wine from California: 2009 Schramsberg Blanc de Blancs.

Panelle with Eggs and Bottarga
ACTIVE: 45 MIN; TOTAL: 3 HR
6 SERVINGS
These crispy chickpea-flour cakes are served with soft-boiled eggs and shavings of bottarga (cured, dried mullet roe), which add a delightfully briny flavor.

Salt
1 cup chickpea flour
6 large eggs
Ice cubes
1 cup pure olive oil
All-purpose flour, for dusting
¼ cup extra-virgin olive oil
1 tablespoon fresh lemon juice
Freshly ground pepper
6 ounces watercress, stems trimmed
Freshly grated bottarga (see Note below left)

1. Lightly oil an 8-by-4-inch loaf pan. In a saucepan, bring 2 cups of water to a boil. Add 1 teaspoon of salt and whisk in the chickpea flour until smooth. Cook over moderate heat just until thickened, 2 minutes. Scrape the mixture into the loaf pan and smooth the surface. Let cool, then refrigerate until firm, at least 2 hours.

2. In a medium saucepan of boiling water, cook the eggs over moderate heat for 6 minutes. Drain and return the eggs to the saucepan; cover with cold water and ice. Lightly crack the shells and let them stand until cooled, 10 minutes. Carefully peel the eggs.

3. Heat the pure olive oil in a skillet. Unmold the chickpea loaf and slice it ½ inch thick. Dust the slices with flour and fry them over high heat, turning, until golden, about 5 minutes. Drain the panelle on paper towels and sprinkle with salt.

4. In a bowl, whisk the extra-virgin olive oil with the lemon juice and season with salt and pepper. Add the watercress, toss to coat with the dressing and transfer to plates. Arrange the panelle and eggs alongside. Garnish with bottarga and serve right away.
—Curtis Di Fede and Tyler Rodde

WINE Clean, mineral-driven white: 2010 Collestefano Verdicchio di Matelica.

Fig, Orange and Pistachio Conserve
ACTIVE: 25 MIN; TOTAL: 1 HR
MAKES THREE ½-PINT JARS ● ●

Three ½-pint canning jars with lids and rings
1¼ pounds Black Mission figs, cut into 1-inch pieces
2 cups sugar
Finely grated zest of 2 oranges
½ cup fresh orange juice
2 tablespoons fresh lemon juice
½ teaspoon cinnamon
⅛ teaspoon ground cloves
⅓ cup raw shelled pistachios

1. Fill a large pot with water, cover and bring to a boil. Add the canning jars, lids and rings along with a set of canning tongs and a ladle and simmer over low heat for about 10 minutes to sterilize. Cover the pot and turn off the heat.

2. Set a metal rack in another large pot. Fill the pot with water, cover and bring to a boil.

3. Meanwhile, in a medium saucepan, combine the figs with the sugar, orange zest and juice, lemon juice, cinnamon and cloves. Bring to a boil, stirring to dissolve the sugar. Boil over moderately high heat, stirring occasionally, until reduced to 3 cups, about 10 minutes. Stir in the pistachios.

4. Using the sterilized canning tongs, carefully remove the jars from the hot water and transfer to a rimmed baking sheet. Ladle the conserve into the jars, leaving ½ inch at the top. Using the tongs, place the lids on the jars, followed by the rings. Screw on the lids securely but not too tightly.

5. Using canning tongs, lower the jars into the boiling water of the pot with the rack at the bottom, making sure they are covered by at least 1 inch of water. Boil over high heat for 15 minutes. Using the canning tongs, transfer the jars to a rack to cool until the lids seal (they will look concave); refrigerate any jars that do not seal. Store the sealed jars in a cool, dark place for up to 6 months.
—Ernest Miller

SERVE WITH Bread and assorted cheeses.

Crispy Potato-and-Sauerkraut Cakes with Smoked Trout

TOTAL: 1 HR • MAKES ABOUT 4 DOZEN
HORS D'OEUVRES ●

2 tablespoons unsalted butter
2 teaspoons caraway seeds
1 cup drained sauerkraut
¼ cup chopped dill, plus more
    for garnish
2 pounds baking potatoes,
    peeled and coarsely shredded
    (4 cups)
Salt and freshly ground pepper
Rendered chicken fat (schmaltz)
    or extra-virgin olive oil, for frying
1 cup crème fraîche
1 smoked trout fillet (about 9 ounces),
    skinned and flaked
Finely grated lemon zest, for garnish

1. In a medium skillet, melt the butter with the caraway seeds and cook over moderate heat until fragrant, about 30 seconds. Add the sauerkraut and cook, stirring, until very dry, about 4 minutes. Transfer to a large bowl, add the ¼ cup of dill and let cool.

2. Meanwhile, in a large pot of salted boiling water, cook the shredded potatoes for 1 minute. Drain well, shaking out the excess water. Add the potatoes to the sauerkraut and stir to combine. Season the potatoes and sauerkraut with salt and pepper and let cool.

3. Heat a large griddle or cast-iron skillet over moderate heat and brush it with schmaltz. Working in batches, spoon 2-tablespoon-size mounds of the potato-and-sauerkraut mixture onto the griddle and flatten them into 2-inch rounds, about ½ inch thick. Cook until the cakes are golden and crispy, 6 to 7 minutes, turning once and adding more schmaltz to the griddle as needed. Reduce the heat to moderately low after the first batch and wipe the griddle occasionally.

4. Arrange the potato cakes on a platter and top with the crème fraîche, smoked trout, lemon zest and dill. Serve.
—Jonathon Sawyer

WINE Frothy, lime-scented Prosecco: NV Drusian Extra Dry.

Lobster-and-Corn Fritters

TOTAL: 1 HR
MAKES ABOUT 25 FRITTERS

One 1½-pound lobster
½ cup basil leaves
½ cup mayonnaise
Salt and freshly ground pepper
1 cup all-purpose flour
½ teaspoon baking powder
½ teaspoon baking soda
¾ cup buttermilk
1 large egg, separated
1 ear of corn, kernels cut from the cob
2 tablespoons minced chives
1 tablespoon unsalted butter, melted
Vegetable oil, for frying
Lemon wedges, for serving

1. Bring a large saucepan of water to a boil. Plunge the lobster into the boiling water head first and cook until bright red all over, about 6 minutes. Transfer the cooked lobster to a large rimmed baking sheet and let cool. Twist the tail from the lobster body and break off the claws. With scissors, cut down the tail shell and remove the meat. Cut down the center of the tail and remove the dark intestinal vein. Crack the claws and knuckles and remove the meat. Coarsely chop the lobster meat and refrigerate.

2. Blanch the basil in a small saucepan of boiling water for 30 seconds. Drain and rinse under cold running water, then squeeze the excess water from the basil and transfer the basil to a blender. Add the mayonnaise and puree. Transfer to a bowl and season with salt and pepper. Refrigerate the basil mayonnaise until lightly chilled.

3. In a large bowl, whisk together the flour, baking powder, baking soda and ½ teaspoon of salt. In a small bowl, whisk the buttermilk with the egg yolk. Make a well in the center of the dry ingredients and add the buttermilk mixture. Stir lightly, then fold in the lobster, corn, chives and melted butter. In a medium bowl, whisk the egg white to soft peaks and fold it into the batter.

4. Preheat the oven to 350°. In a large saucepan, heat 1½ inches of oil to 325°. Drop four

to five 2-tablespoon-size dollops of batter into the hot oil and fry, turning once, until golden brown, about 2 minutes. With a slotted spoon, transfer the fritters to paper towels to drain; season with salt. Transfer the fritters to a baking sheet and keep warm in the oven while you fry the rest. Serve right away, with the basil mayonnaise and lemon wedges. —Nico Monday and Amelia O'Reilly

WINE Minerally, Chardonnay-based Champagne: 2002 Pol Roger Brut Blanc de Blancs.

Butternut Squash Rösti Cakes

⊙ TOTAL: 45 MIN
MAKES 4 DOZEN MINI CAKES ● ●
Adding shredded butternut squash to mini potato pancakes adds a touch of sweetness and a nice orange hue. When fried, the rösti cakes become hot, lacy and crisp.

One 1-pound butternut squash
    neck, peeled and coarsely shredded
    in a processor
1½ pounds baking potatoes,
    peeled and coarsely shredded
    in a food processor
½ cup cornstarch
2 large eggs
½ cup minced onion
Salt and cayenne pepper
Vegetable oil, for frying
Sour cream, salmon caviar and chives,
    for garnish

In a bowl, combine the shredded squash and potatoes with the cornstarch, eggs and onion and season with salt and cayenne. In a large nonstick skillet, heat ⅛ inch of oil until shimmering. Add 2-tablespoon-size mounds of the mixture to the skillet and cook over moderate heat, turning them once, until they are golden and cooked through, 4 to 5 minutes. Drain on paper towels and repeat, adding more oil to the skillet as needed and wiping out the pan occasionally. Top the rösti cakes with sour cream, caviar and chives and serve hot. —Grace Parisi

MAKE AHEAD The fried squash rösti cakes can be kept at room temperature for 4 hours. Recrisp in a warm oven.

● HEALTHY ● MAKE AHEAD ● VEGETARIAN ● STAFF FAVORITE

butternut squash rösti cakes

Crispy Potato Galettes with Smoked Fish and Dill Crème

TOTAL: 50 MIN • 4 SERVINGS ●

In this luxurious dish, star chef Wolfgang Puck tops potato pancakes with smoked salmon, smoked sturgeon and caviar.

½ cup crème fraîche
1 small shallot, minced
2 tablespoons finely chopped dill
2 teaspoons fresh lemon juice, plus more for brushing
Kosher salt and freshly ground pepper
3 baking potatoes (1½ pounds), peeled
4 tablespoons unsalted butter, 2 tablespoons melted
¼ pound thinly sliced smoked salmon
¼ pound thinly sliced smoked sturgeon
Extra-virgin olive oil, for brushing
Freshly snipped chives and caviar, for garnish

1. In a bowl, stir the crème fraîche with the shallot, dill and the 2 teaspoons of lemon juice. Season with salt and pepper. Whisk the mixture until thickened, about 30 seconds.
2. Preheat the oven to 425°. On a box grater, coarsely shred the potatoes. Transfer to a clean kitchen towel and squeeze out as much liquid as possible. In a bowl, combine the potatoes with the 2 tablespoons of melted butter and season with salt and pepper.
3. In a small nonstick skillet, melt 1 tablespoon of the butter. Add half of the potatoes and pat them into a disk about ½ inch thick. Cook over moderately high heat, turning once, until golden, 3 minutes per side. Transfer the potato galette to a baking sheet. Repeat with the remaining 1 tablespoon of butter and potatoes. Bake the galettes for 10 minutes, until cooked through and crisp; transfer to a platter and let stand for 15 minutes.
4. Spoon the dill crème onto the galettes and top with the smoked fish. Lightly brush the fish with olive oil and lemon juice; season with salt and pepper. Garnish with chives and caviar. Serve. —*Wolfgang Puck*

WINE Bright, minerally sparkling wine: NV Quattro Mani Franciacorta Brut.

Herbed Zucchini-Feta Fritters

TOTAL: 50 MIN • 4 TO 6 SERVINGS ● ●

Flecked with chopped parsley and dill, these zucchini-feta fritters are light and crispy.

4 medium zucchini (about 1¾ pounds), coarsely shredded
Kosher salt
2 large eggs, lightly beaten
½ cup all-purpose flour
¼ cup chopped dill
¼ cup chopped parsley
¼ cup plus 2 tablespoons chopped mint
½ cup crumbled feta cheese
Freshly ground pepper
1 medium cucumber—peeled, halved, seeded and coarsely chopped
1 cup plain Greek yogurt
Vegetable oil, for frying

1. Pile the shredded zucchini in a colander and sprinkle with 1 tablespoon of salt. Toss the zucchini well and let stand for 5 minutes. Squeeze out as much liquid as possible and transfer the zucchini to a large bowl. Stir in the eggs, flour, dill, parsley, ¼ cup of the mint and the feta cheese. Stir in ½ teaspoon of freshly ground pepper and refrigerate the batter for about 10 minutes.
2. In a food processor, coarsely puree the cucumber. Transfer to a medium bowl. Stir in the yogurt and the remaining 2 tablespoons of mint; season with salt and pepper.
3. Preheat the oven to 350°. In a medium saucepan, heat ½ inch of oil to 350°. Set a paper towel–covered baking sheet near the stove. Working in batches, drop rounded tablespoons of the fritter batter into the hot oil and fry, turning the fritters a few times, until browned and crisp, about 2 minutes. Using a slotted spoon, transfer the fritters to the prepared baking sheet and repeat with the remaining batter. Discard the paper towels and reheat the fritters in the oven for about 3 minutes. Serve the fritters hot, with the cucumber-yogurt sauce.
—*Didem Senol*

WINE Fruity Spanish sparkling wine: NV Freixenet Cordon Negro Brut Cava.

Chicken-Liver-Pâté Toasts

TOTAL: 1 HR PLUS CHILLING
20 SERVINGS ●

2 pounds chicken livers, trimmed
Kosher salt and freshly ground pepper
1 cup extra-virgin olive oil
1½ cups Marsala
2 tablespoons unsalted butter
2 large white onions, finely chopped
6 garlic cloves, minced, plus halved cloves for rubbing
⅓ cup drained capers
10 oil-packed anchovy fillets, chopped
2 tablespoons chopped sage
2 tablespoons chopped rosemary
½ teaspoon chopped thyme
½ cup crème fraîche
2 tablespoons red wine vinegar
60 toasted baguette rounds
Coarse sea salt, for serving

1. Season the chicken livers with kosher salt and pepper. In a large skillet, heat ¼ cup of the olive oil. Add half of the livers and cook over moderately high heat, turning once, until just barely pink within, 6 minutes. Transfer the livers to a bowl and repeat with the remaining livers and ¼ cup of the olive oil. Add 1 cup of the Marsala to the skillet and cook until reduced to ½ cup, 8 minutes.
2. Add the remaining ½ cup of olive oil to the skillet along with the butter. Add the onions and garlic and cook over moderate heat, stirring frequently, until softened and lightly browned, about 10 minutes. Add the capers, anchovies, sage, rosemary and thyme and cook for 5 minutes. Add the remaining ½ cup of Marsala and cook until nearly evaporated, about 5 minutes. Let cool.
3. Transfer the onion mixture and livers to a food processor. Add the crème fraîche and vinegar and puree until very smooth. Season with kosher salt and pepper. Refrigerate the pâté until chilled.
4. Rub the baguette toasts on one side with garlic, spread the chicken liver pâté on top, sprinkle with sea salt and serve. —*John Adler*

WINE Fresh, focused red Burgundy: 2010 Domaine Louis Boillot & Fils Pommard.

● HEALTHY   ● MAKE AHEAD   ● VEGETARIAN   ● STAFF FAVORITE

crispy potato galette with smoked fish and dill crème

Grape Leaves Stuffed with Pine Nuts and Spiced Rice

ACTIVE: 40 MIN; TOTAL: 1 HR 30 MIN
MAKES 2 DOZEN STUFFED GRAPE LEAVES

● ● ○ ○

These Egyptian stuffed grape leaves are similar to Greek *dolmas* but more fragrant, with cinnamon, cumin and orange zest.

- 30 jarred brined grape leaves, drained
- 2 tablespoons pine nuts
- 2 tablespoons unsalted butter
- 1 medium onion, finely chopped
- One 14-ounce can diced tomatoes, drained
- ½ cup chopped flat-leaf parsley
- ½ cup short-grain rice
- ½ teaspoon cinnamon
- ½ teaspoon ground cumin
- 1 tablespoon finely grated orange zest
- ¼ cup finely chopped mint
- Salt
- 1 tablespoon olive oil

1. Soak the grape leaves in a large bowl of warm water for 20 minutes.

2. In a large skillet, toast the pine nuts over moderate heat until golden, about 4 minutes. Transfer to a medium bowl.

3. In the same skillet, melt the butter. Add the onion and cook over moderate heat, stirring, until softened, about 5 minutes. Stir in the tomatoes and parsley. Add the rice and cook, stirring, until it begins to turn white, 5 minutes. Scrape the mixture into the bowl with the pine nuts, then stir in the cinnamon, cumin, orange zest and mint and season with salt. Let cool slightly.

4. Drain the grape leaves and pat dry, then snip off the stems. Spread 4 leaves on a work surface. Form a 1-tablespoon-size log of the rice filling at the stem end. Fold the sides over the filling, then tightly roll up the leaves to form cylinders, tucking in the sides as you go. Repeat with 20 more grape leaves and the remaining filling.

5. Line a medium saucepan with 3 of the grape leaves. Arrange the stuffed grape leaves in the saucepan in 2 layers. Drizzle with the oil. Top with the remaining 3 grape leaves and a small plate. Add enough water to cover the stuffed grape leaves and bring to a boil. Cover and simmer until the rice is tender, 45 minutes. Turn off the heat and let cool in the saucepan. Arrange the grape leaves on a platter and serve them warm or at room temperature. —*Eric Monkaba*

Crispy Pork, Shrimp and Cabbage Imperial Rolls

TOTAL: 1 HR 45 MIN • MAKES 24 ROLLS

This recipe was inspired by a street food vendor in southern Saigon. To make the rolls, Valerie Luu and Katie Kwan of the San Francisco pop-up café Rice Paper Scissors cook the filling ahead of time and wet the rice paper with their palms. The result: "Crispy, chewy and snowy white rolls!"

ROLLS
- Vegetable oil
- 1 medium shallot, minced
- 2 cups thinly sliced green cabbage
- 3 tablespoons Asian fish sauce
- 1½ tablespoons sugar
- ¼ pound ground pork
- Salt
- 4 medium shrimp—shelled, deveined and minced
- One 4-ounce red-skinned potato or taro root, peeled and cut into matchsticks
- 1 large egg, lightly beaten
- ½ teaspoon freshly ground pepper
- 2 dozen 6-inch rice papers (see Note)

SAUCE
- 1 small garlic clove, minced
- 1 small Thai chile, minced
- 1½ tablespoons sugar
- 1½ tablespoons fresh lime juice
- 2 tablespoons Asian fish sauce

1. MAKE THE ROLLS In a large skillet, heat 1 tablespoon of oil. Add the shallot and cook over moderate heat until softened, about 2 minutes. Add the cabbage and cook, stirring a few times, until just wilted, about 3 minutes. Add ½ tablespoon each of the fish sauce and sugar; cook, stirring, for 1 minute. Transfer the cabbage to a large bowl.

2. Add ½ tablespoon of oil to the skillet. Add the pork and cook over moderately high heat, breaking up the meat with a wooden spoon, until no trace of pink remains, about 3 minutes. Season with salt. Using a slotted spoon, add the pork to the cabbage. Add the shrimp to the skillet and stir-fry for 1 minute. Add the remaining 2½ tablespoons of fish sauce and 1 tablespoon of sugar and cook, stirring to dissolve the sugar. Scrape the shrimp into the bowl of cabbage.

3. Set a steamer basket in a medium saucepan with ½ inch of water and bring to a boil. Add the potato matchsticks, cover and steam until just tender, about 2 minutes. Let cool, then add to the bowl. Mix well. Stir in the egg and ground pepper and mix again.

4. Fill a shallow bowl with water. Working with 2 rice papers at a time and using your palm, rub the rice papers on both sides with water. Let the papers stand for about 1 minute, until softened; do not overmoisten or the papers may tear. Place a rounded tablespoon of the filling on the lower third of each rice paper and bring the bottom up and over the filling. Press tightly to enclose the filling and roll up, folding in the sides as you go. The rolls should seal themselves; if not, moisten with a little water. Place the rolls on a platter seam side down and repeat with the remaining rice papers and filling.

5. MAKE THE SAUCE In a bowl, combine the ingredients with ⅓ cup of water; mix well.

6. Preheat the oven to 375°. In a medium saucepan, heat 1½ inches of vegetable oil to 320° over moderately high heat. Fry 4 to 5 rolls at a time, stirring occasionally to keep them from sticking together, until they're crisp but still white, about 6 minutes. Keep the oil between 320° and 350° during frying. Transfer the rolls to a rack set over a large baking sheet to drain. When all of the rolls have been fried, transfer them to a baking sheet. Warm them in the oven for 2 minutes. Serve the rolls right away, with the dipping sauce. —*Katie Kwan and Valerie Luu*

NOTE Rice papers are available online or at Asian markets.

WINE Lively, juicy sparkling rosé: 2011 Secco Italian Bubbles.

● HEALTHY ● MAKE AHEAD ● VEGETARIAN ● STAFF FAVORITE

Shrimp-and-Pork Dumplings with Bamboo Shoots

⏱ TOTAL: 45 MIN • MAKES 3 DOZEN DUMPLINGS ● ●

TV chef and dim sum guru Martin Yan makes his delicate dumpling wrappers with cornstarch, wheat starch, water and shortening and mixes fresh bamboo shoots into the filling. In this simplified recipe, premade wonton wrappers and canned bamboo shoots are super-quick shortcuts.

10 ounces shelled, deveined medium shrimp, cut into ⅓-inch dice
2 ounces ground pork (¼ cup)
¼ cup finely diced bamboo shoots
2 teaspoons canola oil
1½ teaspoons toasted sesame oil
1 teaspoon salt
Pinch of freshly ground white pepper
One 12-ounce package wonton wrappers
Cornstarch, for dusting
Soy sauce and Chinese chile sauce, for serving

1. In a medium bowl, mix the diced shrimp with the pork, bamboo shoots, canola oil, sesame oil, salt and white pepper.
2. Work with a few wonton wrappers at a time: Brush the edges of each wrapper with water. Spoon a scant tablespoon of the filling into the center of each wrapper and fold the dough over to form triangles. Press the edges to seal. Place the dumplings on a cornstarch-dusted baking sheet. Keep the finished dumplings covered with a lightly dampened towel while you work.
3. Bring a large pot of salted water to a boil. Add the dumplings and boil until they are tender and cooked through, about 5 minutes. Drain the dumplings well and serve with soy sauce and Chinese chile sauce. —Martin Yan

MAKE AHEAD The uncooked dumplings can be frozen on a parchment paper–lined baking sheet in a single layer, then transferred to an airtight container and frozen for up to 1 month.

WINE Medium-bodied, melon-scented white: 2010 Domaine de Pajot Les Quatre Cépages.

Pork Dumplings with Chile-Sesame Sauce

TOTAL: 1 HR 30 MIN • MAKES ABOUT 5 DOZEN DUMPLINGS ●

DUMPLINGS

3 tablespoons vegetable oil
½ pound shiitake mushrooms, stems discarded and caps thinly sliced
6 large scallions, light green parts only, finely chopped
¾ pound baby bok choy, finely chopped
1 medium carrot, coarsely shredded
4 large garlic cloves, finely chopped
2 tablespoons minced fresh ginger
¼ cup low-sodium soy sauce
2 teaspoons mirin or sweet sherry
1 teaspoon Asian chile-garlic sauce
Kosher salt
1 pound ground pork
2 packages wonton wrappers
2 tablespoons cornstarch mixed with 1 cup of water

SAUCE

1 cup low-sodium soy sauce
¼ cup Chinese black bean sauce
¼ cup toasted sesame oil
4 teaspoons minced fresh ginger
4 teaspoons Asian chile-garlic sauce
4 teaspoons mirin or sweet sherry

1. MAKE THE DUMPLINGS In a skillet, heat the oil until shimmering. Add the shiitake, scallions, bok choy and carrot; stir-fry over high heat until tender, 5 minutes. Add the garlic, ginger, soy sauce, mirin and chile-garlic sauce and cook until the liquid is evaporated, about 3 minutes. Season with salt. Transfer the filling to a bowl and refrigerate until chilled, 15 minutes.
2. Line a large baking sheet with wax paper. Add the pork to the filling and mix. On a work surface, brush 3 wonton wrappers with the cornstarch solution; spoon a scant tablespoon of the filling in the center. Fold the wrappers over to form triangles; seal the edges, pressing out any air trapped inside. With scissors, trim the the wrappers, leaving a ¼-inch rim around the filling. Transfer the dumplings to the baking sheet, seam

side up. Keep the dumplings covered with a moist paper towel. Repeat with the remaining wonton wrappers and filling.
3. MAKE THE SAUCE Combine all of the ingredients in a medium bowl.
4. Fill a wok or a large skillet with 2 inches of water and bring to a boil. Working in batches, arrange the dumplings in a double-tiered bamboo steamer lined with oiled wax paper; set the steamer over the boiling water. Cover and steam the dumplings until the filling is cooked through and firm, 6 minutes.
5. Toss the dumplings in 1 cup of the sauce. Using a slotted spoon, transfer the dumplings to a platter. Serve the remaining chile-sesame sauce alongside. —David Burtka

Shumai with Crab and Pork

⏱ TOTAL: 45 MIN • MAKES 2 DOZEN ● ●

These juicy, flavorful dumplings are best served with just a little Chinese mustard and soy sauce for dipping.

¾ pound coarsely ground 80 percent lean pork
4 medium scallions, thinly sliced
2 tablespoons minced fresh ginger
1 tablespoon mirin
1 teaspoon kosher salt
¼ pound lump crabmeat, picked over
Flour, for dusting
24 round gyoza wrappers
6 napa cabbage leaves

1. In a bowl, mix the pork, scallions, ginger, mirin and salt. Gently fold in the crabmeat.
2. Dust a baking sheet with flour. Hold a gyoza wrapper in your palm, keeping the rest covered with plastic. Place about 1½ tablespoons of the filling in the center of the wrapper and pinch the edges all around, forming an open cup. Transfer the dumpling to the baking sheet and cover. Repeat with the remaining wrappers and filling.
3. Fill a wok with 1½ inches of water; bring to a boil. Arrange the cabbage leaves on 2 tiers of a bamboo steamer so they overlap slightly. Add the dumplings and stack the tiers. Cover and steam until just cooked, 8 minutes. Serve. —Sylvan Mishima Brackett

Chicken Satay with Peanut Sauce

ACTIVE: 1 HR; TOTAL: 1 HR 30 MIN
8 SERVINGS ●

SATAY

3 plump lemongrass stalks—bottom 8 inches only, outer layer removed, stalk cut into 2-inch lengths
2 large shallots, coarsely chopped
2 large garlic cloves
⅓ cup light brown sugar
1½ tablespoons ground coriander
1 tablespoon ground cumin
½ teaspoon ground turmeric
2 tablespoons Asian fish sauce
1½ tablespoons kosher salt
2 tablespoons canola oil, plus more for grilling
4 pounds skinless, boneless chicken thighs, cut into 1-inch pieces

PEANUT SAUCE

¼ cup canola oil
4 medium shallots, thinly sliced (¾ cup)
2 garlic cloves, thinly sliced
1 plump lemongrass stalk—bottom 8 inches only, outer layer removed, stalk cut into 2-inch lengths
1 jalapeño, thinly sliced
1 tablespoon minced fresh ginger
1½ cups unsalted roasted peanuts
½ cup unsweetened coconut milk
2 tablespoons light brown sugar
3 tablespoons freshly squeezed lime juice
2 tablespoons Asian fish sauce
1 tablespoon soy sauce
Pinch of crushed red pepper

1. PREPARE THE SATAY In a food processor, combine the lemongrass, shallots, garlic, brown sugar, coriander, cumin, turmeric, fish sauce, salt and the 2 tablespoons of canola oil and process to a paste. Transfer the marinade to a bowl and add the chicken, gently tossing to coat each piece. Thread the coated chicken pieces onto 12-inch skewers and refrigerate them for at least 30 minutes and up to 1 hour.

2. MEANWHILE, PREPARE THE PEANUT SAUCE In a medium saucepan, heat the canola oil. Add the shallots, garlic, lemongrass, jalapeño and ginger and cook over moderate heat, stirring, until the aromatics are softened and browned, about 10 minutes. Scrape the mixture into a food processor. Add all of the remaining ingredients along with ½ cup of water and process until a smooth paste forms.

3. Scrape the peanut paste back into the saucepan and cook over low heat, stirring frequently, until very thick and the fat separates, about 20 minutes. The peanut sauce will turn a deeper shade of brown. Whisk in ½ cup of hot water until incorporated. Keep the peanut sauce warm over very low heat.

4. Light a grill and oil the grates. Grill the chicken skewers over moderately high heat, turning occasionally, until charred in spots and cooked through, 10 to 12 minutes. Serve with the peanut sauce. —*Bryant Ng*
WINE Black cherry–rich red from Piedmont: 2010 Prunotto Dolcetto.

Chicken-Meatball Yakitori

◷ TOTAL: 30 MIN
MAKES 2 DOZEN MEATBALLS ●
Known as *tsukune* in Japanese, these chicken meatballs are brushed with a sweet mirin-and-soy-sauce glaze and then cooked yakitori-style (skewered and grilled).

¼ cup sake
¼ cup soy sauce
¼ cup raw sugar
¼ cup plus 2 tablespoons mirin
1 pound coarsely ground chicken
2 teaspoons kosher salt
1 medium shallot, minced
Finely grated zest of 1 yuzu or lemon
1 tablespoon vegetable oil

1. In a saucepan, combine the sake with the soy sauce, sugar and ¼ cup of the mirin; boil until reduced to ¾ cup, 3 minutes. Let cool.
2. Preheat the oven to 375°. In a bowl, combine the chicken, salt, shallot, zest and the remaining 2 tablespoons of mirin. Lightly coat a rimmed baking sheet with 1 teaspoon

of the vegetable oil. Form the chicken mixture into 24 meatballs. Brush the meatballs with the remaining 2 teaspoons of oil and arrange them on the baking sheet. Bake the meatballs for about 6 minutes, until they are barely cooked through.
3. Light a grill. Thread the meatballs onto 8 bamboo skewers and grill over moderately high heat, turning, until lightly charred, about 2 minutes. Reduce the heat to low and brush the meatballs with the sauce. Grill, turning and brushing, until glazed, 30 seconds longer. Serve with the remaining sauce.
—*Sylvan Mishima Brackett*
SERVE WITH Yuzu or lemon wedges.
WINE Juicy, light-bodied red: 2010 De Forville Dolcetto d'Alba.

Hogs in a Blanket

ACTIVE: 20 MIN; TOTAL: 50 MIN
MAKES 3 DOZEN HORS D'OEUVRES ● ●
In this fun take on pigs in a blanket, spicy andouille sausage stands in for the hot dogs, with sweet mustard chutney as a condiment.

7 ounces all-butter puff pastry, thawed and cut into four 5-inch squares
1 large egg yolk mixed with 1 tablespoon of water
Four 3-ounce andouille sausages
¼ cup Major Grey's chutney
2 tablespoons whole-grain mustard

1. Preheat the oven to 375° and position a rack in the center. Arrange the puff pastry squares on a work surface and brush the top edges with the egg wash. Place the sausages on the bottom edges and roll up the pastry, pressing the edges to seal. Freeze the logs for 10 minutes, or until firm.
2. Cut the logs into ½-inch slices and place them cut side up in 3 mini muffin pans. Bake for 25 minutes, until golden and sizzling. Turn out onto a paper towel–lined rack to cool.
3. Meanwhile, in a mini food processor, pulse the chutney and mustard just until the chutney is chopped. Spoon a dollop of the chutney mustard on each slice and serve.
—*Grace Parisi*

● HEALTHY ● MAKE AHEAD ● VEGETARIAN ● STAFF FAVORITE

chicken satay with peanut sauce

Apples on Horseback

⏱ TOTAL: 30 MIN • MAKES 16 PIECES

16 thin slices of pancetta
1 Pink Lady apple, peeled and
   cut into 16 wedges
3 ounces Manchego cheese,
   sliced ¼ inch thick and cut into
   2-by-½-inch sticks
Sixteen 2-inch rosemary sprigs or
   toothpicks, for skewers

1. Preheat a grill pan. Arrange the pancetta slices on a work surface and place an apple wedge and a cheese stick in the center of each slice. Wrap the pancetta around the filling and secure the rolls with a rosemary sprig or toothpick.
2. Grill the skewers until the pancetta is golden and crispy and the cheese is melted, 5 to 6 minutes. Serve hot.
—*Grace Parisi*
WINE Fruit-forward sparkling wine: NV Juvé y Camps Brut Nature Cava.

Soppressata Bundles with Radicchio and Goat Cheese

⏱ TOTAL: 20 MIN
MAKES 2 DOZEN BUNDLES
The cured Italian salami soppressata acts as a wrap for this delicious hors d'oeuvre.

1 small head of radicchio,
   finely shredded
5 peperoncini—stemmed, seeded
   and chopped
2 ounces fresh goat cheese, softened
1 teaspoon red wine vinegar
1 teaspoon extra-virgin olive oil
3 tablespoons pine nuts, toasted
24 thin slices of soppressata (4 ounces)

In a bowl, toss the radicchio with the peperoncini, goat cheese, vinegar, olive oil and pine nuts. Arrange the soppressata on a work surface and mound the radicchio salad on the sliced soppressata. Roll up like a cone and serve. —*Dante de Magistris*
WINE Lively Italian sparkling wine: NV Nino Franco Prosecco Rustico.

Fried Chicken Wings with Black Bean Sauce

TOTAL: 1 HR • 8 SERVINGS
Chinese black bean sauce flavored with five-spice powder and Sriracha—a nice change from barbecue sauce—coats these crispy fried chicken wings.

½ cup Chinese black bean sauce
   (see Note)
¼ cup low-sodium soy sauce
¼ cup toasted sesame oil
¼ cup water
3 tablespoons Sriracha
2 tablespoons dark brown sugar
2 tablespoons rice vinegar
4 garlic cloves, minced
½ teaspoon Chinese five-spice powder
   (see Note)
6 cups vegetable oil, for frying
4 pounds chicken wings, patted dry

1. In a blender, puree the black bean sauce with the soy sauce, toasted sesame oil, water, Sriracha, brown sugar, rice vinegar, garlic and five-spice powder until smooth. Transfer the black bean sauce to a medium saucepan, bring to a boil and simmer over moderately low heat until thickened and glossy, about 5 minutes.
2. In a large cast-iron skillet or Dutch oven, heat the vegetable oil to 350°. Working in 4 or 5 batches, fry the chicken wings, turning once, until deep golden and crispy, about 12 minutes; be sure to keep the vegetable oil at 350°. Drain the wings on a rack set over a baking sheet.
3. In a large bowl, toss the fried chicken wings with the black bean sauce until they are coated. Transfer the wings to a large platter and serve right away.
—*David Burtka*
NOTE Chinese black bean sauce and Chinese five-spice powder are available online and at Asian markets.
MAKE AHEAD The sauce can be refrigerated for up to 5 days. Rewarm the sauce gently before proceeding with Step 3.
WINE Plush, cassis-inflected California Merlot: 2011 Avalon.

Hot-and-Sticky Lemon-Pepper Chicken Wings

TOTAL: 1 HR • 4 TO 6 SERVINGS ●
Top Chef All-Stars winner Richard Blais uses an unlikely ingredient—lemon curd—plus plenty of black pepper to make these fabulous hot, sticky and sweet chicken wings.

2 tablespoons extra-virgin olive oil
1 tablespoon minced garlic
½ cup prepared lemon curd
2 tablespoons fresh lemon juice
1 teaspoon hot sauce
3 tablespoons coarsely ground
   black pepper
½ cup rice flour
½ cup all-purpose flour
2 tablespoons cornstarch
¾ cup seltzer
½ cup malt liquor (high-alcohol beer)
Salt
2½ pounds chicken wings (about 16)
Vegetable oil, for frying

1. In a saucepan, heat the olive oil. Add the garlic and cook over moderate heat until fragrant, about 1 minute. Whisk in the lemon curd, lemon juice and ¼ cup of water and bring to a boil. Off the heat, stir in the hot sauce and pepper.
2. In a large bowl, whisk both flours with the cornstarch. Add the seltzer and malt liquor; whisk until smooth. Season with salt. Add the wings to the batter and turn to coat.
3. In a large saucepan, heat 2 inches of vegetable oil to 350°. Scrape the excess batter from the wings. Working in batches, fry the wings in the hot oil for 3 minutes, until the crust is just set and pale golden. Drain on a wire rack and air-dry for 10 minutes.
4. Return the oil to 350°. Fry the wings a second time, in batches, until they are deep mahogany and an instant-read thermometer inserted in the thickest part registers 170°, 5 to 6 minutes. Drain the wings on the rack.
5. In a large bowl, gently toss the fried wings with the sauce. Transfer the wings to a platter and serve right away. —*Richard Blais*
BEER Classic malty English bitter: Fuller's London Pride.

● HEALTHY ● MAKE AHEAD ○ VEGETARIAN ● STAFF FAVORITE

hot-and-sticky lemon-pepper chicken wings

Smokin' Sweet Chicken Wings with Cherry Barbecue Glaze

⏱ TOTAL: 40 MIN • 4 SERVINGS

- 2 tablespoons unsalted butter
- ½ medium sweet onion, such as Vidalia, finely chopped
- 1 large habanero chile, seeded and minced
- ¾ cup cherry preserves, preferably sour cherry
- ⅓ cup fresh lime juice
- Salt and freshly ground black pepper
- 3½ pounds chicken wings, tips discarded and wings split

1. In a medium saucepan, melt the butter. Add the chopped sweet onion and cook over moderate heat, stirring occasionally, until the onion is softened and lightly browned, about 5 minutes. Add three-fourths of the minced habanero chile and cook for 1 minute, just until softened. Scrape the onion and habanero into a blender, add the cherry preserves and lime juice and puree until smooth. Return the cherry glaze to the saucepan and bring it to a boil over moderately high heat. Stir in the remaining minced habanero chile and season the glaze with salt and black pepper. Transfer the glaze to a small bowl.

2. Light a grill or preheat a broiler and position a rack 8 inches from the heat source. Season the chicken wings all over with salt and black pepper and grill over moderately high heat, turning occasionally, until lightly charred and crispy, about 20 minutes. Alternatively, broil the wings for about 20 minutes, turning occasionally, until they are crispy.

3. Transfer the chicken wings to a large bowl and toss with one-third of the cherry glaze. Return the wings to the grill or broiler and cook, turning once, just until sticky and caramelized, about 2 minutes. Return the chicken wings to the bowl and toss with another one-third of the cherry glaze. Transfer the glazed chicken wings to a serving platter and serve with the remaining glaze on the side.

—Grace Parisi

WINE Fresh, berry-rich Syrah from Washington state: 2008 Powers.

Japanese-Style Folded Omelet

⏱ TOTAL: 20 MIN • 4 SERVINGS ●

This thick, rolled omelet called *dashimaki tamago* gets its sweet-savory flavor from soy sauce, mirin and dashi (broth made from shavings of dried smoked bonito, a kind of tuna). Usually cut into rectangles to top rice for sushi, it's a fabulous starter served simply with grated daikon and soy sauce.

- ¾ cup bonito shavings (see Note)
- 1 tablespoon sugar
- 1 tablespoon mirin
- 1 teaspoon kosher salt
- 1 teaspoon light soy sauce, plus more for serving
- 8 large eggs, at room temperature
- Vegetable oil, for greasing
- 2 tablespoons lightly drained grated daikon, for serving

1. In a small saucepan, bring ¾ cup of water to a boil. Add the bonito and simmer over low heat for about 1 minute. Cover, remove the saucepan from the heat and let stand for about 10 minutes. Strain the dashi (broth) through cheesecloth and let it cool to warm.

2. In a bowl, whisk ½ cup of the warm dashi with the sugar, mirin, salt and 1 teaspoon of soy sauce. Whisk in the eggs.

3. Heat a large nonstick skillet over moderate heat. Rub the pan with an oil-soaked paper towel. Add a drop of the egg mixture to the pan, and when it sizzles, pour in one-quarter of the egg mixture so that it forms a thin layer. As the egg begins to cook, use chopsticks or a spatula to roll the omelet away from you, popping air bubbles as you go, to form the omelet into a flattened log. Dab more vegetable oil in the skillet and add another quarter of the egg mixture, lifting the rolled omelet and tilting the pan to allow the egg mixture to seep under it. As the layer of egg cooks, roll the omelet with the new layer of egg toward you. Push the log to the opposite edge of the skillet. Repeat the process twice more with the remaining egg to form a large, loose roll.

4. Remove the skillet from the heat and set a lightly moistened wooden sushi mat over the omelet. Invert the omelet onto the mat. Bring the sides of the mat over the omelet and let rest for 5 minutes. Turn the omelet out onto a plate and thickly slice crosswise. Serve with daikon and soy sauce.

—Sylvan Mishima Brackett

NOTE Bonito shavings, also known as bonito flakes, are available at Japanese markets.

Shrimp Cocktail with Singapore Hot Sauce

ACTIVE: 30 MIN; TOTAL: 1 HR

20 HORS D'OEUVRE SERVINGS ● ●

Chef Susan Feniger of the global street food–inspired restaurant Street in Los Angeles likes to quickly simmer raw shrimp in broth or sauté them with garlic and ginger, but you can certainly use precooked shrimp to save time. This sweet-and-spicy dipping sauce was inspired by the ones Feniger sampled at street stalls throughout Singapore.

- 2 tablespoons canola oil
- 1 medium red onion, thinly sliced
- ¾ cup coarsely chopped fresh ginger
- ¾ cup light brown sugar
- 1¼ cups ketchup
- ¼ cup Chinese chile bean sauce
- Lemon wedges, for serving
- 4 pounds cooked large tail-on shrimp, chilled

1. In a medium saucepan, heat the oil. Add the onion and cook over moderately high heat until lightly browned, 4 minutes. Add the ginger and cook over moderately low heat until softened and lightly browned, 3 minutes. Add the sugar, ketchup and chile bean sauce and simmer over low heat until the sauce is thickened, 5 minutes.

2. Transfer the sauce to a blender and add ½ cup of water. Blend until smooth. With the machine on, add another ½ cup of water. Scrape the sauce into the saucepan; simmer over low heat for 3 minutes. Transfer the hot sauce to a bowl and refrigerate until chilled.

3. Squeeze lemon over the shrimp and serve with the sauce and more lemon wedges.

—Susan Feniger

WINE Lively, fruit-forward rosé: 2011 Muga.

● HEALTHY ● MAKE AHEAD ● VEGETARIAN ● STAFF FAVORITE

shrimp cocktail with singapore hot sauce

Kale Chips with Almond Butter and Miso

ACTIVE: 35 MIN; TOTAL: 2 HR 15 MIN
6 SERVINGS ● ● ○

"We have an entire garden bed dedicated to kale that we use for these chips," says Los Angeles chef Sera Pelle. She usually makes them in a dehydrator, but the oven method here works perfectly, too. Flavored with miso, almond butter and nutritional yeast, the kale chips are a delicious and super-healthy snack.

½   cup almond butter
¼   cup warm water
¼   cup chopped onion
3   tablespoons extra-virgin olive oil, plus more for greasing
2   garlic cloves, chopped
1   tablespoon white miso
1   tablespoon nutritional yeast (see Note)
1   tablespoon chopped fresh oregano
1   tablespoon chopped fresh thyme
2   teaspoons cider vinegar
2   teaspoons tamari
¼   teaspoon turmeric
¼   teaspoon crushed red pepper
1½ pounds curly kale, leaves left whole and stems discarded
Sea salt

1. Preheat the oven to 200° and position 3 racks spaced evenly apart. In a blender or food processor, puree all of the ingredients except the kale and salt.
2. Grease 3 large rimmed baking sheets with olive oil and divide the kale leaves among them. Drizzle the almond-butter mixture over the kale and rub each leaf to season evenly. Arrange the kale on the baking sheets in an even layer and season with sea salt. Bake for about 1 hour and 40 minutes, until the leaves are crisp. Switch the pans a few times during baking and rearrange the leaves to help them cook evenly. Let cool, then carefully lift the kale chips off the baking sheets with a spatula and serve.
—*Sera Pelle*
NOTE Nutritional yeast is available at specialty and health-food stores.

Chipotle-Garlic Edamame

🕒 **TOTAL: 15 MIN • 4 SERVINGS** ● ● ○

One 14-ounce bag frozen edamame in the pods
1   tablespoon extra-virgin olive oil
1   chipotle in adobo—stemmed, seeded and minced
1   garlic clove, minced
½   teaspoon ground cumin
Coarse sea salt and freshly ground black pepper

1. Bring a large saucepan of water to a boil. Add the edamame and cook for about 4 minutes. Drain and pat dry.
2. In a large skillet, heat the olive oil with the minced chipotle, minced garlic and ground cumin. Add the edamame pods and cook over moderate heat, stirring occasionally, until the garlic is softened, 1 to 2 minutes. Season the edamame with salt and black pepper and transfer to a bowl. Serve warm or at room temperature. —*Grace Parisi*

Black Pepper Kettle Corn

🕒 **TOTAL: 15 MIN**
MAKES 8 CUPS (6 SERVINGS) ● ● ○

2   tablespoons canola oil
6   tablespoons popping corn
2   tablespoons sugar
1   tablespoon golden flaxseeds
½   teaspoon each of salt and freshly ground black pepper

In a large nonstick saucepan, heat the canola oil with the popping corn over moderately high heat until sizzling. Add the sugar, flaxseeds, salt and pepper; cover and cook, shaking the pan constantly, until nearly all of the kernels are popped, 5 to 6 minutes. Pour the kettle corn onto a rimmed baking sheet and let cool, tossing once or twice. Transfer the kettle corn to a bowl, leaving any unpopped kernels behind. —*Grace Parisi*
MAKE AHEAD The kettle corn can be made up to 4 hours ahead.
WINE Bright sparkling wine from Spain: NV Cristalino Cava Brut.

Smoky Popcorn

🕒 **TOTAL: 20 MIN • 6 SERVINGS** ● ●

¼   cup vegetable oil
½   cup plus 2 tablespoons popping corn
1   teaspoon smoked hot Spanish paprika
½   tablespoon sugar
4   tablespoons unsalted butter, melted and kept warm
½   cup *furikake* mix (see Note)
2   cups Japanese mixed rice crackers
Kosher salt

1. In a large saucepan, combine the oil and popcorn, cover and cook over moderate heat until it starts to pop. Shake the pan and cook until the corn stops popping.
2. Transfer the hot popcorn to a large bowl. Sprinkle with the paprika and sugar and toss well. Drizzle with the butter and toss, adding the *furikake* and rice crackers. Season with salt, toss again and serve.
—*Peter Rudolph*
NOTE *Furikake* is a Japanese seasoning mix that includes seaweed, sesame seeds, sugar, salt and dried bonito (dried fish flakes).

Cristina's Famous Nuts

ACTIVE: 10 MIN; TOTAL: 3 HR 30 MIN
10 TO 12 SERVINGS ● ● ○

4   cups mixed raw nuts, such as pecans, walnuts, almonds and cashews
32 sage leaves, torn into large pieces
One 8-inch rosemary sprig, leaves stripped
3   tablespoons extra-virgin olive oil
Salt and freshly ground pepper

Preheat the oven to 200°. On a large rimmed baking sheet, toss the mixed nuts with the sage, rosemary and olive oil and season with salt and pepper. Spread the nuts in an even layer. Bake for 3 hours; the nuts should not be browned. Let the nuts cool on the baking sheet until they are crisp, then transfer them to a bowl and serve. —*Cristina Salas-Porras*
MAKE AHEAD The nuts can be stored in an airtight container for up to 3 days.

● HEALTHY   ● MAKE AHEAD   ○ VEGETARIAN   ● STAFF FAVORITE

Asian Snack Mix with Nori

**ACTIVE: 10 MIN; TOTAL: 30 MIN PLUS
COOLING • MAKES 6 CUPS (6 SERVINGS)**

● ● ○ ○

In an effort to create a healthy snack that also satisfied cravings for something crispy and salty, F&W's Grace Parisi came up with this Asian-inspired riff on Chex Mix: She tosses rice-flake cereal and toasted pecans with seasoned nori (seaweed flavored with sesame oil and salt), miso and wasabi. The result is a light, munchable snack packed with iodine, iron and protein.

½ cup pecans, broken into large pieces (2 ounces)
6 cups rice-flake cereal, such as Special K (6 ounces)
5 sheets seasoned nori, crumbled (from one .74-ounce bag; see Note)
3 tablespoons yellow or white miso
2 tablespoons agave nectar
1 tablespoon wasabi powder or 1½ teaspoons wasabi paste
1 teaspoon salt
¼ cup canola oil

1. Preheat the oven to 350°. Spread the pecans in a pie plate and toast for about 6 minutes, until fragrant. Transfer to a large bowl and let cool slightly. Add the cereal and nori and toss well.
2. In a mini food processor, combine the miso, agave nectar, wasabi and salt. Add the oil and process until smooth. Dollop the mixture over the flakes, pecans and nori and toss with your hands to coat evenly.
3. Spread the mix on a parchment paper–lined rimmed baking sheet in an even layer. Toast for 18 minutes, stirring and tossing 2 or 3 times, until browned; the mix will crisp as it cools. Transfer to a bowl and serve.
—*Grace Parisi*

NOTE If seasoned nori is unavailable, use plain nori and add 1 teaspoon of toasted sesame oil to the food processor in Step 2.
MAKE AHEAD The cooled snack mix can be stored in an airtight container at room temperature for up to 5 days.
BEER Hoppy IPA: Sixpoint Bengali Tiger.

Spiced Chickpea Nuts

**ACTIVE: 15 MIN; TOTAL: 2 HR 15 MIN
PLUS OVERNIGHT SOAKING
MAKES 3½ CUPS** ● ●

These crunchy spiced chickpea nuts are a great snack for kids; adults will love them with a cold beer.

1 pound dried chickpeas, soaked overnight and drained
Herbamare or sea salt (see Note)
¼ cup extra-virgin olive oil
½ cup nutritional yeast (see Note)
2 teaspoons ground cumin
½ teaspoon granulated garlic

1. In a large pot, cover the chickpeas with 2 inches of water and bring to a boil. Simmer over low heat, stirring, until the chickpeas are almost tender, about 1 hour and 15 minutes; add more water as needed to keep the chickpeas covered. Add a large pinch of salt for the last 15 minutes of cooking. Drain the chickpeas; dry on a rimmed baking sheet lined with a kitchen towel.
2. Preheat the oven to 425°. Line a large rimmed baking sheet with parchment. In a bowl, toss the chickpeas with the oil. Add the nutritional yeast, cumin and garlic; toss well. Spread the chickpeas on the prepared baking sheet and season with salt. Bake for about 45 minutes, stirring a few times, until crisp. Serve hot or warm. —*Sera Pelle*
NOTE Herbamare salt and nutritional yeast are available at health-food stores.

Bacon Candy

🕐 **ACTIVE: 10 MIN; TOTAL: 35 MIN
MAKES 20 STRIPS** ●

"What's better than bacon, except sugar?" asks New York City event planner Bronson van Wyck. He coats thick-cut bacon strips in brown sugar and chile powder, then bakes them in the oven instead of frying, so a lot of the fat drains off.

½ cup packed light brown sugar
1½ teaspoons chile powder
20 slices of thick-cut bacon (1½ pounds)

1. Preheat the oven to 400°. Line 2 rimmed baking sheets with aluminum foil.
2. In a small bowl, whisk the brown sugar with the chile powder.
3. Arrange the bacon strips on the baking sheets and coat the tops with the chile sugar. Bake for 20 to 25 minutes, until caramelized and almost crisp. Transfer the bacon candy to a rack set over a sheet of aluminum foil to cool completely before serving.
—*Bronson van Wyck*

MAKE AHEAD The bacon candy can be kept at room temperature for up to 6 hours.

Sugar-and-Spice Nuts

**ACTIVE: 10 MIN; TOTAL: 1 HR
MAKES 5 CUPS** ● ○

"I like to take something that's generally ordinary and do it really well," says Bronson van Wyck about this sticky cashew-and-almond mix. "With cinnamon, salt and sugar, it hits a lot of spots on the tongue." He gives the nuts a lovely thin crust by tossing them in egg white before baking.

¾ cup sugar
1 tablespoon kosher salt
1 tablespoon chile powder
2 teaspoons cinnamon
2 teaspoons cayenne pepper
1 large egg white
2 cups raw cashews (9 ounces)
2 cups raw almonds (9 ounces)

1. Preheat the oven to 300°. Coat a rimmed baking sheet with nonstick cooking spray.
2. In a small bowl, whisk the sugar with the salt, chile powder, cinnamon and cayenne pepper. In a large bowl, beat the egg white until frothy. Add the cashews, almonds and spiced sugar and toss.
3. Spread out the nuts on the prepared baking sheet and bake for about 45 minutes, stirring once, until browned. Let the nuts cool on the baking sheet, stirring occasionally before serving or storing.
—*Bronson van Wyck*

MAKE AHEAD The spiced nuts can be stored in an airtight container at room temperature for up to 2 days.

As riders make their way from Vail to Aspen, Colorado, chef Kelly Liken prepares rustic meals for them using local ingredients. Dishes include a refreshing pea shoot and arugula salad, OPPOSITE; *recipe, page 42.*

SALADS

Mixed Herb Salad with Pickled Radish Vinaigrette

ACTIVE: 30 MIN; TOTAL: 2 HR 30 MIN
8 TO 10 SERVINGS ● ●

Cleveland chef Jonathon Sawyer pays homage to what he calls "beautiful greens" in this dish. The radishes are what make the salad so delicious; they pickle in the lemony dressing for a couple of hours before being served.

1½ teaspoons finely grated lemon zest
3 tablespoons fresh lemon juice
3 tablespoons extra-virgin olive oil
1½ tablespoons rosé vinegar or
white wine vinegar
¼ teaspoon ground coriander
5 radishes, very finely diced
2 tablespoons minced shallots
Kosher salt and freshly ground pepper
3 ounces brioche, cut into 1-inch
cubes (3 lightly packed cups)
1 head of red leaf lettuce, leaves torn
1 head of Bibb lettuce, leaves torn
One 6-ounce head of frisée,
torn into bite-size pieces
¼ cup lightly packed tarragon leaves
¼ cup lightly packed flat-leaf
parsley leaves
¼ cup lightly packed mint leaves
¼ cup snipped chives
Crushed pink peppercorns, for garnish
(optional)

1. In a small bowl, whisk the lemon zest and juice with the olive oil, vinegar and coriander. Stir in the radishes and shallots and season with salt and pepper. Let the vinaigrette stand at room temperature for 2 hours.
2. Preheat the oven to 350°. Spread the brioche cubes on a baking sheet and bake for 10 minutes, until golden and crisp. Let them cool slightly, then break into coarse crumbs.
3. In a large bowl, toss all of the lettuces with the tarragon, parsley, mint and chives. Add the radish vinaigrette to the salad and toss to coat. Season with salt and pepper and toss again. Transfer the salad to plates. Top with the brioche crumbs, garnish with crushed pink peppercorns and serve.
—Jonathon Sawyer

Blooming Bibb Lettuce Salad

ACTIVE: 30 MIN; TOTAL: 1 HR
4 SERVINGS ●

¼ cup balsamic vinegar
2 tablespoons red wine vinegar
1 tablespoon finely chopped oregano
¾ cup extra-virgin olive oil
4 plum tomatoes—peeled, seeded
and finely diced
Salt and freshly ground pepper
4 heads of Bibb lettuce, separated
into leaves

1. In a small bowl, whisk both vinegars with the oregano. Gradually whisk in the olive oil. Stir in the tomatoes and season with salt and pepper; let stand for 30 minutes.
2. Stack the lettuce leaves on 4 plates, forming a flower-like shape by placing the largest leaves on the bottom and the smallest ones on top. Drizzle with the dressing, distributing the tomatoes among the stacked leaves.
—Scott Conant

Classic Caesar Salad

⏱ **TOTAL: 30 MIN • 6 TO 8 SERVINGS**

½ pound baguette, cut into
1-inch cubes
½ cup plus 2 tablespoons
extra-virgin olive oil
Salt
1 large egg yolk
4 oil-packed anchovy fillets, drained
2 garlic cloves, chopped
2 tablespoons red wine vinegar
2 tablespoons fresh lemon juice
⅛ teaspoon cayenne pepper
1½ pounds romaine lettuce, torn into
bite-size pieces
½ cup freshly grated Parmigiano-
Reggiano cheese (about 1½ ounces)

1. Preheat the oven to 375°. Toss the bread cubes with 2 tablespoons of the olive oil on a large rimmed baking sheet; spread in an even layer and season lightly with salt. Bake the baguette cubes for about 15 minutes, until golden brown and crisp.

2. Meanwhile, in a blender, combine the egg yolk, anchovy fillets, garlic, vinegar, lemon juice and cayenne pepper and puree. With the machine on, slowly add the remaining ½ cup of olive oil and blend until incorporated. Season the dressing with salt.
3. In a large bowl, toss the romaine with the croutons, dressing and cheese, then serve.
—Brian Perrone

Shredded Caesar Salad on Toasts

⏱ **TOTAL: 30 MIN • 8 FIRST-COURSE**
SERVINGS

1 medium oval country loaf, sliced
½ inch thick
¾ cup extra-virgin olive oil, plus
more for brushing
2 garlic cloves—1 minced and 1 halved
¼ cup fresh lemon juice
1½ teaspoons anchovy paste
1 teaspoon Dijon mustard
1 teaspoon Worcestershire sauce
1 teaspoon capers—
rinsed, drained and minced
Kosher salt and freshly ground pepper
3 romaine hearts (1½ pounds),
finely chopped
½ cup freshly shaved Parmigiano-
Reggiano cheese, plus more
for garnish

1. Preheat the broiler. Brush both sides of the bread slices with olive oil and arrange on a rimmed baking sheet. Broil 6 inches from the heat for 3 minutes, turning once, until the bread is crisp and golden on the outside but still slightly soft in the center. Rub one side of each slice with the halved garlic.
2. In a medium bowl, whisk the minced garlic with the lemon juice, anchovy paste, Dijon mustard, Worcestershire sauce and capers. Gradually whisk in the ¾ cup of olive oil and season the dressing with salt and pepper.
3. In a large bowl, toss the romaine with the ½ cup of cheese and the dressing. Season with salt and pepper. Mound the salad on the toasts, garnish with shaved cheese and serve. —Bronson van Wyck

● HEALTHY ● MAKE AHEAD ● VEGETARIAN ● STAFF FAVORITE

shredded caesar salad on toasts

Baby Lettuces with Feta, Strawberries and Almonds

⏱ **TOTAL: 20 MIN • 8 SERVINGS** ● ● ●

San Francisco chef Jeff Banker gives this salad an unexpected twist with strawberries, smoked almonds and French feta, which is milder and creamier than Greek feta.

- 2 teaspoons Dijon mustard
- 1 teaspoon honey
- 1 small shallot, minced
- 2 tablespoons red wine vinegar, preferably Banyuls
- ⅓ cup extra-virgin olive oil
- Salt and freshly ground pepper
- 12 cups packed assorted baby lettuces (about 6 ounces)
- 1 quart strawberries, hulled—small berries halved, large ones quartered
- 4 ounces feta cheese (preferably French), crumbled (1 cup)
- 1 cup smoked almonds, chopped

1. In a small bowl, stir together the mustard, honey, shallot and vinegar. Stir in the olive oil and season with salt and pepper.

2. Put the lettuces in a large bowl. Add the strawberries, feta and almonds. Drizzle the dressing over the salad, toss well and serve. —*Jeff Banker*

WINE Bright, berry-scented rosé: 2011 Villa des Anges Old Vines.

Green Salad with Chorizo Chips

⏱ **TOTAL: 30 MIN • 8 SERVINGS** ●

Instead of the usual croutons or bacon bits, F&W's Grace Parisi makes crisp little chorizo bites to add crunch to a green salad.

- 6 ounces dry chorizo, very thinly sliced
- 1½ tablespoons sherry vinegar
- 1 tablespoon minced shallots
- ¼ cup extra-virgin olive oil
- Salt and freshly ground pepper
- 2 celery ribs, thinly sliced
- 4 large radishes, thinly sliced
- ¾ cup Spanish green olives, sliced
- 4 ounces mesclun
- 2 heads of baby Bibb lettuce, leaves torn

1. Line a large microwave-safe plate with paper towels. Arrange half of the chorizo slices on the plate and cover with a paper towel. Microwave at high power for 1 minute; the fat should be rendered and the chorizo slightly browned. If it is not yet browned, cover and microwave at 20-second intervals until done. Transfer the cooked chorizo to a plate to cool; it will crisp as it cools. Repeat with the remaining chorizo.

2. In a large bowl, whisk the vinegar and the shallots with the olive oil and a generous pinch each of salt and pepper. Add the celery, radishes, olives, mesclun and Bibb lettuce and toss to coat. Sprinkle with the chorizo chips and serve. —*Grace Parisi*

WINE Bright, zippy Portuguese white: 2011 Broadbent Vinho Verde.

Spicy Greens and Pear Salad with Pomegranate Gremolata

⏱ **TOTAL: 30 MIN • 10 TO 12 SERVINGS** ● ● ●

Aida Mollenkamp, host of the Cooking Channel's *Ask Aida*, packs bitter (arugula, watercress), tart (pomegranate) and sweet flavors (honey, pear) into this spicy salad.

- 1 cup pomegranate seeds
- 3 tablespoons finely chopped flat-leaf parsley
- 1 shallot, minced
- ½ teaspoon finely grated orange zest
- Kosher salt and freshly ground black pepper
- ¼ cup extra-virgin olive oil
- 2 tablespoons pomegranate molasses
- 2 tablespoons red wine vinegar
- 1 tablespoon honey
- 1 tablespoon Dijon mustard
- 15 ounces mixed spicy baby greens, such as watercress and arugula
- 3 Bosc pears, thinly sliced lengthwise

1. In a small bowl, combine the pomegranate seeds with the parsley, shallot and orange zest. Season with salt and black pepper.

2. In another small bowl, whisk the oil with the pomegranate molasses, vinegar, honey and mustard; season with salt and pepper.

3. In a large bowl, toss the greens with the dressing and season lightly with salt and black pepper. Transfer the salad to plates or a platter, then top with the pear slices and pomegranate gremolata. Serve right away. —*Aida Mollenkamp*

Spinach Salad with Garlic-Cider Vinaigrette

ACTIVE: 30 MIN; TOTAL: 1 HR 45 MIN 8 SERVINGS ● ●

San Francisco chef Michael Mina tosses raw spinach with a warm, garlicky vinaigrette, lightly wilting the leaves.

- 3 heads of garlic, unpeeled
- ½ pound ciabatta loaf, torn into 1-inch pieces
- ¼ cup extra-virgin olive oil, plus more for brushing and drizzling
- 1 medium red onion, cut into ½-inch dice
- 1 cup apple cider
- 3½ tablespoons cider vinegar
- Salt and freshly ground pepper
- ¾ pound curly spinach leaves— stemmed, washed and dried

1. Preheat the oven to 350°. Wrap the garlic in a sheet of foil and bake for 1½ hours, until tender. Let cool to room temperature.

2. Meanwhile, on a large baking sheet, drizzle the ciabatta pieces with olive oil. Bake for about 12 minutes, until crisp.

3. Peel the roasted garlic. In a large skillet, heat 2 tablespoons of the olive oil. Add the onion and cook over moderate heat until softened, about 5 minutes. Add the apple cider and boil over high heat until reduced to ¼ cup, about 4 minutes. Add the cider vinegar, roasted garlic and the remaining 2 tablespoons of olive oil and season the dressing with salt and pepper.

4. In a large bowl, toss the spinach with the croutons and warm dressing and serve. —*Michael Mina*

MAKE AHEAD The croutons can be kept in an airtight container overnight. The roasted garlic can be refrigerated overnight; bring to room temperature before using.

● HEALTHY ● MAKE AHEAD ● VEGETARIAN ● STAFF FAVORITE

baby lettuces with feta, strawberries and almonds

Red Cabbage Salad with Fennel, Orange and Pepitas

⏲ **TOTAL: 30 MIN · 8 SERVINGS** ●

This crisp, fresh salad is full of healthy ingredients, including earthy hemp seeds, which are packed with protein and antioxidants.

2 cups raw pumpkin seeds (pepitas)
2 tablespoons tamari
¼ cup extra-virgin olive oil
1 tablespoon finely grated lemon zest
¼ cup fresh lemon juice
Sea salt and freshly ground black pepper
4 oranges
One 1½-pound head of red cabbage—halved, cored and very thinly sliced
2 small fennel bulbs—halved, cored and thinly sliced, fronds reserved
¼ cup shelled hemp seeds
1 small bunch of cilantro, leaves picked and stems discarded (about ¼ cup packed)

1. Preheat the oven to 350°. Spread the raw pumpkin seeds on a large rimmed baking sheet and bake them for about 7 minutes, until golden brown. Drizzle with the tamari and toss well. Bake the pumpkin seeds for about 3 minutes longer, tossing them once or twice, until crisp. Let cool.

2. In a small bowl, whisk the ¼ cup of olive oil with the lemon zest and lemon juice and season with salt and pepper.

3. Using a sharp knife, peel the oranges, removing all of the bitter white pith. Working over a bowl, cut in between the membranes to release the sections.

4. In a large bowl, toss the cabbage, sliced fennel, hemp seeds and cilantro with two-thirds of the pumpkin seeds. Add the dressing; toss well. Transfer the salad to a platter; arrange the orange sections and fennel fronds on top. Sprinkle with the remaining pumpkin seeds and serve. —Sera Pelle

MAKE AHEAD The roasted pumpkin seeds, dressing and orange sections can be prepared 1 day in advance; store the roasted pumpkin seeds in an airtight container at room temperature. Refrigerate the dressing and orange sections separately.

Overnight Slaw

TOTAL: 30 MIN PLUS OVERNIGHT CHILLING · 8 SERVINGS ● ● ● ●

Atlanta chef Linton Hopkins calls this vinegary slaw a maceration salad; it sits overnight to develop its superbly tangy flavor.

3½ pounds green cabbage, cut into 1-inch chunks
1 very large Vidalia or other sweet onion (1¼ pounds), cut into 1-inch pieces
1 pound carrots, cut into ½-inch pieces
3 celery ribs, cut into ½-inch pieces
1 cup sugar
1 cup distilled white vinegar
¾ cup peanut oil
1 teaspoon dry mustard powder
1 teaspoon celery seeds
1 teaspoon kosher salt
½ cup chopped flat-leaf parsley leaves

1. Working in batches, add the vegetables to a food processor and pulse until they are finely chopped. Transfer to a large bowl and toss well, then stir in the sugar.

2. In a small saucepan, combine the vinegar, oil, dry mustard, celery seeds and salt and bring to a boil. Pour the dressing over the slaw and toss well. Refrigerate overnight. Just before serving, drain the slaw and stir in the parsley. —Linton Hopkins

Lemony Brussels Sprout Slaw

⏲ **TOTAL: 30 MIN
10 TO 12 SERVINGS** ● ●

½ cup 2 percent plain Greek yogurt
½ cup low-fat mayonnaise
1 teaspoon finely grated lemon zest
⅓ cup fresh lemon juice
½ cup chopped chives
¼ cup chopped dill
Salt and freshly ground pepper
2 pounds raw brussels sprouts, finely shredded in a food processor (12 cups)
¼ cup plus 2 tablespoons salted roasted sunflower seeds

In a bowl, whisk the yogurt with the mayonnaise, lemon zest, lemon juice, chives and dill and season with salt and pepper. Add the brussels sprouts and toss to coat evenly. Fold in the sunflower seeds and serve. —Grace Parisi

MAKE AHEAD The brussels sprout slaw can be refrigerated overnight.

Brussels Sprout Salad with Pepitas and Dates

⏲ **TOTAL: 35 MIN
10 TO 12 SERVINGS** ● ●

TV host Aida Mollenkamp loves finding new ways to prepare slightly bitter ingredients like brussels sprouts. In this salad, she builds up layers of flavor and texture with crunchy pumpkin seeds, plump dried fruit and a tart red wine vinegar dressing.

¾ cup raw pumpkin seeds (pepitas)
Kosher salt
3 pounds brussels sprouts, quartered
⅓ cup extra-virgin olive oil
3 tablespoons freshly squeezed lemon juice
3 tablespoons red wine vinegar
2 small shallots, thinly sliced
1 tablespoon Dijon mustard
Freshly ground pepper
7 Medjool dates, finely chopped

1. In a small skillet, toast the pumpkin seeds over moderate heat, stirring occasionally, until golden, about 5 minutes. Transfer the seeds to a plate and season with salt.

2. Fill a large bowl with ice water. In a large saucepan of salted boiling water, cook half of the brussels sprouts until they are crisp-tender, 4 minutes. Using a slotted spoon, transfer the brussels sprouts to the ice water bath to cool. Repeat with the remaining brussels sprouts. Drain well and pat dry.

3. In a large bowl, whisk the olive oil with the lemon juice, vinegar, shallots and mustard. Add the brussels sprouts, season with salt and pepper and toss to coat. Stir in the pumpkin seeds and dates and serve. —Aida Mollenkamp

red cabbage salad with fennel, orange and pepitas

Farmers' Market Chopped Salad

⏱ **TOTAL: 30 MIN** • **6 SERVINGS** ● ●

Combining crunchy, perfectly in-season vegetables in a creamy, lemony dressing is a fun way to reimagine slaw.

- 4 ounces snow peas, cut into 1-inch pieces
- 1 yellow bell pepper, thinly sliced
- 1 medium zucchini, cut into 1-by-⅓-inch sticks
- 1 medium yellow squash, cut into 1-by-⅓-inch sticks
- 2 medium golden beets, peeled and finely julienned
- 1 bunch of watercress, thick stems discarded and watercress coarsely chopped
- 2 scallions, thinly sliced on the diagonal
- 2 tablespoons fresh lemon juice
- 2 tablespoons light mayonnaise
- ¼ cup canola oil
- Salt and freshly ground pepper

In a large bowl, combine the snow peas, bell pepper, zucchini, yellow squash, beets, watercress and scallions. In a small bowl, whisk the lemon juice with the mayonnaise and oil and season with salt and pepper. Add the dressing to the vegetables and toss. Serve right away. —*Grace Parisi*

Lemon Vinaigrette

⏱ **TOTAL: 10 MIN**

MAKES 1¼ CUPS ● ● ●

"Oil and lemon juice separate, so when you add them to a salad, some leaves have mostly lemon, others mostly oil," says chef Jesse Schenker of Recette in Manhattan. He relies on xanthan gum, a powder that thickens dressings instantly, for perfectly emulsified vinaigrettes that coat evenly.

- 6 tablespoons fresh lemon juice
- 1 gram (¼ teaspoon) xanthan gum (see Note)
- ½ cup grapeseed oil
- ½ cup extra-virgin olive oil
- Salt and freshly ground white pepper

In a blender, mix the lemon juice with 3½ tablespoons of cold water at low speed. With the blender on, add the xanthan gum and blend until the liquid is slightly thickened, about 15 seconds. Increase the blender speed to medium and slowly add the grapeseed oil, then the olive oil, in a thin stream; blend until creamy. Season with salt and white pepper. —*Jesse Schenker*

SERVE WITH Lettuce or vegetable salads, such as a shaved fennel salad with seared octopus or poached shrimp.

NOTE Xanthan gum is available at many grocery stores.

Pea Shoot and Arugula Salad with Radishes and Hazelnuts

📷 PAGE 35

⏱ **TOTAL: 30 MIN** • **6 SERVINGS** ● ●

With their sweet, mild pea flavor and juicy stems, pea shoots are becoming a popular salad addition. In this salad from Colorado chef Kelly Liken, they're the perfect foil for sharp arugula and radishes, herbal fennel and toasty hazelnuts.

- ½ cup hazelnuts
- 1½ tablespoons Champagne vinegar or white wine vinegar
- ¼ teaspoon Dijon mustard
- ¼ teaspoon honey
- ¼ teaspoon minced shallot
- ¼ cup extra-virgin olive oil
- Salt and freshly ground black pepper
- 5 ounces baby arugula
- 3½ ounces pea shoots
- 4 large radishes, trimmed and very thinly sliced on a mandoline
- 1 fennel bulb—halved lengthwise, cored and very thinly sliced on a mandoline

1. Preheat the oven to 375°. Spread the hazelnuts in a pie plate and toast them in the oven until they are fragrant and the skins blister, about 14 minutes. Transfer the toasted hazelnuts to a clean kitchen towel and let them cool slightly, then vigorously rub the nuts together to remove the skins. Coarsely chop the nuts.

2. In a large bowl, whisk the Champagne vinegar with the Dijon mustard, honey and minced shallot. Add the extra-virgin olive oil and whisk until blended. Season the vinaigrette with salt and freshly ground black pepper. Add the arugula, pea shoots, radishes, fennel and chopped hazelnuts and toss well. Season with salt and pepper and serve right away. —*Kelly Liken*

Farmhand Salad with Goat Cheese

⏱ **TOTAL: 30 MIN** • **6 SERVINGS** ● ● ●

Chef Brian Lewis of Elm in New Canaan, Connecticut, sends his staff to apprentice at a local farm for 16 hours a month. In return, Elm receives fresh produce, which Lewis features in this shaved vegetable salad.

- 1 fennel bulb, halved and cored
- 1 large carrot
- 1 small golden or Chioggia beet, peeled
- 3 large radishes
- 1 endive, sliced crosswise ½ inch thick
- 1 cup baby arugula
- 1 tablespoon tarragon leaves
- 1 tablespoon dill
- 1 tablespoon flat-leaf parsley leaves
- 1 tablespoon snipped chives
- 1 tablespoon balsamic vinegar
- 2 tablespoons extra-virgin olive oil
- Salt and freshly ground pepper
- 3 ounces fresh goat cheese, crumbled
- ½ cup chopped marcona almonds
- 4 Medjool dates, pitted and thinly sliced

1. Using a mandoline, very thinly slice the fennel, carrot, beet and radishes and transfer to a large bowl. Add the endive, arugula, tarragon, dill, parsley and chives.

2. In a small bowl, whisk the balsamic vinegar with the olive oil and season with salt and pepper. Add the dressing and half of the goat cheese, almonds and dates to the salad and toss gently. Transfer the salad to plates and garnish with the remaining goat cheese, almonds and dates. Serve right away. —*Brian Lewis*

● HEALTHY   ● MAKE AHEAD   ● VEGETARIAN   ● STAFF FAVORITE

farmers' market chopped salad

Tomato and Pineapple Salad with Garlic Chips

⏱ TOTAL: 40 MIN • 4 TO 6 SERVINGS ● ○

1 tablespoon soy sauce
4 ounces fresh pineapple, cut into ½-inch pieces (about ⅔ cup)
3 tablespoons canola oil
1 tablespoon rice vinegar
1 teaspoon sugar
1 scallion, white and tender green parts only, thinly sliced
½ tablespoon mirin
2 large tomatoes, cored and sliced ¼ inch thick
¼ small sweet onion, very thinly sliced
4 ounces baby arugula
¼ cup Golden Garlic Chips (recipe follows)

1. In a blender or mini food processor, combine the soy sauce with 2 tablespoons of the pineapple pieces and the oil, vinegar, sugar, scallion and mirin; puree until smooth.
2. Arrange the tomatoes on half of a large serving platter; scatter the onion slices on top. Drizzle the vegetables with half of the dressing. In a large bowl, toss the arugula with the remaining pineapple pieces and dressing. Mound the salad alongside the tomatoes and onions and garnish with the Golden Garlic Chips. —*Roy Choi*

GOLDEN GARLIC CHIPS

⏱ TOTAL: 30 MIN • MAKES 1¼ CUPS ● ○

1½ cups peeled plump garlic cloves, thinly sliced
2 cups canola oil

Set a coarse strainer over a heatproof bowl. In a small saucepan, combine the garlic slices with the canola oil and cook over moderate heat, stirring frequently, until the garlic is golden, about 15 minutes. Drain the garlic in the strainer, shaking off any of the excess cooking oil. Spread the garlic chips on a paper towel–lined baking sheet and let them cool. Reserve the strained garlic oil for another use. —*RC*

Heirloom Tomato Salad with Anchovy Vinaigrette

⏱ TOTAL: 30 MIN • 4 SERVINGS ●

The warm, garlicky anchovy dressing here is fantastic with an assortment of juicy, peak-season tomatoes. To finish the dish, chefs Amelia O'Reilly and Nico Monday of the Market Restaurant in Gloucester, Massachusetts, top it with tangy pickled shallots and an oozy soft-boiled egg.

¼ cup extra-virgin olive oil
4 anchovies, minced
1 garlic clove, minced
1 teaspoon finely grated lemon zest
1 medium shallot, thinly sliced
2 tablespoons red wine vinegar
2 large eggs
1½ pounds assorted heirloom tomatoes—large ones sliced, small ones halved
Fleur de sel and freshly ground pepper
Flat-leaf parsley and marjoram leaves, for serving

1. In a small skillet, combine the olive oil, anchovies, garlic and lemon zest.
2. In a small bowl, toss the shallot with the vinegar and let stand for 10 minutes.
3. Bring a small saucepan of water to a boil. Turn the heat to low, and when the water is simmering, gently place the eggs in the water. Cook for 6 minutes, until the eggs are lightly boiled. Have an ice bath ready near the stove. With a slotted spoon, plunge the eggs in the ice bath and let cool for 2 minutes. Peel the eggs.
4. Arrange the tomatoes on 4 plates and season with fleur de sel and freshly ground pepper. Scatter the shallot and vinegar over the tomatoes.
5. Warm the anchovy dressing over moderate heat to a gentle simmer, then pour the dressing over the tomatoes. Cut the eggs in half crosswise and place a half on each plate. Scatter the parsley and marjoram over the salad and serve right away.
—*Nico Monday and Amelia O'Reilly*
WINE Vibrant California Sauvignon Blanc: 2011 Joel Gott.

Grilled Peach, Onion and Bacon Salad with Buttermilk Dressing

⏱ TOTAL: 45 MIN • 8 SERVINGS ●

The combination of grilled onion, smoky bacon and juicy peaches makes this salad from chef Linton Hopkins of Atlanta's Restaurant Eugene delightfully Southern. He favors big, juicy sweet onions like Vidalias, which get nicely charred on the grill.

¼ cup mayonnaise
¼ cup sour cream
¼ cup buttermilk
2 tablespoons chopped mint
2 tablespoons chopped parsley
2 tablespoons snipped chives
1 teaspoon apple cider vinegar
Salt and freshly ground black pepper
1 pound thick-sliced bacon
¼ cup light brown sugar
½ teaspoon cayenne pepper
3 pounds Vidalia or other sweet onions, cut into 1-inch-thick slabs
Extra-virgin olive oil, for brushing
4 large ripe peaches, cut into ½-inch wedges

1. Preheat the oven to 325°. In a small bowl, whisk the mayonnaise, sour cream, buttermilk, mint, parsley, chives and vinegar; season with salt and black pepper. Refrigerate.
2. Line a large rimmed baking sheet with parchment paper. Arrange the bacon slices on the sheet in a single layer and sprinkle with the brown sugar and cayenne. Bake for about 25 minutes, until caramelized (the bacon will crisp as it cools). Let cool, then cut the bacon into bite-size pieces.
3. Meanwhile, light a grill or preheat a grill pan. Brush the onions with olive oil and season with salt and black pepper. Grill over moderate heat, turning occasionally, until softened and browned, 10 minutes. Separate the onions into rings. Brush the peaches with olive oil and grill over moderately high heat until tender, 2 minutes. Transfer to a plate.
4. In a large bowl, toss the onions with the peaches and bacon. Add the buttermilk dressing and toss to coat. Serve right away.
—*Linton Hopkins*

● HEALTHY ● MAKE AHEAD ○ VEGETARIAN ● STAFF FAVORITE

tomato and pineapple salad with garlic chips

Super Sprout Chopped Salad

⏲ TOTAL: 35 MIN • 4 SERVINGS ● ● ●

- 1 pound sweet potatoes, peeled and cut into 2-by-⅓-inch sticks
- 5 tablespoons extra-virgin olive oil

Salt

- 2 tablespoons fresh lemon juice
- 1 tablespoon *ume* vinegar (Japanese plum vinegar)
- 1 tablespoon raspberry vinegar
- 1 tablespoon tamari
- 1 teaspoon honey
- 2 cups lentil, mung or adzuki sprouts (see Sprouting Beans below)
- 1 romaine heart, coarsely chopped
- 4 small Japanese or Persian cucumbers, cut into ½-inch dice
- 2 cups packed mesclun
- 2 large scallions, finely chopped
- 8 oil-cured olives, pitted and chopped
- 1 firm, ripe Hass avocado, diced
- 1 tablespoon black sesame seeds

SPROUTING BEANS

Sprouted beans (or lentils) are super-nutritious and easy to make. Here, a step-by-step guide.

soaking In a wide-mouth 1-quart jar, cover ½ cup dried mung beans or green lentils with water. Cover the jar with a double layer of cheesecloth and secure with a rubber band. Let stand.

draining After 24 hours, drain and rinse the beans through the cheesecloth, then drain them again.

sprouting Store the jar in a dark place on its side, propping up the base so excess water drains onto paper towels. Rinse and drain the beans twice a day.

harvesting After 36 hours, the beans or lentils will grow tails and be ready to eat, but they taste best when the tails are about 1½ times as long as the beans. Rinse well, cover the jar loosely and refrigerate for up to 3 days.

1. Preheat the oven to 450°. Line a large rimmed baking sheet with parchment, add the sweet potato sticks and toss with 1 tablespoon of the olive oil; spread in an even layer. Season with salt and bake for about 12 minutes, until the sweet potatoes are just tender.

2. In a small bowl, combine the lemon juice, *ume* and raspberry vinegars, tamari and honey with the remaining ¼ cup of oil. Season the dressing with salt.

3. In another small bowl, toss the sprouts with 1 tablespoon of the dressing and let stand for 10 minutes, tossing a few times.

4. In a large bowl, combine the romaine, cucumbers, mesclun, scallions, olives and avocado and toss. Add the remaining dressing and toss well. Transfer the salad to a platter and top with the roasted sweet potatoes, followed by the marinated sprouts. Sprinkle with the black sesame seeds and serve. —*Adina Niemerow*

Escarole Salad with Clams and Grilled Corn

TOTAL: 1 HR • 6 SERVINGS ● ●

- 2 ears of corn, shucked
- ¼ cup extra-virgin olive oil, plus more for drizzling

Salt and freshly ground pepper

- ½ cup dry white wine
- 2 small shallots—1 thinly sliced, 1 minced
- 7 garlic cloves—4 smashed, 3 minced
- 1 bay leaf
- 2 dozen Manila clams, scrubbed
- 2 tablespoons fresh lemon juice

Finely grated zest of 1 lemon

- 2 plum tomatoes—peeled, seeded and cut into ¼-inch dice
- ½ pound tender escarole leaves, torn into bite-size pieces (8 cups)
- 4 ounces frisée, torn into bite-size pieces (4 cups)
- 2 celery ribs, peeled and shaved lengthwise with a vegetable peeler

1. Light a grill or preheat a grill pan. Drizzle the corn with oil; season with salt and pepper. Grill over moderately high heat, turning, until lightly charred all over, 15 minutes. Let cool, then cut the kernels off the cobs.

2. In a saucepan, bring the wine, sliced shallot, smashed garlic and bay leaf to a boil. Add the clams, cover and cook over moderately high heat until they open, 4 minutes. Using a slotted spoon, transfer the clams to a bowl; remove the clams from the shells and coarsely chop them.

3. Strain the clam broth into a small saucepan and boil over moderately high heat until reduced to 3 tablespoons, 10 minutes. Transfer to a small bowl and let cool. Add the lemon juice, lemon zest, tomatoes and the minced shallot and garlic. Stir in the ¼ cup of oil and season with salt and pepper.

4. In a bowl, combine the escarole, frisée, celery, corn and clams. Drizzle with the dressing, toss well and serve. —*Karen Nicolas*

WINE Briny, medium-bodied Vermentino: 2011 Poggio al Tesoro Solosole.

Charred Corn Salad with Mint, Parsley and Cilantro

⏲ TOTAL: 30 MIN • 4 SERVINGS ● ● ●

- 4 large ears of corn, shucked

Extra-virgin olive oil

Salt and freshly ground pepper

- ½ small red onion, thinly sliced
- 2½ tablespoons fresh lime juice
- 1 teaspoon pure maple syrup
- 1 jalapeño, seeded and thinly sliced
- 3 tablespoons torn mint leaves
- 3 tablespoons torn parsley leaves
- 3 tablespoons torn cilantro leaves

1. Heat a large grill pan. Brush the corn with olive oil and season with salt and pepper. Grill over moderately high heat, turning, until crisp-tender, about 12 minutes. Let cool.

2. Meanwhile, in a small bowl, combine the onion and lime juice and let stand for 10 minutes. Stir in the syrup, jalapeño and 2 tablespoons of oil and season with salt and pepper.

3. Working in a large bowl, cut the kernels off the cobs in sections. Add the onion dressing and toss. Add the mint, parsley and cilantro and toss again. Serve warm. —*Yotam Ottolenghi*

● HEALTHY ● MAKE AHEAD ● VEGETARIAN ● STAFF FAVORITE

charred corn salad with mint, parsley and cilantro

Beet and Onion Salad with Mint

**ACTIVE: 30 MIN; TOTAL: 1 HR 30 MIN
PLUS OVERNIGHT MACERATING
6 TO 8 SERVINGS** ● ● ○

For this lovely make-ahead salad, beets and onions macerate overnight in a lemony dressing. When they're available, young spring onions are especially delicious here.

- 2 pounds medium beets (about 5), scrubbed
- ¼ cup extra-virgin olive oil
- 3 tablespoons hazelnut oil
- ¼ cup plus 2 tablespoons fresh lemon juice
- 1 tablespoon honey
- Kosher salt
- 1 small white onion, cut into thin slivers
- ¼ cup coarsely chopped mint

1. In a saucepan, cover the beets with water and bring to a boil. Cook over moderate heat, adding more water as needed to keep the beets covered, until they are tender, about 1 hour. Drain the beets and let them cool. Peel the beets and slice into thin wedges.
2. In a bowl, whisk the olive oil and hazelnut oil with the lemon juice and honey. Season with salt. Add the beets and onion and toss to coat. Cover and refrigerate overnight, stirring once or twice. Garnish the salad with mint and serve. *—Eric Monkaba*

Spicy Raw Beet Slaw with Citrus, Scallions and Arugula

⏱ **TOTAL: 35 MIN • 10 TO 12 SERVINGS**
● ○

This tangy raw beet slaw gets a flavor boost from two kinds of citrus juice, cayenne pepper and toasted cumin and caraway seeds.

- 2 garlic cloves, minced
- 2 tablespoons fresh lemon juice
- 2 tablespoons fresh lime juice
- 1 teaspoon finely grated orange zest
- 1 teaspoon finely grated lemon zest
- ¼ teaspoon cayenne pepper
- ½ cup extra-virgin olive oil
- Salt
- ½ teaspoon cumin seeds
- ½ teaspoon caraway seeds
- 2 pounds medium beets, peeled and cut into fine julienne (see Note)
- 12 scallions, thinly sliced
- 1 jalapeño, seeded and minced
- 5 ounces baby arugula

1. In a small bowl, combine the garlic with the lemon and lime juices, orange and lemon zests and cayenne pepper and let stand for 10 minutes. Stir in the olive oil and season the dressing with salt.
2. In a skillet, toast the cumin and caraway seeds over moderate heat until fragrant, about 1 minute. Let cool completely, then grind coarsely in a spice mill or mortar.
3. In a large bowl, toss the ground spices with the beets, scallions and jalapeño. Add the dressing and toss to coat. Season with salt. Spread the arugula on a platter, mound the beet slaw on top and serve.
—David Tanis
NOTE To julienne beets, use a mandoline or the shredding disk of a food processor.

Lemony Beet and Beet Green Salad

**ACTIVE: 25 MIN; TOTAL: 1 HR 15 MIN
4 SERVINGS** ●

Buying beets with the beet greens still attached is like getting two ingredients in one. To turn them into this fabulous salad, roast the beets until they're sweet, blanch the greens until they're tender, toss both with olive oil and lemon, then top it all with white anchovies.

- 3 pounds baby beets with their greens, preferably Chioggia, scrubbed
- ¼ cup extra-virgin olive oil
- 1½ tablespoons freshly squeezed lemon juice
- ½ teaspoon finely grated lemon zest, plus more for garnish
- Salt and freshly ground black pepper
- 12 marinated white anchovies (also called *alici*)

1. Preheat the oven to 375°. Cut the greens from the beets and discard the stems. Put the beets in a small roasting pan and add ½ cup of water. Cover the roasting pan with aluminum foil and bake for about 45 minutes, until the beets are tender. When the beets are cool enough to handle, peel and slice them crosswise ⅓ inch thick.
2. In a large saucepan of salted boiling water, cook the beet greens until they are bright green and just tender, about 2 minutes. Drain the greens and let them cool. Lightly squeeze out the excess water from the greens and coarsely chop them.
3. In a large bowl, combine the olive oil with the lemon juice and the ½ teaspoon of lemon zest; season with salt and pepper. Stir in the sliced beets. Using a slotted spoon, transfer the beets to plates. Add the beet greens to the bowl, season with salt and pepper and toss with the remaining dressing in the bowl. Transfer the greens to the plates along with the white anchovies. Garnish the beet salad with lemon zest and serve.
—Marcia Kiesel
WINE Crisp, berry-scented rosé: 2011 Commanderie de la Bargemone.

DIY HERB PANTRY

herb oil
Blanch fresh herbs (such as basil, mint or tarragon), then puree with olive oil to use in dressings.

herb syrup
Infuse fresh herbs in simple syrup (sugar dissolved in water) for tea.

dried herbs
Tie fresh herbs into bundles, hang them to dry, then crumble into sauces.
—Grace Parisi

● HEALTHY ● MAKE AHEAD ○ VEGETARIAN ● STAFF FAVORITE

Chipotle-Roasted Baby Carrots
ACTIVE: 20 MIN; TOTAL: 1 HR
6 SERVINGS ● ● ● ●

30 thin baby carrots (2 to 3 bunches), tops discarded, carrots scrubbed
2 chipotle chiles in adobo, minced, plus 1 teaspoon of adobo sauce from the can
1 tablespoon unsulfured molasses
2½ tablespoons extra-virgin olive oil
Kosher salt and freshly ground pepper
3 tablespoons sesame seeds
4 ounces watercress, stems discarded
Plain Greek yogurt, for serving

1. Preheat the oven to 350°. Toss the carrots on a rimmed baking sheet with the chipotle chiles, molasses and 2 tablespoons of the olive oil; season with salt and pepper. Roast for 30 to 35 minutes, until the carrots are crisp-tender and browned. Transfer the carrots to a plate and let cool completely.
2. Meanwhile, in a skillet, toast the sesame seeds, tossing, until golden, 3 to 5 minutes. Stir in the remaining ½ tablespoon of oil and season with salt; let cool.
3. On the plate, toss the carrots with the 1 teaspoon of adobo sauce. Arrange the carrots on 6 plates and scatter the watercress on top. Garnish with the sesame seeds and serve with yogurt. —*Alex Stupak*

Moroccan Carrot Salad with Spicy Lemon Dressing
TOTAL: 45 MIN • 20 SERVINGS ● ●

¼ cup harissa (see Note)
⅔ cup fresh lemon juice
½ cup extra-virgin olive oil
Salt and freshly ground pepper
4 pounds carrots, julienned or coarsely shredded (about 12 cups; see Note)
2 cups raisins
4 cups flat-leaf parsley leaves
1 pound feta cheese, crumbled

1. In a large bowl, whisk the harissa with the lemon juice. Gradually whisk in the olive oil and season with salt and pepper.

2. Add the carrots, raisins, parsley and feta to the dressing and toss well. Serve lightly chilled or at room temperature.
—*Susan Feniger*
NOTE Harissa, a chile paste used in Tunisia and Morocco, is available at specialty food shops. Use a mandoline to julienne the carrots or a food processor to shred them.

Cellared-Vegetable Salad
ACTIVE: 25 MIN; TOTAL: 1 HR
4 SERVINGS ● ●

2 medium golden beets (¾ pound), peeled and cut into ½-inch chunks
2 medium turnips (¾ pound), peeled and cut into ½-inch chunks
2 parsnips (¾ pound), peeled and cut into ½-inch chunks
1 celery root (1 pound), peeled and cut into ½-inch chunks
1½ teaspoons chopped rosemary
¼ cup plus 3 tablespoons extra-virgin olive oil
Salt and freshly ground black pepper
1 tablespoon minced shallot
2 tablespoons fresh orange juice
1½ tablespoons white balsamic vinegar
½ teaspoon honey
3 cups packed mizuna

1. Preheat the oven to 400°. Put the beets and turnips on one large rimmed baking sheet and the parsnips and celery root on another. Sprinkle with the rosemary and drizzle 1½ tablespoons of the olive oil over each pan of vegetables; toss well. Arrange the vegetables in an even layer and season with salt and pepper. Bake in the upper and lower thirds of the oven for about 35 minutes, until the vegetables are tender and golden brown. Switch the pans halfway through baking. Let cool slightly.
2. In a bowl, mix the remaining ¼ cup of olive oil with the shallot, orange juice, vinegar and honey and season with salt and pepper.
3. Transfer the roasted vegetables to a serving bowl. Add the vinaigrette and mizuna, toss the salad well and serve.
—*Art Smith*

Four-Herb Tabbouleh
TOTAL: 45 MIN • 6 SERVINGS ● ●
This refreshing tabbouleh, which uses Israeli couscous in place of bulgur, follows the Lebanese tradition of including more herbs than grain. F&W's Grace Parisi adds lovage, which has a light, bright flavor that's similar to celery leaves, as well as parsley.

¼ cup plus 3 tablespoons extra-virgin olive oil
2 large garlic cloves
1 cup Israeli couscous (6 ounces)
Salt
3 tablespoons freshly squeezed lemon juice
Freshly ground pepper
2 cups tender flat-leaf parsley leaves
1 cup lovage leaves or tender light-green celery leaves
½ cup mint leaves
¼ cup snipped chives
1 jalapeño—halved, seeded and thinly sliced crosswise
1 pint grape tomatoes, quartered
1 seedless cucumber, peeled and finely diced

1. In a medium saucepan, heat 1 tablespoon of the olive oil with the garlic cloves and cook over moderate heat until the garlic is lightly browned in spots, about 2 minutes. Add the Israeli couscous and cook, stirring, until lightly browned, about 2 minutes. Add 1¼ cups of water, season with salt and bring to a boil. Cover and cook over low heat until the couscous is tender and the water has been absorbed, about 10 minutes.
2. Pick out the garlic cloves from the couscous and mash them to a paste. Transfer the garlic paste to a large bowl and whisk in the lemon juice and the remaining ¼ cup plus 2 tablespoons of oil. Season with salt and pepper and stir in the couscous. Refrigerate for 10 minutes, just until no longer warm.
3. Add the parsley, lovage, mint, chives, jalapeño, grape tomatoes and cucumber to the couscous and toss well. Season the tabbouleh with salt and pepper and serve.
—*Grace Parisi*

● HEALTHY ● MAKE AHEAD ● VEGETARIAN ● STAFF FAVORITE

four-herb tabbouleh

Melon, Berry and Feta Salad

⏱ **TOTAL: 20 MIN • 6 SERVINGS** ● ● ●

For this versatile salad, you can use whatever melon looks best at the market and swap out the chives for mint.

- 2 tablespoons extra-virgin olive oil
- 2 tablespoons fresh lemon juice
- 1 small shallot, thinly sliced
- ½ teaspoon minced preserved lemon peel or lemon zest
- ¼ teaspoon crushed red pepper

Salt and freshly ground black pepper

- ½ green melon (about 1¼ pounds)—halved, cut into wedges, peeled and thinly sliced
- ½ orange or yellow melon (about 1¼ pounds)—halved, cut into wedges, peeled and thinly sliced
- 1 cup blackberries
- 2 ounces feta cheese, cut into thin slices
- 2 tablespoons snipped chives

1. In a bowl, combine the oil, lemon juice, shallot, preserved lemon and crushed red pepper; season with salt and black pepper.
2. Arrange the melon slices and blackberries on a platter. Drizzle the dressing over the fruit. Garnish the salad with the feta and snipped chives and serve. —*Jenn Louis*
WINE Delicate, berry-scented rosé Champagne: NV Gatinois Brut Rosé.

UTENSIL TIP

serving style These beech wood "serving hands" from Nigella Lawson's Living Kitchen by BlissHome give cooks more control when tossing and serving salad. *$39; amazon.com.*

Pita and Chopped Vegetable Salad

⏱ **TOTAL: 35 MIN • 6 SERVINGS** ● ●

In the Middle East, a salad of fried bits of pita bread and fresh chopped vegetables tossed in a vinaigrette is called *fattoush*. The unconventional version here is from the mother of Sami Tamimi, the head chef at Ottolenghi in London; she bucks tradition by toasting the pita and tossing the salad in a tangy buttermilk dressing.

- ¼ cup extra-virgin olive oil, plus more for drizzling
- 2 garlic cloves, minced
- 2 tablespoons fresh lemon juice
- 2 tablespoons white wine vinegar
- 2 teaspoons dried mint

Salt and freshly ground pepper

- 6 radishes, thinly sliced
- 4 small Turkish or Japanese cucumbers (½ pound), cut into ½-inch dice
- 3 large tomatoes (1½ pounds), cut into 1-inch dice
- 2 scallions, thinly sliced
- ¼ cup torn parsley leaves
- 2 tablespoons torn fresh mint leaves
- 1 large, thin pita or naan, toasted until crisp and torn into bite-size pieces
- 1 cup organic buttermilk
- 1 tablespoon sumac (see Note)

1. In a small bowl, whisk the ¼ cup of olive oil with the garlic, lemon juice, vinegar and dried mint; season the dressing with salt and freshly ground pepper.
2. In a large bowl, toss the radishes, cucumbers, tomatoes, scallions, parsley and fresh mint. Add the pita, drizzle with the dressing and toss well. Let stand for 5 to 10 minutes.
3. Add the buttermilk and toss again. Season with salt and freshly ground pepper. Drizzle the salad with olive oil, sprinkle with the sumac and serve.
—*Yotam Ottolenghi and Sami Tamimi*
NOTE Sumac is a Middle Eastern spice prized for its super-tangy flavor. It is available at specialty stores and *penzeys.com.*

Eggplant, Pear and Pecorino Salad

⏱ **TOTAL: 30 MIN • 4 SERVINGS** ● ●

There's a saying in Italy: Don't tell a farmer just how good his cheese and pears taste together (presumably because if he knew, he would hoard them all). This salad adds eggplant and walnuts to that beloved duo.

- ⅓ cup walnuts

One 1¼-pound eggplant, peeled and sliced lengthwise ¼ inch thick

Extra-virgin olive oil

Salt and freshly ground pepper

- 1 tablespoon unsalted butter
- 2 Bosc pears—peeled, cored and sliced lengthwise ¼ inch thick
- 1 tablespoon Cognac or other brandy
- 1 small garlic clove, minced
- 1½ tablespoons red wine vinegar
- 2 tablespoons chopped parsley
- 1 tablespoon chopped chives
- 1 tablespoon honey

Thin shavings of Pecorino Toscano cheese

1. Preheat the oven to 350°. In a pie plate, toast the walnuts for about 5 minutes, until lightly browned. Let cool, then coarsely chop.
2. Light a grill or preheat a grill pan. Brush eggplant with oil; season with salt and pepper. Grill over moderately high heat until lightly browned and tender, 2 minutes per side.
3. In a large skillet, melt the butter. Add the pear slices and cook over moderate heat, tossing, until just starting to soften, 3 minutes. Add the Cognac and toss the pears to coat thoroughly; remove from the heat.
4. In a small bowl, whisk 3 tablespoons of oil with the garlic, vinegar, 1 tablespoon of the parsley and ½ tablespoon of the chives. Season the vinaigrette with salt and pepper.
5. Arrange the eggplant slices on a platter and drizzle with the vinaigrette. Arrange the pear slices over the eggplant and drizzle with the honey. Scatter the walnuts, cheese and the remaining 1 tablespoon of parsley and ½ tablespoon of chives over the top. Serve. —*Silvana Baranzoni*
WINE Dry, black cherry–scented Lambrusco: 2010 Opera 02 Operapura.

● HEALTHY ● MAKE AHEAD ● VEGETARIAN ● STAFF FAVORITE

melon, berry and feta salad

Brown Butter Chicken Jus with Citrus and Greens

ACTIVE: 45 MIN; TOTAL: 1 HR 15 MIN
4 SERVINGS ●

This dish is loosely based on one that chef René Redzepi makes at Noma, his acclaimed Copenhagen restaurant. Redzepi doesn't serve much meat at Noma; instead, he uses tricks like turning a richly flavored chicken jus into a sauce for salad.

- 2 whole chicken legs, split, or 2 drumsticks and 2 thighs

  Salt and freshly ground black pepper
- 1 tablespoon vegetable oil
- 1 small onion, coarsely chopped
- 1 small carrot, coarsely chopped
- ½ cup dry red wine
- 2 tablespoons unsalted butter
- 12 walnut halves
- 4 mandarin oranges
- 1 large pink grapefruit
- 1 orange
- 1 Meyer lemon (optional)
- 24 paper-thin slices of peeled ginger
- 1 kumquat, very thinly sliced crosswise
- 2 cups small or torn mixed red lettuce and radicchio leaves
- ½ cup mixed flat-leaf parsley and cilantro leaves

  Pinch of cayenne pepper

1. Cut the meat from the chicken legs, then cut the meat and any skin into 1-inch pieces; reserve the bones. Season the meat with salt and black pepper.

2. In a medium skillet, heat the vegetable oil. Add the chicken bones and meat and cook over high heat, stirring occasionally, until richly browned, about 6 minutes. Add the onion and carrot and cook, stirring, until browned, about 4 minutes. Add the wine and boil until reduced to 2 tablespoons, about 2 minutes. Add 1 cup of water and boil until reduced by two-thirds, about 3 minutes. Add another 1½ cups of water and simmer over low heat until reduced to 1 cup, about 25 minutes. Strain the stock into a small saucepan. Skim off the fat and boil the stock over high heat until reduced to ⅓ cup, about 3 minutes.

3. In a small skillet, cook the butter over moderate heat until it becomes nutty brown, about 2 minutes. Pour into the chicken jus.

4. Preheat the oven to 350°. In a pie plate, toast the walnuts for about 6 minutes, until golden. Let cool, then break them in half.

5. Cut the skins and white pith from the mandarins, grapefruit, orange and lemon. Cut in between the membranes to release the sections into a bowl. Cut the grapefruit, orange and lemon sections in thirds.

6. Arrange the citrus pieces on plates along with the walnut pieces, ginger slices and kumquat. Scatter the lettuce, radicchio and herbs around the plate. Bring the brown butter chicken jus to a simmer, whisking, and season with salt, black pepper and cayenne. Drizzle the brown butter sauce over the citrus and garnishes and serve right away. —René Redzepi

WINE Crisp, steely Italian white: 2010 Fontezoppa Verdicchio di Matelica.

Citrus Salad with Creamy Poppy Seed Dressing

TOTAL: 40 MIN • 8 SERVINGS ● ●

Adding limes to this salad gives it a distinctly tart flavor, but feel free to leave them out and use more oranges or grapefruit instead.

- 6 oranges
- 2 red grapefruits
- 2 limes
- 1 large shallot, very thinly sliced
- ½ cup coarsely chopped flat-leaf parsley
- 1 teaspoon finely grated lemon zest
- 2 tablespoons freshly squeezed lemon juice
- ¼ cup crème fraîche or sour cream
- 2 tablespoons pure maple syrup
- 1 teaspoon poppy seeds

  Salt

1. Using a sharp knife, carefully peel the oranges, grapefruits and limes, removing all of the bitter white pith. Working over a small bowl to catch the juices from the fruit, cut in between the membranes to release the citrus sections. Cut the lime and grapefruit

sections into thirds; leave the orange sections whole. Transfer all of the citrus to a serving bowl and add the sliced shallot and chopped parsley. Reserve the citrus juice for another use.

2. In another small bowl, whisk the lemon zest with the lemon juice, crème fraîche, maple syrup and poppy seeds. Season the dressing lightly with salt. Pour the dressing over the fruit, toss the salad gently and serve right away. —Grace Parisi

Fennel and Citrus Salad with Mint

TOTAL: 30 MIN • 4 SERVINGS ● ●

For his light, simple salad, San Francisco chef Matthew Accarrino mixes grapefruit and orange segments with shaved fennel and a sweet-tart honey-lemon dressing.

- 2 red grapefruits
- 2 navel oranges
- 2 tablespoons extra-virgin olive oil
- 1 tablespoon honey
- 1 tablespoon fresh lemon juice

  Salt
- 2 fennel bulbs—halved, cored and thinly sliced on a mandoline, 2 tablespoons of chopped fronds reserved for garnish
- 2 tablespoons small mint leaves
- ½ teaspoon ground coriander

1. Using a sharp knife, cut the skin and white pith from the grapefruits and oranges. Working over a bowl, cut between the membranes to release the sections into the bowl. Squeeze the membranes to extract the juice.

2. In a small bowl, stir the olive oil with the honey and lemon juice. Add 3 tablespoons of the citrus juice and season with salt. Reserve the remaining citrus juice for another use.

3. In a shallow serving bowl, toss the fennel slices and citrus sections with the honey-lemon dressing. Garnish with the chopped fennel fronds, mint leaves and ground coriander and serve the salad right away. —Matthew Accarrino

WINE Lively white from Greece: 2011 Gai'a Thalassitis Assyrtiko.

fennel and citrus salad with mint

Spring Panzanella with Asparagus

⏱ **TOTAL: 45 MIN • 8 SERVINGS** ●

Recipes for panzanella (a Florentine bread salad popular in the summer) typically call for tomatoes, but in the spring, chef Mike Lata of Fig restaurant in Charleston, South Carolina, prefers using seasonal ingredients like asparagus and radishes.

4 large eggs
Four thin slices of peasant bread, torn into 1-inch pieces
¼ cup plus 2 tablespoons extra-virgin olive oil, plus more for brushing
2 pounds fat asparagus, peeled
¼ cup red wine vinegar
Salt and freshly ground pepper
2 cups packed young mustard greens or chicory
½ small red onion, thinly sliced
¼ pound *ricotta salata,* thinly sliced and crumbled
1 watermelon radish or 2 large red radishes, very thinly sliced

1. Preheat the oven to 350°. Put the eggs in a saucepan of water and bring to a simmer over moderately high heat. Simmer for 6 minutes. Drain the saucepan and fill it with cold water. Crack the eggs all over and let them stand in the water for 1 minute. Peel and thickly slice the eggs; the yolks will be barely cooked but not runny.

2. Spread the torn bread pieces on a baking sheet and brush lightly with olive oil. Bake for about 12 minutes, until crisp.

3. Meanwhile, in a large pot of salted boiling water, cook the asparagus until just tender, about 3 minutes. Drain and cool the asparagus, then cut in half lengthwise.

4. In a small bowl, combine the ¼ cup plus 2 tablespoons of olive oil with the vinegar; season with salt and pepper. In a large bowl, toss the asparagus, toasted bread, greens, onion and cheese. Drizzle with the dressing and toss. Garnish with the eggs and radish and serve the panzanella right away.
—*Mike Lata*

WINE Citrusy Sauvignon Blanc: 2010 Teira.

Morel and Asparagus Salad with Frisée and Butter Lettuce

⏱ **TOTAL: 35 MIN • 8 SERVINGS** ●

When morels are in season, chef Siegfried Danler of Pauly Saal restaurant in Berlin prepares them as simply as possible, as in this salad with asparagus, frisée and butter lettuce. The rest of the year, the dish can be made with dried morels that have been rehydrated in hot water.

4 tablespoons unsalted butter
3 dozen small fresh morels, rinsed, or dried morels soaked in boiling water for 30 minutes, drained and rinsed
½ cup chicken stock or low-sodium broth
1 pound asparagus—tough ends discarded, asparagus halved lengthwise and cut into 2-inch lengths
Salt and freshly ground pepper
2 tablespoons extra-virgin olive oil
1 tablespoon fresh lemon juice
5 ounces frisée, torn into bite-size pieces
1 medium head of butter lettuce, torn
2 tablespoons small chervil sprigs
Argan oil, for drizzling (optional; see Note)

1. In a large skillet, melt the butter. Add the morels and stock, cover and cook over moderately high heat until softened, 5 minutes. Add the asparagus, cover and cook until crisp-tender, about 2 minutes. Season with salt and pepper and cook uncovered until the broth is nearly absorbed, 1 minute longer.

2. In a large bowl, whisk the olive oil with the lemon juice and season with salt and pepper. Add the frisée, butter lettuce and chervil and toss to coat. Arrange the morels and asparagus on plates and mound the salad alongside. Drizzle with argan oil, if using, and serve.
—*Siegfried Danler*

NOTE Argan oil, which has an intense, nutty flavor, is available at *zamourispices.com*.

WINE Fresh, concentrated German Riesling: 2010 Mönchhof Mosel Slate Spätlese.

Grilled Asparagus Salad

⏱ **TOTAL: 40 MIN • 6 SERVINGS** ●

Celebrity chef and grilling master Bobby Flay makes this delightful grilled asparagus salad with sweet grape tomatoes, briny kalamata olives and sharp white cheddar cheese. Each bite of salad brings out a different combination of ingredients.

1 pound asparagus
½ cup extra-virgin olive oil, plus more for brushing
Salt and freshly ground pepper
4 cups lightly packed mesclun
1 seedless cucumber, cut into ½-inch dice
1 cup grape tomatoes, halved
1 cup drained and rinsed canned chickpeas
½ cup pitted kalamata olives, coarsely chopped (3 ounces)
8 ounces sharp white cheddar cheese, cut into ¼-inch dice
3 tablespoons fresh orange juice
1 tablespoon fresh lemon juice
1 tablespoon red wine vinegar
1 teaspoon Dijon mustard
1 teaspoon grainy mustard
1 tablespoon chopped tarragon
3 cups pita chips

1. Light a grill or preheat a grill pan. Brush the asparagus with olive oil and season with salt and freshly ground pepper. Grill over high heat, turning, until tender, about 5 minutes. Let cool, then cut the asparagus into 1-inch pieces.

2. In a large bowl, toss the mesclun with the grilled asparagus, cucumber, tomatoes, chickpeas, olives and cheese.

3. In a small bowl, whisk the orange juice with the lemon juice, red wine vinegar, Dijon and grainy mustards and a pinch each of salt and freshly ground pepper. Gradually whisk in the ½ cup of olive oil until emulsified; add the tarragon. Pour the dressing over the salad and toss. Garnish with pita chips and serve. —*Bobby Flay*

WINE Tart, citrusy Spanish white: 2011 Txomin Etxaniz Txakoli.

● HEALTHY ● MAKE AHEAD ● VEGETARIAN ● STAFF FAVORITE

spring panzanella with asparagus

White Asparagus Salad with Creamy Tomato Dressing

⏱ **TOTAL: 30 MIN • 6 SERVINGS** ● ● ●

 5 large plum tomatoes—4 cut into wedges, 1 coarsely chopped
 2 tablespoons fresh lemon juice
 ½ teaspoon Dijon mustard
 ½ teaspoon sugar
 ½ cup mayonnaise
 3 tablespoons extra-virgin olive oil, plus more for drizzling
Salt and freshly ground black pepper
 1 pound green beans, preferably romano beans
 ½ small red onion, thinly sliced
One 12-ounce jar or tin of white asparagus, preferably from Navarra, drained

1. In a blender, puree the coarsely chopped tomato with the lemon juice, mustard and sugar. Add the mayonnaise and the 3 tablespoons of olive oil and blend until thick. Season the dressing with salt and pepper.
2. In a large saucepan of salted boiling water, cook the green beans until tender, 4 minutes. Drain and let cool to room temperature, then drizzle the beans lightly with olive oil and season lightly with salt and pepper.
3. Arrange the beans, tomato wedges, onion and asparagus on a platter. Drizzle the dressing over the vegetables and serve.
—*Alex Raij*

Poached Salmon Salad

⏱ **TOTAL: 30 MIN • 4 SERVINGS** ● ●

 2 shallots, thinly sliced
 ½ cup dill sprigs, plus chopped dill for garnish
 1 pound skinless salmon fillet
 2 cups semidry white wine, such as Riesling
 ¼ cup prepared horseradish, drained
 2 tablespoons mayonnaise
 2 tablespoons canola oil
Salt and freshly ground white pepper
One 15-ounce can butter beans— drained, rinsed and patted dry
 4 cups tender escarole leaves, torn

1. Put the shallots and dill sprigs in a saucepan and top with the salmon fillet. Add the wine and 2 cups of water and bring to a boil. Simmer over very low heat until the salmon is nearly cooked through, 5 minutes; transfer to a plate and let cool slightly. Break the salmon into large flakes and then freeze for 5 minutes to cool.
2. Meanwhile, strain the fish poaching broth, reserving 3 tablespoons of the broth and 2 tablespoons of the shallots; discard the dill. Chop the shallots and transfer to a large bowl. Add the horseradish and mayonnaise, then whisk in the reserved poaching broth and the oil; season with salt and pepper.
3. Add the butter beans and escarole to the dressing and toss. Add the salmon and toss gently. Garnish with chopped dill and serve.
—*Grace Parisi*

WINE Bright, full-bodied Austrian Riesling: 2011 Loimer Kamptal.

Smoked Fish Salad with Pickled Beans and Eggs

⏱ **TOTAL: 40 MIN • 4 SERVINGS** ● ●

 1 pound small Bintje, Yukon Gold or other yellow potatoes, halved but not peeled
Salt
 1 cup pickled green beans or yellow wax beans, drained and cut into 2-inch lengths, plus 2 tablespoons of the pickling liquid
 2 tablespoons cider vinegar
 1 tablespoon plus 1 teaspoon Dijon mustard
 1 tablespoon honey
 ½ teaspoon yellow mustard seeds
Pinch of cayenne pepper
 ¼ cup vegetable oil
Freshly ground black pepper
 4 ounces upland cress or watercress (4 cups)
 ½ cup small parsley sprigs
 2 celery ribs, cut into 1½-inch-by-¼-inch sticks
 ½ pound smoked bluefish, mackerel or trout, skinned and coarsely shredded
 2 hard-cooked eggs, quartered

1. Put the potatoes in a medium saucepan and cover with water. Add a large pinch of salt and bring to a boil. Boil over moderately high heat until just tender, about 10 minutes. Drain and transfer to a large bowl.
2. Meanwhile, in a small bowl, whisk the pickling liquid, vinegar, mustard, honey, mustard seeds and cayenne. Whisk in the oil; season with salt and black pepper.
3. Add 2 tablespoons of the dressing to the warm potatoes and toss. Add the cress, parsley, celery, pickled beans, smoked fish and the remaining dressing and toss well. Transfer the salad to plates, arrange the eggs on top and serve. —*Spike Gjerde*

Grilled Cucumber and Smoked Trout Salad with Hazelnuts

⏱ **TOTAL: 40 MIN • 4 SERVINGS** ● ●

 ¼ cup hazelnuts
 4 mini cucumbers (Persian), sliced diagonally ¼ inch thick
 2 tablespoons canola oil, plus more for grilling
Kosher salt and freshly ground pepper
 1 garlic clove, minced
 1 anchovy fillet, mashed
 1 tablespoon cider vinegar
 1 tablespoon chopped dill
Pinch of sugar
 ½ pound smoked trout fillets, skinned and flaked
 4 cups mesclun (about 2½ ounces)

1. Preheat the oven to 350°. Bake the hazelnuts in a pie plate for 12 minutes, until the skins blister. Let cool, then rub in a kitchen towel to remove the skins; coarsely chop.
2. Preheat a grill pan. Toss the cucumbers with oil and season with salt and pepper. Working in 2 batches, grill over high heat, turning once, until lightly charred, 3 minutes.
3. In a bowl, mash the garlic and anchovy to a paste using the back of a spoon. Add the vinegar, dill and sugar and whisk in the 2 tablespoons of oil. Season with salt and pepper, add the grilled cucumbers and let stand until cool. Add the trout, mesclun and hazelnuts, toss well and serve. —*Paul Berglund*

Kale Salad with Chicken

⏱ ACTIVE: 20 MIN; TOTAL: 45 MIN
4 SERVINGS ● ●

For this hearty main-course salad, Baltimore chef Spike Gjerde tosses raw Tuscan kale, shredded chicken and crunchy croutons in a pungent Caesar-like dressing made with anchovies and Worcestershire sauce. "Kale salads are great with a dressing that relies on cured fish like anchovies or the oysters I salt-cure for 40 days at my restaurant, which I call 'oy-chovies.'"

Four 4-by-½-inch slices of peasant bread
2 garlic cloves—1 peeled, 1 minced
¼ cup freshly grated Parmigiano-Reggiano cheese (1 ounce)
4 anchovies, minced
3 tablespoons malt vinegar
2 tablespoons fresh lemon juice
1 tablespoon Worcestershire sauce
⅓ cup extra-virgin olive oil
Salt and freshly ground pepper
½ pound Tuscan kale, stems trimmed and leaves thinly sliced crosswise
Two 3-ounce jars cocktail onions, drained and halved
3 cups shredded rotisserie chicken

1. Preheat the oven to 350°. Arrange the bread on a baking sheet and toast for about 10 minutes, until crisp. Rub the hot toast with the peeled garlic clove, sprinkle with 2 tablespoons of the cheese and bake for about 10 minutes longer, until the cheese browns. Let cool, then break into 1-inch croutons.
2. In a small bowl, whisk the anchovies, minced garlic, vinegar, lemon juice, Worcestershire sauce and the remaining 2 tablespoons of Parmigiano-Reggiano cheese. Whisk in the olive oil; season the dressing with salt and freshly ground pepper.
3. In a large bowl, toss the kale with 6 tablespoons of the dressing. Let stand for 3 minutes. Add the onions, chicken, croutons and remaining dressing. Toss and serve.
—Spike Gjerde
WINE Zippy California Sauvignon Blanc: 2010 Heron Napa Valley.

Walnut-Cranberry Turkey Salad

⏱ TOTAL: 20 MIN • 6 SERVINGS ● ●

The dressing for this light, delicious turkey salad is made with yogurt, low-fat mayonnaise and chopped herbs.

1 cup walnuts (4 ounces)
¾ cup low-fat plain Greek yogurt
¼ cup low-fat mayonnaise
¼ cup chopped flat-leaf parsley
¼ cup snipped chives
1 tablespoon chopped tarragon
Salt and freshly ground pepper
1¼ pounds roast turkey, diced (4 cups; see Note)
¾ cup dried cranberries
8 ounces mixed greens, such as baby kale, baby arugula and chopped radicchio (8 packed cups)
2 tablespoons extra-virgin olive oil
1 tablespoon fresh lemon juice

1. Preheat the oven to 350°. Spread the walnuts in a pie plate and toast for about 10 minutes, until golden and fragrant. Let cool, then coarsely chop the nuts.
2. In a large bowl, whisk the yogurt with the mayonnaise, parsley, chives and tarragon and season with salt and freshly ground pepper. Fold in the turkey, dried cranberries and chopped walnuts.
3. In another large bowl, toss the mixed greens with the olive oil and lemon juice; season with salt and freshly ground pepper. Mound the mixed green salad on a platter and top with the turkey salad. Serve right away. —Grace Parisi
NOTE You can use any leftover turkey from Grace's Roast Beer-Brined Turkey with Onion Gravy and Bacon (page 161) or store-bought roast turkey

Smoked Duck Salad with Walnuts and Raspberries

⏱ TOTAL: 30 MIN • 4 SERVINGS ●

Traditional southwestern French flavors—meaty duck breasts, duck cracklings, toasted walnuts and nut oil—pair with sweet, tangy raspberries and slightly bitter frisée to make this completely original salad.

½ pound smoked duck breast—skin and fat removed and reserved, breast thinly sliced crosswise
½ cup walnuts
2 tablespoons sherry vinegar
2½ teaspoons Dijon mustard
1 small shallot, very finely chopped
3 tablespoons walnut oil
1 tablespoon vegetable oil
Salt and freshly ground black pepper
6 ounces frisée lettuce, torn into bite-size pieces (6 cups)
3 cups packed torn Boston lettuce
1 cup raspberries

1. Preheat the oven to 350°. Spread the duck skin and fat in a pie plate and bake for about 15 minutes, until crisp. Drain on paper towels, then break into pieces.
2. Meanwhile, spread the walnuts in a pie plate and toast until fragrant, about 8 minutes. Let cool, then coarsely chop the nuts.
3. In a large bowl, mix the vinegar with the mustard and shallot. Gradually whisk in the walnut and vegetable oils. Season generously with salt and pepper. Add the frisée, Boston lettuce and walnuts and toss to coat. Top the salad with the raspberries, sliced duck breast and cracklings and serve.
—Marcia Kiesel
WINE Vibrant, lightly fruity Bordeaux rosé: 2011 Rosé de Haut-Bailly.

SUPER-SIMPLE SALAD

broccoli matchsticks and kale

In a bowl, season 1 pound sliced kale and 3 peeled, julienned broccoli stems with salt; squeeze with your hands to soften. Sauté 2 thinly sliced leeks in ¼ cup olive oil until softened. Add 2 tablespoons fresh lemon juice and pour over the broccoli and kale. Let stand for 2 minutes, then toss with ½ cup toasted, chopped hazelnuts and ½ cup shredded Pecorino Romano.
—Grace Parisi

F&W's Grace Parisi at her home in Brooklyn, New York; she adds toasted angel hair pasta to her quick root-vegetable minestrone, OPPOSITE; recipe, page 68.

SOUPS

Curried Cauliflower Soup with Coconut and Chiles

TOTAL: 1 HR 15 MIN • 6 SERVINGS ● ● ○

Chef Annie Somerville of Greens Restaurant in San Francisco makes this healthy vegan cauliflower soup with southern Indian flavors, including unsweetened coconut milk, cilantro and a sweet, fragrant curry spice blend. The thinly sliced jalapeño served on top adds a bright, fresh heat.

One 1¾-pound head of cauliflower, cored—one-third cut into ¾-inch florets, the rest coarsely chopped
2 tablespoons extra-virgin olive oil
Salt and freshly ground black pepper
1½ teaspoons cumin seeds
1½ teaspoons coriander seeds
1½ teaspoons fennel seeds
½ teaspoon ground turmeric
¼ teaspoon ground cinnamon
⅛ teaspoon ground allspice
¼ teaspoon cayenne pepper
1 large onion, thinly sliced
2 tablespoons coarsely grated peeled fresh ginger
1 tablespoon minced garlic
¼ cup dry white wine
1 baking potato (about 8 ounces), peeled and cut into ½-inch pieces
1 quart vegetable stock, preferably homemade
½ cup unsweetened coconut milk
¼ cup chopped cilantro, 1 seeded and thinly sliced jalapeño and lime wedges, for serving

1. Preheat the oven to 400°. In a medium baking dish, toss the cauliflower florets with ½ tablespoon of the olive oil. Season with salt and black pepper and roast on the top shelf of the oven for about 20 minutes, until tender but not browned.
2. Meanwhile, in a small skillet, combine the cumin, coriander and fennel seeds and toast over moderate heat, shaking the pan, until fragrant, about 2 minutes. Transfer the seeds to a spice grinder and let cool. Add the turmeric, cinnamon, allspice and cayenne pepper and pulse until finely ground.

3. In a large pot, heat the remaining 1½ tablespoons of olive oil. Add the onion and cook over moderate heat, stirring, until softened, about 5 minutes. Add the ginger, garlic and spice blend and cook, stirring, for 1 minute. Add the wine and cook until evaporated, about 2 minutes. Add the chopped cauliflower, potato and stock and bring to a boil. Simmer over moderate heat until the vegetables are very tender, about 20 minutes.
4. Working in batches, puree the soup in a blender until smooth and silky. Return the soup to the pot and add the coconut milk. Season with salt and black pepper and simmer for about 5 minutes.
5. Ladle the soup into bowls and pass the roasted cauliflower, cilantro, jalapeño and lime wedges at the table. —*Annie Somerville*
MAKE AHEAD The soup can be refrigerated for up to 4 days. Reheat gently.
WINE Lively, green apple–inflected Pinot Gris: 2010 Boomtown.

Red Kuri Squash Soup

ACTIVE: 25 MIN; TOTAL: 50 MIN
4 SERVINGS ● ● ○ ○

Legendary chef Alice Waters uses sweet, nutty Red Kuri squash, but her silky soup can be made with any variety of winter squash.

1½ pounds Red Kuri or butternut squash, peeled and cut into 1-inch cubes (3 cups)
½ medium onion, coarsely chopped
1 bay leaf
1 medium fennel bulb, cored and cut into thin wedges
1 tablespoon extra-virgin olive oil, plus more for drizzling
Salt and freshly ground black pepper
1 tablespoon unsalted butter
Chopped toasted pecans and small marjoram leaves, for garnish

1. Preheat the oven to 375°. In a large saucepan, combine the cubed squash with the chopped onion, bay leaf and 3 cups of water and bring to a boil over high heat. Cover and simmer over low heat until the squash is tender, about 20 minutes.

2. Meanwhile, spread the fennel wedges on a large rimmed baking sheet and toss them with the 1 tablespoon of olive oil. Season the fennel with salt and pepper and toss well. Roast for about 25 minutes, until the fennel is tender and starting to brown.
3. Discard the bay leaf from the soup. Working in batches, puree the soup in a blender. Return the soup to the saucepan and warm over low heat. Stir in the butter and season with salt and pepper. Ladle the soup into bowls and garnish with the roasted fennel, pecans, marjoram leaves and a drizzle of olive oil. —*Alice Waters*
WINE Strawberry-and-cinnamon-inflected Pinot Noir: 2008 Mac Forbes Yarra Valley.

Smoky Butternut Squash Soup

ACTIVE: 30 MIN; TOTAL: 1 HR
8 SERVINGS ● ●

2 tablespoons unsalted butter
1 medium onion, finely chopped
One 3-pound butternut squash, peeled and diced (8 cups)
1 small canned chipotle in adobo, chopped
7 cups chicken or turkey stock or low-sodium broth
2 tablespoons honey
Salt
1 cup crème fraîche
¼ cup finely chopped chives, plus more for garnish

1. In a large pot, melt the butter. Add the onion and cook over moderate heat until softened, about 5 minutes. Stir in the squash and chipotle and cook for 1 minute. Add the stock and honey and bring to a boil. Simmer until the squash is tender, about 30 minutes.
2. Puree the soup in a blender until smooth. Season with salt.
3. In a microwave-safe bowl, stir the crème fraîche with the ¼ cup of chopped chives. Microwave until just melted, 30 seconds. Serve the soup with a swirl of chive cream and a sprinkling of chives. —*Grace Parisi*
WINE Juicy, light-bodied Beaujolais: 2011 Terres Dorées L'Ancien.

● HEALTHY ● MAKE AHEAD ○ VEGETARIAN ● STAFF FAVORITE

smoky butternut squash soup

Curried Carrot Soup with Tarragon Oil

ACTIVE: 30 MIN; TOTAL: 1 HR 15 MIN
8 SERVINGS ● ● ●

To make this healthy, low-fat soup especially tasty, chef Naomi Pomeroy of Beast in Portland, Oregon, cooks the carrots with Madras curry powder, ginger and garlic. She adds a little bit of Tabasco sauce and a drizzle of tarragon-infused oil before serving.

- ¾ cup extra-virgin olive oil
- 1 large white onion, coarsely chopped
- 2 garlic cloves, thinly sliced
- 1 tablespoon minced peeled fresh ginger
- 2 teaspoons Madras curry powder
- 1½ pounds carrots, thinly sliced
- 1 teaspoon sugar

Salt and freshly ground pepper

- 2 medium bunches of tarragon
- 1 cup flat-leaf parsley leaves
- ½ teaspoon finely grated lemon zest

Tabasco

Snipped chives, for garnish

1. In a large pot, heat ¼ cup of the olive oil. Add the onion and cook over moderately high heat, stirring frequently, until softened, about 6 minutes. Add the garlic, ginger and curry powder and cook, stirring, until fragrant, about 2 minutes. Add the carrots and cook, stirring, for 2 minutes longer. Add the sugar and 7 cups of water and season with salt and pepper. Simmer over moderately low heat until the carrots are very tender, about 45 minutes.

2. Meanwhile, in a small saucepan of salted boiling water, blanch the tarragon and parsley just until wilted, 30 seconds, then drain. Transfer the herbs to a bowl of ice water and drain again, squeezing out the excess water. Transfer to a blender. Add the remaining ½ cup of olive oil and puree until smooth. Strain the oil through a double layer of cheesecloth without pressing down on the solids.

3. Carefully puree the hot soup in a blender or food processor until smooth. Return the soup to the pot, stir in the lemon zest and season with Tabasco and salt and pepper.

4. Ladle the soup into shallow bowls, drizzle with the tarragon oil and garnish with chives. —Naomi Pomeroy

MAKE AHEAD The soup and tarragon oil can be refrigerated separately overnight. Reheat the soup and let the tarragon oil come to room temperature before serving.

Creamy Piquillo Pepper and Chickpea Soup with Chicken

TOTAL: 7 MIN • 4 SERVINGS ● ●

- 1 cup drained piquillo peppers (8 ounces), ¼ cup cut into thin strips
- ¾ cup hummus (7 ounces)
- 2 cups chicken or beef stock
- ½ cup cooked white rice, homemade or store-bought
- 1 cup shredded rotisserie chicken

Salt and freshly ground pepper

- 2 tablespoons chopped flat-leaf parsley

Olive oil and hot sauce, for serving

In a blender or a food processor, combine the whole piquillos with the hummus and chicken stock and puree until smooth. Transfer the soup to a medium saucepan. Add the rice and chicken, season with salt and pepper and bring to a boil. Ladle the soup into bowls; garnish with the chopped parsley, sliced piquillos, olive oil and hot sauce, then serve. —Grace Parisi

Rich Chicken Stock

TOTAL: 2 HR • MAKES 8 CUPS ● ●

This chicken stock is terrific to use in soups, stews, dressings and stuffings.

One 3-pound chicken, quartered or left whole

- 1 large onion, quartered
- 2 large carrots, chopped
- 2 celery ribs, chopped
- 6 parsley sprigs
- 2 thyme sprigs
- 1 bay leaf
- 1 teaspoon black peppercorns

Salt

1. In a large stockpot, combine the chicken, vegetables, herbs and peppercorns with 4 quarts of water. Cover partially and simmer over very low heat for about 1 hour and 30 minutes, skimming the surface as necessary.

2. Strain the stock into a large bowl and rinse out the pot; reserve the chicken for another use. Return the stock to the pot and boil over moderately high heat until reduced to 8 cups, 30 minutes longer. Season with salt. —Grace Parisi

MAKE AHEAD The stock can be refrigerated for up to 3 days or frozen for up to 1 month.

Egyptian Red Lentil Soup

ACTIVE: 15 MIN; TOTAL: 45 MIN
8 SERVINGS ● ● ●

Known as *shorbet ads,* this vivid red lentil soup is very popular in Egypt.

- 2 tablespoons unsalted butter
- 1 medium onion, chopped
- 2 carrots, finely chopped
- 3 celery ribs, finely chopped
- 3 garlic cloves, thinly sliced
- 1 teaspoon ground cumin
- ½ teaspoon ground coriander
- ½ teaspoon ancho chile powder
- 1 pound tomatoes, seeded and diced
- 2 cups red lentils (14 ounces)

Salt

Plain yogurt, lemon wedges and warm pita, for serving

1. In a large pot, melt the butter. Add the onion, carrots, celery and garlic and cook over moderate heat, stirring, until softened, 5 minutes. Add the cumin, coriander and chile powder and cook until fragrant, 3 minutes. Add the tomatoes and cook just until softened, 2 minutes. Add the lentils and 8 cups of water and season with salt. Simmer over moderately low heat until the lentils are very soft, 30 minutes.

2. Working in batches, puree the soup in a blender. Season with salt and serve with yogurt, lemon wedges and warm pita. —Eric Monkaba

MAKE AHEAD The soup can be refrigerated overnight. Reheat gently.

curried carrot soup with tarragon oil

Creamy Roasted Broccoli Soup

ACTIVE: 20 MIN; TOTAL: 1 HR 15 MIN
6 SERVINGS ●

- 5 garlic cloves, unpeeled
- 2 pounds broccoli—florets cut into 1-inch pieces, stems reserved for another use
- 2 tablespoons extra-virgin olive oil
- 2 tablespoons unsalted butter, melted

Kosher salt and freshly ground black pepper

- 4 ounces cream cheese
- 3 cups low-sodium chicken broth

Croutons, for serving

1. Preheat the oven to 400°. Wrap the garlic in a foil packet and roast for 50 minutes, until softened. Meanwhile, in a small roasting pan, toss the broccoli with the olive oil and butter and season with salt and pepper. Roast for 20 minutes, or until tender.
2. Squeeze the garlic cloves from their skins into a blender, then add the roasted broccoli, cream cheese and chicken broth; puree until smooth. Transfer the soup to a saucepan and bring to a simmer. Season with salt and pepper and serve with croutons.
—*Grace Parisi*

MAKE AHEAD The soup can be refrigerated overnight. Reheat gently before serving.

Beef Goulash Soup

ACTIVE: 10 MIN; TOTAL: 40 MIN
6 SERVINGS ● ● ●

- 2 tablespoons extra-virgin olive oil
- 1 large onion, finely chopped
- 2 garlic cloves, minced
- ¼ cup sweet Hungarian paprika
- 2 teaspoons caraway seeds, chopped
- 1 pound ground beef sirloin
- 2 tablespoons tomato paste

One 14-ounce can diced tomatoes

- 1 cup thinly sliced roasted red peppers
- 1 quart low-sodium beef broth

Kosher salt and freshly ground black pepper

- 4 ounces wide egg noodles (2 cups)

Crème fraîche or sour cream, for serving

1. In a large Dutch oven or pot, heat the oil. Add the onion and garlic and cook over moderate heat until softened. Add the paprika and caraway and cook for 1 minute. Add the beef and cook, breaking up the meat, until no longer pink, 3 minutes. Add the tomato paste, diced tomatoes with their juices, red peppers, broth and 1 cup of water. Season with salt and pepper and bring to a boil. Cover partially and simmer for 25 minutes.
2. Meanwhile, in a saucepan of salted boiling water, cook the noodles until al dente. Drain.
3. Add the noodles to the soup and cook for 2 minutes. Ladle the soup into bowls and garnish with a dollop of crème fraîche.
—*Grace Parisi*

NOTE To speed up this brothy goulash soup, Grace uses quick-cooking ground beef sirloin instead of the more traditional chunks of beef chuck.

WINE Rich, spicy Italian red: 2009 Cantina del Taburno Aglianico.

Creamy Tomato Soup with Shrimp and Jerk Spices

TOTAL: 20 MIN • 4 SERVINGS ● ●

- 2 tablespoons unsalted butter
- 1 medium onion, finely chopped
- 1 teaspoon coarsely chopped thyme
- 1 quart creamy tomato soup, preferably Pacific Natural Foods brand

1 to 1½ teaspoons jerk spice paste, like Walkerswood or Busha Browne's

Salt and freshly ground black pepper

- ½ pound shelled, deveined shrimp
- 2 scallions, thinly sliced

Steamed rice and lime wedges, for serving

In a large saucepan, melt the butter. Add the onion and thyme and cook over high heat until lightly browned, about 5 minutes. Add the soup and jerk paste and season with salt and pepper. Bring to a boil and simmer for about 5 minutes. Add the shrimp and cook just until pink and curled, about 3 minutes. Stir in the scallions and some rice and serve with lime wedges. —*Grace Parisi*

Pork and Kale Soup with Sizzling Puffed Rice

TOTAL: 45 MIN • 6 TO 8 SERVINGS

- 2 tablespoons unsalted butter
- 1 small onion, thinly sliced
- 2 garlic cloves, minced
- 1 cup dry white wine, preferably Pinot Blanc
- 1 pound kale, stemmed and chopped
- 2 quarts chicken stock
- 3 tablespoons soy sauce
- 2 teaspoons toasted sesame oil
- 1 sweet potato, peeled and thinly sliced lengthwise with a vegetable peeler
- 1½ pounds trimmed boneless pork shoulder, cut into thin strips
- 2 tablespoons fresh lemon juice
- 2 teaspoons sugar
- 1 tablespoon extra-virgin olive oil
- 2 puffed rice cakes, crumbled

1. Melt 1 tablespoon of the butter in a pot. Add the onion and garlic and cook over moderate heat until lightly browned, 4 minutes. Add the wine and bring to a boil. Simmer until reduced by half, 5 minutes. Add the kale and stock and bring to a boil. Cover partially and simmer over low heat until the kale is almost tender, about 10 minutes. Add 1½ tablespoons of the soy sauce with the sesame oil and sweet potato. Simmer uncovered until the potato is tender, 10 minutes longer.
2. Meanwhile, in a medium bowl, toss the pork strips with the lemon juice, sugar and the remaining 1½ tablespoons of soy sauce. Let stand for 10 minutes.
3. Melt the remaining 1 tablespoon of butter in a large skillet. Add the pork and cook over high heat until browned and cooked through, about 10 minutes. Add the pork to the soup.
4. Heat the olive oil in a medium skillet until shimmering. Add the rice cakes and cook, stirring, until lightly toasted, about 2 minutes. Ladle the soup into bowls, spoon the sizzling rice on top and serve right away.
—*Edward Lee*

WINE Creamy, full-bodied Alsace white: 2011 Mittnacht Pinot Blanc.

● HEALTHY ● MAKE AHEAD ● VEGETARIAN ● STAFF FAVORITE

creamy roasted broccoli soup

Italian Wedding Soup

⏱ **TOTAL: 40 MIN • 6 SERVINGS** ● ●

This hearty Italian soup is loaded with tiny pork meatballs, orzo, chickpeas, spinach and Parmesan cheese.

- 2 quarts homemade chicken stock or low-sodium broth
- 1 large carrot, finely diced
- 1 celery rib, finely diced
- Kosher salt and freshly ground pepper
- ¼ cup orzo
- 1 pound ground pork
- ¼ cup freshly grated Parmigiano-Reggiano, plus more for serving
- ¼ cup dry bread crumbs
- 5 ounces baby spinach, chopped
- One 15-ounce can chickpeas, drained and rinsed

1. In a large pot, bring the chicken stock to a boil with the carrot and celery. Season with salt and pepper. Add the orzo and cook until al dente, about 7 minutes.

2. Meanwhile, in a bowl, knead the pork with the ¼ cup of cheese, the bread crumbs and ½ teaspoon each of salt and pepper. Form the mixture into 1-inch balls.

3. Simmer the meatballs in the boiling soup for 5 minutes. Stir in the spinach and chickpeas; simmer until the meatballs are cooked through, about 5 minutes longer. Serve, passing extra cheese at the table. —*Grace Parisi*

WINE Fruity, floral northern Italian red: 2008 Andriano Rubeno Lagrein.

COOKWARE TIP

double-duty dish The lid on this 6-quart enameled steel pot—a reissue of a 1950s Dansk classic—also works as a trivet. *$100; crateandbarrel.com.*

Root-Vegetable Minestrone

📷 **PAGE 61**

⏱ **TOTAL: 40 MIN • 6 SERVINGS** ● ●

F&W's Grace Parisi riffs on this Italian classic by using unexpected vegetables like parsnips, butternut squash and broccoli stems. She also stirs in toasted angel hair pasta for additional texture and flavor.

- ¼ cup extra-virgin olive oil
- 1 small onion, finely chopped
- 1 garlic clove, minced
- 1 small rosemary sprig
- 2 carrots, sliced ¼ inch thick
- 2 parsnips, sliced ¼ inch thick
- 3 broccoli stems or 1 kohlrabi, peeled and sliced ¼ inch thick
- 1 pound cubed peeled butternut squash, cut into ¾-inch dice (3 cups)
- 6 cups low-sodium chicken broth
- Salt and freshly ground black pepper
- 4 ounces angel hair pasta, broken into 1-inch lengths
- 1 cup frozen baby lima beans
- ½ cup freshly grated pecorino cheese, plus more for serving

1. In a large Dutch oven or pot, heat 2 tablespoons of the olive oil. Add the onion, garlic and rosemary and cook over moderate heat until the onion is softened, about 5 minutes. Add the carrots, parsnips, broccoli stems and squash and cook for 1 minute. Add the broth, season with salt and pepper and simmer until the vegetables are nearly tender, about 15 minutes.

2. Meanwhile, in a medium skillet, heat the remaining 2 tablespoons of olive oil. Add the pasta and cook over moderately high heat, stirring frequently, until it is deeply golden, about 4 minutes.

3. Add the toasted pasta and the lima beans to the soup; cook until the pasta and vegetables are tender, 5 to 6 minutes. Discard the rosemary. Stir the ½ cup of cheese into the soup and serve, passing extra cheese at the table. —*Grace Parisi*

MAKE AHEAD The minestrone can be refrigerated overnight.

Smoked Fish Chowder

TOTAL: 50 MIN • 6 TO 8 SERVINGS ●

For this creamy chowder, use whatever local smoked fish you can find, from haddock to bluefish or trout. If you can't get any smoked fish, try using fresh cod or sole and adding bacon for smokiness.

- 2 ears of corn, kernels cut from the cobs
- 1½ pounds large red-skinned potatoes, peeled and cut into ½-inch dice
- 3 tablespoons unsalted butter
- 2 fennel bulbs—cored and thinly sliced, fronds reserved and chopped
- 2 large leeks, white and pale green parts only, cut into ¼-inch dice
- 1 large onion, thinly sliced
- 2 thyme sprigs
- 1 bay leaf
- Salt and freshly ground pepper
- 1 quart plus 3 cups milk
- 1 cup heavy cream
- 1 pound smoked fish, such as haddock, mackerel, bluefish or trout, skinned and flaked

1. In a saucepan of salted boiling water, cook the corn until just tender, about 1 minute. With a slotted spoon, transfer the corn to a bowl. Add the potatoes to the boiling water and cook until tender, about 6 minutes. Drain the potatoes and add them to the bowl with the corn.

2. In a large pot, melt the butter. Add the fennel slices, leeks, onion, thyme sprigs and bay leaf and season with salt and pepper. Cover and cook over low heat, stirring occasionally, until the vegetables are softened, about 10 minutes. Add the milk, cream, corn and potatoes and simmer for about 3 minutes, smashing some of the potatoes to thicken the soup. Discard the thyme sprigs and bay leaf. Add the fish and simmer until heated through, about 2 minutes. Season lightly with salt and pepper. Ladle the chowder into bowls, garnish with fennel fronds and serve. —*Nico Monday and Amelia O'Reilly*

WINE Minerally northern Italian white: 2011 Alois Lageder Riff Pinot Grigio.

● HEALTHY ● MAKE AHEAD ○ VEGETARIAN ● STAFF FAVORITE

italian wedding soup

Fava Bean Pasta e Fagioli

TOTAL: 1 HR • 8 SERVINGS ● ●

This spring version of the Italian soup pasta e fagioli uses fresh fava beans in place of traditional borlotti or cannellini beans.

- 3 pounds fava bean pods, shelled
- 1 tablespoon extra-virgin olive oil, plus more for serving
- 2 thick slices of lean, meaty bacon, cut crosswise ½ inch thick
- 1 large carrot, halved lengthwise and cut crosswise into ¼-inch half-moons
- 1 medium onion, cut into ½-inch pieces
- 1 large garlic clove, minced

One 3-inch-long rosemary sprig

- 1 quart chicken stock or low-sodium broth
- 1 cup *tubetti* or other small pasta

Salt and freshly ground pepper

- 2 tablespoons small mint leaves

Freshly grated Parmigiano-Reggiano cheese, for serving

1. Bring a large saucepan of water to a boil. Add the shelled fava beans and blanch until they are bright green, about 1 minute. Drain and peel the favas.

2. In a large saucepan, heat the 1 tablespoon of olive oil. Add the bacon and cook over moderate heat until starting to brown, about 4 minutes. Add the carrot, onion, garlic and rosemary and cook, stirring occasionally, until softened, about 5 minutes. Add the stock, cover and simmer over low heat until the carrot is tender, about 6 minutes.

3. Meanwhile, in a medium saucepan of salted boiling water, cook the pasta until al dente. Drain.

4. Discard the rosemary sprig and season the soup with salt and pepper. Add the fava beans, pasta and mint leaves. Spoon the soup into bowls, drizzle with olive oil and serve, passing the cheese at the table.
—*Mike Lata*

MAKE AHEAD The recipe can be prepared through Step 3 and refrigerated overnight. The blanched and peeled fava beans can be refrigerated separately overnight.

Soupe De Poisson

SERVES 8 ● ●

When veteran chef-TV host Anthony Bourdain was cooking at his Les Halles brasserie in New York City, he would occasionally make this classic French *soupe de poisson* around the holidays. "This soup was my gateway drug to France and French cooking," Bourdain says. "Rough, ugly and absolutely delicious . . . This more than anything else is the flavor of my childhood vacations in France." The recipe below is taken directly from Bourdain's *Les Halles* cookbook.

INGREDIENTS

6 tbsp olive oil
4 garlic cloves
2 small onions, thinly sliced
2 leeks, whites only, washed and thinly sliced
1 fennel bulb, thinly sliced
1 14-ounce can plum tomatoes, chopped
2 lb tiny whole fish (like porgies or whiting), gutted but heads intact
6 cups water
1 bouquet garni (1 parsley sprig, 2 thyme springs, and 1 bay leaf, wrapped in cheesecloth bundle)
2 strips of orange zest
3 strands of saffron
salt and pepper
1 ounce Pernod
croutons
rouille (recipe follows)
grated Parmesan

EQUIPMENT

large, heavy-bottomed pot
wooden spoon
fine strainer
large bowl
food mill

In the large, heavy-bottomed pot, heat the olive oil over medium heat. Add the garlic, onions, leeks, and fennel and let them sweat for about 5 minutes, stirring occasionally with the wooden spoon. Add the tomatoes and cook for another 4 to 5 minutes, then add the small fish. Cook for about 15 minutes, stirring occasionally. Add 6 cups of water, as well as the bouquet garni and orange zest. Stir well; add the saffron, salt and pepper, and Pernod. Lower the heat and simmer for about an hour.

Remove the pot from the heat and let the soup cool slightly. Taking care not to splatter or scald yourself, strain the liquid into the large bowl. In the pot, crush the heads, bones, and vegetables as much as possible, then pass that through the food mill in batches. Return to the pot along with the strained broth.

Bring the soup back up to heat and serve with croutons, rouille, and some grated Parmesan on the side. The idea is to smear a little rouille on the croutons, float them in the soup as a garnish, and allow guests to sprinkle cheese as they wish. —*Anthony Bourdain*

Rouille

YIELDS APPROXIMATELY 1 CUP ●

The garnishes for *soupe de poisson* are central to the experience and should not be omitted, according to Bourdain. He advises using good saffron to make the rouille, a garlicky rust-colored sauce for the croutons.

INGREDIENTS

1 large garlic clove, crushed
½ red bell pepper, roasted, peeled, and seeded
1 egg yolk
1 tsp freshly squeezed lemon juice
small pinch of saffron threads
1 cup extra-virgin olive oil
salt and pepper

EQUIPMENT

food processor

In the bowl of the food processor, combine the garlic, red pepper, egg yolk, lemon juice, and saffron. Pulse until smooth, then slowly drizzle in the oil and process continuously until the mixture thickens. Season with salt and pepper to taste, and use immediately.
—*Anthony Bourdain*

● HEALTHY ● MAKE AHEAD ● VEGETARIAN ● STAFF FAVORITE

fava bean pasta e fagioli

Coconut Laksa with Shrimp

ACTIVE: 1 HR; TOTAL: 1 HR 30 MIN
8 SERVINGS ●

This soothing Southeast Asian noodle soup is sweet, spicy and vibrant; coconut milk lends a tropical creaminess.

1½ **pounds medium shrimp—shelled and deveined, shells reserved**
1 **onion, quartered**
1 **carrot, sliced**
3 **large shallots, quartered**
4 **jalapeños, seeded and coarsely chopped**
⅓ **cup thinly sliced peeled fresh ginger**
¼ **cup macadamia nuts**
1 **teaspoon ground coriander**
½ **teaspoon ground turmeric**
¼ **cup Asian fish sauce**
¼ **cup canola oil**
2 **plump lemongrass stalks—bottom 8 inches only, outer layer removed, stalk cut into 2-inch lengths**
One 14½-ounce can unsweetened **coconut milk**
2 **tablespoons light brown sugar**
1 **pound Thai flat rice noodles (pad thai), soaked in warm water for 10 minutes**
Salt
Lime wedges, for serving

1. In a large saucepan, combine the shrimp shells with the onion, carrot and 8 cups of water and bring to a boil. Simmer over moderate heat until the stock is bright orange and reduced to 5 cups, about 30 minutes. Strain and reserve the stock.

2. In a food processor, combine the shallots, jalapeños, ginger, macadamia nuts, coriander and turmeric with 2 tablespoons of the fish sauce and 2 tablespoons of the canola oil; puree until smooth.

3. In a soup pot, heat the remaining 2 tablespoons of oil. Add the seasoning paste and cook over moderate heat, stirring, until fragrant, about 2 minutes. Add the lemongrass pieces and cook, stirring occasionally, until the mixture darkens slightly and the oil separates, about 10 minutes.

4. Add the reserved shrimp stock, coconut milk, brown sugar and the remaining 2 tablespoons of fish sauce. Simmer over moderate heat until the soup is reduced to 6 cups, about 15 minutes.

5. Meanwhile, in a large pot of boiling water, cook the rice noodles just until pliable, about 1 minute. Drain, shaking out the excess water. Transfer to 8 soup bowls.

6. Add the shrimp to the soup and cook until pink and curled, about 5 minutes. Season the soup with salt and ladle it over the noodles. Garnish with lime wedges and serve.
—Bryant Ng

MAKE AHEAD The recipe can be prepared through Step 2 and refrigerated overnight.
WINE Off-dry sparkling wine: NV Patrick Bottex La Cueille Bugey-Cerdon.

Oxtail Soup with Daikon and Ramen Noodles

ACTIVE: 1 HR; TOTAL: 4 HR 45 MIN
6 SERVINGS ● ●

Oxtail is a popular ingredient in Hawaiian cooking. Los Angeles chef Roy Choi makes it the base for the broth of his noodle soup and adds plenty of the tender braised meat as well. The soup is packed with sliced daikon and leeks, then garnished with crisp, sweet fried garlic chips.

3 **tablespoons vegetable oil**
5 **pounds large, meaty oxtails, cut 2 inches thick**
Salt and freshly ground black pepper
1 **cup coarsely chopped peeled fresh ginger (about 4 ounces)**
1 **cup coarsely chopped garlic (from about 2 large heads)**
¼ **cup sake**
2 **quarts beef stock or low-sodium broth**
1 **large daikon (1 pound), peeled and cut into ¾-inch-thick rounds**
1 **large leek, white and pale green parts only, cut into 1-inch rounds**
1 **pound dried ramen or soba noodles**
½ **cup Golden Garlic Chips (page 44) and ½ cup chopped chives, for serving**

1. In a large enameled cast-iron casserole, heat 2 tablespoons of the vegetable oil. Season the oxtail pieces with salt and freshly ground black pepper and add half of them to the casserole. Cook over moderately high heat until the oxtails are browned all over, about 8 minutes. Transfer the browned meat to a bowl and repeat with the remaining oxtail pieces. Carefully pour off the fat from the casserole.

2. Add the remaining 1 tablespoon of vegetable oil to the casserole. Add the chopped ginger and garlic and cook over moderate heat, stirring a few times, until golden and fragrant, about 5 minutes. Carefully stir in the sake and scrape up any browned bits from the bottom of the casserole. Add the beef stock and bring the mixture to a simmer. Return the oxtails to the casserole, cover and simmer over low heat until the meat is very tender, about 3 hours.

3. Transfer the oxtails to a large rimmed baking sheet and let cool slightly. Remove the meat from the bones and cut into bite-size pieces; discard the bones, fat and gristle. Strain the broth, pressing down on the solids. Skim off the fat.

4. Return the strained broth to the casserole. Add the sliced daikon and leek and bring the broth to a boil. Cover the casserole and simmer over low heat until the daikon is tender, about 45 minutes. Add the oxtail meat, season with salt and freshly ground black pepper and keep hot.

5. In a large pot of salted boiling water, cook the ramen, stirring often, until the noodles are al dente, about 5 minutes. Drain and then return the ramen to the pot. Fill the pot with cold water and drain again. Rinse and drain the ramen one more time.

6. Transfer the ramen to large bowls. Ladle the daikon and leek into the bowls, then the broth and oxtail meat. Serve the soup, passing the Golden Garlic Chips and chopped chives at the table. *—Roy Choi*

MAKE AHEAD The recipe can be prepared through Step 3 and refrigerated overnight. Store the broth and oxtail meat separately.
BEER Hoppy, slightly bitter India pale ale: Bear Republic Racer 5 IPA.

● HEALTHY   ● MAKE AHEAD   ● VEGETARIAN   ● STAFF FAVORITE

coconut laksa with shrimp

Dashi with Crab and Tofu
ACTIVE: 15 MIN; TOTAL: 1 HR 25 MIN
4 TO 6 SERVINGS ●

The key to this quick dashi (broth) is to buy the best-quality bonito (flakes of smoked, dried skipjack tuna) you can find. Look for it at Japanese markets.

One 2-inch piece of kombu (seaweed)
  2 cups bonito shavings (1 ounce)
  3 tablespoons light soy sauce
  1 tablespoon mirin
  6 ounces silken tofu, cut into
     ½-inch cubes
  ½ pound lump crabmeat or the
     meat from 1 steamed Dungeness
     crab, picked over
  4 mitsuba or celery leaves

1. In a medium saucepan, cover the kombu with 4½ cups of water; let stand for 1 hour.
2. Preheat the oven to 350°. Bring the water to a simmer over moderate heat and remove and discard the kombu before it boils. Add the bonito and simmer for 1 minute. Cover the saucepan, remove from the heat and let stand for 10 minutes. Strain the dashi through cheesecloth into another saucepan and add the soy sauce and mirin.

3. Arrange the tofu cubes and crabmeat in ovenproof bowls and warm in the oven for about 3 minutes. Bring the dashi to a simmer. Pour the hot dashi into the bowls, garnish with the mitsuba or celery leaves and serve right away. —*Sylvan Mishima Brackett*
WINE Bright, creamy Alsace Pinot Blanc: 2009 Domaines Schlumberger Les Princes Abbés.

Cold Watermelon Soup
⏱ **ACTIVE: 20 MIN; TOTAL: 40 MIN**
4 SERVINGS ● ● ●

"Watermelon juice has such a mild flavor that most thickeners, like cornstarch, would overpower its taste," says chef Jamie Bissonnette of Coppa in Boston. "But xanthan allows me to turn it into a soup." He adds just a small amount of the industrial powder (now available at many grocery stores) to thicken this easy summer soup.

  5 cups (1½ pounds) diced seedless
     watermelon, chilled
  2 tablespoons fresh lime juice
  1 tablespoon plus 1 teaspoon
     chervil leaves
  2 teaspoons extra-virgin olive oil
  2 grams xanthan gum (½ teaspoon)
Tabasco
Salt
Chervil or shredded shiso leaves,
     for garnish

1. In a blender, puree the watermelon with the lime juice, chervil leaves and olive oil until the mixture is very smooth. Set a fine-mesh strainer over a large bowl and strain the watermelon puree, pressing very lightly on the solids to extract the watermelon juice without pushing the pulp through.
2. Rinse out the blender and then return the strained watermelon juice to it. With the blender on, add the xanthan gum and blend until slightly thickened, about 15 seconds. Transfer the watermelon soup to a pitcher and season with Tabasco and salt. Refrigerate until the soup is well chilled, about 20 minutes. Serve the soup in bowls, garnished with chervil or shredded shiso leaves.
—*Jamie Bissonnette*

White Gazpacho
ACTIVE: 30 MIN; TOTAL: 1 HR
6 SERVINGS ● ● ●

Made with apples, green grapes, almonds and cucumber, this refreshing white gazpacho from Atlanta chef Linton Hopkins is a perfect balance of sweet and tangy.

  1 cup stale, crustless ½-inch
     white country bread cubes
  1 cup white grape juice
1¼ cups blanched sliced almonds
  1 cup peeled, seeded
     and diced cucumber
  1 Granny Smith apple—peeled,
     seeded and chopped
  1 cup seedless green grapes
  1 garlic clove
  3 tablespoons sherry vinegar
  ¼ cup extra-virgin olive oil,
     plus more for garnish
  1 cup buttermilk
Salt and freshly ground pepper
Shredded mint leaves, for garnish

1. Preheat the oven to 350°. In a small bowl, soak the bread in the grape juice for 5 minutes, pressing to soften.
2. Spread the almonds in a pie plate; toast them in the oven for 6 minutes, until lightly golden. Let cool. Transfer 1 cup of the toasted almonds to a blender. Add the bread, cucumber, apple, grapes, garlic, sherry vinegar and ¼ cup of olive oil. Puree until smooth. Strain the soup through a sieve into a large bowl, pressing on the solids. Whisk in the buttermilk and season the soup with salt and pepper. Refrigerate the gazpacho until chilled, at least 30 minutes.
3. Pour the gazpacho into bowls and garnish with the mint and the remaining ¼ cup of almonds. Drizzle with olive oil and serve.
—*Linton Hopkins*
MAKE AHEAD The gazpacho can be made through Step 2 and refrigerated for up to 1 day. The ¼ cup of toasted almonds can be kept in an airtight container at room temperature for up to 3 days.
WINE Zesty, fruit-forward Spanish white: 2011 MartínSancho Verdejo.

EQUIPMENT TIP

electric scale A scale that weighs in 0.1-gram increments is best for accurately measuring xanthan gum for recipes like the chilled watermelon soup at right. A chef favorite is Edlund's Precision Gram Scale shown here (*$495; edlundco.com*). A more affordable option: the Compact Scale from Ohaus (*$45; amazon.com*).

● HEALTHY ● MAKE AHEAD ● VEGETARIAN ● STAFF FAVORITE

Top Chef Masters *star Susan Feniger (in green pants) entertains at her L.A. home; she serves recipes inspired by global street food, such as cold soba salad in banana leaves,* OPPOSITE; *recipe, page 96.*

PASTA & NOODLES

Turkey Meatballs Two Ways

ACTIVE: 30 MIN; TOTAL: 1 HR 15 MIN
8 TO 10 SERVINGS ● ●

These easy baked turkey meatballs can be prepared two ways: mild for kids or spicy (with hot Italian turkey sausage and a pinch of crushed red pepper worked into the meat-ball mixture) for adults.

    4 large eggs
    ¾ cup whole milk
    2 cups panko (Japanese bread crumbs)
    1 tablespoon minced garlic
    ½ cup finely chopped
       flat-leaf parsley
    ½ teaspoon dried oregano, crumbled
    ½ teaspoon dried basil, crumbled
    1 cup freshly grated
       Parmigiano-Reggiano cheese,
       plus more for serving
Kosher salt and freshly ground pepper
    2 pounds ground turkey
    1 pound hot Italian turkey sausage,
       casings removed
Pinch of crushed red pepper
Two 24-ounce jars tomato sauce
    2 pounds dried pasta,
       such as rigatoni or mezzi rigatoni

1. Preheat the oven to 400°. Line 2 large rimmed baking sheets with parchment paper. In a large bowl, whisk the eggs with the milk. Stir in the panko, minced garlic, chopped parsley, oregano, basil, 1 cup of the Parmigiano-Reggiano cheese, 2 teaspoons of salt and ½ teaspoon of freshly ground pepper. Add the ground turkey and gently knead to combine.

2. FOR KIDS Form two-thirds of the meat mixture into thirty-two 1½-inch meatballs and transfer to one of the baking sheets. **FOR ADULTS** Knead the sausage and red pepper into the remaining meat mixture and form into thirty-two 1½-inch meatballs. Transfer to the second baking sheet.

3. Brush the meatballs with 1 cup of the tomato sauce. Bake in the upper and lower thirds of the oven for about 40 minutes, shifting the pans halfway through baking, until the meatballs are cooked through.

4. Meanwhile, in a pot of salted boiling water, cook the pasta until al dente. Drain the pasta and return it to the pot. Add the remaining 5 cups of tomato sauce and cook until heated through, tossing well. Spoon the pasta into 2 large serving bowls; add the mild meatballs to one and the spicy meatballs to the other. Serve, passing additional cheese at the table. —*Katie Workman*

WINE Juicy, ebullient Barbera d'Alba: 2009 Elvio Cogno Bricco dei Merli.

Antipasto Pasta

☼ **TOTAL: 20 MIN • 4 SERVINGS** ● ●

   12 ounces fettuccine
    ¼ cup extra-virgin olive oil
One 2-ounce can anchovies, drained
       and chopped
    4 small garlic cloves, minced
    1 pound broccoli—cut into
       small florets, stems peeled and
       coarsely shredded
    ¼ cup chopped hot Peppadew peppers
    ½ cup freshly grated
       Parmigiano-Reggiano cheese,
       plus more for serving
    ¼ cup chopped flat-leaf parsley

1. In a large pot of salted boiling water, cook the pasta just until al dente. Drain, reserving 1 cup of the cooking water.

2. In a large, deep skillet, heat the olive oil. Add the anchovies and garlic and cook over moderately high heat, stirring, until fragrant, about 1 minute. Add the broccoli florets and stems and cook for 2 minutes, stirring occasionally. Add ½ cup of the reserved pasta water, cover and cook until the broccoli is tender but still bright green, about 2 minutes. Mash the broccoli coarsely.

3. Add the pasta, Peppadews and the ½ cup of Parmigiano to the skillet and toss. Add the remaining ½ cup of pasta water and cook, tossing, until the pasta is coated with a light sauce, about 2 minutes. Stir in the parsley and serve in bowls, passing extra Parmigiano on the side. —*Grace Parisi*

WINE Fresh, minerally California white: 2011 Massican Annia.

$4 Spaghetti That's Almost as Good as $24 Spaghetti

ACTIVE: 30 MIN; TOTAL: 3 HR • 4 TO 6
SERVINGS PLUS 4 CUPS OF SAUCE ● ● ● ●

"The $24 spaghetti from Scott Conant's Scarpetta in NYC is so delicious," says Roy Choi of L.A.'s Kogi empire. "My $4 version tastes *almost* as good." Choi's trick: flavoring tomato sauce with a quick mushroom broth and slow-cooked garlic.

    4 ounces white button mushrooms,
       thinly sliced
    ¾ cup peeled garlic cloves
       (4 ounces, from about 4 heads)
    ⅔ cup extra-virgin olive oil
Two 28-ounce cans peeled Italian
       tomatoes with their juices
Salt and freshly ground pepper
    1 pound spaghetti
    ¼ cup torn basil leaves
Freshly grated Parmigiano-Reggiano
       cheese, for serving

1. In a saucepan, bring the mushrooms and 3 cups of water to a boil. Simmer over moderate heat until the broth is reduced to 1 cup, 1 hour. Strain and discard the mushrooms.

2. Meanwhile, in a small saucepan, bring the garlic and olive oil to a boil. Simmer over moderately low heat, stirring, until the garlic is very tender and golden, about 30 minutes.

3. In a large enameled cast-iron casserole or Dutch oven, bring the tomatoes and the garlic and oil to a boil. Add the mushroom broth and, using an immersion blender, puree the sauce until smooth. Bring the sauce back to a boil, then simmer over moderately low heat until thickened, about 1 hour. Season the sauce with salt and pepper.

4. Cook the spaghetti in a large pot of salted boiling water until al dente. Drain the pasta and return it to the pot. Add 2 cups of the sauce and cook, tossing, for 1 minute. Transfer the spaghetti to bowls, top with the basil and serve with grated cheese. —*Roy Choi*

MAKE AHEAD The sauce can be refrigerated for up to 5 days or frozen for up to 3 months.

WINE Fruit-forward, medium-bodied red: 2010 Vallevò Montepulciano d'Abruzzo.

$4 spaghetti that's almost as good as $24 spaghetti

Kamut Spaghetti with Clams, Chicory and Parsley

◔ **TOTAL: 40 MIN • 4 SERVINGS** ● ●

Paola Budel, the chef at Venissa Ristorante Ostello on the Venetian island of Mazzorbo, updates linguine with clams by using pasta made with kamut (an ancient variety of high-protein wheat) and adding bitter chicory and a bright parsley sauce.

¼ pound chicory or stemmed dandelion greens
2 dozen littleneck clams, scrubbed
½ cup packed flat-leaf parsley leaves
5 tablespoons extra-virgin olive oil
Salt
4 scallions, cut into ½-inch lengths
1 fresh red chile, thinly sliced
10 ounces kamut spaghetti or linguine

1. Bring a large saucepan of salted water to a boil. Add the chicory and cook until tender, about 1 minute. Drain and lightly squeeze out the excess water. Finely chop the chicory.
2. In a large skillet, bring 1 cup of water to a boil. Add the clams, cover and cook over moderately high heat, shaking the pan a few times, until they start to open; transfer the clams to a bowl as they open. When all the clams are open, pour the broth into a heatproof measuring cup; stop before you reach the grit at the bottom. You should have at least ½ cup. Remove the clams from their shells.
3. In a blender, puree the parsley with 4 tablespoons of the olive oil and 1 tablespoon of water. Season with salt.
4. In a large, deep skillet, heat the remaining 1 tablespoon of oil. Add the scallions and chile and cook over moderate heat until softened, about 3 minutes. Add the chicory and stir well. Cover and turn off the heat.
5. Bring a large pot of salted water to a boil. Add the pasta and cook until al dente. Drain and add it to the skillet along with the parsley puree and clams. Slowly pour in the reserved clam broth. Cook the pasta over moderate heat, tossing a few times, until the broth has been absorbed. Serve at once. —*Paola Budel*
WINE Clean, zesty Venetian white: 2011 Fattori Runcaris Soave.

Whole Wheat Fettuccine with Arugula Pesto

ACTIVE: 35 MIN; TOTAL: 1 HR
4 FIRST-COURSE SERVINGS ● ●

Top Chef All-Stars finalist Mike Isabella makes both the silky whole wheat pasta and the simple arugula pesto here, then finishes the dish with sweet cherry tomatoes.

¾ cup whole wheat flour
¾ cup all-purpose flour
Salt
3 large egg yolks
⅓ cup plus 1 teaspoon extra-virgin olive oil
2 tablespoons pine nuts
2 cups packed baby arugula (2 ounces)
¼ cup freshly grated Parmigiano-Reggiano cheese
1 garlic clove, chopped
1 cup halved cherry tomatoes

1. In a food processor, pulse the whole wheat and all-purpose flours with ½ teaspoon of salt. In a bowl, whisk the egg yolks with ⅓ cup of water and 1 teaspoon of the oil. With the processor on, add the egg yolk mixture and process until a ball forms. Transfer the dough to a work surface and knead until smooth. Cover with plastic wrap and let stand at room temperature for 20 minutes. Wipe out the processor.
2. In a small skillet, toss the pine nuts over moderate heat until toasted, about 1 minute; let cool. In the food processor, pulse the arugula, pine nuts, Parmigiano-Reggiano, garlic and the remaining ⅓ cup of olive oil to a paste. Season the pesto with salt and add to a large skillet.
3. Cut the dough into 3 pieces; work with 1 piece at a time and keep the rest covered. Flatten the dough slightly and run it through progressively narrower settings in a pasta machine until you reach the thinnest setting. Cut the pasta into 10-inch lengths. Using the pasta machine, cut each length into fettuccine. Transfer the fettuccine to a baking sheet, leaving space between the pasta so it doesn't stick.
4. In a large pot of salted boiling water, cook the pasta, stirring, until al dente, about 30 seconds. Drain the pasta, reserving ⅓ cup of the cooking water. Stir the reserved water into the pesto. Add the pasta and tomatoes to the pesto, toss over moderate heat and serve. —*Mike Isabella*
WINE Brisk Italian white: 2010 Conti di Buscareto Verdicchio dei Castelli di Jesi.

Whole Wheat Linguine with Walnuts, Orange and Chile

◔ **TOTAL: 25 MIN**
4 FIRST-COURSE SERVINGS ● ●

Calabrian chiles add a fruity, spicy flavor to this earthy pasta dish. If you can't get them, substitute any chile packed in oil or just use crushed red pepper.

½ cup walnuts (2 ounces)
¼ cup extra-virgin olive oil
1 large garlic clove, minced
¾ teaspoon finely grated orange zest
1 tablespoon seeded and chopped Calabrian chiles (see Note)
Salt
¼ cup chopped flat-leaf parsley
8 ounces whole wheat linguine
2 tablespoons freshly grated Parmigiano-Reggiano cheese

1. Preheat the oven to 350°. Spread the walnuts in a pie plate and toast for about 8 minutes, until fragrant. Let cool, then chop.
2. In a large skillet, heat the oil. Add the garlic, orange zest, chiles and toasted walnuts and cook over low heat until fragrant, 2 minutes. Season with salt and stir in the parsley.
3. In a large pot of salted boiling water, cook the linguine until al dente. Reserve ½ cup of the cooking water and drain the pasta. Add the linguine and reserved water to the skillet and simmer until the liquid is just absorbed, 2 minutes. Transfer the pasta to a bowl and sprinkle with the cheese. Toss and serve.
—*Maria Helm Sinskey*
NOTE Calabrian chiles are available at Italian markets and *dipaloselects.com*.
WINE Rich, citrusy Pinot Gris: Robert Sinskey Vineyards 2010 Los Carneros.

● HEALTHY ● MAKE AHEAD ○ VEGETARIAN ● STAFF FAVORITE

kamut spaghetti with clams, chicory and parsley

Spaghettini with Shrimp, Tomatoes and Chile Crumbs

⏱ TOTAL: 45 MIN • 4 SERVINGS ● ●

- 2 large plum tomatoes (about 1¼ pounds), cored and scored on the bottoms with an X
- 1 tablespoon red wine vinegar
- ½ cup plus 1 tablespoon extra-virgin olive oil
- Salt and freshly ground black pepper
- 1 cup coarse, dried sourdough bread crumbs (about 2 ounces)
- 1 teaspoon finely grated lemon zest
- Crushed red pepper
- 12 ounces spaghettini
- 1 pound medium shrimp, shelled and deveined
- 2 tablespoons finely shredded basil
- ½ pound heirloom cherry tomatoes, halved

1. Preheat the oven to 450°. Put the plum tomatoes in a small baking dish and drizzle with the vinegar and 2 tablespoons of the olive oil. Roast just until the skins loosen and the tomatoes are barely softened, about 20 minutes. Let cool slightly, then peel. Using the large holes on a box grater, grate the tomatoes back into the baking dish and stir. Season with salt and black pepper.

2. Meanwhile, heat 2 tablespoons of the olive oil in a large skillet. Add the bread crumbs and cook over moderately low heat, stirring, until golden and crisp, about 5 minutes. Stir in the lemon zest and a pinch of crushed red pepper and season with salt. Transfer the crumbs to a bowl and wipe out the skillet.

3. In a large pot of salted boiling water, cook the pasta until barely al dente. Drain the pasta, reserving ½ cup of the cooking water. Return the pasta to the pot and stir in 2 tablespoons of the olive oil.

4. In the large skillet, heat the remaining 3 tablespoons of oil until shimmering. Season the shrimp with salt and a pinch of crushed red pepper and cook over high heat, tossing once or twice, until barely cooked, about 1½ minutes. Add the basil and pasta along with the reserved pasta cooking water and cook, tossing, until the shrimp are white throughout and the pasta is coated in a light sauce, about 1 minute. Transfer the pasta to bowls and scatter the cherry tomatoes all around. Top with the tomato sauce and bread crumbs. Serve right away. —*Dan Kluger*

MAKE AHEAD The tomato sauce and bread crumbs can be prepared up to 2 days ahead. Refrigerate the tomato sauce and store the bread crumbs in an airtight container at room temperature.

WINE Lively, apple-inflected Chardonnay: 2009 Iron Horse Unoaked.

Orecchiette with Salmon, Arugula and Artichokes

⏱ TOTAL: 25 MIN • 4 SERVINGS ●

- 8 ounces orecchiette
- ¼ cup extra-virgin olive oil
- 1 large garlic clove, minced
- 5 ounces baby arugula
- ½ cup drained marinated artichokes, quartered
- ¼ cup pitted Sicilian green olives, chopped
- 2 tablespoons drained capers
- ¾ pound roast salmon, flaked (2 loose cups; see Note)
- Salt

1. In a large pot of salted boiling water, cook the pasta until al dente. Drain, reserving ½ cup of the cooking water.

2. In a large skillet, heat the olive oil. Add the garlic and cook over high heat until fragrant, about 30 seconds. Add the pasta and ¼ cup of the cooking water and cook, stirring, for 2 minutes. Add the arugula, artichokes, olives, capers and the remaining ¼ cup of cooking water and simmer, stirring, until the pasta is coated in a creamy sauce, about 1 minute. Stir in the salmon and cook just until heated through. Season lightly with salt and serve. —*Grace Parisi*

NOTE Use leftover salmon from Grace's Spice-Rubbed Salmon (page 102) or store-bought roast salmon.

WINE Citrusy Austrian Grüner Veltliner: 2011 Wieninger Vienna Hills.

Fettuccine with Spicy Shellfish

TOTAL: 1 HR • 6 SERVINGS

- ½ cup extra-virgin olive oil
- 1 teaspoon crushed red pepper
- 1 pound fresh fettuccine
- ½ cup freshly grated Parmigiano-Reggiano cheese
- ¼ cup shredded basil leaves
- 6 ounces dry chorizo—quartered lengthwise, thinly sliced crosswise
- 1 large shallot, minced
- 2 large garlic cloves, minced
- 2 plum tomatoes—peeled, seeded and chopped
- 1 dozen littleneck clams, scrubbed
- 1 cup bottled clam juice
- 1 pound mussels, scrubbed
- 1 pound shelled and deveined medium shrimp
- Salt

1. In a small skillet, combine ¼ cup of the olive oil with the crushed red pepper and cook over moderate heat for 2 minutes.

2. Meanwhile, in a large pot of salted boiling water, cook the pasta until it is barely al dente; drain and rinse under cold water to stop the cooking. Return the pasta to the pot and stir in the warm chile oil, ¼ cup of the cheese and 2 tablespoons of the basil.

3. In a very large, deep skillet, heat the remaining ¼ cup of olive oil. Add the chorizo and cook over high heat, stirring occasionally, until the fat is rendered, 2 minutes. Add the shallot and garlic; cook until fragrant, 1 minute. Add the tomatoes, clams and clam juice; cover. Cook until the clams just begin to open, 5 minutes. Add the mussels; cover. Cook until all the shells have opened, 3 minutes. Stir in the shrimp, season with salt and cook until pink and curled, about 2 minutes.

4. Using a ladle, transfer half of the liquid to the pasta in the pot; cook over high heat, tossing, until the pasta is al dente, 2 minutes. Transfer to bowls and ladle the broth and shellfish on top. Garnish with the remaining basil and cheese and serve. —*Emeril Lagasse*

WINE Robust, cherry-rich rosé: 2011 Montes Cherub Rosé of Syrah.

● HEALTHY ● MAKE AHEAD ○ VEGETARIAN ● STAFF FAVORITE

orecchiette with salmon, arugula and artichokes

Strozzapreti with Lamb Ragù

ACTIVE: 45 MIN; TOTAL: 2 HR 15 MIN
8 SERVINGS ● ●

The ridge along the length of the rolled pasta known as *strozzapreti* helps pick up more of the spiced, slow-cooked lamb ragù.

1 tablespoon fennel seeds
1 tablespoon cumin seeds
1 tablespoon Aleppo pepper or
½ tablespoon crushed red pepper
1 teaspoon whole black peppercorns
1 tablespoon extra-virgin olive oil
2 pounds ground lamb
Salt and freshly ground black pepper
6 large garlic cloves, coarsely chopped
1 large onion, coarsely chopped
1 large fennel bulb—halved, cored
and cut into ½-inch dice
½ teaspoon sweet smoked paprika
2 tablespoons harissa
One 14-ounce can whole tomatoes,
chopped, liquid reserved
2 cups chicken stock
1 pound dried *strozzapreti*
1 pint cherry tomatoes, halved
6 scallions, chopped
½ cup thinly sliced mint leaves
Freshly grated sheep-milk cheese, such
as Everona Stony Man or pecorino,
for serving

1. In a large enameled cast-iron casserole, combine the fennel, cumin, Aleppo pepper and peppercorns and cook over moderate heat until fragrant, 2 minutes. Let cool, then wrap in cheesecloth and tie into a bundle.
2. Add the oil to the casserole and heat. Add half of the lamb, season with salt and black pepper and cook over high heat, breaking it up with a spoon, until browned, 3 minutes. With a slotted spoon, transfer the lamb to a bowl. Repeat with the remaining lamb.
3. Pour off all but 2 tablespoons of the fat from the casserole. Add the garlic, onion and fennel and cook over moderate heat until softened, 8 minutes. Stir in the spice bundle, paprika, harissa, tomatoes and their liquid and the stock. Return the lamb and its juices to the casserole and bring to a simmer.

4. Cover the ragù and simmer over low heat for 45 minutes, stirring occasionally. Uncover and simmer until thickened, about 50 minutes longer. Discard the spice bundle and season the ragù with salt and black pepper.
5. In a large pot of salted boiling water, cook the *strozzapreti* until al dente. Drain and return to the pot. Add the ragù and stir. Fold in the cherry tomatoes, scallions and half of the mint. Season with salt and black pepper; transfer to a large bowl. Top with the remaining mint and serve, passing the cheese at the table. —*Michael Mina*
MAKE AHEAD The lamb ragù can be refrigerated for up to 3 days. Reheat gently.
WINE Juicy, spicy Pinot Noir: 2009 Gallo Signature Series Santa Lucia Highlands.

Bucatini all'Amatriciana

📷 PAGE 378
ACTIVE: 20 MIN; TOTAL: 50 MIN
4 SERVINGS ●

This classic Italian pasta recipe features long, hollow noodles in a porky sauce with tomatoes and pecorino cheese. True *amatriciana* sauce is made with *guanciale* (cured pork cheeks), but pancetta (cured pork belly) is a fine, easy-to-find substitute.

¼ cup extra-virgin olive oil
1 medium onion, thinly sliced
¼ pound *guanciale* or pancetta, cut
into ½-by-¼-inch strips (see Note)
1½ tablespoons white wine vinegar
1½ tablespoons dry white wine
One 14.5-ounce can whole peeled
tomatoes with their juices, crushed
Salt and freshly ground pepper
10 ounces bucatini
Freshly grated Pecorino Romano cheese

1. In a large, deep skillet, heat the oil. Add the onion and cook over moderately low heat until very soft, 7 minutes. Add the *guanciale* and cook until translucent, 3 minutes. Add the vinegar, wine, tomatoes and 2 tablespoons of water and simmer until thick, 30 minutes. Season with salt and pepper.
2. In a large pot of salted boiling water, cook the bucatini until al dente; drain, reserving 2

tablespoons of the cooking water. Add the pasta to the sauce along with the reserved cooking water and cook over moderate heat, stirring, for 1 minute. Remove the skillet from the heat and stir in 3 tablespoons of cheese. Serve, passing more cheese at the table.
—*Iside Maria de Cesare and Romano Gordini*
NOTE *Guanciale* is available at Italian markets or online at salumeriarosi.com.
WINE Smoky, peppery red: 2007 Castello Banfi Brunello di Montalcino.

Penne with Asparagus, Peas, Mushrooms and Cream

⏱ **TOTAL: 40 MIN • 8 TO 10 SERVINGS** ●
A simple vegetarian pasta, this dish combines the flavors of spring—mushrooms, peas and asparagus—in a luscious creamy sauce.

1 pound thin asparagus
3 tablespoons extra-virgin olive oil,
plus more for grilling
Salt and freshly ground pepper
3 medium shallots, minced
¾ pound shiitake mushrooms,
stems discarded
and caps thinly sliced
2¼ cups heavy cream
1½ pounds penne rigate
1½ cups frozen baby peas, thawed
¾ cup freshly grated
Parmigiano-Reggiano cheese
3 tablespoons finely chopped
flat-leaf parsley

1. Preheat a cast-iron grill pan. Brush the asparagus with olive oil and season lightly with salt and pepper. Grill the asparagus over high heat, turning, until it is lightly charred and very tender, about 6 minutes. Cut the asparagus into 1-inch lengths.
2. In a very large, deep skillet, heat the 3 tablespoons of olive oil. Add the shallots and cook over moderate heat until fragrant, about 1 minute. Add the shiitake, season with salt and pepper and cook, stirring once or twice, until the mushrooms are golden and tender, about 8 minutes. Add the cream and bring to a boil. Simmer until slightly reduced, about 4 minutes.

3. Meanwhile, in a large pot of salted boiling water, cook the pasta until al dente. Drain, reserving ¾ cup of the cooking water.

4. Add the pasta to the skillet along with the asparagus, peas and grated cheese and toss well. Add the reserved pasta water and simmer, tossing, until the pasta is nicely coated. Season the pasta with salt and pepper and stir in the parsley. Serve right away.
—*Grace Parisi*

WINE Tangy, medium-bodied Pinot Noir: 2009 Educated Guess.

Pasta with Fresh Tomatoes and Grilled Scallions

TOTAL: 25 MIN • 4 SERVINGS ● ●

An uncooked scallion-and-tomato puree comes together in a flash for this easy, three-ingredient recipe (not counting salt, pepper and olive oil).

4 large plum tomatoes—
    peeled, seeded and chopped
14 large scallions, 4 chopped
¼ cup extra-virgin olive oil, plus more
    for drizzling
Salt and freshly ground pepper
10 ounces campanelle or farfalle

1. In a food processor, pulse three-fourths of the tomatoes with the chopped scallions and the ¼ cup of olive oil to a coarse puree; season with salt and pepper.

2. Light a grill or preheat a grill pan. Drizzle the whole scallions with olive oil and season them with salt and pepper. Grill the scallions over high heat until lightly charred and tender, about 1 minute per side. Transfer the grilled scallions to a work surface and cut them into 1-inch pieces.

3. In a large pot of salted boiling water, cook the pasta until al dente. Drain and transfer the pasta to a large serving bowl. Add the tomato-scallion puree and the grilled scallions and toss well. Season with salt and pepper. Top the pasta with the remaining chopped tomatoes and serve.
—*Marcia Kiesel*

WINE Lively, light-bodied red: 2011 Tenuta delle Terre Nere Etna Rosso.

Pasta with Roasted Squash, Sausage and Pecans

ACTIVE: 30 MIN; TOTAL: 50 MIN
6 SERVINGS

2½ pounds butternut squash—peeled,
     seeded and cut into 1-inch dice
3 tablespoons extra-virgin olive oil
Salt and freshly ground pepper
Freshly grated nutmeg
1 tablespoon chopped sage,
    plus 20 whole leaves
½ cup pecans, coarsely chopped
3 tablespoons unsalted butter
1 pound sweet Italian sausage,
    casings removed
1 pound fusilli or other curly pasta
¼ cup freshly grated aged Asiago
    cheese, plus more for serving

1. Preheat the oven to 400°. On a large rimmed baking sheet, drizzle the squash with 2 tablespoons of oil and toss. Arrange in an even layer and season with salt, pepper and nutmeg. Bake until just tender, about 30 minutes. Add the chopped sage and toss.

2. Meanwhile, put the pecans in a pie plate and bake for about 4 minutes, until toasted.

3. In a large skillet, melt the butter. Add the whole sage leaves and cook over moderate heat, turning once, until crisp, 2 minutes. Transfer the leaves to a plate and pour the butter into a bowl. Add the remaining 1 tablespoon of oil and the sausage to the skillet and cook over moderately high heat, breaking up the sausage, until no pink remains, about 7 minutes.

4. In a large pot of salted boiling water, cook the pasta until al dente. Drain, reserving 1 cup of the cooking water. Return the pasta to the pot, then add the sausage and melted butter; gradually stir in the cooking water over moderate heat. Gently fold in the squash, pecans and the ¼ cup of cheese. Season with salt and pepper and transfer to a bowl. Scatter the crispy sage leaves on top and serve with more cheese.
—*Emeril Lagasse*

WINE Minerally, intensely berried Spanish red: 2007 Dominio do Bibei Lalama.

Fusilli with Asparagus, Zucchini and Basil-Mint Pesto

TOTAL: 45 MIN • 8 SERVINGS ●

Actor-turned-chef David Burtka of the Los Angeles catering company Gourmet M.D. created this entirely green dish: He tosses spinach fusilli and green vegetables in a pesto punched up with basil and mint.

¼ cup pine nuts
4 cups packed basil leaves
1 cup mint leaves
2 garlic cloves, smashed
1¼ cups extra-virgin olive oil
¼ cup freshly grated
    Parmigiano-Reggiano cheese,
    plus more for serving
Kosher salt and freshly ground
    black pepper
1 pound spinach fusilli
1 pound asparagus,
    cut into ½-inch pieces
¾ pound small zucchini,
    cut into 1-by-½-inch matchsticks
5 ounces baby spinach

1. In a small skillet, toast the pine nuts over moderate heat until golden, about 2 minutes; transfer to a plate and let cool. In a food processor, combine the pine nuts, basil, mint and garlic and pulse until finely chopped. With the machine on, add 1 cup of the olive oil in a steady stream. Add the ¼ cup of Parmigiano-Reggiano and pulse to incorporate. Season the pesto with salt and pepper.

2. In a large pot of salted boiling water, cook the fusilli until al dente. Drain the pasta and wipe out the pot.

3. Add the remaining ¼ cup of oil to the pot and heat until shimmering. Add the asparagus and zucchini, season with salt and pepper and cook over high heat until crisp-tender and browned in spots, 5 minutes. Stir in the spinach and cook just until wilted, 3 minutes. Add the pasta and pesto and toss well to coat. Season with salt and pepper and serve right away, passing additional grated cheese on the side. —*David Burtka*

WINE Vibrant, zesty white: 2011 Chehalem Grüner Veltliner.

Fregola with Charred Onions and Roasted Cherry Tomatoes

ACTIVE: 20 MIN; TOTAL: 1 HR 30 MIN
8 SERVINGS ● ● ●

San Francisco chef Jeff Banker uses fregola, a nicely chewy, bead-shaped pasta from Sardinia, as the base for this phenomenal summer salad. Roasting the cherry tomatoes in the oven before adding them to the fregola makes them especially sweet.

TOMATOES

- 1 pint cherry tomatoes
- 2 tablespoons extra-virgin olive oil
- 2 rosemary sprigs
- 2 thyme sprigs

Salt and freshly ground pepper

ONIONS

- 2 medium red onions, sliced ½ inch thick
- ¼ cup extra-virgin olive oil, plus more for brushing

Salt and freshly ground pepper

- ¼ cup balsamic vinegar

FREGOLA

- 3 cups fregola
- ¼ cup balsamic vinegar
- 3 tablespoons extra-virgin olive oil

Salt and freshly ground pepper

- 1 cup torn basil leaves

1. PREPARE THE TOMATOES Preheat the oven to 300°. On a rimmed baking sheet, toss the tomatoes with the oil. Add the rosemary and thyme; season with salt and pepper. Bake until the tomatoes are ready to burst, 40 minutes. Strip the crispy leaves from the herb stems; discard the stems. Increase the oven temperature to 350°.

2. PREPARE THE ONIONS Light a grill or preheat a grill pan. Brush the onions with olive oil and season with salt and pepper. Grill over moderately high heat until nicely charred but still crisp in the center, about 3 minutes per side.

3. Transfer the onions to a baking dish. Add the vinegar and the ¼ cup of olive oil and bake for 20 minutes, until tender. Let the onions cool in the liquid, then coarsely chop them. Reserve the liquid.

4. MAKE THE FREGOLA Bring a large pot of salted water to a boil. Add the fregola and cook, stirring occasionally, until the pasta is al dente, about 15 minutes. Drain and transfer to a large bowl.

5. While the fregola is still warm, add the onions and their cooking liquid, the tomatoes and crispy herbs. Stir in the vinegar and olive oil; season with salt and pepper. Garnish with the basil and serve. —*Jeff Banker*
MAKE AHEAD The recipe can be prepared through Step 3 and refrigerated overnight. Serve at room temperature.

Orzo Risotto with Dried Mushrooms and Country Ham

TOTAL: 30 MIN • 4 LARGE SERVINGS

- 2 tablespoons extra-virgin olive oil
- 2 large shallots, finely chopped
- 1¼ cups orzo (8 ounces)
- ½ teaspoon chopped rosemary
- 4 ounces country ham or prosciutto, sliced ¼ inch thick and cut into ¼-inch cubes
- ¾ ounce dried mushrooms, such as shiitake, black trumpet and maitake, pulverized with a mortar and pestle or a stone
- 5 cups water
- 1 ounce grated Parmigiano-Reggiano cheese (6 tablespoons)
- ½ teaspoon finely grated lemon zest

Salt and freshly ground pepper
Hot sauce, for serving

In a medium cast-iron casserole or Dutch oven, heat the olive oil. Add the shallots and cook over moderate heat until softened, about 3 minutes. Add the orzo, rosemary, ham and mushrooms and cook for 1 minute, stirring. Add the water ½ cup at a time and stir constantly, allowing the liquid to be absorbed between additions, until the orzo is al dente, about 20 minutes. Stir in the cheese and lemon zest and season with salt and pepper. Serve with hot sauce.
—*Grace Parisi*

WINE Light, berry-inflected Beaujolais: 2010 Georges Duboeuf Jean Descombes Morgon.

Fregola, Corn and Cherry Tomato Salad with Pancetta

TOTAL: 45 MIN • 8 SERVINGS ●

- 3 tablespoons canola oil
- 3 tablespoons red wine vinegar
- 2 tablespoons extra-virgin olive oil
- 2 tablespoons honey
- 2 teaspoons freshly squeezed lemon juice
- 1 teaspoon thyme leaves
- ½ teaspoon Dijon mustard
- ½ medium shallot, chopped

Salt and freshly ground pepper

- 4 ounces pancetta, sliced ⅛ inch thick and cut into ⅛-inch dice
- 1 pound fregola
- 1 cup fresh corn kernels (from 2 ears)
- 1 pint cherry tomatoes, halved

Four 3-inch stalks of hearts of palm, quartered lengthwise and sliced crosswise into ¼ inch thick
Snipped chives, for garnish

1. In a blender, combine the canola oil with the red wine vinegar, olive oil, honey, lemon juice, thyme, mustard and shallot and blend until smooth. Season the vinaigrette with salt and freshly ground pepper.

2. In a medium skillet, cook the pancetta over moderately low heat, stirring occasionally, until golden and crisp, about 15 minutes. Using a slotted spoon, transfer the pancetta to a paper towel–lined plate. Pour off all but 1 tablespoon of the fat in the skillet.

3. In a large pot of salted boiling water, cook the fregola, stirring, until al dente, 15 minutes. Drain the fregola, rinse under cold water and transfer to a large bowl.

4. Meanwhile, add the corn to the pancetta fat in the skillet and cook over moderate heat, stirring occasionally, until tender, 3 minutes. Add the corn to the fregola.

5. Add the cherry tomatoes, hearts of palm and pancetta to the bowl and toss gently. Add the vinaigrette and toss again. Season the fregola salad with salt and freshly ground pepper. Transfer the salad to a large serving bowl, sprinkle with the snipped chives and serve. —*Tara Lazar*

● HEALTHY ● MAKE AHEAD ● VEGETARIAN ● STAFF FAVORITE

fregola with charred onions and roasted cherry tomatoes

Risotto-Style Ditalini with Mussels, Clams and Saffron

ACTIVE: 45 MIN; TOTAL: 2 HR
4 SERVINGS ●

The pasta here gets cooked slowly in fish stock like risotto, so it absorbs the delicious briny flavors of the mussels and clams. If you can't find the short tube pasta called *ditalini* ("small thimbles" in Italian), look for other small pasta shapes or pearl couscous.

- 3 cups Fish Stock (recipe follows)
- 2 dozen littleneck clams, scrubbed
- 2 pounds mussels, scrubbed
- ½ teaspoon loosely packed saffron threads, crushed
- 1½ cups *ditalini* (8 ounces)
- 1 garlic clove, mashed to a paste
- 2 tablespoons chopped parsley

Extra-virgin olive oil, for serving

1. In a large pot, bring the Fish Stock to a simmer. Add the clams, cover and cook over moderately high heat until nearly all have opened, about 8 minutes. Add the mussels and cook until opened, 2 to 3 minutes. Using a slotted spoon, transfer the clams and mussels to a bowl; remove them from their shells. Discard any clams and mussels that have not opened. Strain the stock into a large heatproof measuring cup. Wipe out the pot and return 3 cups of the strained stock to the saucepan, stopping before you reach the grit at the bottom. Stir in the saffron and let stand for 5 minutes.

2. In a medium saucepan, combine the *ditalini* with ½ cup of the stock and bring to a simmer. Cook over moderate heat, stirring constantly, until the stock is absorbed. Continue adding stock ½ cup at a time, allowing it to be absorbed before adding more. The *ditalini* is done when it is al dente and suspended in a thick, rich sauce, about 25 minutes. Stir in the garlic, mussels and clams and cook 1 minute longer. Transfer the pasta to bowls. Sprinkle with the parsley, drizzle with olive oil and serve.
—*Curtis Di Fede and Tyler Rodde*
WINE Minerally, balanced Chardonnay: 2010 De Forville Piemonte.

FISH STOCK
TOTAL: 1 HR 15 MIN • MAKES ABOUT 9 CUPS ● ●

- ½ cup extra-virgin olive oil
- 2 pounds fish heads and bones, rinsed
- 1 leek, white and tender green parts only, thinly sliced
- 1 medium onion, finely chopped
- 1 fennel bulb, finely chopped

One 750-milliliter bottle dry white wine
- 1 bunch of parsley stems

Salt

In a large pot, heat the oil. Add the fish heads and bones, the leek, onion and fennel; cook over moderately high heat, stirring, until the vegetables are just tender, about 15 minutes. Add the wine and bring to a boil. Cook over moderately high heat until reduced by half, 20 minutes. Add 8 cups of water and the parsley stems and simmer over moderate heat for 30 minutes. Strain the broth and season it lightly with salt. —*CDF and TR*
MAKE AHEAD The stock can be frozen for up to 2 months.

Potato Gnocchi with Pastrami Ragù

ACTIVE: 1 HR; TOTAL: 3 HR • 4 SERVINGS
Making meat ragù out of pastrami is a clever twist on the classic. The ragù is delicious with gnocchi but would be great on any pasta.

Rock salt, for baking
Two 12-ounce Yukon Gold potatoes
- 1 cup all-purpose flour, plus more for dusting
- 2 large eggs, lightly beaten
- 2½ teaspoons kosher salt
- 1 tablespoon extra-virgin olive oil, plus more for drizzling
- 3 tablespoons unsalted butter
- 1 medium onion, minced
- 1 celery rib, minced
- 6 ounces sliced pastrami, finely chopped (1½ cups)
- 1 cup low-sodium chicken broth
- ¼ cup sour cream
- ¼ cup sliced chives

1. Preheat the oven to 350°. Line a small baking pan with rock salt. Pierce the potatoes with a fork and place on the salt. Bake for about 1 hour and 15 minutes, until tender.

2. As soon as the potatoes are cool enough to handle, peel them and pass them through a ricer into a bowl. Let the potatoes cool.

3. Lightly dust a baking sheet with flour. Stir the eggs, the 1 cup of flour and the kosher salt into the riced potatoes. Gently knead a few times to form a dough that just holds together. Divide the dough into 4 equal pieces. On a lightly floured work surface, roll out 1 piece of the dough into a ½-inch-thick rope. Cut the rope into ½-inch pieces and transfer the gnocchi to the prepared baking sheet. Repeat with the remaining dough. Refrigerate the gnocchi for at least 1 hour and up to 4 hours.

4. Bring a large pot of salted water to a boil. Fill a large bowl with ice water. Boil the gnocchi just until they rise to the surface of the water, about 1 minute. With a slotted spoon, transfer the gnocchi to the ice water to chill, then drain on paper towels and pat dry. Transfer the gnocchi to a bowl and drizzle with olive oil.

5. In a large skillet, melt 1 tablespoon of the butter in the 1 tablespoon of oil. Add the onion, cover and cook over moderate heat until translucent, 4 minutes. Add the celery, cover and cook over moderately low heat, stirring, until richly browned, 15 minutes.

6. In a food processor, mince the pastrami. Add the pastrami to the skillet along with 1 cup of water and the chicken broth and bring to a boil. Simmer over low heat until most of the liquid has evaporated, about 1 hour.

7. In a nonstick skillet, melt 1 tablespoon of the butter. When the foam subsides, add half of the gnocchi and cook over moderate heat, turning, until browned all over, 5 minutes. Transfer to a bowl; repeat with the remaining 1 tablespoon of butter and gnocchi.

8. Spoon the sour cream onto 4 plates and top with the gnocchi and pastrami ragù. Garnish with the chives and serve.
—*Mario Carbone and Rich Torrisi*
WINE Vibrant, spicy Barbera d'Alba: 2010 Fantino Coterno Vignota.

potato gnocchi with pastrami ragù

Parsnip Triangoli with Aged Balsamic Vinegar

ACTIVE: 1 HR; TOTAL: 1 HR 30 MIN
6 FIRST-COURSE SERVINGS ●

DOUGH

- 2 cups 00 flour (see Note)
- 3 large eggs
- 2 teaspoons extra-virgin olive oil
- 1 teaspoon kosher salt

FILLING

- 1 tablespoon extra-virgin olive oil
- 1 small onion, thinly sliced
- 1 cup finely diced peeled parsnips
- ¼ cup freshly grated Parmigiano-Reggiano cheese
- 1 teaspoon Champagne vinegar

Kosher salt

- 1 stick unsalted butter

Snipped chives, chopped parsley and aged balsamic vinegar, for serving

1. MAKE THE DOUGH In a food processor, combine all of the ingredients and process until crumbly. Gather the dough and knead until smooth. Wrap tightly in plastic and let stand at room temperature for 30 minutes.

2. MAKE THE FILLING Heat the olive oil in a saucepan. Add the onion and cook until softened. Add the parsnips and ½ cup of water, cover and simmer until tender, about 15 minutes. Uncover and boil to evaporate any water.

3. Transfer the vegetables to the food processor and puree. Stir in the Parmigiano and Champagne vinegar and season with salt. Let the filling cool slightly, then scrape it into a pastry bag fitted with a ½-inch tip.

4. Cut the pasta dough into 4 pieces and keep wrapped. Using a hand-cranked pasta machine and dusting lightly with flour, run each piece of dough through each setting 3 times, beginning at the widest setting and ending at the second-to-narrowest. Place the pasta sheet on a floured work surface and cover with wax paper. Repeat with the remaining 3 pieces of pasta dough.

5. Working with one sheet at a time, cut the pasta into 2-inch squares. Lightly moisten the edges with water and pipe a scant teaspoon of parsnip filling in the center of each square. Fold the pasta corner to corner to form triangles and press out any air. Trim the edges with a fluted pastry wheel. Transfer the *triangoli* to a floured baking sheet.

6. Bring a large pot of generously salted water to a boil. Add the *triangoli* all at once and cook until al dente, about 5 minutes. Drain, reserving ½ cup of the cooking water.

7. In a large skillet, melt the butter in the cooking water; swirl the pan until a creamy sauce forms. Add the *triangoli*; cook over moderately high heat until hot and coated with sauce. Transfer to plates. Garnish with chives and parsley, drizzle balsamic on top and serve. —*Thomas McNaughton*

NOTE *Doppio zero* ("double zero") flour is a fine Italian flour available at *amazon.com*.
WINE Smooth, fruity Italian white: 2010 Villa Matilde Falanghina.

Speedy Baked Ziti

TOTAL: 45 MIN • 8 SERVINGS ●

- 1 pound ziti or penne
- 1 tablespoon extra-virgin olive oil
- 1 medium onion, finely chopped
- 3 garlic cloves, minced
- 1 pound lean ground sirloin
- ¼ teaspoon crushed red pepper
- ½ teaspoon smoked paprika

Salt

One 24-ounce jar marinara sauce (3 cups)

- 1½ cups fresh ricotta (about 12 ounces)
- ½ pound packaged mozzarella, shredded
- ¼ cup freshly grated Parmigiano-Reggiano cheese

1. Preheat the oven to 450° and bring a large pot of salted water to a boil. Boil the ziti until just al dente. Drain and return to the pot.

2. Meanwhile, in a large, deep skillet, heat the oil. Add the onion and garlic, cover and cook until just softened, 2 minutes. Add the sirloin, crushed red pepper and paprika; season with salt. Cook over high heat, stirring to break up the meat, until the meat is no longer pink, 3 minutes. Add the marinara and bring to a boil. Cover partially and cook over moderate heat for 5 minutes.

3. Add the sauce to the ziti in the pot and stir to coat it thoroughly. Add the ricotta in large dollops and stir gently, leaving it in large clumps. Pour half of the ziti into a 9-by-13-inch baking dish and top with half of the mozzarella and Parmigiano. Repeat with the remaining ziti and cheeses.

4. Bake the ziti on the top rack of the oven for about 15 minutes, until it is bubbling and browned. Let the ziti rest for 10 minutes before serving. —*Grace Parisi*

WINE Tart-berried, medium-bodied Barbera d'Asti: 2009 Michele Chiarlo Le Orme.

Crunchy Couscous Galette

TOTAL: 40 MIN • 8 SERVINGS ●

- 4 tablespoons unsalted butter
- ½ cup thinly sliced shallots
- 2 cups couscous
- 2 cups low-sodium chicken broth

Salt

- 3 large eggs
- 7 ounces Gruyère cheese, shredded (2 cups)

Freshly ground pepper

- 2 tablespoons extra-virgin olive oil

1. In a large saucepan, melt 2 tablespoons of the butter. Add the shallots; cook over high heat, stirring, until softened, 2 minutes. Add the couscous; cook, stirring, for 2 minutes. Remove from the heat. Add the broth and a pinch of salt, cover and let stand until the liquid has been absorbed, 5 minutes.

2. Fluff the couscous and scrape it into a large bowl. Let cool for 5 minutes, stirring occasionally. Stir in the eggs and cheese and season with salt and pepper.

3. Preheat the broiler. In a large nonstick skillet, melt 1 tablespoon of the butter in the oil. Spread the couscous mixture in the skillet. Dot with the remaining 1 tablespoon of butter; cook over moderately high heat until golden on the bottom, 5 minutes. Broil the galette 8 inches from the heat until golden and sizzling, about 5 minutes. Using oven mitts, invert a large plate over the skillet. Carefully flip the galette out onto the plate, cut into wedges and serve. —*Grace Parisi*

● HEALTHY ● MAKE AHEAD ○ VEGETARIAN ● STAFF FAVORITE

parsnip triangoli with aged balsamic vinegar

Baked Broccoli Ravioli

TOTAL: 1 HR • 4 SERVINGS ●

These fresh, free-form ravioli are filled with pureed broccoli and cheese, then baked until crisp at the edges.

 1 cup packed basil leaves
 ½ cup plus 2 tablespoons extra-virgin olive oil, plus more for the dish
Salt
 2 garlic cloves, thinly sliced
1½ pounds broccoli, cut into 2-inch florets
 1 tablespoon unsalted butter
 ½ cup fresh ricotta cheese
 ¼ cup plus 3 tablespoons freshly grated pecorino cheese, plus more for serving
 8 ounces fresh lasagna sheets

1. Blanch the basil in boiling water for 20 seconds. Drain and rinse under cold water; squeeze dry. In a mini food processor, puree the basil with ½ cup of the oil. Season with salt and transfer to a small bowl.
2. In a large skillet, heat 2 tablespoons of the oil. Add the garlic and cook for 30 seconds. Add the broccoli, ½ cup of water and the butter, cover and cook over moderately low heat until tender, 10 minutes. Let cool. Coarsely puree the broccoli in a food processor; transfer to a bowl. Stir in the ricotta and ¼ cup of the pecorino and season with salt.
3. Bring a large pot of salted water to a boil. Using a pasta machine, roll the lasagna sheets through the thinnest setting. Cut the sheets into twelve 4-inch squares. Cook the squares in the water until tender, 2 minutes. Drain, pat dry and rub with oil to prevent sticking.
4. Preheat the oven to 425°. Coat a large, shallow baking dish with oil. Place 2 heaping tablespoons of the filling into the center of each pasta square, then fold into triangles; arrange in the dish. Sprinkle with 3 tablespoons of the pecorino. Bake on the top rack for 10 minutes, until the cheese starts to brown. Drizzle with the basil oil; serve, passing more cheese at the table. —*Bill Telepan*
WINE Nutty, apple-scented Italian white: 2010 Palazzone Terre Vineate Orvieto.

Goat Cheese Ravioli with Orange and Fennel

TOTAL: 1 HR • 6 SERVINGS ● ●

 11 ounces fresh goat cheese, softened
 ¼ cup milk
 1 tablespoon chopped flat-leaf parsley
 ¼ teaspoon chopped sage
 ¼ teaspoon chopped rosemary
 ¼ teaspoon chopped thyme
 ¼ teaspoon freshly grated nutmeg
 ½ cup freshly grated Parmigiano-Reggiano cheese
Salt and freshly ground pepper
All-purpose flour, for dusting
One 12-ounce package wonton wrappers
 1 stick unsalted butter
 2 tablespoons coarsely chopped fennel fronds
 ½ teaspoon finely grated orange zest
Pinch of fennel pollen

1. In a bowl, combine the goat cheese, milk, parsley, sage, rosemary, thyme, nutmeg and ¼ cup of the Parmigiano and season with salt and pepper. Refrigerate for 10 minutes.
2. Line a baking sheet with wax paper and dust with flour. Arrange 6 wonton wrappers on a work surface and brush with water. Drop teaspoons of the goat cheese mixture onto the center of each wonton. Fold into triangles, pressing out the air to seal. Transfer the ravioli to the baking sheet and repeat with the remaining wonton wrappers and filling.
3. Bring a pot of salted water to a boil. Add the goat cheese ravioli and cook just until al dente, about 3 minutes. Drain the ravioli, reserving ½ cup of the pasta cooking water.
4. In a very large skillet, melt the butter. Add the reserved ½ cup of cooking water; cook, shaking the pan, until creamy and emulsified. Add the ravioli, fennel fronds and zest; cook, tossing gently, until the ravioli are nicely coated. Transfer to plates, sprinkle with the remaining grated cheese and the fennel pollen and serve. —*Mario Batali*
MAKE AHEAD The uncooked ravioli can be refrigerated for up to 4 hours.
WINE Zippy, grapefruit-scented Sauvignon Blanc: 2010 Fattori Vecchie Scuole.

Four-Cheese Mac and Cheese

ACTIVE: 40 MIN; TOTAL: 1 HR 35 MIN
6 SERVINGS ● ●

 ¼ cup vegetable oil
 ½ cup finely diced onion
 1 garlic clove, minced
 ¼ cup all-purpose flour
 1 quart whole milk
 ½ teaspoon celery seeds
 ⅛ teaspoon ground mace
 3 tablespoons Tabasco
 ¼ teaspoon cayenne pepper
 10 ounces extra-sharp cheddar cheese, shredded (3 cups)
 4 ounces Muenster cheese, shredded (1¼ cups)
 2 ounces Swiss cheese, shredded (¾ cup)
 ¼ cup cream cheese
Salt and freshly ground black pepper
Butter, for the dish
 1 pound medium pasta shells

1. In a large saucepan, heat the oil until shimmering. Add the onion and cook over moderate heat until translucent, 5 minutes. Add the garlic and cook until fragrant, 1 minute. Stir in the flour to make a paste. Gradually whisk in the milk until smooth. Bring to a simmer, whisking, until the sauce thickens. Reduce the heat to low and simmer, whisking often, until no floury taste remains, 7 minutes. Add the celery seeds, mace, Tabasco and cayenne. Stir in the cheeses just until they melt. Remove from the heat and season the sauce with salt and black pepper.
2. Butter a large, shallow baking dish. In a large pot of salted boiling water, cook the pasta shells until almost al dente, about 4 minutes. Drain the pasta and return it to the pot. Stir in the cheese sauce until thoroughly combined. Transfer the mixture to the prepared dish and let stand for 20 minutes.
3. Meanwhile, preheat the oven to 425°. Bake the pasta in the upper third of the oven for 25 minutes, until it's bubbling and starting to brown. Turn the broiler on and broil the pasta for about 1 minute, until it's browned and crisp on top.

● HEALTHY ● MAKE AHEAD ● VEGETARIAN ● STAFF FAVORITE

4. Let the mac and cheese rest for 10 minutes before serving. —*Brian Perrone*

MAKE AHEAD The cheese sauce can be refrigerated overnight and reheated gently; add more milk if it is too thick.

WINE Rich, peppery Zinfandel: 2011 Ravenswood Vintners Blend Old Vine.

Cannelloni with Walnuts and Fried Sage

ACTIVE: 2 HR; TOTAL: 4 HR 15 MIN
6 SERVINGS ● ●

To create his outstanding cannelloni, chef Matthew Accarrino of SPQR in San Francisco fills rectangles of fresh pasta with beef that's been braised in red wine, then bakes the dish in a béchamel sauce. Each bite should include tender shredded beef, creamy sauce, toasted nuts and crispy fried sage.

BRAISED BEEF FILLING

2 tablespoons vegetable oil
1½ pounds trimmed boneless beef chuck, cut into 1-inch pieces
Salt and freshly ground pepper
1 each of onion and carrot, finely diced
2 garlic cloves, minced
1½ teaspoons tomato paste
1 cup dry red wine
2 cups chicken stock
2 thyme sprigs
1 cup fresh ricotta cheese
¼ cup freshly grated Parmigiano-Reggiano cheese
2 tablespoons chopped flat-leaf parsley
1 large egg, lightly beaten

PASTA RECTANGLES

2 cups all-purpose flour
¼ teaspoon salt
3 large eggs, lightly beaten
Olive oil, for coating

BÉCHAMEL SAUCE

4 tablespoons unsalted butter
⅓ cup all-purpose flour
4 cups milk
¼ cup freshly grated Parmigiano-Reggiano cheese
Freshly grated nutmeg
Salt and freshly ground pepper

TO FINISH THE DISH

2 tablespoons unsalted butter, plus more for the dish
3 tablespoons freshly grated Parmigiano-Reggiano cheese
12 sage leaves
½ cup walnuts, toasted and chopped
2 tablespoons freshly squeezed lemon juice

1. MAKE THE BRAISED BEEF FILLING Preheat the oven to 350°. In an enameled cast-iron casserole, heat the vegetable oil. Season the beef with salt and pepper and cook over high heat until browned on two sides, about 7 minutes total. Transfer the meat to a bowl and pour off all but 1 tablespoon of the fat from the casserole.

2. Add the onion, carrot, garlic and a large pinch of salt to the casserole. Cook over moderately low heat until the vegetables soften, 5 minutes. Stir in the tomato paste until shiny, 10 seconds. Stir in the wine; boil over moderately high heat until reduced by half, 4 minutes. Add the chicken stock and thyme sprigs and bring to a boil. Add the beef and any accumulated juices. Cover and braise in the oven until the meat is tender, 1 hour. Discard the thyme sprigs.

3. Transfer the beef and vegetables to a large bowl. Reduce the braising liquid over high heat to ½ cup, about 5 minutes; let cool. Coarsely shred the beef and mix well with the vegetables. Stir in the ricotta, Parmigiano and parsley and season with salt and pepper. Stir in the egg and the cool braising liquid. Cover and refrigerate the filling.

4. MAKE THE PASTA RECTANGLES In a food processor, pulse the flour and salt. With the machine on, add the eggs; process until the dough looks like wet sand. On a work surface, knead the dough until smooth. Wrap in plastic and let stand for 15 minutes.

5. Cut the dough in half and flatten each piece to a ¼-inch thickness; keep one piece covered. Run the other piece through progressively narrower settings on a pasta machine, through the thinnest setting. Cut the sheet into nine 6-by-5½-inch rectangles. Repeat with the second piece of dough.

6. Cook the pasta in a large pot of salted boiling water until al dente, about 1 minute. Transfer the pasta to a bowl of cold water. Drain and pat dry with paper towels; coat the pasta lightly with olive oil.

7. MAKE THE BÉCHAMEL SAUCE In a medium saucepan, melt the butter. Add the flour and whisk over moderately high heat to a thick paste, about 20 seconds. Gradually whisk in the milk and bring to a boil, whisking constantly until the sauce thickens. Reduce the heat to low and simmer, whisking, until no floury taste remains, about 7 minutes. Stir in the Parmigiano-Reggiano; season with nutmeg, salt and pepper.

8. FINISH THE DISH Preheat the oven to 350°. Butter a 9-by-13-inch baking dish. On a work surface, arrange the pasta rectangles with the shorter end facing you. Fill each rectangle with about 3 tablespoons of the braised beef filling and loosely roll them up lengthwise. In the prepared baking dish, spread 1 cup of the béchamel sauce in an even layer. Arrange the cannelloni seam side down on the béchamel in the dish. Pour the remaining béchamel sauce over the cannelloni and sprinkle with the grated Parmigiano-Reggiano cheese.

9. Cover the cannelloni with foil and bake for about 40 minutes, until hot and bubbling. Remove from the oven and uncover. Preheat the broiler. Broil about 6 inches from the heat until golden brown, about 3 minutes. Let rest for 15 minutes.

10. In a medium skillet, melt the 2 tablespoons of butter. Add the sage leaves and cook over moderate heat until crisp, about 1 minute per side. Using a slotted spoon, transfer the fried sage to a paper towel–lined plate. Add the toasted walnuts and lemon juice to the skillet and swirl to blend. Spoon the topping over the cannelloni, sprinkle with the fried sage and serve hot.
—*Matthew Accarrino*

MAKE AHEAD The assembled cannelloni can be wrapped tightly and refrigerated overnight. Let the cannelloni return to room temperature before baking.

WINE Robust, decadent Barolo: 2007 Paolo Scavino Bric dëi Fiasc.

Ricotta-and-Fontina-Stuffed Shells with Fennel and Radicchio

ACTIVE: 45 MIN; TOTAL: 1 HR 45 MIN
6 SERVINGS ● ● ●

F&W's Grace Parisi elevates standard baked stuffed shells by folding Fontina cheese, fennel and radicchio into the ricotta filling.

- 2 tablespoons unsalted butter
- 2 tablespoons extra-virgin olive oil
- 2 pounds fennel bulbs, thinly sliced
- 1 medium sweet onion, thinly sliced
- 2 medium heads of radicchio (10 ounces total), chopped
- 12 ounces jumbo shells
- 2 cups fresh ricotta cheese
- 6 ounces Italian Fontina cheese, shredded (1½ cups)
- ¼ cup chopped parsley
- Salt and freshly ground pepper
- 2 large eggs, beaten
- 3 cups Best-Ever Marinara (recipe follows) or jarred sauce
- ½ cup heavy cream

1. Preheat the oven to 375°. In a large, deep skillet, melt the butter in the olive oil. Add the fennel and onion; cook over moderate heat, stirring occasionally, until lightly browned, about 15 minutes; add water as needed to keep the vegetables from scorching. Add the radicchio and cook until very soft, about 10 minutes, adding water as needed. Scrape the vegetables into a bowl and let cool.

2. Meanwhile, in a large pot of salted boiling water, cook the pasta until al dente. Drain and cool the pasta under running water. Pat the shells dry.

3. Fold the ricotta, 1 cup of the Fontina and the parsley into the vegetables and season with salt and pepper. Stir in the eggs.

4. In another bowl, mix the marinara sauce with the heavy cream. Pour 1½ cups into a 9-by-13-inch baking dish. Stuff each shell with a slightly rounded tablespoon of the filling and nestle the shells in the sauce as close together as possible. Drizzle 1 cup of the remaining sauce on top and sprinkle with the remaining ½ cup of Fontina.

5. Bake the shells for about 40 minutes, until golden. Let rest for 15 minutes. Warm the remaining sauce and serve on the side. —*Grace Parisi*

MAKE AHEAD The recipe can be prepared through Step 4 and refrigerated overnight.
WINE Floral, light-bodied Italian red: 2011 Matteo Correggia Anthos.

BEST-EVER MARINARA
ACTIVE: 10 MIN; TOTAL: 40 MIN
MAKES 3 CUPS ● ● ●

- ¼ cup extra-virgin olive oil
- 3 garlic cloves, halved
- 1 tablespoon tomato paste
- One 35-ounce can whole peeled Italian tomatoes
- Kosher salt and freshly ground black pepper
- Pinch of sugar
- 2 basil sprigs

In a large saucepan, heat the extra-virgin olive oil. Add the garlic cloves and cook over moderate heat, stirring occasionally, until golden, about 5 minutes. Add the tomato paste and cook, stirring, for 1 minute. Add the tomatoes and crush them with the back of a spoon; season with salt and pepper. Stir in the sugar and basil sprigs and bring to a boil. Simmer over low heat, stirring occasionally, until the sauce is thickened and reduced to 3 cups, about 30 minutes. Discard the basil sprigs and garlic. —*GP*

Wild-Mushroom Lasagna

ACTIVE: 45 MIN; TOTAL: 2 HR
8 TO 10 SERVINGS ● ●

- 2 tablespoons unsalted butter
- 2 tablespoons extra-virgin olive oil
- 3 medium shallots, minced
- 2 pounds wild mushrooms, such as chanterelle, stemmed shiitake and oyster, caps thickly sliced
- Salt and freshly ground white pepper
- ½ cup dry white wine
- 2 cups plus 2 tablespoons heavy cream
- ¼ cup finely chopped flat-leaf parsley
- 12 ounces fresh lasagna sheets
- 1 pound Taleggio cheese, rind removed and cheese cut into ½-inch cubes

1. Preheat the oven to 350° and lightly butter a 9-by-13-inch baking dish. In a large, deep skillet, melt the 2 tablespoons of butter in the oil. Add the shallots and cook, stirring, for 1 minute. Add the mushrooms, season with salt and pepper and cook over high heat, stirring occasionally, until the mushrooms are browned, about 18 minutes. Add the wine and boil until evaporated, about 1 minute. Add 2 cups of the cream and bring to a boil. Simmer over moderate heat until slightly reduced, about 5 minutes. Stir in the parsley; season with salt and pepper.

2. Meanwhile, in a large pot of salted boiling water, cook the lasagna sheets until barely al dente. Fill a large bowl with ice water. Drain the sheets and immediately transfer them to the ice water to cool. Drain and pat dry.

3. Arrange one-fourth of the pasta in the baking dish. Top with one-third of the mushroom mixture and one-fourth of the cheese. Repeat this layering twice more, ending with a layer of pasta. Brush with the remaining cream; scatter the remaining cheese on top.

4. Cover the lasagna very loosely with buttered parchment; bake in the upper third of the oven for 15 minutes. Remove the parchment; bake until the top is golden in spots, 15 minutes longer. Cover loosely and let rest for 15 minutes before serving. —*Grace Parisi*
WINE Elegant, raspberry-inflected Pinot Noir: 2010 Etude Estate.

INGREDIENT TIP

marinara sauce We tasted 33 brands of jarred marinara; our overwhelming favorite was the tangy, balanced sauce by Rao's. It's a great time-saving shortcut for pasta recipes like the baked stuffed shells with fennel and radicchio above. *$8 for 24 oz; amazon.com.*

● HEALTHY   ● MAKE AHEAD   ● VEGETARIAN   ● STAFF FAVORITE

ricotta-and-fontina-stuffed shells with fennel and radicchio

Beef Ragù, Mozzarella and Mushroom Timballo

ACTIVE: 1 HR 30 MIN; TOTAL: 4 HR
MAKES TWO 10-INCH PIES; 16 SERVINGS ●

DOUGH

- 5 cups all-purpose flour
- 2½ teaspoons salt
- 5 sticks unsalted butter, cut into ½-inch dice and chilled
- 1 cup plus 2 tablespoons ice water

FILLING

- ½ pound thick-cut bacon, cut crosswise ½ inch thick
- 7 tablespoons extra-virgin olive oil
- 1 large onion, finely chopped
- 4 garlic cloves, minced
- 2 teaspoons each of chopped thyme, rosemary and oregano

Salt and freshly ground pepper
Two 28-ounce cans whole tomatoes

- 2 ounces dried porcini mushrooms
- ¾ pound cremini mushrooms, sliced
- 2½ pounds ground beef sirloin
- ½ pound sweet Italian sausage, casings removed
- 1 cup dry red wine
- 16 ounces veal demiglace
- 1 pound dried thin pappardelle
- 1 cup freshly grated Parmigiano-Reggiano cheese (4 ounces)
- 1 pound fresh mozzarella, thinly sliced
- 1 egg yolk beaten with 2 tablespoons of water
- 8 cups warm tomato sauce (optional)

1. MAKE THE DOUGH In a food processor, pulse the flour and salt. Add the butter and pulse 10 times. Sprinkle on ½ cup plus 1 tablespoon of the ice water and pulse 5 times. Add another ½ cup of the water and pulse 5 times, until the dough just holds together when pinched; add the remaining 1 tablespoon of water if necessary. Divide the dough into thirds. Form 2 pieces into 8-inch disks. Cut the remaining dough in half and form into 2 small disks. Wrap all the disks in plastic and refrigerate them until firm, at least 1 hour.

2. MEANWHILE, MAKE THE FILLING In a saucepan, cook the bacon until crisp. Transfer the bacon to a plate and pour off the fat.
3. Add 2 tablespoons of the oil and the onion to the pan and cook over moderate heat until the onion softens. Add the garlic and herbs; season with salt and pepper. Add the tomatoes with their juice; crush with a potato masher. Cook, stirring occasionally, until the sauce is very thick, about 30 minutes.
4. Bring 2 cups of water to a boil. Add the porcini and let stand until softened, 10 minutes. Drain, reserving 1 cup of the soaking liquid. Rinse and finely chop the porcini.
5. In a large, deep skillet, heat ¼ cup of the olive oil. Add the porcini and cremini and cook over moderately high heat until the cremini are lightly browned, 7 minutes. Add the mushrooms and the bacon to the tomato sauce.
6. Add the ground beef and sausage to the skillet, season with salt and pepper and cook over high heat, breaking up the meat, until lightly browned, 15 minutes. Spoon off as much fat as possible. Add the wine and cook until evaporated. Add the demiglace and the reserved 1 cup of porcini soaking liquid and simmer over moderate heat for 15 minutes. Add the meat to the tomato sauce and simmer until nearly dry, about 10 minutes.
7. Preheat the oven to 350°. On a lightly floured surface, roll out each large piece of the dough into an 18-inch round. Fit the dough into two 10-inch springform pans (2½ to 3 inches deep), allowing it to hang over the rims. Line the dough with parchment and fill with pie weights. Refrigerate until firm, at least 10 minutes. Bake the crusts for 30 minutes; remove the paper and weights and bake until golden, about 15 minutes longer. Let the crusts cool slightly. Carefully trim the overhang flush with the rims. Turn the oven up to 400°.
8. In a large pot of salted boiling water, cook the pappardelle until al dente; drain and toss with the remaining 1 tablespoon of olive oil.
9. Sprinkle ¼ cup of the Parmigiano in each crust. Top with one-fourth of the pasta, 2½ cups of the sauce and one-fourth of the mozzarella. Repeat the layering in each crust, ending with the mozzarella.

10. On a lightly floured surface, roll the two smaller pieces of dough into 11-inch rounds. Brush the rims with the egg wash and invert the rounds over the filling; press the edges to seal and trim the dough as necessary. Brush the tops with egg wash and make several slits to release steam. Bake until the tops are golden and the pies are hot, 30 to 35 minutes: To test, insert a metal skewer into the centers for 5 seconds. If the skewer feels hot, the pie is ready. Let cool for 15 minutes, then unmold. Serve the pies in wedges with warm tomato sauce. —*Daniel Duane*
WINE Robust, dark-fruited Brunello di Montalcino: 2007 Col d'Orcia.

Cold Soba Salad with Dried Shiitake Dressing

📷 PAGE 77

TOTAL: 1 HR • 20 SIDE-DISH SERVINGS
● ● ○

- ½ ounce dried shiitake mushrooms
- 1 cup light soy sauce
- ½ cup mirin
- 1 tablespoon thinly sliced fresh ginger
- 3 tablespoons Thai sweet chile sauce
- ¼ cup canola oil

Kosher salt
Two 14-ounce packages soba noodles

- 4 large carrots, finely julienned
- 1 cup finely julienned pickled daikon (available at Asian markets)
- ½ pound mung bean sprouts
- ¼ cup black sesame seeds

1. In a small saucepan, combine the shiitake, soy sauce, mirin and ginger; simmer over low heat for 10 minutes. Strain into a blender and add the sweet chile sauce and oil. Blend until emulsified. Let the dressing cool.
2. Bring a large pot of lightly salted water to a boil; fill a large bowl with ice water. Boil the soba until tender, 3 minutes. Drain in a colander; set the colander in the ice water. Toss to cool; drain well, shaking out the excess water. Transfer to a bowl. Add the carrots, daikon, bean sprouts, sesame seeds and dressing; toss to coat. Serve lightly chilled or at room temperature. —*Susan Feniger*

● HEALTHY ● MAKE AHEAD ○ VEGETARIAN ● STAFF FAVORITE

beef ragù, mozzarella and mushroom timballo

Asian Noodles with Roast Pork

ACTIVE: 35 MIN; TOTAL: 1 HR

6 SERVINGS ●

This traditional Singaporean dish is a savory mix of fresh noodles, Chinese broccoli and two kinds of pork, roasted and ground.

2 tablespoons canola oil

2 large shallots, finely chopped

2 garlic cloves, minced

1 pound ground pork

1 tablespoon light brown sugar

1½ tablespoons Chinese black bean sauce

4 dried hot chiles

2 teaspoons Maggi sauce (a vegetable-based liquid seasoning) or soy sauce

2 teaspoons Asian fish sauce

1¼ cups low-sodium chicken broth

1½ tablespoons unseasoned rice vinegar

2 tablespoons oyster sauce

1 teaspoon toasted sesame oil

1 tablespoon *sambal oelek* (hot chile sauce)

1 pound Chinese broccoli

1 pound fresh Chinese egg noodles, linguine or spaghetti

½ pound Chinese roast pork, thinly sliced

1 scallion, thinly sliced

1. In a very large nonstick skillet, heat 1 tablespoon of the canola oil. Add the shallots and garlic and stir-fry over moderately high heat until lightly browned, about 2 minutes. Add the ground pork, brown sugar, black bean sauce, dried chiles, Maggi sauce and fish sauce and cook, breaking up the meat with a spoon, until it is browned in spots, about 10 minutes. Add ¾ cup of the chicken broth and cook over moderately low heat until the broth has evaporated, about 8 minutes. Stir in 1 tablespoon of the rice vinegar. Transfer the ground pork mixture to a bowl and wipe out the skillet.

2. In a jar, combine the remaining ½ cup of chicken broth and ½ tablespoon of rice vinegar with the oyster sauce, sesame oil and *sambal oelek*. Seal the jar and shake the sauce to blend.

3. Bring a large pot of water to a boil. Add the Chinese broccoli and cook until it is crisp-tender, about 2 minutes. Using tongs, transfer the broccoli to a work surface and cut it into 1-inch pieces. Return the water to a boil and add the Chinese egg noodles. Cook just until al dente. Drain the noodles, shaking off the excess water.

4. Heat the remaining 1 tablespoon of canola oil in the skillet. Add the roast pork, ground pork mixture, broccoli and noodles and toss to combine. Add the sauce and cook, tossing, until the noodles are evenly coated, 5 minutes. Add the scallion, transfer to a large platter and serve. —*Bryant Ng*

WINE Lightly sweet, full-bodied German Riesling: 2011 Leitz Dragonstone.

Cold Peanut-Sesame Noodles

ACTIVE: 30 MIN; TOTAL: 1 HR 30 MIN

6 SERVINGS ● ● ●

The key to this Sichuan-style noodle recipe from Andrew Zimmern, host of the Travel Channel's *Bizarre Foods* and an F&W contributing editor, is the oil that gets drizzled on top. Called Ma La ("numbing and spicy"), it's made with hot Chinese chiles, Sichuan peppercorns and star anise.

1 tablespoon minced peeled fresh ginger

⅓ cup soy sauce

3 tablespoons toasted sesame oil

3 tablespoons natural unsweetened salted peanut butter

3 tablespoons sugar

3 tablespoons rice vinegar

2 tablespoons rice wine or sake

1 small garlic clove, minced

3 tablespoons Chinese sesame paste or tahini

1 small shallot, minced

5 tablespoons roasted peanut oil (see Note)

1 pound dried Chinese egg noodles

½ large seedless cucumber—peeled, halved lengthwise, seeded and cut into fine matchsticks

4 scallions, thinly sliced

Ma La Oil (recipe follows)

1. In a blender, combine the ginger, soy sauce, sesame oil, peanut butter, sugar, vinegar, rice wine, garlic, sesame paste, shallot and 3 tablespoons of the peanut oil and puree until smooth. Transfer the sauce to a bowl and refrigerate for 45 minutes.

2. In a large pot of boiling water, cook the noodles until al dente. Drain and rinse under cold running water until chilled. Shake out the excess water and blot dry; transfer the noodles to a large bowl and toss with the remaining 2 tablespoons of peanut oil. Add the peanut-sesame sauce and toss well to coat. Garnish with the cucumber and scallions and drizzle with Ma La Oil, leaving the solid spices behind. —*Andrew Zimmern*

NOTE Roasted peanut oil, unlike neutral peanut oil, smells richly nutty. Boyajin's Fragrant Peanut Oil is available at specialty markets and from *mingspantry.com*.

MAKE AHEAD The peanut-sesame sauce can be refrigerated for up to 3 days.

MA LA OIL

🕒 **TOTAL: 30 MIN • MAKES ABOUT 1 CUP**

● ●

¾ cup roasted peanut oil (see Note above)

1 tablespoon minced peeled fresh ginger

1 star anise pod

½ small cinnamon stick

1 small shallot, minced

1 small garlic clove, minced

2 tablespoons Sichuan peppercorns

½ cup dried hot Chinese chiles

¼ cup toasted sesame oil

In a small saucepan, heat the roasted peanut oil over low heat to 175°. Add the ginger, star anise, cinnamon, shallot, garlic, Sichuan peppercorns and chiles and cook over moderately low heat until the oil reaches 225°. Simmer at 225° for 5 minutes, then transfer to a heatproof jar and let cool. Stir in the sesame oil. —*AZ*

MAKE AHEAD The Ma La Oil can be kept in a sealed jar or airtight container at room temperature for up to 1 week.

cold peanut-sesame noodles

Chef Jeff Banker of Baker & Banker in San Francisco prepares for a rooftop party; he serves a grilled feast featuring lemon-dill salmon cooked on cedar planks, OPPOSITE; *recipe, page 106.*

FISH

Spice-Rubbed Salmon with Herb-and-Pomegranate Raita

ACTIVE: 30 MIN; TOTAL: 1 HR PLUS 4 HR
CURING • 16 SERVINGS ●

1½ tablespoons caraway seeds
1½ tablespoons cumin seeds
3   tablespoons ancho chile powder
1½ teaspoons garlic powder
Kosher salt
Three 3-pound (or four 2-pound) salmon
   fillets with skin, pin bones removed
Extra-virgin olive oil, for rubbing
2   cups plain 2 percent Greek yogurt
1   cup pomegranate seeds
½   cup chopped cilantro
½   cup chopped mint
¼   cup minced scallions (about 4)
1   tablespoon fresh lemon juice

1. In a small skillet, toast the caraway and cumin seeds over moderate heat, shaking the pan, until the seeds are fragrant, about 2 minutes. Transfer the toasted seeds to a spice grinder and let them cool completely. Add the chile and garlic powders and 1 tablespoon of salt and grind to a powder.

2. Arrange the salmon fillets skin side down on 2 large rimmed baking sheets. Spread the spice mix on the salmon fillets, cover the fish with plastic wrap and refrigerate for 4 to 6 hours.

3. Preheat the oven to 425° and position racks in the upper and lower thirds. Lightly drizzle the fish all over with olive oil and rub it into the spice mixture to make a paste with the spices. Roast the fish for about 25 minutes (for 3-pound fillets), until the flesh just begins to flake; shift the pans from top to bottom and front to back halfway through roasting.

4. Meanwhile, in a medium bowl, combine the yogurt with the pomegranate seeds, cilantro, mint, scallions and lemon juice and season the raita with salt.

5. Using 2 large spatulas, carefully lift the fish off the pans, leaving the skin behind, and transfer to platters. Serve with the pomegranate raita. —*Grace Parisi*
WINE Lively, light-bodied Sicilian red: 2011 Tami Frappato.

Wild Salmon, Orzo and Arugula Pesto en Papillote

TOTAL: 55 MIN • 6 SERVINGS

Salt
10 ounces baby arugula
1   pound orzo
¾   cup freshly grated Parmigiano-
    Reggiano cheese
3   garlic cloves, coarsely chopped
1   tablespoon grated lemon zest
1   teaspoon distilled white vinegar
½   medium shallot, chopped
¼   teaspoon Tabasco
¼   teaspoon sugar
⅔   cup extra-virgin olive oil
Six 6-ounce skinless center-cut
    wild salmon fillets
6   tablespoons dry white wine
Freshly ground pepper
2   lemons, very thinly sliced

1. Preheat the oven to 375°. Fill a bowl with ice water and bring a pot of salted water to a boil. Add the arugula to the boiling water and stir until just wilted, 20 seconds. Transfer to the ice water to cool; drain and squeeze out as much water as possible. Transfer the arugula to a food processor.

2. Boil the orzo, stirring, until almost al dente, 9 minutes. Drain, rinse under cold water and transfer to a large bowl.

3. Meanwhile, add the cheese, garlic, lemon zest, vinegar, shallot, Tabasco and sugar to the arugula and pulse to chop. With the machine on, drizzle in the olive oil and process until smooth. Season with salt. Add the pesto to the orzo and toss.

4. Arrange six 16-by-12½-inch sheets of parchment paper on a work surface. In the center of each sheet, mound 1 heaping cup of the orzo and top with a salmon fillet. Drizzle 1 tablespoon of wine over each fillet. Season with salt and pepper. Arrange the lemon slices in a single layer on the fish. Bring up 2 opposite sides of the parchment over the fish and orzo and fold to seal.

5. Arrange the papillotes on a baking sheet, leaving space between them. Bake for 18 minutes, until the packets are slightly puffed.

6. Transfer the packets to plates, open them carefully and serve. —*Tara Lazar*
WINE Herbal, lemony Sauvignon Blanc: 2011 Les Roches Touraine Blanc.

Tandoori Salmon

TOTAL: 30 MIN PLUS 2 HR MARINATING
8 SERVINGS ●

The salmon fillets here are marinated in an Indian-spiced yogurt, then grilled. Wrap the succulent salmon in warm flatbread with cucumber salad and cilantro for a delicious, healthy sandwich.

1   large garlic clove, minced
1½ teaspoons minced fresh ginger
1   tablespoon ground coriander
1   teaspoon ground cumin
1   teaspoon sweet paprika
1   teaspoon ground fenugreek
½   teaspoon ground turmeric
¼   teaspoon cayenne pepper
Pinch of ground cloves
Salt and freshly ground black pepper
1½ cups plain low-fat yogurt (not Greek)
¼   cup canola oil, plus more for grilling
Eight 8-ounce skinless center-cut
    salmon fillets
Grilled naan, cilantro sprigs and
    cucumber salad, for serving

1. Using the side of a chef's knife, mash the garlic and ginger to a paste. Scrape the paste into a medium bowl and add the coriander, cumin, paprika, fenugreek, turmeric, cayenne, cloves and ½ teaspoon each of salt and black pepper. Add the yogurt and the ¼ cup of oil and whisk until smooth. In a glass baking dish, coat the salmon with the marinade. Cover and refrigerate 2 to 4 hours.

2. Light a grill. Oil the grill grates and oil a fish basket. Scrape off the excess marinade and lightly brush the fish with oil. Grill over moderate heat, turning once or twice, until golden in spots and nearly cooked through, about 8 minutes. Transfer the salmon to a platter and serve with grilled naan, cilantro sprigs and cucumber salad. —*Grace Parisi*
WINE Citrusy, medium-bodied white: 2011 Telmo Rodriguez Basa.

spice-rubbed salmon with herb-and-pomegranate raita

Potato and Wild Salmon Cakes with Ginger and Scallions

ACTIVE: 40 MIN; TOTAL: 1 HR 15 MIN

MAKES 14 CAKES ● ●

"I started making these fish cakes to use up leftover bits of salmon and potato," says Los Angeles chef Sera Pelle. "But my family began to request them so often, I make them from scratch now."

- 2 **pounds medium red-skinned potatoes, scrubbed**
- **Sea salt**
- 1 **pound skinless wild salmon fillet**
- **Safflower or sunflower oil, for greasing and frying**
- **Freshly ground pepper**
- 1 **bunch of scallions (about 6 scallions), coarsely chopped**
- 3 **large eggs, lightly beaten**
- 3 **garlic cloves, minced**
- 2 **tablespoons minced fresh ginger**
- ½ **medium red onion, finely chopped**
- 1 **tablespoon tamari**
- 1 **tablespoon toasted sesame oil**
- ½ **cup plain dry bread crumbs**
- **Dill Sauce (recipe follows), for serving**

1. Preheat the oven to 350°. In a large saucepan, cover the potatoes with water. Add a large pinch of sea salt and bring to a boil. Simmer over moderately high heat until the potatoes are tender, about 20 minutes. Drain and let cool slightly, then peel. Transfer the potatoes to a large bowl and mash.

2. Meanwhile, put the salmon on a lightly oiled rimmed baking sheet and season with salt and pepper. Bake for about 15 minutes, until the salmon is medium-rare inside.

3. Gently flake the salmon and add it to the potatoes along with the scallions, eggs, garlic, ginger, onion, tamari and sesame oil. Mix well, then fold in the bread crumbs. Season with salt. Form into fourteen ½-cup patties.

4. In a large nonstick skillet, heat ¼ inch of safflower or sunflower oil until shimmering. Working in batches, fry the potato-and-salmon cakes over moderately high heat until browned and crisp, about 2 minutes per side. Transfer to a large baking sheet. Repeat with

the remaining potato-and-salmon cakes; add more oil and adjust the heat as necessary. Bake until heated through, 15 minutes. Serve with the Dill Sauce. —*Sera Pelle*

WINE Citrusy New Zealand Sauvignon Blanc: 2011 Villa Maria Private Bin.

DILL SAUCE

TOTAL: 5 MIN • MAKES 1 CUP ● ●

- 1 **cup reduced-fat vegan mayonnaise or regular mayonnaise**
- 2 **tablespoons fresh lemon juice**
- ¼ **cup chopped dill**
- **Sea salt**

In a bowl, whisk the mayonnaise with the lemon juice and dill and season with salt. Refrigerate until ready to serve. —*SP*

Salmon in Charmoula with Risotto-Style Israeli Couscous

TOTAL: 1 HR PLUS OVERNIGHT MARINATING • 4 SERVINGS ●

Michael Solomonov of Zahav in Philadelphia makes his salmon incredibly tasty by marinating it in *charmoula*, a tangy, cilantro-based Moroccan sauce. For a side dish, he treats Israeli couscous like risotto, simmering the pearl-shaped grains in a tomato sauce until they become rich and creamy.

SALMON

- ¼ **cup chopped cilantro**
- ¼ **cup canola oil**
- 2 **garlic cloves**
- 1 **tablespoon minced fresh ginger**
- 1½ **teaspoons sweet paprika**
- 1 **teaspoon kosher salt**
- ½ **teaspoon turmeric**
- ½ **teaspoon ground cumin**
- **Four 5-ounce skinless salmon fillets**

TAHINI SAUCE

- 1 **tablespoon extra-virgin olive oil**
- ¼ **cup sliced cremini mushrooms**
- 2 **garlic cloves, thinly sliced**
- 1 **tablespoon tahini**
- 1 **tablespoon fresh lemon juice**
- 1 **tablespoon finely chopped dill**
- **Kosher salt**

COUSCOUS

- 1 **cup Israeli couscous (6 ounces)**
- ¼ **cup extra-virgin olive oil**
- ½ **cup finely chopped Spanish onion**
- **Pinch of cinnamon**
- **Kosher salt**
- ½ **cup tomato puree**
- 1½ **cups warm water**

1. PREPARE THE SALMON In a blender, puree the chopped cilantro, canola oil, garlic, minced ginger, paprika, salt, turmeric and cumin until smooth. Pour the marinade into a resealable plastic bag, add the salmon and seal. Refrigerate overnight.

2. MAKE THE TAHINI SAUCE In a skillet, heat the oil. Add the mushrooms and garlic and cook over moderately low heat, stirring, until the mushrooms are well browned, about 10 minutes. Scrape the mushrooms into a blender and let cool. Add the tahini, lemon juice and ⅓ cup of water and puree. Stir in the dill; season with salt.

3. PREPARE THE COUSCOUS In a saucepan, toast the couscous over moderate heat, tossing, until golden, about 10 minutes. Transfer to a bowl. In the same saucepan, heat the oil. Add the onion and a pinch each of cinnamon and salt and cook over moderately low heat, stirring, until the onion is softened and just starting to brown, about 8 minutes. Add the toasted couscous and cook for 1 minute, stirring, then stir in the tomato puree. Add the warm water ½ cup at a time and stir constantly over moderately low heat, allowing the liquid to be absorbed between additions, until the couscous is al dente, about 20 minutes. Season with salt and keep warm; add 1 or 2 tablespoons of water if the couscous seems dry.

4. Light a grill or preheat a grill pan. Scrape the marinade off the salmon fillets, season the fish with salt and grill over high heat, turning once, until nearly cooked through, about 4 minutes. Spoon the couscous onto plates, top with the grilled salmon and tahini sauce and serve right away.
—*Michael Solomonov*

WINE Perfumed, full-bodied Viognier: 2010 Domaine de Triennes Sainte Fleur.

● HEALTHY ● MAKE AHEAD ● VEGETARIAN ● STAFF FAVORITE

potato and wild salmon cakes with ginger and scallions

Cedar-Planked Salmon with Lemon and Dill

📷 PAGE 101

ACTIVE: 45 MIN; TOTAL: 4 HR

8 SERVINGS ● ●

Curing raw salmon fillets in a combination of salt, sugar, dill and lemon zest for 90 minutes, then soaking them in sake for an hour, gives the fish an exceptionally silky texture and delicate flavor. Depending on the size of your grill, you might need to cook the salmon fillets in two batches.

- 1 cup kosher salt
- ⅓ cup light brown sugar
- 1 cup chopped dill, plus 8 large dill sprigs

Finely grated zest of 2 lemons, plus 16 lemon slices

Eight 8-ounce center-cut salmon fillets with skin

- 2 cups sake

Olive oil, for drizzling

1. Soak four 8-by-7-inch cedar planks in water for 2 hours.

2. Meanwhile, in a medium bowl, combine the salt with the light brown sugar, chopped dill and grated lemon zest. Coat the salmon fillets thoroughly with the rub and arrange them in a large, shallow dish in one layer. Cover and refrigerate the salmon for 1 hour and 30 minutes.

3. Rinse the salmon and pat dry. Return the salmon to the dish and cover with the sake. Refrigerate for 1 hour, turning the salmon halfway through.

4. Light a grill, cover and heat for 10 minutes. Grill the cedar planks until grill marks appear, about 30 seconds per side.

5. Drain the salmon from the sake and pat the fillets dry. Brush the salmon with olive oil and place 2 fillets on each cedar plank, spacing them apart. Top each fillet with a large dill sprig and 2 lemon slices and drizzle lightly with more olive oil.

6. Turn off half of the burners on the grill. Carefully set two of the salmon-topped planks on the grill over indirect heat. Cover and grill the salmon for 25 to 30 minutes,

rotating the planks halfway through, just until the salmon is cooked. Tent the salmon with foil to keep warm. Repeat to grill the remaining salmon. Serve. —*Jeff Banker*

WINE Lively, grassy Sauvignon Blanc from Chile: 2012 Lapostolle Casa.

Salmon Carpaccio with Lemon Aioli and Pork Rind Crumble

🕑 **TOTAL: 30 MIN**

4 FIRST-COURSE SERVINGS

- 3 tablespoons finely crushed pork rinds
- 3 tablespoons finely crushed toasted rye-bread crumbs

Kosher salt

- 2 large egg yolks
- 1 small garlic clove
- ¾ teaspoon finely grated lemon zest
- 1½ tablespoons fresh lemon juice
- ½ cup canola or vegetable oil
- 1 tablespoon finely chopped dill
- 4 ounces broccoli rabe, trimmed
- 1 teaspoon extra-virgin olive oil, plus more for brushing
- ½ pound sushi-grade skinless salmon fillet, preferably wild, thinly sliced at a slight angle

1. In a small bowl, toss the crushed pork rinds with the toasted bread crumbs and season with salt.

2. In a blender, combine the egg yolks with the garlic, ¼ teaspoon of the lemon zest and 1 tablespoon of the lemon juice and puree until smooth. With the blender on, drizzle in the canola oil and puree until thickened. Scrape the aioli into a bowl and stir in the chopped dill; season with salt.

3. In a medium pot of salted boiling water, cook the broccoli rabe until crisp-tender, about 2 minutes. Using a slotted spoon, transfer the broccoli rabe to a bowl of ice water to chill. Drain well, pat dry and cut into ½-inch pieces. Transfer the broccoli rabe to a bowl and toss with the 1 teaspoon of olive oil and the remaining ½ teaspoon of lemon zest and ½ tablespoon of lemon juice. Season with salt.

4. Spread a little of the lemon aioli on each of 4 plates and top with the broccoli rabe. Arrange the sliced salmon over the broccoli rabe and brush with olive oil. Sprinkle each serving with some of the pork rind crumble. Serve right away, passing the remaining lemon aioli and pork rind crumble alongside. —*Paul Qui*

WINE Zesty, medium-bodied white: 2011 Cape Mentelle Sauvignon Blanc Semillon.

Roast Salmon with Whole-Grain-Mustard Crust

🕑 **TOTAL: 20 MIN • 4 SERVINGS** ●

In this fast and easy recipe, whole-grain mustard becomes a wonderful crust for salmon fillets. "We use simple crusts so the fish stands out," says chef Ken Norris. He focuses on sustainable seafood like line-caught wild chinook salmon at Riffle NW in Portland, Oregon.

- ¼ cup whole-grain mustard
- 1 tablespoon extra-virgin olive oil
- 1½ tablespoons minced chives

Four 8-ounce wild salmon fillets with skin

Salt and freshly ground pepper

1. Preheat the oven to 400° and line a rimmed baking sheet with aluminum foil. In a small bowl, stir together the mustard, olive oil and chives.

2. Season the salmon fillets with salt and pepper and place them skin side down on the prepared baking sheet. Spread the mustard mixture over the tops of the fillets. Roast the fish for 6 minutes.

3. Preheat the broiler. Broil the salmon 6 inches from the heat for about 4 minutes, until the mustard crust is browned and the salmon is almost cooked through. Using a spatula, carefully slide the salmon fillets off their skins and transfer to plates; leave the skin on, if desired. Serve immediately. —*Ken Norris and Jennifer Quist Norris*

SERVE WITH Brussels sprout leaves sautéed with diced dry chorizo.

WINE Lively, medium-bodied California red: 2010 Unti Petit Frere.

● HEALTHY   ● MAKE AHEAD   ● VEGETARIAN   ● STAFF FAVORITE

Spicy Tuna Burgers with Soy Glaze

⏱ **TOTAL: 45 MIN • MAKES 6 BURGERS** ●

"I like to use soy sauce in pizza dough and burgers," says chef Tim Cushman of Boston's O Ya. "It fills in flavor holes that salt doesn't."

- ½ cup mayonnaise
- ¾ teaspoon soy sauce
- ½ teaspoon toasted sesame oil
- 3 tablespoons Sriracha
- 2 pounds cold sushi-grade yellowfin tuna, cut into 1-inch cubes
- 2½ tablespoons Chinese hot mustard
- 2 small garlic cloves, finely grated

Kosher salt and freshly ground
      black pepper

Canola oil, for brushing
- 6 hamburger buns, split and toasted
- 1 tablespoon julienned pickled ginger (optional)
- 3 tablespoons Soy Glaze (recipe follows)

Thinly sliced scallions, baby lettuces and
      sliced tomatoes, for serving

1. In a small bowl, whisk the mayonnaise with the soy sauce, sesame oil and 2 tablespoons of the Sriracha.
2. In a food processor, pulse one-third of the tuna at a time just until finely chopped; transfer to a bowl. Repeat with the remaining tuna.
3. Light a grill or preheat a grill pan. Mix the Chinese mustard, garlic, 2½ teaspoons of salt and ½ teaspoon of pepper into the chopped tuna. With lightly moistened hands, form the tuna into six 4-inch burgers. Brush with oil and season with salt and pepper. Grill the burgers over high heat, turning once, until lightly charred on the outside and rare in the center, about 3 minutes total.
4. Spread both halves of the buns with the Sriracha mayonnaise. Set the burgers on the buns and top with the pickled ginger. Drizzle 1½ teaspoons of the Soy Glaze and ½ teaspoon of Sriracha on each burger. Top with scallions, lettuce and tomatoes and serve. —*Tim Cushman*
WINE Strawberry-inflected Beaujolais: 2011 Marcel Lapierre Raisins Gaulois.

SOY GLAZE

⏱ **TOTAL: 10 MIN • MAKES 1½ CUPS**
● ● ●

This versatile soy glaze is also great on grilled chicken, pork and portobello mushrooms.

- 2 teaspoons cornstarch
- ½ cup soy sauce
- ½ cup sake
- ½ cup mirin
- ½ cup sugar

In a small bowl, whisk the cornstarch with 1 tablespoon of water. In a small saucepan, whisk the soy sauce with the sake, mirin and sugar. Simmer over moderate heat, stirring, until the sugar is dissolved, about 2 minutes. Whisk in the cornstarch mixture and simmer until the sauce is slightly thickened, about 2 minutes longer. Transfer the glaze to a heat-proof jar and let cool completely. —*TC*
MAKE AHEAD The glaze can be refrigerated for up to 2 weeks.

Grilled Halibut with Herb Pistou and Walnut Butter

TOTAL: 1 HR • 4 SERVINGS ●
Zesty nut butter and a bright herb sauce are the perfect accompaniments for the meaty grilled halibut here.

Four 5-ounce skinless halibut fillets
Kosher salt
- 2 tablespoons sugar
- 2 walnut halves, finely chopped
- 4 tablespoons unsalted butter, softened
- 3 juniper berries, finely chopped (optional)
- ¼ teaspoon finely grated orange zest
- 1½ teaspoons minced serrano ham
- 1 teaspoon fresh lime juice

Pinch of fennel pollen
- 16 garlic cloves
- ¼ cup plus 2 tablespoons extra-virgin olive oil, plus more for grilling
- ¼ cup plus 1 tablespoon grapeseed oil
- 1 cup watercress, leaves and tender sprigs only
- ½ cup baby arugula
- ¼ cup flat-leaf parsley leaves
- ¼ cup basil leaves
- 2 tablespoons chopped dill
- 2 tablespoons freshly grated Parmigiano-Reggiano cheese
- 1 teaspoon finely grated lemon zest
- 1½ teaspoons fresh lemon juice

Freshly ground black pepper

1. Set the fish on a platter. In a small bowl, combine ¼ cup of salt with the sugar and pat it over both sides of the fillets. Let stand for 30 minutes. Rinse the fish and pat dry.
2. Meanwhile, in a small skillet, toast the walnuts over moderate heat for about 3 minutes, until golden. Transfer to a small bowl and let cool. Stir in the butter, juniper berries, orange zest, ham, lime juice and fennel pollen. Scrape the nut butter onto a sheet of wax paper and spread to a 3-by-6-inch rectangle; wrap in the paper. Refrigerate until firm.
3. Put the garlic cloves in a small saucepan, add cold water to cover and bring to a boil. Drain. Repeat this process 3 times, reserving 2 tablespoons of the final water. Transfer the garlic and reserved water to a blender. Add 2 tablespoons of the olive oil and 1 tablespoon of the grapeseed oil and puree until smooth. Scrape the garlic puree into a bowl and reserve.
4. Add the watercress, arugula, parsley, basil and dill to the blender and pulse until finely chopped. With the machine on, pour in the remaining ¼ cup each of olive oil and grapeseed oil and puree until smooth. Add the Parmigiano, lemon zest, lemon juice and the garlic puree and pulse to combine. Season the pistou with salt and pepper and transfer to a bowl.
5. Light a grill or preheat a grill pan and brush it with olive oil. Brush the fish with olive oil and grill over moderately high heat, turning once, until cooked through and lightly charred, 6 minutes. Spoon the pistou onto 4 plates and top with the fish. Unwrap the butter and cut it into 4 rectangles. Place the butter on the fish and serve. —*Danny Grant*
SERVE WITH Heirloom tomato salad.
WINE Creamy, pear-scented Oregon Pinot Gris: 2011 Elk Cove.

● HEALTHY ● MAKE AHEAD ● VEGETARIAN ● STAFF FAVORITE

spicy tuna burger with soy glaze

Halibut with Braised Romaine and Cumin Brown Butter

⏱ **TOTAL: 45 MIN • 4 SERVINGS** ●

To keep this halibut moist, *Top Chef Masters* winner Chris Cosentino sears it in cumin-spiked brown butter. "Brown butter makes everything explode with flavor," he says.

- 1 pound new potatoes
- 2 serrano chiles—1 halved lengthwise, 1 seeded and thinly sliced
- 3 mint sprigs—leaves chopped, stems reserved

Kosher salt

- ¼ cup extra-virgin olive oil
- 12 large radishes, quartered lengthwise

Freshly ground pepper

- 2 small romaine hearts—large inner leaves halved lengthwise and small leaves left whole
- ½ cup low-sodium chicken broth
- 4 tablespoons unsalted butter

Four 6-ounce skinless halibut fillets

- ¾ teaspoon ground cumin
- ½ teaspoon finely grated lemon zest
- 1 tablespoon fresh lemon juice

1. In a medium saucepan, cover the potatoes with water. Add the halved serrano, the mint stems and a generous pinch of salt and bring to a boil. Cook over moderate heat until the potatoes are tender, about 10 minutes. Drain the potatoes and let cool slightly; discard the chile and mint stems. Cut the potatoes in half. **2.** In a very large skillet, heat 2 tablespoons of the oil. Add the radishes and a generous pinch each of salt and pepper and cook over moderately high heat until just softened, 1 to 2 minutes. Fold in all of the romaine and the sliced serrano. Add the broth and cook over moderate heat, tossing, until the lettuce is just wilted and the radishes are crisp-tender, about 4 minutes. Stir in the potatoes and the chopped mint and season with salt and pepper; transfer to a bowl and keep warm. **3.** Wipe out the skillet and melt the butter in the remaining 2 tablespoons of oil. Season the halibut with salt and pepper and cook over moderate heat for 3 minutes, until the butter is golden and the fish is browned on

the bottom. Turn the fish. Add the cumin to the butter and cook, spooning the butter over the fish until just cooked through, about 3 minutes. Transfer to plates; spoon the vegetables alongside. Add the lemon zest and juice to the skillet; season with salt and pepper. Spoon the brown butter over the fish and vegetables and serve. —*Chris Cosentino*
WINE Dry, full-bodied Riesling: 2010 Knebel Riesling Trocken.

Halibut and Corn Hobo Packs with Herbed Butter

⏱ **TOTAL: 40 MIN • 4 SERVINGS**

Chives and tarragon are fantastic with both corn and fish. Here, the herbs are folded into softened butter and grilled with a mix of corn and halibut in a foil hobo pack.

- ¼ cup snipped chives
- 2 tablespoons tarragon leaves
- 1 stick unsalted butter, softened

Salt and freshly ground white pepper

- 2 ears of corn, kernels cut from the cobs
- 4 large shiitake mushrooms, stemmed and caps thinly sliced

Four 6-ounce skinless halibut fillets

- 8 baguette slices, cut on the diagonal

1. In a mini food processor, pulse the chives and tarragon leaves until chopped. Add the butter and a pinch each of salt and white pepper and pulse just until the butter is bright green with flecks of herbs. Transfer the herb butter to a sheet of plastic wrap and form into a log. Freeze for about 5 minutes, until the butter is slightly firm. Cut the butter into 16 pieces. **2.** Arrange four 12-inch sheets of heavy-duty foil on a work surface and spray evenly with vegetable oil spray. In a medium bowl, toss the corn with the shiitake and season with salt and pepper. Mound the mixture in the center of the foil sheets and top each mound with a piece of the herb butter. Top with the halibut fillets and another piece of the herb butter and season with salt and pepper. Fold up the foil on all sides and pinch the seams to seal the packets.

3. Light a grill. Place the foil packets on the grill, close the lid and cook over high heat until the fish is cooked through and the mushrooms are tender, 8 to 10 minutes; let the packets rest for 2 minutes. **4.** Grill the baguette slices for 2 minutes, turning once. Top with the remaining herb butter, allowing it to melt. Open the packets carefully and serve the fish and vegetables with the buttered baguette toasts.
—*Grace Parisi*
WINE Zippy, herbal Sauvignon Blanc from New Zealand: 2011 Whitehaven.

Herb Sauce

⏱ **TOTAL: 20 MIN • MAKES 2¼ CUPS** ● ●

To maintain the fresh flavor of the herbs in this simple sauce, chef Jason Fox of Commonwealth in San Francisco uses xanthan gum, an industrial powder that thickens sauces and dressings in an instant. The sauce is delicious with roasted or steamed fish, poached eggs or chicken breast.

- 2 cups flat-leaf parsley leaves
- 1 cup loosely packed snipped chives
- ½ cup loosely packed chervil leaves
- ½ cup loosely packed tarragon leaves
- 0.5 gram (⅛ teaspoon) xanthan gum (see Note)
- 4 teaspoons freshly squeezed lemon juice

Salt and freshly ground white pepper

1. Bring a large saucepan of salted water to a boil and fill a bowl with ice water. Add the parsley, chives, chervil and tarragon to the saucepan and blanch for 15 seconds. Drain and immediately transfer the herbs to the ice water to cool. Drain, gently squeezing out the excess water. **2.** Transfer the herbs to a blender. Add 2¼ cups of cold water and puree until smooth. With the blender on, add the xanthan gum and puree until slightly thickened, about 15 seconds. Blend in the lemon juice and season with salt and white pepper. Use the sauce right away. —*Jason Fox*
NOTE Xanthan gum is available in many grocery stores.

● HEALTHY ● MAKE AHEAD ● VEGETARIAN ● STAFF FAVORITE

EASY GLAZES AND SAUCES

F&W's **Marcia Kiesel** creates three quick mayonnaise-based glazes to brush on fish fillets before roasting or broiling. As an alternative, she also transforms each one into a fast sauce.

start with ½ cup mayonnaise

SESAME & SRIRACHA

for the glaze

Blend 3 tablespoons toasted sesame seeds, 1 tablespoon mirin, 2 teaspoons Sriracha, salt and pepper.

HAZELNUT & PORCINI

for the glaze

Blend ½ cup dried porcini mushrooms, ground to a powder; ¼ cup skinned roasted hazelnuts, finely chopped; salt and pepper.

SAFFRON, ORANGE & TOMATO

for the glaze

Infuse 1 teaspoon heated dry white wine with a pinch of saffron for 10 minutes, then blend with 2 teaspoons tomato paste and 1½ teaspoons finely grated orange zest.

for the sauce

Add 4 thinly sliced scallions, 2 tablespoons soy sauce and 2 teaspoons mirin.

for the sauce

Add 2 tablespoons dry Marsala.

for the sauce

Add 2 tablespoons fresh orange juice.

Olive Oil–Poached Cod with Mussels, Orange and Chorizo

TOTAL: 1 HR • 4 SERVINGS ●

At the French Laundry in Napa Valley, star chef Thomas Keller serves this dish with an orange gelée flavored with Espelette peppers. In this simplified version, he pairs the olive oil–poached cod with an orange *sauce vierge*, a classic French sauce typically made with olive oil and lemon juice.

- 4 ounces dry chorizo—quartered lengthwise, thinly sliced crosswise
- 1 tablespoon grapeseed oil
- 1 large shallot, thinly sliced
- ½ cup finely chopped fennel, fronds reserved
- 2 pounds mussels, scrubbed
- ½ cup dry white wine
- 1 cup fresh orange juice, plus 1 whole orange
- 1 cup homemade chicken stock
- ¼ teaspoon piment d'Espelette
- 4¼ cups extra-virgin olive oil
- Four 6-ounce skinless cod fillets, each cut into 3 pieces
- ¼ cup kosher salt

1. In a large saucepan, cook the chorizo in the grapeseed oil over moderate heat until the fat is rendered, 4 minutes. Remove the chorizo with a slotted spoon, leaving as much of the oil as possible in the pan—about 3 tablespoons. Reserve the chorizo.
2. Add the shallot and chopped fennel to the saucepan and cook over moderately high heat, stirring, until softened, about 7 minutes. Add the mussels and wine, cover and cook until the shells have opened, 6 minutes. Transfer the mussels to a large bowl. Strain the cooking juices into a heatproof bowl.
3. Wipe out the saucepan and return the cooking juices to it, stopping before you reach the grit at the bottom. Add the orange juice, chicken stock and piment d'Espelette to the saucepan and simmer over moderate heat until reduced to ½ cup, about 15 minutes. Add ¼ cup of the olive oil and keep the sauce warm. Remove the mussels from their shells and add them to the sauce.

4. In a large saucepan, heat the remaining 4 cups of olive oil to 180°. Meanwhile, on a plate, sprinkle the cod all over with the salt; let stand for 5 minutes. Rinse the cod and pat dry. Poach the cod in the oil, adjusting the heat as necessary to keep the temperature constant, until just cooked, 10 minutes. If the cod is not completely submerged in oil, turn it halfway through poaching. Using a slotted spatula, transfer the cod to a paper towel–lined plate and blot dry.
5. Using a sharp knife, peel the orange, removing all of the bitter white pith. Working over a bowl, cut in between the membranes to release the sections into the bowl. Heat the sauce just until warm. Transfer the cod to 4 shallow bowls and spoon the mussels and sauce all around. Garnish the fish with the orange sections, fennel fronds and fried chorizo and serve. —*Thomas Keller*
WINE Orange-scented Sauvignon Blanc: 2011 Shannon Ridge Ranch Collection.

Sea Bass Carpaccio with Coriander and Grapefruit

TOTAL: 20 MIN • 4 FIRST-COURSE SERVINGS ●

Like all raw fish dishes, this one is about the freshness of the sea bass. Good-quality olive oil is also key.

- 3 tablespoons fresh grapefruit juice
- 2 tablespoons fresh orange juice
- ¼ cup extra-virgin olive oil
- ¼ teaspoon ground coriander
- Salt and freshly ground pepper
- Two 6-ounce skinless black sea bass fillets, thinly sliced crosswise on the diagonal
- 4 grapefruit sections, cut into 3 pieces each (see Note)
- 2 orange sections, cut into 3 pieces each (see Note)
- 1 small scallion, thinly sliced
- 1 tablespoon chopped dill
- Toasted thin baguette slices, for serving

1. In a small bowl, combine the grapefruit and orange juices with the oil and coriander. Season the dressing with salt and pepper.

2. Arrange the fish on a platter. Drizzle with the dressing and scatter the citrus sections, scallion and dill on top. Let stand for 3 minutes. Serve with toasts. —*Didem Senol*
NOTE To make the citrus sections, use a sharp knife to cut off all of the skin and bitter white pith from the fruit. Cut between the membranes to release the sections.
WINE Minerally, light-bodied white: 2011 Santiago Ruiz Albariño.

Mahimahi with Sauerkraut-Pickle Beurre Blanc

TOTAL: 35 MIN • 4 SERVINGS ●

- 6 tablespoons cold unsalted butter, cut into tablespoons
- 1 large shallot, minced
- ½ cup bottled clam juice
- ¾ cup sauerkraut
- 1 large half-sour pickle, halved crosswise and cut into thin sticks
- Salt and freshly ground pepper
- 1½ tablespoons vegetable oil
- Four 7-ounce skinless mahimahi fillets
- 1 tablespoon finely chopped parsley

1. In a medium skillet, melt 1 tablespoon of the butter. Add the shallot and cook over low heat until softened, 5 minutes. Add the clam juice and ¼ cup of water; boil until reduced to ½ cup, 4 minutes. Add the sauerkraut and cook just until heated through. Remove the skillet from the heat and swirl in the remaining 5 tablespoons of butter, 1 tablespoon at a time, putting the skillet back over moderate heat briefly once or twice as necessary. Stir in the pickle; season with salt and pepper.
2. In a large skillet, heat the oil. Season the mahimahi fillets with salt and pepper and cook over moderately high heat until they are nicely browned on the bottom, 3 minutes. Turn the fish and cook until just white throughout, 2 minutes longer.
3. Very gently rewarm the sauce, whisking constantly over low heat. Stir in the parsley and spoon the sauce onto plates. Set the fillets on the sauce and serve. —*Marcia Kiesel*
WINE Fruit-forward Oregon Pinot Gris: 2009 Cloudline Cellars.

● HEALTHY ● MAKE AHEAD ● VEGETARIAN ● STAFF FAVORITE

olive oil–poached cod with mussels, orange and chorizo

Fried Beer-Battered Fish and Chips with Dilled Tartar Sauce

ACTIVE: 40 MIN; TOTAL: 2 HR

4 SERVINGS ●

1¼ pounds baking potatoes, peeled and cut into 2½-by-⅓-inch sticks
Vegetable oil, for frying
1½ cups all-purpose flour, plus more for dredging
Kosher salt
1¾ cups cold lager or pilsner
1¾ pounds skinless center-cut cod or haddock fillet, cut into four 6-by-2-inch pieces
Freshly ground pepper
Malt vinegar and Dilled Tartar Sauce (recipe follows), for serving

1. In a large bowl, cover the potatoes with water; let soak for 1 hour. Drain the potatoes and pat dry thoroughly with paper towels.
2. Set a rack over a rimmed baking sheet. In a large, wide pot, heat 2 inches of oil to 330°. Add the potatoes and fry until tender, about 12 minutes. Using a long-handled wire scoop, transfer the potatoes to the rack to drain. Let cool for at least 15 minutes.
3. Meanwhile, in a large bowl, whisk the 1½ cups of flour with 1½ teaspoons of salt. Whisk in 1½ cups of the cold beer until the batter is almost smooth; it should be a little lumpy. Refrigerate for 15 minutes. Stir in the remaining ¼ cup of beer.
4. Preheat the oven to 350° and heat the oil to 375°. Add half of the potatoes and fry until crisp, 2 minutes; transfer to the rack to drain while you fry the remaining potatoes. Spread the fries on a large rimmed baking sheet.
5. Reduce the oil temperature to 325°. Season the fish with salt and pepper. Mound flour in a wide, shallow bowl. Working with 2 pieces at a time, dredge the fish in the flour, shaking off the excess. Dip the floured fish in the beer batter; allow any excess batter to drip off. Add the battered fish to the hot oil and fry, turning a few times, until richly browned and crunchy and the fish is cooked through, 8 to 10 minutes. Drain on the rack, blot dry with paper towels and keep warm.

6. Reheat the fries in the oven. Batter and fry the remaining fish. Serve the fried fish and chips hot with malt vinegar and Dilled Tartar Sauce. —*Marcia Kiesel*
BEER Malty, slightly bitter English pale ale: Old Speckled Hen.

DILLED TARTAR SAUCE

TOTAL: 10 MIN • MAKES 1 CUP ● ●

In a bowl, blend ¾ cup mayonnaise with 3 tablespoons sweet pickle relish, 1 diced sour pickle and 1 tablespoon chopped dill. Season the tartar sauce with salt and pepper and serve cold. —*MK*

Fried-Fish Reuben Tacos

TOTAL: 30 MIN • 4 SERVINGS

A cross between a fish taco and a Reuben sandwich, this fun dish features fried flounder wrapped in a flour tortilla with Jarlsberg cheese, sauerkraut and Russian dressing.

1 cup all-purpose flour
¾ cup cornstarch
1 tablespoon baking powder
Salt
1¾ cups club soda
½ cup mayonnaise
1 large dill pickle, coarsely chopped
2 tablespoons ketchup
Vegetable oil, for frying
Four 6-ounce flounder fillets
Four 8-inch flour tortillas
¾ cup drained sauerkraut
¾ cup shredded Jarlsberg cheese (about 3 ounces)
1 cup microgreens or baby arugula

1. In a large bowl, whisk together the flour, cornstarch, baking powder and a pinch of salt. With a fork, blend in the club soda until incorporated; it's OK if the batter is lumpy. Let rest at room temperature for 10 minutes.
2. Preheat the oven to 350°. In a small bowl, combine the mayonnaise, pickle and ketchup and season with salt. In a deep fryer or a very large saucepan, heat 1½ inches of vegetable oil to 375°. Pat the flounder dry and season lightly with salt. Dip 2 of the fillets in the batter and let any excess drip off. Fry the fish,

turning once, until golden brown and crisp, about 2½ minutes. Drain the fish on a rack set over a baking sheet and repeat with the remaining fish fillets and batter.
3. Warm the tortillas in the oven for about 40 seconds, until hot and pliable. Spread the Russian dressing on the tortillas. Top with the sauerkraut, fried flounder, Jarlsberg and microgreens. Fold the tortillas over the fillings and serve. —*Amanda Hallowell*
WINE Spritzy, lime-scented white from Portugal: 2011 Broadbent Vinho Verde.

Grilled Black Cod with Red Wine–Miso Butter Sauce

TOTAL: 30 MIN • 4 SERVINGS ●

1½ cups dry red wine
1 large shallot, minced
1 stick cold unsalted butter, diced
1 tablespoon white miso
¼ teaspoon soy sauce
Salt and freshly ground pepper
Four 6-ounce skinless black cod fillets
Vegetable oil
6 cups packed assorted baby lettuces

1. In a small skillet, boil the wine and shallot over moderately high heat until reduced to ¼ cup, 10 minutes. Reduce the heat to moderate. Gradually add the butter to the skillet and whisk constantly on and off the heat until the sauce is creamy. Remove from the heat and whisk in the miso and soy sauce; season with salt and pepper.
2. Light a grill or heat a grill pan. Brush the cod fillets with oil and season with salt and pepper. Brush the grill with oil and cook the fish over high heat, turning once, until lightly charred and just cooked, 4 to 5 minutes.
3. In a large skillet, heat 1 teaspoon of the oil until shimmering. Add the lettuces; toss over high heat until barely wilted, about 30 seconds. Transfer the lettuces to plates and top with the fish. Briefly rewarm the sauce, whisking, over moderate heat. Spoon some of the sauce over the fish and serve. Pass the remaining sauce separately. —*Marcia Kiesel*
WINE Concentrated, currant-driven red Bordeaux: 2009 Château Jonqueyres.

grilled black cod with red wine–miso butter sauce

Grilled Mackerel with Apple-and-Onion Relish

⏱ TOTAL: 35 MIN • 4 SERVINGS

Mackerel has a wonderful flavor and a great, firm texture, but it definitely gets a bad rap as a "fishy" fish. Maybe that's why it's always so reasonably priced. In the recipe here, the Dijon mustard, dill and caramelized apple in the relish flatter the rich, almost smoky-tasting grilled fillets.

3 tablespoons extra-virgin olive oil, plus more for drizzling
1 medium onion, cut into ¼-inch dice
2 small Granny Smith apples, peeled and cut into ¼-inch dice
2 teaspoons Dijon mustard
2 teaspoons chopped dill
1 teaspoon freshly squeezed lemon juice
Kosher salt and freshly ground black pepper
Four 7-ounce Spanish mackerel fillets

1. In a large skillet, heat 1 tablespoon of the olive oil. Add the diced onion and cook over high heat until starting to brown, about 2 minutes. Stir in the diced apples and the remaining 2 tablespoons of olive oil. Spread the apples in an even layer and cook over moderate heat, without stirring, until tender and nicely browned on the bottom, about 3 minutes. Remove the skillet from the heat and stir in the mustard, chopped dill and lemon juice. Scrape the apple-and-onion relish into a bowl and season with salt and freshly ground pepper.

2. Light a grill or preheat a grill pan. Drizzle the mackerel fillets with olive oil and season with salt and freshly ground pepper. Grill the fillets skin side down over high heat until the skin is nicely charred and crisp, about 2 minutes. Turn the fillets and grill until just cooked through, about 2 minutes longer. Transfer the fillets to plates, skin side down. Top with the relish and serve right away.
—*Marcia Kiesel*

WINE Minerally, cold-climate white: 2011 San Michele All'Adige Müller-Thurgau.

Fried Haddock with Onion Fonduta

TOTAL: 1 HR 15 MIN • 6 SERVINGS ●

4 onions, thinly sliced
1 stick unsalted butter
Kosher salt and freshly ground pepper
1 cup plain Greek yogurt
1 tablespoon chopped dill
1 tablespoon chopped cilantro
1 cup all-purpose flour
1 cup semolina flour
1 tablespoon dried harissa (see Note)
½ teaspoon ground cumin
Pinch of ground allspice
4 juniper berries, finely crushed
Six 8-ounce haddock or hake fillets
1½ cups buttermilk
Vegetable oil, for frying

1. In an enameled cast-iron casserole, combine the onions and butter with 1½ cups of water; boil. Season with salt and pepper, cover and cook over moderate heat until the onions are softened, 10 minutes. Uncover and cook over moderately low heat, stirring, until the onions are soft and just beginning to caramelize, 40 minutes longer. Add a few tablespoons of water as the pan dries out. The *fonduta* will be thick and creamy.

2. Meanwhile, in a small bowl, combine the yogurt with the dill and cilantro. Season with salt and pepper.

3. In a bowl, mix the all-purpose flour, semolina flour, harissa, cumin, allspice and juniper with 1 tablespoon of salt. Soak the fish in the buttermilk for 5 minutes. Drain and dredge the fillets in the flour mixture and transfer to a wax paper–lined baking sheet.

4. In a very large skillet, heat ¼ inch of oil. Fry the fish in batches over moderate heat, turning once, until golden and just cooked through, 6 to 8 minutes. Drain the fish on paper towels and transfer to plates. Serve with the *fonduta* and yogurt.
—*Curtis Di Fede and Tyler Rodde*

NOTE Dried harissa is available online at zamourispices.com.

WINE Powerful, spicy Alto Adige Sylvaner: 2010 Abbazia di Novacella Praepositus.

Pan-Seared Trout with Serrano Ham and Chile-Garlic Oil

⏱ TOTAL: 25 MIN • 6 SERVINGS ● ●

Using only a few ingredients, this fish dish from chef Alex Raij of La Vara in New York City is easy, elegant and full of flavor. "The Spanish ham keeps the fish from drying out, basting it with its inimitable fat," says Raij.

Six 8-ounce trout fillets with skin
Salt and freshly ground pepper
6 thin slices of Spanish serrano or Ibérico ham
¼ cup plus 2 tablespoons extra-virgin olive oil
6 garlic cloves, thinly sliced
1 fresh red chile, thinly sliced crosswise
3 tablespoons chopped parsley
2 tablespoons sherry vinegar

1. Preheat the oven to 325°. Season the trout fillets with salt and freshly ground pepper. Press 1 slice of Spanish ham onto the skinless side of each fillet.

2. In a large nonstick skillet, heat 1 tablespoon of the olive oil until shimmering. Carefully add 3 of the trout fillets, ham side down, and cook them over moderately high heat until the ham is crisp, about 3 minutes. Turn the fillets and cook until the skin is crisp, about 1 minute longer. Transfer the trout fillets to a large rimmed baking sheet, ham side up. Cook the remaining trout fillets in 1 more tablespoon of olive oil and transfer them to the baking sheet. Keep the fish warm in the oven.

3. In the same skillet, heat the remaining ¼ cup of olive oil. Add the sliced garlic and cook over moderate heat until golden, about 2 minutes. Add the sliced chile and cook for 1 minute. Add the chopped parsley, sherry vinegar and a pinch of salt, then remove the skillet from the heat.

4. Transfer the trout fillets to plates, ham side up. Spoon the chile-garlic oil over the fish and serve right away.
—*Alex Raij*

WINE Fragrant, minerally white blend from Spain: 2011 Licia Albariño.

● HEALTHY ● MAKE AHEAD ● VEGETARIAN ● STAFF FAVORITE

grilled mackerel with apple-and-onion relish

Trout Schnitzel with Lemon-Chile Butter

⏱ TOTAL: 35 MIN • 4 SERVINGS ●

In this ingenious schnitzel recipe, trout fillets replace the usual veal or pork cutlets. If you can't find large enough trout fillets, use half-pound butterflied trout instead.

6 tablespoons unsalted butter, softened
6 anchovy fillets, minced
1 fresh red chile, minced
1 medium shallot, minced
1½ teaspoons finely grated lemon zest
Salt and freshly ground pepper
2 large eggs
3 cups soft, fresh, coarsely ground brioche bread crumbs
Four 8-ounce skinless trout fillets
Vegetable oil, for frying
Lemon wedges, for serving

1. Preheat the oven to 325°. In a bowl, blend the butter with the anchovies, chile, shallot and lemon zest. Season the lemon-chile butter with salt and pepper.
2. In a large, shallow bowl, beat the eggs. Put the bread crumbs in another large, shallow bowl. Season the trout with salt and pepper and dip each fillet in the egg, letting the excess drip off. Dredge the trout in the bread crumbs, pressing to help them adhere.
3. Set a plate lined with paper towels and a baking sheet with a rack near the stove. In a large nonstick skillet, heat ¼ inch of oil until shimmering. Add 2 of the trout fillets and cook over moderately high heat, turning once, until browned and crisp, 1½ to 2 minutes per side; reduce the heat to moderate if the fillets brown too quickly. Drain the trout on the paper towels, transfer the fillets to the rack and keep warm in the oven. Using a slotted spoon, discard any dark crumbs in the skillet and add more oil if needed to fry the remaining 2 trout fillets. Serve the trout schnitzel with the lemon-chile butter and lemon wedges. —*Marcia Kiesel*

SERVE WITH Sautéed or steamed spinach.
WINE Slinky, brightly acidic Grüner Veltliner: 2010 Nikolaihof Im Weingebirge Federspiel.

Japanese-Style Trout with Dashi

⏱ TOTAL: 45 MIN • 4 SERVINGS ●

The trout here is broiled and glazed with the same sweet and salty sauce that's served with *unagi* (eel) at sushi bars.

1 cup soy sauce
1 cup mirin
½ cup sugar
½ cup unseasoned rice vinegar
1 teaspoon instant dashi
2 carrots, finely julienned
2 leeks, white and light green parts only, finely julienned
Four 6-ounce rainbow trout fillets, bones removed
Steamed sushi rice and crumbled nori, for serving

1. In a medium saucepan, combine the soy sauce, mirin, sugar and rice vinegar and bring to a boil. Simmer over moderate heat until the glaze is reduced to about 1½ cups, about 10 minutes.
2. Meanwhile, in another medium saucepan, combine the dashi with 1½ cups of water and bring to a boil. Add the carrots and leeks and simmer just until crisp-tender, about 1 minute. Remove the saucepan from the heat and let stand.
3. Preheat the broiler and position a rack 6 to 8 inches from the heat. Arrange the trout fillets on a sturdy baking sheet, skin side up, and broil for about 2 minutes, until the skin begins to sizzle. Carefully peel off the skin. Brush the fish with some of the glaze and broil for 3 minutes, brushing once or twice more, until the sauce is lightly caramelized. Turn the fillets, brush liberally with more glaze and broil for 3 minutes longer, brushing once or twice, until the trout is cooked through and lacquered.
4. Mound rice in shallow bowls and drizzle lightly with the glaze. Using a slotted spoon, add the carrots and leeks. Top with the fish and nori and spoon the dashi into the bowls. Serve with the remaining glaze on the side. —*Grace Parisi*

WINE Lightly sweet, full-bodied Riesling: 2010 Dr. Loosen Dr. L.

North African Fish Stew

TOTAL: 50 MIN • 6 SERVINGS

¼ cup extra-virgin olive oil
2 medium red onions, thinly sliced
2 tablespoons golden raisins
¼ cup salted roasted cashews
1 red bell pepper, thinly sliced
1 yellow bell pepper, thinly sliced
4 medium tomatoes—peeled, seeded and sliced crosswise 1 inch thick
1 tablespoon *ras el hanout* (Moroccan spice blend)
1½ cups vegetable stock
1½ pounds catfish or tilapia fillets, cut into 1½-inch cubes
Salt and freshly ground pepper
2 cups couscous
½ teaspoon cinnamon
½ teaspoon ground cumin
1 tablespoon unsalted butter
2 scallions, thinly sliced

1. In a large, deep skillet, heat 2 tablespoons of the oil. Add half of the onion and cook over moderate heat, stirring, until browned, 8 minutes. With a slotted spoon, transfer to a plate. Add the raisins and cashews to the skillet and cook for 1 minute. Transfer to the plate with the onion.
2. Add the remaining 2 tablespoons of oil to the skillet along with the remaining onion and both peppers. Cook until softened, about 7 minutes. Add the tomatoes, *ras el hanout* and vegetable stock, cover and cook over low heat for 10 minutes. Season the fish with salt and pepper and add to the skillet. Cook over moderately high heat until the fish is cooked, 5 minutes.
3. Bring 2 cups of water to a boil. Put the couscous in a heatproof bowl and toss with the cinnamon and cumin. Pour the boiling water over the couscous, cover and let stand for 10 minutes. Stir in the butter and season with salt and pepper. Spoon the couscous into bowls and top with the stew. Garnish with the onion, raisins, cashews and scallions. —*Cat Cora*

WINE Full-bodied, tropical California Chardonnay: 2010 Bishop's Peak Central Coast.

● HEALTHY ● MAKE AHEAD ● VEGETARIAN ● STAFF FAVORITE

trout schnitzel with lemon-chile butter

Chef Linton Hopkins's family goes clamming on Georgia's Cumberland Island before a casual July Fourth cookout featuring Southern dishes like a shrimp stew with lima beans and sausage, OPPOSITE; recipe, page 124.

SHELLFISH

Shrimp Salad with Sherry Vinaigrette

TOTAL: 50 MIN • 4 SERVINGS ●

 5 tablespoons extra-virgin olive oil
1¼ pounds medium shrimp—shelled and deveined, shrimp halved lengthwise, shells reserved
Salt and freshly ground pepper
 2 tablespoons sherry vinegar
 6 ounces watercress (10 cups packed), thick stems discarded

1. In a medium saucepan, heat 1 tablespoon of the olive oil. Add the shrimp shells, season with salt and pepper and cook over moderately high heat, stirring occasionally, until the shells start to brown, about 3 minutes. Add 2 cups of water and bring to a boil. Cover and simmer over low heat for 15 minutes.
2. Strain the shrimp stock and return it to the saucepan. Boil over high heat until reduced to 2 tablespoons, about 10 minutes. Pour the reduction into a small bowl. Stir in the vinegar and 3 tablespoons of the olive oil; season the dressing with salt and pepper.
3. In a large skillet, heat the remaining 1 tablespoon of oil. Add the shrimp and season with salt and pepper. Cook over moderate heat, tossing, until just cooked, 3 minutes.
4. In a bowl, toss the watercress with the dressing. Add the shrimp and toss. Mound the salad on plates; serve. —*Marcia Kiesel*
WINE Zesty New Zealand Sauvignon Blanc: 2011 Babich Marlborough.

Sweet-and-Sour Shrimp

TOTAL: 25 MIN • 4 TO 5 SERVINGS ●

 2 tablespoons ketchup
 2 tablespoons low-sodium soy sauce
 ¾ cup chicken broth
 2 teaspoons sugar
 1 teaspoon Chinese chile sauce
 1 teaspoon cornstarch
1½ tablespoons rice vinegar
 2 tablespoons vegetable oil
 2 tablespoons minced fresh ginger
 1 garlic clove, minced
1½ pounds medium shrimp, peeled

1. In a small bowl, whisk the ketchup with the soy sauce, chicken broth, sugar, chile sauce, cornstarch and vinegar.
2. Heat a large skillet until very hot. Add the oil and swirl to coat the pan. Add the ginger and garlic and cook for 10 seconds, until fragrant. Add the shrimp and cook until curled but not cooked through, 1 to 2 minutes. Whisk the sauce and add it to the pan. Cook, stirring, until the sauce is thickened and the shrimp are cooked through, about 3 minutes. —*Grace Parisi*
SERVE WITH Snow peas and steamed rice.
WINE Fresh, light-bodied Spanish white: 2010 Ameztoi Txakoli.

Shrimp and Scallops with Lemony Soy

TOTAL: 30 MIN PLUS 30 MIN MARINATING
MAKES 16 SKEWERS ●
The Japanese-style marinade here works especially fast, thanks to the combination of tart citrus and salty soy sauce.

1½ cups low-sodium soy sauce
 1 cup mirin
 1 cup sake
 2 lemons, very thinly sliced
 2 jalapeños, very thinly sliced
 1 pound medium shrimp, shelled and deveined
 1 pound large sea scallops
Vegetable oil, for grilling

1. In a glass or ceramic baking dish, combine the soy sauce with the mirin, sake, lemon slices and jalapeños.
2. Thread the shrimp onto 8 pairs of bamboo skewers and add them to the marinade, turning to coat. Repeat with the scallops. Refrigerate the seafood for 30 minutes, turning once halfway through, then drain.
3. Light a grill and oil the grates. Brush the shrimp and scallops with oil and grill over high heat, turning once or twice, until lightly charred, about 4 minutes. Serve right away. —*Grace Parisi*
SERVE WITH Grilled eggplant and scallions.
WINE Vibrant, strawberry-rich rosé: 2011 Domaine de Fenouillet.

Mofongo with Shrimp

TOTAL: 45 MIN • 4 SERVINGS
Mofongo is a Puerto Rican comfort food that's made with garlicky mashed green plantains. Like mashed potatoes, it's a delicious vehicle for all kinds of savory toppings, such as the sautéed shrimp here.

 3 garlic cloves, minced
 ¾ ounce fried pork rinds, crushed (½ packed cup)
 ½ cup extra-virgin olive oil
Vegetable oil for frying
 2 large green plantains (about 12 ounces each), peeled and cut into 1-inch-thick rounds
Salt and freshly ground pepper
 1 pound medium shrimp, shelled and deveined
 ½ cup dry white wine

1. In a small bowl, combine two-thirds of the minced garlic cloves with the pork rinds and 1 tablespoon of the olive oil and mash to combine.
2. In a large saucepan, heat 1 inch of vegetable oil to 350°. Add the plantains and fry, keeping the oil at about 300°, until they are very tender but not browned, about 15 minutes. Drain the plantains on paper towels, then transfer them to a large bowl. Using a potato masher, mash the plantains to a coarse puree with 1 tablespoon of the olive oil. Add the garlic–pork rind mixture and mash until evenly combined. Season the *mofongo* with salt and pepper; keep warm.
3. In a large skillet, heat the remaining ¼ cup plus 2 tablespoons of olive oil until shimmering. Add the shrimp and remaining garlic, season with salt and pepper and cook over high heat, stirring occasionally, until curled, about 2 minutes. Add the white wine and boil until the wine is nearly evaporated and the shrimp are cooked through, about 2 minutes longer.
4. Spoon the *mofongo* into bowls and top with the shrimp. Serve right away. —*Benny Ojeda*
WINE Robustly fruity rosé: 2010 Domaine Faillenc Sainte Marie.

● HEALTHY   ● MAKE AHEAD   ● VEGETARIAN   ● STAFF FAVORITE

shrimp salad with sherry vinaigrette

Fresh Corn Grits with Shrimp

⏱ **TOTAL: 45 MIN • 4 SERVINGS** ●

Top Chef Season 5 star Jeff McInnis makes corn grits by grating the kernels from just-shucked ears to serve with his delicious shrimp-and-country-ham sauté.

GRITS

- 5 large ears of corn, shucked and coarsely grated on a box grater (2 cups pulp and juice)
- ¼ cup milk, plus more for stirring
- Salt and freshly ground pepper
- ¼ cup unsweetened roasted pecan butter (see Note)

SHRIMP SAUTÉ

- 6 tablespoons unsalted butter
- 3 ounces thinly sliced country ham or prosciutto, cut into strips
- ½ large sweet onion, thinly sliced
- 6 ounces sugar snap peas, trimmed
- 1 cup fresh corn kernels (from 2 ears)
- Salt and freshly ground pepper
- 1 pound shelled and deveined large shrimp
- 1 cup lager

1. MAKE THE GRITS In a saucepan, simmer the grated corn and juices with the ¼ cup of milk over moderate heat, stirring, until thick, 4 minutes. Season with salt and pepper and fold in the pecan butter; keep warm.

2. MAKE THE SHRIMP SAUTÉ In a large, deep skillet, melt 4 tablespoons of the butter. Add the ham and cook over moderately high heat, stirring, until lightly browned, about 5 minutes. Add the onion, snap peas and corn, season with salt and pepper and cook until crisp-tender, about 5 minutes. Add the shrimp and cook, stirring, until they just begin to curl, about 3 minutes. Add the lager and bring to a boil. Simmer, stirring frequently, until the shrimp are cooked through and the liquid is slightly reduced, 3 minutes. Swirl in the remaining butter.

3. Whisk a little milk into the grits so it's the consistency of polenta; heat until warm. Spoon the grits into shallow bowls, top with the shrimp and serve at once. —*Jeff McInnis*
SERVE WITH Lemon wedges.

NOTE To make your own pecan butter, process 1 cup toasted pecans in a mini food processor with ½ teaspoon canola oil until smooth, about 2 minutes. Season with salt.
WINE Crisp, medium-bodied white Bordeaux: 2011 Chateau Magneau.

Shrimp-and-Sausage Stew

📷 PAGE 122
ACTIVE: 30 MIN; TOTAL: 1 HR
6 TO 8 SERVINGS

- ¼ cup extra-virgin olive oil
- 1 pound andouille sausage, cut into 1-inch rounds
- 1 medium onion, finely chopped
- 1 large celery rib, finely chopped
- ½ green bell pepper, chopped
- 8 garlic cloves, minced
- ½ teaspoon cayenne pepper
- 3 tomatoes, chopped (2 cups)
- 1 cup chicken stock or low-sodium broth
- 1 cup bottled clam juice
- One 10-ounce bag fresh or frozen baby lima beans, thawed if frozen
- ¼ cup chopped flat-leaf parsley
- 2 pounds large shrimp in the shell
- Steamed rice and hot sauce, for serving

1. In a large, deep skillet, heat the oil. Add the sausage and cook over moderately high heat, stirring, until lightly browned, 5 minutes. Using a slotted spoon, transfer to a plate.
2. Add the onion, celery and green pepper to the skillet and cook over moderate heat, stirring frequently, until softened, 5 minutes. Add the garlic and cayenne; cook for 1 minute. Add the tomatoes; cook, stirring, until their liquid is nearly evaporated, 5 minutes. Add the stock and clam juice; bring to a boil. Scatter the sausage, lima beans and half of the parsley on top. Add the shrimp and cover tightly; simmer, stirring occasionally, for 15 minutes, until the shrimp are pink and cooked through. Let the stew rest for 5 minutes, then sprinkle with the remaining parsley. Serve with rice and hot sauce. —*Linton Hopkins*
BEER Lively summer beer: Sierra Nevada Summerfest.

Grilled Jumbo Shrimp with Kimchi-Miso Butter

⏱ **TOTAL: 25 MIN**
4 FIRST-COURSE SERVINGS ●

Quick and elegant, these sweet Asian shrimp are glazed with a delightfully savory butter seasoned with miso and kimchi.

- 1 stick unsalted butter, softened
- 1½ tablespoons yellow miso paste
- ¼ teaspoon toasted sesame oil
- Pinch of salt
- ¼ cup kimchi—drained, pressed dry and finely chopped
- 12 plump scallions, bottom 6 inches only, white parts halved lengthwise
- Canola oil, for brushing
- 12 jumbo shrimp in the shell, butterflied (see Note)
- ¼ cup shredded seasoned nori

1. In a microwave-safe bowl, using a wooden spoon, beat the softened butter with the miso paste, toasted sesame oil and salt. Add the chopped kimchi and beat until blended. Microwave at high power for about 10 seconds, just until the butter is melted.
2. Preheat the broiler and position a rack 6 inches from the heat. Preheat a cast-iron grill pan. Brush the scallions with canola oil and grill over moderately high heat, turning, until tender and browned in spots, about 3 minutes. Transfer the scallions to a plate. Lightly brush the shrimp with canola oil and place on the grill, shell side down. Drizzle each shrimp with a scant tablespoon of the seasoned butter and grill for 3 minutes. Transfer the grill pan to the oven rack and broil for about 1 minute, until the shrimp are cooked through and glazed with the butter. Transfer the shrimp and scallions to plates and drizzle with more of the butter. Garnish with the shredded nori and serve right away. —*Grace Parisi*

NOTE To butterfly the shrimp, using a sharp knife, carefully cut through the underside of the shrimp almost all the way through. Pull out and discard the intestinal vein.
WINE Full-bodied Central Coast Chardonnay: 2010 Talley Rincon Vineyard.

● HEALTHY ● MAKE AHEAD ● VEGETARIAN ● STAFF FAVORITE

fresh corn grits with shrimp

Shrimp in Tomato Sauce with Onion and Green Pepper

ACTIVE: 1 HR; TOTAL: 1 HR 45 MIN
8 SERVINGS ● ●

2 tablespoons unsalted butter
3 pounds large shrimp—shelled and deveined, shells reserved
1 chopped sweet onion, plus 2 cups finely diced sweet onion
Kosher salt and freshly ground pepper
3 tablespoons extra-virgin olive oil
1 green bell pepper, finely diced
3 tablespoons minced garlic
⅓ cup dry white wine
Two 15-ounce cans tomato sauce
2 tablespoons Worcestershire sauce
¼ teaspoon cayenne pepper
Steamed white rice, for serving

1. In a saucepan, melt the butter. Add the shrimp shells and cook over moderate heat, stirring, until pink, about 3 minutes. Add the 1 chopped onion and cook until softened, 3 minutes. Add 5 cups of water and bring to a boil. Simmer over moderately low heat until the stock is reduced to 2 cups, 40 minutes. Strain the shrimp stock through a fine sieve.
2. Season the shrimp lightly with salt and pepper. In a very large, deep skillet, heat 2 tablespoons of the olive oil until shimmering. Add half of the shrimp and cook over moderately high heat, turning once, until lightly browned, about 2 minutes. Transfer to a plate and repeat with the remaining shrimp.
3. In the same skillet, heat the remaining 1 tablespoon of oil. Add the green pepper, garlic and the 2 cups of diced onion; cook over moderately low heat, stirring, until softened, 8 minutes. Add the wine; simmer for 2 minutes. Stir in the stock, tomato sauce, Worcestershire and cayenne; bring to a boil. Simmer over moderate heat, stirring often, until the sauce has reduced by half, 15 minutes. Season with salt and pepper.
4. Add the shrimp to the sauce and simmer over moderately low heat until the shrimp are just cooked through, about 5 minutes. Serve over steamed rice. —*David Guas*
WINE Zesty Sauvignon Blanc: 2011 Steenberg.

Scallops with Snow Peas, Cauliflower and Peanut Panade

ACTIVE: 30 MIN; TOTAL: 1 HR
4 SERVINGS

2 teaspoons Madras curry powder
½ cup plus 1 tablespoon grapeseed oil
2 tablespoons fresh lime juice
Salt and freshly ground pepper
½ pound cauliflower, cut into florets
4 ounces snow peas
2 tablespoons dry bread crumbs
1½ tablespoons salted peanuts, minced
¼ cup plus 2 tablespoons creamy peanut butter, such as Skippy
16 large sea scallops (1½ pounds)
Cilantro sprigs, for garnish

1. Preheat the oven to 450°. In a small bowl, stir the curry powder into ¼ cup of the oil and let stand for 15 minutes. Let the spices settle, then pour the oil into another small bowl, stopping before you reach the solids. Whisk the lime juice into the curry oil and season the vinaigrette with salt and pepper.
2. In a small baking dish, toss the cauliflower with 2 tablespoons of the oil and season with salt. Roast on the top rack of the oven, stirring once, until the cauliflower is tender and lightly browned in spots, about 18 minutes.
3. Meanwhile, bring a pot of salted water to a boil. Add the snow peas and cook for 1 minute, until crisp-tender and bright green. Drain, cool under running water and pat dry.
4. In a skillet, toast the bread crumbs in 1 tablespoon of the oil until golden, 1 minute. Transfer the bread crumbs to a small bowl and let cool. Stir in the peanuts and peanut butter and season the *panade* with salt.
5. Preheat the broiler. Heat the remaining 2 tablespoons of oil in a large ovenproof skillet until smoking. Season the scallops with salt and pepper, add them to the pan and cook over high heat until well browned and crusty on the bottom, 4 minutes. Flip the scallops and spoon a dollop of the peanut *panade* onto each one. Broil for 10 seconds, until the *panade* is heated through.
6. Transfer the scallops to plates and arrange the cauliflower and snow peas around them.

7. Drizzle the curry vinaigrette all around, garnish with cilantro sprigs and serve. —*Grant Achatz*
WINE Vibrant, citrusy Riesling from New Zealand: 2010 Huia Dry Riesling.

Scallops with Grapefruit and Bacon

🕓 TOTAL: 35 MIN • 4 SERVINGS

1 large grapefruit
3 ounces slab bacon, cut into 1-by-¼-inch matchsticks
1¼ pounds sea scallops (about 20)
Salt and freshly ground pepper
¼ cup minced onion
½ cup Sauvignon Blanc
2 tablespoons drained capers
2 tablespoons unsalted butter

1. Using a sharp knife, peel the grapefruit, removing all of the bitter white pith. Working over a bowl, cut in between the membranes to release the sections. Squeeze the juice from the membrane into another bowl; you should have about 3 tablespoons of juice.
2. In a large skillet, cook the bacon over moderate heat until crisp, 3 minutes. Using a slotted spoon, transfer it to a small plate. Pour off all but 1 tablespoon of the bacon fat.
3. Season the scallops with salt and pepper, add to the skillet and cook over moderately high heat until browned, about 3 minutes. Turn the scallops, add the onion and cook over moderate heat until the scallops are just cooked through, 3 minutes longer. Transfer to a plate.
4. Add the wine and grapefruit juice to the skillet and bring to a simmer over moderate heat. Cook, scraping up any browned bits. Strain the liquid into a heatproof cup, then return it to the skillet. Add the capers and butter and cook, shaking the pan, until the sauce is thickened, 2 to 3 minutes. Add the scallops and any juices to the skillet; turn to coat them with the sauce. Add the grapefruit sections and bacon and serve right away. —*Grace Parisi*
WINE Grapefruit-scented California Sauvignon Blanc: 2011 Honig.

● HEALTHY ● MAKE AHEAD ● VEGETARIAN ● STAFF FAVORITE

scallops with grapefruit and bacon

Mussels on the Half Shell with Curried Crumbs

⏱ **TOTAL: 30 MIN**
6 FIRST-COURSE SERVINGS ● ●

This starter was inspired by *mouclade,* the classic Bordelais dish of steamed mussels in saffron or curry cream. Here, plump mussels are topped with buttery garlic-curry bread crumbs and broiled until they are golden brown and sizzling.

4 tablespoons unsalted butter, softened
1 large garlic clove, minced
1½ teaspoons curry powder
1 tablespoon chopped parsley
A few dashes of hot pepper sauce
1½ cups coarse fresh bread crumbs
Salt and freshly ground pepper
2 pounds medium mussels, scrubbed

1. In a skillet, melt 1 tablespoon of the butter. Add the garlic and cook over low heat until fragrant, 1 minute. Add the curry powder and cook, stirring, until fragrant, 1 minute. Scrape the mixture into a bowl and let cool. Stir in the remaining 3 tablespoons of butter and the parsley and hot sauce. Fold in the bread crumbs and season with salt and pepper.

2. In a large pot, bring 1 cup of water to a boil. Add the mussels, cover and cook over moderately high heat, shaking the pot a few times, until the mussels open, 3 minutes. Using a slotted spoon, transfer the mussels to a large rimmed baking sheet. Let cool, then break off 1 shell of each mussel. Pry each mussel loose, leaving it in the shell. Spoon a little of the mussel cooking liquid over each mussel.

3. Preheat the broiler. Dot each mussel with 1 teaspoon of the bread crumb topping. Broil the mussels 6 inches from the heat, rotating the pan a few times, until the crumbs are browned and crisp, 2 minutes. Serve.
—Marcia Kiesel

MAKE AHEAD The mussels can be prepared through Step 2 and refrigerated overnight.
WINE Lively white Bordeaux blend: 2010 Château de Tourtes Blanc Tradition.

Summer Squid Sauté

⏱ **TOTAL: 30 MIN • 4 SERVINGS** ●

2½ tablespoons extra-virgin olive oil
1 pound sugar snap peas, trimmed
Salt and freshly ground pepper
4 thin slices of pancetta (1½ ounces), finely diced
1¼ pounds cleaned small squid— bodies cut crosswise into ¼-inch rings, tentacles left whole

1. In a large skillet, heat 1½ tablespoons of the olive oil. Add the snap peas, season with salt and pepper and cook over moderately high heat, tossing, until blistered in spots and crisp-tender, about 3 minutes. Transfer the snap peas to a bowl.

2. Add the remaining 1 tablespoon of olive oil to the skillet along with the pancetta. Cook over low heat until the pancetta fat has rendered and starts to brown, about 3 minutes. Add the squid, season with salt and pepper and cook over high heat, tossing, until just cooked, about 2 minutes. Return the snap peas to the skillet and toss for about 1 minute. Serve. *—Marcia Kiesel*
WINE Minerally northern Italian white: 2010 Venica & Venica Friulano.

Grilled Oysters with Spiced Tequila Butter

⏱ **TOTAL: 25 MIN**
6 FIRST-COURSE SERVINGS

Blaine Wetzel, the chef at Willows Inn on Lummi Island in Washington, grills oysters, then drizzles them with warm butter flavored with sage, oregano, lemon juice and tequila.

½ teaspoon fennel seeds
¼ teaspoon crushed red pepper
7 tablespoons unsalted butter
¼ cup small to medium sage leaves, plus 36 small leaves for garnish
1 teaspoon dried oregano
2 tablespoons fresh lemon juice
2 tablespoons tequila
Kosher salt
Rock salt, for serving
3 dozen medium oysters, scrubbed

1. In a skillet, toast the fennel seeds and crushed red pepper over moderate heat until fragrant, 1 minute. Transfer to a mortar and let cool completely. With a pestle, grind the spices to a coarse powder; transfer to a bowl.

2. In the same skillet, cook 3½ tablespoons of the butter over moderate heat until it starts to brown, 2 minutes. Add the ¼ cup of sage and cook, turning once, until crisp, 2 minutes. With a slotted spoon, transfer the sage to a plate. Pour the browned butter into the bowl with the spices. Repeat with the remaining butter and the 36 sage leaves; reserve the leaves for garnish.

3. Add the first batch of fried sage leaves to the mortar and crush them with the pestle. Add the crushed sage to the butter along with the oregano, lemon juice and tequila and season with salt. Keep warm.

4. Light a grill. Line a platter with rock salt. Grill the oysters, flat side up, over high heat until they open, 1 to 2 minutes. Discard the flat top shell and place the oysters on the rock salt, being careful not to spill their liquor. Spoon the warm tequila butter over the oysters, garnish each one with a crisp sage leaf and serve. *—Blaine Wetzel*

WINE Bright, floral Loire white: 2011 Domaine de la Noblaie Chinon Blanc.

INGREDIENT TIP

oysters This bag of 100 Island Creek oysters is a great deal for anyone willing to shuck. *$150; available online at islandcreekoysters.com.*

● HEALTHY   ● MAKE AHEAD   ○ VEGETARIAN   ● STAFF FAVORITE

mussels on the half shell with curried crumbs

Okra Gumbo with Blue Crabs and Shrimp

ACTIVE: 35 MIN; TOTAL: 1 HR 15 MIN
8 SERVINGS ●

In this recipe from *The Dooky Chase Cookbook*, New Orleans chef Leah Chase—a.k.a. the Queen of Creole Cuisine—uses okra (and lots of it) to thicken the dish.

- ¼ cup vegetable oil
- 3 pounds okra, thinly sliced crosswise
- 4 live blue crabs
- 1½ cups finely chopped onion
- ½ cup finely chopped green bell pepper
- ½ cup finely chopped celery
- 2 tablespoons tomato paste
- 1 teaspoon minced garlic
- 1 teaspoon crushed red pepper
- 1 teaspoon paprika
- ½ teaspoon cayenne pepper
- ½ teaspoon dried thyme
- 2 bay leaves

Kosher salt
- 1 pound medium shrimp, shelled and deveined

Steamed white rice, for serving

1. Heat the vegetable oil in a large pot. Add the okra and cook over low heat, stirring, until softened, about 20 minutes. Add the crabs, onion, bell pepper and celery; cover and cook, stirring to prevent the okra from sticking to the bottom of the pot, until the vegetables are tender and the crabs are partially cooked, about 15 minutes.
2. Stir in the tomato paste, garlic, crushed red pepper, paprika, cayenne pepper, thyme, bay leaves and 1½ quarts of water; season with salt. Bring to a boil. Reduce the heat to moderate and simmer until the crabs are bright red, about 10 minutes. Stir in the shrimp and cook until pink, about 10 minutes longer.
3. Transfer the crabs to a work surface and pull off the triangular shell on the underside of each one. Using a sharp knife, cut each crab in half and transfer to bowls. Ladle the gumbo into the bowls and serve with rice. —*Leah Chase*
BEER Clean, mellow pale ale: Geary's.

Grilled Shellfish and Vegetables al Cartoccio

ACTIVE: 45 MIN; TOTAL: 1 HR 10 MIN
4 SERVINGS ● ●

- 1 bunch of Broccolini
- 8 fat asparagus spears
- 8 small carrots with some stem attached
- 8 large red radishes with some stem attached, halved lengthwise
- 4 medium tomatoes, halved crosswise
- 1 red onion, cut into ½-inch-thick wedges through the root end

Extra-virgin olive oil, for drizzling
Salt
- 16 small oysters, such as Wellfleet, scrubbed
- 16 littleneck clams, scrubbed
- 24 large mussels, scrubbed
- 4 large basil sprigs

Warm crusty bread, for serving

1. Light a grill. In a large bowl, toss all of the vegetables with olive oil and season with salt. Pull out the Broccolini and grill over moderately high heat until lightly charred, about 1 minute per side. Transfer to a large plate. Pull out the asparagus and carrots and grill for about 1 minute, until lightly charred; transfer to the plate. Grill the radishes, tomatoes and onion wedges, cut side down, until lightly charred, about 2 minutes. Add to the other vegetables.
2. Tear off eight 16-by-18-inch pieces of heavy-duty aluminum foil. Layer the sheets in pairs. Divide the oysters, clams and mussels among the four pairs of foil and drizzle with olive oil. Arrange the vegetables over the shellfish and drizzle with more olive oil. Add a pinch of salt, a basil sprig and 1 tablespoon of water to each. Fold the foil tightly into neat rectangular packets.
3. Arrange the packets on the grill. Cover and cook over moderately high heat, rotating once or twice, until the packets are puffed and sizzling, about 25 minutes. Serve right away, with bread. —*Cesare Casella*
WINE Zesty, citrusy Sauvignon Blanc from Austria: 2010 Neumeister.

Shellfish-Tomato Stew on Soft-Cooked Polenta

⏱ TOTAL: 45 MIN • 6 SERVINGS

- 1 tablespoon extra-virgin olive oil
- 1 small onion, diced
- 6 garlic cloves, minced

One 28-ounce can diced tomatoes
- ¾ cup dry white wine

Salt and freshly ground pepper
- 1½ cups chicken stock
- 1 cup milk
- 1 cup instant polenta
- 3 tablespoons unsalted butter
- 1 pound large shrimp, shelled and deveined
- 1 pound cleaned small squid—bodies cut crosswise into ½-inch rings, tentacles left whole
- 2 pounds mussels, scrubbed
- 2 tablespoons chopped flat-leaf parsley

1. In a large pot, heat the oil. Add the onion and cook over moderately low heat until softened, 5 minutes. Add the garlic and cook, stirring, until fragrant, 2 minutes. Add the tomatoes and bring to a simmer. Stir in the wine and cook over moderate heat for 2 minutes. Season with salt and pepper; set aside.
2. In a saucepan, bring the stock, milk and 2 cups of water to a boil. Gradually whisk in the polenta. Cook over moderate heat, whisking, until the polenta is slightly thickened, 2 minutes. Stir in 2 tablespoons of the butter and season with salt and pepper. Cover and keep warm.
3. Bring the tomato sauce back to a simmer. Add the shrimp and squid and simmer over moderately high heat until barely cooked, about 2 minutes. Add the mussels, cover and cook until they open, 4 minutes. Swirl in the remaining 1 tablespoon of butter and the parsley. Season with salt and pepper.
4. Whisk the polenta and ladle it into bowls. Spoon the stew over the polenta and serve. —*Sophie Heaulme*
WINE Spicy, cherry-inflected Sangiovese: 2010 Poderi San Lazzaro Polesio.

● HEALTHY ● MAKE AHEAD ● VEGETARIAN ● STAFF FAVORITE

okra gumbo with blue crabs and shrimp

FIRE-POWERED PAELLA

Rich stock, a wide pan and a grill are key to creating an authentic version of the iconic Spanish dish. Chef **Seamus Mullen** of New York City's Tertulia demonstrates how.

FIRST, PREPARE THE STOCK

Lobster-Infused Chicken Stock

ACTIVE: 35 MIN; TOTAL: 3 HR
MAKES ABOUT 10 CUPS ●

Two 1¼-pound lobsters
- 2 dried ñora or ancho chiles (see Note below right), stemmed and seeded
- ½ cup boiling water
- 2 tablespoons vegetable oil
- ¼ cup tomato paste
- ½ cup brandy
- 2 medium onions, quartered
- 2 medium carrots, quartered
- 2 fennel bulbs, quartered and cored
- 4 garlic cloves, quartered
- 2 quarts plus 3 cups chicken stock or low-sodium broth
- 2 bunches of basil
- ¼ teaspoon loosely packed saffron threads

1. Boil the lobsters until just red but still undercooked, 4 minutes; let cool. Remove the meat from the tails, claws and knuckles; discard the intestinal veins and cut the tails into thick slices. Put the meat in a bowl and refrigerate. Chop the body and leg shells.
2. In a heatproof bowl, cover the chiles with the boiling water and let stand for 15 minutes. Meanwhile, in a pot, heat the oil. Add the chopped shells and cook over high heat for 1 minute. Reduce the heat to moderate and cook, stirring, until browned. Stir in the tomato paste and cook for 1 minute. Add the brandy and simmer for 2 minutes, scraping up any browned bits. Add the onions, carrots, fennel and garlic; cook over low heat for 5 minutes.
3. Mince the chiles; add with the soaking liquid to the pot. Add the stock and basil; bring to a boil. Cover partially; simmer for 2 hours. Strain, add the saffron and let stand for 20 minutes.

THEN, MAKE THE SOFRITO (SAUTÉED MINCED VEGETABLES)

In a small heatproof bowl, cover 1 **DRIED ÑORA CHILE** with ½ cup **BOILING WATER**; let stand until softened, 15 minutes. Finely chop the chile; return to the soaking liquid. In a medium skillet, heat 2 tablespoons **EXTRA-VIRGIN OLIVE OIL.** Add 1 small minced **ONION**; cook over moderate heat until translucent, 4 minutes. Add 2 minced **GARLIC CLOVES**, ½ minced **RED BELL PEPPER**, 2 **PLUM TOMATOES** that have been grated on a box grater, 1 tablespoon **WHITE WINE VINEGAR** and the chile and its soaking liquid. Simmer over low heat, stirring occasionally, until the liquid has evaporated and the vegetables are very soft and browned, 20 minutes. Season with salt and pepper. You should have about 1 cup.

FINALLY, GRILL THE PAELLA

Chicken-and-Seafood Paella

TOTAL: 1 HR 10 MIN • 8 SERVINGS

- 2 tablespoons extra-virgin olive oil
- 8 each of chicken drumsticks and thighs (about 6 pounds)
- Salt and freshly ground pepper
- 10 cups warm Lobster-Infused Chicken Stock (recipe at left)
- 1 cup Sofrito (recipe above)
- 2¼ cups Bomba or Calasparra rice (see Note)
- ½ pound romano beans or green beans, cut into ½-inch pieces
- 2 pounds littleneck clams, scrubbed
- 1 pound mussels, scrubbed
- Allioli (recipe opposite) and lemon wedges, for serving

1. Light a hardwood charcoal or wood fire in a covered grill. When the fire is very hot, set a 17-inch paella pan on the grill. Add the oil and heat until shimmering. Season the chicken with salt and pepper and cook until browned, about 4 minutes per side. Transfer to a plate. Add 3 cups of the warm stock to the pan, scraping up any browned bits. Whisk in the 1 cup of *sofrito* and bring to a rolling boil. Add the rice and beans, shaking the pan to distribute them evenly. Season with salt; return to a vigorous boil. Cook for 4 minutes, stirring as little as possible; add more lit coals and/or wood to the fire to maintain the temperature. Bury the chicken pieces skin side up in the rice and cook until the stock is nearly evaporated, about 6 minutes.
2. Reduce the heat to a simmer; if necessary, use cast-iron trivets to lift the pan higher off the grill. Add 3 more cups of the stock, 1 cup at a time, shaking the pan occasionally and waiting until the stock is nearly absorbed between additions, 10 minutes. The rice should be lightly browned and crisp on the bottom, but not burned. Continue to cook, adding as much of the remaining stock as necessary ½ cup at a time, until the rice is almost tender and still very moist, 5 minutes. Nestle the clams and mussels into the rice, cover the grill and cook until they start to open, 6 minutes. Arrange the lobster all over the paella. Cover and cook until the clams and mussels are wide open and the lobster is heated through, 3 minutes longer.
3. Transfer the paella to the table, cover with a kitchen towel and let stand for 5 minutes. Serve with the *allioli* and lemon wedges.
NOTE Dried ñora chiles and Calasparra and Bomba rice are available at *tienda.com.*
WINE Crisp, bright Spanish white: 2011 Burgáns Albariño.

STEP-BY-STEP GUIDE TO GRILLED PAELLA

1. SEAR Heat olive oil until shimmering. Season the chicken with salt and pepper and cook until browned. Set the chicken aside.

2. DEGLAZE Add the hot lobster-infused chicken stock to the paella pan, and scrape up the browned bits on the bottom.

3. WHISK Add the *sofrito* to the paella pan, whisking to break it up and distribute evenly throughout the lobster-infused chicken stock.

4. SPRINKLE Bring the stock to a rolling boil. Sprinkle in the rice and beans, gently stirring and shaking the pan to distribute evenly.

5. BOIL Return the stock to a vigorous boil. Stirring as little as possible, allow the boiling stock to agitate the rice.

6. SIMMER Bury the seared chicken pieces in the rice and simmer, waiting until the stock is nearly absorbed before adding more stock.

7. COOK Continue adding small amounts of hot stock as the rice absorbs it. Arrange the littleneck clams all over the rice.

8. SCATTER Add the mussels to the pan, nestling them in the rice. Cover and grill until the clams and mussels start to open.

9. FINISH Add the lobster, cover and cook until the clams and mussels are wide open and the lobster is warmed through.

MAKE THE ALLIOLI (GARLIC MAYONNAISE)

In a blender, puree 3 **GARLIC CLOVES**, 1 **EGG**, ¼ cup **LEMON JUICE**, 2 teaspoons **WHITE WINE VINEGAR** and a pinch of **SALT**. At low speed, add ¼ cup **CANOLA OIL** in a thin stream until creamy, then drizzle in ½ cup **EXTRA-VIRGIN OLIVE OIL** until blended.

Buttery Crab Bread Pudding

ACTIVE: 25 MIN; TOTAL: 1 HR 15 MIN
8 SERVINGS ●

A decadent mix of custardy bread and sweet crabmeat, this savory bread pudding is from *The River Cottage Fish Book* by British chef Hugh Fearnley-Whittingstall. The recipe is quite easy to prepare: Fearnley-Whittingstall simply layers baguette slices and lump crabmeat, then bakes it all in a rich custard.

 1 stick unsalted butter, softened, plus more for greasing the dish
10 ounces lump crabmeat, picked over
 1 tablespoon finely chopped flat-leaf parsley
 1 tablespoon finely chopped chives
 2 teaspoons fresh lemon juice
Pinch of cayenne pepper
Kosher salt and freshly ground black pepper
One 24-inch day-old baguette—ends trimmed, bread cut into ¾-inch slices
 4 large eggs
 1 cup milk
 1 cup half-and-half

1. Preheat the oven to 350° and butter a 9-by-13-inch ceramic baking dish. In a medium bowl, toss the crabmeat with the parsley, chives, lemon juice and cayenne pepper. Season with salt and black pepper.
2. Butter each baguette slice and stand the slices in the prepared baking dish. Using a spoon, tuck the crab mixture evenly between the slices of bread.
3. In a medium bowl, whisk the eggs with the milk, half-and-half, 1 teaspoon of salt and ½ teaspoon of black pepper. Pour the custard evenly over the bread and let stand for 10 minutes.
4. Bake the bread pudding for 30 minutes, until the top is lightly browned and the custard is set. Let stand for 10 minutes before serving. —*Hugh Fearnley-Whittingstall*
SERVE WITH A crisp, bitter salad of chicory, radicchio and arugula.
WINE Concentrated white Burgundy: 2009 Domaine de la Cadette La Châtelaine.

Crab Imperial with Red Pepper

⏱ TOTAL: 40 MIN • 8 SERVINGS

 1 stick unsalted butter—6 tablespoons melted—plus more for greasing
 2 tablespoons all-purpose flour
1½ cups milk
Salt and freshly ground pepper
 1 tablespoon extra-virgin olive oil
 1 small onion, finely diced
 ½ red bell pepper, cut into ¼-inch dice
 2 large egg yolks
 2 tablespoons fresh lemon juice
Finely grated zest of 1 lemon
Hot sauce, such as Crystal or Tabasco
 1 pound lump crabmeat, picked over

1. In a saucepan, melt 2 tablespoons of the butter over moderate heat. Stir in the flour to make a paste. Gradually whisk in the milk until smooth and simmer, whisking, until thickened. Reduce the heat to low and cook, whisking, until no floury taste remains, 7 minutes. Season the béchamel with salt and pepper. Cover and remove from the heat.
2. In a skillet, heat the oil. Add the onion and cook over moderate heat until translucent. Add the bell pepper and cook until softened, 5 minutes. Season with salt and pepper.
3. In a stainless steel bowl, whisk the egg yolks with the lemon juice. Set the bowl over (not in) a saucepan of simmering water; whisk constantly until thickened, 2 minutes. Remove from the heat; slowly whisk in the melted butter until a smooth sauce forms. Fold in the béchamel and lemon zest. Season with salt, pepper and hot sauce.
4. Preheat the broiler. Set one rack 6 inches from the heat and another 10 inches from the heat. Butter a 9-by-9-inch ceramic baking dish. In a bowl, combine the crabmeat, onion and bell pepper. Gently fold in the sauce. Scrape into the prepared baking dish and broil on the upper rack for 3 minutes, until browned. Transfer the baking dish to the lower rack and broil for 4 minutes longer, until hot throughout. Serve. —*Michael Mina*
SERVE WITH Toasted baguette slices.
WINE Creamy Russian River Valley Chardonnay: 2009 Gallo Signature Series.

Korean Seafood Pancakes

⏱ TOTAL: 45 MIN • 4 FIRST-COURSE SERVINGS ●

These crispy seafood pancakes get a spicy tang from the kimchi that's mixed into the batter. To add more heat to the dish, thinly slice a hot chile pepper and add it to the soy-vinegar dipping sauce.

 ¾ cup all-purpose flour
 ¼ cup rice flour
 1 large egg, beaten
 ¾ cup plus 2 tablespoons seltzer or sparkling water
 ½ teaspoon toasted sesame oil
Salt
 ½ cup kimchi—drained, pressed dry and chopped
 4 ounces medium shrimp—shelled, deveined and split horizontally
 4 ounces baby squid—bodies cut into ¼-inch rings, tentacles halved
 4 large scallions, thinly sliced
Vegetable oil, for frying
 ¼ cup soy sauce
 ¼ cup unseasoned rice vinegar

1. In a large bowl, whisk the all-purpose flour and the rice flour with the egg, seltzer, toasted sesame oil and ¾ teaspoon of salt. Add the kimchi, shrimp, squid and scallions to the batter.
2. In 2 medium nonstick skillets, heat ¼ inch of vegetable oil. Spoon 2 mounds of the batter into each skillet and gently spread them into 4- to 5-inch rounds; be sure to distribute the seafood evenly in the pancakes. Cook over moderately high heat until the pancakes are golden and crisp on the bottom, 4 to 5 minutes. Carefully flip and cook over moderate heat until the pancakes are golden and crisp and the batter is cooked through, about 3 minutes longer. Using a slotted spatula, transfer to a paper towel–lined plate to drain.
3. In a small bowl, combine the soy sauce and rice vinegar. Cut the seafood pancakes into wedges and serve them with the dipping sauce. —*Grace Parisi*
WINE Unoaked, medium-bodied Chardonnay: 2011 Bishop's Peak.

● HEALTHY   ● MAKE AHEAD   ● VEGETARIAN   ● STAFF FAVORITE

buttery crab bread pudding

At the pop-up café Rice Paper Scissors in San Francisco, Valerie Luu (below) and Katie Kwan serve dishes inspired by Vietnamese street food like caramelized ginger chicken with sticky rice, OPPOSITE; recipe, page 142.

Chicken Caprese Salad

TOTAL: 30 MIN PLUS 1 HR MARINATING
4 SERVINGS ●

½ pound spicy marinated
    bocconcini (mozzarella balls), plus
    the oil from the container
4 skinless, boneless chicken breast
    halves, pounded ½ inch thick
Salt and freshly ground pepper
1 pint heirloom cherry
    or grape tomatoes, halved
Olive oil, for grilling

1. Pick the *bocconcini* out of the marinade.
Transfer half of the marinade to a medium
baking dish. Add the chicken, season with
salt and pepper and let stand at room temperature for 1 hour or refrigerate for 4 hours.
2. Quarter the *bocconcini* and transfer to a
bowl. Add the remaining marinade and the
tomatoes and season with salt and pepper.
3. Light a grill and oil the grate or preheat a
grill pan. Grill the chicken over high heat, turning once, until lightly charred and cooked
through, about 8 minutes. Cut the chicken
into bite-size pieces and add to the bowl with
the *bocconcini* and tomatoes. Toss and serve.
—*Grace Parisi*

WINE Juicy rosé: 2011 Maysara Roseena.

Chicken Teriyaki Plate

ACTIVE: 45 MIN; TOTAL: 1 HR 45 MIN
4 SERVINGS ●

1 cup lemon-lime soda
½ cup plus 2 tablespoons soy sauce
¾ cup rice vinegar
1 medium onion—½ grated,
    ½ thinly sliced
1 tablespoon grated fresh ginger
4 garlic cloves, smashed
1 tablespoon sugar
2 pounds boneless chicken thighs
    with skin
3 tablespoons canola oil
1 tablespoon unsalted butter
2 tablespoons chopped cilantro
Steamed white rice and hot sauce,
    for serving

1. In a bowl, mix the soda, soy, vinegar, grated
onion, ginger, garlic and sugar, then add the
chicken; turn to coat. Let stand at room temperature for 1 hour or refrigerate overnight.
2. Remove the chicken from the marinade
and pat very dry. Reserve 1 cup of the marinade. Heat 1½ tablespoons of the oil in a
large, deep skillet. Add the chicken skin side
down and cook over moderately high heat,
turning once, until it is browned and cooked
through, 7 to 8 minutes. Transfer to a plate.
3. Wipe out the skillet; heat the remaining
1½ tablespoons of oil. Add the sliced onion
and cook over moderate heat, stirring, until
browned, 5 minutes. Add the reserved marinade and boil until slightly reduced, 2 minutes. Swirl in the butter and add the cilantro.
Return the chicken and any juices to the skillet and cook until heated through, 1 minute.
Serve with rice and hot sauce. —*Roy Choi*
WINE Fruity, minerally Beaujolais: 2010 Guy
Breton Vieilles Vignes Morgon.

Chicken Stir-Fry with Corn, Pineapple and Red Pepper

⏲ **TOTAL: 35 MIN • 4 SERVINGS**

3 tablespoons vegetable oil
1¼ pounds skinless, boneless
    chicken breasts, sliced crosswise
    into ⅓-inch strips
1 small red onion, thinly sliced
2 teaspoons minced fresh ginger
1 red bell pepper, cut into thin strips
½ teaspoon ground cumin
¼ cup chicken stock
½ cup corn kernels, thawed if frozen
½ cup diced fresh pineapple
2 teaspoons Sriracha
Salt and freshly ground pepper

In a large nonstick skillet, heat 1 tablespoon
of the oil. Stir-fry the chicken over moderately high heat for 3 minutes; transfer to a
plate. Heat the remaining 2 tablespoons of
oil. Add the onion and ginger and cook for
3 minutes. Add the red pepper, cumin and
stock, cover and cook over moderately low
heat, stirring a few times, for 4 minutes. Add
the corn, pineapple and Sriracha and stir-fry

over moderately high heat until hot. Add the
chicken and stir-fry for 1 minute. Season with
salt and pepper and serve. —*Marcia Kiesel*
WINE Oaky, full-bodied white: 2010 Bonny
Doon Le Cigare Blanc.

Chicken in Pineapple Sauce

TOTAL: 1 HR • 4 SERVINGS

½ cup all-purpose flour
One 3-pound chicken, cut into 8 pieces
Salt and freshly ground black pepper
1 teaspoon sweet paprika
¼ cup extra-virgin olive oil
1 sweet onion, finely chopped
1 green bell pepper, finely chopped
4 garlic cloves, minced
1 cup dry white wine
1 cup chicken stock
½ cup pineapple juice
¼ cup fresh lime juice
1 bay leaf
Steamed white rice, for serving

1. Put the flour in a shallow bowl. Season the
chicken with salt and black pepper and sprinkle with the paprika. Dredge the chicken in
the flour, tapping off the excess.
2. In a large, deep skillet, heat the oil until
shimmering. Cook the chicken over moderately high heat, turning once or twice, until
golden brown, 6 minutes. Transfer to a plate.
Pour off all but 1 tablespoon of the fat.
3. Add the onion, green pepper and garlic to
the skillet and cook over moderate heat, stirring, until softened, 5 minutes. Add the wine
and boil until reduced by half, scraping up
any browned bits from the bottom of the skillet, 5 minutes. Add the stock, pineapple juice,
lime juice and bay leaf and bring to a boil.
4. Nestle the chicken in the skillet and add
any accumulated juices. Cover and cook over
very low heat, turning the chicken once, until
cooked through, about 25 minutes. Uncover
and cook over high heat until the sauce is
thickened and glossy, about 5 minutes. Discard the bay leaf; serve the chicken with rice,
spooning the sauce on top. —*David Guas*
WINE Substantial California Chardonnay:
2010 Clos Julien.

● HEALTHY ● MAKE AHEAD ● VEGETARIAN ● STAFF FAVORITE

chicken caprese salad

Classic Chicken Teriyaki

TOTAL: 30 MIN • 4 SERVINGS ●

Iconic chef Nobu Matsuhisa of the Nobu restaurants worldwide makes a chicken teriyaki that outdoes every other interpretation out there. Here, his best-ever version simplified for home cooks.

- 1 cup chicken stock or low-sodium broth
- ⅓ cup low-sodium soy sauce
- ⅓ cup sugar
- 2 tablespoons mirin
- 2 tablespoons sake

Four 6-ounce skinless, boneless chicken breasts, lightly pounded

Salt and freshly ground pepper

- 2 tablespoons canola oil
- 2 large Italian frying peppers, cut into ½-inch strips

Steamed short-grain rice, for serving

1. In a medium saucepan, combine the stock with the soy sauce, sugar, mirin and sake and bring the mixture to a boil over high heat, stirring to dissolve the sugar. Reduce the heat to moderate and simmer until the teriyaki sauce is reduced to ½ cup and syrupy, about 20 minutes.

2. Meanwhile, season the chicken with salt and pepper. In a large nonstick skillet, heat 1 tablespoon of the canola oil. Add the chicken and cook over moderately high heat, turning once, until browned all over and cooked through, 8 to 9 minutes. Transfer the chicken to a plate and let stand for 5 minutes.

3. Wipe out the skillet. Add the remaining 1 tablespoon of canola oil and heat until shimmering. Add the pepper strips and cook over high heat, stirring occasionally, until crisp-tender and lightly charred, about 3 minutes. Transfer the peppers to plates. Slice the chicken breasts crosswise and transfer to the plates. Drizzle the teriyaki sauce over the chicken and serve with rice.

—*Nobu Matsuhisa*

MAKE AHEAD The teriyaki sauce can be refrigerated for up to 1 month.

WINE Medium-bodied, raspberry-rich Grenache: 2010 The Show.

Coconut Chicken with Pickled-Pepper Collards

TOTAL: 45 MIN PLUS 2 HR MARINATING
4 SERVINGS ●

These delicious fried chicken cutlets from star chef Marcus Samuelsson have a crisp coconut crust; on the side, he serves sautéed collard greens with pickled jalapeños.

COCONUT CHICKEN

- 2 cups buttermilk
- ¾ cup unsweetened coconut milk
- 2 garlic cloves, minced
- 8 thin chicken cutlets (1¾ pounds)
- 3 cups panko (6 ounces)
- 3 tablespoons unsweetened shredded coconut

Salt and freshly ground pepper

Canola oil, for frying

COLLARDS

- 3 tablespoons extra-virgin olive oil
- 2 large garlic cloves, halved
- 2 pounds young collard greens, stems and inner ribs removed and leaves thinly sliced
- 1 cup chicken stock

Salt and freshly ground pepper

- 4 pickled jalapeños, seeded and thickly sliced

1. **MAKE THE COCONUT CHICKEN** In a large bowl, combine the buttermilk, coconut milk and garlic. Add the chicken and refrigerate for at least 2 hours and up to 4 hours.

2. In a shallow bowl, combine the panko and coconut; season with salt and pepper. Drain the chicken and season with salt and pepper. Dip the cutlets into the panko, pressing to help it adhere. Refrigerate for 10 minutes.

3. **MAKE THE COLLARDS** Heat the olive oil in a large skillet. Add the garlic and cook over moderate heat until golden, 2 minutes. Add the collards and cook, stirring, until wilted, 2 minutes. Add the stock and season with salt and pepper. Cook, stirring, until the liquid is nearly evaporated and the collards are tender, about 8 minutes. Discard the garlic and stir in the sliced jalapeños; keep warm.

4. In a large nonstick skillet, heat ½ inch of canola oil until shimmering. Working in batches, fry the chicken over moderately high heat, turning once, until crispy, 6 minutes. Drain on paper towels and season with salt. Serve with the collards.

—*Marcus Samuelsson*

WINE Balanced, fruit-forward Spanish white: 2011 Paso a Paso Verdejo.

Chicken Thighs Marinated with Homemade Ssam Paste

TOTAL: 25 MIN PLUS 8 HR MARINATING
4 SERVINGS ●

- ⅓ cup yellow miso
- ¼ cup plus 2 tablespoons sugar
- ¼ cup plus 2 tablespoons toasted sesame oil
- ¼ cup Asian fish sauce
- ¼ cup white vinegar
- 1½ tablespoons Korean red chile powder (*gochugaru*, available at Asian markets and *TriFood.com*)
- 4 garlic cloves, minced
- 2 tablespoons minced fresh ginger
- 8 large boneless chicken thighs with skin
- 1 medium onion, sliced ½ inch thick

Vegetable oil, for brushing

- 4 scallions, thinly sliced

Bibb or Boston lettuce leaves, for serving

1. In a bowl, whisk together the miso, sugar, sesame oil, fish sauce, vinegar, chile powder, garlic and ginger. Put the chicken and onion in a large, shallow dish, add half of the marinade and turn to coat the chicken completely. Cover and refrigerate for 8 to 12 hours. Refrigerate the remaining marinade.

2. Light a grill or preheat a grill pan. Remove the chicken from the marinade, discarding the onions; brush with oil. Grill the chicken over moderate heat, turning once, until it is browned and cooked through, 10 minutes.

3. Stir the scallions into the reserved marinade and brush some on the chicken. Grill for 10 seconds per side, until glazed. Brush a little more marinade on the skin. Serve with lettuce leaves for wrapping. —*Bill Kim*

WINE Spice-inflected, pear-scented Alsace Gewürztraminer: 2011 Albert Mann.

● HEALTHY ● MAKE AHEAD ● VEGETARIAN ● STAFF FAVORITE

Caramelized Ginger Chicken with Sticky Rice

📷 PAGE 137

ACTIVE: 45 MIN; TOTAL: 3 HR PLUS OVERNIGHT SOAKING • 4 SERVINGS

Inspired by the ginger chicken sold by a street hawker in Vietnam, this recipe from the San Francisco pop-up café Rice Paper Scissors is sweet and sticky, with lots of great ginger flavor.

½ cup plus 2 tablespoons light brown sugar
⅓ cup plus 2 tablespoons Asian fish sauce, such as *nuoc mam*
4 whole chicken legs
¼ cup vegetable oil
6 scallions, white and green parts, thinly sliced
3 tablespoons soy sauce
1½ tablespoons white vinegar
1 tablespoon honey
1 cup very finely chopped shallots
4 garlic cloves, very finely chopped
½ cup minced peeled fresh ginger
3 Thai chiles, very finely chopped
½ cup sliced pickled daikon (see Note)
2½ cups Chinese sticky rice (about 18 ounces), soaked overnight in water and drained (see Note)
Salt

1. In a large, shallow baking dish, combine 2 tablespoons of the brown sugar with 2 tablespoons of the fish sauce and stir until the sugar is dissolved. Add the chicken legs and coat them thoroughly with the marinade. Let the chicken stand at room temperature for 2 hours or refrigerate overnight.

2. Preheat the oven to 450°. In a small saucepan, heat the vegetable oil. Add the scallions and cook over high heat until they sizzle, about 30 seconds. Remove from the heat.

3. Meanwhile, in a medium enameled cast-iron casserole, combine the remaining ½ cup of brown sugar with 1 tablespoon of water and cook over moderately high heat, stirring a few times, until bubbling, about 3 minutes. Gradually stir in 1½ cups of water, then stir in the remaining ⅓ cup of fish sauce along with the soy sauce, vinegar, honey and half of the scallion oil. Bring to a boil and simmer the sauce over moderately high heat until slightly reduced, about 5 minutes. Add the shallots, garlic, ginger and chiles and simmer over moderately low heat for 5 minutes.

4. Roast the chicken in the upper third of the oven for about 25 minutes, until browned.

5. Nestle the chicken legs in the sauce in the casserole, then tuck in the pickled daikon slices. Cover the casserole and simmer over low heat for about 15 minutes, basting the chicken a few times, until it is cooked through; add a few tablespoons of water if the sauce gets too thick and dark.

6. Meanwhile, in a wide stainless steel or bamboo steamer, bring 1½ inches of water to a boil. Moisten a double layer of cheesecloth that is large enough to cover the basket of the steamer and reach partway up the side; line the steamer basket with it. Add the drained rice to the basket; pat into an even layer. Cover and steam the rice over moderate heat until tender, 15 minutes.

7. Uncover the rice and season lightly with salt. Spoon the remaining scallion oil over the rice and stir gently. Serve the chicken with the rice. —*Katie Kwan and Valerie Luu*

NOTE Pickled daikon and Chinese sticky rice are available online or at Asian markets.

WINE Rich, minerally German Riesling: 2011 Merkelbach Ürziger Würzgarten Kabinett.

Chicken and Golden Rice

🕐 TOTAL: 40 MIN • 4 SERVINGS ● ●

1 garlic clove, minced
½ tablespoon vegetable oil
⅛ teaspoon turmeric
1 cup jasmine rice, rinsed
1 cup chicken broth
Salt and freshly ground pepper
3 cups shredded cooked chicken
½ small white onion, thinly sliced
½ cup torn Thai basil
½ cup cilantro leaves
1 tablespoon fresh lemon juice, plus lemon wedges for serving
¼ cup soy sauce
1 tablespoon Sriracha

1. In a saucepan, cook the garlic in the oil over moderate heat for 1 minute. Add the turmeric and rice; cook for 1 minute. Add the broth; bring to a boil. Cover and cook over low heat for 10 minutes. Remove from the heat and let stand for 5 minutes. Fluff the rice, season with salt and pepper and cover.

2. In a bowl, toss the chicken, onion, basil, cilantro and lemon juice; transfer to plates. In a small bowl, combine the soy sauce and Sriracha. Serve the chicken with the rice, dipping sauce and lemon. —*Anita Lo*

WINE Minerally, herb-scented Italian white: 2010 Fontezoppa Verdicchio di Matelica.

Chicken Katsu

🕐 TOTAL: 30 MIN • 4 SERVINGS

Eight 6-ounce skinless, boneless chicken thighs
Salt
1 cup all-purpose flour
3 large eggs, lightly beaten with 3 tablespoons of water
3 cups panko bread crumbs
3 cups vegetable oil
Tonkatsu sauce (Japanese barbecue sauce; see Note), Dijon mustard and steamed sushi rice, for serving

1. Lightly pound the chicken thighs ½ inch thick and season with salt. Put the flour, eggs and panko in 3 separate pie plates and season each one lightly with salt. Dredge 1 piece of chicken in the flour, tapping off the excess. Dip in the egg, allowing the excess to drip off, then coat the chicken with the panko, pressing to help the crumbs adhere. Transfer the chicken to a wax paper–lined baking sheet. Repeat with the remaining chicken.

2. Divide the oil between 2 large skillets and heat until shimmering. Fry the chicken over moderately high heat, turning once, until golden and crispy, 3 minutes per side. Drain on paper towels. Serve with *tonkatsu* sauce, mustard and rice. —*Roy Choi*

NOTE *Tonkatsu* sauce is available in the Asian section of most supermarkets.

BEER Crisp lager-style beer: Kona Brewing Co. Longboard Island Lager.

● HEALTHY   ● MAKE AHEAD   ● VEGETARIAN   ● STAFF FAVORITE

chicken katsu

Tuscan Chicken with Grilled Fennel and Onions

TOTAL: 1 HR 15 MIN • 4 SERVINGS ●

This chicken from Cesare Casella of Manhattan's Salumeria Rosi has a triple hit of fennel: fennel seeds in the marinade, fennel pollen in the vinaigrette and grilled fennel on the side.

Four 8-ounce boneless chicken breasts
    with skin
Four 6-ounce boneless chicken thighs
    with skin
Salt and freshly ground pepper
  ½ cup plus 2 tablespoons extra-virgin
    olive oil, plus more for brushing
  1 tablespoon fennel seeds
  1 tablespoon plus ½ teaspoon
    crushed red pepper
  2 fennel bulbs, cut lengthwise through
    the cores into ¼-inch-thick slices,
    fronds reserved
  2 red onions, cut into ½-inch-thick
    wedges through the root ends
  4 medium tomatoes, halved crosswise
  4 garlic cloves, minced
Finely grated zest of 2 lemons
  3 tablespoons fresh lemon juice
  1 teaspoon fennel pollen

1. Season the chicken breasts and thighs with salt and freshly ground pepper. In a large bowl, combine 2 tablespoons of the olive oil with the fennel seeds and 1 tablespoon of the crushed red pepper. Add the chicken pieces and turn to coat well with the marinade.
2. Bring a large saucepan of salted water to a boil. Add the fennel slices and blanch over moderately high heat for 2 minutes. With a slotted spoon, transfer the fennel to paper towels to drain. Add the onions to the boiling water and blanch for 1 minute; drain well. Brush the fennel, onion and tomatoes with olive oil and season with salt and pepper.
3. Light a grill or preheat a grill pan. Grill the fennel slices and onions over moderately high heat until lightly charred and tender, about 3 minutes per side. Transfer to a platter; cover loosely with foil. Grill the tomato halves cut side down until lightly charred, about 2 minutes per side; add to the platter.

4. In a small bowl, combine the remaining ½ cup of olive oil and ½ teaspoon of crushed red pepper with the garlic, lemon zest, lemon juice and fennel pollen; season the dressing with salt and pepper.
5. Remove the chicken from the marinade. Grill the chicken skin side down over moderately high heat, basting once with 2 tablespoons of the lemon-fennel dressing, until charred, about 12 minutes. Turn the chicken and grill until cooked through, about 8 minutes longer for the breasts and 12 minutes longer for the thighs.
6. Arrange the chicken on the platter with the grilled vegetables. Spoon the remaining lemon-fennel dressing over the chicken and vegetables, garnish with the fennel fronds and serve. —*Cesare Casella*

MAKE AHEAD The blanched vegetables and lemon-fennel dressing can be refrigerated overnight. Bring them to room temperature before proceeding.

WINE Fruit-forward, light-bodied Italian red: 2010 Casale della Ioria Cesanese del Piglio.

Tunisian Chicken Kebabs with Currants and Olives

TOTAL: 1 HR 30 MIN PLUS 4 HR MARINATING • 20 SERVINGS ● ●

Sweet and tangy, these chicken skewers are flavorful enough to eat on their own, but they're even better with the chunky currant-and-olive relish.

  2 medium red bell peppers
  1 cup dried currants
One 14-ounce jar sweet Peppadew
    or other sweet pickled red peppers,
    ½ cup of the juices from the jar
    reserved
  1 cup extra-virgin olive oil,
    plus more for grilling
Kosher salt
  3 pounds skinless, boneless chicken
    breasts, lightly pounded and cut
    lengthwise into 1-inch-wide strips
  3 pounds skinless, boneless chicken
    thighs, trimmed and cut lengthwise
    into 1-inch-wide strips
Tunisian Relish (recipe follows)

1. Roast the bell peppers directly over a gas flame or under the broiler, turning, until they are charred all over. Transfer to a bowl, cover with plastic wrap and let cool. Peel, seed and core the peppers.
2. Meanwhile, soak the currants in ½ cup of hot water until plump, about 5 minutes. Drain and transfer the currants to a blender. Add the roasted peppers, Peppadews and their liquid and the 1 cup of olive oil and puree. Season the marinade lightly with salt.
3. Thread the chicken breast and thigh strips separately onto 30 to 40 bamboo skewers and transfer to a large rimmed baking sheet. Pour half of the marinade over the chicken, turning to coat completely. Refrigerate for 4 hours. Refrigerate the remaining half of the marinade in a serving bowl.
4. Light a grill and oil the grates or preheat a grill pan. Remove the chicken from the marinade, letting the excess drip off. Season the chicken with salt. Grill the chicken over high heat, in batches if necessary and turning with tongs, until lightly charred and cooked through, about 8 minutes for the breasts and 10 minutes for the thighs. Serve the kebabs hot or at room temperature along with the reserved marinade and the Tunisian Relish. —*Susan Feniger*

WINE Apple-scented, full-bodied Spanish white: 2010 Ludovicus Blanco.

TUNISIAN RELISH

☉ **TOTAL: 20 MIN • MAKES ABOUT 3 CUPS** ● ● ●

  1 cup dried currants
  2 cups pitted green olives, chopped
  1 cup sweet Peppadew peppers,
    chopped
  ½ cup extra-virgin olive oil
  ¼ cup sherry vinegar
Kosher salt

In a medium bowl, soak the dried currants in hot water until plump, about 5 minutes. Drain, pressing out the excess water. Return the currants to the bowl and add the olives, Peppadews, olive oil and vinegar. Season the relish with salt and serve. —*SF*

tuscan chicken with grilled fennel and onions

Crispy Corn Tortillas with Chicken and Cheddar

⏱ **TOTAL: 40 MIN • 4 SERVINGS**

For these quick flautas, F&W's Grace Parisi rolls corn tortillas around shredded rotisserie chicken, cheddar cheese and roasted jalapeños, then pan-fries them in just ¼ inch of oil until they're crisp.

- 2 jalapeños
- 2 cups finely shredded roast chicken
- 4 ounces sharp cheddar cheese, shredded (1 cup)
- ½ teaspoon cumin seeds
- Salt and freshly ground pepper
- 12 corn tortillas
- Vegetable oil, for frying
- 4 radishes, very thinly sliced
- ¼ cup chopped cilantro
- 2 tablespoons finely chopped red onion
- 1 teaspoon fresh lime juice

1. Skewer the jalapeños on a metal skewer or fork and roast over a flame until blackened, 3 minutes. Wrap in foil and let cool slightly. Rub off the skins and remove the seeds, then finely chop. Transfer the jalapeños to a bowl and add the chicken, cheese and cumin. Season with salt and pepper; toss well.

2. Wrap half of the tortillas in a towel and microwave at high power for 1 minute, until pliable. Arrange the tortillas on a surface and pack half of the chicken filling into cylinders across the bottoms. Tightly roll the tortillas around the filling, securing with toothpicks. Repeat to form the remaining flautas.

3. In a large skillet, heat ¼ inch of oil. Line a baking sheet with paper towels. Fry half of the flautas over moderate heat, turning, until golden and crisp all over and heated through, about 4 minutes. Drain on paper towels. Fry the remaining flautas.

4. In a small bowl, toss the radishes with the cilantro, onion and lime juice; season with salt and pepper. Remove the toothpicks from the flautas and serve with the radish salad.
—*Grace Parisi*

SERVE WITH Sour cream.

BEER Malty brown ale: Big Sky Moose Drool.

Chicken Tamales with Tomatillo-Cilantro Salsa

ACTIVE: 2 HR; TOTAL: 6 HR
MAKES ABOUT 30 TAMALES ● ●

Anna Zepaltas, owner of a meal-delivery service in Santa Rosa, California, learned to prepare these light, fluffy tamales from her Mexican-born mother. Zepaltas carries on the teaching tradition by giving her friends a tamale tutorial on Fridays; everyone goes home with several ready-made meals for the week ahead.

- 6 ounces dried corn husks (about 35; see Note on page 237)
- 1½ pounds tomatillos, husked and halved
- 1 Spanish onion, cut into 1-inch wedges
- 3 garlic cloves, peeled
- 2 serrano chiles, stemmed
- 1 tablespoon vegetable oil
- ⅓ cup fresh lime juice
- ¼ cup packed cilantro leaves
- Salt and freshly ground pepper
- One 4½- to 5-pound chicken, cut into 8 pieces
- 6 cups Tamale Dough (page 237)
- Tomatillo-Cilantro Salsa (recipe follows)

1. Soften the corn husks (for the method, see page 237).

2. Preheat the oven to 500°. In a medium roasting pan, toss the tomatillos, onion, garlic and chiles with the oil. Roast for about 30 minutes, stirring twice, until the vegetables are very soft and browned in spots. Transfer the vegetables and any juices to a blender or food processor. Add the lime juice and cilantro and puree until smooth. Season the sauce with salt and pepper. Reduce the oven temperature to 350°.

3. In a large enameled cast-iron casserole or Dutch oven, pour the sauce over the chicken pieces. Cover and braise in the oven for about 1 hour and 15 minutes, until chicken is cooked through. Remove the chicken from the pot and let cool slightly.

4. Set the pot over moderately high heat and boil the sauce, stirring frequently, until reduced to 2½ cups, about 15 minutes.

5. Discard the chicken skin and shred the meat into bite-size pieces. Add the chicken to the sauce and let cool completely.

6. Fill, fold and steam the tamales (method, page 237). Serve the tamales with the Tomatillo-Cilantro Salsa. —*Anna Zepaltas*

MAKE AHEAD The uncooked tamales can be refrigerated for up to 5 days or frozen for up to 1 month; steam them while still frozen.

WINE Bright, concentrated Chardonnay: 2011 Healdsburg Ranches.

TOMATILLO-CILANTRO SALSA

⏱ **ACTIVE: 15 MIN; TOTAL: 30 MIN**
MAKES 2½ CUPS ● ●

"We always choose a lighter, green salsa like this one for poultry or vegetable dishes," says Zepaltas. "With a strong-flavored red salsa, you would lose the taste of the chicken."

- ½ pound tomatillos (about 4), husked
- 1 large beefsteak tomato or 2 medium ones (about 1 pound)
- 2 serrano chiles, stemmed
- 1 dried pasilla chile, stemmed and seeded
- 1 medium onion, cut into 1-inch wedges
- 1 garlic clove, peeled
- ½ cup packed cilantro sprigs
- 1 tablespoon fresh lime juice
- Salt

1. Preheat the oven to 500°. On a rimmed baking sheet, spread the tomatillos, beefsteak tomato, serranos, pasilla, onion and garlic. Roast the vegetables in the center of the oven for about 15 minutes, turning them once or twice, until they are softened and lightly browned in spots.

2. Peel and core the beefsteak tomato and cut the flesh into quarters. Crumble the pasilla chile into a blender or food processor and add the remaining roasted vegetables and any juices. Add the cilantro sprigs and lime juice and puree until smooth. Season the salsa with salt. —*AZ*

NOTE Dried pasilla chiles are available at Latin American markets.

MAKE AHEAD The Tomatillo-Cilantro Salsa can be refrigerated overnight.

● HEALTHY ● MAKE AHEAD ● VEGETARIAN ● STAFF FAVORITE

crispy corn tortillas with chicken and cheddar

Latin-Spiced Chicken in Lettuce Cups

ACTIVE: 30 MIN; TOTAL: 1 HR 20 MIN
PLUS 4 HR MARINATING • 4 SERVINGS

New York City chef Bill Telepan's easy spiced chicken in lettuce cups is a great combination of meaty, crunchy and fresh.

Kosher salt and freshly ground pepper
- 1 tablespoon chile powder
- 1 tablespoon dried oregano
- 3 garlic cloves, minced
- 2 tablespoons fresh orange juice
- ¼ cup plus 2 tablespoons fresh lime juice
- ¼ cup plus 2 tablespoons extra-virgin olive oil
- 6 whole chicken legs (about 4½ pounds), excess fat trimmed and skin scored
- 1 pound Savoy cabbage, finely shredded (8 cups)
- ½ small red onion, very thinly sliced
- 2 jalapeños, seeded and minced
- 3 tablespoons chopped cilantro
- 16 large Boston lettuce leaves

1. In a small bowl, combine 1 tablespoon each of salt and pepper with the chile powder, oregano, garlic, orange juice and 2 tablespoons each of the lime juice and olive oil. Put the chicken legs on a large rimmed baking sheet and coat all over with the spiced oil. Cover and refrigerate for 4 hours.

2. Meanwhile, in a large bowl, combine the remaining ¼ cup each of lime juice and olive oil. Add the cabbage, onion, jalapeños and cilantro. Season the slaw with salt and pepper and refrigerate for at least 2 hours and up to 5 hours, tossing occasionally.

3. Preheat the oven to 400°. Roast the chicken legs skin side up for about 40 minutes, until browned and cooked through. When cool enough to handle, discard the skin and bones and shred the chicken.

4. Arrange the lettuce on a platter and fill with the chicken; top with the slaw and serve.
—*Bill Telepan*

WINE Vibrant, citrusy New Zealand Sauvignon Blanc: 2010 Kato.

Poulet Basquaise

SERVES 4 ●

This chicken recipe is a personal favorite of Anthony Bourdain's, the intrepid explorer and irreverent TV host. Excerpted directly from his classic *Les Halles* cookbook, it is written in his inimitable style.

INGREDIENTS
1 whole chicken, about 4 lb, cut into 8 pieces
salt and pepper
pinch of cayenne pepper or piment d'Espelètte
2 tbsp olive oil
1 tbsp butter
2 red bell peppers, cut into fine julienne
2 green bell peppers, cut into fine julienne
1 onion, thinly sliced
16 ounces canned Italian plum tomatoes
½ cup white wine
½ cup water
½ cube chicken bouillon or ½ cup light chicken stock or broth (this is one dish that can handle a bouillon cube)
3 sprigs of flat parsley, finely chopped
rice pilaf

EQUIPMENT
large pot with cover
plate
wooden spoon
serving platter

Season the chicken all over with salt, pepper, and cayenne. Heat the large pot over medium-high heat and add the oil. When the oil is hot, add the butter. When the butter has foamed and subsided, add the chicken, skin side down, and brown on that side only. Remove the chicken and set aside on the plate. Add the peppers and onion to the pot and reduce the heat to medium low. Cook for about 10 minutes, then add the tomatoes and cook until the liquid is reduced by half. Stir in the wine, scraping, scraping—as always—to get the good stuff up. Cook until the wine is reduced by half, then add the water and the bouillon. Return the chicken to the pot, making sure to add all the juice on the plate. Cover the pot and cook on low heat for about 25 minutes. Remove the chicken to the platter. Crank up the heat to high and reduce the sauce for 5 minutes. Season with salt and pepper and add the parsley. Pour the sauce over the chicken and serve with rice pilaf. —*Anthony Bourdain*

Arroz con Pollo

🕐 **TOTAL: 35 MIN • 4 SERVINGS**

This delicious mix of chicken drumsticks, spicy sausage and fragrant jasmine rice improves upon the classic Latin dish with baby peas, roasted red peppers and broken bits of angel hair pasta.

- 1 tablespoon extra-virgin olive oil
- ½ cup broken angel hair pasta or thin egg noodles
- 1 small onion, finely chopped
- 4 chicken drumsticks
- 1 pound fresh chorizo or hot Italian sausage, halved crosswise
- 1 cup jasmine rice
- 1 cup low-sodium chicken broth
Kosher salt and freshly black ground pepper
- ¼ cup sliced roasted red peppers
- ½ cup frozen baby peas, thawed
Hot sauce and lemon slices, for serving

1. In a large, deep nonstick skillet, heat the olive oil. Add the broken pasta and cook over high heat until very lightly browned, about 1 minute. Add the onion, chicken and chorizo and cook over high heat until lightly browned in spots, about 5 minutes. Add the rice and cook for 1 minute, stirring.

2. Add the broth and 1 cup of water, season with salt and freshly ground black pepper and bring to a boil. Cover the skillet and cook over low heat until the rice is tender and the chicken and sausage are cooked, about 15 minutes. Stir in the peppers and peas, cover and let rest for about 5 minutes. Serve with hot sauce and lemon slices.
—*Grace Parisi*

WINE Blackberry-scented, peppery Zinfandel: 2009 Ridge Three Valleys.

latin-spiced chicken in lettuce cup

Roast Chicken Thighs with Lentil Stew

ACTIVE: 30 MIN; TOTAL: 1 HR 10 MIN
4 SERVINGS

¼ cup plus 2 tablespoons extra-virgin olive oil
2 slices of thick-cut bacon, diced
1 small onion, finely chopped
1 quart chicken stock or broth
8 garlic cloves, plus 1 tablespoon chopped garlic
1 medium carrot, halved lengthwise
1 small leek, white and pale green parts only, halved lengthwise
1 large green bell pepper, quartered
1 cup green lentils
1 thyme sprig
4 large chicken thighs (2 pounds)
Salt
Pimentón de la Vera
2 teaspoons sherry vinegar

1. Preheat the oven to 450°. In a large saucepan, heat 1 tablespoon of the oil. Add the bacon and cook over moderate heat until golden brown, about 4 minutes. Add the onion and cook, stirring, for 3 minutes. Add the stock, whole garlic cloves, carrot, leek, bell pepper, lentils and thyme and bring to a boil. Simmer over low heat for 30 minutes.
2. Meanwhile, in a baking dish, drizzle the chicken with 1 tablespoon of oil and season with salt and pimentón. Roast on the top rack for about 40 minutes, until cooked through.
3. Discard the thyme sprig from the lentils. Transfer the garlic cloves, carrot, leek and bell pepper to a blender. Add ¼ cup of the cooking liquid and puree. Drain the lentils and return them to the saucepan, then stir in the pureed vegetables.
4. In a small skillet, heat the remaining ¼ cup of oil. Add the chopped garlic and cook over low heat for 1 minute. Add 1 teaspoon of pimentón. Scrape the mixture into the lentils and simmer for 5 minutes. Add the vinegar and season with salt. Serve the lentils in bowls topped with the chicken.
—*José Andrés*
WINE Rich, plummy Merlot: 2009 Parcel 41.

Chicken Bouillabaisse with Rouille

ACTIVE: 30 MIN; TOTAL: 1 HR 15 MIN
4 SERVINGS ●

BOUILLABAISSE

1 tablespoon extra-virgin olive oil
1 small onion, chopped
1 celery rib, chopped
1 carrot, chopped
3 garlic cloves, chopped
1 teaspoon finely grated lemon zest
½ teaspoon saffron threads
¼ teaspoon fennel seeds
¼ teaspoon herbes de Provence
Salt and freshly ground pepper
4 large skinless chicken thighs (about 2 pounds)
One 14-ounce can diced tomatoes, drained
½ cup dry white wine
3 medium Yukon Gold potatoes, peeled and cut into 4 pieces each
1 kielbasa (about 10 ounces), cut into ⅓-inch-thick rounds
2 tablespoons chopped tarragon

ROUILLE

2 large garlic cloves, smashed
¼ teaspoon sweet paprika
⅛ teaspoon cayenne pepper
¼ cup mayonnaise
¼ cup extra-virgin olive oil
Salt

1. MAKE THE BOUILLABAISSE In a large enameled cast-iron casserole or Dutch oven, combine the olive oil with the onion, celery, carrot, garlic, lemon zest, saffron threads, fennel seeds and herbes de Provence; season with salt and pepper. Add the chicken thighs, toss to coat and let stand at room temperature for 15 minutes.
2. Add the tomatoes, wine, potatoes and ¾ cup of water to the casserole. Cover and bring to a boil over high heat. Cover partially and simmer over low heat until the potatoes are half-cooked, 25 minutes. Add the kielbasa and simmer until the chicken is cooked through and the potatoes are tender, 10 minutes longer. Stir in the tarragon; keep warm.

3. MAKE THE ROUILLE Transfer 2 of the potato chunks to a food processor along with ¼ cup of the cooking liquid from the stew. Add the garlic, paprika and cayenne and pulse to combine. Add the mayonnaise and puree. With the machine on, add the olive oil in a thin stream and process until smooth and creamy. Season the rouille with salt.
4. Serve the bouillabaisse in shallow bowls and spoon the rouille on top.
—*Jacques Pépin*
MAKE AHEAD The stew and rouille can be refrigerated separately overnight.
WINE Strawberry-inflected Provençal rosé: 2011 Mas des Bressades Cuvée Tradition.

Italian Sweet-and-Sour Chicken

ACTIVE: 30 MIN; TOTAL: 1 HR 15 MIN
4 SERVINGS

One 4-pound chicken, cut into 10 pieces (each breast split crosswise)
Salt and freshly ground pepper
¼ cup extra-virgin olive oil
1 large onion, cut into ½-inch dice
2 carrots, halved lengthwise and sliced crosswise ¼ inch thick
2 celery ribs, cut into ½-inch dice
8 garlic cloves, peeled
¼ cup sugar
1 cup dry, light-bodied red wine, such as Chianti
½ cup red wine vinegar
½ cup fresh orange juice
2 tablespoons capers, drained
¼ cup sliced almonds

1. Season the chicken with salt and pepper. In a large, deep skillet, heat 2 tablespoons of the olive oil. Add the chicken and cook over moderately high heat until browned, about 4 minutes per side. Transfer the chicken to a plate and pour off the oil.
2. Add the remaining 2 tablespoons of olive oil to the skillet and add the onion, carrots, celery and garlic. Cook over moderate heat, stirring occasionally, until starting to brown, about 8 minutes. Add the sugar, wine, vinegar, orange juice, capers and almonds and bring to a boil. Return the chicken to the

● HEALTHY ● MAKE AHEAD ● VEGETARIAN ● STAFF FAVORITE

skillet, skin side up. Cover partially and simmer over low heat until the chicken is cooked through, about 35 minutes.

3. Transfer the chicken to a plate. Boil the pan sauce over high heat until thickened, 3 minutes. Season the sauce with salt and pepper. Return the chicken to the skillet until warmed through. Transfer to a plate, spoon the sauce on top and serve. —*Mario Batali*
SERVE WITH A salad of bitter greens.
WINE Smooth Malbec: 2009 Durigutti.

Chicken Cacciatore

⏱ **TOTAL: 45 MIN • 4 SERVINGS** ● ●

- 2 tablespoons extra-virgin olive oil
- 2 pounds skinless, boneless chicken thighs, trimmed and cut into 2-inch pieces
- Salt and freshly ground pepper
- 1 large onion, finely chopped
- 3 garlic cloves, minced
- 8 ounces cremini mushrooms, thinly sliced
- 1 teaspoon finely chopped rosemary
- 2 tablespoons tomato paste
- One 28-ounce can peeled Italian tomatoes, pureed
- 1 tablespoon balsamic vinegar
- Crusty bread, for serving

1. In a large, deep skillet, heat the olive oil until shimmering. Season the chicken with salt and pepper, add it to the skillet and cook over high heat until browned, about 8 minutes. Transfer the chicken to a plate.
2. Add the onion, garlic, mushrooms and rosemary to the skillet. Season with salt and pepper; cook, stirring occasionally, until softened and lightly browned in spots, 5 minutes. Stir in the tomato paste, then add the pureed tomatoes and ¼ cup of water. Add the chicken and any juices and bring to a boil.
3. Cover partially and simmer over moderately low heat until the chicken is cooked through and the sauce is thickened, about 15 minutes. Stir in the balsamic vinegar and serve with crusty bread. —*Grace Parisi*
WINE Earthy, spiced Chianti: 2009 Coltibuono RS Chianti Classico.

Tangy Sort-Of Jerk Chicken

ACTIVE: 1 HR; TOTAL: 2 HR
PLUS OVERNIGHT MARINATING
6 SERVINGS ● ●

- Twelve 7-ounce chicken thighs
- Kosher salt
- 1 small white onion, chopped
- 3 scallions, sliced
- 1 small habanero, stemmed
- 5 garlic cloves
- ½ tablespoon minced peeled fresh ginger
- 2 teaspoons ground allspice
- 1 tablespoon thyme leaves
- 1 tablespoon sugar
- ½ tablespoon cayenne pepper
- ½ tablespoon freshly ground black pepper
- ¾ teaspoon freshly grated nutmeg
- ¾ teaspoon cinnamon
- ½ cup white wine vinegar
- ½ cup fresh orange juice
- ⅓ cup fresh lime juice
- ¼ cup soy sauce
- 2 tablespoons Coke
- ¼ tablespoon liquid smoke (optional)
- ¼ cup canola oil, plus more for brushing

1. Arrange the chicken on a large baking sheet and season generously with salt. Let stand at room temperature for 30 minutes. Rinse the chicken and pat dry.
2. Meanwhile, in a blender, puree the onion, scallions, habanero, garlic and ginger until chunky. Add the allspice, thyme, sugar, cayenne, black pepper, nutmeg and cinnamon; puree until very smooth. Transfer the puree to a large bowl and whisk in the white wine vinegar, orange juice, lime juice, soy sauce, Coke and liquid smoke, then whisk in the ¼ cup of oil. Add the chicken and turn to coat thoroughly. Cover and refrigerate overnight.
3. Light a grill and brush the grates with oil or preheat a grill pan. Transfer the chicken to a large plate. Transfer the marinade to a medium saucepan and boil until reduced by half, about 15 minutes.

4. Brush the chicken with canola oil and grill over moderate heat for 25 minutes, until lightly charred and cooked through. Brush the chicken with some of the marinade and grill for 1 minute. Serve the chicken with the remaining reduced marinade.
—*Steven Brown*
WINE Juicy, fruit-forward rosé: 2011 Abacela.

Thai Chicken with Hot-Sour-Salty-Sweet Sauce

ACTIVE: 25 MIN; TOTAL: 1 HR 15 MIN
4 SERVINGS ● ●

MARINATED CHICKEN
- ¼ cup chopped cilantro
- 2 tablespoons Asian fish sauce
- 1½ teaspoons freshly ground pepper
- 4 whole chicken legs, skinned

DIPPING SAUCE
- ½ teaspoon tamarind concentrate (see Note) dissolved in 1 teaspoon water
- ¼ cup Asian fish sauce
- 2 tablespoons fresh lime juice
- 1 small garlic clove, minced
- 1 small Thai chile, seeded and minced
- 2 teaspoons sugar
- ½ tablespoon vegetable oil
- ½ cup chopped cilantro

1. MARINATE THE CHICKEN In a mini food processor, process the cilantro, fish sauce and freshly ground pepper to a coarse puree. Coat the chicken with the marinade. Let stand at room temperature for 20 minutes.
2. MAKE THE DIPPING SAUCE In a bowl, combine the tamarind, fish sauce, lime, garlic, chile, sugar and 1 tablespoon of water.
3. Preheat the oven to 400°. Light a grill. Rub the chicken with the oil and rub the grill with an oiled paper towel. Grill the chicken over moderately high heat, turning, until charred, 12 minutes. Transfer the chicken to a baking sheet and roast for 30 minutes, until cooked.
4. Stir the cilantro into the dipping sauce and serve with the chicken. —*Naomi Duguid*
NOTE Tamarind concentrate is available at Indian and Latin food shops.
WINE Full-bodied, raspberry-rich Zinfandel: 2009 Grayson Zinfandel.

Chicken and Barley Stew with Dill and Lemon

ACTIVE: 40 MIN; TOTAL: 1 HR 15 MIN
6 SERVINGS ● ●

"My mother-in-law passed a version of this recipe along to me several years ago, and it remains a staple in my kitchen when the weather turns cold," says F&W's Gail Simmons. An enriched take on classic chicken soup with rice, this one-pot dinner is at once hearty and comforting.

½ cup all-purpose flour
Kosher salt and freshly ground
    black pepper
2 pounds skinless, boneless chicken
    breasts, cut into 1½-inch pieces
¼ cup plus 1 tablespoon vegetable oil
2 carrots, sliced ¼ inch thick
2 celery ribs, sliced ¼ inch thick
1 large leek, white and pale
    green parts only, thinly sliced
1 garlic clove, minced
1¾ cups pearled barley
6 cups chicken stock
¼ cup chopped dill
2 tablespoons fresh lemon juice
¼ cup chopped tarragon
½ cup freshly grated Parmigiano-
    Reggiano cheese (1½ ounces)

1. In a shallow bowl, combine the flour with 1 teaspoon each of salt and pepper. Dredge the chicken in the flour; shake off the excess.
2. In a medium enameled cast-iron casserole, heat 2 tablespoons of the vegetable oil. Add half of the chicken and cook over moderately high heat until golden, about 2 minutes per side. Transfer the chicken to a bowl, then brown the remaining chicken in 2 more tablespoons of the vegetable oil.
3. Pour off the fat. Add the remaining 1 tablespoon of oil and the carrots to the casserole and cook over moderate heat for 3 minutes. Add the celery, leek and garlic and cook until starting to soften, about 2 minutes. Add a large pinch each of salt and pepper and the barley. Cook over moderately high heat, stirring constantly, until the barley starts to toast, about 1 minute.

4. Add the chicken stock and 1 cup of water and bring to a boil. Cover and simmer over low heat, stirring occasionally, until the barley is almost tender, about 20 minutes.
5. Return the chicken to the stew; cover and simmer until the chicken is cooked through and the stew has thickened, about 10 minutes. Stir in the dill and lemon juice and season with salt and pepper. Spoon the stew into deep bowls, sprinkle with the tarragon and grated Parmigiano-Reggiano and serve.
—*Gail Simmons*

MAKE AHEAD The chicken and barley stew can be refrigerated overnight. Reheat gently.
WINE Ripe, floral South African Chenin Blanc: 2010 Badenhorst Secateurs.

Chicken Alambre

TOTAL: 30 MIN • 8 SERVINGS

Using bacon, chorizo, chicken and cheese, this Mexican griddle dish from chef Veronica Salazar of El Huarache Loco in San Francisco and Larkspur, California, is fantastic heaped onto flour tortillas like a fajita filling.

1 tablespoon vegetable oil
6 ounces ⅓-inch-diced slab bacon
12 ounces fresh chorizo, casings
    removed and meat crumbled
12 ounces skinless, boneless chicken
    thighs, cut into strips
2 red bell peppers, cut into strips
1 large red onion, thinly sliced
8 ounces Oaxaca cheese
    or mozzarella cheese, torn
Flour tortillas, avocado slices, cilantro,
    salsa and lime wedges, for serving

1. Heat the vegetable oil on a large griddle. Add the bacon and chorizo and cook over high heat, stirring, until browned in spots, about 5 minutes. Add the chicken strips and cook, stirring, until cooked through.
2. Add the bell peppers and onion and cook until softened, about 8 minutes. Scatter the cheese on top and stir until it just starts to melt, then serve with the flour tortillas, avocado, cilantro, salsa and lime wedges.
—*Veronica Salazar*

BEER Nutty brown ale: Avery Ellie's.

Braised Chicken with Cilantro, Mint and Chiles

ACTIVE: 15 MIN; TOTAL: 45 MIN
4 SERVINGS ● ●

The vibrant, herb-packed sauce for this stew from F&W's Grace Parisi gets a little heat from poblano and jalapeño chiles. Grace serves the stew with pickled jalapeños and rice as well as warm flatbread, which is great for scooping up the fresh, green sauce.

4 chicken drumsticks
4 skinless, boneless chicken thighs
1 tablespoon ground coriander
Salt and freshly ground white pepper
2 tablespoons canola oil
1 cup packed cilantro, plus leaves
    for garnish
½ cup packed mint leaves
1 small onion, quartered
2 poblano chiles, stemmed
    and seeded
1 jalapeño, stemmed and seeded
½ cup light cream or half-and-half
Sliced pickled jalapeños, cooked rice
    and warm naan, for serving

1. Make 3 slashes to the bone in each drumstick. Rub the chicken all over with the coriander and season with salt and white pepper.
2. In a large Dutch oven or enameled cast-iron casserole, heat the oil. Add the chicken and cook over high heat, turning occasionally, until browned all over, about 8 minutes.
3. Meanwhile, in a blender or food processor, combine the 1 cup of cilantro with the mint leaves, onion, poblanos and jalapeño and blend until finely chopped. Add the cream and ½ cup of water and puree until smooth.
4. Pour the green sauce over the chicken and bring to a boil. Cover partially and simmer over moderately low heat until the chicken is cooked through, about 30 minutes. Sprinkle the chicken with cilantro and serve with pickled jalapeños, rice and naan.
—*Grace Parisi*

MAKE AHEAD The stew can be refrigerated for up to 2 days.
WINE Lemony, herb-scented New Zealand Sauvignon Blanc: 2011 Momo.

braised chicken with cilantro, mint and chiles

Roast Chicken Thighs with Tomato-Tapioca Porridge

⏱ ACTIVE: 30 MIN; TOTAL: 45 MIN
4 SERVINGS

Wylie Dufresne, the chef and owner of Manhattan's acclaimed WD-50, is known for his avant-garde techniques. When F&W challenged him to create a fast recipe, he simplified a chicken confit dish he makes at the restaurant. It takes three chefs 12 hours to prepare the WD-50 dish, but less than an hour for a home cook to make this delicious crisp-skinned chicken with a simple, flavorful tomato-tapioca porridge.

> 2 pounds red heirloom
>   tomatoes, quartered
> 6 thyme sprigs
> Salt and freshly ground white pepper
> 6 medium unpeeled carrots, trimmed
> 6 tablespoons extra-virgin olive oil
> ¼ cup plus 2 tablespoons medium
>   pearl tapioca (2 ounces); see Note
> 8 boneless chicken thighs with skin
>   (about 2½ pounds)
> 2 tablespoons chopped pistachios

1. Preheat the oven to 425°. In a blender, puree the tomatoes until fairly smooth. Strain through a fine sieve into a saucepan, pressing on the solids; you should have about 2½ cups of puree. Add 3 thyme sprigs and simmer over moderate heat, scraping down the sides, until thick and glossy, 15 minutes. Season with salt and pepper; discard the thyme.
2. Meanwhile, in a flameproof roasting pan, toss the carrots with 3 tablespoons of the oil; season with salt and pepper. Cook over high heat until lightly browned, 3 minutes. Roast the carrots in the oven for 40 minutes, turning, until browned and very tender. Halve the carrots lengthwise. Leave the oven on.
3. Rinse the tapioca. In a large saucepan of boiling water, cook the tapioca over high heat, stirring, until al dente with a small white core at the centers, 17 minutes. Drain and rinse the tapioca and stir into the tomato puree.
4. Heat the remaining 3 tablespoons of oil in a large ovenproof skillet until nearly smoking. Season the chicken with salt and pepper and add to the skillet, skin side down, with the remaining 3 thyme sprigs. Cook over high heat just until the skin is lightly browned, 5 minutes, then roast in the oven for 15 minutes, until cooked through; discard the thyme.
5. Preheat the broiler. Broil the chicken skin side up until it is golden and crispy, about 3 minutes. Arrange the chicken and carrots on plates. Spoon off the fat from the pan juices. Add the juices to the tomato-tapioca porridge and spoon it around the chicken. Top with the chopped pistachios and serve. —Wylie Dufresne

NOTE Medium pearl tapioca is available at specialty food stores and Asian markets.
WINE Full-bodied Rhône-style white: 2010 Tablas Creek Côtes de Tablas Blanc.

Chicken and Biscuits in a Pot

ACTIVE: 15 MIN; TOTAL: 55 MIN
6 SERVINGS

> 6 tablespoons unsalted butter
> 2 shallots, thinly sliced
> ½ pound shiitake mushrooms,
>   stemmed and thinly sliced
> 1 large carrot, cut into ⅓-inch chunks
> ½ cup dry white wine
> 1¼ cups plus 1 tablespoon
>   self-rising flour
> 2½ cups low-sodium chicken broth
> Salt and freshly ground pepper
> 3 cups shredded rotisserie chicken
> ½ cup frozen baby peas
> 1 tablespoon each of chopped
>   sage and thyme
> ½ cup plus 2 tablespoons whole milk

1. Preheat the oven to 425°. In a large Dutch oven or enameled cast-iron casserole, melt 2 tablespoons of the butter. Add the shallots, mushrooms and carrot chunks and cook over moderate heat, stirring, until the shallots and mushrooms are softened, about 8 minutes. Add the wine and cook until completely evaporated, about 1 minute. Stir in 1 tablespoon of the flour and the broth and bring to a boil. Season with salt and pepper. Simmer until thick, about 3 minutes. Stir in the chicken and peas.
2. In a food processor, combine the remaining 1¼ cups of flour with the remaining 4 tablespoons of butter and the chopped sage and thyme; pulse 5 times. Add the whole milk; pulse just until a soft dough forms.
3. Using a small ice cream scoop or a tablespoon, scoop 20 balls of biscuit dough over the chicken stew. Bake in the center of the oven for 25 minutes. Turn on the broiler and broil the chicken stew for 1 to 2 minutes, until the biscuits are golden. Let rest for 5 minutes before serving. —Grace Parisi

WINE Floral, ripe California white: 2010 Bonterra Viognier.

Butternut Squash–Chicken Pan-Roast

ACTIVE: 20 MIN; TOTAL: 1 HR 40 MIN
6 SERVINGS

This super-easy one-pot recipe is a perfect dinner-party dish: All you do is set chicken on top of squash, apples and sage and roast it.

> One 1½-pound butternut squash,
>   peeled and cut into ¾-inch dice
> 3 Fuji apples, peeled and cut into
>   ¾-inch dice
> 1 tablespoon chopped sage
> ¼ cup extra-virgin olive oil
> Salt and freshly ground pepper
> 6 whole chicken legs (3 pounds)
> 2 tablespoons unsalted butter,
>   thinly sliced

1. Preheat the oven to 400°. In a large roasting pan, toss the squash, apples and sage with the olive oil and season with salt and pepper. Season the chicken legs and set them on top. Dot with the butter and roast for about 1 hour and 15 minutes, until the squash and apples are tender and the chicken is browned and cooked through.
2. Transfer the chicken legs to a plate and keep warm. Place the roasting pan over a burner and boil, stirring, until the pan juices are reduced, about 5 minutes. Return the chicken to the roasting pan and serve. —Grace Parisi

WINE Elegant, balanced Chardonnay: 2009 Domaine Leroy Bourgogne Blanc.

● HEALTHY ● MAKE AHEAD ○ VEGETARIAN ● STAFF FAVORITE

Vinegar-Braised Chicken with Leeks and Peas

🕐 TOTAL: 45 MIN • 8 SERVINGS

8   whole chicken legs
Salt and freshly ground pepper
3   tablespoons unsalted butter
3   tablespoons extra-virgin olive oil
3   large leeks, halved lengthwise
     and cut into 1-inch pieces
1   cup low-sodium chicken broth
¼   cup white balsamic vinegar
One 10-ounce package frozen
     baby peas, thawed
2   tablespoons chopped tarragon
2   tablespoons chopped parsley
½   cup crème fraîche

1. Preheat the oven to 425° and position a rack in the upper third. Turn the chicken legs skin side down on a work surface and cut halfway through the joint. Season the chicken generously with salt and pepper.
2. In each of 2 large nonstick skillets, heat half of the butter and oil. Add the chicken to the skillets, skin side up, and cook over high heat until browned, 5 minutes. Turn and cook the chicken for 1 minute, then pile all of the chicken into one skillet.
3. In the other skillet, cook the leeks over high heat until just beginning to soften, about 2 minutes. Add the chicken broth and balsamic vinegar and bring to a boil. Season with salt and pepper, then pour the mixture into a medium roasting pan.
4. Set the chicken on the leeks, skin side up; roast for about 25 minutes, until it is cooked through. Turn on the broiler and broil for about 2 minutes, until the skin is golden and crisp. Transfer the chicken to a platter.
5. Place the roasting pan over a burner and boil over high heat until the liquid is reduced by half, about 5 minutes. Add the peas, herbs and crème fraîche and simmer until the sauce is hot and slightly thickened, about 2 minutes. Season with salt and pepper. Pour the sauce over the chicken and serve.
—*Grace Parisi*
WINE Rhône white: 2010 Kermit Lynch Sunflower Cuvée Côtes-du-Rhône Blanc.

Braised Chicken with Apples and Calvados

ACTIVE: 45 MIN; TOTAL: 1 HR 15 MIN
4 SERVINGS

¼   cup extra-virgin olive oil
½   pound shiitake mushrooms—stems
     discarded, caps sliced ¼ inch thick
Salt and freshly ground pepper
One 4-pound chicken, cut into 8 pieces
2   Granny Smith apples,
     peeled and coarsely chopped
2   large shallots, minced
2   garlic cloves, minced
1   tablespoon all-purpose flour
¼   cup Calvados
2   cups chicken stock
½   cup apple cider
½   teaspoon caraway seeds
Pinch of crushed red pepper
2   tablespoons cold unsalted butter,
     cut into 2 pieces
2   tablespoons minced chives

1. Preheat the oven to 350°. In a large, deep ovenproof skillet, heat 2 tablespoons of the olive oil. Add the mushrooms and season with salt and pepper. Cover and cook over moderate heat, stirring a few times, until browned and tender, about 5 minutes. Transfer the mushrooms to a large bowl.
2. Heat the remaining 2 tablespoons of oil in the skillet. Season the chicken with salt and pepper; add to the skillet, skin side down. Cook over moderately high heat until browned, about 4 minutes. Turn the chicken and brown the other side, about 3 minutes longer. Add the chicken to the mushrooms and pour off all but 2 tablespoons of fat from the skillet.
3. Add the apples to the skillet and cook over moderately high heat until browned, about 2 minutes. Add the shallots and garlic and cook over low heat, stirring a few times, until softened, about 3 minutes. Stir in the flour. Add the Calvados and cook for 1 minute. Stir in the stock, cider, caraway and crushed red pepper and bring to a simmer.
4. Return the chicken to the skillet, skin side up, along with any accumulated juices. Braise in the oven for about 20 minutes, until the breast meat is just cooked. Transfer the breast pieces to a large ovenproof platter. Continue braising the remaining chicken until cooked through, about 10 minutes longer. Add to the platter and keep warm.
5. Boil the pan juices and apples over moderately high heat until slightly thickened, about 6 minutes. Add the shiitake mushrooms. Remove the skillet from the heat and swirl in the butter, 1 piece at a time. Season the sauce with salt and pepper and add half of the minced chives. Spoon the sauce over and around the chicken. Garnish with the remaining chives and serve right away.
—*Matthew Accarrino*
WINE Herbal Loire Valley Cabernet Franc: 2010 Philippe Alliet Chinon.

Chardonnay-Braised Chicken Thighs with Parsnips

🕐 TOTAL: 45 MIN • 4 SERVINGS ●

2   tablespoons unsalted butter
2   tablespoons extra-virgin olive oil
8   medium chicken thighs
     (about 2¾ pounds)
Salt and freshly ground black pepper
¼   cup all-purpose flour
4   small shallots, peeled and quartered
1   pound parsnips, peeled and
     cut into 3-by-½-inch batons
1   rosemary sprig (about 6 inches)
1   cup California Chardonnay
     or other dry white wine
1½ cups low-sodium chicken broth
Chopped flat-leaf parsley, for garnish

1. Preheat the oven to 425°. In a large, deep ovenproof skillet, melt the butter in the oil. Season the chicken with salt and pepper and dust with the flour, tapping off the excess. Add the chicken to the skillet skin side down and cook over high heat, turning once, until browned, 6 minutes. Transfer to a plate.
2. Add the shallots, parsnips and rosemary to the skillet and cook, stirring, for 1 minute. Add the wine and boil until reduced by half, about 3 minutes. Add the broth and bring to a boil. Nestle the chicken skin side up in the skillet, tucking it between the parsnips.

● HEALTHY ● MAKE AHEAD ● VEGETARIAN ● STAFF FAVORITE

Transfer the skillet to the middle rack of the oven and braise the chicken uncovered for about 25 minutes, until cooked through.

3. Turn the broiler on. Broil the chicken until the skin is crisp, 3 minutes. Return the skillet to high heat; boil the sauce until it has thickened, 3 minutes. Discard the rosemary. Transfer the chicken and vegetables to bowls, garnish with parsley; serve. —*Grace Parisi*

WINE Fresh, peach-scented Chardonnay: 2009 Alma Rosa Santa Barbara County.

Molokhia with Spiced Chicken

ACTIVE: 30 MIN; TOTAL: 2 HR
4 TO 5 SERVINGS

One 3½-pound chicken
  1 large onion, finely chopped
  1 rosemary sprig
One 4-inch cinnamon stick
  1 bay leaf
One 14-ounce package frozen *molokhia* (see Note) or two 10-ounce packages chopped frozen spinach
  1 tablespoon minced garlic
  1 tablespoon plus ½ teaspoon ground coriander
  3 tablespoons unsalted butter
Salt and freshly ground black pepper
  ½ teaspoon ground cinnamon
  ½ teaspoon ground cumin
  ¼ teaspoon sweet paprika
Steamed short-grain rice, for serving

1. In a large, deep pot, cover the chicken with the chopped onion, rosemary sprig, cinnamon stick, bay leaf and 12 cups of water. Top with a small plate to keep the chicken submerged and bring to a boil. Simmer over low heat until the chicken is cooked through, 45 minutes. Transfer the chicken to a platter and let cool slightly, then cut into wings, breasts, thighs and drumsticks and pat dry.

2. Strain the broth into a heatproof bowl. Skim off the fat. Return 2 cups of the broth to the pot; reserve the remaining broth for another use. Add the *molokhia* to the pot and simmer for 10 minutes.

3. Meanwhile, using the side of a knife, mash the minced garlic to a paste with 1 tablespoon

of the coriander. In a small skillet, melt 1 tablespoon of the butter. Add the garlic paste and cook over moderately high heat until golden and fragrant, 1 minute. Scrape the paste into the *molokhia* and simmer for 5 minutes longer. Season with salt and pepper.

4. In a small bowl, combine the remaining ½ teaspoon of coriander with the ground cinnamon, cumin, paprika and ½ teaspoon each of salt and pepper. Sprinkle the chicken all over with the spices. In a large nonstick skillet, melt the remaining 2 tablespoons of butter. Add the chicken and cook over high heat, turning once, until golden and heated through and the skin is crisp, 4 minutes.

5. Mound rice in the center of 4 or 5 shallow bowls and top with the chicken. Ladle the *molokhia* around the chicken and serve. —*Eric Monkaba*

NOTE *Molokhia,* a dark leafy green, is available at Middle Eastern markets.

WINE Fruit-forward white: 2010 La Vieille Ferme Luberon Blanc.

Yucatán Chicken with Orange-Guajillo Glaze

ACTIVE: 1 HR; TOTAL: 3 HR
2 TO 4 SERVINGS ●

CHICKEN
One 4-pound chicken, backbone removed
  ¼ **cup plus 2 tablespoons Adobo Rub (see Latin Grilled Rib Eye Steak on page 194)**
SAUCE
  2 **dried guajillo chiles, stemmed and seeded (see Note)**
Finely grated zest of 1 orange
  1 **cup fresh orange juice**
  ¾ **cup apple cider vinegar**
  ¼ **cup light corn syrup**
  ¼ **cup light brown sugar**
  2 **tablespoons honey**
  ½ **mango, peeled and chopped, plus mango slices for serving**
  ¼ **cup chopped peeled fresh ginger**
  1 **habanero chile, coarsely chopped**
  ½ **teaspoon ground coriander**
Salt
Vegetable oil, for grilling

1. MARINATE THE CHICKEN On a large rimmed baking sheet, flatten the chicken by pressing on the breastbone. Sprinkle the chicken all over with the Adobo Rub. Cover and refrigerate for at least 30 minutes or up to 2 hours. Bring the chicken to room temperature before grilling.

2. MEANWHILE, MAKE THE SAUCE In a glass measuring cup, cover the guajillo chiles with ⅓ cup of boiling water. Cover and let stand until softened, about 15 minutes.

3. In a saucepan, combine the orange zest, orange juice, apple cider vinegar, corn syrup, brown sugar, honey, chopped mango, ginger, habanero chile and ground coriander. Add the guajillo chiles along with their soaking liquid and bring to a boil. Boil over moderately high heat until the liquid is reduced by half, about 7 minutes. Transfer the sauce to a blender and puree. Scrape the puree back into the saucepan and simmer over moderate heat until reduced to 1½ cups, about 15 minutes. Season with salt.

4. Light a grill. Oil the grill grate and put the chicken on it, skin side down. Grill over moderately high heat until charred, about 7 minutes. Turn the chicken and cook until charred on the other side, about 5 minutes. Turn off the heat in half of the grill or rake the coals to one side, away from the chicken. Cover and grill over indirect heat, turning the chicken over halfway through, until an instant-read thermometer inserted in the inner thigh registers 160°, about 1 hour.

5. Brush half of the sauce all over the chicken. Grill the chicken skin side down over direct heat until richly glazed, about 1 minute. Turn the chicken skin side up and grill until glazed, about 1 minute longer. Let the chicken rest for 15 minutes, then serve with the remaining sauce and the mango slices. —*Jose Garces*

NOTE Guajillo chiles are available at Latin American markets, specialty food stores and some supermarkets.

MAKE AHEAD The sauce can be refrigerated for up to 1 week. Let it return to room temperature before using.

WINE Orange-scented Argentinean white: 2011 Finca las Nubes Torrontes.

Grilled Chicken with Spiced Red-Pepper Paste

ACTIVE: 45 MIN; TOTAL: 2 HR
PLUS OVERNIGHT MARINATING
2 TO 4 SERVINGS

- 3 red bell peppers
- 2 red jalapeños or fresno chiles, coarsely chopped
- 4 garlic cloves, coarsely chopped
- 2½ tablespoons white wine vinegar
- 1 teaspoon ground cumin
- 1 teaspoon kosher salt
- ½ teaspoon freshly ground black pepper
- ¼ cup extra-virgin olive oil

One 4-pound chicken, backbone removed and chicken halved through the breastbone
Vegetable oil, for grilling

1. Roast the red bell peppers on a hot grill or over an open flame, turning, until charred all over. Transfer the peppers to a bowl to cool, then peel, stem, seed and coarsely chop them. Transfer the peppers to a food processor and add the jalapeños, garlic, vinegar, cumin, salt and pepper and puree. With the machine on, slowly pour in the olive oil.

2. With a small knife, make ½-inch-deep slits all over the chicken halves. Transfer to a large resealable plastic bag and add the marinade. Refrigerate the chicken overnight. Bring to room temperature before grilling.

3. Light a grill. Wipe off most of the marinade from the chicken. Oil the grill grate and put the chicken on it, skin side down. Cover and cook over moderately high heat until lightly charred, about 7 minutes. Turn the chicken and cook until charred on the other side, about 7 minutes. Turn off the heat in half of the grill or rake the coals to one side, away from the chicken. Cover and grill, turning the chicken halfway through, until an instant-read thermometer inserted in the inner thigh registers 160°, about 1 hour.

4. On a work surface, let the chicken rest for 10 minutes, then serve. —*Silvena Rowe*
WINE Lively Spanish rosé: 2011 Bodegas Bleda Castillo de Jumilla Monastrell.

Chicken Wings with Molasses Barbecue Sauce

TOTAL: 1 HR 15 MIN PLUS 14 HR
MARINATING • 4 TO 6 SERVINGS

These super-flavorful crusty wings come from chef Adam Perry Lang, founder of Daisy May's BBQ in New York City. They are fantastic with or without Lang's sweet-and-sticky barbecue sauce.

- 3 cups freshly squeezed orange juice
- 1 cup freshly squeezed lime juice
- ½ cup sea salt or kosher salt
- 8 garlic cloves, smashed
- 2 tablespoons sugar
- 2 tablespoons soy sauce
- 2 tablespoons dried oregano
- 1 tablespoon black peppercorns
- 2 lemons, halved
- 1 teaspoon ground cumin
- 5½ pounds chicken wings, tips discarded and wings separated at the joints
- 2 tablespoons garlic salt
- 1 tablespoon freshly ground black pepper
- 1 teaspoon cayenne pepper
- ¼ cup each of chopped scallion and cilantro leaves, for garnish

Molasses Barbecue Sauce (recipe follows), for serving

1. In a large pot, combine 1 quart of water with the orange juice and lime juice, salt, smashed garlic, sugar, soy sauce, oregano, peppercorns, lemon halves and cumin and bring to a boil. Let the marinade cool to room temperature.

2. Add the chicken wings to the marinade, cover and refrigerate for 14 to 16 hours.

3. Light a grill. In a small bowl, combine the garlic salt with the freshly ground black pepper and cayenne pepper. Remove the chicken wings from the marinade and pat them dry with paper towels. Sprinkle the wings with the seasoning salt and grill them over moderately high heat, turning often, until they are charred and cooked through, about 30 minutes.

4. Transfer the grilled chicken wings to a serving platter and sprinkle them with the scallions and cilantro. Serve the Molasses Barbecue Sauce at the table.
—*Adam Perry Lang*
VARIATION Light a hardwood charcoal fire. The coals are ready when they have a strong red glow and a thin coating of white ash. Working in batches, remove the wings from the marinade and put them in a hinged grill basket, leaving space between them. With a hair dryer or chimney bellow, blow as much ash as possible from the coals. Set the grill basket directly on the hot coals and cook the wings for 3 minutes. Turn the basket and cook for 3 minutes. Repeat twice more (a total of 18 minutes) until the wings are nicely charred and cooked through.
WINE Dark berry–inflected Malbec: 2010 Pascual Toso.

MOLASSES BARBECUE SAUCE
⟳ TOTAL: 20 MIN
MAKES ABOUT 1½ CUPS ● ○

- ½ cup ketchup
- ⅓ cup dark brown sugar
- ¼ cup unsulfured blackstrap molasses
- ¼ cup apricot preserves
- 2 tablespoons yellow mustard
- 2 tablespoons apple cider vinegar
- 2 tablespoons vegetable oil
- 1 garlic clove, minced
- 1½ teaspoons chile powder
- ½ teaspoon freshly ground black pepper
- ½ teaspoon hot sauce

Pinch of ground cloves
Pinch of ground allspice
Salt

In a medium saucepan, combine all of the ingredients except the salt with ½ cup of water and bring to a boil, stirring well. Let the barbecue sauce cool and season with salt. —*APL*
MAKE AHEAD The barbecue sauce can be refrigerated in a jar or another airtight container for up to 1 week.

● HEALTHY ● MAKE AHEAD ○ VEGETARIAN ● STAFF FAVORITE

chicken wings with molasses barbecue sauce

Lemon-Brined Smoked Chickens

ACTIVE: 1 HR 30 MIN; TOTAL: 3 HR
PLUS 8 HR BRINING • 8 SERVINGS

- ¾ cup kosher salt
- ¾ cup fresh lemon juice (from about 4 lemons)
- 2 tablespoons Frank's RedHot or other hot sauce
- 2 teaspoons freshly ground black pepper
- 2 teaspoons poultry seasoning
- Two 4-pound chickens, backbones removed and chickens split through the breast (see Note)
- ¼ cup plus 2 tablespoons Paprika-Ancho Spice Rub (page 186)
- 1 cup hardwood chips, soaked in water for 1 hour and drained

1. In a pot, combine the salt, lemon juice, hot sauce, pepper and poultry seasoning with 2½ quarts of water. Bring to a boil, stirring to dissolve the salt. Let the brine cool to room temperature.

2. Put 2 chicken halves in each of two 1-gallon resealable plastic bags. Pour half of the brine into each bag, seal and refrigerate the chicken for 8 hours.

3. Drain the chickens and pat dry. Sprinkle all over with the Paprika-Ancho Spice Rub, massaging it into the meat.

4. Light a charcoal fire in a starter chimney. Add the lit coals to a grill and set it up for indirect grilling: Carefully push the hot coals to the edges all around the grill, leaving a large open space in the center. Place a drip pan in the open space and fill the pan with water. Alternatively, add the lit coals to the firebox of a smoker. Scatter half of the soaked hardwood chips over the coals.

5. Arrange the chickens skin side down on the grill over the drip pan. Cover and cook the chickens for about 1 hour at 250°, rotating them a few times, until the skin is crisp. Turn the chickens skin side up and continue to cook for about 1½ hours longer, rotating them a few times, until an instant-read thermometer inserted in the inner thigh registers 165°. Monitor the grill throughout and add more lit coals, soaked hardwood chips and water to the drip pan as needed to maintain the temperature and smoke level. Let the chickens rest for 10 minutes, then serve. —Brian Perrone

NOTE Ask your butcher to remove the backbones and split the chickens in half.

WINE Full-bodied Chenin Blanc from the Loire Valley: 2010 Champalou Vouvray.

Asian-Brined Cornish Hens

TOTAL: 1 HR PLUS 24 HR BRINING
6 SERVINGS ●

The salt and sugar in a brine help season meat all the way to the bone. Chiles, kaffir lime and star anise make these hens so flavorful that they don't even need a sauce.

- 1 cup kosher salt
- ¾ cup sugar
- ½ pound firm unpeeled ginger, sliced lengthwise ¼ inch thick
- 6 whole star anise
- ½ cup dried red chiles (about 25)
- 24 kaffir lime leaves
- 2 heads of garlic, halved horizontally
- Six 2-pound Cornish hens
- Canola oil, for grilling

1. In a pot, combine the salt, sugar, ginger, star anise, chiles, lime leaves and garlic with 5 quarts of water and bring just to a simmer. Stir to dissolve the sugar and salt. Remove from the heat and let the brine cool. Put the hens in a large container and pour the brine on top. Cover and refrigerate for 24 hours.

2. Light a grill and oil the grates. Drain the hens. Using poultry shears, cut the hens in half. Pat the hens dry, brush them with oil and arrange on the grill. Cover and grill over moderate heat, turning occasionally, until lightly charred in spots and an instant-read thermometer inserted in the thighs registers 160°, about 35 minutes. Transfer the hens to platters and serve them hot or at room temperature. —Grace Parisi

SERVE WITH Cabbage slaw, cilantro, lime, chiles, Thai sticky rice and Bibb lettuce.

WINE Dry, fruit-forward Riesling: 2010 Chateau Ste. Michelle Dry Riesling.

Roast Cornish Hens with Morels and Leeks

ACTIVE: 25 MIN; TOTAL: 2 HR
4 SERVINGS ●

"I like to roast these Cornish hens in a large skillet instead of a roasting pan, because it allows more of the skin to get crispy," says F&W's Marcia Kiesel. She cooks the birds over morels and leeks simmered in Riesling to create a deeply savory sauce.

- ½ cup small dried morels (½ ounce)
- 1½ cups boiling water
- 2 tablespoons unsalted butter
- 1 tablespoon vegetable oil
- 3 large leeks, white and pale green parts only, sliced crosswise 1 inch thick
- ½ teaspoon hot paprika, plus more for seasoning
- 1 cup dry Riesling
- 1 cup chicken stock
- Salt
- Four 1-pound Cornish hens, legs tied with kitchen twine
- Freshly ground pepper
- ¼ teaspoon finely grated lemon zest
- 2 tablespoons fresh lemon juice
- 1 tablespoon chopped tarragon

1. Preheat the oven to 350°. In a small heatproof bowl, cover the morels with the boiling water. Let stand for about 20 minutes, until softened. Lift the morels from the water and rinse well. Let the soaking liquid stand so the grit settles to the bottom of the bowl.

2. In a very large, deep skillet, melt the butter in the oil. Add the leeks and the ½ teaspoon of paprika, cover and cook over moderate heat, stirring, until softened, about 5 minutes. Add the Riesling and simmer until reduced to ⅓ cup, about 4 minutes. Add the stock and slowly pour in the mushroom soaking liquid, stopping before you reach the grit. Add the morels and a pinch of salt.

3. Season the hens with salt, pepper and paprika. Set them on top of the leeks and morels, breast side up, cavities facing outward. Roast in the upper third of the oven for about 1 hour, until the juices in the cavities run clear and an instant-read thermometer inserted in the inner thighs registers 160°.

4. Transfer the hens to a carving board and let rest for 10 minutes. Simmer the pan juices over moderate heat until the liquid is reduced to ½ cup, 6 minutes. Add the lemon zest and juice and remove from the heat. Stir in the tarragon; season with salt and pepper.

5. Transfer the hens to plates and serve with the leeks, morels and sauce. —*Marcia Kiesel*
WINE Minerally, concentrated Riesling: 2010 Maximin Grünhaus QbA Trocken.

Roast Guinea Hens with Prosciutto and Endives
ACTIVE: 30 MIN; TOTAL: 1 HR
8 SERVINGS
Siegfried Danler of Berlin's Pauly Saal restaurant prefers guinea hens to chickens because their meat is firmer and has a deep flavor. To showcase the hens, he roasts them simply with a little rosemary, then serves them with crisped prosciutto and sautéed endives and dandelion greens.

Four 2½-pound guinea hens, quartered (see Note)
Salt and freshly ground pepper
 ½ cup extra-virgin olive oil
 4 rosemary sprigs, broken into 1-inch pieces
 8 slices of prosciutto (about 4 ounces)
 2 tablespoons unsalted butter
 6 Belgian endives (about 1¼ pounds), quartered lengthwise
 4 ounces baby dandelion greens or arugula
Creamy boiled fingerling potatoes, for serving

1. Preheat the oven to 425°. Season the hens all over with salt and pepper and arrange them on 2 large rimmed baking sheets, skin side up. Drizzle with ¼ cup of the oil and scatter the rosemary all around. Roast the hens in the upper and middle thirds of the oven for 40 minutes, until cooked through, shifting the pans from top to bottom and front to back halfway through. Pour the cooking juices into a gravy boat.

2. Meanwhile, in a large skillet, heat the remaining ¼ cup of olive oil until shimmering. Arrange 4 slices of the prosciutto in the skillet in a slightly overlapping layer and cook them over moderately high heat, turning once, until crisp, about 3 minutes. Transfer to a paper towel–lined plate. Repeat with the remaining prosciutto.

3. Pour off all but 2 tablespoons of the fat from the skillet and add the butter. Add the endives cut side down and cook them over moderately high heat, turning, until browned and tender, about 12 minutes. Season the endives with salt and pepper. Add the greens to the skillet and cook, stirring, just until wilted, about 2 minutes.

4. Transfer the hens to plates and surround with the endives, greens and crispy prosciutto. Serve with boiled potatoes, passing the reserved cooking juices at the table. —*Siegfried Danler*
NOTE You can ask your butcher to quarter the guinea hens for you. Chicken can be substituted for guinea hens, but it will need to cook for about 15 minutes longer.
WINE Lively, earthy German Pinot Noir: 2010 August Kesseler Pinot N.

Roast Beer-Brined Turkey with Onion Gravy and Bacon
ACTIVE: 30 MIN; TOTAL: 3 HR 30 MIN
PLUS 24 HR BRINING • 12 SERVINGS ●
Adding Guinness (or any dark beer) to the brine gives turkey a toasty flavor and helps give the skin a dark brown color.

 ¼ cup yellow mustard seeds
 2 tablespoons black peppercorns
 8 bay leaves
 1 cup dark brown sugar
 1 cup kosher salt
 2 onions, cut into thick wedges
 1 pound slab bacon, skin removed and meat sliced ⅓ inch thick
Six 12-ounce bottles Guinness stout
One 12- to 14-pound turkey
 1 cup turkey stock or low-sodium chicken broth
 1 tablespoon unsalted butter
 1 tablespoon all-purpose flour

1. In a very large pot, combine the mustard seeds, peppercorns and bay leaves and toast over moderate heat until fragrant, about 2 minutes. Add the brown sugar and salt and remove from the heat. Add 4 cups of water and stir until the sugar and salt are dissolved; let cool completely.

2. Add the onion wedges, bacon slices, Guinness stout and 16 cups of cold water to the pot. Add the turkey to the brine, breast side down, and top with a heavy lid to keep it submerged. Cover and keep in the refrigerator for 24 hours.

3. Preheat the oven to 350° and position a rack on the bottom shelf. Lift the turkey from the brine, pick off any peppercorns, mustard seeds and bay leaves and pat dry. Transfer the turkey to a large roasting pan, breast side up. Scatter the onion wedges in the pan and add 1 cup of water. Using toothpicks, secure the bacon slices over the breast. Roast the turkey for about 2 hours, turning the pan occasionally, until an instant-read thermometer inserted deep into a turkey thigh registers 150°. Remove the bacon and return the turkey to the oven. Roast for about 1 hour longer, until the breast is browned and an instant-read thermometer inserted in a thigh registers 170°. Transfer the turkey to a carving board.

4. Pour the pan juices along with the onion wedges into a saucepan and boil until the mixture is reduced to 3 cups, about 5 minutes. Add the turkey stock and return to a boil. In a small bowl, mash the butter to a paste with the flour. Whisk the paste into the gravy and boil until it has thickened slightly, about 5 minutes.

5. Meanwhile, cut the bacon crosswise into ½-inch pieces. In a large skillet, fry the bacon over high heat, stirring occasionally, until browned and crisp, about 3 minutes.

6. Carve the roast turkey and serve with the onion gravy and bacon.
—*Grace Parisi*
NOTE Use any leftover turkey to make Grace's Walnut-Cranberry Turkey Salad (page 59) or her Turkey Quesadillas (page 162).
WINE Smoky, peppery California Syrah: 2009 Terre Rouge Les Cotes de l'Ouest.

Herb-Roasted Turkey with Wild Mushroom Gravy

ACTIVE: 1 HR; TOTAL: 4 HR
10 TO 12 SERVINGS ●

TURKEY

1   stick unsalted butter, softened
2   garlic cloves, minced
1   tablespoon chopped thyme, plus 4 large sprigs
1   tablespoon chopped sage, plus 4 large sprigs
Salt and freshly ground pepper
One 12- to 14-pound turkey, neck and gizzard reserved
½   large apple
1   medium onion, cut into 1-inch-thick wedges
1   large carrot, cut into 1-inch pieces
1   large celery rib, cut into 1-inch pieces
Extra-virgin olive oil, for rubbing

GRAVY

1   tablespoon small dried porcini pieces
1   tablespoon unsalted butter
1   tablespoon extra-virgin olive oil
1   pound golden chanterelles or a mix of cremini and oyster mushrooms, sliced ½ inch thick
3   medium shallots, minced
Salt and freshly ground pepper
¼   cup plus 1 tablespoon all-purpose flour
4   cups chicken stock

1. **PREPARE THE TURKEY** Preheat the oven to 400°. In a small bowl, beat the butter with the garlic, chopped thyme and chopped sage and season with salt and pepper.

2. Season the turkey inside and out with salt and pepper. Rub two-thirds of the herb butter inside the cavity and under the neck flap. Place the remaining herb butter in the cavity along with the thyme and sage sprigs. Tuck the wing tips under the bird and tie the legs together with kitchen string. Tuck the apple half, rounded side out, under the neck flap. Fold the neck skin under the body and secure with a skewer.

3. Put the onion, carrot and celery in a large roasting pan. Set the turkey in the pan and add the neck and gizzard. Rub the turkey all over with olive oil. Roast the turkey in the lower third of the oven for 30 minutes. Reduce the oven temperature to 325° and continue to roast the turkey, basting occasionally, for 2 hours and 35 minutes longer, until an instant-read thermometer registers 165° when inserted in an inner thigh. Transfer the roast turkey to a carving board and let rest in a warm place for at least 25 minutes and up to 1 hour.

4. **MEANWHILE, MAKE THE GRAVY** In a small bowl, cover the porcini with ¼ cup of hot water. Let stand until softened, about 10 minutes. In a large skillet, melt the butter in the olive oil. Add the sliced chanterelle mushrooms and the minced shallots and season with salt and pepper. Cook over moderate heat, stirring occasionally, until the mushrooms are golden brown and tender, about 8 minutes. Lift the porcini from the soaking liquid and add them to the skillet. Cover and remove the skillet from the heat.

5. Set a coarse strainer over a medium bowl. Pour in the cooking juices and vegetables from the roasting pan and press on the solids to extract as much liquid as possible. Skim the fat off of the juices and reserve 2 tablespoons of the fat.

6. In a large saucepan, combine the reserved 2 tablespoons of fat with the flour and stir until smooth; cook over moderate heat until lightly browned, about 2 to 3 minutes. Gradually whisk in the strained juices and the chicken stock and bring to a simmer, whisking. Stir in the mushroom mixture and simmer over low heat, whisking often, until no floury taste remains, about 10 minutes. Season the gravy with salt and pepper.

7. Carve the turkey and serve with the gravy.
—*David Tanis*

SERVE WITH Tanis's Tomato-Ginger Chutney (recipe follows).

WINE Intense, spiced Syrah: 2010 Hudson Vineyards Carneros.

Tomato-Ginger Chutney

ACTIVE: 25 MIN; TOTAL: 40 MIN PLUS
OVERNIGHT MELLOWING
MAKES ABOUT 2½ CUPS ● ●

This Indian-style condiment from cookbook author David Tanis provides the sweetness of traditional cranberry sauce along with less conventional spice from fennel seeds, ginger and jalapeño.

2   teaspoons fennel seeds
2   teaspoons brown mustard seeds
1   teaspoon cumin seeds
1½ pounds tomatoes, chopped
1   cup granulated sugar
½   cup light brown sugar
4   garlic cloves, thinly sliced
3   tablespoons finely julienned peeled fresh ginger
1   jalapeño, seeded and minced
Salt
Cayenne pepper

1. In a small saucepan, toast the fennel, mustard and cumin seeds over moderate heat until fragrant, about 1 minute. Transfer to a plate; let cool.

2. In the same saucepan, cook the tomatoes with the granulated and brown sugars over moderate heat, stirring, until the sugars dissolve. Add the garlic, ginger and toasted seeds and simmer over moderate heat, stirring, until the chutney is thick and reduced to 2½ cups, 15 minutes. Stir in the jalapeño; transfer to a bowl to cool. Season with salt and cayenne. Refrigerate overnight before serving at room temperature.
—*David Tanis*

SUPER-FAST IDEA FOR LEFTOVER TURKEY

turkey quesadilla Sprinkle shredded Fontina cheese, shredded roast turkey, chopped roasted red peppers, caramelized onions, sliced pickled jalapeños and chopped cilantro on a large flour tortilla in a cast-iron skillet. Cook over moderate heat until the cheese melts. Slide the tortilla onto a plate; fold in half. Serve with black beans, sour cream and hot sauce. —*Grace Parisi*

● HEALTHY   ● MAKE AHEAD   ● VEGETARIAN   ● STAFF FAVORITE

herb-roasted turkey with wild mushroom gravy

Crispy Duck Legs with Toasted Hazelnut and Garlic Sauce

ACTIVE: 45 MIN; TOTAL: 2 HR
4 SERVINGS ●

¼ cup extra-virgin olive oil
1 large Spanish onion, chopped
One 3-inch cinnamon stick, broken
Salt and freshly ground black pepper
2 cups chopped plum tomatoes
1 cup dry red wine
1 cup chicken stock
Eight 8-ounce Pekin duck legs, trimmed of excess fat
⅓ cup hazelnuts
1 cup finely diced crustless baguette
2 large garlic cloves, chopped
1 tablespoon unsalted butter

1. Preheat the oven to 325°. In a large skillet, heat 2 tablespoons of the oil. Add the onion, cinnamon and a pinch of salt; cover and cook over moderately low heat, stirring, until the onion is softened, 8 minutes. Add the tomatoes and cook over moderate heat, stirring, until very soft, 8 minutes. Add the wine and boil over high heat for 2 minutes. Add the stock and bring to a boil, then pour into a 9-by-13-inch baking dish.
2. Season the duck with salt and pepper and set the legs skin side up on the vegetables; keep the skin out of the liquid. Bake the duck legs in the top third of the oven for 1½ hours, until the meat is tender and the skin is crisp.
3. Meanwhile, spread the hazelnuts in a pie plate and toast until golden, 10 minutes. Transfer to a towel and rub to remove the skins, then transfer to a mini food processor.
4. In a medium skillet, heat the remaining 2 tablespoons of oil. Cook the bread over moderately high heat, stirring, until browned, 2 minutes. Reduce the heat to low; add the garlic. Cook, stirring, until the garlic is golden. Transfer the bread, garlic and oil to the processor; grind coarsely with the nuts.
5. Transfer the duck to a rimmed baking sheet and keep warm in the oven. Strain the pan sauce through a coarse sieve set over a saucepan, pressing on the solids; scrape the vegetables on the underside of the sieve into the sauce. Skim off the fat. Boil the sauce over high heat until reduced to 2 cups.
6. Whisk the nut mixture into the sauce; bring to a simmer. Remove from the heat and whisk in the butter. Season with salt and pepper; serve with the duck. —*Marcia Kiesel*
WINE Bold, berry-dense Spanish red: 2009 Alvaro Palacios Camins del Priorat.

Wood-Smoked Turkey

ACTIVE: 30 MIN; TOTAL: 6 HR PLUS
24 HR BRINING • 8 SERVINGS

1½ cups fine sea salt
¾ cup pure maple syrup
12 thyme sprigs
5 dried bay leaves
1 head of garlic, halved crosswise
One 10-pound turkey, neck and giblets reserved for another use
2 pounds cherry or other fruitwood chips, soaked in water overnight

1. In a very large pot, combine the salt, syrup, thyme, bay leaves and garlic with 3 gallons of water. Stir the brine until the salt is completely dissolved. Add the turkey, breast side down, top it with a plate to keep it submerged and refrigerate for 24 hours.
2. Light a hardwood charcoal or wood fire in the firebox of a smoker. Heat the smoker to 200°. Scatter some of the soaked wood chips around the coals; the chips should smolder but not flare. Set a drip pan filled with water on the bottom of the smoke box.
3. Remove the turkey from the brine and pat dry inside and out with paper towels. Tuck the wing tips under the turkey and tie the legs together with string. Set the turkey over the drip pan. Smoke the turkey for about 5 hours, until an instant-read thermometer inserted in an inner thigh registers 165°; monitor the coals throughout the smoking process and add more coals and/or wood, soaked chips and water as needed to maintain the temperature and smoke level. Transfer the turkey to a carving board and let rest for 20 minutes before serving. —*Josh Vogel*
WINE Fresh, berry-rich California red: 2009 Unti Petit Frere.

Turkey-and-Pinto-Bean Chili

ACTIVE: 30 MIN; TOTAL: 1 HR 15 MIN
6 TO 8 SERVINGS ●

This chili from Art Smith of Chicago's Table Fifty-Two is rich with ground turkey, beans and spices. "It's a big favorite of Oprah's," says Smith, who was once the TV mogul's personal chef.

¼ cup extra-virgin olive oil
3 pounds ground turkey
1 medium onion, cut into ½-inch dice
3 garlic cloves, minced
1½ tablespoons chile powder
1 teaspoon ground cumin
1 teaspoon dried oregano
¾ teaspoon chipotle powder
1 large carrot, cut into ¼-inch dice
1 red bell pepper, cut into ½-inch dice
One 28-ounce can tomato puree
Three 15-ounce cans pinto beans, drained
¾ cup lager
1 cup chicken stock
1 tablespoon cider vinegar
1 teaspoon chopped thyme
Salt and freshly ground black pepper
Chopped chives, for garnish

1. In a large Dutch oven, heat 1 tablespoon of the oil until shimmering. Add half of the turkey and cook over high heat, undisturbed, until browned on the bottom, about 3 minutes. Stir the turkey and cook until no pink remains, about 2 minutes longer. Transfer to a bowl and repeat with 1 more tablespoon of oil and the remaining turkey.
2. Add the remaining 2 tablespoons of oil and the onion to the pot. Cook over moderate heat until softened, about 5 minutes. Add the garlic, chile powder, cumin, oregano and chipotle powder and cook, stirring, until fragrant, about 2 minutes. Return the turkey to the pot. Stir in the carrot, bell pepper, tomato puree, beans and lager and bring to a boil. Stir in the chicken stock and vinegar, cover and simmer over low heat for 45 minutes. Add the thyme, season with salt and pepper and serve, garnished with chives. —*Art Smith*
BEER Crisp, malty beer: Blue Point Brewing Company Toasted Lager.

● HEALTHY ● MAKE AHEAD ● VEGETARIAN ● STAFF FAVORITE

Slows Bar BQ in Detroit's Corktown serves local craft beers and fantastic smoked meat like slow-cooked baby back ribs rubbed with paprika, brown sugar and ancho chile powder, OPPOSITE; *recipe, page 186.*

crispy duck legs with toasted hazelnut and garlic sauce

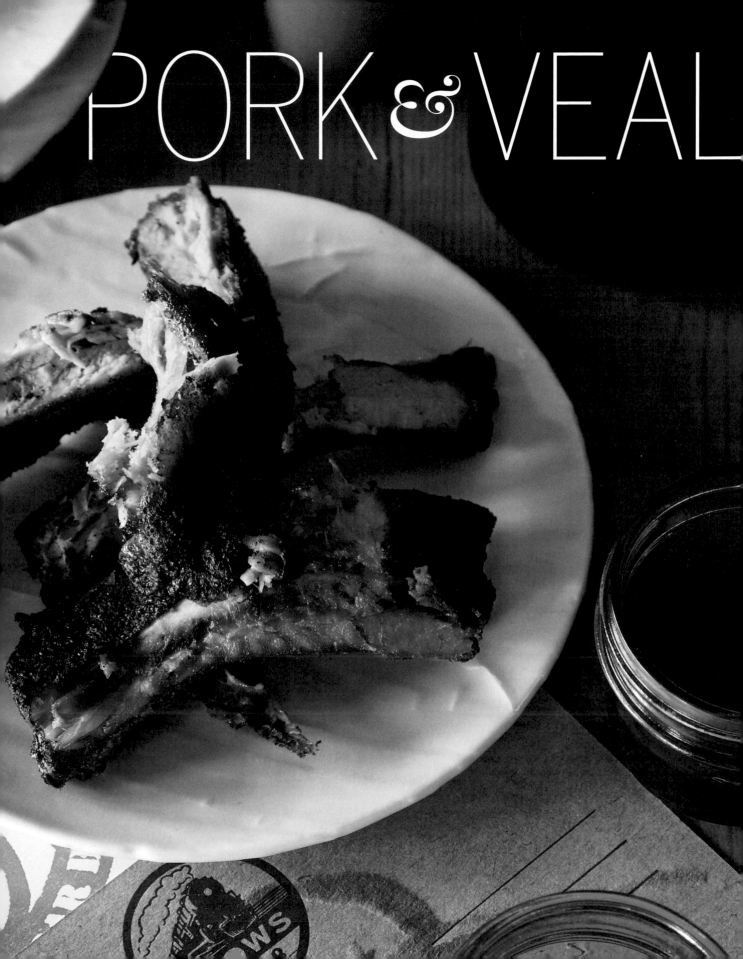

PORK & VEAL

Seaweed-Dusted Pork Chops with Quick-Pickled Carrots

ACTIVE: 30 MIN; TOTAL: 1 HR
4 SERVINGS

San Francisco chef Daniel Patterson (an F&W Best New Chef 1997) uses dried seaweed as a rub to coat thick pork chops before pan-roasting them. The odd combination—briny seaweed with succulent pork—works. This is a simplified version of the dish Patterson created, in which he cooked seaweed with garam masala and soy sauce, then dehydrated and ground it.

¼ cup fresh lime juice
½ teaspoon crushed red pepper
Kosher salt
4 large carrots, cut into ribbons with a vegetable peeler
Three 1-pound double-rib pork chops
1 ounce dried seaweed such as hijiki or wakame, ground in a spice grinder (about 3 tablespoons)
2 tablespoons extra-virgin olive oil
Cilantro sprigs, for garnish

1. Preheat the oven to 350°. In a bowl, stir the lime juice, crushed red pepper and 1 teaspoon of salt until the salt dissolves. Add the carrots; toss to coat. Let stand for 20 minutes or up to 1 hour, tossing occasionally.
2. Meanwhile, season the pork with salt. Spread the ground seaweed on wax paper and coat both sides of the chops with seaweed. In a large ovenproof skillet, heat the oil. Add the pork and cook over moderately high heat, turning once, until the seaweed crust is slightly darkened, about 6 minutes. Transfer the chops to the oven and roast for 20 minutes, turning once or twice, until an instant-read thermometer inserted near the bone registers 145°. Transfer the chops to a cutting board and let rest for 10 minutes.
3. Cut the pork off the bone, slice the meat and transfer to plates. Drain the carrots and mound alongside the pork. Garnish with cilantro sprigs and serve.
—*Daniel Patterson*

WINE Rich Rhône-style white blend: 2010 Boekenhoutskloof Wolftrap White.

Pork Chops with Charred Vegetable Puree

ACTIVE: 15 MIN; TOTAL: 1 HR
4 SERVINGS

"This puree is a cinch," says chef Matthew Accarrino of San Francisco's SPQR. "You roast the tomatoes with the carrots, onion and chile in the oven, and then you transfer the vegetables to the blender." The puree is fantastic with his lemony, thyme-coated baked pork chops.

3 plum tomatoes, halved lengthwise
2 small carrots, halved lengthwise
1 large white onion, sliced ½ inch thick
1 large jalapeño, halved and seeded
2 garlic cloves, unpeeled
2 tablespoons vegetable oil
Salt and freshly ground pepper
¼ cup extra-virgin olive oil
3 tablespoons freshly squeezed lime juice
Four bone-in 1-inch-thick pork rib chops
1 tablespoon chopped thyme
Finely grated zest of 1 lemon

1. Preheat the oven to 450°. Set the tomatoes and carrots cut side down on a large rimmed baking sheet. Add the onion, jalapeño and garlic. Drizzle with the vegetable oil and season with salt and pepper. Roast in the bottom third of the oven for about 30 minutes, until well browned.
2. Peel the garlic cloves. Coarsely chop all of the roasted vegetables and transfer to a blender. Add 2 tablespoons of olive oil and the lime juice and puree until smooth. Season with salt and pepper. Leave the oven on.
3. Set the chops on the rimmed baking sheet and drizzle with the remaining 2 tablespoons of olive oil. Rub the chops with the thyme and lemon zest and season with salt and pepper. Bake in the top third of the oven for about 15 minutes, or until an instant-read thermometer inserted near the bone registers 145°. Let the pork chops rest for 5 minutes. Serve with the charred vegetable puree.
—*Matthew Accarrino*

WINE Bold red from Spain's Ribera del Duero: 2009 Tinto Pesquera Crianza.

Grilled Pork Tenderloin with Herb Salsa

TOTAL: 45 MIN • 4 SERVINGS ●

Butterflying and pounding pork tenderloin maximizes the amount of surface area that gets deliciously charred on the grill.

1 cup flat-leaf parsley leaves
2 tablespoons oregano leaves
¼ cup pitted green olives
¾ cup extra-virgin olive oil, plus more for brushing
¼ cup dried currants
2 tablespoons fresh lemon juice
Salt and freshly ground pepper
1 sweet onion, cut into ½-inch-thick slabs
1 pound Broccolini
1 large pork tenderloin (about 1¼ pounds)
½ teaspoon smoked paprika

1. In a food processor, combine the parsley, oregano, olives and the ¾ cup of olive oil and process to a fine paste. Add the currants and lemon juice, season with salt and pepper, then pulse to blend.
2. Light a grill and oil the grates or preheat a grill pan. Brush the onion slabs and Broccolini all over with olive oil and season with salt and pepper. Grill over high heat, turning once or twice, until charred and tender, about 5 minutes for the Broccolini and 8 to 10 minutes for the onion.
3. Meanwhile, butterfly the pork, cutting halfway through the meat; open the meat on a work surface. Using a meat pounder, pound the tenderloin to a ½-inch thickness. Brush the pork with olive oil and season with the paprika and salt and pepper. Grill over high heat, turning the pork once or twice, until browned and cooked through, about 8 minutes. Let the pork rest for 5 minutes and then cut into thick slices. Serve with the grilled Broccolini and onion and pass the herb salsa alongside. —*Grace Parisi*

MAKE AHEAD The herb salsa can be refrigerated for up to 2 days.

WINE Concentrated, peppery South African Syrah: 2008 Noble Hill.

● HEALTHY   ● MAKE AHEAD   ● VEGETARIAN   ● STAFF FAVORITE

seaweed-dusted pork chops with quick-pickled carrots

PERFECT PORK CHOP CONDIMENT

pickled figs in balsamic vinegar

These vinegar-infused figs are fabulous with grilled pork chops. To guarantee that the figs remain whole, use firm fruit, since the double-cooking process would break down very ripe figs.

Fill a large pot with water, cover and bring to a boil. Add four ½-pint canning jars along with their lids and rings, a set of tongs and a ladle and simmer over low heat for about 10 minutes to sterilize, then cover and turn off the heat. Set a metal rack in another large pot, then fill with water, cover and bring to a boil. In a medium saucepan, combine 1¼ cups of sugar and ¾ cup of balsamic vinegar with 2 cups of water and bring to a boil, stirring to dissolve the sugar. Add 1¼ pounds of small ripe but firm Black Mission figs (about 24) and simmer over low heat, stirring a few times, until they are barely tender, about 10 minutes. Using the sterilized tongs, remove the jars from the hot water and transfer to a large rimmed baking sheet. Pack the figs into the hot jars and ladle the hot balsamic vinegar over them, leaving ½ inch of space at the top. Using the tongs, place the lids on the jars followed by the rings. Screw on the lids securely but not too tightly. Using the canning tongs, carefully lower the jars onto the rack in the pot of boiling water, making sure that the tops of the jars are covered by at least 1 inch of water, and boil the jarred figs over high heat for 15 minutes. Using the canning tongs, carefully transfer the jars to a rack to cool until the lids seal (they will look concave); refrigerate any jars that do not seal. Store the sealed jars in a cool, dark place for up to 6 months.
—*Ernest Miller*

Sage-Rubbed Pork Chops with Pickled-Peach Relish

ACTIVE: 35 MIN; TOTAL: 2 HR
4 SERVINGS

For the sweet-savory peach relish served with these big, juicy pork chops, chef Amelia O'Reilly of the Market Restaurant in Gloucester, Massachusetts, says it's important to use fruit that's ripe but firm so it won't get mushy during pickling.

- 2 cups white wine vinegar
- ¼ cup sugar
- 2 tablespoons yellow mustard seeds
- 1 bay leaf
- 1 tablespoon whole black peppercorns, plus 1 tablespoon coarsely ground black pepper
- Kosher salt
- 4 large ripe but firm peaches, pitted and cut into ½-inch dice
- 3 tablespoons extra-virgin olive oil
- 20 small sage leaves, plus 1 tablespoon chopped sage
- Four 1-inch-thick bone-in pork rib chops (10 to 12 ounces each)

1. In a large saucepan, combine the white wine vinegar with the sugar, mustard seeds, bay leaf, 1 tablespoon of whole peppercorns, 2 tablespoons of salt and 1½ cups of water; bring the mixture to a boil to dissolve the sugar. Put the diced peaches in a large, heatproof bowl and pour the hot brine over them. Let the peaches stand for 1 hour, then refrigerate them for about 30 minutes, until the peaches are chilled.

2. Meanwhile, in a small bowl, combine 1 tablespoon of the olive oil with the chopped sage, coarsely ground pepper and 1 tablespoon plus 1 teaspoon of salt. Rub the mixture all over the pork chops and let stand for 30 minutes.

3. Preheat the oven to 400°. In a large ovenproof skillet, heat 1 tablespoon of the olive oil until shimmering. Add the pork chops to the skillet and cook over moderately high heat until browned, about 3 minutes per side. Transfer the skillet to the oven and roast the pork chops for about 5 minutes, until an instant-read thermometer inserted in the thickest part of the meat nearest the bone registers 145°. Transfer the chops to a plate to rest for 10 minutes.

4. Meanwhile, in a medium skillet, heat the remaining 1 tablespoon of oil. Add the sage leaves and cook over moderate heat until crisp, about 1 minute per side.

5. Put a pork chop on each plate. Using a slotted spoon, top each chop with about ½ cup of the pickled peaches. Garnish with the fried sage leaves and serve.
—*Nico Monday and Amelia O'Reilly*

MAKE AHEAD The pickled peaches can be refrigerated for up to 1 week.

WINE Medium-bodied Pinot Noir from Oregon: 2011 Cooper Hill.

Milk-Braised Pork Chops with Mashed Potatoes and Gravy

ACTIVE: 1 HR 15 MIN; TOTAL: 3 HR
6 SERVINGS ●

Braising pork in milk, a method that Jimmy Bannos, Jr., of Chicago's Purple Pig learned while cooking in Florence, results in supertender meat and an incredibly rich and flavorful gravy. Although the dish is rooted in Tuscan tradition, Bannos adds an American comfort-food spin by serving it with creamy mashed potatoes.

- 2 tablespoons extra-virgin olive oil
- Six 8-ounce well-marbled boneless pork loin chops
- Kosher salt and freshly ground black pepper
- 1 large onion, chopped
- 1 large carrot, chopped
- 2 celery ribs, chopped
- 5 garlic cloves, smashed
- 2 cups chicken stock or low-sodium broth
- 5 thyme sprigs
- 5 bay leaves
- 2½ cups whole milk
- 3 pounds baking potatoes, peeled and cut into 1-inch pieces
- 1 cup heavy cream
- 6 tablespoons unsalted butter
- 2 tablespoons all-purpose flour

● HEALTHY ● MAKE AHEAD ● VEGETARIAN ● STAFF FAVORITE

1. In a large enameled cast-iron casserole, heat the olive oil until shimmering. Season the pork chops with salt and freshly ground pepper and add them to the casserole. Cook the chops over moderately high heat, turning them once, until they are golden, about 7 minutes total. Transfer the chops to a plate.

2. Add the chopped onion, carrot and celery, the smashed garlic and a generous pinch each of salt and freshly ground pepper to the casserole and cook over moderately high heat, stirring occasionally, until the vegetables just start to soften, about 5 minutes. Add the chicken stock, thyme sprigs, bay leaves and 2 cups of the milk and bring to a simmer. Return the pork chops to the casserole, cover and braise over very low heat until the pork chops are tender, about 2 hours.

3. Meanwhile, in a large saucepan, cover the potatoes with water and bring to a boil. Add a generous pinch of salt and simmer over moderate heat until the potatoes are tender, about 20 minutes. Drain the potatoes. Add the heavy cream and 4 tablespoons of the butter to the saucepan and warm over low heat until the butter is melted. Pass the drained potatoes through a ricer into a large bowl and then stir in the warm cream-butter sauce. Season the mashed potatoes with salt and pepper; keep warm.

4. Transfer the braised pork chops to a serving platter and cover them with aluminum foil. Spoon 4 cups of the braising liquid and vegetables into a blender, discarding the bay leaves, thyme sprigs and remaining vegetables and liquid. Puree the vegetable sauce until smooth.

5. In a medium saucepan, melt the remaining 2 tablespoons of butter over moderately high heat. Whisk in the flour and cook until bubbling. Whisk in the vegetable sauce and the remaining ½ cup of milk and cook over moderate heat, whisking, until the gravy is thickened and no floury taste remains, about 10 minutes. Season the gravy with salt and freshly ground black pepper. Serve the pork chops with the mashed potatoes and gravy. —Jimmy Bannos, Jr.

WINE Bright, medium-bodied Barbera d'Alba: 2010 Sottimano Pairolero.

Braised Pork Chops with Cipollini and Olives

ACTIVE: 45 MIN; TOTAL: 2 HR 30 MIN
4 SERVINGS

"When I think of Piedmont, I think of rustic wild boar dishes," F&W's Marcia Kiesel says about the inspiration behind this hearty dish. She cooks inexpensive pork shoulder chops slowly with bacon, rosemary and red wine until they're tender.

¼ cup extra-virgin olive oil
Four ¾-pound pork shoulder blade chops, each 1¼ inches thick
Salt and freshly ground black pepper
6 ounces Black Forest bacon, sliced ½ inch thick and cut into 1-inch pieces
1 medium onion, finely chopped
5 large garlic cloves, finely chopped
2 rosemary sprigs
4 cloves
½ cup plus 1 tablespoon dry red wine
2 cups chicken stock
1 pound unpeeled baby cipollini onions
⅔ cup assorted olives, including Niçoise olives, rinsed
3 tablespoons chopped parsley

1. Preheat the oven to 325°. In a skillet, heat 1 tablespoon of the olive oil. Season the pork chops with salt and pepper and add 2 chops to the skillet. Cook over moderately high heat, turning once, until browned, about 6 minutes total. Transfer the pork chops to a roasting pan and repeat with 1 more tablespoon of oil and the remaining 2 chops.

2. Add the bacon and the remaining 2 tablespoons of olive oil to the skillet and cook over moderate heat until the bacon is lightly browned. Add the onion and garlic, cover and cook over low heat, stirring, until softened. Add the rosemary and cloves and cook for 1 minute. Add ½ cup of the wine and boil over high heat for 1 minute. Add the chicken stock and bring to a boil.

3. Pour the bacon mixture over the chops in the roasting pan, then cover with foil and bake for 45 minutes. Turn the chops, cover and cook for 30 minutes longer.

4. Meanwhile, in a large saucepan of salted boiling water, cook the unpeeled baby cipollini onions until barely tender, about 4 minutes. Transfer to a plate and let cool, then trim and peel the cipollini onions.

5. Add the cipollini onions and olives to the roasting pan, nestling them in the liquid. Bake uncovered for 20 minutes.

6. Transfer the pork chops, cipollini onions and olives to a platter, cover with aluminum foil and keep warm.

7. Discard the cloves. Set the pan over high heat and boil the liquid until reduced to ¾ cup, about 5 minutes. Add the remaining 1 tablespoon of red wine to the sauce and pour it over the chops. Sprinkle with the parsley and serve. —Marcia Kiesel

MAKE AHEAD The recipe can be prepared through Step 4 one day ahead. Refrigerate the pork chops in sauce separately from the cipollini onions. Reheat the pork, covered, in the oven and proceed with Step 5.

WINE Robust Nebbiolo from Piedmont: 2009 Vietti Perbacco.

SUPER-FAST PORK CONDIMENT

savory apple compote This compote is terrific alongside pork chops or ham steaks, but it can also be spread on burgers or turkey sandwiches.

In a medium saucepan, melt 1 tablespoon butter. Add ⅓ cup minced Vidalia onion and cook until soft. Add 4 peeled and finely chopped Empire apples, ¼ cup water, 1½ teaspoons minced crystallized ginger, a pinch of dried sage and 2 tablespoons each of cider vinegar and sugar. Bring to a boil, cover and cook over low heat, mashing and stirring occasionally, until the apples are tender, about 10 minutes. Season with salt and serve. —Grace Parisi

Pork Larb Lettuce Wraps

⏱ TOTAL: 25 MIN • 4 SERVINGS ●

- 1 tablespoon long-grain rice
- 1 tablespoon vegetable oil
- 4 large garlic cloves, thinly sliced
- 1 tablespoon plus 1 teaspoon sugar
- ½ pound ground pork or beef
- 2 tablespoons plus 1 teaspoon Asian fish sauce

Salt and freshly ground pepper

- 2 tablespoons fresh lime juice
- 3 Thai chiles, very thinly sliced with seeds

Boston lettuce leaves, for serving

- ¼ small red onion, thinly sliced
- ¼ cup torn Thai basil leaves
- ¼ cup torn mint leaves
- ¼ cup torn cilantro leaves

1. In a medium skillet, toast the rice over moderate heat, shaking the pan often, until browned, 3 minutes. Transfer the rice to a plate and let cool completely. Put the toasted rice in a spice grinder and grind to a powder.
2. In the skillet, heat the oil. Add the garlic and cook over moderately low heat, stirring a few times, until golden brown, about 1 minute. Add 1 teaspoon of the sugar and cook for about 20 seconds. Add the pork and cook over moderately high heat, breaking up the meat finely, until no pink remains, about 3 minutes. Add 1 teaspoon of the fish sauce and season with salt and pepper. Set aside.
3. In a small bowl, combine the lime juice with the remaining 2 tablespoons of fish sauce, the remaining 1 tablespoon of sugar, two-thirds of the chiles and 1 tablespoon of water. Stir to dissolve the sugar.
4. Arrange the lettuce leaves on a platter with the dipping sauce. Reheat the pork. Remove from the heat and stir in the onion, basil, mint, cilantro and the remaining chile. Sprinkle the pork with the rice powder. Transfer to a bowl and place on or near the platter. Let everyone spoon the pork onto the lettuce leaves and season with the dipping sauce.
—*Ryan Lowder*
WINE Vibrant, citrusy Grüner Veltliner: 2011 Leth Steinagrund.

Peanut Noodle Salad with Cucumber and Roast Pork

TOTAL: 45 MIN PLUS 1 HR MARINATING
6 SERVINGS ● ●

One 0.2-ounce jar dried chopped chives
- ½ teaspoon freshly ground black pepper

Cayenne pepper
- 3 tablespoons vegetable oil

One 1-pound pork tenderloin

Salt
- ½ cup smooth natural peanut butter (without sugar)
- ¼ cup cider vinegar
- 2 tablespoons Worcestershire sauce
- 1 tablespoon honey
- 10 ounces dried linguine

One 4-ounce cucumber—peeled, halved, seeded and thinly sliced on the diagonal (½ cup)
- ½ cup torn basil leaves
- 2 ounces pea shoots or tendrils (2 cups)

1. In a mini food processor, combine the dried chives, black pepper, a pinch of cayenne pepper and 1 tablespoon of the oil. Process to a moist powder. Season the pork with salt and spread the chive mixture all over. Cover and refrigerate for 1 hour.
2. Preheat the oven to 350°. In a small bowl, whisk the peanut butter with the vinegar, Worcestershire sauce, honey and a pinch of cayenne. Season with salt.
3. In an ovenproof nonstick skillet, heat the remaining 2 tablespoons of oil. Add the pork and cook over moderately high heat for 2 minutes. Reduce the heat to moderate and cook until browned, 2 minutes longer. Turn the pork and cook for 2 minutes more. Transfer the skillet to the oven and roast the tenderloin for about 15 minutes for medium meat, turning halfway through. Transfer the pork to a board and let rest for 10 minutes.
4. Meanwhile, in a pot of salted boiling water, cook the linguine until al dente. Drain, reserving 3 tablespoons of the cooking water. Rinse the noodles under cold water until cool; toss to remove the excess water and pat dry with paper towels. Transfer the noodles to a bowl.

5. Stir the pasta cooking water into the peanut dressing and pour the sauce over the noodles. Toss well. Stir in the cucumber, basil and half the pea shoots. Transfer the noodles to bowls and garnish with the remaining pea shoots. Slice the pork ⅓ inch thick and serve with the noodle salad. —*Spike Gjerde*
WINE Bright, orange-scented off-dry Riesling: 2010 Chateau Ste. Michelle Eroica.

Crunchy Pork-Kimchi Burgers

⏱ TOTAL: 30 MIN • 4 SERVINGS ●

- 1 tablespoon minced fresh ginger
- 1 large garlic clove, minced
- 2 scallions, minced
- 1 pound ground pork
- ¾ cup finely chopped kimchi

Kosher salt

All-purpose flour, for dusting
- 2 large eggs, beaten
- 1 cup panko, lightly crushed

Vegetable oil, for frying

Two 5-ounce bags baby spinach
- ¼ cup plus 2 tablespoons mayonnaise
- ½ teaspoon toasted sesame oil
- 1 tablespoon soy sauce

Toasted sesame seeds, for garnish

1. In a bowl, combine the ginger, garlic, scallions, pork and kimchi with 1 teaspoon of salt. Form the mixture into eight 3-inch patties, ½ inch thick. Dust the patties with flour.
2. Put the eggs and panko in 2 shallow bowls. Dip the patties in the egg and then in the panko, pressing to help the crumbs adhere.
3. In a large skillet, heat ¼ inch of vegetable oil. Fry the patties over moderate heat, turning, until golden and cooked through, 5 to 6 minutes. Drain on paper towels.
4. Pour off all but 1 tablespoon of the oil in the skillet. Add the spinach in batches, season with salt and cook over high heat until wilted, about 1 minute.
5. In a bowl, mix the mayonnaise, sesame oil and soy sauce. Mound the spinach on plates and top with the burgers. Drizzle with the sauce, sprinkle with sesame seeds and serve.
—*Grace Parisi*
WINE Juicy Spanish rosé: 2011 Yellow + Blue.

● HEALTHY ● MAKE AHEAD ● VEGETARIAN ● STAFF FAVORITE

pork larb lettuce wraps

Shanghai Stir-Fried Pork with Cabbage

TOTAL: 30 MIN • 4 SERVINGS ●

¾ pound boneless pork loin, trimmed of fat
8 dried shiitake mushrooms
2 teaspoons cornstarch
1½ tablespoons dry sherry
1 tablespoon soy sauce
¼ teaspoon freshly ground white pepper
¼ cup peanut oil
Kosher salt
1 pound napa cabbage— halved lengthwise, cored and thinly sliced crosswise
Cooked rice and Chinese chile sauce, for serving

1. Freeze the pork for 15 minutes. Meanwhile, in a microwave-safe bowl, cover the shiitake mushrooms with hot water and a paper towel. Microwave at high power for 3 minutes. Let the shiitake stand until softened, about 15 minutes. Drain and press out the water. Cut off and discard the stems, then thinly slice the shiitake caps.
2. Slice the pork loin ¼ inch thick. Stack the slices and cut them into ¼-inch-wide strips. Transfer the pork to a medium bowl and toss with the cornstarch, sherry, soy sauce, white pepper and 1 tablespoon of the oil.
3. Heat a large skillet until it's almost smoking. Add 1½ tablespoons of the oil and heat until small puffs of smoke appear around the edge. Add the pork and stir-fry over high heat until nearly cooked, 30 seconds; transfer to a plate. Add the remaining oil to the skillet, then add 1 teaspoon of salt and swirl to combine. When the oil is shimmering, add the shiitake caps and half of the cabbage and stir-fry over high heat until just wilted. Add the remaining cabbage and stir-fry until crisp-tender, 1½ minutes longer. Return the pork to the skillet and cook until just heated through, 1 minute. Serve right away, with rice and chile sauce. —*Cecilia Chiang*
WINE Dark, peppery Syrah: 2009 Lafond Santa Rita Hills.

Pork-and-Cheese Arepas with Tangy Cabbage Slaw

TOTAL: 45 MIN • 4 SERVINGS ● ●

2 cups masa harina, preferably Maseca brand
Kosher salt
2 cups finely shredded red cabbage
¼ small red onion, very thinly sliced
2 tablespoons red wine vinegar
½ pound roast pork, shredded
4 ounces sharp cheddar cheese, shredded (1 cup)
Hot sauce, for seasoning
Vegetable oil, for frying
Sliced pickled jalapeños, cilantro sprigs and sour cream, for serving

1. In a bowl, mix the masa harina with 1¾ cups plus 2 tablespoons of warm water and 1 teaspoon of salt to form a soft dough. Cover with plastic wrap and let stand for 15 minutes.
2. Meanwhile, in another bowl, toss the cabbage, onion and vinegar. Season with salt.
3. In a small bowl, combine the pork and cheddar and season with salt and hot sauce. Form the pork filling into 4 compact balls.
4. Form the dough into 4 balls and cover with plastic wrap. Working with 1 ball at a time, flatten it on a sheet of plastic wrap to a 7-inch round. Place a pork filling ball in the center of the dough. Bring the dough up to cover the filling. Gently flatten the ball into a 4-inch patty and patch any holes or tears. Repeat with the remaining dough and filling.
5. In a large skillet, heat ¼ inch of vegetable oil until shimmering. Add the arepas and fry over high heat, turning once, until golden, crisp and heated through, about 6 minutes. Drain on paper towels and transfer to plates. Using a slotted spoon, mound the cabbage slaw on top of the arepas and serve with jalapeños, cilantro and sour cream.
—*Grace Parisi*
MAKE AHEAD The uncooked arepas can be stacked between sheets of plastic wrap and refrigerated overnight. Bring them to room temperature before frying.
WINE Spicy, cherry-rich California red blend: 2009 Purple Cowboy Tenacious Red.

Pork with Grapes and Tarragon

TOTAL: 30 MIN • 8 SERVINGS ● ●

This dish tastes surprisingly indulgent for something so low in fat, thanks in part to the tannins in black and red grapes. "If you make the sauce with less tannic green grapes, it just won't have the same texture," says California chef Maria Helm Sinskey. When she can find them, Sinskey uses fragrant black muscat grapes in the recipe.

2 tablespoons extra-virgin olive oil
Eight 4-ounce boneless pork loin chops
Kosher salt and freshly ground pepper
2 cups black or red seedless grapes (12 ounces), halved
2 tablespoons minced shallots
1 tablespoon sugar
1 tablespoon red wine vinegar
½ cup dry, fruity red wine
1 cup chicken stock or low-sodium broth
2 teaspoons chopped tarragon

1. In a very large skillet, heat the olive oil until shimmering. Season the pork with salt and pepper and add the chops to the skillet. Cook over moderately high heat, turning once, until lightly browned and nearly cooked through, about 6 minutes. Transfer the pork to a platter, cover loosely and keep warm.
2. Add the grapes to the skillet and cook until lightly browned, about 3 minutes. Add the shallots and sugar and cook, stirring, until the sugar dissolves, about 1 minute. Add the vinegar and cook until nearly evaporated, about 1 minute. Add the wine and boil over high heat until reduced by half, about 3 minutes. Add the stock and boil until reduced by half, about 4 minutes.
3. Return the pork chops and any juices to the skillet and simmer until the chops are just cooked, about 2 minutes. Transfer the pork to plates. Boil the sauce until thick and glossy, about 2 minutes. Stir in the tarragon and pour the sauce over the pork. Serve right away. —*Maria Helm Sinskey*
SERVE WITH Brown rice or roasted potatoes.
WINE Round, elegant Merlot from Sonoma: 2007 Medlock Ames.

● HEALTHY ● MAKE AHEAD ● VEGETARIAN ● STAFF FAVORITE

shanghai stir-fried pork with cabbage

Pork Tinga

ACTIVE: 45 MIN; TOTAL: 1 HR 45 MIN
4 SERVINGS ●

Star chef Rick Bayless's pork stew is smoky and satisfying, especially when topped with avocado, cheese and onion.

- 1¼ **pounds trimmed boneless pork shoulder, cut into 1½-inch cubes**
- ¼ **teaspoon dried marjoram**
- ¼ **teaspoon dried thyme**
- 3 **bay leaves**
- ¾ **pound red potatoes, cut into ½-inch dice**
- 2 **tablespoons vegetable oil**
- 1 **large fresh chorizo, casing removed**
- 1 **medium onion, finely chopped**
- 1 **garlic clove, minced**

One 28-ounce can peeled Italian tomatoes, chopped and drained
- 2 **chipotle chiles in adobo, seeded and minced, plus 4 teaspoons sauce**

Salt and sugar, for seasoning

1. In a large saucepan, simmer the pork, marjoram, thyme and bay leaves in 4 cups of salted water, partially covered, until the meat is tender, 45 minutes. Using a slotted spoon, transfer the pork to a plate; let it cool slightly, then tear it into smaller pieces. Skim the fat from the pork broth; reserve 1½ cups.
2. In a large saucepan of salted boiling water, cook the potatoes until just tender, about 8 minutes. Drain well.
3. In a medium, deep skillet, heat the oil. Add the chorizo and stir over moderately low heat, breaking it up, until cooked through, 10 minutes; transfer to a plate. Add the pork and onion to the skillet and cook over moderate heat, stirring, until well browned, 10 minutes. Add the garlic and cook for 1 minute. Stir in the tomatoes and chorizo; cook for 5 minutes. Add the potatoes, chipotle, adobo sauce and the 1½ cups of pork broth; simmer for 10 minutes. Season with salt and a pinch of sugar and serve. —*Rick Bayless*

SERVE WITH Flour tortillas, sliced avocado, red onion and *queso fresco.*

WINE Fruity, orange-inflected Syrah: 2010 Andezon Côtes-du-Rhône.

Pork Shoulder Roast with Citrus Mojo and Green Sauce

ACTIVE: 45 MIN; TOTAL: 8 HR PLUS 8 HR MARINATING • 8 TO 10 SERVINGS ● ●

On *Man vs. Food* and *Man vs. Food Nation,* Adam Richman travels around the US eating huge quantities of hearty food. One of his favorite dishes is this Caribbean-style pork roast served at Minneapolis's Brasa, which is as filling as anything he eats on TV. Along with a citrusy *mojo* and a garlicky cilantro mayonnaise, it's a great dish for a crowd.

- 1 **tablespoon extra-virgin olive oil**
- ½ **cup minced onion**
- 2 **large garlic cloves, minced**
- 1 **cup fresh lemon juice**
- 1 **cup fresh orange juice**
- 2 **tablespoons distilled white vinegar**
- 2 **tablespoons garlic powder**
- 2 **tablespoons onion powder**
- 2 **tablespoons freshly ground pepper**
- 1½ **teaspoons ground cumin**
- 1 **tablespoon Worcestershire sauce**

Salt
One 5-pound bone-in Boston butt (pork shoulder, butt end)
Creamy Cilantro-Lime Sauce (recipe follows), for serving

1. In a small saucepan, heat the olive oil. Add the onion and cook over moderate heat until softened, about 5 minutes. Add the garlic and cook until fragrant. Add the lemon and orange juices and simmer for about 2 minutes. Add the vinegar and stir to combine. Transfer half of the *mojo* to a blender and let cool. Refrigerate the remaining *mojo.*
2. Meanwhile, in a jar, shake the garlic and onion powders with the ground pepper and cumin. Add 2 tablespoons of the dry rub to the *mojo* in the blender. Add the Worcestershire sauce and 1 tablespoon of salt to the blender and puree the marinade.
3. Put the pork in a resealable 1-gallon plastic bag; add the marinade and turn to coat. Seal the bag, pressing out the air, and refrigerate for at least 8 hours or up to 24 hours, turning occasionally. Bring the pork to room temperature before roasting.

4. Preheat the oven to 350° and set a rack in a roasting pan. Remove the pork from the marinade and pat dry. Rub the meat all over with the remaining dry rub and set it on the rack. Roast for 3 hours, until an instant-read thermometer inserted into the thickest part of the meat registers 150°. Reduce the oven temperature to 275° and roast for about 3 hours longer, until the meat is very tender and an instant-read thermometer registers 180°. Remove the roast from the oven and cover with foil; let rest for 30 minutes.
5. Shred the meat, discarding the bones and excess fat. Serve the roast with the remaining *mojo* and Creamy Cilantro-Lime Sauce. —*Alex Roberts*

SERVE WITH Guacamole and tortilla chips.
MAKE AHEAD The whole roast can be covered and refrigerated for up to 2 days. Bring to room temperature and shred, then cover and reheat gently in a 300° oven.
WINE Wild-berry-inflected Rioja red: 2008 Mencos Crianza.

CREAMY CILANTRO-LIME SAUCE
TOTAL: 15 MIN • MAKES 1¾ CUPS
● ● ●

Versions of this punchy mayonnaise-based cilantro sauce are served all over Latin America with roasted meats.

- 2 **large jalapeños, seeded and coarsely chopped**
- 2 **large garlic cloves, smashed**
- 2 **tablespoons minced fresh ginger**
- 2 **tablespoons minced white onion**
- 1 **tablespoon freshly squeezed lime juice**
- 1 **cup mayonnaise**
- ¼ **cup finely chopped cilantro**

Salt

In a blender, puree the jalapeños, garlic, ginger, onion, lime juice and ¼ cup of water until smooth. Add the mayonnaise and cilantro and pulse a few times. Season the sauce with salt and serve. —*AR*

MAKE AHEAD The sauce can be refrigerated for up to 3 days. Let return to room temperature before serving.

● HEALTHY   ● MAKE AHEAD   ● VEGETARIAN   ● STAFF FAVORITE

pork tinga

Pork Carnitas with Garlic and Orange

ACTIVE: 40 MIN; TOTAL: 5 HR 30 MIN

4 TO 6 SERVINGS ● ●

The trick to these luscious *carnitas* is to pull the meat into successively smaller pieces as it roasts, exposing more and more surface to the oven's heat for crisping. The result is meat that is super-savory and tender, with a crisp exterior—perfect for tacos.

3½ pounds boneless pork shoulder, in 1 piece

Vegetable oil, for drizzling

Salt and freshly ground pepper

1 teaspoon pure ancho chile powder

20 unpeeled garlic cloves

3 jalapeños, seeded and diced

½ cup fresh orange juice

Warm tortillas, for serving

1. Preheat the oven to 325°. In a small roasting pan, rub the pork shoulder all over with vegetable oil and season with salt and pepper. Turn the meat fat side down and sprinkle with the ancho powder. Add ½ cup of water, cover with foil and bake for 2 hours.

2. Turn the pork over and scatter the garlic cloves and jalapeños around it. Cover and bake for 1 hour longer. Transfer the garlic cloves and jalapeños to a plate. Peel the garlic cloves.

3. Increase the oven temperature to 375°. Cut the pork into 4 thick slices and then into large chunks. Arrange the chunks in the pan and roast the pork for 45 minutes. Pull the chunks into smaller pieces and roast for about 1 hour longer, until the meat is well browned and crisp.

4. Transfer the pork to a large platter and scatter the jalapeños and garlic on top.

5. Pour off all but 1 tablespoon of fat from the roasting pan. Set the pan over moderate heat, add the orange juice and boil, scraping up the browned bits; pour over the pork and toss to coat. Season with salt and pepper and serve with warm tortillas.
—*Marcia Kiesel*

WINE Full-bodied, lightly sweet Riesling: 2010 Dr. Loosen Erdener Treppchen Kabinett.

Pork-and-Green-Chile Stew

ACTIVE: 25 MIN; TOTAL: 45 MIN

6 SERVINGS ● ●

A mix of mild chiles (poblano, Anaheim) and hot ones (serrano) gives body and heat to this quick braise made with boneless pork shoulder (ask your butcher to trim it for you).

¼ cup extra-virgin olive oil

2 pounds trimmed boneless pork shoulder, cut into ¾-inch cubes

Salt and freshly ground black pepper

1 large sweet onion, such as Vidalia, quartered lengthwise and thinly sliced crosswise

1 pound mild green chiles, such as poblanos and Anaheims—halved lengthwise, cored and thinly sliced

3 serrano chiles, seeded and thinly sliced (keep some seeds for spicier flavor)

6 garlic cloves, thinly sliced

2 cups low-sodium chicken broth

¼ cup chopped cilantro, plus more for garnish

Lime wedges, warm corn tortillas and rice, for serving

1. In a large enameled cast-iron casserole, heat the olive oil until almost smoking. Season the pork cubes with salt and black pepper and add them to the casserole. Cook the pork over high heat, stirring once or twice, until lightly browned in spots, about 5 minutes. Add the onion, green chiles, serrano chiles and garlic. Cover and cook over high heat, stirring once or twice, until the vegetables are softened, about 5 minutes. Add the chicken broth and bring to a boil. Cover partially and simmer the stew over moderately low heat until the pork is just tender and the broth is reduced by about half, about 20 minutes.

2. Stir in the ¼ cup of cilantro and season with salt and black pepper. Garnish the stew with cilantro and serve with lime wedges, corn tortillas and rice. —*Grace Parisi*

MAKE AHEAD The stew can be refrigerated for up to 3 days.

BEER Fresh, hoppy pale ale: Tröegs.

Braised Pork with Cherry Gravy

ACTIVE: 1 HR; TOTAL: 5 HR 30 MIN PLUS OVERNIGHT CHILLING · 6 SERVINGS ● ●

4 pounds boneless pork shoulder, tied

Salt and freshly ground pepper

7 tablespoons vegetable oil

6 celery ribs, coarsely chopped

2 carrots, coarsely chopped

3 large onions, coarsely chopped

¼ cup tomato paste

1 cup dry red wine

6 cups chicken stock or broth

1 cup dried sour cherries

2 large fennel bulbs, thinly sliced

2 large leeks, white and pale green parts, sliced crosswise ½ inch thick

1½ cups heavy cream

¼ cup grated young pecorino cheese

¼ cup chives, cut into ½-inch lengths

1. Preheat the oven to 350°. Season the pork with salt and pepper. In a large Dutch oven, brown the pork in 2 tablespoons of the oil. Remove the pork and pour off the fat. Add 2 tablespoons of the oil to the pot. Add the celery, carrots and 2 of the onions and cook over moderate heat until golden, 15 minutes. Add the tomato paste, wine and stock; bring to a boil. Add the pork and cherries, cover and braise in the oven for 4 hours. Let cool, then refrigerate overnight.

2. Skim the fat from the liquid and remove the pork. Boil the gravy until it's reduced to 1½ cups, 25 minutes. Strain the gravy into a saucepan and season with salt and pepper. Untie the pork; slice into 6 medallions.

3. In a skillet, combine 2 tablespoons of the oil with the fennel, leeks and remaining onion. Cover and cook over moderate heat until the vegetables are softened, about 7 minutes. Add the cream and simmer until thickened, about 10 minutes. Add the cheese and chives; season with salt and pepper.

4. In a nonstick skillet, heat the remaining 1 tablespoon of oil. Add the pork and brown well. Serve with the gravy and vegetables.
—*Michel Nischan*

WINE Tart cherry–scented, medium-bodied Chianti: 2009 Selvapiana.

● HEALTHY ● MAKE AHEAD ● VEGETARIAN ● STAFF FAVORITE

braised pork with cherry gravy

DIY PORCHETTA

With a couple of smart tweaks, Miami chef **Michael Pirolo** transforms this classic Italian dish—traditionally a whole pig—into a striking main course for a crowd.

Porchetta

ACTIVE: 45 MIN; TOTAL: 4 HR 30 MIN
PLUS 2 DAYS BRINING AND SEASONING
10 SERVINGS ● ●

BRINE

- 10 rosemary sprigs
- 10 bay leaves
- 3 heads of garlic, smashed
- ⅓ cup juniper berries
- 3 tablespoons black peppercorns
- 2 tablespoons fennel seeds
- 1 tablespoon crushed red pepper
- 1¼ cups kosher salt
- ¼ cup sugar
- 2 tablespoons honey

One 9-pound meaty pork belly
  with skin (see Note)

RUB

- 1½ tablespoons fennel seeds
- 1 teaspoon juniper berries
- ¾ teaspoon black peppercorns
- ¾ teaspoon freshly grated nutmeg
- ¾ teaspoon crushed red pepper
- 3 tablespoons very
  finely chopped rosemary
- 4 large garlic cloves, minced

Roasted potatoes, for serving

1. BRINE THE BELLY In a large pot, add the rosemary, bay leaves, garlic, juniper, peppercorns, fennel seeds, crushed red pepper and 1 gallon of water. Bring to a simmer over high heat, cover and cook for 10 minutes. Add the salt, sugar and honey and stir until dissolved.
2. Pour the brine into a large roasting pan and let cool completely. Add the pork belly to the brine, skin side up. Cover with plastic wrap and refrigerate overnight.
3. MAKE THE RUB In a small skillet, toast the fennel seeds, juniper berries and black peppercorns over moderate heat until they are fragrant, about 1 minute. Let cool, then

grind them to a powder in a spice grinder. Transfer the spice blend to a small bowl and stir in the grated nutmeg, crushed red pepper, rosemary and garlic.
4. Drain the pork belly and pat dry, then pick off any spices. Turn the belly skin side down and rub the meaty side with the spice blend. Transfer the pork belly to the roasting pan, skin side up, and pierce the skin all over with the tip of a knife. Refrigerate the pork uncovered overnight.
5. Preheat the oven to 400° and position a rack in the lower third. Set the pork belly skin side down on a clean work surface. Roll up the pork belly lengthwise to form a tight cylinder and tie it tightly at 2-inch intervals with kitchen twine.

6. Return the pork to the pan and roast for 1 hour. Lower the heat to 300° and roast for 2 hours and 15 minutes longer, until the skin is deep brown and crisp and an instant-read thermometer inserted in the center registers 185°. Transfer the *porchetta* to a cutting board and let rest for 20 minutes. Remove the twine and slice the *porchetta* ½ inch thick, using a serrated knife to cut through the skin. Serve with roasted potatoes.
NOTE Pork belly can be a very fatty cut; be sure to ask your butcher for one that is very meaty, at least 50 percent lean.
MAKE AHEAD The *porchetta* can be prepared through Step 5 and refrigerated overnight.
WINE Spicy, dark-fruited Tuscan red: 2009 Capezzana Barco Reale di Carmignano.

toast In a small skillet, toast fennel seeds, juniper berries and black peppercorns until fragrant.

blend Grind the spices, then mix with nutmeg, crushed red pepper, rosemary and minced garlic cloves.

season Remove the belly from the brine; dry it and rub with the spices, then marinate for at least 12 hours.

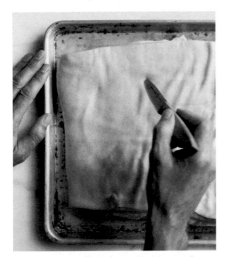

score Pierce the skin all over with the tip of a knife, which will help render some of the fat and crisp the skin.

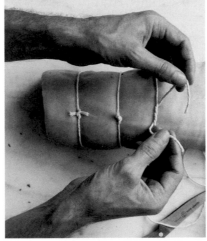

tie Roll up the belly lengthwise to form a tight cylinder and tie tightly at 2-inch intervals with kitchen twine.

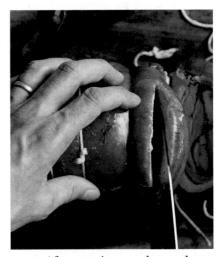

serve After roasting, cut the *porchetta* into slices using a serrated knife, which can help cut through the crisp skin.

IDEAS FOR LEFTOVERS

According to Pirolo, Italians love to make use of leftover porchetta. Here are a few ways he likes to use it up.
salumi Serve the *porchetta* cold and thinly sliced on a *salumi* board.
sandwich Make a sandwich with *porchetta*, melted provolone and sautéed broccoli rabe on toasted ciabatta bread.
omelet Fold the *porchetta* into an omelet with goat cheese and scallions.

Spicy Korean Grilled Pork

TOTAL: 45 MIN PLUS 24 HR MARINATING
4 SERVINGS ●

- 1 cup Chinese fermented black beans (5 ounces; see Note)
- 1 head of garlic, cloves peeled and coarsely chopped
- One 4-inch piece of fresh ginger, peeled and coarsely chopped
- ½ cup Korean chile paste (*gochujang*; see Note)
- ¼ cup plus 2 tablespoons rice vinegar
- ¼ cup soy sauce
- 3 tablespoons toasted sesame oil
- ¾ cup light brown sugar
- One 3-pound trimmed boneless pork shoulder roast, cut crosswise into twelve ¼-inch-thick slices
- Vegetable oil, for brushing

1. Put the fermented black beans in a bowl and cover with water. Let stand for 15 minutes. Drain and coarsely chop the beans.
2. In a food processor, combine the black beans, garlic and ginger and pulse until finely chopped. Add the chile paste, vinegar, soy sauce, sesame oil and sugar and blend well.
3. On a work surface, pound the pork slices ⅛ inch thick. Lay one-fourth of the pork slices in a large, shallow dish and coat with one-fourth of the black bean marinade. Repeat with the remaining pork and marinade for three more layers. Cover and refrigerate for up to 24 hours.
4. Light a grill or preheat a grill pan. Remove the pork from the marinade, leaving just a thin coating on the meat. Brush the pork with oil and grill over moderate heat, turning every 2 minutes, until nicely charred and cooked through, about 6 minutes. —*Bill Kim*
SERVE WITH Vegetables or chilled noodles.
NOTE Chinese fermented black beans and *gochujang* are available at Asian markets and online from *amazon.com*. Or substitute an equal amount of Chinese black bean sauce or any kind of Asian chile paste.
WINE Fruit-forward Grenache-based red: 2010 Camille Cayran Le Pas de la Beaume Côtes du Rhône.

Coffee-Cured Pulled Pork

ACTIVE: 30 MIN; TOTAL: 7 HR PLUS
12 HR CURING
MAKES ABOUT 2½ POUNDS ● ●

- ½ cup sugar
- ¼ cup coarsely ground coffee
- Kosher salt
- One 4-pound bone-in pork butt
- ⅓ cup sorghum or molasses
- ⅓ cup apple cider vinegar
- Freshly ground pepper

1. In a large bowl, combine the sugar, coffee and ½ cup of salt. Add the pork and rub the mixture all over. Cover with plastic wrap and refrigerate for 12 to 24 hours.
2. Preheat the oven to 300°. Rinse off the pork and set in a roasting pan. Roast the pork for 6 hours, basting with pan juices, until an instant-read thermometer inserted in the thickest part registers 200°; cover with foil for the last 2 hours of cooking. Transfer the pan to a rack and let rest for 30 minutes. Increase the oven temperature to 500°.
3. In a saucepan, boil the sorghum and vinegar; season with salt and pepper. Simmer until slightly reduced, 10 minutes. Pour the glaze over the pork and roast for 15 minutes, until glazed. Let cool, then shred the pork and serve. —*Linton Hopkins*
SERVE WITH Slider buns, Aunt Julia's Barbecue Sauce and Sunchoke Pickle Relish (recipes follow).
WINE Very ripe Syrah from Australia: 2010 Yalumba Y Series Shiraz Viognier.

SUNCHOKE PICKLE RELISH

ACTIVE: 30 MIN; TOTAL: 2 HR
MAKES 2 QUARTS ● ● ● ●

- ½ cup kosher salt
- 1¼ pounds sunchokes, scrubbed and cut into ½-inch dice
- 1 large Vidalia or other sweet onion (about 1¼ pounds), finely diced
- 1 large red bell pepper, cut into ¼-inch dice
- ½ cup dry mustard
- ¼ cup all-purpose flour
- 1 quart apple cider vinegar
- 2 cups sugar
- 1 tablespoon turmeric
- 1 teaspoon yellow mustard seeds
- 1 teaspoon freshly ground pepper
- 1 teaspoon celery seeds

1. In a bowl, combine the salt with 4 cups of water. Add the sunchokes; let stand for 1 hour.
2. Drain the sunchokes and return them to the bowl. Add the onion and red pepper and toss. Transfer the vegetables to 2 heated, sterile, quart-size canning jars.
3. In a small bowl, combine the dry mustard and flour with ½ cup of water and stir to make a paste. In a large saucepan, combine all of the remaining ingredients and bring to a boil. Whisk in the mustard-flour paste until smooth. Simmer until thickened, 10 minutes. Pour the hot liquid over the vegetables and tap to release any air bubbles.
4. Cover the jars (not too tightly) and transfer them to a deep pot filled with very hot water. Boil the jars for 25 minutes. Carefully remove the jars from the water and let cool. —*LH*

AUNT JULIA'S BARBECUE SAUCE

TOTAL: 30 MIN; MAKES 1 QUART ● ●

- ½ cup plus 2 tablespoons ketchup
- ½ cup plus 2 tablespoons tomato puree
- ½ cup water
- ½ cup Worcestershire sauce
- ½ cup apple cider vinegar
- ½ cup finely chopped sweet onion
- ¼ cup tomato juice
- ¼ cup Heinz chile sauce
- ¼ cup Tabasco
- ¼ cup brown sugar
- 4 tablespoons unsalted butter
- 3 tablespoons fresh lemon juice
- 1 tablespoon crushed red pepper
- 1 tablespoon kosher salt
- 1 tablespoon dried mustard powder
- 1 tablespoon ground black pepper

Combine all of the ingredients in a large saucepan. Bring to a boil, then simmer for 10 minutes. Let cool, then transfer to a jar. —*LH*

● HEALTHY   ● MAKE AHEAD   ● VEGETARIAN   ● STAFF FAVORITE

coffee-cured pulled pork with sunchoke pickle relish and aunt julia's barbecue sauce

Sausage Burgers with Mustard-Thyme Sauce

ACTIVE: 25 MIN; TOTAL: 1 HR 10 MIN
4 SERVINGS

- 3 cups chicken stock or low-sodium broth
- ½ cup heavy cream
- 3 tablespoons Dijon mustard
- 2 teaspoons chopped thyme
- Salt and freshly ground black pepper
- 1½ pounds sweet Italian sausage, without fennel
- 3 large garlic cloves, minced
- 2 tablespoons dry white wine
- ¼ teaspoon ground allspice
- ⅛ teaspoon ground cloves
- All-purpose flour, for dredging
- 2 large eggs, lightly beaten
- 2 cups coarse fresh bread crumbs
- Vegetable oil, for frying

1. In a small saucepan, boil the chicken stock until reduced to 1 cup, about 25 minutes. Add the heavy cream and simmer for 4 minutes. Remove from the heat and whisk in the Dijon mustard and thyme; season with salt and freshly ground black pepper.

2. Meanwhile, preheat the oven to 350°. Remove the sausage meat from its casing and break it up in a large bowl. In a small bowl, combine the garlic with the wine, allspice, cloves, ¼ teaspoon of salt and ½ teaspoon of black pepper. Pour the garlic mixture over the sausage and knead gently to incorporate. Shape the sausage into four 4½-inch-wide patties.

3. Put the flour, eggs and bread crumbs in 3 large, shallow bowls. Dredge the patties in the flour, patting off the excess. Dip them in the beaten egg, then coat with the bread crumbs.

4. In a large nonstick skillet, heat ¼ inch of vegetable oil. Add the patties and fry over moderately high heat until browned on the bottom, 4 minutes. Turn the patties and cook for 1 minute on the second side. Transfer the skillet to the oven and bake for 15 minutes, until the patties are cooked through. Set the skillet over high heat to brown the patties on the bottom, about 1 minute.

5. Gently reheat the mustard sauce. Set a patty on each plate, spoon some of the sauce around them and serve. Pass the remaining sauce separately. —Marcia Kiesel

WINE Melony white Bordeaux: 2009 Château Le Thil Comte Clary Blanc.

Pressure-Cooker Honey-Glazed Spareribs

ACTIVE: 15 MIN; TOTAL: 1 HR 30 MIN
4 SERVINGS ● ●

- ½ cup hoisin sauce
- ¼ cup soy sauce
- 1 tablespoon unsulfured molasses
- 3½ tablespoons coarsely chopped peeled fresh ginger
- 6 garlic cloves
- ¾ cup honey
- 1 tablespoon *sambal oelek* or Chinese chile-garlic sauce
- 2 racks pork spareribs or baby back ribs (4 pounds), halved lengthwise

1. In a blender, combine the hoisin with the soy sauce, molasses, ginger, garlic and ½ cup of the honey; puree until smooth. Add the *sambal oelek* and pulse to combine.

2. Cut the spareribs into 2 rib sections and transfer to a pressure cooker. Add the hoisin puree and let stand, turning the ribs occasionally, for 45 minutes.

3. Add ¼ cup of water to the cooker. Cover and cook at high pressure for 20 minutes.

4. Line a rimmed baking sheet with foil. Run cold water over the cooker to release the pressure. Transfer the ribs to the lined baking sheet, meaty side up. Boil the cooking juices until reduced to 2 cups, 5 minutes. Transfer the hoisin pan sauce to a bowl.

5. Preheat the broiler and position a rack 8 inches from the heat. Brush the ribs all over with the remaining ¼ cup of honey and broil, turning once, until the ribs are glazed and browned, about 5 minutes. Transfer the rib sections to a cutting board and slice them into individual ribs. Serve the ribs with the hoisin pan sauce. —Grace Parisi

WINE Juicy, black cherry–scented Australian Shiraz: 2010 Paringa.

Asian Fried and Glazed Baby Back Ribs

📷 PAGE 6

ACTIVE: 45 MIN; TOTAL: 1 HR 45 MIN
PLUS 4 HR CHILLING • 6 SERVINGS ●

These sticky ribs from L.A. chef Roy Choi are made with a mixture of staple Asian sauces, including hoisin, black bean and Sriracha.

- 2 racks baby back ribs (about 3 pounds each)
- Salt and freshly ground pepper
- ½ cup hoisin sauce
- ½ cup Chinese chile-garlic sauce
- ½ cup oyster sauce
- ½ cup fresh orange juice
- ¼ cup Chinese black bean sauce
- 1 tablespoon Sriracha
- Vegetable oil, for frying
- 4 scallions, very thinly sliced on the diagonal, and 2 tablespoons toasted sesame seeds, for garnish

1. Bring a large pot of water to a boil. Score the underside of the ribs, making 4 long, deep slits across the backs of the bones. Cut each rack in half and season with salt and pepper. Add the ribs to the boiling water and simmer over moderately low heat until tender, about 1 hour. Transfer the ribs to a rack set over a rimmed baking sheet and let cool, then refrigerate uncovered for at least 4 hours or overnight. Cut the racks into individual ribs and bring to room temperature.

2. In a medium bowl, combine the hoisin with the chile-garlic sauce, oyster sauce, orange juice, black bean sauce and Sriracha. Transfer the glaze to a wide, shallow dish.

3. Preheat the oven to 200°. In a large, deep skillet, heat 2½ inches of oil to 350°. Working in batches, fry the ribs until nicely browned and crisp, 3 minutes. Add the fried ribs to the glaze and turn to coat. Transfer the glazed ribs to a baking sheet and keep warm in the oven while you fry and glaze the remaining ribs. Transfer the ribs to a platter, garnish with the scallions and sesame seeds and serve. —Roy Choi

WINE Fruit-forward Shiraz from Australia's McLaren Vale: 2010 Mitolo Jester.

pressure-cooker honey-glazed spareribs

Paprika-and-Ancho-Rubbed Smoked Baby Back Ribs

📷 PAGE 167

ACTIVE: 2 HR; TOTAL: 5 HR

4 TO 6 SERVINGS

Two 3-pound racks pork baby back ribs
¼ cup plus 2 tablespoons Paprika-Ancho Spice Rub (recipe follows)
1 cup hardwood chips, soaked in water for 1 hour and drained

1. Using a kitchen towel, grasp a corner of the membrane on the underside of each rack and pull off the membrane. If necessary, cut the racks so that they will fit on your grill. Sprinkle the racks all over with the Paprika-Ancho Spice Rub and gently massage it into the meat. Let the racks stand at room temperature for 1 hour.

2. Meanwhile, light a charcoal fire in a starter chimney. Add the lit coals to a grill and set it up for indirect grilling: Carefully push the hot coals to one side and place a drip pan on the opposite side and fill it with water. Alternatively, add the lit coals to the firebox of a smoker. Scatter half of the soaked hardwood chips over the coals.

3. Arrange the rib racks on the grill over the drip pan. Cover the grill and cook for about 4 hours, maintaining a temperature of 225° to 250°, turning and rotating the ribs occasionally, until the rib racks are tender. Monitor the grill throughout the smoking process and add more lit coals, soaked hardwood chips and water to the drip pan as needed to maintain the temperature and smoke level. Cut the racks into ribs and serve.
—*Brian Perrone*

WINE Bold red blend from southern France: 2010 Eric Texier Côtes du Rhône.

PAPRIKA-ANCHO SPICE RUB

⏱ TOTAL: 5 MIN • MAKES 1 CUP ● ○

"The ideal rub should have enough spice that you notice it, but not so much that it overpowers the meat," says Brian Perrone, the chef at Slows Bar BQ in Detroit. He rubs this smoky-sweet spice blend on baby back pork ribs before loading them into the smoker.

⅓ cup light brown sugar
¼ cup sweet paprika
2 tablespoons kosher salt
1 tablespoon plus 1 teaspoon ancho chile powder
1 tablespoon dried oregano
1½ teaspoons ground allspice
1½ teaspoons cayenne pepper
1½ teaspoons ground cumin
1 teaspoon cinnamon

In a bowl, stir the ingredients together. —*BP*
MAKE AHEAD The rub can be kept in a jar at room temperature for up to 2 months.

Smoky Glazed Ham with Red Pepper Jelly

ACTIVE: 1 HR 20 MIN; TOTAL: 3 HR 30 MIN

8 TO 10 SERVINGS

3 cups chicken stock or low-sodium broth
2 cups cola, preferably GuS Dry Cola
1½ cups Pinot Noir or other dry red wine
½ cup turbinado sugar
½ cup buckwheat honey or other dark honey
¼ cup red wine vinegar
½ sweet onion, thinly sliced
½ cup thinly sliced fresh ginger (2 ounces)
1 carrot, thinly sliced
5 small dried red chiles
1½ teaspoons coriander seeds, crushed
1½ teaspoons fennel seeds, crushed
1½ teaspoons black peppercorns, crushed
One 8-pound bone-in smoked ham
Red Pepper Jelly (recipe follows), for serving

1. In a large saucepan, combine the chicken stock, cola, wine, sugar, honey, vinegar, onion, ginger, carrot, chiles and 3 cups of water and bring to a boil. Simmer over moderately high heat for 20 minutes. Add the coriander and fennel seeds and the peppercorns and simmer until reduced to 4½ cups, 15 to 20 minutes longer. Strain the sauce through a fine sieve into a heatproof bowl.

2. Meanwhile, preheat the oven to 375°. Set the ham skin side up in a 12-by-15-inch roasting pan and pour half of the sauce on top. Roast the ham for 1 hour, basting with the sauce in the pan every 15 minutes.

3. Pour the remaining sauce over the ham and roast for about 1 hour and 30 minutes longer, basting the ham every 15 minutes, until glazed and an instant-read thermometer inserted in the thickest part registers 120°. Transfer the ham to a carving board and let rest for 15 minutes. Discard the skin from the ham before slicing. Serve the ham with the Red Pepper Jelly. —*Jonathon Sawyer*
WINE Balanced, berry-rich Oregon Pinot Noir: 2011 Evesham Wood Willamette Valley.

RED PEPPER JELLY

TOTAL: 45 MIN PLUS 12 HR CHILLING

MAKES 5 CUPS ● ○

3 red bell peppers (1½ pounds), finely diced (⅛ inch)
2 Anaheim chiles (6 ounces), finely diced (⅛ inch)
4 cups sugar
1 cup white wine vinegar
½ teaspoon salt
One 3-ounce pouch of liquid fruit pectin (do not use low-sugar pectin; see Note)

1. In a large saucepan, combine the bell peppers, Anaheims, sugar, vinegar and salt and bring to a boil. Simmer over moderately high heat, stirring occasionally, until the peppers are softened, 20 to 25 minutes.

2. Increase the heat to high and quickly stir in the pectin. Boil for 1 minute, then remove from the heat. Using a wooden spoon, stir the mixture just until the foam subsides, then immediately ladle the jelly into a heatproof bowl or jars. Let cool completely, then cover and refrigerate until set, at least 12 hours.
—*JS*
NOTE Pectin is a natural, water-soluble substance used as a thickener. It is available at most supermarkets.
MAKE AHEAD The Red Pepper Jelly can be refrigerated for up to 3 weeks.

● HEALTHY   ● MAKE AHEAD   ● VEGETARIAN   ● STAFF FAVORITE

smoky glazed ham with red pepper jelly

Bollito Misto

**ACTIVE: 2 HR; TOTAL: 5 HR PLUS
OVERNIGHT BRINING • 20 SERVINGS** ●

In this classic Italian dish, chicken, beef brisket, pork shanks and garlic pork sausages are poached in a flavorful broth until tender.

SALTED AND BRINED MEATS
Two 4-pound chickens
2¾ **cups kosher salt**
1½ **cups sugar**
16 **dried hot red chiles**
6 **bay leaves**
4 **heads of garlic, halved horizontally**
2 **large white onions, sliced**
2 **tablespoons black peppercorns**
1½ **tablespoons coriander seeds**
1 **teaspoon fennel seeds**
1 **star anise pod, crushed**
**Eight 1¼-pound whole fresh pork
shanks or one 6-pound veal shank,
cut into 4 sections by the butcher**
One 6-pound beef brisket
BOLLITO
5 **pounds garlic pork sausages**
6 **celery ribs, cut into thirds**
6 **carrots, cut into thirds**
4 **heads of garlic, cloves smashed**
6 **dried hot red chiles**
6 **bay leaves**
3 **large onions, quartered**
2 **cups parsley**
1 **fennel bulb, thickly sliced**
One 1-ounce package thyme sprigs
1 **tablespoon black peppercorns**
1 **tablespoon coriander seeds**
2 **bottles dry white wine**

1. SALT AND BRINE THE MEATS In a baking dish, rub the chickens with ¼ cup of the salt. Cover and refrigerate overnight.

2. In a large pot, combine the remaining 2½ cups of salt and the sugar with 1 gallon of water and boil, stirring, until the salt and sugar dissolve, about 5 minutes. Turn off the heat and add the dried hot red chiles, bay leaves, garlic, onions, peppercorns, coriander seeds, fennel seeds and star anise. Add another 2 gallons of water, the shanks and the brisket and refrigerate overnight.

3. MAKE THE BOLLITO Rinse the chickens. Drain the brined meat and discard the garlic, onion and seasonings. Halve the brisket lengthwise along the grain, then divide the chicken, pork shanks, brisket and sausages between 2 pots. Divide the remaining ingredients between the pots and add enough water to cover the meats. Bring both pots to a boil, then reduce the heat and simmer until the chicken and sausages are cooked through, 1 hour; transfer to a roasting pan and cover loosely with foil.

4. Continue to simmer the *bollito* until the shanks and brisket are very tender, 1 hour and 20 minutes. Add the shanks and brisket to the roasting pan. Strain the broth; discard the vegetables and spices. Spoon off the fat. Return the chicken and sausages to the broth to rewarm.

5. Pull large pieces of meat from the shanks; discard bones. Thinly slice the brisket across the grain. Cut off the chicken thighs, drumsticks and wings; thickly slice the breast. Slice the sausages. Arrange the meats on platters and ladle broth on top to moisten. Serve the remaining broth with the meats, or reserve for another use. *—John Adler and Tamar Adler*
SERVE WITH Salsa Verde and Salsa Rossa (recipes follow).

WINE Firm, robust Cabernet Sauvignon: 2008 Mount Eden Domaine Eden.

SALSA VERDE

◌ **TOTAL: 15 MIN • MAKES 3 CUPS** ●

8 **oil-packed anchovy fillets**
4 **large garlic cloves**
2 **tablespoons drained capers**
4 **cups lightly packed flat-leaf parsley**
2 **cups extra-virgin olive oil**
3 **tablespoons fresh lemon juice**
Salt

In a food processor, pulse the anchovies, garlic and capers until finely chopped. Add the parsley and olive oil and pulse until the parsley is finely chopped. Stir in the lemon juice and season with salt. *—JA and TA*
MAKE AHEAD The Salsa Verde can be refrigerated for up to 3 days.

SALSA ROSSA

**ACTIVE: 40 MIN; TOTAL: 1 HR 15 MIN
MAKES 4 CUPS** ● ●

2 **cups oil-packed sun-dried
tomatoes (12 ounces), drained**
1¼ **cups red wine vinegar**
5 **large hot red chiles**
¾ **cup extra-virgin olive oil,
plus more for brushing**
2 **tablespoons minced garlic**
1 **medium sweet onion, thinly sliced**
2 **pounds ripe plum tomatoes,
peeled and chopped**
Pinch of sugar
Salt

1. In a medium saucepan, combine the sun-dried tomatoes, red wine vinegar and 1½ cups of water and bring to a boil. Remove the saucepan from the heat, cover and let stand until the tomatoes are very soft, about 1 hour. Drain the tomatoes, reserving ½ cup of the soaking liquid.

2. Meanwhile, preheat the broiler. Brush the chiles with olive oil and broil 6 inches from the heat, turning occasionally, until they are lightly charred all over, about 10 minutes. Transfer the chiles to a bowl, cover with plastic wrap and let stand until cool. Peel and seed the chiles.

3. In a medium, deep skillet, heat ½ cup of the olive oil. Add the garlic and cook over moderate heat until softened, about 2 minutes. Add the onion and cook until softened, about 5 minutes. Add the plum tomatoes and the sugar and cook until the liquid has evaporated and the tomatoes begin to break down, about 5 minutes.

4. Scrape the tomato-and-onion mixture into a food processor. Add the chiles, sun-dried tomatoes and the reserved ½ cup of soaking liquid and process until smooth. Strain the puree through a fine-mesh sieve to remove the tomato seeds. Stir the remaining ¼ cup of olive oil into the puree, season the salsa with salt and serve.
—JA and TA
MAKE AHEAD The Salsa Rossa can be refrigerated for up to 1 week.

● HEALTHY   ● MAKE AHEAD   ○ VEGETARIAN   ● STAFF FAVORITE

Spam-and-Kimchi Musubi

TOTAL: 1 HR • MAKES 2 DOZEN PIECES ●

"This is the peanut butter and jelly sandwich of Hawaii," says L.A. chef Roy Choi about the sushi-like *musubi:* seared Spam, sushi rice and pureed kimchi, all wrapped up in nori. "If you've been swimming, if you've been hanging on the beach, it's the perfect snack."

2 cups sushi rice, rinsed
Salt
¼ cup kimchi
1 tablespoon vegetable oil
One 12-ounce can of Spam, cut into
    8 slices
Four 8-by-7½-inch sheets of nori
1 tablespoon toasted sesame oil
Sriracha
1 scallion, thinly sliced, for garnish

1. In a large saucepan, cover the rinsed rice with 2 cups of water. Season with salt and bring to a boil. Cover and cook over low heat for 17 minutes. Uncover and place a clean kitchen towel over the pot. Replace the lid and let stand off the heat for 10 minutes. Fluff the rice and let cool slightly.
2. Meanwhile, add the kimchi and 1 tablespoon of water to a blender or mini food processor and puree.
3. Heat the oil in a large nonstick skillet. Add the Spam slices and cook them over moderate heat, turning once, until browned, about 4 minutes. Transfer to paper towels to drain.
4. Arrange 1 sheet of nori with the longer side facing you and rub with a little sesame oil. Mound ⅓ cup of the warm sushi rice on the bottom and pat into an 8-by-2-inch rectangle. Spread 1 scant tablespoon of the kimchi puree on the rice and top with 2 slices of Spam, then another ⅓ cup of the sushi rice. Fold up the rice in the nori, pressing it into a rectangle. Repeat with the remaining nori sheets, sesame oil, rice, kimchi puree and Spam; there may be a little rice left over. Using a sharp, moistened knife, cut each roll into 6 pieces, wiping the knife with a damp towel between slices. Arrange the *musubi* on a platter, dot with Sriracha, garnish with the sliced scallion and serve. —*Roy Choi*

Hungarian Sausage Stew with Ale

ACTIVE: 35 MIN; TOTAL: 1 HR
6 SERVINGS ●

Beer lends deep, rich flavor to this recipe for *lecsó* (LEH-tcho), a traditional sausage, tomato and bell pepper stew from Hungary.

8 ounces skinless slab bacon,
    sliced ¼ inch thick and cut into
    ¼-inch strips
1 large Vidalia onion, thinly sliced
3 large yellow bell peppers,
    thinly sliced
3 large garlic cloves, thinly sliced
12 ounces spicy Hungarian sausage
    (*kolbász*) or chorizo, thickly sliced
1½ teaspoons crushed red pepper
1 tablespoon sweet paprika
1¾ pounds plum tomatoes, coarsely
    chopped
1 cup red ale or lager
1 bay leaf
Kosher salt and freshly ground
    black pepper
Grilled sourdough bread, for serving

In a large enameled cast-iron casserole or Dutch oven, cook the bacon strips over moderately low heat, stirring occasionally, until lightly browned, about 8 minutes. Add the onion and cook over moderate heat, stirring, until very lightly browned, about 5 minutes. Stir in the bell peppers and garlic and cook, stirring occasionally, until lightly browned and softened, about 5 minutes longer. Stir in the sausage slices, crushed red pepper and paprika and cook for 2 minutes. Add the chopped tomatoes and cook until beginning to break down, about 5 minutes. Add the beer and bay leaf and bring to a boil. Cover partially and cook over low heat until the vegetables are very tender and the sauce is slightly reduced, about 15 minutes. Season the stew with salt and black pepper and serve with grilled sourdough bread.
—*Nicolaus Balla*

MAKE AHEAD The stew can be refrigerated for up to 3 days; reheat gently before serving.
BEER Rich, malty brown ale: Abita Turbodog.

Pressure-Cooker Veal Ragù

TOTAL: 50 MIN • 6 SERVINGS ● ●

⅓ cup dried porcini
¼ cup extra-virgin olive oil
2½ pounds trimmed boneless veal
    shoulder, cut into 1½-inch pieces
Salt and freshly ground pepper
¼ cup all-purpose flour
1 large carrot, finely diced
2 small onions, finely diced
2 garlic cloves, minced
6 sage leaves, finely chopped
¼ cup dry white wine
2 tablespoons white wine vinegar
½ cup beef stock or low-sodium broth
Polenta, noodles or crusty bread,
    for serving

1. In a microwave-safe bowl, cover the porcini with 1 cup of water. Cover and microwave at high power for 1 minute, until just softened. Drain, reserving the soaking liquid. Rinse and chop the mushrooms.
2. In a large skillet, heat 2 tablespoons of the oil. Season the veal with salt and pepper and dust with the flour, tapping off any excess. Add half of the veal to the skillet and cook over moderate heat, turning once or twice, until browned, about 8 minutes. Transfer the veal to the pressure cooker. Repeat with the remaining 2 tablespoons of oil and veal.
3. Add the carrot, onions, garlic, sage and porcini to the skillet and cook over low heat until slightly softened, 2 minutes. Add the wine and vinegar and scrape up any browned bits. Scrape the mixture into the pressure cooker. Add the stock and ½ cup of the porcini soaking liquid, stopping before you reach the grit at the bottom. Season lightly with salt and pepper; bring to a boil.
4. Cover and close the pressure cooker. Cook at moderately low heat, maintaining high pressure for 25 minutes. Gently release the pressure by depressing the valve or by running cold water over the top. Transfer the ragù to a bowl and serve over polenta, noodles or crusty bread. —*Grace Parisi*
WINE Powerful, full-bodied northern Italian white: 2011 Elena Walch Pinot Bianco.

Panko-Crusted Veal Chops with Sorrel Cream

ACTIVE: 25 MIN; TOTAL: 1 HR
4 SERVINGS ●

- 1 cup crème fraîche
- 2 cups packed sorrel leaves (4 ounces), stemmed and leaves sliced into ⅓-inch strips
- 1 tablespoon fresh lemon juice

Salt and freshly ground black pepper
All-purpose flour, for dredging

- 2 large eggs
- 1 tablespoon milk
- 1½ cups panko (Japanese bread crumbs)

Finely grated zest of 1 lemon
Four 1-inch-thick veal rib chops

- 3 tablespoons extra-virgin olive oil
- 3 tablespoons vegetable oil

1. Preheat the oven to 350°. In a small saucepan, simmer the crème fraîche over moderately low heat until reduced to ½ cup, about 15 minutes. Stir in the sorrel and lemon juice; simmer until the sorrel melts into the sauce, 5 minutes. Season the sorrel cream with salt and pepper; remove from the heat.
2. Put the flour in a shallow bowl. In another, beat the eggs with the milk. In a third, toss the panko and lemon zest. Season the chops with salt and pepper, dredge in the flour and shake off the excess. Dip the chops in the egg mixture; let the excess drip off, then coat with panko; press to help the crumbs adhere.
3. In a large skillet, heat both oils until shimmering. Add 2 of the veal chops and cook over moderately high heat until browned and crisp on the bottom, 2 minutes. Reduce the heat to moderate, turn the chops and cook until browned and crisp on the other side, 2 minutes. Transfer to a large rimmed baking sheet. Repeat with the remaining chops.
4. Bake the veal chops for 15 minutes, turning once, until an instant-read thermometer inserted near the bone registers 140°. Gently rewarm the sorrel cream. Place the veal chops on plates, spoon the sorrel cream on top and serve. —Amanda Hallowell
WINE Fragrant, light-bodied Beaujolais: 2010 Clos de la Roilette Fleurie.

Stuffed Veal Breast with Gigante Beans

TOTAL: 4 HR PLUS OVERNIGHT SOAKING AND MARINATING • 6 TO 8 SERVINGS

One 5-pound boneless trimmed veal breast
Salt and freshly ground black pepper

- 1½ tablespoons chopped rosemary, plus 2 rosemary sprigs

Two 1-inch-thick slices of peasant bread

- ¼ cup extra-virgin olive oil, plus more for brushing and drizzling
- 2 medium onions—1 thinly sliced, 1 sliced ½ inch thick
- 1 cup golden raisins
- 1 cup dry white wine
- 1 tablespoon plus 1 teaspoon chopped thyme, plus 2 thyme sprigs

One 2-ounce can anchovies, drained and minced
Pinch of crushed red pepper

- 6 unpeeled garlic cloves
- 6 plum tomatoes, halved
- 1 pound gigante beans or large lima beans, soaked overnight and drained
- 2 tablespoons chopped parsley
- 1 tablespoon fresh lemon juice

1. Lay the veal on a work surface, fat side down. Season the meaty side with 1 tablespoon of salt, 2 teaspoons of black pepper and the chopped rosemary. Fold the veal in half, wrap in plastic and refrigerate overnight.
2. Preheat the oven to 350°. Brush the bread with olive oil and bake for about 15 minutes, until crisp. Let the bread cool completely, then tear it into pieces and transfer to a food processor. Process to coarse crumbs.
3. In a large skillet, heat 2 tablespoons of the olive oil. Add the thinly sliced onion and a pinch of salt, cover and cook over moderately low heat, stirring a few times, until soft, about 8 minutes. Add the raisins, wine and 1 tablespoon of the chopped thyme and boil over moderate heat until the liquid is reduced to 2 tablespoons, about 5 minutes. Remove the skillet from the heat and stir in the anchovies, crushed red pepper and bread crumbs; season with salt.

4. Reduce the oven to 300°. Lay the veal on a work surface, fat side down. Spoon the bread stuffing down the center of the meat and roll up the breast. Tie the veal at 1-inch intervals. Season with salt and black pepper.
5. Heat a roasting pan over 2 burners on moderate heat. Add the remaining 2 tablespoons of olive oil; when the oil is hot, add the veal. Cook, turning, until browned all over, about 5 minutes. Add the thick onion slices, garlic cloves and thyme and rosemary sprigs and turn the veal seam side down. Add 3 cups of water and bring to a simmer. Cover with foil and bake in the middle of the oven for about 2 hours and 30 minutes, until an instant-read thermometer inserted in the thickest part of the meat registers 185°.
6. Meanwhile, arrange the halved tomatoes on a rimmed baking sheet, cut side up. Drizzle them with oil, season with salt and black pepper and sprinkle with the remaining 1 teaspoon of chopped thyme. Bake on the bottom rack of the oven for 1 hour, until soft.
7. Put the gigante beans in a large pot; add enough water to cover by 2 inches. Bring to a boil and simmer over low heat, stirring, until tender, 1 hour. Add more water as needed to maintain the water level. About 10 minutes before the beans are done, add a large pinch of salt. Drain the beans, transfer to a bowl and drizzle with olive oil; keep covered.
8. When the veal is done, transfer it to a work surface and cover loosely with foil. Strain the pan juices and aromatics through a coarse strainer set over a medium saucepan. Press on the solids to extract as much liquid as possible. Skim the fat from the juices and boil over high heat until reduced to 2 cups, 20 minutes. Season with salt and pepper.
9. Peel the roasted tomatoes and coarsely chop. Add the tomatoes to the beans with ½ cup of the veal jus. Add the parsley and lemon juice and season with salt and pepper.
10. Remove and discard the strings from the veal, slice and transfer to plates. Spoon the beans alongside and drizzle with more oil. Pass the remaining jus at the table.
—Cormac Mahoney
WINE Medium-bodied, peppery red from Austria: 2010 Ecker Zweigelt.

stuffed veal breast with gigante beans

Château Curé in France's Bordeaux region makes great wines to pair with hearty beef dishes like grilled hanger steak topped with garlic-brandy butter, OPPOSITE; recipe, page 196.

BEEF, LAMB & GAME

Latin Grilled Rib Eye Steak with Green Chile Aioli

ACTIVE: 40 MIN; TOTAL: 1 HR 20 MIN

2 SERVINGS ●

ADOBO RUB

- 2 tablespoons allspice berries
- 2 tablespoons black peppercorns
- 1 tablespoon cumin seeds

One 1½-inch cinnamon stick, broken

- 7 whole cloves
- 2 tablespoons sweet paprika
- 1 tablespoon chipotle powder
- 1 tablespoon ancho chile powder
- ¼ cup kosher salt
- ¼ cup sugar

One 1¼-pound bone-in rib eye steak (about 1½ inches thick)

GREEN CHILE AIOLI

- 4 large unpeeled garlic cloves
- 1 large poblano
- 3 tablespoons fresh lime juice
- 1 large egg yolk
- 1 serrano or jalapeño, chopped
- ½ teaspoon cumin seeds
- 1 cup cilantro leaves
- ½ cup vegetable oil, plus more for grilling

Salt

1. MAKE THE RUB In a small skillet, toast the allspice, peppercorns, cumin seeds, cinnamon and cloves over moderately high heat until fragrant. Transfer to a spice grinder and let cool completely. Grind to a powder and transfer to a small bowl. Stir in the paprika, chipotle and ancho powders, salt and sugar. Sprinkle 2 tablespoons of the adobo rub all over the rib eye and let stand at room temperature for 30 minutes.

2. MEANWHILE, MAKE THE AIOLI Preheat the oven to 350°. Wrap the garlic in foil and bake for about 30 minutes, until soft.

3. Over an open flame or under a preheated broiler, roast the poblano until charred all over; let cool. Peel, seed and stem the poblano and coarsely chop it, then transfer to a blender. Squeeze the soft garlic cloves from their skins into the blender. Add the lime juice, egg yolk, serrano, cumin and cilantro and puree. With the machine on, slowly pour in the ½ cup of vegetable oil until emulsified. Season the green chile aioli with salt.

4. Light a grill. Oil the grate. Grill the steak over moderately high heat for 6 minutes per side, until charred outside and medium-rare within. Let the steak rest for 5 minutes. Slice and serve with the aioli. —*Jose Garces*

MAKE AHEAD Any leftover adobo rub can be stored in an airtight container at room temperature for up to 1 month.

WINE Lush Washington state Merlot: 2010 Charles Smith Wines The Velvet Devil.

Quick-Aged Grilled Rib Eyes

ACTIVE: 45 MIN; TOTAL: 6 DAYS

2 SERVINGS ●

In this brilliant trick from his most recent book, *Modernist Cuisine at Home,* Nathan Myhrvold simulates the taste of weeks-old dry-aged beef by marinating fresh steaks in fish sauce for three days, then air-drying them for three more.

Two 12-ounce boneless rib eye steaks (1 inch thick)

1½ tablespoons Asian fish sauce

Kosher salt and ground pepper

1. In a resealable plastic bag, arrange the rib eye steaks in a single layer. Add the fish sauce and turn to coat. Seal the bag, pressing out as much air as possible. Refrigerate the steaks for 3 days.

2. Remove the steaks from the plastic bag and tightly wrap each one in a double layer of cheesecloth. Set the steaks on a rack set over a plate and refrigerate for 3 days.

3. Unwrap the steaks, discarding the cheesecloth. Let the steaks stand at room temperature for 30 minutes.

4. Light a grill or preheat a grill pan. Season the steaks with salt and pepper and grill them over high heat, turning once, until well browned outside and medium-rare within, about 8 minutes. Transfer the steaks to a cutting board and let rest for 5 minutes before serving. —*Nathan Myhrvold*

WINE Generous, blackberry-scented Shiraz: 2009 Kilikanoon Killerman's Run.

Southeast Asian Rib Eye Steaks

TOTAL: 30 MIN PLUS 2 HR MARINATING

4 SERVINGS ●

At the Spice Table in Los Angeles, chef Bryant Ng (an F&W Best New Chef 2012) uses his custom-made *sate* grill to cook outstanding dishes that pay homage to the Singaporean home cooking he grew up with as well as the Vietnamese flavors of his wife's heritage. Here he includes anchovies and dry mustard in the marinade for rib eye steaks, giving them a salty, almost umami-like flavor.

Four 1-inch-thick rib eye steaks (about 3½ pounds)

Salt

- 1 tablespoon plus 1 teaspoon dry mustard
- 1 tablespoon dark brown sugar
- 2 tablespoons warm water
- 10 anchovy fillets, minced
- 2 teaspoons onion powder
- 2 teaspoons garlic powder
- 2 teaspoons ground ginger
- 2 teaspoons freshly ground black pepper
- 1 teaspoon freshly ground white pepper

1. Season the rib eye steaks with salt and let them stand at room temperature for about 10 minutes.

2. In a small bowl, combine the dry mustard with the brown sugar and warm water and stir until the sugar is dissolved. Stir in the anchovies, onion powder, garlic powder, ginger, black pepper and white pepper.

3. Spread the paste on both sides of the steaks and refrigerate for 2 hours.

4. Let the steaks return to room temperature. Light a grill. Grill the steaks over moderately high heat for about 3 minutes per side, until they are nicely charred outside and medium-rare within. Let the steaks rest for about 5 minutes before serving. —*Bryant Ng*

SERVE WITH Sautéed bok choy.

WINE Cherry-rich Cabernet Sauvignon–based red blend from the Napa Valley: 2009 Chappellet Mountain Cuvée.

southeast asian rib eye steak

Grilled Skirt Steak with Green Sriracha

TOTAL: 1 HR • 20 SERVINGS ●

Los Angeles chef Susan Feniger purees poblano chiles, kaffir lime leaves and four kinds of herbs to create a green version of Sriracha to pair with slices of grilled skirt steak.

> 3 large poblano chiles
> 2 serrano chiles, stemmed
> 3 large peeled garlic cloves, smashed
> ½ cup thinly sliced fresh ginger
> One ½-inch piece of fresh turmeric (see Note), sliced, or ½ teaspoon ground turmeric
> 1 cup shredded unsweetened coconut
> 2 loose cups basil leaves
> 2 loose cups mint leaves
> 1½ cups snipped chives
> ½ cup chopped cilantro
> 4 kaffir lime leaves, shredded
> 1 lemongrass stalk— tender inner bulb, bottom 4 inches peeled and thinly sliced
> 1 cup canola oil, plus more for grilling
> 6 tablespoons fresh lime juice
> Kosher salt
> 5 pounds skirt steak, cut into 4-inch pieces

1. Roast the poblano chiles directly over a gas flame, turning, until charred and tender. Transfer to a bowl, cover with plastic wrap and let cool. Peel, core and seed the poblanos, then transfer to a blender. Add the serranos, garlic, ginger, turmeric, coconut, basil, mint, chives, cilantro, lime leaves and lemongrass and pulse to chop. With the machine on, add the 1 cup of oil and puree. Add the lime juice and season with salt.

2. Light a grill. Brush the steak with oil and season with salt. Oil the grill grates and grill the steak in batches over high heat, turning once or twice, until the meat is lightly charred and medium-rare, 5 to 6 minutes. Transfer the steak to a carving board and let rest for 5 minutes before slicing across the grain. Serve the steak with the green Sriracha.
—*Susan Feniger*

NOTE Fresh turmeric is available at Indian markets and at many Whole Foods stores.
MAKE AHEAD The steak can be grilled earlier in the day and refrigerated. The green Sriracha can be refrigerated for up to 3 days.
WINE Berry-rich California red blend: 2009 Clayhouse Adobe Red.

Grilled Skirt Steak with Poblano-Corn Sauce and Salsa

TOTAL: 30 MIN • 4 SERVINGS ●

In this ingenious recipe, grilled fresh corn and poblano chile are used in two ways: Half of the mixture gets pureed into a sauce that's served under slices of seared skirt steak, and the rest becomes a chunky salsa that's spooned on top.

> 2 ears of corn, husked
> 1 large poblano chile
> ¼ cup extra-virgin olive oil, plus more for grilling
> Salt and freshly ground pepper
> 1¾ pounds skirt steak, cut into 5-inch pieces

1. Light a grill or preheat a grill pan. Rub the corn and poblano lightly with oil and grill over high heat just until the corn is lightly browned and the poblano is lightly charred all over but still firm, about 3 minutes.

2. Peel and core the poblano, then finely dice it. Cut the kernels from the corn cobs. Transfer half of the poblano and corn to a blender. Add 2 tablespoons of the olive oil and 2 tablespoons of water and puree to a chunky sauce. Season with salt and pepper.

3. In a bowl, toss the remaining diced poblano and corn kernels with the remaining 2 tablespoons of oil; season with salt and pepper.

4. Rub the steaks with oil, season generously with salt and pepper and grill over high heat, turning once or twice, until lightly charred, 6 minutes. Transfer the steaks to a cutting board and let rest for 5 minutes, then thinly slice across the grain. Spoon the sauce onto plates and top with the steak. Spoon the salsa on the meat and serve. —*Grace Parisi*
WINE Black cherry–scented, concentrated Malbec: 2009 Catena.

Grilled Hanger Steak with Garlic-Brandy Butter

📷 PAGE 192

ACTIVE: 30 MIN; TOTAL: 50 MIN
4 SERVINGS ●

F&W's Marcia Kiesel created this dish with inexpensive but well-marbled hanger steak. She melts flavorful *persillade* butter (*persil* is French for "parsley") spiked with brandy over the charred beef.

> 6 tablespoons unsalted butter, softened
> 3 tablespoons chopped parsley
> 2 medium garlic cloves, minced
> 1 tablespoon Cognac or other brandy
> Kosher salt and freshly ground black pepper
> 3 tablespoons extra-virgin olive oil, plus more for brushing
> 3 large leeks, white and pale green parts only, sliced 1 inch thick
> 2 pounds trimmed hanger steaks

1. In a small bowl, mash the softened butter with the parsley, garlic and Cognac; season the garlic-brandy butter with salt and freshly ground pepper.

2. In a large skillet, heat the 3 tablespoons of olive oil. Add the leeks and season with salt. Cover and cook over moderately low heat, stirring occasionally, until the leeks are tender, about 10 minutes.

3. Light a grill or preheat a grill pan. Brush the hanger steaks with olive oil and season them with salt and freshly ground pepper. Grill the steaks over high heat, turning once, until they are nicely charred outside and medium-rare within, about 5 to 6 minutes per side. Transfer the grilled steaks to a carving board and let them rest for 5 minutes. Slice the steaks across the grain and spread the garlic-brandy butter all over the meat, letting it melt in. Serve with the leeks.
—*Marcia Kiesel*

MAKE AHEAD The garlic-brandy butter can be refrigerated overnight.
WINE Robust, smoky red Bordeaux from the St-Émilion region: 2008 Château La Grâce Dieu des Prieurs.

● HEALTHY ● MAKE AHEAD ● VEGETARIAN ● STAFF FAVORITE

grilled skirt steak with green sriracha

Grilled Short Ribs with Anchovy Vinaigrette

TOTAL: 30 MIN • 6 SERVINGS ●

"This type of dressing is in my blood," says New York chef Alex Raij. "It's like the chimichurri I grew up eating when visiting family in Argentina." The thinly sliced short ribs here are perfect for quick grilling—they take less than two minutes to cook. Ask your butcher to cut them flanken-style, or look for the ribs at Asian markets.

- 1 red bell pepper
- One 2-ounce tin of anchovies—
  - 1 tablespoon of oil reserved, fillets drained and minced
- 2 large garlic cloves, minced
- ¼ cup plus 1 tablespoon fresh lemon juice
- ½ teaspoon crushed red pepper
- 1 cup chopped flat-leaf parsley
- ¾ cup extra-virgin olive oil
- Salt and freshly ground black pepper
- 6 pounds flanken-cut beef short ribs (cut across the bones), about ¼ inch thick
- Vegetable oil, for rubbing

1. Light a grill. Grill the red bell pepper over high heat, turning frequently, until charred all over. When the pepper is cool enough to handle, discard the skin, seeds and stem. Thinly slice the pepper.

2. In a bowl, whisk the anchovies and their oil with the garlic, lemon juice and crushed red pepper. Stir in the parsley and olive oil and season with salt and black pepper. Stir in the sliced bell pepper.

3. Rub the ribs with vegetable oil and season with salt and black pepper. Grill over high heat until nicely charred and cooked to medium, about 50 seconds per side. Serve the ribs right away, passing the vinaigrette at the table. —*Alex Raij*

SERVE WITH Crusty bread.

MAKE AHEAD The anchovy vinaigrette can be covered and refrigerated overnight. Bring to room temperature before serving.

WINE Lively, juicy Garnacha: 2010 Bodegas Nekeas Vega Sindoa El Chaparral.

Sweet-and-Salty Korean Barbecued Short Ribs

TOTAL: 30 MIN PLUS OVERNIGHT MARINATING • 4 SERVINGS ●

"Some people follow Texas or American barbecue. Me, I'm a connoisseur of Korean barbecue," says L.A. chef Roy Choi. He especially loves these thinly sliced short ribs, known as *kalbi* in Korea, that are a staple at Hawaiian plate-lunch joints; they're marinated overnight in a garlic, soy sauce and sugar mixture, then quickly grilled, so they're charred all over. On the side, Choi serves kimchi, steamed white rice and the ubiquitous Hawaiian side dish, macaroni salad.

- 1 small onion, coarsely chopped
- 4 scallions, coarsely chopped
- ½ cup peeled garlic cloves
- 1 cup soy sauce
- 1 cup fresh orange juice
- ½ cup mirin
- ½ cup toasted sesame oil
- ¼ cup sugar
- 2 tablespoons toasted sesame seeds
- 3 pounds thinly sliced bone-in beef short ribs (*kalbi* or flanken-style)
- Vegetable oil, for brushing
- Steamed white rice, macaroni salad and kimchi, for serving (optional)

1. In a blender, puree the onion, scallions, garlic, soy sauce, orange juice, mirin, sesame oil, sugar and sesame seeds until smooth. Transfer the marinade to a large baking dish. Add the short ribs and turn to coat. Cover and refrigerate overnight. Bring the short ribs to room temperature before cooking.

2. Preheat the oven to 200°. Light a grill or preheat a grill pan and brush with vegetable oil. Working in batches, grill the short ribs over high heat, turning once, until nicely browned and charred in spots, about 2 minutes per side. Transfer the ribs to a rimmed baking sheet and keep warm in the oven while you grill the remaining ribs. Serve with white rice, macaroni salad and kimchi. —*Roy Choi*

WINE Ripe, dark-cherry fruit–inflected Malbec: 2011 Viña Cobos Felino.

Grilled Beef Ribs with Smoky-Sweet Barbecue Sauce

ACTIVE: 45 MIN; TOTAL: 2 HR 30 MIN 8 SERVINGS ●

RIBS
- 15 pounds beef back rib racks— membrane removed, racks cut into individual ribs (about 25 ribs)
- 1 liter Coca-Cola
- 1½ teaspoons whole black peppercorns
- Kosher salt

SAUCE
- 1 cup dark brown sugar
- 1 cup ketchup
- ½ cup cider vinegar
- ½ cup canned tomato sauce
- ½ cup unsulfured molasses
- ¼ cup tomato paste
- 2 tablespoons hot sauce
- 2 tablespoons liquid smoke
- 1 tablespoon onion powder
- 1 tablespoon garlic powder
- 1 tablespoon Worcestershire sauce
- 1½ teaspoons yellow mustard
- 1½ teaspoons pure ancho chile powder

1. COOK THE RIBS Put the beef ribs in a very large pot or roasting pan; add the Coca-Cola and about 1 quart of water, enough to just cover the ribs. Bring the liquid to a boil, skimming off any scum from the surface. Add the peppercorns and 1 tablespoon of salt. Cover and simmer over low heat until the meat is tender but not falling off the bone, about 2 hours; drain the ribs.

2. MEANWHILE, MAKE THE SAUCE In a medium saucepan, combine all of the sauce ingredients and bring to a boil. Simmer over very low heat, stirring frequently, until thick and glossy, about 15 minutes.

3. Light a grill or preheat the broiler. Working in batches, arrange the ribs on baking sheets and brush them with the sauce. Grill the ribs or broil 10 inches from the heat, turning and brushing with sauce, until lightly charred, 12 minutes. Serve with the remaining sauce. —*David Burtka*

WINE Robust Washington state Syrah: 2007 Chateau Ste. Michelle Canoe Ridge Estate.

● HEALTHY ● MAKE AHEAD ● VEGETARIAN ● STAFF FAVORITE

grilled short ribs with anchovy vinaigrette

BEST VALUE CUTS OF BEEF

Jeremy Stanton of the Meat Market in Great Barrington, Massachusetts, shares recipes for his favorite cuts from the chuck, which are just as delicious as pricey premium steaks.

TERES MAJOR

Beef Medallions with Bacon and Morels

⏱ TOTAL: 35 MIN • 4 SERVINGS

  8 slices of bacon
Two 1-pound beef teres majors, cut into 8 medallions
Salt and freshly ground pepper
  2 tablespoons vegetable oil
16 fresh morels, rinsed, or dried morels—soaked in boiling water for 30 minutes, drained and rinsed
  4 large scallions, cut into ½-inch lengths
½ cup Madeira
¾ cup mushroom stock or low-sodium broth
  2 tablespoons cold unsalted butter

Wrap a slice of bacon around each beef medallion and secure with toothpicks. Season with salt and pepper. In a skillet, heat the oil until shimmering. Add the medallions and cook over moderately high heat until browned on the bottom, 2 minutes; turn and cook for 1 minute. Add the morels and scallions and cook over moderate heat until the scallions are tender. Transfer the meat to a plate. Cook the vegetables for 2 minutes more, add the Madeira and simmer for 2 minutes. Add the meat and stock and simmer over moderately low heat, turning, until an instant-read thermometer inserted in the center of the meat registers 140°, about 3 minutes. Transfer the meat to plates; discard the toothpicks. Remove the skillet from the heat and swirl in the butter. Season with salt and pepper, spoon over the meat and serve.
WINE Tart cherry–inflected, earthy Barolo: 2007 Boroli.
CARROT-AND-ONION VARIATION Substitute 2 medium carrots that have been cut into 1-inch matchsticks and 1 halved and sliced medium onion for the morels and scallions; ½ cup dry white wine for the Madeira; and ¾ cup beef stock for the mushroom stock. Garnish with parsley.

teres major
*This ultra-lean steak, sometimes referred to as the **mock tender**, sits on the shoulder blade. Its similarity to the tenderloin makes it a great substitute for filet mignon.*

chuck eye roast
This 2- to 4-pound roast comes from the chuck portion of the rib eye muscle. Ask the butcher to trim connective tissue and tie the meat for uniform cooking.

flat iron steak
*Great for marinating and grilling, the flat iron sits on the shoulder blade next to the teres major—in fact, it's known as a **blade steak** when sliced against the grain.*

CHUCK EYE ROAST

Beef Chuck Eye Roast with Paprika-Herb Rub
ACTIVE: 25 MIN; TOTAL: 1 HR 45 MIN • 8 SERVINGS

- 1 tablespoon ground bay leaves
- 1 tablespoon freshly ground pepper
- 1 tablespoon chopped thyme
- 2 teaspoons sweet paprika
- ½ teaspoon ground cumin
- One 3-pound chuck eye roast
- Extra-virgin olive oil, for drizzling
- Salt
- 4 garlic cloves, minced
- 3 tablespoons vegetable oil

1. Preheat the oven to 375°. In a small bowl, mix the bay leaves, pepper, thyme, paprika and cumin. Drizzle the roast generously with olive oil and season with salt. Rub the garlic and the spice mixture over the roast and let stand for 10 minutes.

2. Using butcher's twine, tie the roast to give it a uniform shape. In an ovenproof skillet, heat the vegetable oil. Add the roast and cook over moderate heat until lightly browned all over, 12 minutes.

3. Transfer the skillet to the upper third of the oven and roast the meat for 1 hour, until an instant-read thermometer inserted in the center registers 130°. Transfer the roast to a carving board and let rest for 10 minutes. Discard the twine. Using a thin, sharp knife, thinly slice the beef across the grain and serve.

WINE Herb-and-cassis-scented Cabernet Sauvignon: 2009 Buehler.

SUMAC-ROSEMARY RUB VARIATION Combine ¼ cup dried ground sumac (available online at *penzeys.com*), 2 tablespoons chopped rosemary leaves, 1 tablespoon freshly ground pepper and 4 minced garlic cloves; rub all over the roast with a small amount of olive oil.

FLAT IRON STEAK

Lemon-and-Garlic-Marinated Flat Iron Steak
TOTAL: 30 MIN PLUS 24 HR MARINATING • 2 SERVINGS

- One 1-pound beef flat iron steak
- Salt and freshly ground pepper
- 2 tablespoons extra-virgin olive oil
- 6 garlic cloves, minced
- 4 scallions, chopped
- 4 bay leaves, broken into pieces
- 2 lemons, very thinly sliced
- Vegetable oil, for the grill

In a glass baking dish, season the steak with salt and pepper and rub with the olive oil. Spread the garlic, scallions and bay leaves all over the steak. Cover both sides of the steak with lemon slices. Cover and refrigerate for 24 hours. Light a grill and brush with vegetable oil. Scrape off the seasonings and bring the steak to room temperature. Season with salt and pepper and grill over moderately high heat until medium-rare within, 3½ minutes per side. Transfer the steak to a carving board and let rest for 5 minutes. Thinly slice across the grain and serve.

WINE Juicy, berried Syrah: 2010 Amavi Cellars.

RED WINE MARINADE VARIATION In a resealable plastic bag, combine ¼ cup extra-virgin olive oil, 3 tablespoons red wine vinegar, ½ teaspoon crushed red pepper and ¼ cup chopped parsley; add the steak seasoned with salt and pepper to the bag and refrigerate for at least 6 hours and up to 12 hours.

Roast Beef with Oven-Roasted Tomato Salsa

ACTIVE: 30 MIN; TOTAL: 2 HR 45 MIN
8 SERVINGS ●

This roast beef browns beautifully because of the sugar in the mustard-seed crust, which helps the meat caramelize. The salsa, made with oven-roasted plum tomatoes, is a great sauce, though you can serve the beef with a drizzle of balsamic instead.

SALSA

- 3 pounds plum tomatoes, sliced crosswise ⅓ inch thick
- 1 tablespoon extra-virgin olive oil

Kosher salt and freshly ground pepper

- 2 teaspoons whole thyme leaves, plus 2 teaspoons chopped
- 2 tablespoons chopped parsley
- 2 tablespoons aged balsamic vinegar

BEEF

- ½ tablespoon yellow mustard seeds
- ½ tablespoon coriander seeds
- ¼ teaspoon allspice berries
- 1½ teaspoons sugar

Kosher salt

One 2¾-pound beef eye of round roast, trimmed of all visible fat

- 1 tablespoon vegetable oil

Watercress, for garnish

1. PREPARE THE SALSA Preheat the oven to 250°. On 2 large rimmed baking sheets, toss the plum tomato slices with the olive oil. Arrange the slices in a single layer, season with salt and pepper and sprinkle with the whole thyme leaves. Bake the tomatoes for about 1 hour and 30 minutes, until they are very firm and partially dried; rotate the sheets halfway through baking. Let the tomatoes cool slightly, then coarsely chop them.
2. In a bowl, combine the chopped tomatoes, chopped thyme, parsley and the balsamic vinegar. Season with salt and pepper.
3. PREPARE THE BEEF In a small skillet, toast the mustard and coriander seeds with the allspice berries over moderate heat until fragrant and lightly browned, about 1½ minutes. Transfer to a spice grinder and let cool completely, then grind to a powder. Stir in

the sugar and 1½ teaspoons of salt. Rub the spice mixture all over the roast and let stand at room temperature for about 30 minutes, turning occasionally.
4. Preheat the oven to 400°. In an ovenproof skillet just large enough to hold the roast, heat the vegetable oil until shimmering. Add the beef and cook over moderate heat until browned all over, about 3 minutes per side. Transfer the skillet to the oven. Cook the roast, turning a few times, for about 30 minutes, until an instant-read thermometer inserted in the center registers 120° for rare. Transfer the roast to a carving board to rest for 15 minutes.
5. Thinly carve the roast beef across the grain and arrange on a platter. Garnish with the watercress and serve with the tomato salsa. —*Naomi Pomeroy*

SERVE WITH Boiled new potatoes.
WINE Concentrated Oregon Pinot Noir: 2009 Anne Amie Vineyard Willamette Valley.

Beef and Radish Rolls with Buttermilk Dunk

TOTAL: 30 MIN PLUS CHILLING
6 SERVINGS

- 8 ounces radishes, thinly sliced
- ¼ cup white wine vinegar
- 2 tablespoons sugar
- 1 tablespoon kosher salt
- 2 tablespoons light mayonnaise
- 1 cup buttermilk
- ½ teaspoon freshly ground pepper
- ¼ teaspoon celery salt
- 1½ pounds sliced roast beef
- ½ cup cilantro sprigs
- 1 head of green-leaf lettuce, leaves separated

1. Put the radishes in a heatproof bowl. In a small saucepan, combine the vinegar, sugar, salt and ¼ cup of water and simmer until the sugar and salt are dissolved. Pour the warm brine over the radishes, weight them down with a plate and let stand for 10 minutes. Drain the radishes, reserving 2 tablespoons of the brine. Refrigerate the pickled radishes until chilled.

2. In a small bowl, whisk the reserved radish brine with the mayonnaise, buttermilk, pepper and celery salt.
3. Roll the roast beef, cilantro sprigs and pickled radishes in the lettuce leaves and transfer to a platter. Divide the buttermilk dunk between 6 small bowls for dipping and serve. —*Grace Parisi*

WINE Vibrant, blueberry-inflected Dolcetto: 2010 Anna Maria Abonna Sorí dij But.

Balsamic-Marinated Flank Steak

TOTAL: 30 MIN PLUS 4 HR MARINATING
8 SERVINGS

- 2 garlic cloves, sliced
- 1 tablespoon rosemary leaves
- 1 tablespoon dried oregano
- 2 tablespoons whole-grain mustard
- ½ cup balsamic vinegar
- 1 cup extra-virgin olive oil, plus more for grilling

Kosher salt and freshly ground pepper
One 3-pound flank steak

1. In a blender, combine the garlic, rosemary, oregano, mustard and vinegar and puree until the garlic is minced. With the machine on, gradually add the 1 cup of oil; blend until creamy. Season lightly with salt and pepper.
2. Place the meat in a glass or ceramic baking dish and pour all but ¼ cup of the vinaigrette on top; turn the meat to coat. Cover with plastic wrap and refrigerate for at least 4 hours and up to 24 hours.
3. Light a grill and oil the grates. Remove the steak from the marinade, letting the excess drip off. Season with salt and pepper. Grill the steak over moderate heat, turning occasionally, until the meat is lightly charred and an instant-read thermometer inserted in the thickest part registers 125°, 10 to 12 minutes. Transfer the steak to a carving board and let it rest for 5 minutes. Thinly slice the meat against the grain and serve, passing the remaining vinaigrette at the table to drizzle over the steak. —*Grace Parisi*

WINE Spicy Portuguese red: 2010 Quinta do Vallado Quadrifolia.

roast beef with oven-roasted tomato salsa

Red-Wine-Braised Beef Shanks

ACTIVE: 35 MIN; TOTAL: 4 HR 30 MIN PLUS 24 HR MARINATING • 8 SERVINGS ● ●

Chef Michael Mina of San Francisco's Michael Mina restaurant loves beef shanks because the marrow in the bones creates the most amazing braising juices.

1	bottle dry red wine, such as Côtes du Rhône
1	cup ruby port
8	large garlic cloves, smashed and peeled
2	celery ribs, cut into ½-inch dice
2	carrots, cut into ½-inch dice
1	large onion, cut into ½-inch dice
2	large thyme sprigs
1	bay leaf

Eight 14-ounce meaty beef shanks, cut 2 inches thick

¼ cup vegetable oil

Salt and freshly ground black pepper

2 tablespoons tomato paste

6 cups low-sodium beef broth

Parsley sprigs, for garnish

1. In a large roasting pan or 2-gallon resealable plastic bag, combine the wine, port, garlic, celery, carrots, onion, thyme and bay leaf. Add the beef shanks and turn to coat with the marinade. Refrigerate for 24 hours.
2. Preheat the oven to 300°. Remove the beef shanks from the marinade and pat them dry. Strain the marinade into a bowl, reserving the vegetables and marinating liquid.
3. In each of 2 large skillets, heat 1 tablespoon of the oil until shimmering. Season the shanks with salt and pepper and add 4 to each skillet. Cook over high heat until browned, 3 minutes per side. Transfer the shanks to a large roasting pan and arrange them in a single layer.
4. Add the remaining 2 tablespoons of vegetable oil to the skillets. Divide the vegetables between the skillets and cook them over moderate heat, stirring, until they start to brown, about 4 minutes. Stir 1 tablespoon of tomato paste into each skillet and cook for 1 minute. Add 3 cups of beef broth to each skillet and bring to a boil, scraping up

the browned bits from the bottom. Pour the vegetables, broth and reserved marinade over the shanks and cover the roasting pan with aluminum foil.
5. Braise the shanks for 2½ hours, until just tender. Uncover and braise for 30 minutes longer, until the shanks are glazed on top. With a spatula, transfer the shanks to a large rimmed baking sheet; cover with foil.
6. Strain the braising liquid through a coarse sieve set over a large saucepan, pushing the vegetables through as much as possible. Skim the fat off the sauce and boil the sauce over high heat until reduced to 4 cups, about 35 minutes. Season with salt and pepper.
7. Return the shanks to the roasting pan and pour the sauce over and around them. Cover with foil and simmer over moderate heat for a few minutes to rewarm the shanks. Transfer the shanks to serving plates, spoon the sauce on top, garnish with parsley and serve. —*Michael Mina*

MAKE AHEAD The braised shanks can be prepared through Step 6 and refrigerated for up to 3 days. Skim off any fat, return to room temperature, cover and reheat in a 325° oven for about 25 minutes, or until heated through.
WINE Bold, tannic California red: 2008 Buena Vista Winery The Count.

Beef Tenderloin with Parmesan-Prosciutto Crisps

ACTIVE: 40 MIN; TOTAL: 2 HR 12 SERVINGS

½	pound thinly sliced prosciutto
1	tablespoon each of chopped thyme and rosemary
1½	teaspoons chopped sage
½	cup panko bread crumbs, crushed
1	cup freshly grated Parmigiano-Reggiano cheese
¼	cup extra-virgin olive oil

Salt and freshly ground pepper

One 4- to 4½-pound trimmed and tied beef tenderloin roast

4	tablespoons unsalted butter
2	shallots, minced
¾	cup ruby port
1	cup beef demiglace

1. Tear two 12-inch-long sheets of wax paper. On each sheet, arrange half of the prosciutto slices to form a 12-by-6-inch rectangle, overlapping the slices slightly. Transfer to 2 large, flat cookie sheets.
2. In a bowl, combine the thyme, rosemary and sage with the panko, grated cheese and 3 tablespoons of the olive oil; season with salt and pepper. Pat the herbed crumbs evenly over the prosciutto. Place a sheet of plastic wrap on top of each rectangle and, using a rolling pin, press the crumbs onto the prosciutto. Freeze the prosciutto crusts for 10 minutes, until firm.
3. Preheat the oven to 425°. Cut the beef tenderloin into 2 even roasts and season them with salt and pepper. In a large skillet, heat the remaining 1 tablespoon of olive oil. Add the roasts and cook them over moderately high heat until they are lightly browned all over, about 6 minutes. Transfer the roasts to a baking sheet and let them cool.
4. Add 2 tablespoons of the butter to the skillet along with the shallots and cook over moderate heat until they are softened, about 3 minutes. Add the port and simmer over moderately low heat until syrupy, scraping up any browned bits, about 6 minutes. Add the beef demiglace and simmer until slightly reduced, about 5 minutes, then swirl in the remaining 2 tablespoons of butter.
5. Invert the prosciutto crusts onto a work surface and gently peel off the wax paper. Place the crusts over the roasts, prosciutto side down. Discard the plastic wrap. Roast the meat for about 40 minutes, or until an instant-read thermometer inserted in the thickest part registers 130° for medium-rare. Let the roasts rest for 20 minutes.
6. Meanwhile, remove the prosciutto crusts from the roasts and place them on a baking sheet, crumb side up. Press to flatten and bake for 6 to 7 minutes, just until the crumbs are golden and the prosciutto is crispy. Let cool, then break the crusts into shards. Rewarm the sauce. Cut the roast into slices and serve with the Parmesan-prosciutto crisps and the sauce. —*Grace Parisi*
WINE Robust California red blend: NV Marietta Old Vine #58.

● HEALTHY ● MAKE AHEAD ● VEGETARIAN ● STAFF FAVORITE

Beef Stroganoff

⏱ TOTAL: 45 MIN • 6 SERVINGS

"In my quest to be a chef, I first attempted beef Stroganoff at age 12, with a recipe from a cookbook," says Jonathan Waxman, the 1970s California cooking pioneer and chef-owner of New York City's Barbuto. "This version is more luxurious: I make it with beef tenderloin and crème fraîche."

    4 tablespoons unsalted butter
    1 large onion, thinly sliced
    1 pound white mushrooms, sliced
Salt and freshly ground pepper
    2 tablespoons Cognac
    1 cup chicken stock
    ½ cup crème fraîche
    1 tablespoon Dijon mustard
    2 tablespoons extra-virgin olive oil
    1¼ pounds beef tenderloin,
       sliced ¼ inch thick and cut into
       2-by-½-inch strips

1. In each of 2 large skillets, melt 1½ tablespoons of the butter. Add the onion to one skillet and the mushrooms to the other. Season both with salt and pepper and cook over high heat until the onion is softened and the mushrooms are browned and tender, about 5 minutes. Off the heat, add the Cognac to the mushrooms. Cook over high heat until evaporated, about 10 seconds. Add the mushrooms to the onion and wipe out the skillet. Add the stock to the mushrooms and boil until nearly evaporated, 5 minutes. Stir in the crème fraîche and mustard and simmer until thickened, about 5 minutes; keep warm.

2. In the empty skillet, melt the remaining butter in the oil. Season the meat with salt and pepper and add it to the hot skillet. Cook over high heat, turning once, until lightly browned in spots but still rare, about 2 minutes. Scrape the meat and any juices into the mushroom sauce and simmer just until heated through, 1 minute. Serve right away. —Jonathan Waxman

SERVE WITH Rice pilaf or noodles.

WINE Balanced, raspberry-scented Tuscan red: 2009 Antinori Santa Cristina.

Chicken-Fried Steak with Redeye Curry Gravy

⏱ TOTAL: 40 MIN • 4 SERVINGS ●

    1 large egg, lightly beaten
    ½ cup milk
    1½ cups all-purpose flour
Salt and freshly ground pepper
Twelve ¼-inch-thick slices of top-round
       beef (about 18 ounces)
Vegetable oil
    1 small onion, thinly sliced
    2 garlic cloves, minced
    1 tablespoon minced fresh ginger
    1 tablespoon mild Madras
       curry powder
    1½ tablespoons Sriracha
    ½ cup strong-brewed coffee
One 13-ounce can unsweetened
       coconut milk
    2 tablespoons lime juice,
       plus lime wedges for serving
    1½ teaspoons sugar

1. In a pie plate, whisk the egg with the milk. In another pie plate, generously season the flour with salt and pepper. Dredge the beef in the flour, tap off the excess, then dip in the egg. Dredge again in the flour; lightly pat the coating to help it adhere.

2. In a large cast-iron skillet, heat ½ inch of oil until shimmering. Working in 2 batches, fry the steak over moderate heat, turning once, until golden and crispy, 5 minutes. Drain on paper towels; season lightly with salt.

3. Pour the cooking oil into a heatproof cup; wipe out the skillet. Return 2 tablespoons of the oil to the skillet; cook the onion, garlic and ginger over moderate heat, stirring, until softened and browned, 5 minutes. Add the curry powder and Sriracha; cook, stirring, for 2 minutes. Add the coffee; boil until reduced by half, 3 minutes. Add the coconut milk, lime juice and sugar, season with salt and pepper and simmer until thickened, 5 minutes.

4. Put the chicken-fried steaks in shallow bowls. Top with the curry gravy and serve with lime wedges. —Dale Talde

WINE Spicy, coffee-scented Argentinean Syrah: 2010 Elsa Bianchi.

Caprese Burgers

⏱ TOTAL: 30 MIN • 6 SERVINGS

In this play on the classic Italian salad, F&W's Grace Parisi kneads basil pesto into ground beef before grilling the patties. She then tops the burgers with fresh mozzarella, sliced tomatoes and even more pesto.

    2 cups basil leaves
    ¼ cup salted roasted almonds
    1 garlic clove
    ½ cup extra-virgin olive oil, plus
       more for brushing
    ¼ cup grated Pecorino Romano
       cheese
Salt and freshly ground pepper
    1 pound ground beef chuck
    1 pound ground beef sirloin
    8 ounces fresh mozzarella, cut into
       6 slices
    6 brioche hamburger buns, split
    2 tomatoes, sliced

1. In a food processor, combine the basil with the almonds and garlic and pulse until the almonds are finely chopped. Add the ½ cup of olive oil and process to a paste. Add the grated Pecorino and pulse to combine. Season the pesto with salt and pepper. You should have about 1 cup.

2. Transfer ¼ cup of the pesto to a bowl. Add the ground chuck and ground sirloin and a pinch of salt and gently knead to blend. Form the mixture into six 4-inch patties, about ¾ inch thick. Brush the burger patties lightly with olive oil.

3. Light a grill and oil the grates. Grill the burgers over moderately high heat for 3 minutes. Flip the burgers, top them with the mozzarella slices and close the grill. Cook for 3 minutes longer for medium-rare burgers. Grill the buns until lightly toasted, then spread some of the pesto on the bottoms. Top with the burgers, the tomato slices and the remaining pesto. Close the burgers and serve right away. —Grace Parisi

MAKE AHEAD The pesto can be refrigerated for up to 3 days.

WINE Juicy, medium-bodied Piedmontese red: 2010 Tintero Rosso.

Short Rib Burgers
with Shallot–Red Wine Jam

⏱ **TOTAL: 45 MIN • 4 SERVINGS** ●

At Chicago's Blackbird restaurant, chef Paul Kahan cooks his delectable burgers sous vide before grilling them. He also makes his own American cheese. Here, the burgers are grilled and topped with deli cheese.

1 tablespoon unsalted butter, plus more for brushing
2 medium shallots, thinly sliced
1 cup dry red wine
1 tablespoon honey
1 teaspoon red wine vinegar
Pinch of herbes de Provence
Pinch of crushed red pepper
Salt
14 ounces ground chuck
14 ounces ground short ribs (ask your butcher to do this)
Vegetable oil, for brushing
4 brioche burger buns, split
8 slices of deli-quality American cheese (about 4 ounces)

1. In a saucepan, melt the 1 tablespoon of butter. Add the shallots and cook over moderate heat, stirring occasionally, until lightly browned and tender, 5 minutes. Add the red wine, honey, vinegar, herbes de Provence and crushed red pepper; cook over moderately low heat, stirring occasionally, until a thick jam forms, 15 minutes. Season with salt.

2. Meanwhile, lightly mix the ground meats. Divide into 4 mounds and pack loosely into 5-inch patties. Season generously with salt and make a slight depression in the center of each burger to help the patties retain their shape while they cook.

3. Light a grill or preheat a grill pan; brush with oil. Brush the cut sides of the buns with butter and grill until toasted. Grill the burgers over high heat until browned and crusty, about 4 minutes. Flip the burgers and cook for 2 minutes longer. Top with the cheese, cover the grill and let the cheese melt, about 1 minute. Transfer the burgers to the buns and top with the shallot jam. Close the burgers and serve. —*Paul Kahan*

MAKE AHEAD The shallot jam can be refrigerated for up to 5 days. Bring to room temperature before serving.

WINE Bold, spicy Australian Shiraz: 2010 Torbreck Woodcutter's.

Smoked-Gouda-and-Bacon
Burgers with Barbecue Sauce

ACTIVE: 40 MIN; TOTAL: 1 HR 40 MIN
4 SERVINGS

Brian Perrone, the chef at Slows Bar BQ in Detroit, was reluctant to put a burger on the menu because he wanted to focus on barbecue. At the insistence of his partners, he came up with this patty melt–style burger topped with Gouda, sweet house-made barbecue sauce and hot sauce–spiked onions. He's glad he did: It was an instant hit.

2 tablespoons vegetable oil
One 1-pound onion, halved and thinly sliced
Salt
¼ cup Frank's RedHot or other hot sauce
¼ cup beef broth
6 tablespoons unsalted butter, softened
Eight ½-inch-thick slices of firm white bread
8 slices of thick-cut bacon
2 pounds ground beef chuck (20 percent fat), formed into 4 patties the same size as the bread slices
3 ounces smoked Gouda, shredded (1 cup)
¼ cup Sweet Barbecue Sauce (recipe follows)

1. In a large skillet, heat the vegetable oil. Add the sliced onion and a pinch of salt, cover and cook, stirring a few times, until the onion is crisp-tender and just turning translucent, about 5 minutes. Stir in the hot sauce and beef broth and remove from the heat. Season with salt.

2. Heat a large griddle. Spread the butter on 1 side of each bread slice and griddle buttered side down over moderate heat until toasted, about 2 minutes. Transfer the toasts to a plate. Add the bacon to the griddle and cook over moderate heat until crisp, about 4 minutes per side; drain on paper towels. Wipe off the griddle.

3. Season the beef patties with salt and cook on the griddle over moderately high heat until medium-rare, about 2 minutes per side. Top each burger with ¼ cup of the shredded smoked Gouda and cook until the cheese melts, 1 minute.

4. Set the burgers on the unbuttered sides of 4 toasts. Top with the bacon, onion and Sweet Barbecue Sauce. Close the burgers and serve, passing more barbecue sauce at the table. —*Brian Perrone*

MAKE AHEAD The onion can be refrigerated overnight and reheated gently before serving.

BEER Herbal, hoppy IPA: New Holland Brewing Mad Hatter.

SWEET BARBECUE SAUCE
ACTIVE: 20 MIN; TOTAL: 1 HR
MAKES 2 CUPS ● ●

2 tablespoons vegetable oil
1 large onion, thinly sliced
Salt
2 tablespoons unsalted butter
1 cup ketchup
½ cup dark brown sugar
½ cup apple juice
3 tablespoons fresh lemon juice
2 tablespoons chopped peeled fresh ginger
2 tablespoons unsulfured molasses

In a large skillet, heat the vegetable oil. Add the sliced onion and a pinch of salt. Cover and cook over moderately low heat, stirring occasionally, until the onion is richly browned, about 20 minutes. Add the butter and melt. Add the ketchup, brown sugar, apple juice, lemon juice, ginger and molasses. Simmer over low heat, stirring occasionally, until the sauce is thickened and reduced to 2 cups, about 25 minutes. Transfer the sauce to a blender and puree. Season the barbecue sauce with salt and serve. —*BP*

MAKE AHEAD The barbecue sauce can be refrigerated for up to 2 weeks.

smoked-gouda-and-bacon burgers with barbecue sauce

Nacho Burgers

⏱ TOTAL: 35 MIN • 4 SERVINGS ●

SALSA

- 3 tablespoons red wine vinegar
- 1 tablespoon vegetable oil
- 1 chipotle chile in adobo, seeded and minced
- 3 plum tomatoes, finely diced
- 2 tablespoons red onion, finely diced
- 3 tablespoons chopped cilantro

Salt

CHEESE SAUCE

- 1 tablespoon unsalted butter
- 1 tablespoon all-purpose flour
- 1½ cups milk
- ½ pound Monterey Jack cheese, shredded
- 2 tablespoons freshly grated pecorino cheese

Salt and freshly ground pepper

BURGERS

- 1½ pounds ground beef chuck

Vegetable oil, for brushing

Salt and freshly ground pepper

- 4 hamburger buns, split and toasted

Sliced pickled jalapeños and blue corn tortilla chips, for topping

1. MAKE THE SALSA In a bowl, combine all of the ingredients and season with salt.

2. MAKE THE CHEESE SAUCE In a small saucepan, melt the butter. Stir in the flour and cook over moderate heat for 30 seconds. Whisk in the milk and cook, whisking, until smooth and thickened, 5 minutes. Stir in the Jack cheese until melted, then stir in the pecorino; season with salt and pepper. Let cool until very thick and spreadable.

3. MAKE THE BURGERS Light a grill. Form the beef into 4 patties and brush with oil; season with salt and pepper. Grill over moderately high heat until browned outside and medium within, about 4 minutes per side.

4. Place the burgers on the buns. Top with the cheese sauce, salsa, pickled jalapeños and chips. Close the burgers and serve. —*Bobby Flay*

WINE Bold, berry-rich Zinfandel: 2009 Four Vines Old Vine Cuvee.

Double Cheeseburgers with Caramelized Onions

⏱ TOTAL: 45 MIN • 6 SERVINGS

- 2 tablespoons unsalted butter
- 1 sweet onion, thinly sliced

Salt and freshly ground black pepper

- ½ cup mayonnaise
- 1 tablespoon fresh lemon juice
- 1 small garlic clove, mashed
- 1½ teaspoons smoked paprika
- ½ teaspoon cayenne pepper
- ¼ cup extra-virgin olive oil
- 1 tablespoon chopped cornichons
- 1 tablespoon chopped flat-leaf parsley
- 6 ounces shredded Gruyère cheese
- 6 ounces shredded sharp cheddar cheese
- 3 pounds ground beef chuck, shaped into twelve ½-inch-thick patties

Toasted brioche buns, bread-and-butter pickles and shredded lettuce, for serving

1. In a skillet, melt the butter. Add the onion, cover and cook over moderately low heat, stirring, until softened, 15 minutes. Uncover and cook over moderate heat, stirring, until the onion is caramelized, 20 minutes; add water if necessary to keep the onion from burning. Season with salt and black pepper.

2. In a small bowl, whisk the mayonnaise with the lemon juice, garlic, paprika and cayenne. In a steady stream, whisk in the olive oil and season with salt and black pepper. Fold in the cornichons and parsley.

3. Heat a griddle. In a bowl, mix the Gruyère and cheddar. Season the patties with salt and black pepper and cook over high heat for 2 minutes. Flip the burgers and top with the mixed cheeses. Carefully cover the burgers with a large inverted roasting pan and cook for 2 minutes longer, until the meat is medium-rare and the cheese is melted.

4. Spread the paprika mayonnaise on the bottom halves of the buns and stack 2 patties on each. Top with the onions, pickles and lettuce and serve. —*Ron Boyd*

WINE Fruit-forward, medium-bodied Côtes du Rhône: 2010 Les Garrigues.

Campfire Feijoada

⏱ TOTAL: 45 MIN • 4 TO 5 LARGE SERVINGS ●

In Brazil, cooks make feijoada—the national dish of stewed, smoked meats and black beans—with dried beef called *carne seca.* Beef jerky is a clever approximation.

- 2 tablespoons vegetable oil, plus more for brushing
- 1 red onion, finely chopped
- 2 large garlic cloves, minced
- 12 ounces andouille sausage, cut into ⅓-inch-thick rounds
- 4 ounces spicy smoked beef jerky, cut into ½-inch squares
- 2½ cups plus 2 tablespoons low-sodium beef broth
- 1 bay leaf
- ½ teaspoon dried oregano, crumbled

Two 15-ounce cans black beans with their liquid

- 1 pound cooked rice
- 2 very ripe plantains, peeled and sliced on the diagonal ½ inch thick

1. In a large flameproof cast-iron casserole, heat the 2 tablespoons of oil. Add the onion and garlic and cook over moderate heat until softened. Stir in the andouille and beef jerky. Add 2½ cups of the broth, the bay leaf and oregano and bring to a boil. Cook for 10 minutes, stirring frequently. Add the beans and their liquid and simmer for 15 minutes longer. Discard the bay leaf.

2. Meanwhile, light a grill. Mound the rice on the bottom half of a large sheet of nonstick heavy-duty aluminum foil. Fold the foil over the rice, then fold up 2 of the sides and crimp them. Pour the remaining 2 tablespoons of beef broth into the rice packet and crimp the remaining side. Set the packet on the grill and heat the rice until warm.

3. Brush the plantains with oil; grill over moderately high heat, turning once or twice, until lightly charred and tender, 5 minutes. Carefully open the rice packet and serve with the feijoada and plantains. —*Grace Parisi*

WINE Red cherry–scented Grenache: 2010 Bonny Doon Clos de Gilroy.

● HEALTHY   ● MAKE AHEAD   ● VEGETARIAN   ● STAFF FAVORITE

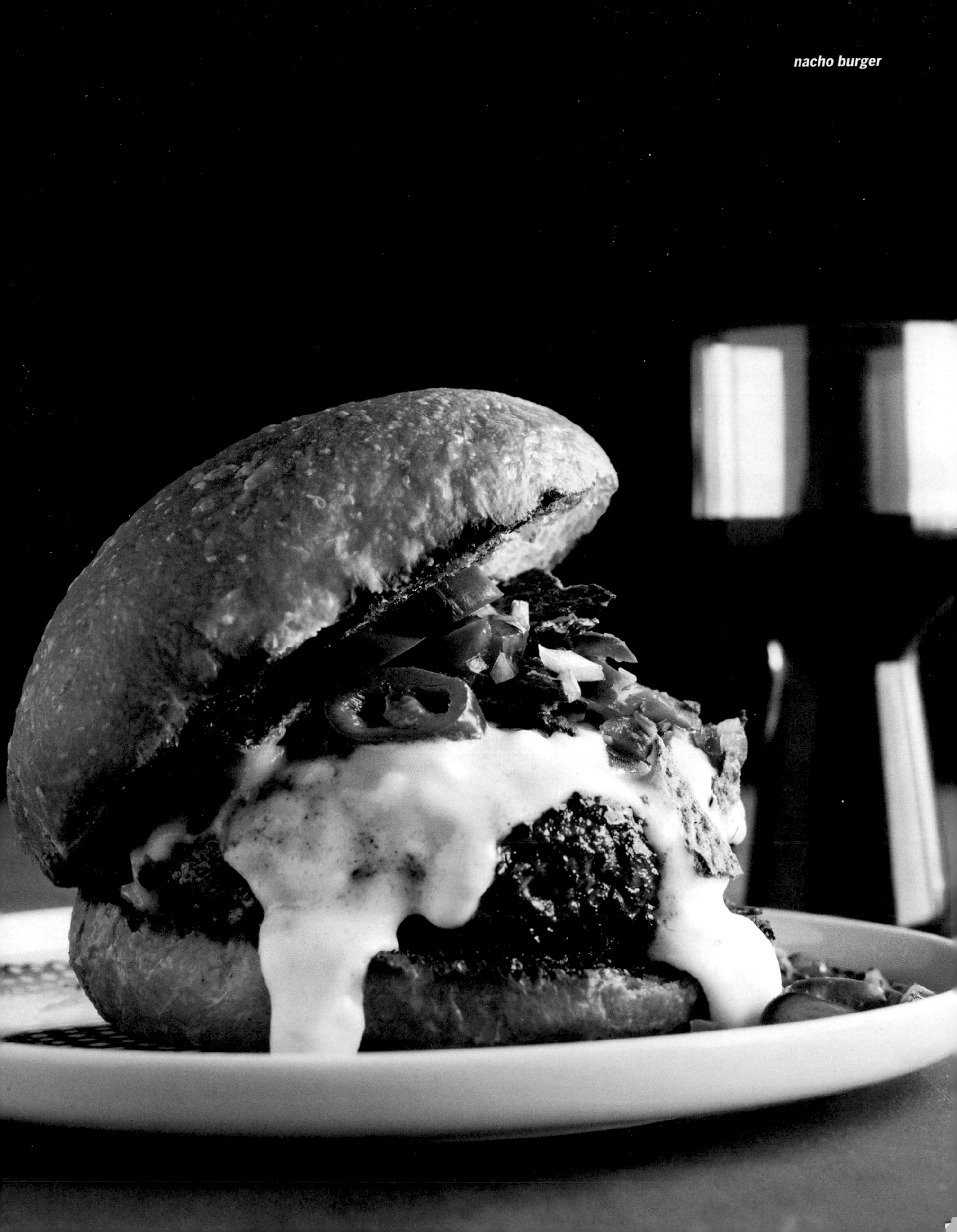

nacho burger

Picadillo

⏱ ACTIVE: 25 MIN; TOTAL: 45 MIN
6 SERVINGS ●

Chef David Guas describes this traditional Cuban ground-beef stew with raisins, onions, olives and tomato as an "à la minute chili." According to Guas, it's a simple dish with countless variations. "Now that I've tasted versions of it in Cuba, I'm able to get my head around some of these slight differences."

 3 tablespoons extra-virgin olive oil
 1 teaspoon cumin seeds
 1 small sweet onion, chopped
 1 medium red bell pepper, chopped
 4 garlic cloves, minced
 1½ pounds ground beef chuck
 ½ cup sliced pitted green olives
 ⅓ cup raisins
 1 tablespoon dried oregano, crumbled
 ¼ cup Worcestershire sauce
One 15-ounce can tomato sauce
 1 cup beef stock or low-sodium broth
Salt and freshly ground pepper
Steamed rice, for serving

1. In a large, deep skillet, heat the olive oil until shimmering. Add the cumin seeds and cook them over moderate heat until fragrant, about 30 seconds. Add the onion, bell pepper and garlic and cook, stirring occasionally, until the vegetables are softened, about 5 minutes. Add the ground beef, olives, raisins and oregano and cook, breaking up the meat with a wooden spoon, until the meat is no longer pink, about 8 minutes. Add the Worcestershire sauce, tomato sauce and stock and season with salt and pepper.

2. Cover the skillet and simmer the stew over low heat for 20 minutes. Serve the *picadillo* with steamed rice. —*David Guas*

SERVE WITH Guas's Fried Green Plantains (page 242).

MAKE AHEAD The *picadillo* can be covered and refrigerated for up to 3 days. Reheat gently over low heat.

BEER Refreshing, easygoing pilsner: Sixpoint The Crisp.

Shaking Beef

TOTAL: 30 MIN PLUS 5 HR MARINATING
6 SERVINGS ● ●

Cubes of beef tenderloin are super-tender in this wonderfully spiced version of the Vietnamese classic. The dish is called "shaking beef" because you shake the skillet to toss the beef while cooking it.

MEAT
 6 garlic cloves, minced
 3 tablespoons medium-dry sherry
 3 tablespoons soy sauce
 1 tablespoon sugar
 1 teaspoon freshly ground black pepper
 ¼ teaspoon Chinese five-spice powder
 1 tablespoon vegetable oil, plus more for cooking the meat
 2 pounds beef tenderloin, cut into 1-inch cubes

VINAIGRETTE
 2 tablespoons soy sauce
 2 tablespoons vegetable oil
 1 tablespoon medium-dry sherry
 1 tablespoon red wine vinegar
 2 teaspoons minced fresh ginger
 2 teaspoons sugar
 1 garlic clove, minced
 1 lemongrass stalk, lower third of the tender inner bulb only, minced
 6 ounces watercress (10 packed cups)
 ½ small red onion, very thinly sliced

1. **MARINATE THE MEAT** In a large bowl, combine the garlic, sherry, soy sauce, sugar, pepper and five-spice powder with the 1 tablespoon of oil. Add the beef and turn to coat with the marinade. Cover and refrigerate for at least 5 hours or overnight.

2. **MAKE THE VINAIGRETTE** In a small bowl, combine the soy sauce with the vegetable oil, sherry, red wine vinegar, ginger, sugar, garlic and lemongrass. Let stand for 30 minutes, stirring a few times.

3. Mound the watercress and red onion on a platter and toss with half of the vinaigrette. Set 2 large skillets over high heat until very hot, about 2 minutes. Add 1 tablespoon of oil to each skillet; when shimmering, add the meat to both skillets in an even layer. Let cook undisturbed until richly browned on the bottom, about 1½ minutes. Shake the skillet to release the meat and cook for about 30 seconds longer, until it is medium-rare. Scrape the beef onto the watercress. Drizzle with the remaining vinaigrette, toss lightly and serve right away. —*Marcia Kiesel*

WINE Balanced, herb-scented Napa Cabernet: 2008 Groth.

Fried Calf's Liver with Onion-and-Tomato Salad

⏱ TOTAL: 25 MIN • 4 SERVINGS

 2 tablespoons extra-virgin olive oil
 1 tablespoon fresh lemon juice
Salt and freshly ground pepper
 1 small red onion, thinly sliced
 2 plum tomatoes, thinly sliced crosswise
 ¼ cup flat-leaf parsley leaves
Four 4-ounce slices of calf or lamb liver (sliced ⅓ inch thick)
 2 tablespoons vegetable oil
 2 teaspoons chopped thyme
 1 small fresh hot red chile, minced

1. In a small bowl, combine the olive oil with the lemon juice. Season the dressing with salt and pepper. On one half of a serving platter, season the onion and tomato slices with salt and pepper and add the parsley. Spoon 2 tablespoons of the lemon dressing on top and toss lightly.

2. Season the liver slices with salt and pepper. In a large nonstick skillet, heat the vegetable oil until shimmering. Add the liver and cook over high heat until browned, about 2 minutes. Reduce the heat to moderate and continue cooking for 1 minute longer. Turn the liver slices and cook until rosy in the center, about 3 minutes longer. Transfer the liver to the platter with the tomato salad and drizzle with the remaining lemon dressing. Sprinkle the liver with the chopped thyme and minced chile and serve right away. —*Cavit Saatci*

WINE Cherry-rich Tempranillo: 2009 Torremilanos Los Cantos.

● HEALTHY ● MAKE AHEAD ● VEGETARIAN ● STAFF FAVORITE

picadillo

Asian Beef with Basil

ACTIVE: 45 MIN; TOTAL: 3 HR

6 SERVINGS ● ●

MARINADE

- 3 garlic cloves, chopped
- 3 lemongrass stalks, lower third only, chopped
- 2 tablespoons soy sauce
- 2 tablespoons vegetable oil
- 1 teaspoon kosher salt
- 1 teaspoon sugar
- ⅛ teaspoon Chinese five-spice powder
- 3½ pounds beef chuck, cut into 1½-inch cubes

STEW

- 2½ tablespoons vegetable oil
- 1 medium onion, cut into ½-inch pieces
- 2 garlic cloves, minced
- 1 tablespoon minced fresh ginger
- ¼ teaspoon crushed red pepper
- 2 tablespoons tomato paste
- 5 cups beef broth
- 4 carrots, cut into 2-inch lengths
- 3 star anise pods
- 1 whole lemongrass stalk, cut into 3-inch lengths and lightly smashed

Kosher salt

Cooked medium-thick rice noodles, for serving

- ½ cup torn basil leaves
- 1 long fresh red chile, thinly sliced

1. MARINATE THE MEAT In a mini food processor, mince the garlic and lemongrass. Add the soy sauce, oil, salt, sugar and five-spice powder; pulse to combine. In a large bowl, toss the beef with the marinade. Let marinate at room temperature for 30 minutes.

2. MAKE THE STEW In an enameled cast-iron casserole, heat 1 tablespoon of the oil over moderate heat. Add half of the meat; cook until lightly browned. Transfer to a bowl. Repeat with 1 tablespoon of the oil and the remaining meat.

3. Add the remaining ½ tablespoon of oil to the casserole along with the onion, garlic, ginger and crushed red pepper. Add 1 tablespoon of water, cover and cook over low heat, stirring occasionally, until softened, about 5

minutes. Add the tomato paste; cook over moderately high heat, stirring, until glossy, 1 minute. Add the broth and bring to a boil, scraping up any browned bits.

4. Return the meat to the casserole. Add the carrots, star anise and lemongrass. Simmer over low heat, stirring occasionally, until the meat is tender, 1 hour and 45 minutes. Using a slotted spoon, transfer the beef to a bowl. Boil the sauce over high heat until reduced to 4 cups, 3 minutes. Discard the star anise and lemongrass. Return the beef to the casserole. Season the stew with salt and serve over noodles. Garnish with the basil and red chile. —*Marcia Kiesel*

WINE Ripe, berry-saturated California Cabernet: 2010 Guenoc.

Keema Beef Curry

⏱ **TOTAL: 45 MIN • 4 TO 6 SERVINGS** ●

- 1 tablespoon canola oil
- 1½ pounds lean ground sirloin
- 1 large onion, finely chopped
- 2 tablespoons minced fresh ginger
- 2 large garlic cloves, minced
- 1½ tablespoons Madras curry powder

Salt and freshly ground pepper

- 1 large Yukon Gold potato, peeled and cut into ½-inch dice
- 1½ cups low-sodium chicken broth

One 14-ounce can unsweetened coconut milk

One 14-ounce can diced tomatoes with their juices

- 1½ cups frozen baby peas

Chopped cilantro, warm naan and steamed rice, for serving

1. In a large, deep skillet, heat the oil. Add the meat and cook over high heat, stirring to break up the lumps, until no longer pink, about 5 minutes. Add the onion, ginger, garlic and curry powder; season with salt and pepper. Cook over high heat, stirring, until the onion is softened, about 3 minutes. Add the potato, broth, coconut milk and the tomatoes and their juices; bring to a boil. Cook over moderate heat, stirring occasionally, until the potato is tender, about 15 minutes.

2. Using the back of a spoon, lightly crush some of the potato. Add the peas and cook just until heated through. Serve in bowls with cilantro, naan and rice. —*Grace Parisi*

WINE Aromatic, fruit-forward Malbec: 2009 Renacer Punto Final Reserva.

Fragrant South Indian Beef Curry

ACTIVE: 20 MIN; TOTAL: 1 HR 50 MIN

4 SERVINGS ●

- 2 tablespoons canola oil
- 1 medium onion, thinly sliced
- 12 fresh curry leaves or 2 bay leaves
- 6 garlic cloves, grated
- 4 teaspoons finely grated peeled fresh ginger
- 1 tablespoon tomato paste dissolved in ½ cup of water
- 2 teaspoons ground coriander
- 1 teaspoon garam masala
- 1 teaspoon cayenne pepper
- ½ teaspoon ground turmeric
- 4 small dried hot chiles
- 4 star anise pods

Two 3-inch cinnamon sticks

- 1¾ pounds boneless beef short ribs, cut into ¾-inch pieces

Salt

In a medium enameled cast-iron casserole, heat the oil until shimmering. Add the onion and curry leaves and cook over moderate heat until lightly browned, about 7 minutes. Add the garlic and ginger and cook until fragrant, 1 minute. Stir in the dissolved tomato paste along with the ground coriander, garam masala, cayenne, turmeric, dried chiles, star anise and cinnamon sticks. Add the ribs, season with salt and stir until coated with spices. Cover partially and cook over very low heat until the meat is tender, about 1 hour and 30 minutes. Spoon off as much fat as possible and discard the star anise, cinnamon sticks and bay leaves, if using, then serve. —*Asha Gomez*

SERVE WITH Steamed rice.

WINE Spiced, dark-berried red: 2010 Bodegas Tarima Monastrell.

● HEALTHY ● MAKE AHEAD ● VEGETARIAN ● STAFF FAVORITE

fragrant south indian beef curry

Microwaved Chile-Lime-Ginger Beef Jerky

ACTIVE: 40 MIN; TOTAL: 3 HR • MAKES
ABOUT 3 CUPS (4 OUNCES) ● ● ●

Making beef jerky at home is surprisingly easy, especially when you use a microwave oven, which cuts down the marinating and drying time to a couple of hours. You'll need either a microwave-safe bacon rack or two silicone ice cube trays.

    3 garlic cloves, minced
    3 tablespoons minced peeled
       fresh ginger
    3 tablespoons light brown sugar
    3 tablespoons soy sauce
    3 tablespoons freshly squeezed
       lime juice
 1¼ teaspoons salt
    1 teaspoon finely grated lime zest
    ¾ teaspoon crushed red pepper
    1 pound flank steak, sliced crosswise
       ¼ inch thick

1. In a blender, combine the garlic, ginger, brown sugar, soy sauce, lime juice and salt and puree until smooth. Add the lime zest and crushed red pepper and pulse to combine. Transfer the marinade to a large bowl.
2. On a cutting board, using the tenderizer side of a meat pounder, lightly pound the steak strips to a scant ⅛-inch thickness. Add the strips to the marinade and turn to coat thoroughly. Let stand at room temperature for 2 hours or refrigerate overnight.
3. Arrange half of the flank steak strips on a microwave-safe bacon rack or over 2 inverted silicone ice cube trays and cover them with dry paper towels. Microwave at high power for about 2 minutes. Repeat once or twice more (depending on the strength of the microwave), turning the steak strips once or twice, until they begin to caramelize and appear leathery. If the strips aren't yet leathery, microwave them in 1-minute bursts at high power until they are. Transfer the beef jerky to a plate and repeat with the remaining steak strips. —*Grace Parisi*
MAKE AHEAD The beef jerky can be refrigerated for up to 2 weeks.

Lamb-and-Spinach-Stuffed Onions

ACTIVE: 1 HR; TOTAL: 3 HR
4 SERVINGS ●

STUFFED ONIONS
Two 1½-pound sweet onions, such
       as Vidalia or Walla Walla, unpeeled
       and root ends trimmed
Vegetable oil, for rubbing
    5 ounces curly-leaf spinach, washed
       but not dried
    1 pound ground lamb
    2 teaspoons ancho chile powder
    ⅛ teaspoon cinnamon
    2 cups coarse fresh bread crumbs
    ¾ cup shredded Gruyère cheese
    1 cup beef broth
    1 cup canned crushed tomatoes
Salt and freshly ground black pepper
    ¼ cup plus 2 tablespoons heavy cream
TOPPING
    ¾ cup coarse fresh bread crumbs
    1 tablespoon vegetable oil
    ¼ teaspoon ancho chile powder
    ¼ cup shredded Gruyère cheese

1. PREPARE THE ONIONS Preheat the oven to 350°. Put the onions in a small baking dish root ends down, and rub with oil. Add ½ inch of water. Cover with foil and bake for about 1½ hours, until tender. Let cool slightly.
2. Meanwhile, heat a large skillet. Add the spinach in batches, tossing until wilted. Transfer to a colander and squeeze out the water. Coarsely chop the spinach.
3. In the same skillet, cook the lamb over moderately high heat, breaking it up, until no pink remains, 3 minutes. Pour off all but 1 tablespoon of the fat; add the chile powder and cinnamon. Cook over moderately high heat, stirring, for 1 minute. Stir in the spinach. Transfer the lamb filling to a large bowl. Stir in the bread crumbs, Gruyère, ¼ cup of the broth and ½ cup of the tomatoes.
4. Cut ½ inch off the top and bottom of the baked onions. Separate the layers, trying not to break them. You will need 10 onion cups: some large, some medium and 2 small. Finely chop enough of the onion scraps to make

½ cup; fold into the lamb filling and season with salt and pepper.
5. Stand the stuffed onion cups in a buttered medium baking dish. Season the insides with salt and fill with the lamb.
6. In a large skillet, combine the cream with the remaining ¾ cup of beef broth and ½ cup of tomatoes and bring to a boil. Pour the sauce over and around the onions.
7. MAKE THE TOPPING In a bowl, combine all of the ingredients. Mound the topping on the onions. Cover with foil and bake for 40 minutes, until hot. Uncover and increase the oven temperature to 425°. Bake for 5 minutes, until the topping is crisp. Let rest for 5 minutes before serving. —*Marcia Kiesel*
WINE Peppery, berry-rich Zinfandel: 2009 Dashe Dry Creek Valley.

Ground Lamb Kebabs with Pine Nuts and Tahini Sauce

⏱ TOTAL: 45 MIN • 8 SERVINGS

    2 pounds ground lamb
    ¾ cup pine nuts (4 ounces)
    ¼ cup finely chopped mint
    ¼ cup finely chopped flat-leaf parsley
    2 teaspoons ground cumin
    ½ teaspoon cinnamon
    2 garlic cloves, minced
    1 onion, finely chopped (½ cup)
Kosher salt and freshly ground pepper
Olive oil, for brushing
Tahini Sauce (recipe follows), lemon
       wedges and warm pita, for serving

1. Light a grill. In a bowl, mix the lamb with the pine nuts, mint, parsley, cumin, cinnamon, garlic, onion, 1 tablespoon of salt and 1 teaspoon of pepper. Form the mixture into 16 ovals and thread them onto 8 skewers.
2. Brush the lamb kebabs with olive oil and season with salt and pepper. Grill over moderately high heat, turning occasionally, until the kebabs are lightly charred in spots and just slightly pink in the center, 8 to 10 minutes. Serve with the Tahini Sauce, lemon wedges and warm pita. —*Eden Grinshpan*
WINE Juicy, citrusy, full-bodied white: 2011 Indaba Chenin Blanc.

TAHINI SAUCE

✦ **TOTAL: 10 MIN • MAKES 1¼ CUPS** ● ●

½ cup tahini
1¼ tablespoons fresh lemon juice
1 garlic clove, minced
1 tablespoon finely chopped
flat-leaf parsley
1 tablespoon finely chopped mint
Kosher salt

In a food processor, combine the tahini with the lemon juice and garlic. Add ¾ cup of water and puree until smooth. Transfer the sauce to a bowl and whisk in up to ½ cup more of water, until the sauce is pourable. Stir in the chopped parsley and mint, season with salt and serve. —EG

MAKE AHEAD The tahini sauce can be refrigerated for up to 2 days.

Stuffed Eggplant with Lamb and Pine Nuts

ACTIVE: 35 MIN; TOTAL: 1 HR 30 MIN
4 SERVINGS ●

Four 1-pound eggplants, halved
lengthwise
1 tablespoon extra-virgin olive oil,
plus more for brushing
Salt and freshly ground pepper
1 tablespoon ground cinnamon
1½ teaspoons ground cumin
1½ teaspoons sweet paprika
1 large onion, finely chopped
1 pound ground lamb
3 tablespoons pine nuts
2 teaspoons tomato paste
¼ cup chopped parsley
1 tablespoon sugar
1 tablespoon freshly squeezed
lemon juice
1 teaspoon tamarind concentrate
One 1½-inch cinnamon stick

1. Preheat the oven to 425° and arrange the eggplants in a large baking dish, cut side up. Brush with olive oil and season with salt and pepper. Bake in the upper third of the oven for about 20 minutes, until browned.

2. Meanwhile, in a small bowl, mix the ground cinnamon, cumin and paprika. In a large skillet, heat the 1 tablespoon of olive oil. Add the onion and half of the spice mixture, cover and cook over moderate heat, stirring a few times, until softened, about 7 minutes. Add the lamb and cook, breaking up the meat with a wooden spoon, until no pink remains, about 4 minutes. Pour off all but 1 tablespoon of the fat in the skillet. Stir in the pine nuts, tomato paste, half of the parsley and 1 teaspoon of the sugar and season the lamb with salt and pepper.

3. Spoon the lamb filling onto the eggplants. In the small bowl with the remaining spices, combine ½ cup of water, the lemon juice, tamarind concentrate, the remaining 2 teaspoons of sugar and a pinch each of salt and pepper and pour into the baking dish. Add the cinnamon stick and cover the dish with aluminum foil. Bake for about 50 minutes, basting twice with the pan juices, until the eggplants are very tender.

4. Transfer the eggplants to plates or a platter and discard the cinnamon stick. Pour the pan juices over the eggplants, sprinkle with the remaining parsley and serve.
—Yotam Ottolenghi and Sami Tamimi
WINE Juicy, red berry–inflected Pinot Noir: 2009 Cloudline Cellars.

Spice-Glazed Lamb Chops with Red Wine–Coffee Pan Sauce

TOTAL: 1 HR • 4 SERVINGS

2 teaspoons ancho chile powder
(see Note)
1 teaspoon freshly ground
black pepper
⅛ teaspoon cinnamon
Eight 6 to 8 ounce lamb loin chops,
cut 1¼ inches thick
Salt
24 red and white pearl onions
1 tablespoon vegetable oil
⅓ cup dry red wine
⅔ cup beef broth
⅓ cup strong-brewed coffee
1½ tablespoons tomato paste
1 tablespoon cold unsalted butter

1. In a small bowl, combine the ancho chile powder with the freshly ground black pepper and the cinnamon. Sprinkle the seasoning mix all over the lamb loin chops and let them stand at room temperature for 30 minutes.

2. Meanwhile, bring a medium saucepan of salted water to a boil. Add the pearl onions and cook until they are barely tender, about 4 minutes, then drain them. When the onions are cool enough to handle, cut off both ends and carefully peel them, keeping the onions intact.

3. Preheat the oven to 375°. Season the lamb chops with salt. In a large ovenproof skillet, heat the vegetable oil. Add the lamb chops fat side down (the edge of the chops) and cook them over moderate heat until they are lightly browned, about 2 minutes. Turn the chops to one (flat) side and cook until lightly browned, about 2 minutes longer. Turn the chops over and add the onions to the skillet. Transfer the skillet to the upper third of the oven and roast the chops and onions for 8 minutes. Turn the chops and roast for 2 minutes longer, until the meat is medium-rare. With a slotted spoon, transfer the chops and onions to a warm platter.

4. Tilt the skillet and carefully spoon off most of the fat, leaving the lamb juices behind. Add the red wine to the skillet and bring to a boil, stirring to scrape up the browned bits, about 1 minute. Stir in the beef broth, coffee and tomato paste and boil, stirring, until the liquid is reduced to ¾ cup, about 3 minutes. Tilt the platter with the lamb and pour any accumulated juices into the skillet. Remove the skillet from the heat and swirl the butter into the sauce. Season with salt and pour the red wine–coffee sauce over the chops. Serve the lamb chops right away.
—Marcia Kiesel

SERVE WITH Mashed vegetables, such as potatoes, rutabagas and carrots.
NOTE Ancho chile powder, which ranges from mild to hot, is made from poblano chile peppers ripened to a deep red, dried until reddish brown and then ground. It is available at specialty food stores and penzeys.com.
WINE Smooth, blackberry-scented Zinfandel: 2009 Dashe Cellars Florence Vineyard.

Lamb Burgers with Green Harissa

⏱ TOTAL: 40 MIN • 4 SERVINGS ●

Harissa, a staple in Tunisian and Moroccan cooking, ordinarily contains dried red chiles. The green version here includes mild Anaheim chiles and hot serranos to add bright flavor to grilled lamb burgers.

- 1 pound ground lamb
- ½ cup cooked white rice
- 1 large egg, beaten
- ½ cup chopped cilantro

Kosher salt and freshly ground
    black pepper
- ¼ cup extra-virgin olive oil,
    plus more for grilling
- 4 hot green chiles, such as serranos
    or jalapeños, thinly sliced
- 2 mild green chiles, such as Anaheim
    or yellow wax chiles, seeded and
    coarsely chopped
- 2 scallions, coarsely chopped
- 1 garlic clove, smashed

Warm naan, chopped tomatoes and
    feta cheese, for serving

1. Light a grill or preheat a grill pan. In a medium bowl, combine the ground lamb with the cooked rice, beaten egg and ¼ cup of the cilantro. Add 1 teaspoon of kosher salt and ½ teaspoon of black pepper and gently knead the meat to blend. Using lightly moistened hands, form the meat into 12 patties, about ½ inch thick. Brush the lamb patties with olive oil.

2. Grill the patties over moderate heat, turning occasionally, until browned and cooked through, about 6 minutes.

3. Meanwhile, in a food processor, combine the hot and mild chiles with the scallions, garlic and the remaining ¼ cup of cilantro and pulse until chopped. Add the ¼ cup of olive oil and process to a chunky puree. Season the harissa with salt. Wrap the lamb in the warm naan with tomatoes and feta cheese. Spoon some of the green harissa on top and serve. —*Grace Parisi*

WINE Lively, cassis-inflected red Côtes du Rhône: 2010 Domaine Pélaquié.

Garlic-and-Herb-Crusted Leg of Lamb

ACTIVE: 25 MIN; TOTAL: 2 HR 25 MIN
8 SERVINGS

This leg of lamb is perfectly juicy in the center, with a fantastic crust. The recipe is surprisingly easy, making it ideal for a dinner party.

- ¼ cup extra-virgin olive oil,
    plus more for drizzling
- 2 heads of garlic, cloves separated
    but not peeled, plus 3 minced
    garlic cloves
- 1 tablespoon minced rosemary,
    plus 3 sprigs
- 1 tablespoon minced thyme

One 6-pound bone-in leg of lamb,
    aitch bone removed

Salt and freshly ground pepper
- 1 large sweet onion, cut into
    ½-inch-thick wedges
- 2 large carrots, cut on the diagonal
    ½ inch thick
- 2 large celery ribs, cut on the
    diagonal ½ inch thick

1. Preheat the oven to 400°. In a small bowl, combine the ¼ cup of oil with the minced garlic, rosemary and thyme.

2. Score the fatty top side of the lamb about ¼ inch deep. Season the lamb all over with salt and pepper. On a large rimmed baking sheet, toss the whole garlic cloves, onion, carrots and celery with a generous drizzle of olive oil. Arrange the vegetables in an even layer and season with salt and pepper. Scatter the rosemary sprigs over the vegetables and set the leg of lamb on top, fatty side up. Spread half of the garlic-and-herb rub all over the lamb, making sure to rub it into the score marks. Roast for 20 minutes.

3. Spread the remaining rub over the lamb and add ¼ cup of water to the baking sheet. Roast the lamb for about 1 hour and 20 minutes longer, rotating the baking sheet a few times, until an instant-read thermometer inserted in the thickest part of the meat registers 145° for medium. Add a few more tablespoons of water to the baking sheet at any point if the vegetables start to get quite dark.

4. Transfer the lamb to a carving board and let it rest for 20 minutes. Discard the rosemary sprigs. Carve the leg of lamb into ½-inch-thick slices and serve with the roasted vegetables. —*Mike Lata*

WINE Black cherry–scented California red: 2009 Coturri Carignane.

Provençal Leg of Lamb

ACTIVE: 20 MIN; TOTAL: 1 HR PLUS 24 HR MARINATING • 8 SERVINGS

Meaty cuts like leg of lamb can sit in a wine-based marinade for a couple of days, soaking up lots of flavor without getting tough. The marinade here, infused with Provençal herbs, is a classic with lamb.

One 6-pound boneless leg of lamb,
    butterflied
- 1 bottle dry red wine
- 12 rosemary sprigs, broken
- 12 thyme sprigs

Zest strips removed from ½ orange
- 2 large shallots, thinly sliced
- 1 teaspoon cracked black peppercorns
- 1 teaspoon dried lavender

Extra-virgin olive oil, for brushing
Salt

1. Put the lamb into a 2-gallon resealable plastic bag. Add the wine, rosemary, thyme, orange zest strips, shallots, peppercorns and lavender. Seal the bag, pressing out the air. Turn to coat the lamb. Refrigerate for at least 24 hours and up to 48 hours, turning the bag occasionally.

2. Drain the lamb, picking off any solids from the marinade. Return to room temperature.

3. Light a grill and oil the grates. Brush the lamb with oil and season with salt. Grill over moderate heat, turning occasionally, until an instant-read thermometer inserted into the thickest part registers 125° for medium-rare meat, 35 to 40 minutes. Transfer the lamb to a board and let rest for 10 minutes. Thinly slice the meat against the grain and serve. —*Grace Parisi*

SERVE WITH Grilled onions and squash.

WINE Peppery, herbal Cabernet Franc: 2010 Lang & Reed North Coast.

lamb burgers with green harissa

Honey-Glazed Lamb with Herbes de Provence

ACTIVE: 40 MIN; TOTAL: 2 HR
6 SERVINGS

One 3½-pound trimmed boneless leg
    of lamb roast with at least ⅛ inch
    of fat on one side, butterflied
Salt and freshly ground black pepper
  ¼ cup plus 1 tablespoon mild honey,
    such as clover
  3 tablespoons herbes de Provence
  ½ cup plus 1 tablespoon dry red wine
  2 heads of garlic, separated
    into unpeeled cloves
Extra-virgin olive oil
Four 12-ounce Asian eggplants,
    sliced crosswise 1 inch thick
  ½ cup chicken stock

1. Preheat the oven to 400°. Spread the leg
of lamb roast out on a work surface, fat side
down. Season with salt and pepper and rub
2 tablespoons of the honey on the lean side
of the lamb. Sprinkle with 1 tablespoon of
the herbes de Provence. Loosely roll the lamb
into a neat oval shape and stitch together
by crisscrossing short skewers at the bottom
of the roast. Transfer the lamb to a shallow
roasting pan, fat side up, and season with
salt and pepper. Rub the remaining 3 tablespoons of honey all over the roast and then
sprinkle with the remaining 2 tablespoons
of herbes de Provence.

2. Add ½ cup of the red wine and ½ cup of
water to the roasting pan. Roast the lamb in
the upper third of the oven for about 1 hour
and 15 minutes, rotating the pan halfway
through, until an instant-read thermometer
inserted into the thickest part of the meat
registers 145° for medium meat.

3. Meanwhile, put the unpeeled garlic cloves
on a sheet of heavy-duty aluminum foil and
drizzle lightly with olive oil. Wrap the garlic
in the foil. Spread the eggplant slices on a
large rimmed baking sheet and brush both
sides generously with olive oil. Roast the
eggplant and the garlic in the lower third
of the oven for 45 to 50 minutes, until the
eggplant is very tender and browned on the
bottom and the garlic is very soft. Using a
thin spatula, loosen the eggplant from the
pan, then cover with foil and keep warm. Peel
the garlic cloves.

4. Transfer the lamb to a carving board and
let rest for 10 minutes. Remove the skewers.
Add the chicken stock and the peeled garlic cloves to the pan juices. Set the pan over
moderately high heat just until the juices
are bubbling; scrape up the browned bits
from the bottom of the pan. Strain the pan
juices through a coarse sieve set over a small
saucepan; press to push the garlic through.
Skim off the fat. Season the sauce with salt
and pepper and stir in the remaining 1 tablespoon of red wine.

5. Slice the lamb ⅓ inch thick and serve with
the roasted garlic sauce and eggplant.
—*Marcia Kiesel*

WINE Powerful, earthy Rhône red: 2008 Château de Beaucastel Châteauneuf-du-Pape.

Slow-Roasted Lamb Shoulder with Homemade Harissa

ACTIVE: 30 MIN; TOTAL: 8 HR
6 SERVINGS ● ●

When chef Peter Hoffman makes his sen-
sational harissa-coated lamb at Back Forty
West in Manhattan, he roasts it slowly for 10
hours. In this quicker version, the lamb cooks
at higher heat for half the time: five hours.
It's still falling-apart tender.

  ¼ teaspoon caraway seeds
  ¼ teaspoon coriander seeds
  ¼ teaspoon cumin seeds
  2 ounces ancho chiles (about 4),
    stemmed and seeded
  1 tablespoon smoked sweet paprika
  1 tablespoon freshly squeezed
    lemon juice
  3 large garlic cloves, 1 clove mashed
    to a paste
  ¼ cup extra-virgin olive oil
Kosher salt
One 3-pound lamb shoulder roast
    on the bone
  1 cup plain Greek yogurt
  2 tablespoons chopped cilantro
Freshly ground pepper

1. In a spice grinder, combine the caraway
seeds, coriander seeds and cumin seeds
and finely grind them.

2. In a microwave-safe bowl, cover the ancho
chiles with water and microwave at high
power for 2 minutes. Let the ancho mixture
cool slightly, then transfer the softened chiles
and 2 tablespoons of the soaking liquid to a
blender. Add the ground spices, the smoked
sweet paprika, lemon juice, the 2 whole garlic cloves, 2 tablespoons of the olive oil and
1 tablespoon of kosher salt. Puree until the
harissa is smooth.

3. Set the lamb shoulder roast in a medium
roasting pan and rub ½ cup of the harissa
all over the meat; let the lamb stand at room
temperature for 2 hours or refrigerate it overnight.

4. Preheat the oven to 325°. Add ½ cup of
water to the roasting pan and cover the pan
loosely with aluminum foil. Roast the lamb
for 2½ hours, adding water to the pan a few
times as necessary to prevent scorching.
Remove the aluminum foil and roast the lamb
for about 2½ hours longer, until the meat is
very brown and tender; occasionally spoon
the pan juices on top. Let the lamb stand for
20 minutes.

5. Meanwhile, in a small bowl, combine the
yogurt with the chopped cilantro, mashed
garlic clove and the remaining 2 tablespoons
of olive oil. Season the yogurt sauce with salt
and freshly ground pepper.

6. Using 2 forks or tongs, pull the roasted
lamb off the bone in large chunks. Then,
using your fingers, pull the meat into smaller
shreds and serve it with the yogurt sauce
and the remaining harissa.
—*Peter Hoffman*

SERVE WITH Warm naan and soft lettuce
leaves (such as Boston, green-leaf or red-
leaf) for wrapping.

MAKE AHEAD The harissa can be covered
and refrigerated for up to 1 week (it makes
a great accompaniment or marinade for
most poultry, meat and hearty fish). The
whole roasted lamb shoulder can be refrigerated overnight; rewarm before serving.

WINE Smooth, red-berried Shiraz: 2011
Grant Burge GB56.

● HEALTHY ● MAKE AHEAD ● VEGETARIAN ● STAFF FAVORITE

Leg of Lamb Shawarma

ACTIVE: 30 MIN; TOTAL: 2 HR 45 MIN
PLUS OVERNIGHT MARINATING
6 TO 8 SERVINGS ●

This grilled lamb is Silvena Rowe's signature dish at Quince in London. It can be set out on a buffet, or sliced and served in grilled flatbread with dilled yogurt and cucumbers.

- **1 head of garlic,** top fourth cut off
- **2 tablespoons extra-virgin olive oil,** plus more for drizzling
- Finely grated **zest and juice of 2 lemons**
- **1 teaspoon sweet paprika**
- **1 teaspoon ground cumin**
- **1 teaspoon ground coriander**
- **½ teaspoon cinnamon**
- Kosher **salt** and freshly ground **black pepper**
- One 5-pound **butterflied leg of lamb**
- **Grilled flatbread,** plain **yogurt** mixed with dill and sliced **cucumbers,** for serving

1. Preheat the oven to 350°. Put the garlic on a double piece of foil and drizzle with olive oil. Wrap the garlic in the foil and bake for about 1 hour and 15 minutes, until very soft.
2. Squeeze the garlic cloves into a bowl; mash them with a fork. Stir in the lemon zest, lemon juice, paprika, cumin, coriander, cinnamon and the 2 tablespoons of olive oil. Add 1 teaspoon of salt and ½ teaspoon of pepper.
3. Lay the lamb on a work surface and make ½-inch-deep slits all over it. Transfer the lamb to a rimmed baking sheet and spread the spice paste all over, rubbing it into the meat. Cover and refrigerate overnight.
4. Light a grill. Bring the lamb to room temperature; season with salt and pepper. Grill the lamb fat side down over moderately high heat until charred, 20 minutes. Turn and grill for 20 minutes longer, until an instant-read thermometer inserted in the thickest part registers 130° for medium. Transfer the lamb to a work surface to rest for 15 minutes.
5. Carve the lamb into thin slices and serve it with grilled flatbread, dilled yogurt and sliced cucumbers. —*Silvena Rowe*

WINE Spicy, dense California Syrah: 2009 Big House The Slammer.

Herb-Crusted Rack of Lamb with Gremolata Pesto

ACTIVE: 1 HR; TOTAL: 2 HR
6 SERVINGS ●

Lamb is Colorado chef Kelly Liken's favorite food in the world. To show it off, she makes a pesto-like sauce by combining gremolata—a mixture of parsley, lemon zest and garlic—with pine nuts and olive oil. Liken often cooks lamb from start to finish over a wood fire, but this home-cook-friendly version calls for starting the racks on the grill and then finishing them in the oven.

LAMB AND SAUCE

- **1 tablespoon extra-virgin olive oil,** plus more for drizzling
- Three 8-bone **racks of lamb** (1½ pounds each), bones frenched and trimmings reserved (see Note)
- **1 carrot,** chopped
- **1 celery stalk,** chopped
- **1 small onion,** chopped
- **6 large garlic cloves,** chopped (about 3 tablespoons)
- **1 medium tomato,** chopped
- **½ cup dry red wine**
- **1 quart low-sodium beef broth**
- **¼ cup chopped flat-leaf parsley,** stems reserved
- **2 tablespoons chopped thyme,** stems reserved
- **Salt** and freshly ground **black pepper**

GREMOLATA PESTO

- **¼ cup pine nuts**
- **1 cup flat-leaf parsley leaves**
- **2 garlic cloves,** smashed
- Finely grated **zest of 1 lemon**
- **½ cup extra-virgin olive oil**
- **Salt** and freshly ground **black pepper**

1. PREPARE THE LAMB AND SAUCE In a large saucepan, heat the 1 tablespoon of olive oil. Add the reserved lamb trimmings along with the chopped carrot, celery and onion and cook over moderately high heat, stirring occasionally, until the vegetables are lightly browned, about 10 minutes. Add 1 tablespoon of the chopped garlic and the chopped tomato and cook until softened,

about 5 minutes. Add the red wine and bring to a boil. Add the low-sodium beef broth and the reserved parsley and thyme stems and simmer over moderate heat until reduced to 1¼ cups, about 1 hour. Strain the lamb sauce into a small saucepan and spoon off the fat. Season the sauce with salt and freshly ground pepper and keep warm.
2. Preheat the oven to 400°. Light a grill or preheat a grill pan. In a small bowl, combine the chopped parsley, chopped thyme and the remaining 2 tablespoons of chopped garlic. Season the racks of lamb with salt and freshly ground black pepper and then coat them with the herb mixture. Drizzle the lamb with olive oil and oil the grill or the grill pan. Grill the racks of lamb over moderately high heat, turning once, until they are browned all over, about 5 minutes. Transfer the racks to a sturdy baking sheet.
3. Roast the racks of lamb in the oven for about 15 minutes, until an instant-read thermometer inserted in the center of the meat registers 130° to 135° for medium-rare. Let the racks rest for 15 minutes.
4. MEANWHILE, MAKE THE GREMOLATA PESTO In a medium skillet, toast the pine nuts over moderate heat, stirring, until they are golden, about 5 minutes. Let the toasted pine nuts cool slightly. Transfer the toasted pine nuts to a blender. Add the parsley leaves, garlic and grated lemon zest and pulse to combine. Add the olive oil and process until smooth. Season the gremolata pesto with salt and pepper.
5. Reheat the sauce. Carve the racks of lamb into chops and serve the chops with the sauce and gremolata pesto. —*Kelly Liken*

SERVE WITH Liken's Sautéed Baby Squash with Scallions (page 232).

NOTE Ask your butcher to french the racks of lamb (meaning scrape the fat and gristle from the bones); also be sure to ask the butcher to reserve all trimmings.

MAKE AHEAD The sauce and gremolata pesto can be refrigerated overnight. Reheat the sauce gently and bring the pesto back to room temperature before serving.

WINE Cassis-inflected Cabernet Sauvignon: 2009 Louis M. Martini Sonoma County.

Ethiopian Spiced Lamb Stew

⏱ TOTAL: 45 MIN • 8 SERVINGS ●

- 2 tablespoons red wine
- 1 tablespoon fresh lemon juice
- 1 tablespoon *berbere* (see Note)
- 1 teaspoon smoked paprika
- 1 teaspoon Dijon mustard
- 3½ pounds trimmed boneless leg of lamb, cut into 1-inch cubes

Kosher salt and freshly ground pepper

- ¼ cup extra-virgin olive oil
- 2 red onions, halved and thinly sliced
- 6 garlic cloves, minced
- 2 teaspoons finely chopped rosemary
- 2 teaspoons finely chopped thyme
- 2 plum tomatoes, cut into ¾-inch dice
- 1 yellow bell pepper, cut into ½-inch dice
- 1 large shallot, thinly sliced

1. In a small bowl, whisk the wine with the lemon juice, *berbere*, paprika and mustard.

2. Season the lamb with salt and pepper. In a large enameled cast-iron casserole, heat the olive oil until shimmering. Add half of the lamb to the casserole and cook over moderately high heat, turning, until browned all over, 6 to 8 minutes. Using a slotted spoon, transfer the lamb to a medium bowl. Repeat with the remaining lamb.

3. Add the onions, garlic, rosemary, thyme and a generous pinch each of salt and pepper to the casserole and cook over moderate heat, stirring occasionally, until the onions have softened, about 8 minutes.

4. Add the lamb and any accumulated juices to the casserole along with the wine mixture, tomatoes, bell pepper and shallot. Cook over moderate heat, stirring, until the tomatoes and bell pepper have softened and the lamb is just cooked through, about 10 minutes. Season with salt and pepper and serve. —*Hiyaw Gebreyohannes*

NOTE *Berbere* is a mild Ethiopian spice blend. It is available online at *kalustyans.com* and *nirmalaskitchen.com*.

WINE Peppery, olive-scented, medium-bodied Côtes du Rhône: 2009 Sélection Laurence Féraud Séguret.

Mini-Meatball Indian Curry

ACTIVE: 30 MIN; TOTAL: 1 HR
6 SERVINGS ●

MEATBALLS

- 1¼ pounds ground lamb
- 1 jalapeño, seeded and minced
- 1 tablespoon minced peeled fresh ginger
- 1 large garlic clove, minced
- 1 cup cooked rice
- 1 large egg
- 2 tablespoons chopped cilantro
- 1 teaspoon garam masala

Kosher salt and freshly ground pepper
Canola oil, for greasing

CURRY

- 2 tablespoons canola oil
- 1 large onion, finely chopped
- 1 tablespoon minced peeled fresh ginger
- 1 large garlic clove, minced
- 2 teaspoons medium-hot Madras curry powder
- 6 tablespoons raw cashew butter
- 1½ cups tomato juice (12 ounces)

Kosher salt and freshly ground pepper

- ¼ cup cilantro leaves

Basmati rice and warm naan, for serving

1. MAKE THE MEATBALLS Preheat the broiler and position a rack 8 inches from the heat. In a medium bowl, knead the lamb with the jalapeño, ginger, garlic, rice, egg, cilantro, garam masala, 1 teaspoon of salt and ½ teaspoon of pepper. Roll the mixture into 18 balls and place on an oiled baking sheet. Broil for about 10 minutes, until the lamb meatballs are nearly cooked through and the tops are lightly browned.

2. MEANWHILE, MAKE THE CURRY In a medium enameled cast-iron casserole, heat the oil. Add the onion, cover and cook over high heat, stirring once or twice, until lightly browned, about 3 minutes. Add the ginger, garlic and curry powder and cook until fragrant, 1 minute. Stir in the cashew butter and cook for 1 minute. Add the tomato juice and 2 cups of water, season with salt and pepper and bring to a boil.

3. Add the meatballs and any pan drippings to the sauce, cover partially and simmer over moderate heat, stirring frequently, until the meat is tender and the sauce is very thick, about 30 minutes. Stir in the cilantro; serve with rice and warm naan. —*Grace Parisi*

WINE Fruit-forward, medium-bodied southern French red blend: 2009 Domaine Rimbert Les Travers de Marceau Saint-Chinian.

Zinfandel-Braised Lamb Chops with Dried Fruit

TOTAL: 1 HR • 4 SERVINGS ●

- 2 tablespoons extra-virgin olive oil

Four 8-ounce lamb shoulder chops (cut 1 inch thick)

Salt and freshly ground pepper

- 1 tablespoon ground coriander
- 8 garlic cloves, halved
- 10 thyme sprigs, plus more for garnish
- 1 cup big, jammy red wine, such as California Zinfandel
- ½ cup dried cherries (3 ounces)
- ½ cup dried California apricots (3 ounces), quartered
- 2 cups low-sodium beef broth

1. In a large, deep skillet, heat the olive oil. Season the lamb chops with salt and pepper and rub them all over with the coriander. Add the lamb chops to the skillet along with the garlic cloves and 10 thyme sprigs and cook over high heat, turning once, until the lamb chops are browned and the garlic cloves are browned in spots, about 6 minutes.

2. Add the red wine, dried cherries and dried apricots to the skillet and bring to a boil. Cook over moderate heat until the wine is reduced by half, about 5 minutes. Add the beef broth and bring to a boil. Cover partially and simmer over moderately low heat until the lamb is tender and the sauce is thick and glossy, about 35 minutes; turn the lamb chops once or twice during cooking. Discard the thyme sprigs. Serve the lamb chops at once, garnished with fresh thyme. —*Grace Parisi*

WINE Ripe, concentrated red from Italy's Veneto region: 2008 Allegrini Amarone.

● HEALTHY ● MAKE AHEAD ● VEGETARIAN ● STAFF FAVORITE

zinfandel-braised lamb chops with dried fruit

Curried Lamb Potpie

ACTIVE: 1 HR; TOTAL: 3 HR 15 MIN
6 SERVINGS ●

PASTRY

1½ cups all-purpose flour
½ teaspoon salt
1 stick cold unsalted butter, diced
¼ cup ice water

CURRY

3 tablespoons extra-virgin olive oil
2 pounds trimmed boneless lamb
   shoulder, cut into ¾-inch cubes
Salt and freshly ground pepper
1 medium onion, chopped
2 teaspoons curry powder
2½ tablespoons all-purpose flour
⅓ cup dry white wine
2 cups chicken stock
2 cups cubed (1-inch) peeled
   butternut squash (10 ounces)
2 cups chopped Tuscan kale
1 medium carrot, chopped
1 cup unsweetened coconut milk
2 tablespoons chopped parsley
1 large egg lightly beaten with
   1 teaspoon of water

1. MAKE THE PASTRY In a food processor, pulse the flour with the salt. Add the butter and pulse until it is the size of peas. Sprinkle the ice water over the mixture and pulse until the pastry starts to come together. On a work surface, gently knead the pastry a few times. Shape into a disk, wrap in plastic and refrigerate until firm, 1½ hours.

2. MAKE THE CURRY In a Dutch oven, heat 1 tablespoon of the oil. Season the lamb with salt and pepper and add half to the casserole. Cook over high heat until browned on 2 sides, about 3 minutes. Using a slotted spoon, transfer the lamb to a bowl; repeat with 1 more tablespoon of oil and the remaining lamb. Pour off the oil in the casserole.

3. Add the remaining 1 tablespoon of oil and the lamb to the casserole. Add the onion and cook over moderate heat, stirring, until softened. Add the curry powder and cook, stirring, for 1 minute. Stir in the flour, then slowly stir in the wine until smooth. Add the stock

and bring to a boil, stirring, until thickened, 1 minute. Cover and simmer over low heat until the lamb is very tender, 1 hour.

4. Add the squash, kale, carrot and coconut milk to the casserole and simmer over moderately low heat until the vegetables are tender, 10 minutes. Season with salt and pepper. Stir in the parsley and let cool.

5. Preheat the oven to 375°. Spoon the curry into a buttered 8-by-11-inch baking dish. Brush the dish rim with beaten egg. On a lightly floured surface, roll out the pastry to a 14-by-12-inch rectangle. Fold the pastry in half, unfold it over the curry and gently press onto the edge of the dish. Brush with beaten egg; cut 4 small steam vents in the top.

6. Bake the potpie for 40 minutes. Raise the heat to 450°; bake for 20 minutes longer, until the pastry is browned and cooked through. Let rest for 20 minutes, then serve.
—*Matthew Accarrino*

WINE Rich, juicy Sicilian red: 2010 Tenuta Rapitalà Nero d'Avola.

Stir-Fried Goat with Basil and Egg

TOTAL: 30 MIN • 4 SERVINGS ● ● ●

¼ cup plus 3 tablespoons canola oil
10 garlic cloves, minced
4 large shallots, thinly sliced
1½ pounds coarsely ground lean goat
10 Thai bird chiles, 4 thinly sliced
½ cup Asian fish sauce
3 tablespoons palm sugar or
   light brown sugar
¼ cup shredded basil leaves
4 large eggs
Steamed rice, for serving

1. In a large skillet, heat 3 tablespoons of the oil. Add the garlic and shallots and cook over moderately high heat, stirring occasionally, until softened. Add the goat and cook, stirring, until lightly browned, about 8 minutes. Tilt the pan and spoon off as much fat as possible. Add the whole Thai chiles, ¼ cup of the fish sauce, the palm sugar and ½ cup of water and simmer until the sugar is dissolved. Stir in the basil; keep warm.

2. In a small bowl, combine the sliced chiles with the remaining ¼ cup of fish sauce.

3. In a large nonstick skillet, heat the remaining ¼ cup of oil. Fry the eggs, 2 at a time, over high heat, tilting the pan and spooning the hot oil over the eggs to puff them up.

4. Spoon the stir-fried goat over steamed rice and top with the fried eggs. Serve the chile-fish sauce on the side. —*Johnny Monis*

WINE Juicy, concentrated Garnacha: 2010 Bodegas Borsao Monte Oton.

Bison Steaks with Fig Balsamic Sauce

ACTIVE: 25 MIN; TOTAL: 45 MIN
4 SERVINGS ●

2 cups dry red wine
2 tablespoons fig balsamic or
   plain balsamic vinegar
2 tablespoons beef or veal demiglace
   (see Note)
Salt and freshly ground pepper
4 tablespoons unsalted butter
Four 5-ounce bison tenderloin steaks
4 large garlic cloves, lightly smashed

1. In a small saucepan, combine the wine, vinegar and demiglace and bring to a boil. Simmer over moderate heat until the sauce is reduced to a thick glaze (about ½ cup), about 20 minutes. Season the glaze lightly with salt and pepper.

2. In a heavy skillet, melt the butter. Lightly season the steaks with salt and pepper and add them to the pan along with the garlic. Cook over moderate heat, turning the steaks occasionally, until the meat is browned and crusty all over and an instant-read thermometer inserted in the center registers 130° for medium-rare, about 14 minutes. Transfer the steaks to a platter and let rest for 5 minutes; discard the garlic. Transfer the steaks to plates and serve with the fig balsamic sauce.
—*Garrett Weber-Gale*

NOTE Frozen demiglace, a kind of concentrated stock, is available at Whole Foods and online at *dartagnan.com*.

WINE Earthy, dried fruit–scented Barolo: 2007 Casa E. di Mirafiore.

Guinness-Marinated Bison Steak Sandwiches

TOTAL: 50 MIN PLUS OVERNIGHT
MARINATING • 4 SERVINGS

1 cup Guinness or other dark stout
½ cup finely chopped red onion, plus 1 large red onion sliced into ½-inch-thick rings
⅓ cup soy sauce
2 tablespoons light molasses
1 tablespoon finely chopped thyme
1 tablespoon minced garlic
½ teaspoon Worcestershire sauce
Salt and freshly ground black pepper
Four 6- to 8-ounce boneless bison rib eye steaks, about 1½ inches thick (see Note)
Extra-virgin olive oil, for brushing
24 cremini mushrooms, stemmed
Four ½-inch-thick slices of rye toast

1. In a bowl, whisk the Guinness, chopped onion, soy sauce, molasses, thyme, garlic, Worcestershire sauce and 2 teaspoons of pepper. Pour the marinade into a large resealable plastic bag. Add the steaks and turn to coat. Seal and refrigerate overnight.
2. Light a gas grill; set it up for both direct and indirect grilling by turning off half of the burners. Remove the steaks from the marinade and pat dry. Brush with oil; season with salt and pepper. Grill over moderately high heat, turning once, until lightly charred, 6 minutes. Move the steaks to indirect heat, close the grill and cook until medium-rare, 8 to 10 minutes. Let rest on a carving board for 10 minutes. Slice ½ inch thick.
3. Brush the onion rings and mushrooms with olive oil and season with salt and pepper. Grill over moderately high heat, turning occasionally, until softened, 6 minutes.
4. Arrange the toasts on plates or a platter and top with the grilled onions, sliced steak and mushrooms. Drizzle with any juices from the bison steaks and serve. —*Bruce Aidells*
NOTE Boneless bison rib eye steaks are available at *dartagnan.com.*
WINE Robust, juicy Spanish red: 2009 Capçanes Costers del Gravet Montsant.

Green Curry of Rabbit, Butternut Squash and Dill

ACTIVE: 30 MIN; TOTAL: 1 HR 45 MIN
4 SERVINGS ● ● ●

This warming rabbit curry, inspired by a northern Thai recipe, is light, tangy and very fragrant from the kaffir lime leaves, lemongrass, fresh dill and basil.

3 large lemongrass stalks, tender inner bulb only, minced
6 large shallots, thinly sliced
10 garlic cloves, finely chopped
6 Thai bird chiles, sliced
¼ cup canola oil
One 2½-pound rabbit, cut into 8 pieces
½ cup Asian fish sauce
One 1¼-pound butternut squash— peeled, seeded and cut into 1½-inch chunks
¼ cup fresh lime juice
10 kaffir lime leaves, inner ribs removed and leaves very thinly sliced
6 scallions, thinly sliced
¾ cup chopped dill
½ cup shredded basil or whole Thai basil leaves
Steamed rice, for serving

1. In a food processor, combine the lemongrass, shallots, garlic and chiles and process to a paste. In a large enameled cast-iron casserole or Dutch oven, heat the canola oil. Add the lemongrass paste and cook over moderate heat, stirring frequently, until fragrant and just beginning to brown, about 5 minutes. Add the rabbit, fish sauce and 8 cups of water and bring to a boil. Simmer over low heat, partially covered, until the rabbit is tender, about 1 hour.
2. Transfer the rabbit to a plate and add the butternut squash to the casserole. Cook over moderate heat until the squash is tender but not mushy, about 15 minutes. Return the rabbit to the pot and stir in the lime juice, lime leaves, scallions, dill and basil. Cook just until the rabbit is heated through. Serve with rice. —*Johnny Monis*
WINE Full-bodied, yellow apple–inflected white: 2010 Château de Campuget Tradition.

Braised Wild Boar Shanks with Sweet Soy and Star Anise

ACTIVE: 30 MIN; TOTAL: 2 HR 30 MIN
6 SERVINGS ● ●

Wild boar shanks are a great alternative to farmed pork. Johnny Monis, the chef at Komi and Little Serow in Washington, DC, braises the meat in an aromatic broth loaded with garlic, star anise, cloves and cinnamon.

¼ cup canola oil
6 wild boar shanks (about 5 pounds)
12 garlic cloves, lightly smashed
8 star anise pods
3 whole cloves
Two 4-inch cinnamon sticks
1 cup low-sodium soy sauce
¼ cup *kecap manis* (sweet Indonesian soy sauce) or 2 tablespoons molasses
1 cup palm sugar or light brown sugar
Steamed rice and cilantro leaves, for serving

1. In a very large skillet, heat the canola oil. Add the boar shanks in a single layer and cook over moderately high heat, turning occasionally, until browned, about 10 minutes. Transfer the shanks to a large enameled cast-iron casserole or Dutch oven.
2. Add the smashed garlic cloves, star anise pods, whole cloves and cinnamon sticks to the skillet and cook over low heat, stirring occasionally, until fragrant, about 1 minute. Add 10 cups of water, the soy sauce, *kecap manis* and sugar and scrape up any browned bits stuck to the pan.
3. Pour the liquid from the skillet into the casserole and bring to a boil. Simmer over low heat, partially covered, until the meat is tender and nearly falling off the bone, about 2 hours; turn the shanks occasionally.
4. Transfer the boar shanks to shallow bowls and strain the broth. Spoon off as much fat as possible. Serve the braised boar shanks with steamed rice and cilantro and spoon some of the fragrant broth on top.
—*Johnny Monis*
WINE Robust, meaty Syrah: 2009 Domaine Alain Graillot Crozes-Hermitage.

Chef Naomi Pomeroy of Portland,
Oregon's Beast restaurant cooks for a
dinner party at Esque glass studio.
A table set with Esque glassware sur-
rounds dishes cooked in the studio's
super-hot ovens, like blistered snap peas
with mint, OPPOSITE; *recipe, page 226.*

VEGETABLES
& TOFU

Haricots Verts and White Beans with Shallot Vinaigrette

ACTIVE: 35 MIN; TOTAL: 2 HR PLUS
OVERNIGHT SOAKING • 10 TO 12 SERVINGS

● ●

- 2 cups dried white beans, such as cannellini, soaked overnight and drained
- 1 small onion, halved
- 1 bay leaf
- 1 large thyme sprig

Kosher salt

- 2 pounds haricots verts, trimmed
- 2 large shallots, minced
- 2 garlic cloves, minced
- 1 tablespoon Dijon mustard
- 2 tablespoons sherry vinegar
- 2 tablespoons red wine vinegar
- ½ cup extra-virgin olive oil

Freshly ground pepper

- ¼ cup chopped parsley

1. In a large pot, cover the dried beans with 3 inches of water. Add the onion, bay leaf and thyme and bring to a boil. Simmer over low heat, stirring occasionally, until the beans are tender, about 1 hour and 15 minutes. Add more water as needed to maintain the water level. Add 2 teaspoons of salt and remove the pot from the heat. Let the beans cool in the cooking water.

2. In a large pot of salted boiling water, cook the haricots verts until crisp-tender, about 3 minutes. Drain the beans and spread them on a large rimmed baking sheet to cool.

3. In a small bowl, combine the shallots with the garlic, mustard and both vinegars. Add a pinch of salt and let the vinaigrette stand for 10 minutes. Whisk in the olive oil and season with salt and pepper.

4. Drain the beans and discard the onion, bay leaf and thyme. Transfer the beans to a large bowl; add the haricots verts and vinaigrette and toss well. Season with salt and pepper and transfer to a platter. Sprinkle with the parsley and serve. —*David Tanis*

MAKE AHEAD The dried beans can be prepared through Step 1 and refrigerated in their liquid overnight.

Green Beans Two Ways

⏱ TOTAL: 30 MIN • 8 SERVINGS ●

- 2 tablespoons chopped tarragon
- ¾ teaspoon chopped rosemary
- 1 teaspoon finely grated lemon zest plus 1 tablespoon fresh lemon juice
- ½ teaspoon finely grated orange zest plus 2 tablespoons fresh orange juice

Salt and freshly ground pepper

- 1 large garlic clove, minced
- 4 tablespoons unsalted butter
- 2½ pounds green beans
- ¾ cup low-sodium chicken broth

1. In a small bowl, combine the tarragon, rosemary, lemon zest and orange zest. Season the gremolata with salt and pepper.

2. In a large skillet, cook the garlic in the butter over moderately high heat until just fragrant, 1 minute. Add the green beans, toss to coat and cook for 2 minutes. Add the broth, cover tightly and bring to a boil. Cook until the beans are crisp-tender, about 3 minutes. Remove the lid and cook, tossing occasionally, until the broth is nearly evaporated and the beans are tender, 4 minutes longer.

3. FOR KIDS Transfer half of the beans to a bowl and season with salt and pepper.

FOR ADULTS Add the gremolata to the beans in the skillet and toss until fragrant. Stir in the orange and lemon juices and transfer the green beans to a bowl. Serve right away. —*Katie Workman*

Garlicky Potatoes, Green Beans and Cauliflower

⏱ TOTAL: 30 MIN • 4 TO 6 SERVINGS ● ●

- 1 pound fingerling potatoes, scrubbed but not peeled

Salt

- 3 cups cauliflower florets
- 1 pound green beans
- 3 tablespoons extra-virgin olive oil
- 4 garlic cloves, finely chopped
- ½ teaspoon spicy pimentón de la Vera (hot smoked Spanish paprika)
- 1 tablespoon sherry vinegar

1. In a large pot, cover the fingerling potatoes with 2 inches of salted water and bring to a boil over high heat. Reduce the heat to moderate and cook until the potatoes are almost tender, about 8 minutes. Add the cauliflower and green beans to the pot and simmer until tender, about 5 minutes.

2. Meanwhile, in a small skillet, heat the olive oil. Add the garlic and cook over low heat until golden brown, about 1 minute. Add the pimentón de la Vera and a large pinch of salt and remove from the heat.

3. Drain the vegetables well and transfer to a serving bowl. Season with salt and drizzle with the garlic oil. Sprinkle with the vinegar, toss well and serve. —*José Andrés*

Blistered Snap Peas with Mint

📷 PAGE 225

⏱ TOTAL: 15 MIN • 8 SERVINGS ● ●

Get a skillet really, really hot before adding the snap peas (they make a fun popping sound when they hit the pan), then put the skillet straight into a very hot oven, carefully tossing the snap peas every few minutes so that they don't burn.

- 1 tablespoon pure olive oil
- 2 pounds sugar snap peas, ends trimmed and strings discarded
- 1½ tablespoons lemon olive oil (see Note)

Flaky sea salt, such as Maldon

- ¼ cup mint leaves, torn

Preheat the oven to 500°. Set a large oven-proof skillet over high heat until very hot, about 2 minutes. Add the pure olive oil and swirl to coat the pan. Add the snap peas, toss a few times and transfer the skillet to the oven. Cook for 2 minutes, then carefully toss the peas a few times. Return the skillet to the oven and cook for 2 minutes longer, until the peas are crisp-tender. Toss the peas with the lemon oil and season with salt. Transfer to a serving bowl. Scatter the mint on top and serve. —*Naomi Pomeroy*

NOTE Olive oil pressed or infused with lemon is available at most supermarkets and specialty food stores.

garlicky potatoes, green beans and cauliflower

Peas and Pea Shoots with Spring Onions and Mint

⏱ TOTAL: 20 MIN • 8 SERVINGS ● ●

"Come March, it's no longer possible to be inspired by root vegetables," says chef Mike Lata of Fig restaurant in Charleston, South Carolina. "You've done everything you can." When spring finally arrives, he uses delicate peas and pea shoots in this simple side dish.

- 1 pound frozen peas (4 cups)
- 1½ tablespoons extra-virgin olive oil
- 3 medium spring onions (bulbing), sliced ¼ inch thick (3 cups)

Salt

- 3 tablespoons unsalted butter
- 3 cups lightly packed tender pea shoots or small watercress sprigs
- ⅓ cup fresh mint leaves

Freshly ground black pepper

1. In a large saucepan of salted boiling water, cook the peas until they are just tender, about 3 minutes. Drain.
2. In the same saucepan, heat the olive oil. Add the spring onions and a pinch of salt, cover and cook over moderately low heat, stirring occasionally, until softened, about 5 minutes. Stir in the peas, cover and cook until heated through, about 1 minute. Stir in the butter, 1 tablespoon at a time. Remove the peas and spring onions from the heat and stir in the pea shoots until they are wilted. Stir in the mint leaves, season with salt and freshly ground pepper and serve.
—*Mike Lata*

PAIRING TIP

wines for spring vegetables Spring vegetables like artichokes and asparagus can be tricky to pair with because they can make wine taste oddly sweet or even metallic. One wine that works is a citrusy Sauvignon Blanc, like the 2010 Silvertap, which acts like a squeeze of lemon with the dish.

Singaporean Sautéed Asparagus with Ginger

⏱ TOTAL: 35 MIN • 6 SERVINGS ●

Asparagus sautéed with garlic, ginger, sweet Chinese sausage and sauerkraut is terrific with a creamy Singapore-style sauce.

- 1½ tablespoons canola oil, plus more for grilling
- 1 Thai chile, thinly sliced
- 1 tablespoon minced fresh ginger, plus about 20 thin matchsticks
- 2 garlic cloves, minced
- 4 tablespoons unsalted butter, cut into tablespoons
- 1 hard-cooked egg yolk, mashed to a paste
- ¼ cup heavy cream

Salt and freshly ground pepper

- ¾ pound medium asparagus
- 1 Chinese sausage link (2 to 3 ounces), thinly sliced (see Note)
- 1 tablespoon sauerkraut, squeezed dry
- 1 scallion, thinly sliced

1. In a medium saucepan, heat ½ tablespoon of the oil. Add the Thai chile, minced ginger and half of the garlic and cook over moderate heat until softened, about 2 minutes. Add the butter and swirl until melted. Add the egg yolk; whisk until blended. Add the cream, season with salt and pepper and simmer just until the sauce is slightly thickened, about 2 minutes.
2. Light a grill or preheat a grill pan; oil the grates. Grill the asparagus, turning occasionally, until crisp-tender, about 5 minutes. Transfer the asparagus to a work surface and cut them into 2-inch lengths. In a large skillet, heat the remaining 1 tablespoon of oil. Add the Chinese sausage, sauerkraut, ginger matchsticks and the remaining garlic and cook over moderate heat, stirring occasionally, until lightly browned, about 2 minutes. Add the asparagus and scallion and stir-fry until heated through, about 1 minute. Remove from the heat and stir in half of the sauce. Transfer the asparagus to a platter and drizzle with the remaining sauce. Serve right away. —*Bryant Ng*

NOTE Chinese sausage is available at Asian markets and many large supermarkets.
WINE Bright, grassy Sauvignon Blanc: 2010 Domaine du Salvard Cheverny.

Braised Dandelion Greens

ACTIVE: 20 MIN; TOTAL: 1 HR 20 MIN
6 SERVINGS ● ● ●

In his first cookbook, called *Beginnings,* chef Chris Cosentino focuses on Italian-inspired, vegetable-focused dishes like these healthy dandelion greens simmered with a pecorino rind rather than the offal-centric food he is well known for serving at his San Francisco restaurant, Incanto.

- 2 tablespoons extra-virgin olive oil, plus more for drizzling
- 1 medium onion, finely chopped
- 1 head of garlic, halved crosswise and most of skin discarded
- 2 ancho chiles, broken and seeds discarded
- 3 guajillo chiles—stemmed, seeded and broken into pieces
- 1 pound dandelion greens, thick ends trimmed and leaves cut crosswise into 2-inch-thick strips
- 5½ cups chicken stock or low-sodium broth

One 4-inch piece of pecorino rind, plus shavings for garnish

Salt

- 12 grilled baguette slices
- 1 whole lemon

1. In a large pot, heat the 2 tablespoons of oil. Add the onion and garlic and cook over moderate heat until softened, 5 minutes. Add the chiles and cook until sizzling, 1 minute. Add the dandelion greens and cook, stirring, until wilted, 1 minute. Add the stock and pecorino rind and bring to a boil. Simmer over low heat until the greens are very tender, about 1 hour. Season with salt.
2. Rub the grilled bread with the lemon. Place a slice in each of 6 bowls. Ladle in the greens and broth, drizzle with olive oil and garnish with pecorino shavings. Serve with the remaining toasts. —*Chris Cosentino*

peas and pea shoots with spring onions and mint

Grilled Summer Squash with Bagna Cauda and Fried Capers

⏱ **TOTAL: 45 MIN • 8 SERVINGS** ● ●

This fast recipe is an excellent way to dress up summer squash, Italian-style: Slices of grilled zucchini and yellow squash are drizzled with bagna cauda, the simple Piedmontese sauce of olive oil, anchovies and garlic, then topped with crispy fried capers.

½ cup extra-virgin olive oil, plus more for brushing

One 3½-ounce jar capers, drained and patted dry with paper towels

8 anchovy fillets, minced

6 garlic cloves, minced

Four 8-ounce zucchini, sliced lengthwise ¼ inch thick

Four 8-ounce yellow squash, sliced lengthwise ¼ inch thick

Salt and freshly ground pepper

Finely grated zest and juice of 1 lemon

1 tablespoon minced flat-leaf parsley, plus 1 cup parsley leaves

1. In a medium skillet, heat the ½ cup of olive oil. Add the capers in an even layer and cook over moderate heat until the capers start to sizzle, about 2 minutes; stand back, as the capers may spatter. Reduce the heat to moderately low and continue to cook until the capers are crisp, about 4 minutes longer. With a slotted spoon, transfer the capers to paper towels to drain.

2. Stir the anchovies and garlic into the olive oil in the skillet. Simmer over low heat until the garlic starts to turn golden, about 10 minutes. Remove from the heat.

3. Light a grill. Brush the slices of zucchini and squash with olive oil and season them with salt and pepper. Grill over high heat until they are just tender and nicely charred, about 2 minutes per side. Transfer the zucchini and squash to a platter.

4. Rewarm the anchovy dressing and add the lemon zest, lemon juice and minced parsley. Drizzle the warm bagna cauda over the grilled zucchini and squash, sprinkle with the fried capers and parsley leaves and serve. —*Jeff Banker*

Zucchini Ribbons and Peaches with Macadamia Cream

TOTAL: 40 MIN PLUS OVERNIGHT SOAKING • 6 SERVINGS ● ●

Chef Alyssa Gorelick of Fern, a vegetarian restaurant in Charlotte, North Carolina, uses macadamia nuts two ways in this summery zucchini-and-peach salad: coarsely chopped, for crunch, and also pureed to make a dairy-free cream. She likes to drizzle any leftover macadamia cream on stir-fries.

3 zucchini (1½ pounds total), sliced lengthwise ¼ inch thick

3 peaches, halved

¼ cup extra-virgin olive oil

Salt and freshly ground pepper

2 tablespoons chopped parsley

2 tablespoons finely chopped mint

2 tablespoons macadamia nuts, toasted and coarsely chopped

¼ cup Macadamia Cream (optional; recipe follows)

1. Light a grill or preheat a grill pan. Brush the zucchini and peaches with half of the oil and season with salt and pepper. Grill them over moderate heat until slightly softened, 4 minutes. Cut the peaches into wedges. Stack the zucchini and thinly slice lengthwise into ribbons.

2. In a bowl, toss the zucchini, parsley and mint with the remaining oil; season with salt and pepper. Transfer to a platter and top with the peaches and chopped nuts. Drizzle with the Macadamia Cream and serve.

—*Alyssa Gorelick*

WINE Floral, peach-scented Viognier: 2010 Calera Central Coast.

MACADAMIA CREAM

TOTAL: 15 MIN PLUS OVERNIGHT SOAKING

MAKES ABOUT ⅔ CUP ● ●

½ cup raw macadamia nuts (2 ounces)

1 tablespoon fresh lime juice

1 tablespoon agave nectar

½ teaspoon xanthan gum (see Note)

Salt

1. In a bowl, cover the macadamia nuts with 1 cup of water. Cover the bowl with plastic wrap and let the nuts stand at room temperature overnight.

2. Pour the nuts and water into a blender and puree. Strain the nut milk through a fine sieve into a bowl, pressing on the solids to extract as much milk as possible.

3. Rinse out the blender and return the strained milk to it. Add the lime juice and agave nectar. With the machine on, add the xanthan gum and blend until the cream is light and airy, about 1 minute. Scrape the cream into a bowl and season with salt. —*AG*

NOTE Xanthan gum is an industrial powder that's now available at many supermarkets.

MAKE AHEAD The cream can be refrigerated for up to 3 days.

Grilled Okra with Red Curry–Lime Dressing

⏱ **TOTAL: 20 MIN • 4 SERVINGS** ● ● ●

Okra is usually fried or simmered in soups. Here it gets charred and tender on the grill, then tossed with a simple dressing of lime juice and store-bought curry paste. Be sure to double-skewer the okra before grilling—it makes the pods easier to turn.

1 tablespoon Thai red curry paste

¼ cup extra-virgin olive oil, plus more for brushing

2 tablespoons fresh lime juice

Salt

1 pound okra, trimmed

1. Light a grill or preheat a grill pan. In a small bowl, whisk the curry paste with the ¼ cup of olive oil and the lime juice; season the dressing with salt. Double-skewer the okra crosswise onto 4 pairs of bamboo skewers. Brush the okra with oil and season with salt.

2. Brush the grill grates with olive oil. Grill the okra over high heat, turning once or twice, until lightly charred in spots and tender, about 10 minutes. Brush with some of the curry dressing and grill until the okra is sizzling, about 1 minute longer. Drizzle the okra with the remaining dressing and serve warm. —*Grace Parisi*

grilled okra with red curry–lime dressing

Sautéed Baby Squash with Scallions

⏱ TOTAL: 20 MIN • 6 SERVINGS ● ●

This quick side dish is a great showcase for summer-fresh baby squash like pattypan and baby zucchini.

2 tablespoons unsalted butter
1¼ pounds baby squash, halved
1 bunch of scallions, finely chopped
1 large shallot, finely chopped
Salt and freshly ground pepper
3 tablespoons chopped flat-leaf parsley

In a large skillet, melt the butter. Add the squash, scallions and shallot and season with salt and pepper. Cover and cook over moderate heat, stirring occasionally, until the squash is tender and lightly browned, 8 minutes. Stir in the parsley and serve right away. —Kelly Liken

Garlic-Mashed Butternut Squash

ACTIVE: 30 MIN; TOTAL: 2 HR
6 SERVINGS ● ● ●

Two 2-pound butternut squash, peeled and sliced ¾ inch thick
12 garlic cloves, peeled
¼ cup extra-virgin olive oil
1 rosemary sprig
1 jalapeño, halved and seeded
Salt and freshly ground pepper
2 tablespoons unsalted butter, melted

1. Preheat the oven to 400°. In a large bowl, toss the squash with the garlic, olive oil, rosemary and jalapeño and season with salt and pepper. Spread the squash mixture on a large baking sheet, cover with foil and roast for about 45 minutes, until the squash is tender. Uncover and roast until lightly browned in spots, about 45 minutes longer.
2. Discard the rosemary; mince the jalapeño. Transfer the squash, garlic and jalapeño to a bowl. Add the butter, season with salt and pepper and mash, then serve. —Grace Parisi
MAKE AHEAD The mashed squash can be refrigerated for up to 2 days.

Roasted Winter Squash with Herbs and Garlic

ACTIVE: 30 MIN; TOTAL: 2 HR 15 MIN
10 TO 12 SERVINGS ● ●

7 pounds winter squash, such as butternut—peeled, halved, seeded and cut into 1-inch cubes
½ cup extra-virgin olive oil
6 garlic cloves, minced
2 tablespoons chopped sage
2 tablespoons chopped thyme
Salt and freshly ground pepper

Preheat the oven to 350°. In a large bowl, toss the squash cubes with the olive oil, garlic, sage and thyme. Season with salt and pepper and toss again. Spread the squash in 2 large rectangular baking dishes about 1½ inches deep. Bake in the upper third of the oven for about 1½ hours, until the squash is tender and browned around the edges. Let rest for 10 minutes before serving. —David Tanis

Coffee-Baked Squash with Crème Fraîche

ACTIVE: 10 MIN; TOTAL: 1 HR 10 MIN
4 SERVINGS ● ●

You don't need to buy good-quality coffee beans for this dish. The beans that the squash bake in cannot be reused, so be sure to get inexpensive ones.

1 pound unflavored coffee beans
4 small, thin-skinned winter squash, such as Delicata, scrubbed
½ cup crème fraîche
Salt and freshly ground pepper

1. Preheat the oven to 350°. Spread the coffee beans in a medium roasting pan and nestle the squash into the beans. Roast the squash for about 1 hour, until very tender; turn them halfway through cooking.
2. Cut each squash in half and scoop out the seeds. Spoon 1 tablespoon of the crème fraîche into each squash half, season with salt and pepper and serve.
—Daniel Patterson and René Redzepi

Sautéed Radishes with Orange Butter

⏱ TOTAL: 30 MIN • 6 SERVINGS

"Radishes grow just about anywhere. People think, 'Oh it's just a radish.' But radishes are delicious, and people don't really think of cooking them," says superstar chef Emeril Lagasse. He sautés radishes and their greens with bacon, shallots and orange juice until they're perfectly crisp-tender.

¼ pound applewood-smoked bacon, cut into 1-inch dice
6 tablespoons unsalted butter
3 pounds radishes with their greens— radishes quartered lengthwise with some stem still attached, greens coarsely chopped
Salt and freshly ground black pepper
3 large shallots, thinly sliced
1 tablespoon sugar
1 cup freshly squeezed orange juice

1. In a large, deep skillet, cook the bacon over moderate heat until crisp, about 4 minutes. Using a slotted spoon, transfer the bacon to paper towels to drain. Pour off the bacon fat in the skillet.
2. Add 2 tablespoons of the butter to the skillet and melt over moderately high heat. Add the radish greens, season them with salt and freshly ground pepper and cook, stirring, until wilted, about 3 minutes. Scrape the greens into a bowl.
3. Melt the remaining 4 tablespoons of butter in the skillet. Add the quartered radishes, sliced shallots and crisp bacon and cook over moderately high heat, stirring a few times, until the radishes are golden brown, about 6 minutes. Add the sugar and cook for about 2 minutes, until the sugar is dissolved. Add the orange juice and bring the liquid to a boil, stirring a few times, until the radishes are barely tender and the sauce is lightly thickened, about 2 minutes. Stir in the radish greens and season with salt and freshly ground pepper.
4. Transfer the radishes and greens to a platter and serve them right away.
—Emeril Lagasse

sautéed radishes with orange butter

Tomato, Chard and Gruyère Casserole

ACTIVE: 45 MIN; TOTAL: 2 HR 15 MIN
8 SERVINGS ●

5½ pounds Swiss chard, stemmed
¼ cup extra-virgin olive oil
2 large onions, thinly sliced
1 tablespoon chopped thyme
1 cup dry white wine
Salt and freshly ground pepper
3 cups chicken stock or
    low-sodium broth
One 1-pound loaf of day-old peasant
    bread, sliced ½ inch thick
3 pounds beefsteak tomatoes,
    sliced ½ inch thick
9 ounces Gruyère cheese, shredded
    (3 cups)
3 tablespoons unsalted butter,
    melted

1. In a large pot of boiling water, cook the chard for 2 minutes; drain. When the leaves are cool enough to handle, squeeze out the excess water. Coarsely chop the chard.
2. In the same pot, heat the olive oil. Add the onions and thyme and cook over moderately low heat, stirring occasionally, until softened, about 12 minutes. Add the chard and wine and simmer over moderately high heat until the wine is reduced to ¼ cup, about 5 minutes. Season with salt and pepper.
3. Preheat the oven to 400°. In a small saucepan, bring the chicken stock to a simmer. Butter a 10-by-15-inch baking dish. Line the bottom of the dish with one-third of the bread, overlapping the slices slightly and cutting the bread to fit. Top with half of the tomato slices and season with salt and pepper. Spread half of the chopped chard on top, then sprinkle with half of the shredded cheese. Repeat the layering once and finish with the remaining bread. Pour the hot stock over the casserole and press with a spatula. Brush the top with the melted butter.
4. Cover the dish with foil and bake in the upper third of the oven for 1 hour. Uncover the dish and bake for about 10 minutes longer, until the top is browned and crisp.

5. Let the casserole rest for at least 10 minutes before serving.
—Nico Monday and Amelia O'Reilly
WINE Bright, light-bodied Beaujolais: 2010 Guy Breton Morgon.

Japanese-Style Swiss Chard and Spinach

TOTAL: 25 MIN • 4 SERVINGS ● ●
"I love to serve dishes on the menu that you wouldn't expect to find on this little island [North Haven] in Maine, where you're expecting things like fried clams," says Nebo Lodge chef Amanda Hallowell. So when she has a surplus of Swiss chard and spinach, instead of sautéing them, she makes this variation on the classic Japanese dish called *oshitashi*.

½ pound Swiss chard, stems removed
    and reserved for another use
½ pound baby spinach
¼ cup soy sauce
1 tablespoon Asian fish sauce
1 tablespoon toasted sesame oil
1 tablespoon unsalted butter
Toasted sesame seeds and dried bonito
    flakes (see Note), for garnish

1. In a large saucepan of salted boiling water, cook the Swiss chard leaves until they are bright green and tender, about 1 minute. With a slotted spoon, transfer the chard to a colander to drain. Repeat with the spinach. When the greens are cool enough to handle, gently squeeze out the excess water, then coarsely chop them.
2. In a small bowl, combine the soy sauce, fish sauce and sesame oil. In a large skillet, melt the butter and remove from the heat. Add 3 tablespoons of the soy mixture and the chopped greens to the skillet and toss to coat. Transfer the greens to a large plate to cool slightly.
3. Form the greens into 8 mounds on a platter. Spoon the remaining soy mixture over the mounds, garnish with the toasted sesame seeds and bonito flakes and serve.
—Amanda Hallowell
NOTE Bonito flakes are available at Asian or specialty food markets.

Spinach and Parmesan Sformati

ACTIVE: 35 MIN; TOTAL: 1 HR 45 MIN
6 FIRST-COURSE SERVINGS ● ●

4 tablespoons unsalted butter,
    plus more for coating
½ cup freshly grated Parmigiano-
    Reggiano cheese, plus
    more for coating and sprinkling
⅓ cup all-purpose flour
2 cups whole milk
⅛ teaspoon freshly grated nutmeg
Kosher salt and freshly ground pepper
¾ pound curly spinach leaves, stemmed
4 large eggs
1 large egg yolk
Extra-virgin olive oil, for drizzling

1. Preheat the oven to 325°. Butter six 6-ounce ramekins, dust with cheese and set them in a large baking dish.
2. In a small saucepan, melt the 4 tablespoons of butter. Over moderate heat, stir in the flour until incorporated, then gradually whisk in the milk until smooth and thick. Cook, whisking often, until no floury taste remains, about 5 minutes. Add the nutmeg and season with salt and pepper. Transfer to a bowl, press plastic wrap directly onto the surface and let stand until warm.
3. Meanwhile, in a large pot of boiling water, cook the spinach until just tender, about 1 minute. Drain the spinach and let it cool slightly, then squeeze out as much water as possible. Transfer the spinach to a food processor and puree. Add the white sauce and process until blended. Add the eggs, egg yolk, ½ cup of cheese and 1 teaspoon of salt and process until smooth. Pour the *sformato* mixture into the prepared ramekins. Carefully pour enough hot water into the baking dish to reach halfway up the sides of the ramekins.
4. Cover the baking dish with foil and bake the *sformati* for about 1 hour and 5 minutes, until just set. Transfer the ramekins to a work surface; let stand for 5 minutes. Run a small, thin knife around the edges of the ramekins and invert the *sformati* onto plates. Drizzle with olive oil, sprinkle with cheese and serve.
—Lachlan Mackinnon-Patterson

● HEALTHY ● MAKE AHEAD ● VEGETARIAN ● STAFF FAVORITE

Swiss Chard with Ginger and Cumin

⏲ **TOTAL: 35 MIN • 6 SERVINGS** ● ● ○ ○

¼ cup plus 2 tablespoons vegetable oil
1 teaspoon cumin seeds
2 jalapeños, minced
1½ tablespoons minced fresh ginger
3 pounds Swiss chard—rinsed, stems cut into ½-inch pieces, leaves cut into 1-inch ribbons
Salt
1½ tablespoons fresh lemon juice

In a large, deep skillet, heat the oil. Add the cumin and cook over moderately high heat until slightly darkened, 10 seconds. Add the jalapeños and ginger and cook, stirring, until fragrant, 1 minute. Stir in the chard leaves and stems with the water that clings to the leaves and a pinch of salt. Cover and cook over low heat, stirring, until the chard is tender, 12 minutes. Uncover and cook over high heat until most of the liquid has evaporated, 2 minutes. Add the lemon juice, season the chard with salt and serve. —*Madhur Jaffrey*

Braised Vegetable Hash

⏲ **TOTAL: 45 MIN • 4 SERVINGS** ○

1 cup extra-virgin olive oil
2 thyme sprigs
1 garlic clove
¾ pound Yukon Gold potatoes, peeled and cut into ½-inch dice
Salt
1 fennel bulb, cut into ¼-inch dice, fronds reserved for garnish
1 medium red onion, diced
1 medium red bell pepper, diced
2 tablespoons red wine vinegar

1. In a saucepan, combine the oil, thyme and garlic. Heat the potatoes slowly until they begin to sizzle. Cook over moderate heat until the potatoes are barely cooked, 5 minutes. Remove from the heat; let stand for 10 minutes. Using a slotted spoon, transfer the potatoes to a plate; season with salt. Discard the garlic and thyme; reserve the oil.

2. Transfer 2 tablespoons of the reserved oil to a large skillet. Add the fennel, onion and red pepper and season with salt. Cover and cook over low heat, stirring, until the vegetables are softened, 10 minutes. Add the vinegar and cook until evaporated, about 2 minutes. Scrape the vegetables into a bowl.
3. Wipe out the skillet. Add 2 tablespoons of the reserved oil and heat until shimmering. Add the blanched potatoes and cook over moderately high heat, stirring once or twice, until crisp, about 5 minutes. Return all of the vegetables to the skillet and cook over moderately high heat, stirring, for about 2 minutes. Season with salt. Transfer the vegetables to a bowl, garnish with fennel fronds and serve. —*Thomas Keller*

Fried Artichokes with Citrus and Parsley

⏲ **TOTAL: 40 MIN**
4 FIRST-COURSE SERVINGS ● ● ○

4 large artichokes
½ lemon
Vegetable oil, for frying
2 tablespoons minced flat-leaf parsley
1 teaspoon finely grated lemon zest
1 teaspoon finely grated orange zest
½ teaspoon Aleppo pepper (see Note)
Maldon sea salt

1. Working with 1 artichoke at a time, using a serrated bread knife, cut off all but 2 inches of the leaves. Pull off and discard the dark green outer leaves, then peel and trim the bottom and the stem. Quarter the artichoke and scrape out the hairy choke. Rub the artichoke quarters all over with the lemon half, squeeze the extra lemon juice into a small bowl of water and add the quartered artichoke to the lemon water. Repeat with the remaining artichokes.
2. In a medium saucepan of salted boiling water, blanch the artichokes until they are crisp-tender, about 3 minutes. Drain, transfer to a plate and pat dry.
3. In a medium saucepan, heat 1 inch of oil to 350°. Fry the artichokes until crisp, 3 to 5 minutes. Transfer to paper towels to drain.

4. In a bowl, toss the artichokes with the parsley, lemon zest, orange zest and Aleppo pepper. Season with sea salt and serve right away. —*Justin Smillie*

NOTE Aleppo pepper is a moderately hot crushed dried chile from Turkey and Syria. It is available at gourmet markets and online at *penzeys.com*.

Marinated Baby Artichokes with Dill and Fresh Ginger

TOTAL: 45 MIN PLUS 4 HR MARINATING
4 SERVINGS ● ● ○

1 lemon, halved, plus
1 tablespoon fresh lemon juice
20 baby artichokes
Salt
½ cup extra-virgin olive oil
4 garlic cloves, crushed
2 tablespoons capers, drained
2 tablespoons chopped dill
1 tablespoon finely grated fresh ginger

1. Squeeze the juice from a lemon half into a large bowl of water and add the half to the bowl. Working with 1 artichoke at a time, cut off and discard the stem. Pull off the dark outer leaves and trim any dark green patches from the base. Using a serrated knife, cut off the top third of the artichoke. Rub all over with the remaining lemon half and add to the lemon water.
2. Bring a medium saucepan of water to a boil and add a large pinch of salt. Drain the artichokes and add them to the boiling water. Cover and simmer over moderate heat until tender, about 15 minutes, then drain the artichokes and pat them dry.
3. In a shallow serving dish, combine the lemon juice with the olive oil, garlic, capers, dill and ginger. Add the artichokes and toss so that they're thoroughly coated with the marinade. Cover and refrigerate the artichokes, stirring occasionally, for at least 4 hours or overnight. Let the artichokes return to room temperature before serving. —*Salih Yildiz*

MAKE AHEAD The marinated artichokes can be refrigerated for up to 3 days.

DIY TAMALES

Anna Zepaltas learned to make tamales from her Mexican-born mother. She carries on the teaching tradition by giving friends tamale tutorials and sharing tips and recipes here.

MAKE THE FILLING

Mushroom and Kale Tamales

ACTIVE: 2 HR; TOTAL: 5 HR
MAKES ABOUT 30 TAMALES ●

- 6 ounces dried corn husks (about 35; see Note on opposite page)
- 1 ounce dried porcini mushrooms
- 2 tablespoons unsalted butter
- 1 tablespoon extra-virgin olive oil
- 1 medium onion, finely chopped
- ½ pound shiitake mushrooms, stems discarded and caps thinly sliced
- ½ pound cremini mushrooms, thinly sliced
- 2 serrano chiles, minced
- 1 garlic clove, minced
- ¾ pound kale, stems discarded and leaves finely chopped (4 cups)
- Salt and freshly ground pepper
- 1½ cups chicken stock
- ½ cup dry white wine
- ½ teaspoon finely grated lime zest
- 1 tablespoon fresh lime juice
- 6 ounces *queso fresco,* crumbled (about 1 cup)
- 2 tablespoons chopped cilantro
- 6 cups Tamale Dough (recipe opposite)

1. Soften the corn husks (see Assemble & Steam the Tamales, opposite).

2. In a heatproof bowl, soak the porcini mushrooms in 2 cups of boiling water until softened, about 15 minutes; drain. Rinse the porcini, then finely chop them.

3. In a large, deep skillet, melt the butter in the olive oil. Add the onion and cook over moderate heat, stirring, until softened, 5 minutes. Stir in the porcini, shiitake and cremini. Add the chiles and garlic and cook, stirring, until tender and lightly browned, 10 minutes.

4. Add the kale, season with salt and pepper and cook until wilted. Add the stock and wine and bring to a boil. Cover and cook over low heat until the kale is very tender, about 30 minutes. Add the lime zest and juice and cook over high heat until the liquid evaporates. Remove from the heat and let the filling cool, then stir in the *queso fresco* and cilantro and season with salt and pepper.

5. Fill, fold and steam the tamales (see the instructions in Assemble & Steam the Tamales, opposite).

SERVE WITH Chile Rojo Salsa (at right).

MAKE AHEAD The uncooked tamales can be refrigerated for up to 5 days or frozen for up to 1 month; steam them while still frozen.

WINE Cherry-scented Sonoma Pinot Noir: 2010 Pali Wine Co. Huntington.

CHILE ROJO SALSA

:) **TOTAL: 30 MIN • MAKES ABOUT 2½ CUPS** ● ● ●

Zepaltas likes to serve this powerful, complex-tasting red salsa with beef, pork, lamb or hearty mushroom tamales.

- 4 dried pasilla chiles (1½ ounces), stemmed and seeded (see Note)
- 2 dried guajillo chiles (½ ounce), stemmed and seeded (see Note)
- ¼ cup golden raisins
- 1 teaspoon sesame seeds
- ½ teaspoon cumin seeds
- 1 large tomato, coarsely chopped
- 1 medium onion, quartered
- 1 garlic clove, smashed
- 2 tablespoons freshly squeezed lime juice
- **Salt**

1. In a large heatproof bowl, cover the dried chiles and raisins with 3 cups of boiling water; set a plate on top to submerge the chiles. Let them stand until they are softened, about 15 minutes. Drain the chiles and raisins, reserving ¼ cup of the soaking liquid. Transfer the chiles and raisins to a blender.

2. In a small skillet, toast the sesame seeds and cumin seeds over moderately high heat until fragrant and golden, shaking the pan, about 2 minutes. Transfer the seeds to the blender. Add the tomato, onion, garlic, lime juice, ¼ cup of reserved soaking liquid and ½ cup of water and puree until smooth. Strain the salsa through a fine sieve, pressing hard on the solids. Season the salsa with salt.

NOTE Dried pasilla and guajillo chiles are available at Latin American markets, specialty food stores and some supermarkets or online at *mexgrocer.com.*

MAKE AHEAD The salsa can be refrigerated for up to 4 days.

MAKE THE DOUGH

Tamale Dough (Masa)

ACTIVE: 20 MIN; TOTAL: 50 MIN
MAKES 6 CUPS (30 TAMALES) ●

Anna Zepaltas recommends real lard—pure rendered pig fat—for making authentic masa. "Go to any Mexican restaurant and ask if you can buy theirs," she says. "They may not be advertising it, but they'll probably sell it. Or try to get it at your butcher shop." She sometimes makes masa with half lard and half butter. It's not traditional, she admits, but the flavor is superb. The dough here can be used for her Mushroom and Kale Tamales (at left) or her Chicken Tamales with Tomatillo-Cilantro Salsa (page 146).

3½ cups masa harina for tamales
    (20 ounces)
½ pound lard
5 tablespoons unsalted butter,
    softened
2 teaspoons salt
1½ teaspoons baking powder
1 cup chicken stock

1. In a large bowl, stir the masa harina with 3 cups of very hot water until evenly moistened. Knead the mixture several times to make a smooth dough.

2. In a standing mixer fitted with the paddle, beat the lard with the butter at medium speed until smooth, about 2 minutes. Add the salt and baking powder and beat at medium-low speed until incorporated. With the machine on, add the masa in 4 batches, beating until smooth and scraping down the bowl occasionally. Pour in the stock in a steady stream and beat until the dough is fluffy and soft, about 2 minutes; it should have the consistency of thick corn bread batter. Refrigerate the tamale dough in the bowl for 30 minutes.

3. Return the bowl to the mixer and beat the dough at high speed for 1 minute before assembling the tamales.

MAKE AHEAD The Tamale Dough can be covered in plastic wrap and refrigerated for up to 3 days.

ASSEMBLE & STEAM THE TAMALES

1. SOFTEN THE CORN HUSKS Bring a large pot of water to a boil. Add the corn husks, remove from the heat and let stand, turning the husks once or twice, until softened, about 2 hours. Drain the corn husks and shake off as much water as possible.

2. FILL AND FOLD Select 30 of the largest husks without tears or large holes. Arrange 1 husk on a work surface with the narrow end pointing away from you. On the wide end, spread 3 tablespoons of the Tamale Dough in a 5-by-3-inch rectangle, leaving a ½-inch border of husk at the bottom. Spoon 2 tablespoons of the cooled filling in the center of the Tamale Dough. Fold in the long sides of the corn husk, overlapping them to enclose the filling, then fold the narrow end

toward you, over the tamale; it will be open at the wide end. Stand the tamale, open end up, in a very large steamer insert. Repeat the process with the remaining corn husks, Tamale Dough and filling.

3. STEAM Fill the bottom of the steamer with 4 inches of water and bring to a boil. Add the tamales, spread some of the remaining corn husks over the top and cover with the lid; wrap foil around the edge if necessary to make a tight seal. Steam the tamales over moderately low heat for 1½ hours. Uncover the steamer and let the tamales cool for about 15 minutes before serving.

NOTE Dried corn husks are available at specialty food shops, Latin American markets and online at *mexgrocer.com*.

Spice-Braised Gingered Eggplant with Mint Yogurt

ACTIVE: 1 HR 15 MIN; TOTAL: 2 HR PLUS
COOLING • 4 MAIN-COURSE OR
6 FIRST-COURSE SERVINGS ● ●

Nico Monday and Amelia O'Reilly serve this baked eggplant at the Market Restaurant in Gloucester, Massachusetts, both as a first course and as a main with couscous, chickpeas and the punchy, cilantro-based Moroccan sauce called *charmoula*.

- 1 cup plain whole-milk yogurt
- ¼ cup finely chopped mint
- 1 teaspoon red wine vinegar
- Kosher salt
- Vegetable oil, for frying
- Six 6-ounce Italian or Japanese eggplants, halved lengthwise
- 1 tablespoon cumin seeds
- 1 tablespoon coriander seeds
- 1 teaspoon yellow mustard seeds
- Two 14-ounce cans diced tomatoes
- 2 ounces fresh ginger, peeled and coarsely chopped
- 6 garlic cloves, very finely chopped
- 1 jalapeño, seeded and finely chopped
- ½ cup chopped cilantro, plus more for garnish
- ½ cup chopped parsley, plus more for garnish

1. In a medium bowl, whisk the yogurt with the mint and vinegar and season with salt. Cover and refrigerate.

2. Preheat the oven to 400°. In a large, deep skillet, heat ½ inch of vegetable oil until shimmering. Add half of the eggplant cut side down and fry over moderate heat, turning once, until lightly golden, about 10 minutes. Transfer the eggplant to paper towels to drain and season with salt. Repeat with the remaining eggplant.

3. In a small skillet, toast the cumin and coriander seeds over moderate heat, stirring, until fragrant, about 2 minutes. Transfer to a spice grinder and let cool completely, then finely grind the spices. Add the mustard seeds to the skillet and toast over moderate heat until they start to pop, about 2 minutes.

4. In a 9-by-13-inch ceramic baking dish, mix the tomatoes with the ground spices, toasted mustard seeds, ginger, garlic, jalapeño, 2 teaspoons of salt, 1 cup of water and the ½ cup each of chopped cilantro and parsley. Arrange the eggplant halves cut side down in the sauce and cover the dish tightly with aluminum foil. Bake for 30 minutes, turning the eggplant once, until it is tender. Remove the foil and bake the eggplant for 15 minutes longer. Let the eggplant cool completely in the tomato sauce.

5. Transfer the eggplant to plates. Spoon the tomato sauce on top and drizzle with the yogurt sauce. Garnish with chopped cilantro and parsley and serve.
—*Nico Monday and Amelia O'Reilly*

WINE Fresh, raspberry-rich Pinot Noir: 2010 Hirsch Vineyards Bohan-Dillon.

Silky Burmese-Style Eggplant

ACTIVE: 20 MIN; TOTAL: 1 HR 20 MIN
4 SERVINGS ● ●

This soft, custardy eggplant puree is delicious alongside grilled steak and rice.

- 2 pounds Asian eggplant
- 1 large egg, lightly beaten
- 1½ tablespoons vegetable oil
- 1 dried red chile
- 1 shallot, minced
- Salt
- 1 tablespoon minced mint
- 1 tablespoon minced cilantro

1. Preheat the oven to 450°. Prick the eggplants all over and transfer them to a rimmed baking sheet. Roast for 50 minutes, until the eggplants are very soft. Let cool to warm. Halve the eggplants lengthwise and scoop the soft flesh into a bowl. Using a fork, beat in the egg until the mixture is fluffy.

2. In a large nonstick skillet, heat the oil. Add the chile and shallot and cook over moderately high heat for 30 seconds. Add the eggplant mixture and cook, stirring constantly, until very smooth, 1 minute. Season with salt and transfer to a bowl. Discard the chile. Top the eggplant with the herbs and serve.
—*Naomi Duguid*

Grilled Eggplant Caponata

ACTIVE: 25 MIN; TOTAL: 1 HR
8 SERVINGS ● ●

A summery, California-inspired version of Italian sweet-and-sour caponata, this relish features plenty of mint and eggplant that's grilled instead of fried.

- ¼ cup pine nuts
- Two 1-pound eggplants, peeled and sliced lengthwise ½ inch thick
- ¼ cup extra-virgin olive oil, plus more for brushing
- Salt and freshly ground pepper
- 1 large onion, cut into ¼-inch dice
- 2 celery ribs, cut into ¼-inch dice
- ¼ cup currants
- 1 teaspoon crushed red pepper
- One 28-ounce can crushed tomatoes
- ¼ cup light brown sugar
- ¼ cup balsamic vinegar
- ½ cup pitted kalamata olives, quartered
- ¼ cup chopped mint

1. Preheat the oven to 350°. Put the pine nuts in a pie plate and toast for about 4 minutes, until golden brown. Let cool.

2. Light a grill or preheat a grill pan. Brush the eggplant slices with olive oil and season with salt and pepper. Grill over moderately high heat until nicely charred and tender, about 4 minutes per side. Cut the eggplant into ½-inch dice.

3. In a large, deep skillet, heat the ¼ cup of oil. Add the onion, celery, currants, crushed red pepper and toasted pine nuts and cook over moderate heat, stirring occasionally, until the onion and celery are softened, about 10 minutes. Add the crushed tomatoes, light brown sugar and balsamic vinegar and simmer, stirring a few times, until most of the liquid has evaporated, about 8 minutes.

4. Add the grilled eggplant and the olives to the skillet and season with salt and pepper. Serve at room temperature, garnished with the chopped mint. —*Jeff Banker*

MAKE AHEAD The caponata can be refrigerated for up to 5 days. Serve lightly chilled or at room temperature.

● HEALTHY ● MAKE AHEAD ● VEGETARIAN ● STAFF FAVORITE

spice-braised gingered eggplant with mint yogurt

Roasted Eggplant with Tomato Dressing

ACTIVE: 35 MIN; TOTAL: 1 HR 15 MIN
4 TO 6 SERVINGS ● ● ●

Two 1½-pound eggplants
1 pound plum tomatoes
Salt
3 long green Korean peppers
  or 1 large poblano chile
1 garlic clove, minced
1 tablespoon white wine vinegar
½ teaspoon sugar
¼ cup plus 1 tablespoon extra-virgin
  olive oil, plus more for drizzling
Freshly ground pepper
2 tablespoons thinly sliced basil

1. Preheat the oven to 450°. Set the eggplants on a large rimmed baking sheet and pierce all over. Roast the eggplants for 45 minutes, until very soft.

2. Meanwhile, peel the tomatoes with a vegetable peeler. Working over a coarse sieve set over a bowl, cut the flesh from the tomatoes and transfer to a shallow bowl. Allow the seeds, core and juices to fall into the sieve. Crush the tomato cores and press the juice through the sieve. Add the juice to the bowl with the tomato flesh; discard the seeds and cores. Season the tomato with ½ teaspoon of salt and let stand until more juices are released, about 25 minutes.

3. Roast the peppers directly over a gas flame or under the broiler, turning frequently, until charred all over. Transfer the peppers to a bowl and let them cool. Peel, core, seed and coarsely chop the peppers.

4. Cut the tomato sections into small dice. Return them to the bowl and then stir in the chopped peppers, garlic, vinegar, sugar and the ¼ cup plus 1 tablespoon of olive oil. Season with pepper.

5. Peel the roasted eggplants, leaving the stem attached. Cut down the center of each eggplant and discard any large seed sacs; lightly drizzle with olive oil. Season well with salt. Spoon the tomato dressing over the eggplants, sprinkle with the basil and serve.
—*Ferit Sarper*

Buckwheat Crêpes with Corn, Tomatoes and Goat Cheese

TOTAL: 1 HR
MAKES 12 STUFFED CRÊPES ● ●

These savory crêpes are made with buckwheat flour, but they'd be just as good with whole wheat or other whole-grain flour.

2 cups whole milk
2 large eggs
2 tablespoons unsalted butter, melted
½ cup buckwheat flour
½ cup all-purpose flour
1 tablespoon sugar
Salt
1 pint cherry tomatoes, halved
½ teaspoon minced garlic
1 teaspoon smoked sweet paprika
1½ tablespoons extra-virgin olive oil
Freshly ground pepper
1 large leek, halved lengthwise and
  thinly sliced crosswise
1½ cups corn kernels (cut from
  2 large ears of corn)
3 tablespoons chopped parsley
3 ounces goat cheese, crumbled
3 tablespoons snipped chives

1. Preheat the oven to 325°. In a blender, blend the milk, eggs and 1 tablespoon of the melted butter. Add the buckwheat flour, all-purpose flour, sugar and ¼ teaspoon of salt; blend until smooth. Let the batter stand while you prepare the filling.

2. On a rimmed baking sheet, toss the tomatoes with the garlic, paprika and 1 tablespoon of the oil. Season with salt and pepper and roast for about 25 minutes, until the tomatoes are slightly dried.

3. In a skillet, cook the leek over moderate heat in the remaining ½ tablespoon of oil for 4 minutes. Add the corn; cook for 1 minute. Add the tomatoes and parsley; cook for 1 minute. Season with salt and pepper.

4. Line a plate with wax paper. Heat a 10-inch nonstick skillet and lightly brush it with some of the remaining 1 tablespoon of butter. If the batter is too thick, whisk in enough water so it is pourable. For each crêpe, add ¼ cup of the batter to the skillet and swirl to coat the pan. Cook over moderate heat until the surface is dry and the underside is golden, about 2 minutes. Flip the crêpe; cook for 1 minute longer. Transfer the crêpe to the prepared plate. Repeat with the remaining batter, brushing the pan with butter as needed. You should have 12 to 14 crêpes.

5. Spoon the filling down the center of each of 12 crêpes. Sprinkle the goat cheese on top and roll each crêpe into a cylinder. Transfer to plates, garnish with the chives and serve. —*Sara Forte*

WINE Light, fruity red: 2011 Le Tel Quel.

Butter-Braised Corn with Dried Shrimp

⏱ **TOTAL: 45 MIN • 4 TO 6 SERVINGS**
This Asian take on buttered summer corn gets marvelous flavor from dried shrimp, Thai chile, scallions and fish sauce.

10 small dried shrimp
4 tablespoons unsalted butter
5 scallions, white and green parts
  thinly sliced separately
1 red Thai chile, thinly sliced
6 ears of corn, shucked,
  kernels cut off the cobs
2 teaspoons sugar
2 teaspoons Asian fish sauce,
  preferably *nuoc mam* (see Note)
Salt

1. Put the dried shrimp in a bowl and cover with hot water. Let stand for 30 minutes. Drain and finely chop the shrimp.

2. In a large skillet, melt 3 tablespoons of the butter. Add the shrimp, scallion whites and sliced chile and cook over moderate heat until the scallion is softened, about 2 minutes. Add the corn kernels and stir well. Add the sugar and fish sauce and cook, stirring occasionally, for about 5 minutes, until the corn is crisp-tender. Stir in the remaining 1 tablespoon of butter and the scallion greens, season with salt and serve.
—*Katie Kwan and Valerie Luu*

NOTE *Nuoc mam* is Vietnamese for fish sauce. Some good-quality brands are Flying Lion, Three Crabs and Squid.

● HEALTHY   ● MAKE AHEAD   ● VEGETARIAN   ● STAFF FAVORITE

butter-braised corn with dried shrimp

Fried Green Plantains

⏱ TOTAL: 30 MIN • 6 SERVINGS ●

4 large green plantains
    (about 10 ounces each)
Vegetable oil, for frying
Salt

1. Cut off the ends of the plantains. Using a knife, score each plantain lengthwise in 3 places; use your thumb to pry off the peel. Slice the plantains crosswise 1 inch thick.

2. In a saucepan, heat 2 inches of oil to 350°. Working in batches, fry the plantains just until pale golden, 4 minutes. Using a slotted spoon, transfer the fried plantains to a paper towel–lined baking sheet. Using a meat pounder, flatten the plantain slices to a ½-inch thickness.

3. Heat the oil to 375°. Working in batches, fry the plantains until they are crisp and golden, about 4 minutes. Drain on paper towels and sprinkle with salt. Serve right away. —*David Guas*

Vegan Enchiladas

ACTIVE: 1 HR 30 MIN; TOTAL: 3 HR
6 SERVINGS ● ● ● ●

Stuffed with butternut squash, mushrooms, kale and corn, these vegan enchiladas are baked in a tangy tomatillo sauce, then topped with a rich cashew *crema*.

CREMA
1 cup raw cashews (4 ounces)
2 tablespoons fresh lime juice
1 teaspoon white vinegar
1 teaspoon smoked paprika
½ teaspoon salt
SAUCE
2 pounds fresh tomatillos, husked
   and quartered
1 medium white onion, coarsely
   chopped
2 garlic cloves, chopped
1 jalapeño, seeded and coarsely
   chopped
2 cups vegetable stock
½ cup chopped cilantro
Salt and freshly ground pepper

ENCHILADAS
2 cups diced (½-inch) butternut
   squash
2 tablespoons extra-virgin olive oil
Salt and freshly ground pepper
1 medium onion, finely chopped
2 shallots, minced
2 cups thinly sliced shiitake caps
2 cups frozen corn kernels
2 cups finely chopped Tuscan kale
1 cup canola oil
12 corn tortillas

1. MAKE THE CREMA In a medium heatproof bowl, cover the cashews with hot water and let stand for about 2 hours. Drain and transfer the cashews to a food processor. Add the lime juice, white vinegar, smoked paprika, salt and ¼ cup of water and puree until the *crema* is smooth and creamy.

2. MEANWHILE, MAKE THE SAUCE In a large saucepan, combine the tomatillos, onion, garlic, jalapeño and stock and bring to a simmer. Cook over moderate heat until the vegetables are tender, about 15 minutes. Transfer the mixture to a food processor, add the cilantro and puree until smooth. Season with salt and pepper.

3. MAKE THE ENCHILADAS Preheat the oven to 400°. In a small baking pan, toss the squash pieces with 1 tablespoon of the olive oil and season with salt and pepper. Roast for 15 minutes, until tender. Remove the squash from the oven and lower the temperature to 375°.

4. Meanwhile, in a large skillet, heat the remaining 1 tablespoon of olive oil. Add the onion and shallots and cook over moderate heat until softened, 5 minutes. Add the shiitake and cook until lightly browned, about 6 minutes. Add the corn and kale and cook until the kale is wilted, 5 minutes. Add the squash and season with salt and pepper.

5. In a large nonstick skillet, heat the canola oil. Dip 1 tortilla into the hot oil and cook just until pliable, turning once, about 10 seconds. Drain the tortilla on paper towels and repeat with the remaining tortillas.

6. Spoon 1 cup of the tomatillo sauce into a 9-by-13-inch glass or ceramic baking dish.

7. Arrange all of the tortillas on a work surface and divide the filling between them. Roll up the enchiladas and arrange them in the baking dish, seam side down. Spoon 2 cups of the sauce on top. Cover the dish with foil and bake for about 25 minutes, until the enchiladas are heated through. Spoon the *crema* on top and serve. —*Akasha Richmond*

SERVE WITH Sliced avocado and red onion, cilantro leaves and toasted pumpkin seeds.

MAKE AHEAD The enchiladas can be kept at room temperature for up to 4 hours. The cashew *crema* can be refrigerated overnight. Serve at room temperature.

WINE Light, tart-berried Sonoma Pinot Noir: 2010 Heron.

Flash-Roasted Broccoli with Spicy Crumbs

⏱ TOTAL: 30 MIN • 6 SERVINGS ● ●

2 ounces sliced pepperoni
1 garlic clove, sliced
1 cup panko (Japanese bread crumbs)
¼ cup plus 2 tablespoons
   extra-virgin olive oil
2 pounds broccoli, trimmed and
   cut into long spears
Salt
2 tablespoons Dijon mustard

1. Preheat the oven to 425°. In a mini food processor, pulse the pepperoni with the garlic until finely chopped. Add the panko and pulse just to combine.

2. In a medium skillet, heat 2 tablespoons of the olive oil. Add the crumb mixture and cook over moderate heat, stirring, until crisp and golden, about 5 minutes. Scrape onto a plate and let cool.

3. Meanwhile, in a bowl, toss the broccoli with the remaining ¼ cup of olive oil and season with salt. Spread the broccoli on a baking sheet and roast for about 15 minutes, turning once, until tender and browned in spots. Spread the mustard on one side of the broccoli, then press the broccoli into the crumbs. Transfer the broccoli to a platter, sprinkle with any remaining crumbs and serve. —*Grace Parisi*

Spinach and Grape Leaf Pie

ACTIVE: 1 HR; TOTAL: 4 HR 30 MIN
8 SERVINGS ● ● ●

DOUGH

2 cups all-purpose flour,
plus more for dusting
1 teaspoon salt
2 sticks cold unsalted butter,
cut into small pieces
1 cup heavy cream

FILLING

4 large whole eggs, plus 1 large egg
lightly beaten
¼ cup extra-virgin olive oil
1 medium onion, minced
Salt
4 garlic cloves, minced
One 10-ounce jar grape leaves,
stems removed and leaves thinly
sliced (about 3 cups)
2 bunches of scallions, thinly sliced
Six 10-ounce packages frozen leaf
spinach, thawed and squeezed dry,
or 3 pounds fresh spinach,
stemmed and blanched
2 cups frozen peas, thawed
8 ounces fresh ricotta (1 cup)
1 ounce Parmigiano-Reggiano cheese,
freshly grated (¼ cup)
Juice of 1 lemon
½ teaspoon freshly grated nutmeg
½ cup finely chopped mint
Freshly ground pepper
1 large egg yolk beaten with
1 tablespoon of milk, for glazing

1. **MAKE THE DOUGH** In a food processor, combine the 2 cups of flour and the salt and pulse a few times to blend. Add half of the butter and pulse until it is the size of large peas. Add the remaining butter and pulse until all of the butter is the size of baby peas. Make holes in the flour mixture and drizzle in the heavy cream. Pulse until the dough starts to come together.

2. Scrape the dough onto a lightly floured work surface. Gently knead it a few times and form the dough into a ball. Cut off one-third of the dough and gently form it into a disk. Gently flatten the larger piece of dough into a disk. Wrap both disks tightly in plastic and refrigerate until they are firm, at least 2 hours or up to 24 hours.

3. **MAKE THE FILLING** In a medium saucepan, cover the 4 whole eggs with warm water and bring to a boil. Boil for 2 minutes, then drain the eggs and cover with cold water. Lightly crack the shells, and when the eggs are cool, carefully peel them.

4. In a large, deep skillet, heat the olive oil. Add the onion and a large pinch of salt and cook over moderate heat until the onion is translucent, about 7 minutes. Add the garlic and cook until fragrant, about 3 minutes. Add the grape leaves, cover and cook over low heat, stirring occasionally, until tender, about 10 minutes. Add the scallions and cook over moderate heat until softened, about 3 minutes. Stir in the spinach. Cover the skillet and cook, stirring occasionally, until the spinach is heated through and thoroughly incorporated, about 5 minutes.

5. Scrape the greens from the skillet into a large bowl and let cool to room temperature. Stir in the peas, ricotta, Parmigiano, beaten egg, lemon juice, nutmeg and mint. Season the filling with salt and pepper.

6. Preheat the oven to 425° and place a large rimmed baking sheet in the oven to heat. On a lightly floured work surface, roll out the large piece of dough to a 16-inch round slightly less than ¼ inch thick. Fold the dough in half and transfer it to a 10-inch springform pan. Unfold the dough and gently press it into the pan and up the side. Trim the overhang to ½ inch. Refrigerate the dough in the pan. Roll out the smaller piece of dough to a 10-inch round slightly less than ¼ inch thick. Slide the round onto a cookie sheet and chill for 5 minutes, until firm. Trim the chilled round to 9 inches.

7. Arrange the whole cooked eggs in the dough-lined pan and cover with the filling, smoothing the top. Place the 9-inch dough round on top and brush the edge with some of the egg-milk glaze. Fold the overhanging dough over the center round and pinch the edges together to seal. Brush the top and edge of the pie with the glaze.

8. Transfer the pie to the hot baking sheet in the oven and bake for 10 minutes. Reduce the oven temperature to 375° and bake for about 50 minutes, until the crust is richly browned and the filling is hot. Transfer the pie to a rack and let cool to warm.

9. Remove the side of the pan. Cut the pie into wedges and serve warm or at room temperature. —*Alex Raij*

MAKE AHEAD The baked pie can be kept at room temperature for up to 4 hours or refrigerated for up to 2 days; reheat at 375°.

WINE Green apple–scented, full-bodied white Rioja: 2011 Ostatu Blanco.

Thai Chile Relish

🕐 TOTAL: 45 MIN • MAKES 2 CUPS ● ●
Chef Kris Yenbamroong of Night+Market in L.A. created this northern Thai–style chile relish. Made with relatively mild Anaheim chiles, the relish is smoky, not too spicy and fabulous with steamed vegetables.

5 garlic cloves, unpeeled
6 Anaheim chiles
4 medium shallots, unpeeled
½ cup chopped cilantro
3 tablespoons Asian fish sauce
1 tablespoon light brown sugar
1½ tablespoons fresh lime juice

1. Light a grill or preheat a grill pan. Thread the garlic cloves on a skewer. Grill the garlic, chiles and shallots over moderately high heat, turning often, until charred and tender, 8 to 10 minutes for the garlic and chiles and 20 minutes for the shallots.

2. Transfer the vegetables to a bowl and let them cool. Peel the garlic and shallots and transfer them to a mortar or a food processor. Peel, seed and core the chiles (or leave in some seeds for extra heat). Add the chiles to the garlic and shallots and pound or pulse to a coarse puree. Stir or pulse in the cilantro, fish sauce, sugar and lime juice and serve. —*Kris Yenbamroong*

SERVE WITH Steamed vegetables or plain grilled chicken, fish or meat.

MAKE AHEAD The relish can be refrigerated for up to 3 days.

Grilled Broccoli with Chipotle-Lime Butter and Queso Fresco

🕐 **TOTAL: 25 MIN • 8 SERVINGS** ● ●

6 tablespoons unsalted butter, softened
Finely grated zest and juice of 1 lime
1 tablespoon Tabasco Chipotle Sauce
1 teaspoon honey
1 garlic clove, finely grated on a Microplane
Salt
4 heads of broccoli—cut into large florets, stems trimmed
Olive oil, for drizzling
1 cup crumbled *queso fresco* (see Note)

1. In a bowl, stir the softened butter with the lime zest, lime juice, Tabasco, honey and garlic and season lightly with salt.
2. Light a grill. Drizzle the broccoli florets with olive oil and season with salt. Grill the florets over moderately high heat, turning them occasionally, until crisp-tender and lightly charred, about 8 minutes.
3. Transfer the grilled broccoli florets to a platter and toss with the lime butter. Garnish with the *queso fresco* and serve.
—*Jeff Banker*

NOTE *Queso fresco* is a creamy, crumbly white cheese from Mexico that can be found at specialty food shops. Farmers' cheese is a fine substitute.

Roasted Cauliflower with Turmeric and Cumin

ACTIVE: 20 MIN; TOTAL: 1 HR 20 MIN
8 SERVINGS ● ● ● ●

1 cup safflower or sunflower oil
1 tablespoon ground cumin
2 teaspoons turmeric
2 teaspoons crushed red pepper
Sea salt
4 heads of cauliflower—halved, cored and cut into 1-inch florets
¼ cup pine nuts
2 tablespoons chopped cilantro
1 tablespoon chopped mint

1. Preheat the oven to 425°. In a small bowl, combine the oil, cumin, turmeric, crushed red pepper and ½ teaspoon of salt.
2. On 2 large rimmed baking sheets, drizzle the cauliflower with the spiced oil and toss well to coat; season with salt. Spread the cauliflower in an even layer and bake for about 1 hour, until browned and tender; switch the baking sheets halfway through cooking.
3. Meanwhile, in a pie plate, bake the pine nuts for about 1 minute, until toasted. Let cool.
4. Transfer the roasted cauliflower to a large serving bowl and sprinkle with the pine nuts, cilantro and mint. Serve.
—*Sera Pelle*

MAKE AHEAD The cauliflower can be prepared through Step 2 and refrigerated overnight; reheat before combining with the pine nuts and herbs.

Red Cabbage Stir-Fry with Coconut

🕐 **TOTAL: 25 MIN • 4 SERVINGS** ●

2 tablespoons canola oil
1 teaspoon mustard seeds
1 teaspoon cumin seeds
10 fresh curry leaves or 2 bay leaves
One 2-pound red cabbage, cored and coarsely chopped (8 cups)
½ teaspoon ground turmeric
Salt
3 garlic cloves, smashed
1 serrano chile, stemmed and coarsely chopped
½ cup finely shredded dried coconut (1½ ounces)

1. In a large, deep skillet, heat the canola oil. Add the mustard seeds and cook over moderate heat just until they begin to pop, about 30 seconds. Add the cumin seeds and curry leaves and cook until fragrant, about 30 seconds. Add the chopped cabbage and turmeric and season with salt. Cook, stirring occasionally, until the cabbage is crisp-tender, about 3 minutes. Add ½ cup of water and cook until the water is evaporated and the cabbage is tender, 5 to 6 minutes longer. Discard the bay leaves, if using.

2. Meanwhile, in a mini food processor, add the garlic, chile, coconut and ¼ cup of water and pulse to a paste.
3. Scrape the paste into the skillet and toss to coat the red cabbage. Cook, stirring, for 2 minutes. Season with salt and serve.
—*Asha Gomez*

Grilled Kale with Garlic, Chile and Bacon

🕐 **TOTAL: 35 MIN • 4 TO 6 SERVINGS** ●
Grilling kale gives it a toasty flavor; blanching it before grilling makes the kale tender and keeps it from burning.

1 pound kale, thick stems discarded
2 tablespoons vegetable oil
1 large garlic clove, thinly sliced
1 small fresh red chile, thinly sliced
Salt and freshly ground pepper
2 thick slices of bacon, cut into ⅓-inch pieces
1 tablespoon extra-virgin olive oil
Finely grated zest of 1 lemon
1 tablespoon freshly squeezed lemon juice

1. In a large pot of salted boiling water, blanch the kale until it is just tender, about 3 minutes. Drain and lightly squeeze out the excess water. Blot the kale dry and transfer to a bowl. Add the vegetable oil, garlic and chile, season with salt and pepper and toss well to coat.
2. In a skillet, cook the bacon over moderate heat, stirring, until crisp, 5 minutes. Drain on paper towels.
3. Light a grill. Place a 10-inch springform ring (not the bottom) on the grill to contain the kale. Carefully pat the kale inside the ring, pressing down to form an even layer. Grill until lightly charred on the bottom, 3 minutes. With tongs, turn the kale over and grill on the other side for 3 minutes. Alternatively, grill the kale on a perforated grill pan, tossing occasionally.
4. Transfer the kale to a bowl and immediately toss with the bacon, olive oil, lemon zest and lemon juice; season with salt. Serve right away. —*Adam Perry Lang*

grilled kale with garlic, chile and bacon

Root Vegetable and Cauliflower Tagine with Parsley Yogurt

ACTIVE: 40 MIN; TOTAL: 1 HR 30 MIN
10 TO 12 SERVINGS ● ● ●

1½ cups plain whole-milk yogurt
¼ cup finely chopped parsley,
 plus more for garnish
Kosher salt and freshly ground pepper
¼ cup extra-virgin olive oil
1 medium onion, finely chopped
8 garlic cloves, thinly sliced
3 tablespoons tomato paste
1 tablespoon ground cumin
2 teaspoons ground coriander
2 teaspoons crushed red pepper
1 teaspoon caraway seeds
¾ teaspoon cinnamon
2 pounds turnips, peeled and
 cut into ¾-inch dice
1 pound parsnips, peeled and
 cut into ¾-inch dice
One 28-ounce can diced tomatoes
1 quart low-sodium vegetable broth
Pinch of saffron threads
1 pound sweet potatoes,
 peeled and cut into ½-inch dice
½ cauliflower (1 pound),
 cut into bite-size florets
Two 15-ounce cans chickpeas, drained
 and rinsed
½ cup dried currants
1½ cups pitted green olives, quartered

1. In a bowl, whisk the yogurt with the ¼ cup of parsley and season with salt and pepper. Cover and refrigerate until chilled.
2. In a large enameled cast-iron casserole, heat the olive oil. Add the onion, garlic and a generous pinch each of salt and pepper and cook over moderate heat, stirring occasionally, until softened and just starting to brown, about 8 minutes. Stir in the tomato paste, cumin, coriander, crushed red pepper, caraway and cinnamon and cook, stirring, until fragrant and glossy, about 3 minutes.
3. Add the turnips, parsnips, tomatoes and their liquid, broth, saffron and 1 cup of water to the pot and bring to a boil. Cover and simmer over moderately low heat, stirring occasionally, until the turnips and parsnips are beginning to soften, about 20 minutes.
4. Add the sweet potatoes, cauliflower, chickpeas and currants to the pot. Cover partially and simmer over moderately low heat, stirring occasionally, until the vegetables are tender, about 20 minutes. Stir in the olives and season with salt and pepper. Transfer the tagine to a serving bowl, garnish with parsley and serve with the parsley yogurt.
—Aida Mollenkamp

WINE Bright, medium-bodied Spanish white: 2011 Marqués de Irún Verdejo.

Warm Brussels Sprouts with Honey, Caraway and Lime

ACTIVE: 20 MIN; TOTAL: 1 HR
4 TO 6 SERVINGS ● ● ●
Tossed in a sweet-tart dressing with cilantro, mint and chiles, these caramelized brussels sprouts are from chef Nicolaus Balla of San Francisco's Bar Tartine.

2 pounds brussels sprouts,
 halved lengthwise
3 tablespoons extra-virgin olive oil
Kosher salt
¼ teaspoon caraway seeds
One ¼-inch piece of star anise
¼ cup shredded carrot
2 tablespoons fresh lime juice
2 tablespoons honey
1 small garlic clove, very finely
 chopped
¼ cup thinly sliced scallions
¼ cup chopped mint
¼ cup chopped cilantro
2 serrano chiles, seeded and
 thinly sliced

1. Preheat the oven to 425°. In a large bowl, toss the brussels sprouts with the olive oil and season them with salt. Spread on a large rimmed baking sheet and roast for about 40 minutes, stirring once or twice, until tender and crisp on the edges.
2. In a small skillet, toast the caraway seeds and star anise until fragrant, about 1 minute. Transfer to a spice grinder; let cool completely, then grind to a fine powder.
3. In a small bowl, whisk the carrot, lime juice, honey, garlic and spice powder. In the large bowl, toss the brussels sprouts with the dressing, scallions, mint, cilantro and chiles; season with salt. Serve. —Nicolaus Balla

Jerk-Spiced Brussels Sprouts, Cauliflower and Chickpeas

⏱ TOTAL: 40 MIN • 8 SERVINGS ● ●
The chickpeas, cauliflower and brussels sprouts here are roasted until browned and crispy, then sprinkled with a fantastic jerk spice blend. You'll have some of the spice blend left over, but it keeps for months and is also great on shrimp and chicken.

1 whole dried habanero chile,
 stemmed and crushed
1 tablespoon whole allspice berries
1 tablespoon coriander seeds
1 tablespoon black peppercorns
½ teaspoon whole cloves
1 tablespoon dried thyme
½ teaspoon ground ginger
¼ teaspoon freshly grated nutmeg
½ cup extra-virgin olive oil
One 15-ounce can chickpeas, drained
 and patted dry
1 pound small brussels sprouts,
 halved lengthwise
4 cups cauliflower florets (from 1 head)
Salt

1. Preheat the oven to 425°. In a medium skillet, combine the habanero, allspice, coriander, peppercorns and cloves and toast over low heat, shaking the pan, until fragrant, about 2 minutes. Let cool, then transfer to a spice grinder. Add the thyme, ginger and nutmeg and grind to a powder.
2. Heat a roasting pan over high heat. Add the oil and chickpeas and cook until browned and slightly crispy, about 5 minutes. Add the brussels sprouts and cauliflower, season with salt and cook, stirring, until lightly browned, about 5 minutes. Transfer the pan to the oven and roast the vegetables for about 15 minutes, until tender. Sprinkle with 1 teaspoon of the spice mixture and serve right away. —Jonathon Sawyer

jerk-spiced brussels sprouts, cauliflower and chickpeas

Sautéed Cabbage and Carrots with Turmeric

ACTIVE: 35 MIN; TOTAL: 1 HR 20 MIN
8 SERVINGS ● ● ●

Cooking onions until they're softened, then stirring in spices and aromatics like garlic and ginger, is the foundation of many Ethiopian recipes, from vegetables and lentils to meat and chicken. In this delicately spiced vegetarian dish, chunks of carrots and cabbage are added to the base and cooked until the cabbage is sweet and silky. Turmeric, the main seasoning, lends an earthy flavor.

⅓ cup extra-virgin olive oil
3 medium red onions, finely chopped (2 cups)
Salt
10 garlic cloves, minced
One 2-inch piece of fresh ginger, peeled and minced
2 tablespoons ground turmeric
1 pound carrots, quartered lengthwise and cut into 1½-inch lengths
5 pounds green cabbage, cored and cut into ¾-inch pieces

1. In a large enameled cast-iron casserole, heat the olive oil. Add the onions and a generous pinch of salt and cook over moderate heat, stirring occasionally, until softened, about 8 minutes. Add the garlic, ginger and turmeric and cook, stirring, until the vegetables are fragrant and just starting to brown, about 5 minutes.
2. Add the carrots to the casserole along with ½ cup of water and cook over moderate heat, stirring, until the carrots are just starting to soften, about 7 minutes. Stir in the cabbage in large handfuls, letting each batch wilt slightly before adding more. When all of the cabbage has been added, cover and cook over moderately low heat, stirring occasionally, until the cabbage is tender, 40 to 45 minutes. Season with salt and serve.
—Hiyaw Gebreyohannes

MAKE AHEAD The cooked cabbage can be refrigerated for up to 2 days. Reheat gently before serving.

Roasted Cabbage with Warm Walnut-Rosemary Dressing

ACTIVE: 30 MIN; TOTAL: 1 HR 45 MIN
18 SERVINGS ● ● ●

Three 1¾-pound heads of green cabbage, each cut into 6 wedges through the core
¾ cup extra-virgin olive oil
Salt and freshly ground pepper
8 garlic cloves, halved
6 rosemary sprigs
1½ cups walnuts (4½ ounces)
1 stick unsalted butter
¼ cup apple cider vinegar
2 tablespoons Moscatel vinegar (see Note) or white balsamic vinegar

1. Preheat the oven to 400°. In a large roasting pan, toss the cabbage wedges with the olive oil and season with salt and pepper. Arrange the wedges cut side down in a single layer and scatter the garlic and rosemary sprigs around them. Cover tightly with foil. Bake for about 45 minutes, until the cabbage cores are tender. Uncover and bake for about 20 minutes longer, turning once, until the cabbage is brown around the edges.
2. Arrange the cabbage on a platter and tent with foil. Strip the rosemary leaves from the stems; discard the stems and garlic.
3. In a medium skillet, toast the walnuts over moderate heat, tossing, until lightly browned, 5 minutes. Let cool, then coarsely chop.
4. In the same skillet, melt the butter. Add the chopped toasted walnuts and cook them over moderate heat, stirring, until the butter turns medium brown and smells nutty, about 5 minutes. Add the rosemary needles and cook, stirring, until they are crisp, about 1 minute. Reduce the heat to low, stir in both of the vinegars and cook until the dressing is slightly reduced, about 2 minutes. Season with salt and pepper. Spoon the dressing over the cabbage wedges and serve.
—John Adler

NOTE Moscatel vinegar, a lightly sweet and tangy, Spanish white balsamic–like vinegar, is available at specialty food stores and online at taylorsmarket.com.

Grilled Bok Choy with Braised Mushrooms

ACTIVE: 1 HR; TOTAL: 2 HR PLUS
OVERNIGHT SOAKING · 4 SERVINGS ●

2½ ounces dried shiitake mushrooms (about 5 cups)
3 tablespoons canola oil, plus more for brushing
One 1-inch piece of peeled fresh ginger—½ inch smashed, ½ inch cut into thin matchsticks
½ ounce rock sugar, crushed, or 1 tablespoon granulated sugar
1 scallion, cut into 3-inch lengths
2 cups plus 2 tablespoons chicken stock or low-sodium broth
¼ cup plus 1 tablespoon oyster sauce
Kosher salt
1 teaspoon unaged whiskey or other grain alcohol
1 pound bok choy, quartered lengthwise

1. In a large bowl, cover the shiitake with water and let soak overnight at room temperature. Drain the mushrooms and discard the stems.
2. In a large saucepan, heat 2 tablespoons of the oil until shimmering. Add the smashed ginger, sugar and scallion; cook over moderate heat, stirring, until the sugar dissolves and starts to caramelize, 4 to 5 minutes. Add the mushrooms and 2 cups of the chicken stock and bring to a boil. Cover partially and simmer over low heat, stirring occasionally, until the mushrooms are tender and most of the stock has evaporated, 1 hour and 15 minutes. Stir in 1 tablespoon of the oyster sauce and season the mushrooms with salt.
3. Meanwhile, in a small saucepan, heat the remaining 1 tablespoon of canola oil until shimmering. Add the ginger matchsticks and cook over moderately high heat, stirring, until lightly golden, 1 minute. Add the whiskey and cook for 30 seconds. Add the remaining 2 tablespoons of chicken stock and ¼ cup of oyster sauce and simmer over moderately low heat until thickened, about 5 minutes. Keep the sauce warm.

● HEALTHY ● MAKE AHEAD ● VEGETARIAN ● STAFF FAVORITE

4. Bring a large pot of salted water to a boil. Add the bok choy and blanch until crisp-tender, about 2 minutes. Drain and cool the bok choy under running water; pat dry.

5. Light a grill or preheat a grill pan. Brush the bok choy with canola oil and grill over high heat, turning, until lightly charred, about 5 minutes. Transfer the bok choy to plates or a platter and top with the mushrooms. Drizzle the ginger-oyster sauce over the bok choy and mushrooms and serve.
—*Bryant Ng*

Roasted King Oyster Mushrooms

ACTIVE: 10 MIN; TOTAL: 1 HR
8 SERVINGS ● ●

The king oyster mushroom, a large variety of oyster mushroom with a long, thick stem and relatively small cap, is perfect for cutting into meaty slices. Here they're oven-roasted in butter and chicken stock for a rich, concentrated flavor.

1½ pounds king oyster mushrooms, sliced ¼ inch thick
4 tablespoons cold unsalted butter, diced
½ cup chicken stock or low-sodium broth
¼ cup extra-virgin olive oil
Salt and freshly ground black pepper
2 tablespoons chopped flat-leaf parsley

1. Preheat the oven to 425°. Arrange the mushroom slices on a large rimmed baking sheet in a slightly overlapping layer. Dot the mushrooms with the butter and drizzle with the chicken stock and olive oil. Season with salt and freshly ground pepper. Roast the mushrooms in the center of the oven for about 50 minutes, turning them occasionally, until the chicken stock has evaporated and the mushrooms are tender and lightly browned in spots.

2. Blot the mushrooms with paper towels and transfer to a plate. Sprinkle the mushrooms with the parsley and serve.
—*Siegfried Danler*

Mixed Crudités with Green Goddess Dressing

⏱ **TOTAL: 40 MIN • 8 TO 10 SERVINGS** ●

DRESSING
1 cup lightly packed flat-leaf parsley
½ English cucumber—halved lengthwise, seeded and chopped
½ Hass avocado
1 small shallot, chopped
2 tablespoons full-fat plain yogurt
1 tablespoon snipped chives
1 garlic clove, crushed
2 teaspoons rosé or white wine vinegar
1 teaspoon Asian fish sauce
3 tablespoons extra-virgin olive oil
Kosher salt and freshly ground pepper
CRUDITÉS
½ teaspoon finely grated lemon zest
2 tablespoons fresh lemon juice
2 tablespoons extra-virgin olive oil
1 tablespoon finely chopped chives
1 tablespoon finely chopped flat-leaf parsley
½ small rutabaga (6 ounces), peeled and cut into 2-by-½-inch batons
½ head of cauliflower, cut into bite-size florets
2 kohlrabi bulbs (½ pound), peeled and cut into 2-by-½-inch batons
1 crispy sweet apple, such as Granny Smith or Honey Crisp—halved, cored and thinly sliced
½ cup shaved aged Pecorino Romano cheese
2 tablespoons sliced toasted almonds
Kosher salt and freshly ground pepper
1 head of Bibb lettuce, leaves separated, for serving

1. MAKE THE DRESSING In a food processor, combine all of the ingredients except the olive oil, salt and pepper. Pulse until very finely chopped. With the machine on, drizzle in the olive oil and process until the dressing is nearly smooth. Season with salt and pepper. Scrape the dressing into a bowl, cover and refrigerate until chilled, 30 minutes.

2. MEANWHILE, PREPARE THE CRUDITÉS In a large bowl, whisk the lemon zest and

juice with the oil, chives and parsley. Add the rutabaga, cauliflower, kohlrabi, apple, pecorino and almonds and toss well. Season with salt and pepper. Serve the crudités in the lettuce cups with the Green Goddess dressing on the side. —*Jonathon Sawyer*
MAKE AHEAD The Green Goddess dressing can be refrigerated for up to 3 days.

Roasted Beets with Pistachios, Herbs and Orange

📷 PAGE 4
ACTIVE: 20 MIN; TOTAL: 1 HR 20 MIN
8 SERVINGS ● ●

3 pounds medium beets, preferably a mix of colors
One 3-inch cinnamon stick, broken into 3 or 4 pieces
2 bay leaves
1 large shallot, minced
¼ cup white wine vinegar
Salt
Finely grated zest of 1 orange
¼ cup chopped tarragon
¼ cup chopped flat-leaf parsley
¼ cup chopped chives
¼ cup plus 2 tablespoons extra-virgin olive oil
¼ cup chopped unsalted roasted pistachios
¼ cup celery leaves, for garnish

1. Preheat the oven to 375°. Arrange the beets in a roasting pan and add the cinnamon stick pieces, bay leaves and 1 cup of water. Cover tightly with foil and bake for 1 hour, until the beets are tender; transfer to a large rimmed baking sheet and let cool; discard the liquid and spices.

2. Meanwhile, in a bowl, mix the shallot, vinegar and a large pinch of salt. Let stand for 10 minutes. Stir in the orange zest, tarragon, parsley, chives and oil; season with salt.

3. Peel and trim the beets and slice them ¼ inch thick. Arrange the beet slices in overlapping rows on a platter. Stir the herb dressing and spoon it over the beets. Scatter the pistachios and celery leaves on top and serve.
—*Naomi Pomeroy*

Sweet Cauliflower-and-Carrot Pickles

TOTAL: 35 MIN PLUS OVERNIGHT PICKLING • MAKES 6 CUPS ● ● ○

"These pickles came from an overzealous trip to the farmers' market," says Portland, Oregon chef Naomi Pomeroy. "When I see something beautiful like purple cauliflower, I can't resist." She marinates the vegetables in a mixture that includes sugar and Cointreau, and sometimes honey, too. The sweet, slightly tangy pickles can be served in salads, on a charcuterie plate or alone as a snack.

    1   tablespoon fennel seeds
    1   tablespoon coriander seeds
    1   teaspoon allspice berries
    1   whole clove
    ½   teaspoon anise seeds
    One 2-inch cinnamon stick, broken
    1   tablespoon fennel pollen
    1   bay leaf
    ½   teaspoon crushed red pepper
    1   cup white balsamic vinegar
    1   cup white wine vinegar
    1½ cups sugar
    ½   cup plus 2 tablespoons kosher salt
    ¼   cup Cointreau or other triple sec
    6   carrots, sliced diagonally
        ¼ inch thick
    1   head of purple or white cauliflower,
        cut into 1½-inch florets

1. In a large saucepan, combine the fennel and coriander seeds, allspice berries, clove, anise seeds and cinnamon stick; toast over moderate heat until fragrant, 1½ minutes. Transfer to a small bowl to cool. Stir in the fennel pollen, bay leaf and crushed red pepper. Wrap the spice mixture in a double layer of cheesecloth and tie with kitchen string.

2. Add 6 cups of water to the saucepan along with the balsamic and white wine vinegars, sugar, salt and Cointreau. Add the spice bag and bring to a boil, stirring to dissolve the sugar. Cover the saucepan and simmer over moderate heat for 5 minutes.

3. Add the carrot slices to the simmering liquid and cook until they are barely tender, about 3 minutes.

4. Using a slotted spoon, transfer the carrots to a medium bowl. Repeat the process with the cauliflower and transfer to another bowl. Discard the spice bag and let the pickling liquid cool to warm. Pour the pickling liquid over the carrots and cauliflower. Cover and refrigerate the pickles overnight. Drain the carrots and cauliflower and serve together in a bowl. —*Naomi Pomeroy*

MAKE AHEAD The drained pickles can be refrigerated separately for up to 1 week.

Fall Vegetable Giardiniera

TOTAL: 30 MIN PLUS OVERNIGHT PICKLING • MAKES 2 QUARTS ● ● ○ ○

    4   ounces *shishito* peppers, pricked
        with a fork, or 2 Italian frying
        peppers, cut into thin strips
    4   carrots, cut into matchsticks
    4   ounces sunchokes, scrubbed and
        thinly sliced, or broccoli stems,
        peeled and thinly sliced
    4   cups cauliflower florets (12 ounces)
    ¼   cup plus 2 tablespoons kosher salt
    1   teaspoon coriander seeds
    1   teaspoon black peppercorns
    2   bay leaves
    2   cups distilled white vinegar
    1   cup olive oil
    2   teaspoons dried oregano, crumbled

1. Place the *shishitos*, carrots, sunchokes and cauliflower in a large, tall glass or plastic container. In a large jar, combine the salt, coriander seeds, peppercorns and bay leaves with 6 cups of water. Pour the brine over the vegetables and top with a plate to keep the vegetables submerged. Cover with plastic wrap and refrigerate overnight.

2. Drain the vegetables and discard the coriander seeds, bay leaves and peppercorns. Pack the vegetables into two 1-quart jars. Add 1 cup of the vinegar, ½ cup of the olive oil, 1 teaspoon of the oregano and ½ cup of water to each jar and seal. Shake gently and refrigerate overnight before serving. —*Grace Parisi*

MAKE AHEAD The *giardiniera* can be refrigerated for up to 2 weeks.

Grilled Vegetables with Roasted-Chile Butter

⏱ **TOTAL: 35 MIN • 6 TO 8 SERVINGS** ●

Fresno chiles are similar in shape and heat to jalapeños, but they're red and a little less meaty. Roasting them over an open flame tames their spice and brings out their natural sweetness. F&W's Grace Parisi likes folding them into softened butter, then melting a little on grilled vegetables or steaks or spreading some on bread.

    5   red Fresno chiles or jalapeños
    ½   teaspoon minced Scotch bonnet
        chile or ¼ teaspoon cayenne pepper
    1   stick unsalted butter, softened
    2   tablespoons minced chives
    ½   pound king oyster or portobello
        mushrooms, sliced lengthwise
        ⅓ inch thick
    1   pound Japanese eggplants
        or baby eggplants, sliced on the
        diagonal ⅓ inch thick
    ¾   pound small zucchini (about 2),
        thinly sliced on the diagonal
    2   ears of corn, shucked, cobs cut
        crosswise into 1½-inch-thick rounds
    Extra-virgin olive oil, for grilling
    Salt and freshly ground black pepper

1. Light a grill or preheat a grill pan. Grill the Fresno chiles over high heat, turning, until blackened and softened, 4 to 5 minutes. Transfer the chiles to a bowl, cover with plastic wrap and let cool slightly. Peel, seed and mince the chiles and then return them to the bowl. Add the Scotch bonnet, butter and chives and stir until combined.

2. Lightly brush the mushrooms, eggplant, zucchini and corn with olive oil and season with salt and pepper. Grill the vegetables over moderately high heat, turning once or twice, until lightly charred and tender, about 5 minutes. Arrange the vegetables on a platter and immediately dot with the chile butter. Serve right away. —*Grace Parisi*

MAKE AHEAD The chile butter can be refrigerated for up to 3 days or frozen for 1 month.

WINE Bright, green apple–scented Chardonnay: 2010 Peter Lehmann Art Series.

sweet cauliflower-and-carrot pickles

Sunflower-Seed Risotto

⏱ TOTAL: 40 MIN • 6 SERVINGS

Chefs Andy Ticer and Michael Hudman of Memphis's Andrew Michael Italian Kitchen worked together to make this ingenious interpretation of risotto. Their secret weapon: a pressure cooker.

2 tablespoons unsalted butter
Extra-virgin olive oil
1 small onion, minced
1¼ pounds shelled raw sunflower seeds (4 cups)
½ cup dry white wine
1 quart chicken stock or low-sodium broth
1 ounce thickly sliced country ham, finely diced
Salt and freshly ground pepper
1 cup frozen baby peas, thawed
¼ cup freshly grated Parmigiano-Reggiano cheese

1. In a pressure cooker, melt the butter in 2 tablespoons of oil. Add the onion and cook over moderate heat until softened, 3 minutes. Add the sunflower seeds and cook, stirring, for 4 minutes. Add the wine; cook until evaporated. Add the stock and ham. Season with salt and pepper; bring to a boil.
2. Cover the cooker and bring it up to pressure. Maintain pressure over low heat for 7 minutes. Set the cooker in the sink and run cold water over the lid to cool and depressurize it; remove the lid once you can release it without force.
3. Drain the sunflower seeds, reserving 1 cup of the cooking liquid. Transfer ½ cup of the seeds to a blender along with the 1 cup of reserved cooking liquid and puree until the mixture is creamy.
4. Transfer the whole seeds to a skillet. Add the puree, peas and cheese and cook over moderate heat, stirring, until the seeds are coated with a creamy sauce, about 2 minutes. Spoon the "risotto" into bowls, drizzle with olive oil and serve.
—*Michael Hudman and Andy Ticer*
WINE Apple-scented, balanced Chardonnay: 2009 Estancia Pinnacles Ranches.

Roasted Sunchokes with Buttery Bagna Cauda

⏱ ACTIVE: 20 MIN; TOTAL: 45 MIN

8 SIDE-DISH OR STARTER SERVINGS ● ●

Sunchokes, which are also known as Jerusalem artichokes, are small, knobby, nutty-tasting tubers that can be eaten raw or cooked. When roasted, they make a great change of pace from the usual crudités served with bagna cauda, the garlicky Italian olive oil–anchovy sauce. The combination of butter and olive oil in the bagna cauda here makes it especially luxurious.

2 tablespoons vegetable oil
2 pounds young sunchokes, scrubbed and halved lengthwise
3 tablespoons extra-virgin olive oil
4 large anchovy fillets, minced
2 large garlic cloves, minced
¼ teaspoon crushed red pepper
3 tablespoons unsalted butter
1 tablespoon freshly squeezed lemon juice
Salt and freshly ground black pepper
1 tablespoon chopped flat-leaf parsley
Lemon wedges, for serving

1. Preheat the oven to 400°. In a large ovenproof skillet, heat the vegetable oil. Add the sunchokes cut side down and cook them over moderately high heat for 1 minute, then transfer the skillet to the oven and bake for about 25 minutes, until the sunchokes are golden brown and tender.
2. Meanwhile, in a small saucepan, heat the olive oil. Add the anchovy fillets, minced garlic and crushed red pepper and cook over low heat until the anchovies are sizzling, about 1 minute. Remove the saucepan from the heat and stir in the butter, 1 tablespoon at a time, then stir in the lemon juice; season with salt and freshly ground black pepper. Transfer the bagna cauda to a shallow bowl and keep warm.
3. Spoon the sunchokes onto a platter. Garnish with the parsley and serve with the warm bagna cauda and lemon wedges.
—*Mike Lata*

Vidalia Onion Soufflés

ACTIVE: 30 MIN; TOTAL: 1 HR 45 MIN

8 SERVINGS ● ●

Vidalia onion soufflé was a fixture at Thanksgiving and Christmas meals when Sarah Simmons was growing up in Fayetteville, North Carolina. Simmons, the founder of the Manhattan supper club (or "culinary salon," as Simmons calls it) City Grit, now cooks her own version—lighter and airier than the one her mother makes. The soufflé mixture can be prepared in individual gratin dishes or in one big baking dish. Feel free to use any sweet onion you can get, such as Vidalia, Walla Walla or Oso Sweet.

1 stick unsalted butter, plus more for greasing
4 pounds Vidalia or other sweet onions, thinly sliced
Salt
3 tablespoons all-purpose flour
2 teaspoons baking powder
6 large eggs
2 cups heavy cream
¾ cup freshly grated Parmigiano-Reggiano cheese

1. In a very large skillet, melt the stick of butter over moderately low heat. Add the sliced onions and a generous pinch of salt and cook, stirring occasionally, until the onions are soft and golden, about 40 minutes. Let the onions cool completely.
2. Preheat the oven to 350° and butter eight 5½-inch gratin dishes (see Note). In a small bowl, whisk the flour with the baking powder and 1 teaspoon of salt. In a large bowl, beat the eggs with the heavy cream and grated Parmigiano-Reggiano cheese. Whisk in the dry ingredients until incorporated, then fold in the onions. Spoon the soufflé mixture into the prepared gratin dishes and bake for about 20 minutes, until the soufflés are set and golden on top. Serve right away.
—*Sarah Simmons*
NOTE The onion soufflé mixture can also be baked in a buttered 9-by-13-inch glass or ceramic baking dish. Bake it at the same temperature for 45 minutes.

Braised Carrots with Lamb

ACTIVE: 40 MIN; TOTAL: 3 HR

4 SERVINGS ●

In this brilliant recipe from chef Dan Barber of New York's Blue Hill, carrots are the star and shredded lamb the sauce.

One 1½-pound lamb shank
Salt and freshly ground pepper
2 tablespoons vegetable oil
2 large onions, coarsely chopped
5 garlic cloves, smashed
1 celery rib, coarsely chopped
1 cup dry red wine
½ cup ruby port
1 rosemary sprig
6 large carrots, peeled
¼ cup mixed chopped parsley, chervil and mint
Finely grated zest of 1 lemon

1. Preheat the oven to 325°. Season the lamb with salt and pepper. In a large skillet, heat 1 tablespoon of the oil. Add the lamb and cook over moderately high heat until browned on all sides, about 8 minutes. Transfer the lamb to a plate and pour off the oil.
2. Add the remaining 1 tablespoon of oil to the skillet and add the onions, garlic and celery. Cook over moderate heat until browned, 12 minutes. Add the wine and port and boil until reduced to ⅓ cup, about 4 minutes. Transfer to a roasting pan and add the rosemary. Arrange the lamb shank and carrots in the pan, add ¾ cup of water and cover with foil. Bake for 2 hours, turning the lamb and carrots once, until the lamb is very tender.
3. Transfer the lamb to a bowl. Reserve 2 of the carrots for the Cracked Emmer and Carrot Porridge (page 268). Transfer the 4 remaining carrots to a serving platter. Keep warm
4. Strain the pan juices into a saucepan. Boil over high heat until reduced to ½ cup, 7 minutes. Shred the shank meat and add it to the pan juices; season with salt and pepper.
5. Sprinkle the herbs and lemon zest over the carrots. Surround the carrots with the lamb and sauce and serve. —Dan Barber
WINE Bold Italian red: 2008 Santadi Rocca Rubia Carignano del Sulcis Riserva.

Five-Spice Tofu with Barley and Kale

ACTIVE: 45 MIN; TOTAL: 1 HR 15 MIN

4 SERVINGS ● ● ●

1 cup pearled barley, rinsed
Salt
One 14-ounce block extra-firm tofu, drained on paper towels for 10 minutes
2 tablespoons grapeseed oil or coconut oil
2 teaspoons toasted sesame oil
½ teaspoon Chinese five-spice powder
4 scallions, white and tender green parts only, thinly sliced
Freshly ground pepper
1 lemongrass stalk, bottom 6 inches only, peeled and minced
4½ packed cups shredded stemmed Tuscan kale
1½ tablespoons prepared horseradish
2 tablespoons tamari or soy sauce
2 tablespoons seasoned rice vinegar
2 tablespoons sweetened shredded coconut, toasted
1 tablespoon toasted sesame seeds
2 tablespoons chopped cilantro

1. In a saucepan, cover the barley with 2 cups of water, add a pinch of salt and bring to a boil. Cover and simmer over low heat until the barley is just tender, about 25 minutes.
2. Meanwhile, cut the tofu into 1-inch cubes. In a large nonstick skillet, heat 1 tablespoon of the grapeseed oil with the sesame oil until shimmering. Add the tofu cubes and five-spice powder and cook over moderately high heat, stirring, until the tofu is lightly browned, about 7 minutes. Add the scallions and cook for 1 minute. Season with salt and pepper and transfer the tofu to a plate.
3. Add the remaining 1 tablespoon of grapeseed oil to the skillet. Add the lemongrass and cook over moderately high heat for 1 minute. Add the kale and cook, stirring, until wilted, about 2 minutes. Add the barley and cook for 1 minute, then add the horseradish, tamari and vinegar. Cook, stirring, until the pan is nearly dry, about 2 minutes.

4. Transfer the barley and kale to a platter. Top with the tofu, coconut, sesame seeds and cilantro. Serve right away. —Sara Forte
WINE Rich Pinot Blanc: 2010 Charles Baur.

Keralan Vegetable Stew

ACTIVE: 20 MIN; TOTAL: 50 MIN

4 SERVINGS ● ●

For this lovely vegetarian stew, carrots, potatoes and green beans simmer in an Indian-flavored coconut milk broth for 30 minutes.

2 tablespoons canola oil
2 tablespoons finely julienned peeled fresh ginger
4 garlic cloves, thinly sliced
12 fresh curry leaves or 2 bay leaves
2 serrano chiles, finely chopped
1 teaspoon ground turmeric
Coarsely ground black pepper
1 cup frozen pearl onions, thawed
Salt
1 medium Yukon Gold potato, peeled and cut into 1-inch cubes
2 medium carrots, cut into ½-inch dice
½ pound green beans, cut into ½-inch pieces
½ cup vegetable stock or broth
1 cup unsweetened coconut milk

In a large saucepan, heat the canola oil. Add the ginger, garlic, curry leaves, chiles, turmeric, 1½ teaspoons of black pepper and ½ cup of the pearl onions. Season with salt and cook over moderate heat, stirring occasionally, until the onions are softened, about 8 minutes. Add the potato cubes, diced carrots, green beans, vegetable stock and the remaining ½ cup of pearl onions and bring to a boil. Add the coconut milk and simmer, partially covered, until the vegetables are tender and the coconut milk is slightly reduced, about 30 minutes. Season with salt and black pepper. Discard the bay leaves, if using, and serve. —Asha Gomez
SERVE WITH Steamed rice.
MAKE AHEAD The vegetable stew can be refrigerated overnight.
WINE Fragrant, medium-bodied Spanish white: 2011 Bodegas Protos Verdejo.

Tofu and Vegetable Tacos with Eggplant-Ancho Spread

ACTIVE: 45 MIN; TOTAL: 1 HR 45 MIN
6 SERVINGS ● ●

An eggplant-and-ancho-chile spread gives these grilled-vegetable and tofu tacos a rich, smoky taste. The spread can also double as a dip to be served with pita chips.

One 14-ounce block extra-firm tofu, cut crosswise into 6 slabs
¼ cup dry white wine
¼ cup extra-virgin olive oil
2 tablespoons chopped mint
2 tablespoons chopped flat-leaf parsley
Salt and freshly ground pepper
1 yellow squash, thinly sliced lengthwise
1 zucchini, thinly sliced lengthwise
1 small red onion, cut into wedges
1 red bell pepper—cored, seeded and cut into strips
3 small tomatoes, halved
6 flour tortillas, warmed
¼ cup plus 2 tablespoons Smoky Eggplant-Ancho Spread (recipe follows)

1. Arrange the slabs of extra-firm tofu on a baking sheet and top with another baking sheet and several plates. Let the tofu stand for 1 hour to press out some of the excess water. Pat the slabs of tofu dry.

INGREDIENT TIP

tofu "I like firm tofu for sautéing, grilling, scrambling and in burgers; silken for desserts and salad dressings. I love the artisanal tofu company Hodo Soy Beanery (*hodosoy.com*) in Oakland, California."
—*Akasha Richmond, chef at Akasha restaurant in Los Angeles, where she creates excellent dishes for both vegans and omnivores.*

2. In a large bowl, combine the white wine, olive oil, mint and parsley and season with salt and pepper. Add the squash, zucchini, onion, bell pepper, tomatoes and tofu; let stand for 5 minutes.

3. Light a grill and oil the grates. Grill the vegetables in a grill basket over moderately high heat, turning occasionally, until tender, about 10 minutes. Grill the tofu directly on the grates, turning, until charred all over, about 8 minutes.

4. Spread each flour tortilla with 1 tablespoon of the Smoky Eggplant-Ancho Spread. Add the grilled tofu and vegetables, fold up the tacos and serve right away.
—*Alyssa Gorelick*

WINE Balanced, citrusy Oregon Pinot Gris: 2009 Willamette Valley Vineyards.

SMOKY EGGPLANT-ANCHO SPREAD
⏱ **ACTIVE: 15 MIN; TOTAL: 45 MIN**
MAKES 1½ CUPS ● ● ●

This luscious spread gets a triple hit of smoky flavor from grilled eggplant, ancho chiles and sweet smoked paprika.

One 12-ounce eggplant
¼ cup extra-virgin olive oil, plus more for rubbing
2 ancho chiles
Boiling water
1 teaspoon sweet smoked paprika
1 teaspoon ground cumin
½ tablespoon light brown sugar
Salt and freshly ground pepper

1. Light a grill or preheat a grill pan. Rub the eggplant with olive oil and grill over high heat, turning occasionally, until the skin is charred and the eggplant is very tender, 20 minutes. Let the eggplant cool slightly, then scoop the flesh into a colander and let stand for 10 minutes to drain.

2. Meanwhile, soak the chiles in boiling water until pliable, about 15 minutes. Drain them and discard the stems and seeds, then transfer the chiles to a blender. Add the eggplant, paprika, cumin, brown sugar and ¼ cup of olive oil and puree. Season with salt and pepper and serve. —*AG*

Spiced-Tofu Sandwiches

TOTAL: 30 MIN PLUS 4 HR MARINATING
8 SERVINGS ●

The robust spices in the paste here are especially good on the smoky, grilled tofu.

2 tablespoons coriander seeds
1½ teaspoons fennel seeds
1 teaspoon whole black peppercorns
1 teaspoon crushed red pepper
1 dried bay leaf, crumbled
1 tablespoon sweet paprika
½ cup extra-virgin olive oil, plus more for the grill
4 large garlic cloves, minced and mashed to a paste with a pinch of salt
Two 14-ounce blocks firm tofu—drained, each one cut crosswise into 4 slabs
Salt
8 brioche buns, split
½ cup mayonnaise
¼ cup barbecue sauce
Lettuce, sliced pickles, red onion and tomatoes, for serving

1. In a skillet, combine the coriander and fennel seeds, peppercorns, crushed red pepper and bay leaf and cook over moderate heat, shaking the pan, until fragrant, 1 minute. Transfer the spices to a grinder and let cool. Add the paprika and finely grind the spices, then transfer them to a bowl and stir in the ½ cup of olive oil. Stir in the garlic paste.

2. Arrange the tofu in a baking dish. Spread all but 1 tablespoon of the spice paste over the tofu. Cover with plastic wrap and refrigerate for at least 4 hours or up to 48 hours.

3. Light a grill and oil the grates. Season the tofu with salt and grill over moderate heat, turning, until just heated through, 10 minutes.

4. Grill the buns until toasted. In a bowl, mix the mayonnaise and barbecue sauce with the remaining 1 tablespoon of spice paste. Spread the mayonnaise sauce on the buns and top with the tofu, lettuce, pickles, red onion and tomatoes. Close the sandwiches and serve. —*Grace Parisi*

WINE Fruity, dry Provençal rosé: 2011 Jean-Luc Colombo Cape Bleue.

● HEALTHY ● MAKE AHEAD ● VEGETARIAN ● STAFF FAVORITE

tofu and vegetable tacos with eggplant-ancho spread

POTATOES, GRAINS & BEANS

Healthy Potato Gratin with Herbs

ACTIVE: 30 MIN; TOTAL: 2 HR
8 SERVINGS ●

Inspired by a potato gratin at Restaurant Daniel in New York City, this creamy—but creamless—recipe gets great flavor from thyme and rosemary.

1½ tablespoons extra-virgin olive oil, plus more for the cake pan
1 large shallot, minced (about ⅓ cup)
1½ teaspoons chopped thyme
½ teaspoon chopped rosemary
2 cups low-sodium chicken broth
2 pounds medium red potatoes, very thinly sliced
Salt and freshly ground pepper

1. Preheat the oven to 400° and oil an 8-inch round cake pan, preferably of dark metal. Line the bottom of the pan with parchment paper and oil the paper.

2. In a medium saucepan, heat the 1½ tablespoons of oil. Add the shallot and cook over moderate heat, stirring occasionally, until softened, 3 minutes. Add the thyme and rosemary; cook for 1 minute. Add the broth and bring to a boil. Cook over moderately high heat until reduced to ¾ cup, 10 minutes.

3. Arrange an overlapping layer of potato slices in the cake pan. Season lightly with salt and pepper and spoon a small amount of the reduced broth on top. Repeat the layering with the remaining potato slices and reduced broth, seasoning each layer lightly. Pour any remaining broth on top. Cover the pan with a sheet of oiled parchment paper and then a sheet of foil.

4. Bake the gratin in the center of the oven until the potatoes are very tender, about 1 hour. Remove the foil and paper and bake until the top is dry, about 10 minutes longer.

5. Turn the broiler on. Remove the gratin from the oven and let it rest for 5 minutes. Invert the gratin onto a heatproof plate. Carefully remove the parchment. Broil the gratin 6 inches from the heat until the surface is lightly browned, about 2 minutes. Cut into wedges; serve. —*Garrett Weber-Gale*

Pizzoccheri Gratin

ACTIVE: 45 MIN; TOTAL: 1 HR 15 MIN
8 SERVINGS ● ○ ○

1 stick unsalted butter
2 tablespoons chopped sage
1 teaspoon poppy seeds
½ teaspoon caraway seeds
One ½-pound baking potato, peeled and cut into ½-inch pieces
1 pound fresh lasagna sheets, cut into 6-by-1½-inch strips, or fresh pappardelle
1 small head of napa cabbage, thinly sliced (6 packed cups)
Salt and freshly ground pepper
5 ounces imported Fontina cheese, shredded (1½ cups)
½ cup freshly grated Parmigiano-Reggiano cheese
½ cup dry bread crumbs
2 tablespoons chopped parsley

1. Preheat the oven to 350°. In a small skillet, melt 6 tablespoons of the butter with the sage, poppy seeds and caraway seeds; cook over moderate heat, stirring, until nutty and fragrant, about 5 minutes. Transfer to a bowl.

2. Meanwhile, bring a large pot of salted water to a boil. Add the potato and cook until tender, 5 minutes. Using a slotted spoon, transfer the potato to a bowl. Add the pasta to the pot and cook, stirring, until al dente, 2 minutes. Using a slotted spoon, transfer the pasta to a colander. Add the cabbage to the pot and cook until just wilted, 3 minutes. Drain the cabbage; shake out the excess water. Pour off the water and return the cabbage to the pot along with the pasta and potato. Add the browned butter, season with salt and pepper and toss well. Stir in 1 cup of the Fontina and half of the Parmigiano; transfer the mixture to a 9-by-13-inch baking dish.

3. In the small skillet, melt the remaining butter, then add the bread crumbs and parsley. Cook over moderate heat, stirring, until golden and toasted, 3 minutes. Stir in the remaining Fontina and Parmigiano; sprinkle over the pasta. Bake for 35 minutes, until golden brown. Serve hot. —*Jonathon Sawyer*

Tartiflette

SERVES 6 ●

"Damn delicious—and idiot-proof!" That's what Anthony Bourdain says about his *tartiflette*, a decadent French bacon-studded potato gratin. Excerpted from his classic *Les Halles* cookbook, the recipe is written in Bourdain's characteristic style.

INGREDIENTS
2½ lb potatoes, peeled
½ lb slab bacon, cut in small dice
1 medium onion, thinly sliced
¾ cup dry white wine
salt and pepper
1 lb Reblochon-style cheese, sliced

EQUIPMENT
large pot
paring knife
strainer
large sauté pan
wooden spoon
10-inch round, ovenproof dish

Preheat the oven to 350° F. Place the potatoes in the pot, cover with water, and bring to a boil. Cook for about 20 minutes, or until the potatoes are easily pierced with the knife. Remove from the heat, drain, and let sit until they are cool enough to handle. Cut the potatoes into small dice and set aside.

In the sauté pan, cook the bacon over high heat until browned. Drain, leaving 1 tablespoon of fat in the skillet and add the onion. Cook over moderately high heat for about 5 minutes until golden brown then add the bacon and wine and cook for another 5 minutes, stirring occasionally. Add the potatoes and season with salt and pepper.

Remove the potato mixture from the heat and place half of it in the ovenproof dish. Spread half the cheese slices atop the potato mixture. Cover this with the other half of the potato mixture. Top with the remainder of the cheese. Bake in the hot oven for 20 minutes, or until golden brown and bubbling. Serve hot. —*Anthony Bourdain*

● HEALTHY ● MAKE AHEAD ○ VEGETARIAN ● STAFF FAVORITE

healthy potato gratin with herbs

Potatoes, Corn and Avocado with Horseradish Dressing

⏱ TOTAL: 45 MIN • 6 SERVINGS ● ●

1 cup plain rice milk

2 tablespoons finely grated fresh horseradish, plus more for garnish

1 tablespoon cornstarch dissolved in 2 tablespoons of water

½ teaspoon finely grated lemon zest, plus 2 teaspoons fresh lemon juice

Salt and freshly ground pepper

2 ears of corn, shucked and kernels cut from the cob (about 2 cups)

1½ pounds fingerling potatoes

1 fennel bulb—halved, cored and very thinly sliced

1 Hass avocado, thinly sliced

¼ cup chopped dill

¼ cup snipped chives

1. In a small saucepan, combine the plain rice milk with 1½ tablespoons of the horseradish and bring to a boil. Whisk in the cornstarch mixture and return to a boil. Cook, whisking, until slightly thickened, about 1 minute. Strain into a small heatproof bowl and let cool. Add the lemon zest and lemon juice and the remaining ½ tablespoon of horseradish. Season the horseradish dressing with salt and freshly ground pepper.

2. Bring a large saucepan of water to a boil. Set the corn kernels in a strainer and submerge the strainer in the boiling water. Cook the corn for 1 minute. Shake off any excess water and let the corn cool completely.

3. Return the water to a boil and add the potatoes. Cook until the potatoes are tender, about 12 minutes. Drain and let cool completely. Cut the potatoes into ½-inch-thick coins and arrange them in an even layer on a large, deep platter. Season lightly with salt and freshly ground pepper. Scatter the corn on top of the potatoes, followed by the fennel and avocado slices, lightly seasoning each layer with salt and pepper. Spread the horseradish dressing on top and garnish with the dill and chives. Finely grate more fresh horseradish over the salad and serve right away. —Garrett Weber-Gale

French Fries with Bulgogi and Caramelized Kimchi

TOTAL: 1 HR PLUS OVERNIGHT MARINATING
4 SERVINGS ●

Austin is a city with tons of food trucks, and the Korean-Mexican-Texan mash-up called Chi'Lantro is a favorite among locals. For his famous late-night snack, Chi'Lantro chef and owner Jae Kim tops hot french fries with caramelized kimchi, grilled Korean-style beef and a mayonnaise spiked with Sriracha.

BULGOGI

1 small onion, minced

3 garlic cloves, minced

1 tablespoon minced fresh ginger

½ cup soy sauce

2 tablespoons sugar

1 tablespoon distilled white vinegar

1 teaspoon toasted sesame oil

1 pound boneless rib eye steak, cut into very thin 3-inch slices

2 tablespoons vegetable oil

TOPPINGS

½ cup sugar

¼ cup distilled white vinegar

2 tablespoons Korean chile paste (gochujang)

2 tablespoons soy sauce

1 cup kimchi

½ cup mayonnaise

3 tablespoons Sriracha, plus more for serving

1 pound hot french fries

Shredded cheddar cheese, chopped white onion, toasted sesame seeds and cilantro, for serving

1. MAKE THE BULGOGI In a large resealable plastic bag, combine the onion, garlic, ginger, soy sauce, sugar, white vinegar and sesame oil. Add the rib eye and toss to coat. Seal the bag and refrigerate overnight.

2. Drain the bulgogi, pick off the solids and pat dry. In a large skillet, heat the vegetable oil until smoking. Add the meat and cook over high heat, turning once, until it is lightly browned, 4 minutes. Transfer the meat to a plate and keep warm. Rinse out the skillet and wipe dry.

3. PREPARE THE TOPPINGS In a medium bowl, combine the sugar, vinegar, chile paste and soy sauce. Add the kimchi and toss to coat. Heat the skillet until very hot. Add the kimchi and cook over high heat until the liquid is thickened and glossy and the kimchi is browned in spots, about 5 minutes.

4. In a small bowl, whisk the mayonnaise with the 3 tablespoons of Sriracha.

5. Scatter the fries on a platter; top with the bulgogi and kimchi. Drizzle with some of the Sriracha mayonnaise and sprinkle with cheddar, onion, sesame seeds and cilantro. Serve with additional Sriracha. —Jae Kim

BEER Crisp pilsner: Avery Brewing Co. Joe's.

Baked Mustard Dressing

⏱ TOTAL: 25 MIN • MAKES 1½ CUPS ● ●

Alex Guarnaschelli, host of the TV show Alex's Day Off, coats warm new potatoes with this ingenious dressing instead of mayonnaise or an oily vinaigrette.

½ cup Dijon mustard

¼ cup fresh lemon juice

2 tablespoons sherry vinegar

1 teaspoon capers, minced, plus 1 teaspoon of brine from the jar

⅓ cup extra-virgin olive oil

⅓ cup canola oil

2 tablespoons whole-grain mustard

Kosher salt

1. Preheat the oven to 325° and line a baking sheet with foil. Spread 6 tablespoons of the Dijon mustard on the prepared baking sheet a scant ¼ inch thick. Bake the mustard for 10 to 12 minutes, until a crust forms on the surface and the mustard feels slightly firm.

2. In a blender, combine the baked mustard, lemon juice, vinegar, capers and brine with the remaining 2 tablespoons of Dijon mustard; blend until smooth. With the blender on, drizzle in the olive oil and canola oil until thick. Transfer the dressing to a jar; stir in the whole-grain mustard, season with salt and serve. —Alex Guarnaschelli

SERVE WITH Warm new potatoes.

MAKE AHEAD The dressing can be refrigerated for up to 3 days.

baked mustard dressing on warm new potatoes

Potato, Baby Artichoke and Mushroom Sauté

📷 PAGE 257

TOTAL: 1 HR • 2 TO 4 SERVINGS ●

3 medium red potatoes
   (about ½ pound total)
Salt
4 baby artichokes
½ lemon
4 tablespoons unsalted butter
¼ cup dry white wine
½ pound shiitake mushrooms, stems
   discarded and caps quartered
1 medium shallot, minced
1 ounce aged hard goat cheese, such
   as Etude or goat Gouda, shaved
   with a vegetable peeler (⅓ cup)

1. In a small saucepan, cover the potatoes with water. Add a large pinch of salt and bring to a boil. Simmer the potatoes over moderately high heat until they are just tender when pierced with a knife, about 8 minutes. Drain and let cool. Peel and cut the potatoes into ½-inch-thick wedges.

2. Working with one artichoke at a time, pull off and discard the dark green outer leaves. Using a small, sharp knife, trim off about ½ inch of the leaves and peel and trim the stem. Quarter the artichoke and scrape out the hairy choke. Rub the artichoke all over with the lemon half and squeeze the extra lemon juice into a small bowl of water. Add the quartered artichoke to the lemon water. Repeat with the remaining artichokes.

3. In a small skillet, melt 1 tablespoon of the butter. Drain the artichokes. Add them to the skillet and cook over moderate heat, stirring a few times, until they are golden brown, about 2 minutes. Add the white wine and bring to a boil. Add ¼ cup of water, cover and cook over moderate heat, stirring occasionally, until the artichokes are just tender, about 12 minutes.

4. In a large skillet, melt 1 tablespoon of the butter. Add the shiitake mushrooms and season with salt. Cover and cook over moderate heat, stirring occasionally, until the mushrooms are browned and tender, about

4 minutes. Push the mushrooms to one side of the skillet and add the remaining 2 tablespoons of butter. Add the minced shallot and cook until softened, about 4 minutes. Add the potatoes, season with salt and turn to coat with the butter. Cook until the potatoes are golden brown, about 2 minutes per side. Gently fold in the mushrooms along with the artichokes and their cooking liquid. Season with salt and transfer the vegetables to a shallow serving bowl. Garnish with the cheese shavings and serve.
—*Daniel Patterson*

MAKE AHEAD The whole cooked potatoes and artichoke quarters can be refrigerated separately overnight. Gently reheat the artichokes and bring the potatoes to room temperature before proceeding.

Potato Salad with Radishes and Sweet Pickle Relish

**ACTIVE: 30 MIN; TOTAL: 1 HR PLUS 4 HR
CHILLING • 6 TO 8 SERVINGS** ● ● ● ● ●

3 pounds medium Yukon Gold
   potatoes, halved but not peeled
Salt
½ cup mayonnaise
¼ cup sweet pickle relish
1 tablespoon white vinegar
1 teaspoon dry mustard powder
½ teaspoon sweet smoked paprika
½ teaspoon freshly ground
   black pepper
¼ teaspoon cayenne pepper
6 red radishes, cut into ⅓-inch dice
3 celery ribs, cut into ⅓-inch dice
½ medium red onion, cut into
   ⅓-inch dice

1. In a large pot, cover the potatoes with water, add a large pinch of salt and bring to a boil. Cook over moderately high heat until tender, about 20 minutes. Drain the potatoes and return them to the pot. Shake the pot over moderately high heat for about 10 seconds to dry the potatoes. Transfer the potatoes to a large rimmed baking sheet and let cool completely. Peel the potatoes and cut them into 1-inch pieces.

2. In a large bowl, blend the mayonnaise with the relish, vinegar, mustard powder, paprika, black pepper, cayenne, radishes, celery and onion. Gently fold in the potatoes and season with salt. Refrigerate the potato salad for at least 4 hours or overnight. Serve cold or lightly chilled. —*Brian Perrone*

MAKE AHEAD The potato salad can be refrigerated for up to 2 days.

Fried Rice with Shallots

⏱ **TOTAL: 25 MIN • 4 SERVINGS** ● ●

The Burmese make a simple breakfast dish by stir-frying leftover rice with crispy fried shallots, sweet peas and earthy turmeric. To make the dish more substantial, Naomi Duguid, author of the cookbook *Burma*, likes to top the rice with fried eggs.

3 tablespoons peanut oil,
   plus more for frying
3 shallots, thinly sliced (¾ cup)
¼ teaspoon ground turmeric
4½ cups cold cooked jasmine rice
   (see Note)
Salt
1 cup frozen petite peas, thawed
Lime wedges, for serving

1. In a small skillet, heat ¼ inch of peanut oil until shimmering. Add ¼ cup of the sliced shallots and fry over moderately high heat, stirring occasionally, until they are golden brown and crisp, about 2 minutes. Using a slotted spoon, transfer the fried shallots to paper towels to drain.

2. In a wok or large skillet, heat the 3 tablespoons of oil until shimmering. Add the turmeric and the remaining ½ cup of shallots and stir-fry over moderately high heat until the shallots are softened, about 5 minutes. Add the rice and 1 teaspoon of salt and stir-fry over high heat for 1 minute. Add the peas and stir-fry until the rice and peas are hot, 2 to 3 minutes. Stir in the fried shallots and season with salt. Transfer the rice to a bowl and serve with lime wedges.
—*Naomi Duguid*

NOTE If you don't have leftover rice on hand, you'll need to cook 1½ cups of rice.

● HEALTHY ● MAKE AHEAD ● VEGETARIAN ● STAFF FAVORITE

fried rice with shallots

Turkey Fried Rice with Crushed Potato Chips

🕐 TOTAL: 30 MIN • 4 SERVINGS

"The key to great fried rice is starting with cooked rice that's had time to cool and dry out, so it stays firm in the pan," says chef Angelo Sosa of Social Eatz in New York City. He makes his clever version with ground turkey punched up with ginger and lemongrass and garnished with lightly crushed potato chips for crunch.

- 3 tablespoons vegetable oil
- 2 tablespoons minced fresh ginger
- 1 tablespoon minced garlic
- 1 tablespoon minced lemongrass, tender inner white bulb only
- 4 ounces ground turkey
- ½ teaspoon kosher salt
- 2 large eggs, lightly beaten
- 2 cups leftover (cold) cooked rice
- ¼ cup low-sodium soy sauce
- 1 tablespoon toasted sesame oil
- 2 scallions, thinly sliced
- ¼ cup chopped mint
- ½ cup plain potato chips, lightly crushed, for garnish

Asian-style hot sauce, such as Sriracha, for serving (optional)

1. Heat a wok until very hot. Add the vegetable oil, ginger, garlic and lemongrass and stir-fry over high heat until fragrant but not browned, about 1 minute. Add the ground turkey and salt and break up the meat into small clumps. Stir-fry until the turkey is just cooked through, about 3 minutes.

2. Make a well in the center of the ground turkey. Add the eggs and stir-fry over high heat until just set into large curds, about 2 minutes. Add the cold rice and stir-fry until heated through and the grains are separated, about 3 minutes. Add the soy sauce and stir-fry until absorbed, about 2 minutes. Stir in the sesame oil and transfer to bowls. Stir in the scallions and mint and garnish with the potato chips. Serve with hot sauce. —Angelo Sosa

WINE Bright, slightly sweet German Riesling: 2011 Leitz Leitz Out.

Chicken Livers with Bacon, Watercress and Dirty Rice

TOTAL: 1 HR 10 MIN • 4 SERVINGS

- 1¼ cups long-grain rice, rinsed and drained
- ½ pound bacon, sliced crosswise ¼ inch thick
- 1 medium onion, finely diced
- 1 large celery rib, finely diced
- ½ teaspoon dried thyme
- ½ teaspoon cayenne pepper
- ¾ cup chicken stock

Salt and freshly ground black pepper
- ⅓ cup all-purpose flour

Vegetable oil, for frying
- 1 pound chicken livers, trimmed and halved
- 2 cups small watercress sprigs

Pickled red onion slices (see Note)
- 1 tablespoon extra-virgin olive oil

1. In a medium saucepan, cover the rice with 1¾ cups of water and bring to a boil. Cover and cook over low heat for 13 minutes. Remove the saucepan from the heat and let the rice steam, covered, for 5 minutes. Lightly fluff the rice and cover.

2. Meanwhile, in a deep skillet, cook the bacon over moderate heat until crisp; transfer to paper towels. Pour off all but 2 tablespoons of the fat in the skillet. Add the onion, celery, thyme and ⅛ teaspoon of the cayenne. Cover and cook over moderately low heat, stirring, until the onion is softened, 7 minutes. Add the stock; bring to a simmer over moderately high heat. Add the rice and bacon; stir well. Remove from the heat, season with salt and black pepper and cover.

3. In a bowl, combine the flour with ½ teaspoon of salt, ¼ teaspoon of black pepper and the remaining cayenne. In another large skillet, heat ¼ inch of vegetable oil until shimmering. Pat the livers dry with paper towels, dredge in the flour mixture and add to the skillet. Cover with a splatter screen and fry over high heat until the livers are browned outside and rosy within, about 1½ minutes per side. Transfer the livers to a plate and sprinkle lightly with salt.

4. Transfer the rice mixture to a platter. In a bowl, toss the watercress with the pickled onions and olive oil, then season with salt and black pepper. Arrange the watercress and livers over the rice and serve. —Marcia Kiesel

NOTE To pickle, soak 1 thinly sliced small red onion in ½ cup vinegar with ¼ cup sugar and a pinch of salt for about 1 hour.

WINE Lively, juicy sparkling red: NV Gemma Rubia Lambrusco Secco.

Mixed Grains with Green Beans and Crispy Bacon

ACTIVE: 20 MIN; TOTAL: 1 HR 10 MIN
4 SERVINGS

A packaged rice-and-grain blend (like those with barley, wheat berries and oats) allows you to cook the grains in one pot at the same time. Adding bacon makes it super-tasty.

- 1 cup rice-and-grain blend, such as SooFoo
- 6 ounces smoky slab bacon, cut into 1-inch cubes
- ½ pound green beans, cut into 1-inch pieces

Salt
- 2 tablespoons extra-virgin olive oil

Freshly ground pepper

1. In a large saucepan, combine the rice-and-grain blend with the bacon cubes and 2 cups of water and bring to a boil. Cover and simmer over very low heat until the grains are tender and the water is absorbed, 45 to 50 minutes, depending on the brand. Scrape the grains into a medium bowl. Slice the bacon cubes in half.

2. Meanwhile, steam the green beans until they are crisp-tender, about 3 minutes. Season with salt.

3. In a medium nonstick skillet, heat the olive oil. Add the bacon and cook over high heat until crispy, about 2 minutes. Add the green beans, season with salt and pepper and stir-fry for about 1 minute. Scrape the mixture into the grains and toss, then season with salt and pepper and serve. —Grace Parisi

● HEALTHY ● MAKE AHEAD ○ VEGETARIAN ○ STAFF FAVORITE

Coconut Jasmine Rice

⏱ TOTAL: 20 MIN • 8 SERVINGS ● ●

Coconut and kaffir lime are high on the list of favorite flavors in Los Angeles chef Sera Pelle's household. She has a kaffir lime tree on the balcony right off the kitchen and uses the fragrant leaves in everything from vegetable stews to Thai-style soups.

- 1 cup unsweetened coconut milk
- 1 teaspoon sea salt
- 2½ cups jasmine rice, rinsed
- 2 kaffir lime leaves

In a large saucepan, combine the coconut milk and salt with 3 cups of water. Add the rinsed rice and lime leaves and bring to a boil. Cover and simmer over low heat for 12 minutes. Keeping the pan covered, turn off the heat and let the rice stand for 5 minutes. Uncover and fluff the rice. Discard the lime leaves and serve. —*Sera Pelle*

Butternut Squash Basmati Rice

⏱ ACTIVE: 15 MIN; TOTAL: 45 MIN
4 TO 5 SERVINGS ● ●

Adding diced butternut squash and aromatic spices is an excellent way to jazz up rice.

- 1 tablespoon unsalted butter
- 1 teaspoon whole cumin seeds
- 1 teaspoon mustard seeds
- 1 cup basmati rice
- ¾ pound peeled butternut squash, cut into ¼-inch dice (2 cups)
- 2 teaspoons kosher salt

1. In a medium saucepan, melt the butter. Add the cumin and mustard seeds and cook over high heat until the mustard seeds begin to pop, about 30 seconds. Add the rice and diced squash and stir to coat with the butter. Add the salt and 2 cups of water and bring to a boil. Cover and cook over very low heat until the squash is tender and the water is completely absorbed, about 15 minutes.

2. Remove the saucepan from the heat and let the rice stand, covered, for 5 minutes. Fluff the rice with a fork and serve right away. —*Asha Gomez*

Kamut Salad

ACTIVE: 25 MIN; TOTAL: 1 HR 15 MIN
6 SERVINGS ● ●

After cooking in the Google cafeteria, Nate Keller and Mirit Cohen started Gastronaut, a San Francisco catering company that prepares healthy lunches for tech companies. For this wholesome salad, Keller uses kamut, an heirloom wheat with a naturally sweet, almost buttery flavor.

- ½ vanilla bean
- 1 small carrot, halved lengthwise
- 1 small celery rib, halved
- 6 tablespoons olive oil
- 2 cups dried kamut berries
- 1 small onion, halved
- 2 blood oranges
- 1 medium shallot, minced
- 2 tablespoons fresh lemon juice
Salt and freshly ground pepper
- 10 strawberries, quartered
- 2 packed cups baby spinach

1. Split the vanilla bean half lengthwise and scrape the seeds into a small bowl. Using kitchen twine, tie the vanilla bean, carrot and celery together. In a medium saucepan, heat 1 tablespoon of the olive oil. Add the kamut and cook over moderately high heat, stirring, until toasted, 1 minute. Add 6 cups of water and bring to a boil. Add the vegetable bundle and onion halves. Cover partially and simmer over low heat, stirring occasionally, until the kamut is just tender, about 1 hour. Drain the kamut and discard the vegetables.

2. Meanwhile, finely grate the zest of 1 blood orange into the bowl with the vanilla seeds. Add the shallot and lemon juice. Using a knife, remove the peel and white pith from both of the oranges. Cut in between the membranes to release the sections into a large bowl. Squeeze the juice from the membranes into the small bowl and let stand for 10 minutes. Whisk in the remaining 5 tablespoons of olive oil.

3. Add the kamut to the orange sections in the large bowl. Stir in the dressing and season with salt and pepper. Fold in the strawberries and spinach and serve. —*Nate Keller*

Grilled Polenta with Spinach and Robiola Cheese

ACTIVE: 15 MIN; TOTAL: 50 MIN
4 SERVINGS ●

Superstar chef Mario Batali grills wedges of polenta until they're crisp and lightly charred, then tops them with creamy, tangy robiola cheese and garlicky sautéed spinach.

- 2 tablespoons extra-virgin olive oil, plus more for brushing
Salt
- 1 cup instant polenta
- 2 large garlic cloves, thinly sliced
- 1 pound baby spinach
Freshly ground pepper
- ¼ pound robiola cheese, cut into 8 slices, at room temperature

1. Lightly oil a 9-inch round glass baking dish. In a medium saucepan, bring 3 cups of water to a boil. Add 1½ teaspoons of salt and slowly whisk in the polenta. Cook over low heat, whisking constantly, until the polenta is thick, about 5 minutes. Carefully pour the hot polenta into the baking dish and cover the surface directly with plastic wrap. Let stand until firm, about 25 minutes.

2. In a large, deep skillet, heat the 2 tablespoons of olive oil. Add the garlic and cook over moderate heat until golden brown, about 30 seconds. Increase the heat to moderately high and add the spinach, stirring to wilt it. Season with salt and pepper. Keep the spinach warm.

3. Light a grill and oil the grates or preheat a grill pan. Cut the polenta into 8 wedges and grill over moderately high heat until crisp and lightly charred, about 5 minutes per side. Place 2 polenta wedges on each plate; top each with 2 robiola slices. Spoon the warm spinach on top and serve. —*Mario Batali*

MAKE AHEAD The polenta can be prepared through Step 1, wrapped in plastic and refrigerated overnight. Slice the polenta and let it return to room temperature before proceeding with the recipe.

WINE Intense, smoky southern Italian red: 2010 Librandi Cirò Rosso.

● HEALTHY ● MAKE AHEAD ● VEGETARIAN ● STAFF FAVORITE

grilled polenta with spinach and robiola cheese

Farro Salad with Smoked Trout

ACTIVE: 25 MIN; TOTAL: 1 HR 15 MIN
6 FIRST-COURSE SERVINGS ● ●

- 3 small beets (½ pound)
- ⅓ cup extra-virgin olive oil, plus more for drizzling
- 2 garlic cloves, crushed
- 2 thyme sprigs
- 1 rosemary sprig

Kosher salt

- 1½ cups semi-pearled farro (8 ounces)
- 1 large shallot, minced
- 3 tablespoons fresh lemon juice
- 1 tablespoon honey

Freshly ground pepper

- 6 ounces skinless smoked trout fillet, flaked
- ½ pound beet greens or Swiss chard— stems removed, leaves washed and finely chopped (1 cup)

1. Preheat the oven to 375°. In a small baking dish, lightly drizzle the beets with olive oil and rub to coat. Cover with foil and roast for about 1 hour, until tender. Let cool, then peel the beets and cut into ½-inch dice.

2. Meanwhile, in a medium saucepan, combine the garlic, thyme, rosemary, 4 cups of water and 2 teaspoons of salt and bring to a boil. Stir in the farro and simmer over moderate heat until just tender, about 15 minutes. Drain well. Transfer the farro to a bowl and discard the garlic and herbs. Let cool to room temperature, stirring occasionally.

3. In a small bowl, combine the shallot with the lemon juice and honey. Gradually whisk in the ⅓ cup of oil and season the dressing with salt and pepper.

4. In a medium bowl, toss 2 tablespoons of the dressing with the trout. Add the beets, greens and the remaining dressing to the farro and toss gently. Season with salt and pepper and let stand at room temperature for 20 minutes. Transfer the salad to a serving platter, scatter the trout on top and serve.
—*Daniel Klein*

WINE Clean, minerally Grüner Veltliner from Austria: 2011 Sepp.

Farro Salad with Turnips and Greens

ACTIVE: 45 MIN; TOTAL: 1 HR 30 MIN
20 SERVINGS ● ● ●

To get the most out of turnips, buy them with their greens attached. Both parts are used in this easy-to-make grain salad.

- 2 pounds farro (4½ cups)
- 2 bay leaves

Salt

- 2½ pounds turnips, peeled and cut into ½-inch dice, plus 3 pounds turnip greens, mustard greens or Swiss chard, stems discarded and leaves chopped
- ¾ cup extra-virgin olive oil
- 2 tablespoons chopped thyme

Freshly ground pepper

- ¼ cup red wine vinegar
- 1 cup chopped flat-leaf parsley

1. Preheat the oven to 375°. Spread the farro in a roasting pan; toast for about 15 minutes, shaking the pan occasionally, until fragrant.

2. In a large pot, combine the farro with the bay leaves and 12 cups of water and bring to a boil. Simmer the farro over moderately low heat until al dente, about 25 minutes; season the water generously with salt about 10 minutes before the farro is done. Let cool slightly. Drain the farro, discard the bay leaves and transfer the farro to a large serving bowl.

3. In the same roasting pan, toss the diced turnips with ½ cup of the olive oil and the chopped thyme. Set the roasting pan over 2 burners and cook over moderate heat, stirring occasionally, until the turnips are browned and nearly tender, about 10 minutes. Add the chopped greens, season with salt and freshly ground pepper and cook, tossing, until the greens are just wilted, about 5 minutes. Cover with aluminum foil and cook until tender, about 5 minutes longer. Stir in the vinegar and parsley.

4. Scrape the turnips and turnip greens into the farro. Add the remaining ¼ cup of olive oil and season with salt and pepper; toss well. Serve warm or at room temperature.
—*Tamar Adler*

Cracked Emmer and Carrot Porridge

TOTAL: 30 MIN • 4 TO 6 SERVINGS
● ● ●

Dan Barber, the chef at New York's Blue Hill and Blue Hill at Stone Barns, is a big proponent of cooking with whole grains, which are healthier and more flavorful than the processed kinds. One of the grains he's most keen on is emmer wheat, also known as farro, which he uses in this savory, carrot-rich dish.

- 1 cup cracked emmer wheat (see Note)
- 1½ cups whole milk
- 2 large braised carrots (from Barber's Braised Carrots with Lamb on page 253), chopped, or other steamed or roasted carrots
- 2 teaspoons sherry vinegar
- 1 teaspoon honey

Salt

- 2 tablespoons salted roasted pumpkin seeds
- 2 tablespoons freshly grated Parmigiano-Reggiano cheese
- ½ teaspoon crushed cumin seeds

1. In a medium saucepan, cook the cracked emmer wheat over moderate heat, stirring, until it is toasted, about 1 minute. Whisk in the milk and 2 cups of water and cook over low heat, whisking often, until the porridge is thick and the emmer wheat is al dente, about 20 minutes.

2. Meanwhile, quarter the braised carrots and puree them in a food processor.

3. Stir the carrot puree into the emmer porridge along with the vinegar and honey and season with salt. Spoon the porridge into shallow bowls. Top with the roasted pumpkin seeds, grated Parmigiano-Reggiano cheese and crushed cumin seeds and serve.
—*Dan Barber*

NOTE The sweet, nutty-tasting emmer wheat called for in this recipe is slightly cracked, so it cooks more quickly than whole emmer. It's available at *bluebirdgrainfarms.com*. If you are using whole emmer, crack the grains in a blender for 15 to 20 seconds.

● HEALTHY ● MAKE AHEAD ● VEGETARIAN ● STAFF FAVORITE

farro salad with smoked trout

Risotto with Shiitake, Squid and Tomatoes

TOTAL: 1 HR • 4 SERVINGS ●

¼ cup extra-virgin olive oil
¾ pound shiitake mushrooms—stems discarded, caps sliced ⅓ inch thick
Salt and freshly ground pepper
½ pound cleaned squid—bodies sliced crosswise ¼ inch thick, large tentacles halved
3 cups bottled clam juice (24 ounces)
½ cup finely chopped onion
2 garlic cloves, minced
1 cup plus 2 tablespoons arborio rice
¼ cup rosé wine
Pinch of saffron threads
1 tablespoon unsalted butter
1 tablespoon fresh lemon juice
½ teaspoon finely grated lemon zest
12 cherry tomatoes, quartered
2 tablespoons chopped basil
1 teaspoon chopped sage

1. In a large skillet, heat 2 tablespoons of the oil. Add the shiitake; season with salt and pepper. Cover and cook over moderate heat, stirring occasionally, until tender and starting to brown, 6 minutes; uncover and cook until browned, 2 minutes. Transfer to a bowl.
2. Heat 1 tablespoon of the olive oil in the same skillet. Add the squid, season with salt and pepper and stir over high heat for 1 minute. Scrape the squid and any juices into another bowl; cover.
3. In a medium saucepan, bring the clam juice and 3 cups of water to a boil. Cover and keep hot over low heat. In another medium saucepan, heat the remaining 1 tablespoon of oil. Add the onion and garlic; cook over low heat, stirring occasionally, until softened, about 4 minutes. Add the rice; stir over moderate heat until coated with the oil. Add the wine and saffron and simmer until almost evaporated. Add enough of the hot clam broth to just cover the rice; cook, stirring, until the broth is almost absorbed. Repeat until the rice is al dente and bound in a creamy sauce, about 25 minutes. Keep the remaining ½ cup of broth hot.

4. Stir the shiitake and butter into the rice, then stir in the squid and its juices. Add the remaining clam broth and the lemon juice and zest and stir well. Remove from the heat and stir in the tomatoes, basil and sage. Season the risotto with salt and pepper, spoon into shallow bowls and serve.
—Marcia Kiesel

WINE Berry-scented rosé: 2011 Clarendelle.

Lemony Bulgur-Stuffed Swiss Chard Leaves

ACTIVE: 40 MIN; TOTAL: 1 HR
4 SERVINGS ● ● ● ●

24 medium Swiss chard leaves, stems and ribs removed
1 cup coarse bulgur (about 6 ounces)
3 tablespoons extra-virgin olive oil, plus more for drizzling
1 medium onion, finely chopped
2 long green Korean peppers or 1 poblano chile, seeded and finely chopped
1 tablespoon Turkish red pepper paste (see Note)
1 plum tomato, cut into ¼-inch dice
½ cup mixed chopped herbs, such as parsley, dill and mint
2 tablespoons fresh lemon juice
Salt and freshly ground pepper

1. Bring a large pot of salted water to a boil. Add the chard leaves and blanch until bright green, 1 minute. Drain the leaves and rinse under cold water. Drain again and carefully pat the leaves dry with paper towels.
2. In a medium heatproof bowl, cover the bulgur with 2 cups of boiling water. Cover the bowl and let stand until the water has been absorbed and the bulgur is tender, about 15 minutes.
3. In a skillet, heat the 3 tablespoons of oil. Add the onion and cook over moderate heat until translucent, 4 minutes. Add the peppers and cook until softened, 5 minutes. Stir in the red pepper paste. Add the diced tomato and cook until sizzling, 1 minute. Remove from the heat. Stir in the bulgur, herbs and lemon juice and season with salt and pepper.

4. Spread a chard leaf out on a work surface; overlap the leaf to fill the space where the rib was. Mound 3 tablespoons of the filling on the lower third of the leaf. Bring the lower end of the leaf up and over the filling and roll up tightly, folding in the sides as you go. Repeat with the remaining chard leaves and filling. Arrange the stuffed leaves on a platter. Drizzle with oil, season with salt and serve.
—Semsa Denizsel

NOTE Turkish red pepper paste, also known as biber salcasi, is available at Middle Eastern groceries and specialty food stores.

Farro Salad with Winter Fruit, Pistachios and Ginger

ACTIVE: 25 MIN; TOTAL: 1 HR
6 SERVINGS ● ●

Salt
1½ cups farro (10 ounces)
1 teaspoon finely grated orange zest
1 tablespoon fresh orange juice
1 tablespoon fresh lemon juice
1 tablespoon finely grated ginger
¼ cup extra-virgin olive oil
¼ cup golden raisins
¼ cup dried sour cherries
2 scallions, thinly sliced
⅓ cup salted roasted pistachios, chopped
¼ cup chopped mint
2 tablespoons chopped cilantro

1. Bring a large saucepan of lightly salted water to a boil. Add the farro and simmer over moderate heat until al dente, about 35 minutes. Drain the farro well, shaking off the excess water.
2. Meanwhile, in a large bowl, combine the orange zest, orange juice, lemon juice, ginger and oil and whisk to blend. Season with salt.
3. Add the warm farro to the dressing along with the raisins and cherries and toss well. Let stand until the farro is almost cool. Just before serving, fold in the scallions, pistachios, mint and cilantro and season with salt.
—Annie Somerville

MAKE AHEAD The salad can be kept at room temperature for up to 4 hours.

● HEALTHY ● MAKE AHEAD ● VEGETARIAN ● STAFF FAVORITE

farro salad with winter fruit, pistachios and ginger

Rice and Sweet Corn Porridge with Dried Scallops

**ACTIVE: 45 MIN; TOTAL: 1 HR 30 MIN
PLUS OVERNIGHT SOAKING
6 SERVINGS** ● ●

8 small dried scallops (1 ounce; see Note)

6 small dried wood ear mushrooms (½ ounce; see Note)

2 ears of corn—kernels cut off, cobs cut crosswise into 1-inch pieces

2 quarts plus 1 cup low-sodium chicken broth

1 large chicken thigh (7 ounces)

One 2-inch piece of fresh ginger, peeled and thinly sliced

1 celery rib, sliced ½ inch thick, plus ½ cup celery leaves

1½ cups short-grain or sushi rice, rinsed

1 tablespoon tamari

2 tablespoons freshly grated Parmigiano-Reggiano cheese

Salt

1. Put the scallops and mushrooms in 2 small separate bowls and cover with water. Let stand at room temperature overnight.
2. In a small saucepan of salted boiling water, cook the corn kernels until just tender, about 2 minutes. Drain.
3. In a large saucepan, combine the chicken broth, corn cobs, chicken thigh, ginger and sliced celery; bring to a simmer. Cover partially and simmer over low heat until the chicken is cooked through, about 30 minutes. Strain the broth; reserve the chicken thigh. You should have about 5½ cups of broth.
4. Preheat the oven to 325°. Measure out 1 cup of the broth and reserve. In a 3- to 4-quart casserole or Dutch oven, combine the remaining 4½ cups of broth with the rice and bring to a simmer over moderate heat. Cover and bake for about 20 minutes, stirring occasionally, until the rice is tender and a thick porridge has formed.
5. Drain the scallops and transfer them to a small saucepan. Add ½ cup of the reserved broth and bring to a simmer. Cover and simmer over low heat for 10 minutes. Using a slotted spoon, transfer the scallops to a plate. Remove any membranes, then thickly shred the scallops; cover. Add the tamari to the cooking liquid in the pan and cover.
6. Drain the mushrooms and cut off the knob ends. Cut the mushrooms into ½-inch pieces. Remove the meat from the chicken thigh and cut into ½-inch pieces. Add the chicken, mushrooms, corn, the remaining ½ cup of reserved broth, half of the celery leaves and the cheese to the porridge. Season with salt.
7. Spoon the porridge into bowls. Top with a little of the scallop-tamari broth. Scatter the shredded scallop and remaining celery leaves over the porridge and serve.
—*Corey Lee*

NOTE Dried scallops and wood ear mushrooms are available at well-stocked Asian markets and online.

WINE Rich, apple-scented Chardonnay: 2010 Louis Latour Mâcon-Villages Chameroy.

Golden Semolina-Quinoa-Spinach Cakes

**TOTAL: 1 HR PLUS 4 HR CHILLING
MAKES 12 CAKES** ● ● ●

These healthy panko-coated patties crisp up nicely in the skillet. For a great meatless main course, serve them with a poached egg or a mixed green salad.

½ cup quinoa

6 tablespoons extra-virgin olive oil

1 tablespoon minced shallot

10 ounces baby spinach

Salt and freshly ground pepper

1 cup low-fat milk

¾ cup finely ground semolina

¼ cup freshly grated Parmigiano-Reggiano cheese

1 large egg, beaten

1½ cups panko (Japanese bread crumbs)

3 large egg whites

1. In a small saucepan, combine the quinoa with 1 cup of water and bring to a boil. Cover and cook over low heat until the water has been absorbed, about 15 minutes. Lightly fluff the quinoa with a fork and cover it again.
2. Meanwhile, in a large skillet, heat 1 tablespoon of the olive oil. Add the shallot and cook over moderate heat, stirring, until softened, about 1 minute. Add the spinach and cook until most of the liquid has evaporated, about 5 minutes. Season with salt and pepper. Transfer the spinach to a strainer and let cool slightly; press out any remaining liquid and finely chop the spinach.
3. In a large saucepan, combine the milk, 1½ cups of water, 1 tablespoon of the olive oil and 2 teaspoons of salt and bring to a boil. Remove the pan from the heat and gradually whisk in the semolina until very smooth. Cook over moderate heat, stirring constantly with a wooden spoon, until the semolina is thick enough to hold soft peaks when the spoon is lifted, about 7 minutes. Remove the semolina from the heat and stir in the quinoa and Parmigiano. Season with salt and pepper and let cool for 15 minutes.
4. Stir the beaten whole egg and spinach into the quinoa mixture and spread in an ungreased 7-by-11-inch pan; it will be about 2 inches thick. Let cool at room temperature, then cover loosely with plastic wrap and refrigerate for at least 4 hours or overnight.
5. Preheat the oven to 250°. Cut the chilled semolina mixture into 12 squares. Put the panko in a shallow dish and season with 1 teaspoon of salt. In another shallow dish, whisk the egg whites with ½ teaspoon of salt and 1 tablespoon of water. Dip the cakes into the whites and turn to coat, letting the excess drip off. Coat the cakes in the panko and shake off excess crumbs. Transfer to a clean baking sheet.
6. In a large skillet, heat 2 tablespoons of the olive oil. Add half of the cakes and cook over moderately high heat until golden on both sides and on the edges, about 6 minutes; adjust the heat as necessary to prevent the cakes from burning. Drain the cakes on a paper towel–lined plate, then transfer to a baking sheet and keep them warm in the oven. Wipe out the skillet and cook the remaining cakes in the remaining 2 tablespoons of olive oil. Serve the cakes hot.
—*Maria Helm Sinskey*

WINE Zesty Sauvignon Blanc: 2010 Voss.

Warm Quinoa Salad with Carrots and Grilled Chicken

⏱ TOTAL: 35 MIN • 4 SERVINGS ●

6 ounces red or black quinoa (1 cup)
Salt and freshly ground black pepper
¼ cup pine nuts
3 tablespoons extra-virgin olive oil, plus more for drizzling
3 garlic cloves, minced
½ medium red onion, finely chopped
2 medium carrots, halved lengthwise and sliced crosswise into half-moons
2 teaspoons ground cumin
1 tablespoon plus 1 teaspoon sherry vinegar
Two 6-ounce skinless, boneless chicken breast halves, cut into 1-inch cubes
2 tablespoons small mint leaves

1. Put the quinoa in a small saucepan and cover with 2 cups of water. Add a large pinch of salt and pepper and bring to a boil. Cover and cook over low heat until the water has been absorbed and the quinoa is tender, about 15 minutes.
2. Meanwhile, in a large skillet, toast the pine nuts over moderate heat, stirring, until fragrant, about 2 minutes. Transfer to a plate. Heat the 3 tablespoons of olive oil in the skillet. Add the garlic and onion and cook over moderate heat until softened, about 5 minutes. Add the carrots and cumin, cover and cook over low heat until the carrots are just tender, about 5 minutes. Stir in the quinoa and sherry vinegar and season the salad with salt and pepper.
3. Light a grill or preheat a grill pan. Drizzle the chicken cubes with olive oil and thread them onto 4 skewers. Season with salt and pepper and grill over moderately high heat, turning, until browned and cooked through, about 5 minutes total.
4. Mound the quinoa salad on plates. Garnish with the toasted pine nuts and mint leaves and serve the chicken skewers alongside. —Cat Cora

WINE Spiced, black cherry–inflected Pinot Noir: 2009 Cambria Julia's Vineyard.

Quinoa and Brown Rice Bowl with Vegetables and Tahini

ACTIVE: 45 MIN; TOTAL: 1 HR
6 SERVINGS ● ● ●

F&W's Gail Simmons makes this vegan rice bowl when she craves something especially healthy to eat.

1 cup long-grain brown rice
1 cup red quinoa
¼ cup extra-virgin olive oil
1 small onion, finely diced
1 carrot, sliced crosswise ¼ inch thick
¼ pound shiitake mushrooms, stems discarded and caps thinly sliced
1 small zucchini, halved lengthwise and sliced crosswise ¼ inch thick
Salt
1 head of broccoli—stems peeled and sliced into coins, heads cut into small florets
One 12-ounce bunch of kale, large stems discarded
¼ cup tahini, at room temperature
½ cup fresh lemon juice
2 garlic cloves, minced
¼ teaspoon crushed red pepper
1 ripe avocado, cut into ½-inch dice
1 cup mung bean sprouts

1. In a medium saucepan, cover the brown rice with 2 inches of water and bring to a boil. Cover and cook over low heat until the rice is just tender, about 40 minutes. Drain and return the rice to the saucepan; keep the saucepan covered.
2. Meanwhile, in a small saucepan, combine the quinoa with 2 cups of water and bring to a boil. Cover the saucepan and simmer over low heat until the quinoa is tender and all of the water has been absorbed, 20 minutes.
3. In a large skillet, heat 2 tablespoons of the oil. Add the onion and cook over moderate heat until translucent, about 4 minutes. Add the carrot and cook until starting to soften, about 3 minutes. Add the shiitake, cover and cook until tender, about 4 minutes. Add the zucchini, season with salt and cook, stirring a few times, until tender, about 3 minutes. Transfer to a bowl.

4. Add the remaining 2 tablespoons of olive oil to the skillet. Add the broccoli, cover and cook over moderate heat, stirring a few times, until deep green, about 5 minutes. Add the kale, cover and cook, stirring a few times, until the broccoli and kale are just tender, 4 minutes longer. Season with salt, then stir in the other vegetables.
5. In a small bowl, whisk the tahini with the lemon juice, garlic, crushed red pepper and 2 tablespoons of warm water. Season the tahini sauce with salt.
6. Spoon the brown rice and quinoa into bowls. Top with the cooked vegetables, diced avocado and bean sprouts. Serve right away, passing the tahini sauce at the table. —Gail Simmons

WINE Fresh, grapefruit-scented New Zealand Sauvignon Blanc: 2011 Lobster Point.

Quinoa-Leek Pilaf

ACTIVE: 20 MIN; TOTAL: 50 MIN
10 TO 12 SERVINGS ● ● ●

3 tablespoons extra-virgin olive oil
2 pounds leeks, white and light green parts only, halved lengthwise and thinly sliced crosswise
Kosher salt and freshly ground black pepper
2½ cups quinoa (1 pound), rinsed and drained
2 cups low-sodium vegetable broth

1. In a large, deep skillet, heat the olive oil. Add the leeks and a generous pinch each of salt and pepper and cook over moderately low heat, stirring occasionally, until the leeks are softened, 10 to 12 minutes. Add the quinoa and cook over moderate heat, stirring, until dry, about 5 minutes.
2. Add the vegetable broth and 2 cups of water to the skillet and bring to a boil. Cover and simmer over moderately low heat until the quinoa is tender and the liquid has been absorbed, about 20 minutes. Remove the skillet from the heat and let stand for 10 minutes. Fluff the pilaf with a fork, season with salt and pepper and serve. —Aida Mollenkamp

Roasted Carrot and Red Quinoa Salad

ACTIVE: 30 MIN; TOTAL: 1 HR
8 SERVINGS ● ●

Anna Zepaltas, owner of a meal-delivery service in Santa Rosa, California, combines roasted carrots, walnuts and dried cranberries with red quinoa, which has a crunchier texture than the more common white quinoa. Cumin, coriander and cardamom punch up this salad, inspired by a favorite dish at Chloé's French Café in Santa Rosa.

- 2 teaspoons sweet paprika
- 1 teaspoon ground turmeric
- 1 teaspoon ground cumin
- 1 teaspoon ground ginger
- 1 teaspoon ground coriander
- 1 teaspoon ground cinnamon
- ½ teaspoon cayenne pepper
- ¼ teaspoon ground cardamom
- Salt and freshly ground black pepper
- 4 large carrots, thinly sliced lengthwise
- 1 small red onion, thinly sliced
- 7 tablespoons extra-virgin olive oil
- ½ cup walnuts
- 1 cup red quinoa
- 2 tablespoons fresh lemon juice
- 5 ounces mixed salad greens
- ½ teaspoon finely grated lemon zest
- 1 teaspoon Dijon mustard
- ½ cup dried cranberries
- 2 tablespoons chopped flat-leaf parsley

1. Preheat the oven to 400°. In a small bowl, whisk the paprika with the turmeric, cumin, ginger, coriander, cinnamon, cayenne pepper, cardamom and 1 teaspoon each of salt and black pepper. In a medium bowl, toss the carrots with the onion and 2 tablespoons of the olive oil. Add 1 tablespoon of the spice mix and toss to coat. Spread the vegetables on a rimmed baking sheet and roast for 20 to 25 minutes, stirring them once or twice, until they are tender.

2. Meanwhile, spread the walnuts in a pie plate and bake them for about 7 minutes, until golden. Let cool, then coarsely chop.

3. In a medium saucepan, combine the quinoa with 2 teaspoons of the spice mix and 2 cups of water and bring to a boil. Cover and simmer over low heat until the water is absorbed and the quinoa is tender, about 17 minutes. Uncover the saucepan, fluff the quinoa with a fork and let cool slightly.

4. In a large bowl, whisk 2 tablespoons of the oil with 1 tablespoon of the lemon juice and season with salt and black pepper. Add the salad greens and toss to coat. Spread the greens on a large platter. In the same bowl, whisk the remaining 3 tablespoons of oil with the remaining 1 tablespoon of lemon juice and the zest, mustard and 1 teaspoon of the spice mix; season with salt. Add the quinoa, walnuts, cranberries, parsley and roasted vegetables and toss well. Spoon the quinoa salad on the greens and serve.

—*Anna Zepaltas*

Quinoa-Stuffed Poblanos with Grilled Romesco Sauce

ACTIVE: 45 MIN; TOTAL: 1 HR 30 MIN
6 SERVINGS ● ● ○ ●

To boost the smoky flavors in this dish, chef Alyssa Gorelick of the vegetarian restaurant Fern in Charlotte, North Carolina, grills both the stuffed poblanos and the vegetables for the *romesco* sauce served alongside. The grilled poblano chiles are fabulous with the nutty quinoa filling.

- ½ cup red quinoa
- 6 very large poblano chiles
- 2 ears of corn, shucked
- Extra-virgin olive oil, for grilling
- ½ cup walnuts, toasted and finely chopped
- 3 scallions, thinly sliced
- 2 tablespoons chopped cilantro, plus sprigs for garnish
- ¼ cup finely diced fresh mozzarella
- Salt and freshly ground pepper
- 1½ cups Grilled Romesco Sauce (recipe follows), for serving

1. In a medium saucepan, combine the quinoa with 1 cup of water and bring to a boil. Cover and simmer until the quinoa is tender,

18 minutes. Remove the saucepan from the heat and let it stand for 5 minutes; uncover and let the quinoa cool.

2. Light a grill or preheat a grill pan. Rub the poblanos and corn with olive oil and grill over high heat, turning occasionally, until the poblanos are charred all over and the corn is charred and tender, about 5 minutes. Transfer the poblanos to a bowl, cover with plastic wrap and let stand for 5 minutes. Rub off the poblano skins with a paper towel. Cut off the tops and reserve them, then pull out and discard the cores.

3. In a large bowl, cut the corn kernels off the cobs. Add the walnuts, scallions, chopped cilantro, mozzarella and quinoa and season with salt and pepper. Lightly pack the quinoa into the poblanos. Replace the tops and secure with toothpicks.

4. Rub the poblanos with oil and grill over moderate heat, covered, turning the chiles occasionally, until tender, 15 minutes. Transfer the chiles to plates and remove the toothpicks. Garnish with cilantro sprigs and serve with the Grilled Romesco Sauce.

—*Alyssa Gorelick*

WINE Zippy Vinho Verde: 2011 Vera.

GRILLED ROMESCO SAUCE

⏲ **TOTAL: 30 MIN • MAKES 2¼ CUPS** ● ●
Any extra sauce is terrific with roasted or grilled potatoes or on a veggie burger.

- 2 large red bell peppers—halved, cored and seeded
- 1 large tomato, halved
- ½ medium onion, thickly sliced
- ¼ cup raw almonds
- ½ teaspoon crushed red pepper
- Salt

1. Light a grill or preheat a grill pan. Wrap the red peppers, tomato and onion in a large sheet of heavy-duty aluminum foil. Grill over moderate heat for about 25 minutes, until the vegetables are softened and charred.

2. Transfer the vegetables to a blender. Add the almonds and crushed red pepper and puree. Season the *romesco* sauce with salt and serve. —*AG*

● HEALTHY ● MAKE AHEAD ○ VEGETARIAN ● STAFF FAVORITE

roasted carrot and red quinoa salad

Quinoa Salad with Sweet Potatoes and Apples

ACTIVE: 30 MIN; TOTAL: 1 HR 30 MIN
10 TO 12 SERVINGS ● ●

Toasting the quinoa in olive oil before cooking it brings an extra layer of flavor to this healthy fall salad. A great meal-in-one, it makes an ideal vegetarian option for any occasion.

½ cup extra-virgin olive oil
1½ cups quinoa
Salt
1½ pounds sweet potatoes, peeled and cut into ¾-inch dice
Freshly ground pepper
¼ cup apple cider vinegar
2 large Granny Smith apples, cut into ½-inch dice
½ cup chopped flat-leaf parsley
½ medium red onion, thinly sliced
8 packed cups baby greens, such as arugula or kale (about 6 ounces)

1. Preheat the oven to 400°. In a large saucepan, heat 1 tablespoon of the olive oil. Add the quinoa and toast over moderate heat, stirring constantly, for 2 minutes. Add 3 cups of water, season with salt and bring to a boil. Cover the saucepan and simmer the quinoa for 16 minutes. Remove the saucepan from the heat and let the quinoa stand for 10 minutes. Fluff the quinoa, then spread it out on a baking sheet and refrigerate until it is chilled, about 20 minutes.

2. Meanwhile, on a large rimmed baking sheet, toss the sweet potatoes with 1 tablespoon of the olive oil and season with salt and pepper. Roast the sweet potatoes for about 25 minutes, stirring once, until golden and softened. Let them cool.

3. In a large bowl, whisk the remaining ¼ cup plus 2 tablespoons of olive oil with the vinegar; season with salt and pepper. Add the quinoa, sweet potatoes, apples, parsley, onion and greens and toss well. Serve right away. —Grace Parisi

MAKE AHEAD The quinoa and sweet potatoes can be refrigerated for up to 2 days. Assemble the salad just before serving.

Red Quinoa and Lentil Pilaf

TOTAL: 1 HR • 6 SERVINGS ● ● ● ●

Chopped marcona almonds (a buttery Spanish variety) add a super crunch to this fantastic cauliflower-flecked pilaf; coconut oil lends an unexpected tropical flavor.

1 cup French green lentils, rinsed
1 bay leaf
1 thyme sprig
1 garlic clove
¼ onion
2 tablespoons coconut oil
1 shallot, minced
1 celery rib, minced
1 carrot, minced
½ cup red quinoa, rinsed
1 cup vegetable stock
Salt and freshly ground pepper
1 pound cauliflower, coarsely grated
¼ cup chopped flat-leaf parsley
⅓ cup coarsely chopped marcona almonds

1. Put the lentils in a medium saucepan and cover with cold water. Add the bay leaf, thyme sprig, garlic and onion and bring to a boil. Simmer over moderately low heat until the lentils are tender, about 18 minutes. Drain and discard the bay leaf, thyme, garlic and onion. Wipe out the pot.

2. Add 1 tablespoon of the coconut oil to the saucepan. Add the shallot, celery and carrot and cook over low heat until softened, about 8 minutes. Add the quinoa and cook, stirring, for about 2 minutes. Add the stock, season with salt and pepper and bring to a boil. Cover and cook over low heat until the grains are tender and plump and the liquid is absorbed, about 18 minutes. Cover and let stand for 5 minutes.

3. In a large nonstick skillet, heat the remaining 1 tablespoon of coconut oil. Add the cauliflower and cook over moderately high heat until lightly browned in spots, about 5 minutes. In a large bowl, toss the lentils with the quinoa, cauliflower, parsley and almonds. Season the pilaf with salt and pepper and serve hot or at room temperature.
—Akasha Richmond

Red Lentil Dal with Tamarind and Asparagus

TOTAL: 45 MIN • 4 SERVINGS ● ● ● ●

During her stay in Bangladesh, cookbook author Naomi Duguid fell in love with dals (soupy lentil dishes) known as tok dal, or tart dal. While asparagus isn't a traditional ingredient, Duguid was inspired to add it because Bangladesh is so fertile, and many green vegetables grow there.

1 cup masur dal (red lentils), rinsed
¼ teaspoon turmeric
¼ cup vegetable oil
½ teaspoon yellow mustard seeds
½ teaspoon fennel seeds
½ teaspoon ground coriander
1 serrano chile, halved lengthwise
3 garlic cloves, minced
1 medium red onion, thinly sliced
½ pound thin asparagus, cut into 1-inch lengths
1 teaspoon tamarind concentrate blended with 1 tablespoon hot water
Salt

1. In a medium saucepan, combine the lentils with 1 quart of water and bring to a boil. Skim off the foam from the surface and stir in ⅛ teaspoon of the turmeric. Cover partially and simmer over moderately low heat, stirring occasionally, until the lentils break down, about 20 minutes.

2. Meanwhile, in a large skillet, heat the vegetable oil. Add the mustard seeds and cook over moderate heat until they start to pop, 1 minute. Add the fennel seeds, coriander, serrano chile and the remaining ⅛ teaspoon of turmeric and stir until fragrant, 30 seconds. Add the garlic and onion and cook over low heat, stirring occasionally, until softened, about 8 minutes.

3. Add the asparagus pieces to the skillet, then cover and cook until they are crisp-tender, about 3 minutes. Add the cooked lentils and dissolved tamarind and bring to a simmer. Season the dal with salt and serve.
—Naomi Duguid

SERVE WITH Lime wedges and rice.
WINE Vibrant Grüner Veltliner: 2011 Etz.

● HEALTHY ● MAKE AHEAD ● VEGETARIAN ● STAFF FAVORITE

Spiced Red Lentils

ACTIVE: 25 MIN; TOTAL: 1 HR
8 SERVINGS ● ● ○ ○

The heat in this deeply satisfying red lentil dish—called *misir wat* in Amharic, the language of Ethiopia—comes mainly from *berbere,* the ground Ethiopian spice blend that includes chile pepper, cardamom, coriander, fenugreek and *ajwain,* a thyme-like seed.

½ cup extra-virgin olive oil
3 medium red onions,
    finely chopped (2 cups)
10 garlic cloves, minced
One 3-inch piece of fresh ginger,
    peeled and minced
3 tablespoons *berbere,* plus more
    for sprinkling (see Note)
2 teaspoons nigella seeds,
    finely ground
1 teaspoon ground cardamom
Kosher salt and freshly ground pepper
3 cups red lentils (1¼ pounds)

1. In a large enameled cast-iron casserole, heat the olive oil. Add the onions and cook over moderate heat, stirring occasionally, until they are softened and just starting to brown, about 8 minutes. Add the garlic, ginger, *berbere,* nigella seeds, cardamom and a generous pinch each of salt and black pepper and cook until fragrant and deeply colored, about 10 minutes.

2. Add the red lentils with 8 cups of water to the casserole and bring to a boil. Cover and cook over moderately low heat, stirring occasionally, until the lentils have cooked down and thickened, about 25 minutes. Season the lentils with salt and freshly ground pepper. Ladle the lentils into bowls, sprinkle with *berbere* and serve right away.
—*Hiyaw Gebreyohannes*

NOTE The spices in Ethiopian cooking, such as nigella seeds and *berbere,* are available at *kalustyans.com* and *nirmalaskitchen.com.*

MAKE AHEAD The cooked lentils can be refrigerated overnight. Reheat the dish gently before serving.

WINE Spiced, lively Italian white: 2010 Capestrano Passerina.

Italian Butter Beans with Meyer Lemon and Tarragon

ACTIVE: 30 MIN; TOTAL: 3 HR PLUS
OVERNIGHT SOAKING • 6 SERVINGS ● ● ○

Marinating big, creamy Italian butter beans in their dressing for half an hour makes them ultra-flavorful. If you can't find butter beans, you can use any large white bean.

1½ cups dried Italian butter beans
    or gigante beans (10 ounces),
    soaked overnight and drained
1 bay leaf
Salt
½ cup finely chopped red onion
1 tablespoon Champagne vinegar
2 teaspoons finely grated Meyer lemon
    zest or 1 teaspoon lemon zest
3 tablespoons fresh Meyer lemon
    juice or 2 tablespoons fresh
    lemon juice
¼ cup plus 2 tablespoons extra-
    virgin olive oil
Freshly ground pepper
2 tablespoons chopped
    flat-leaf parsley
1 tablespoon chopped tarragon

1. Rinse the butter beans and transfer them to a large saucepan. Add the bay leaf and 3 quarts of water and bring to a boil. Simmer over low heat until nearly tender, about 1½ hours. Season the beans with salt and simmer until they are tender but still hold their shape, about 45 minutes longer.

2. Meanwhile, bring a small saucepan of water to a boil. Add the onion and blanch for 30 seconds. Drain the onion and transfer to a large bowl. Stir in the vinegar, lemon zest, lemon juice and olive oil.

3. Drain the beans. Add them to the dressing in the large bowl, season with salt and pepper and toss. Let the beans stand for 30 minutes, stirring occasionally. Just before serving, fold in the parsley and tarragon.
—*Annie Somerville*

MAKE AHEAD The dressed beans can be refrigerated overnight. Let them return to room temperature and fold in the chopped herbs just before serving.

Warm White Bean Salad with Smoked Trout

⏱ ACTIVE: 15 MIN; TOTAL: 45 MIN
6 SERVINGS ● ●

After a 30-minute quick-soak in a pressure cooker, these dried white beans become scented with garlic and rosemary and are ready to eat in just 7 minutes.

½ pound Great Northern or
    other small dried white beans,
    sorted and rinsed
2 ounces thickly sliced pancetta or
    bacon, chopped
1 garlic clove, minced
1 large carrot, cut into ½-inch dice
1 teaspoon finely chopped rosemary
¼ cup plus 1 tablespoon extra-
    virgin olive oil
1½ tablespoons fresh lemon juice
Salt and freshly ground black pepper
5 ounces skinless smoked trout, flesh
    flaked, or 1 jar imported Italian tuna
    in olive oil, drained and flaked
2 tablespoons chopped parsley

1. To quick-soak the beans, put them in the pressure cooker and cover with 3 inches of water. Cover and bring to high pressure. Turn off the heat and let the pressure release naturally, about 5 minutes. Uncover and let cool, about 20 minutes.

2. Drain and rinse the beans, then return them to the pressure cooker. Add the pancetta, garlic, carrot, rosemary and 1 tablespoon of the olive oil. Add 3 cups of water and bring to a boil. Cover and close the pressure cooker according to the manufacturer's instructions. Cook over very low heat, maintaining high pressure for 7 minutes. Let the pressure release naturally, then uncover and drain the beans.

3. Transfer the beans to a large, wide bowl or deep platter. Add the lemon juice and remaining ¼ cup of olive oil and season with salt and pepper. Arrange the trout on top, sprinkle with the parsley and serve right away or at room temperature. —*Grace Parisi*

WINE Floral, minerally Chenin Blanc: 2010 Champalou Vouvray.

Dandelion and White Bean Salad with Mint and Olives

ACTIVE: 40 MIN; TOTAL: 2 HR 30 MIN PLUS OVERNIGHT SOAKING • 4 SERVINGS ● ● ○

Dandelion greens, mint, olives and lemon zest are all a little bitter, which is why they work so well together. Mild white beans soften the robust flavors in this perfect-for-late-fall salad.

1¼ cups dried white beans
     (½ pound), such as cannellini,
     soaked overnight and drained
1   bay leaf
Salt
½   pound dandelion greens, stemmed
⅓   cup extra-virgin olive oil
1   teaspoon finely grated lemon zest
2   tablespoons fresh lemon juice
3   tablespoons chopped mint
½   small onion, finely diced
8   pitted green olives, sliced crosswise
     ¼ inch thick
Freshly ground black pepper

INGREDIENT TIP

dried beans like the Rosa de Castillas below will last for years, but the newer the crop, the more delicious the beans are and the more evenly they cook. So it's best to buy from a trusted source, like Rancho Gordo (*ranchogordo.com*), and cook the beans soon after buying.

1. Put the white beans and bay leaf in a large saucepan and add enough water to cover by 2 inches; bring to a boil. Simmer over low heat, stirring, until the beans are tender, 50 minutes; add water to maintain the water level. Remove from the heat; stir in 1 tablespoon of salt. Let stand for 5 minutes. Drain the beans, discard the bay leaf and let cool.

2. In a large pot of salted boiling water, cook the dandelion greens until tender, about 4 minutes. Drain the greens and let cool, then lightly squeeze out excess water. Coarsely chop the dandelion greens.

3. In a small bowl, combine the olive oil, lemon zest, lemon juice and mint. In a large bowl, combine the beans and dandelion greens. Add the onion, olives and dressing and toss well. Season with salt and pepper and toss again. Cover and refrigerate for 1 hour. Serve the salad lightly chilled.
—Marcia Kiesel

WINE Zesty white with bright acidity: 2011 Martinshof Lobster Grüner Veltliner.

Cannellini Bean Gratin with Herbed Bread Crumb Topping

ACTIVE: 45 MIN; TOTAL: 2 HR 30 MIN PLUS OVERNIGHT SOAKING 20 SERVINGS ● ● ○

"Beans are incredibly easy to scale up: Cooking enough beans for 20 people is not really any harder than cooking them for four," says New York writer and chef Tamar Adler. Here, she lightly flavors them with mustard, garlic and vinegar and tops them with crisp herbed bread crumbs.

3   pounds dried cannellini beans
     (6½ cups), soaked overnight
     and drained
2   carrots
2   celery ribs
1   small onion, halved
4   bay leaves
1   head of garlic, halved horizontally,
     plus 7 cloves minced
Bouquet garni made with 20 parsley
     stems, 10 thyme sprigs, 2 sage
     sprigs and 2 rosemary sprigs tied
     with twine

1½   cups extra-virgin olive oil, plus
     more for drizzling
Salt
4   cups fresh bread crumbs
     (from 1 baguette, crusts removed)
½   cup chopped flat-leaf parsley
1   tablespoon chopped sage
1   tablespoon chopped rosemary
2   tablespoons Dijon mustard
2   tablespoons red wine vinegar

1. In a large pot, combine the cannellini beans with the carrots, celery, onion, bay leaves, garlic head, bouquet garni and ½ cup of the olive oil. Add 6 quarts of water and bring to a boil. Simmer the beans over low heat until tender, about 1 hour; generously season the beans with salt about 10 minutes before they are done. Let cool.

2. Meanwhile, preheat the oven to 375°. On a rimmed baking sheet, toss the fresh bread crumbs with ½ cup of the olive oil and bake, stirring frequently, until golden and crisp, about 8 minutes. Let cool, then transfer the bread crumbs to a bowl and toss with the chopped parsley, sage and rosemary.

3. Using the side of a chef's knife, mash the minced garlic to a paste with a generous pinch of salt. Scrape the garlic paste into a small bowl and stir in the Dijon mustard. Stir half of the garlic-mustard mixture into the toasted bread crumbs.

4. Drain the beans and reserve 1 cup of the cooking liquid; discard the carrots, celery, onion, bay leaves, garlic and bouquet garni. Transfer the beans to 2 large, shallow baking dishes. Whisk the vinegar and the remaining ½ cup of olive oil into the remaining garlic-mustard mixture, then stir in the reserved bean cooking liquid. Pour the mixture over the beans and stir. Sprinkle the bread crumbs on top and bake on the top shelf for 15 minutes, until hot and crusty. Drizzle with olive oil and serve warm. *—Tamar Adler*

MAKE AHEAD The beans can be refrigerated in their cooking liquid for up to 3 days; the toasted bread crumbs can be kept in an airtight container at room temperature without the herbs for up to 3 days. Return the beans to room temperature before baking.

● HEALTHY   ● MAKE AHEAD   ○ VEGETARIAN   ● STAFF FAVORITE

dandelion and white bean salad with mint and olives

Chefs Curtis Di Fede (left) and Tyler Rodde in the open kitchen at Napa's Oenotri; the duo create stellar Cal-Ital dishes like pizza with garlic cream and nettles, OPPOSITE; *recipe, page 290.*

BREADS, PIZZAS & SANDWICHES

Crispy Whole Wheat–Maple Crackers

ACTIVE: 30 MIN; TOTAL: 2 HR 30 MIN
MAKES FOUR 12-INCH ROUNDS ● ○ ○

To make these lightly sweet crackers, F&W's Justin Chapple works both maple syrup and maple sugar into the dough, then breaks the baked pastry into shards.

1½ cups all-purpose flour, plus
   more for dusting
1 cup whole wheat flour
¼ cup maple sugar (see Note),
   plus more for sprinkling
1 teaspoon salt
1 stick cold unsalted butter, cut
   into ½-inch pieces
¼ cup pure maple syrup, plus
   more for brushing

1. In a food processor, combine both flours with the ¼ cup of maple sugar and the salt and pulse to mix. Scatter the butter pieces on top and pulse until a coarse meal forms. Add ⅓ cup of water and the ¼ cup of maple syrup; pulse until the dough comes together when you pinch it. Scrape out onto a work surface and press together. Divide the dough into 4 equal pieces and shape into disks; wrap the disks in plastic and refrigerate until well chilled, about 1 hour.

2. Preheat the oven to 400° and line 2 baking sheets with parchment paper. On a floured work surface, dust 1 disk of dough with flour. Roll out the dough to a 12-inch round and transfer it to one of the prepared baking sheets. Repeat with 1 more disk of dough. Brush the rounds of dough with maple syrup and sprinkle with maple sugar.

3. Bake the crackers for about 18 minutes, until crisp; shift the baking sheets from top to bottom and front to back halfway through baking. Transfer the crackers to racks to cool completely. Repeat with the remaining 2 disks of dough. Break the crackers into large shards and serve. —*Justin Chapple*

NOTE Maple sugar is made from reduced syrup; it is available at specialty food stores.

MAKE AHEAD The crackers can be stored in an airtight container for up to 2 weeks.

Linseed Crisps

ACTIVE: 15 MIN; TOTAL: 1 HR 15 MIN
4 SERVINGS ● ● ●

At Fäviken, his hyper-local restaurant in the Swedish countryside, chef Magnus Nilsson adds super-healthy linseeds (flaxseeds) to the batter for these ethereal chips.

¼ cup linseeds (flaxseeds)
1 tablespoon potato starch
½ teaspoon kosher salt

1. Preheat the oven to 300° and line a baking sheet with a nonstick baking mat. In a small bowl, whisk the linseeds with the potato starch and salt. Add ¾ cup of boiling water and whisk until the starch dissolves. Let the batter stand until slightly thickened, about 10 minutes.

2. Scrape the batter onto the baking mat. Using an offset spatula, spread the batter into a very thin 11-by-15-inch rectangle. Bake for 25 to 30 minutes, until it is very dry and no longer sticky. Let cool completely, about 20 minutes, then break the crisp into large shards and serve within 20 minutes.
—*Magnus Nilsson*

MAKE AHEAD The baked linseed crisps can be kept at room temperature for up to 2 hours. Recrisp them in a 300° oven for about 5 minutes before serving.

Parker House Rolls Topped with Cheddar and Old Bay

ACTIVE: 30 MIN; TOTAL: 1 HR PLUS 2 HR
RISING • MAKES 15 LARGE ROLLS ● ○ ○

1 cup milk
1 envelope active dry yeast
   (2½ teaspoons)
3 tablespoons sugar
1 large egg, beaten
1 stick unsalted butter, melted,
   plus more for greasing the pan
3½ cups all-purpose flour,
   plus more for kneading
1½ teaspoons table salt
¾ cup shredded sharp cheddar cheese
   (about 2 ounces)
1 teaspoon Old Bay seasoning

1. In a microwave-safe cup, heat the milk in the microwave until it is warm but not hot, about 20 seconds. Add the yeast and sugar and let the mixture stand until foamy, about 5 minutes. Scrape the mixture into the bowl of a standing electric mixer fitted with the dough hook. Add the beaten egg and 6 tablespoons of the melted butter and beat at low speed just until combined. Add the 3½ cups of flour and the salt and beat at low speed until the dough is evenly moistened, about 2 minutes. Increase the speed to medium and knead until a soft, smooth dough forms, about 10 minutes.

2. Transfer the dough to a floured work surface and pat it into a 10-inch square. Fold one-third of the dough into the center and the other third on top, like folding a letter. Turn the dough around and fold it the same way again; you should now have a small square. Butter the mixer bowl and return the dough to it. Cover with plastic wrap and let the dough stand in a warm place until it has doubled in bulk, about 1 hour.

3. Butter a 9-by-13-inch baking pan. On a well-floured work surface, roll out the dough to a 15-inch square. Working from the bottom, tightly roll the dough into a log. Using a floured knife, cut the log into thirds. Cut each third into 5 slices. Arrange the rolls spiral side up in the prepared baking pan in 3 rows of 5. Cover loosely with buttered plastic wrap and let rise for about 1 hour, until the rolls are billowy.

4. Preheat the oven to 375°. Remove the plastic wrap from the baking pan and bake the rolls for 15 minutes. Sprinkle the cheddar cheese on top and bake for about 15 minutes longer, until the rolls are golden and cooked through; cover the rolls with aluminum foil for the last 5 minutes of baking to prevent them from overbrowning. Brush the rolls with the remaining 2 tablespoons of melted butter and sprinkle them with the Old Bay seasoning. Transfer the baking pan to a rack to let the rolls cool before serving.
—*Jonathon Sawyer*

MAKE AHEAD The baked rolls can be kept at room temperature overnight. Rewarm them before serving.

● HEALTHY ● MAKE AHEAD ○ VEGETARIAN ● STAFF FAVORITE

Sausage, Apple and Cranberry-Nut-Bread Dressing

ACTIVE: 40 MIN; TOTAL: 2 HR
12 SERVINGS ● ●

Using cubes of store-bought cranberry-pecan bread in this classic sausage-apple dressing is a clever shortcut.

- 2 pounds sliced cranberry-pecan bread, cut into cubes
- 6 tablespoons unsalted butter
- 3 Granny Smith apples—peeled, cored and cut into 1-inch pieces
- 2 shallots, thinly sliced
- 1 celery rib, finely chopped
- 2 tablespoons chopped sage
- 1 pound bulk breakfast sausage, broken into pieces
- 6 cups chicken stock or low-sodium broth

Salt and freshly ground pepper

1. Preheat the oven to 350°. Spread the bread cubes in a large roasting pan and toast for about 15 minutes, stirring once or twice, until slightly dry. Transfer to a large bowl.

2. In a large, deep skillet, melt 4 tablespoons of the butter. Add the apples, shallots, celery and sage and cook over high heat, stirring occasionally, until the apples are lightly browned in spots, about 8 minutes. Add the sausage pieces and cook over high heat, breaking them up with a spoon, until they're browned and cooked through, about 5 minutes. Add 3 cups of the stock and boil until nearly evaporated, about 6 minutes. Season with salt and pepper.

3. Add the sausage mixture to the bread in the large bowl along with the remaining 3 cups of stock. Stir until evenly moistened. Transfer the dressing to a large, buttered baking dish and dot with the remaining 2 tablespoons of butter.

4. Cover the dressing with foil and bake for 30 minutes. Remove the foil and bake for 30 minutes longer, until the dressing is browned around the edges. Let rest for 15 minutes before serving. —*Grace Parisi*

MAKE AHEAD The recipe can be prepared through Step 3 and refrigerated for 3 days.

Corn Bread Stuffing with Bacon and Greens

ACTIVE: 1 HR; TOTAL: 2 HR 30 MIN
10 TO 12 SERVINGS ●

- 1 stick plus 6 tablespoons unsalted butter, plus more for brushing
- Two 8-inch loaves Stone-Ground Corn Breads (recipe follows), cut into 1-inch cubes
- 1 pound Tuscan kale, stems discarded
- 1 pound lean thick-cut bacon, sliced crosswise ½ inch thick
- 4 celery ribs, cut into ¼-inch dice
- 2 large onions, cut into ¼-inch dice
- Pinch of crushed red pepper
- Salt and freshly ground black pepper
- 2 large eggs
- 4 cups chicken stock or low-sodium broth

1. Preheat the oven to 350°. Brush 2 large, shallow baking dishes with butter. Spread the corn bread cubes on 2 large rimmed baking sheets and bake for about 30 minutes, until golden brown and crisp. Let cool.

2. Meanwhile, in a large saucepan of salted boiling water, cook the kale until bright green, about 1 minute. Using a slotted spoon, transfer the kale to a colander and drain. Lightly squeeze dry the kale and coarsely chop. Add the bacon to the boiling water and blanch for 1 minute. Drain and pat dry.

3. In a large skillet, melt the 1 stick of butter. Add the bacon and cook over moderate heat until it is browned and crisp, about 10 minutes. Using a slotted spoon, transfer the bacon to paper towels to drain. Add the celery, onions and crushed red pepper to the skillet and season with salt and black pepper. Cover and cook over low heat, stirring occasionally, until the vegetables are softened, about 15 minutes. Transfer the mixture to a large bowl. Add the kale, bacon and corn bread and gently toss to mix. Season with salt and black pepper.

4. In a small saucepan, melt the remaining 6 tablespoons of butter over moderate heat. In a medium bowl, lightly beat the eggs, then gradually beat in the stock. Gently fold the egg mixture into the stuffing, then fold in the melted butter. Spread the stuffing in the prepared baking dishes and cover with foil.

5. Bake the stuffing in the upper third of the oven for 20 minutes. Uncover and bake for about 20 minutes longer, until hot throughout and crisp on top. Transfer the baking dishes to racks and let the stuffing rest for about 10 minutes before serving. —*David Tanis*

MAKE AHEAD The corn bread stuffing can be prepared through Step 4 and refrigerated overnight, before baking.

STONE-GROUND CORN BREADS

ACTIVE: 15 MIN; TOTAL: 1 HR
MAKES TWO 8-INCH LOAVES ● ●

- 2½ cups stone-ground cornmeal
- 2½ cups all-purpose flour
- 3½ tablespoons sugar
- 2 tablespoons baking powder
- 2¼ teaspoons salt
- ¾ cup vegetable oil
- 3 large eggs
- 2½ cups milk
- 2 tablespoons unsalted butter

1. Preheat the oven to 375°. Put two 8-inch cast-iron skillets or round cake pans in the oven to heat up. In a large bowl, whisk the cornmeal with the flour, sugar, baking powder and salt. In a medium bowl, whisk the vegetable oil with the eggs and milk. Using a flexible spatula, gently fold the wet ingredients into the dry ingredients until just blended; do not overmix.

2. In each hot skillet, melt 1 tablespoon of the butter, swirling to coat the bottoms and sides. Divide the batter between the skillets and shake to smooth the tops. Bake the corn breads in the center of the oven for 35 minutes, until springy when lightly pressed in the center. Transfer the corn breads in the pans to racks to cool. Turn them out onto a baking sheet. Cover with plastic wrap and keep at room temperature overnight. —*DT*

MAKE AHEAD The corn breads can be made several days ahead and refrigerated, or frozen for up to 1 month.

Injera

**TOTAL: 20 MIN PLUS OVERNIGHT
FERMENTING • MAKES ABOUT EIGHT
12-INCH CRÊPES** ● ●

This spongy, crêpe-like Ethiopian flatbread is made from teff, tiny ancient gluten-free whole grains ground into flour.

- 4 cups teff flour (about 5 ounces)
- 1½ teaspoons salt

1. In a large bowl, whisk the teff flour with 5 cups of water until a smooth batter forms. Cover the bowl with plastic wrap and let it stand at room temperature overnight; the batter will be slightly foamy.

2. Heat a 12-inch nonstick skillet over high heat. Whisk the salt into the batter. Ladle ¾ cup of the batter into the skillet; swirl to coat the bottom with batter. Cook over moderately high heat until the *injera* just starts to bubble, about 30 seconds. Cover the skillet and cook for 30 seconds longer, until the *injera* is cooked through and the surface is slightly glossy. Invert the skillet onto a work surface, letting the *injera* fall from the pan. Repeat with the remaining batter and serve.
—Hiyaw Gebreyohannes

Garlic Bread "Fries" with Marinara "Ketchup"

**ACTIVE: 20 MIN; TOTAL: 1 HR
8 TO 10 SERVINGS**

In this imaginative party snack, garlicky bread sticks and smoky, bacon-laced tomato sauce stand in for french fries and ketchup.

- 10 tablespoons extra-virgin olive oil
- 2 ounces thick-cut bacon
- 1 small onion, minced
- ½ teaspoon crushed red pepper
- 2 tablespoons tomato paste
- 1½ teaspoons sugar
- One 28-ounce can whole peeled tomatoes with juices, pureed
- 4 tablespoons unsalted butter
- 3 large garlic cloves, minced
- ½ cup finely chopped flat-leaf parsley
- 1 large baguette, halved and split
- ½ cup freshly grated Pecorino Romano

1. In a saucepan, heat 2 tablespoons of the oil. Add the bacon and cook over high heat until golden, 6 minutes. Add the onion and crushed red pepper and cook, stirring, until softened, 4 minutes. Stir in the tomato paste and sugar and cook for 1 minute. Add the pureed tomatoes and cook over low heat until the sauce is very thick and reduced to 2 cups, 30 minutes. Discard the bacon.

2. Meanwhile, preheat the oven to 450°. In a medium skillet, melt the butter in the remaining ½ cup of olive oil. Add the garlic and cook over moderate heat for 1 minute. Remove from the heat and add the parsley.

3. Place the bread on a baking sheet, cut side up, and spoon the garlic butter on top. Sprinkle with the cheese and bake in the middle of the oven for 10 minutes. Light the broiler and broil for 1 minute, just until golden. Cut the bread into ½-inch "fries" and serve in paper cones, with the marinara ketchup.
—Grace Parisi

Spicy Carrot Sandwiches

🕐 **TOTAL: 25 MIN • 4 SERVINGS** ● ●

British chef Nick Sandler created this sandwich for Paul, Stella and Mary McCartney's *The Meat Free Monday Cookbook.*

- 1 tablespoon extra-virgin olive oil
- 2 large carrots, coarsely grated
- 2 garlic cloves, thinly sliced
- 1 teaspoon caraway seeds
- Salt and crushed red pepper
- ½ cup plus 2 tablespoons hummus
- 4 slices of sourdough bread or two 8-inch whole wheat baguettes, split lengthwise and grilled
- ¼ cup Greek yogurt
- Cilantro leaves
- Freshly ground black pepper

1. In a skillet, heat the olive oil. Add the carrots, garlic and caraway; season with salt and crushed red pepper. Cook until the carrots are just wilted, 4 minutes. Let cool.

2. Spread the hummus on the bread. Sprinkle with the carrot mixture and dollop on the yogurt. Top with cilantro, season with black pepper and serve. *—Nick Sandler*

Hummus with Whole Wheat Flatbreads

**ACTIVE: 1 HR; TOTAL: 1 HR 30 MIN PLUS
OVERNIGHT SOAKING • 4 TO 6 SERVINGS**
● ● ● ●

Alice Waters's wholesome flatbreads take only 4 minutes to cook in a cast-iron skillet.

HUMMUS

- ¾ cup dried chickpeas, soaked overnight and drained
- ¼ preserved lemon, rind only, chopped
- ¼ cup tahini
- ¼ cup extra-virgin olive oil
- 3 tablespoons fresh lemon juice
- 2 garlic cloves, smashed
- ½ teaspoon ground cumin
- Salt

FLATBREADS

- 2 cups whole wheat flour
- 1 teaspoon salt
- ½ teaspoon baking powder
- 3 tablespoons extra-virgin olive oil

1. MAKE THE HUMMUS In a saucepan, cover the chickpeas with 2 inches of water and bring to a boil. Simmer over low heat until the chickpeas are tender, about 1 hour; add more water as needed to keep them covered. Reserve ¼ cup of the cooking liquid and drain the chickpeas. Transfer the chickpeas to a food processor. Add the reserved cooking liquid and the remaining hummus ingredients; process until smooth. Season with salt.

2. MEANWHILE, MAKE THE FLATBREADS In a large bowl, whisk the flour, salt and baking powder. Stir in ¾ cup of warm water and the oil; knead to form a moist dough. Cover with a kitchen towel and let rest for 30 minutes.

3. Heat a 10-inch cast-iron skillet. Divide the dough into 16 balls. On a lightly floured work surface, roll out each ball to a 6-by-3-inch oval. Cook 2 flatbreads at a time in the skillet over moderate heat until they start to brown on the bottom, 2 minutes. Flip and cook until browned in spots on the other side, 2 minutes. Just before serving, turn each flatbread over an open flame until it is lightly charred, 1 minute. Serve with the hummus. *—Alice Waters*

hummus with whole wheat flatbreads

Brussels Sprout, Pancetta and Parmesan Flatbreads

ACTIVE: 30 MIN; TOTAL: 2 HR • MAKES TWO 13-BY-15-INCH FLATBREADS ●

DOUGH

- 1 envelope (¼ ounce) instant dry yeast
- 1 teaspoon sugar
- 1 tablespoon extra-virgin olive oil, plus more for brushing
- 1 teaspoon kosher salt
- 2½ cups all-purpose flour, plus more for dusting

TOPPING

- ½ cup extra-virgin olive oil, plus more for brushing
- 1 large white onion, halved and thinly sliced
- 1 pound brussels sprouts, thinly sliced (5 cups)
- 5 ounces Parmigiano-Reggiano cheese, finely grated (1½ cups)
- ¼ pound thinly sliced pancetta, torn into 2-inch strips

Salt and freshly ground pepper

Lemon wedges and Asian chile oil, for serving

1 MAKE THE DOUGH In a bowl, combine the yeast with 1 cup of warm water and the sugar and let stand until foamy, 5 minutes. Add the 1 tablespoon of oil, the salt and 2 cups of the flour and stir until a soft dough forms. Knead in the remaining ½ cup of flour, then turn the dough out onto a lightly floured work surface and knead until it's firm yet supple, about 5 minutes. Lightly brush the bowl with oil, add the dough and cover with plastic wrap; let stand until doubled in bulk, about 1 hour.

2. MEANWHILE, MAKE THE TOPPING In a medium skillet, heat 2 tablespoons of the olive oil. Add the onion, cover and cook over moderately high heat until softened, about 5 minutes; reduce the heat and cook, stirring, until very soft and lightly caramelized, about 15 minutes longer. Transfer the onion to a large bowl and let cool slightly. Add the brussels sprouts, cheese and pancetta to the bowl and season with salt and pepper. Stir in ¼ cup of the olive oil.

3. Preheat the oven to 450° and position racks in the upper and lower thirds. Lightly brush 2 rimmed baking sheets with olive oil. On a lightly floured work surface, cut the dough in half and shape each piece into a 13-by-15-inch rectangle ¼ inch thick. Transfer the dough to the baking sheets and brush with the remaining 2 tablespoons of olive oil. Spread the topping on the flatbreads and bake for 25 minutes, until golden and crispy. Shift the pans from top to bottom and front to back halfway through. Slide the flatbreads onto a work surface, cut into rectangles and serve with lemon wedges and Asian chile oil. —*Sara Vaughn*

WINE Lively California rosé: 2011 Bonny Doon Vin Gris de Cigare.

Whole Wheat Pizzas with Onions and Bitter Greens

ACTIVE: 1 HR; TOTAL: 2 HR

MAKES THREE 10-INCH PIZZAS ● ●

Olympic swimmer Garrett Weber-Gale, who interned at a pizzeria in Umbria, Italy, tops these healthy pizzas with radicchio, kale and sweet, silky caramelized onions.

DOUGH

- ¾ teaspoon active dry yeast
- ¼ teaspoon sugar
- 1 cup whole wheat flour
- 1 cup all-purpose flour, plus more for dusting
- ½ teaspoon salt
- 2½ teaspoons extra-virgin olive oil, plus more for oiling and rubbing

TOPPINGS

- 2 tablespoons canola oil
- 2 large onions, halved and thinly sliced
- 10 thyme sprigs

Salt and freshly ground pepper

- ¼ cup pine nuts
- 1 large garlic clove, minced
- 2 tablespoons extra-virgin olive oil
- 1 head of radicchio (6 ounces), thinly sliced
- 2 cups thinly sliced kale leaves (3 ounces)
- 1 tablespoon thinly sliced sage leaves
- 5 ounces fresh mozzarella, thinly sliced

1. MAKE THE DOUGH In the bowl of a standing electric mixer fitted with the dough hook, combine the yeast with ¼ cup of warm water and the sugar and let stand for 5 minutes. Add another ½ cup of warm water, the whole wheat and all-purpose flours, the salt and the 2½ teaspoons of olive oil and beat at medium speed until a soft, supple dough forms, about 8 minutes. Roll the dough into a ball, rub it with olive oil and return it to the bowl. Cover the dough and let stand until doubled in bulk, about 1 hour.

2. Preheat the oven to 500° and place a pizza stone on the bottom rack of the oven, allowing at least 30 minutes for it to preheat. Punch down the dough and divide it into 3 pieces; form them into 3 balls and transfer to a lightly oiled baking sheet. Cover the dough balls with oiled plastic wrap and let stand for 20 to 30 minutes.

3. MEANWHILE, PREPARE THE TOPPINGS In a large skillet, heat the canola oil. Add the onions and thyme and season with salt and pepper. Cover and cook over moderate heat, stirring once or twice, until the onions soften, about 5 minutes. Uncover and cook until the onions are very soft and golden, about 15 minutes longer; add water as needed to prevent scorching. Discard the thyme.

4. Spread the the pine nuts in a pie plate and toast in the oven until golden, 2 minutes.

5. In a large bowl, combine the garlic and olive oil. Add the radicchio, kale and sage, season lightly with salt and pepper and toss.

6. Turn the broiler on. Roll or stretch 1 ball of dough to a 10-inch round and transfer it to a floured pizza peel. Mound one-third of the greens on top, followed by one-third each of the onions, pine nuts and cheese. Carefully slide the pizza onto the hot stone and bake until the crust is browned and the toppings are sizzling, 8 to 10 minutes. Cut the pizza into wedges and serve right away. Repeat to make the remaining 2 pizzas. —*Garrett Weber-Gale*

MAKE AHEAD The caramelized onions can be refrigerated overnight. Bring them to room temperature before proceeding.

WINE Juicy, fruit-forward Piedmontese red: 2010 Elio Altare Dolcetto d'Alba.

brussels sprout, pancetta and parmesan flatbread

Grilled Flatbreads with Mushrooms, Ricotta and Herbs

⏱ TOTAL: 45 MIN

MAKES TWO 12-INCH FLATBREADS ● ●

"The main challenge of backcountry cooking is being limited to wood-burning stoves and fire pits. There's no low, medium or high on those," says Colorado chef Kelly Liken. "Luckily, one of my favorite things to make is grilled flatbread, which doesn't require an oven." For these flatbreads she gathers wild mushrooms, but cultivated ones like shiitake and oyster mushrooms are also delicious.

- ¼ cup extra-virgin olive oil, plus more for brushing and drizzling
- ½ pound oyster and shiitake mushrooms, thinly sliced (2 cups)
- 1 shallot, minced
- 1 garlic clove, minced
- ¼ cup dry white wine
- Salt and freshly ground pepper
- Two 8-ounce balls of pizza dough, at room temperature
- 1 cup fresh ricotta cheese (8 ounces)
- 2 tablespoons coarsely chopped chervil
- 2 tablespoons coarsely chopped chives
- 2 tablespoons coarsely chopped flat-leaf parsley
- 2 tablespoons coarsely chopped tarragon

1. In a medium skillet, heat the ¼ cup of olive oil. Add the mushrooms and cook over moderately high heat, stirring occasionally, until lightly browned, about 5 minutes. Add the shallot and garlic and cook until fragrant, about 1 minute. Add the wine and cook until evaporated, about 1 minute. Season the mushrooms with salt and pepper.

2. Light a grill or preheat a grill pan. Lightly oil a rimless baking sheet. On the baking sheet, stretch each ball of pizza dough out to a 12-inch round; brush with extra-virgin olive oil. Carefully slide the dough rounds onto the grill and cook over moderately high heat, shifting the rounds to prevent scorching, until lightly browned on the bottom,

about 2 minutes. Flip the rounds and spread ½ cup of the fresh ricotta cheese over each one. Scatter the sautéed mushrooms and herbs over the flatbreads and grill until they are heated through, about 2 minutes.

3. Transfer the flatbreads to a work surface, drizzle lightly with olive oil and season with salt and pepper. Cut into wedges and serve right away. *—Kelly Liken*

MAKE AHEAD The cooked mushrooms can be refrigerated for up to 3 days. Rewarm gently before proceeding with Step 2.

WINE Earthy Spanish Tempranillo: 2008 Dominio de Eguren Protocolo.

White Bean Flatbreads with Prosciutto and Cheese

⏱ TOTAL: 10 MIN • MAKES 4 FLATBREADS

These white bean flatbreads are a quick and satisfying late-night snack that can be made in just 10 minutes. Simply top toasted pitas with mashed cannellini beans, prosciutto and Fontina, then broil until the cheese is melted and gooey.

- 4 pocketless pitas
- 2 tablespoons extra-virgin olive oil, plus more for drizzling
- One 15-ounce can cannellini beans, drained and rinsed
- 1 teaspoon crushed red pepper
- 1 teaspoon chopped rosemary
- 2 ounces chopped sliced prosciutto
- ¼ cup chopped salted roasted almonds
- 6 ounces imported Fontina cheese, shredded (1½ cups)

Preheat a large skillet; preheat the broiler. Position a rack 6 inches from the heat. Brush the pitas on both sides with the 2 tablespoons of olive oil. Cook in the skillet over high heat until browned, about 3 minutes. In a bowl, mash the cannellini beans with the red pepper, rosemary and prosciutto; spread on the pitas. Top with the almonds and cheese and transfer the skillet to the broiler. Broil for about 2 minutes, until the cheese is melted and the pitas are golden. Drizzle with oil, cut into wedges and serve. *—Grace Parisi*

Chris Bianco's Pizza Rosa

TOTAL: 45 MIN PLUS 30 MIN PREHEATING
6 SERVINGS ●

At Pizzeria Bianco in Phoenix, Chris Bianco was among the first chefs in the country to make pizza an art form, using stellar ingredients and a custom-built wood-burning oven that heats up to 800°. For home cooks, preheating a pizza stone in a 500° oven for half an hour before baking the pizza creates a charred, crisp crust. Store-bought pizza dough is a perfectly fine base for Bianco's pizza, which is topped with Parmigiano-Reggiano cheese, red onion, rosemary and chopped pistachios.

- Three 8-ounce balls of pizza dough, thawed if frozen
- All-purpose flour, for dusting
- 6 ounces freshly grated Parmigiano-Reggiano cheese (1½ cups)
- 1 large red onion, thinly sliced
- 1 tablespoon chopped rosemary
- ¼ cup plus 2 tablespoons unsalted raw pistachios, coarsely chopped
- Extra-virgin olive oil, for drizzling

1. Place a pizza stone in the oven and preheat the oven to 500°, allowing at least 30 minutes for the stone to preheat.

2. Work with 1 piece of dough at a time: On a floured surface, roll or stretch the dough out to a 12-inch round. Transfer the dough to a floured pizza peel. Spread one-third of the cheese on top, leaving a ½-inch border all around. Lightly press the cheese into the dough. Top with one-third of both the onion and the rosemary.

3. Slide the pizza onto the hot stone and bake for about 4 minutes, until lightly golden and bubbling. Carefully sprinkle one-third of the pistachios over the pizza and bake for 2 minutes longer, until the crust is browned and the onions are very soft. Slide the pizza onto a work surface. Drizzle with olive oil, cut into wedges and serve. Repeat with the remaining dough and toppings. *—Chris Bianco*

WINE Crisp, floral sparkling wine from Oregon: 2007 Argyle Brut.

● HEALTHY ● MAKE AHEAD ● VEGETARIAN ● STAFF FAVORITE

white bean flatbreads with prosciutto and cheese

Turkish Ground-Lamb Pizzas

ACTIVE: 40 MIN; TOTAL: 1 HR 40 MIN
4 SERVINGS

At Kantin Dükkan, Semsa Denizsel's take-out shop in Istanbul, she tops her pizzas with ground lamb (flavored with sweet sun-dried tomatoes and a little spicy red pepper), but you can substitute ground beef instead. To make the pizza even more substantial, bake it with an egg on top; the runny yolk is terrific with the whole wheat crust.

DOUGH

- 1 cup whole wheat flour
- 1 cup all-purpose flour
- ½ teaspoon salt
- ½ tablespoon honey
- 1 tablespoon active dry yeast
- ½ tablespoon extra-virgin olive oil, plus more for brushing

TOPPING

- 1 tablespoon extra-virgin olive oil
- 1 small onion, finely chopped
- 1 pound ground lamb or beef
- 1 garlic clove, minced

Kosher salt and freshly ground black pepper

- ¼ cup chopped drained oil-packed sun-dried tomatoes
- 1 tablespoon Turkish red pepper paste (see Note) or 2 jarred hot cherry peppers, minced
- ½ teaspoon ground cumin
- 4 large eggs (optional)
- 2 tablespoons flat-leaf parsley leaves

1. MAKE THE DOUGH In a small bowl, whisk the whole wheat flour with the all-purpose flour and salt. In a large bowl, combine ¾ cup of warm water with the honey. Sprinkle the yeast over the water and let stand for about 5 minutes, until foamy. Stir in the olive oil and then the flour mixture. Gently knead the dough on a work surface until it forms a smooth, somewhat sticky ball. Lightly oil another bowl and add the dough. Cover with plastic wrap and let stand in a warm place until doubled in bulk, about 1 hour.

2. PREPARE THE TOPPING In a skillet, heat the 1 tablespoon of olive oil. Add the onion and cook over moderate heat until translucent, 4 minutes. Add the lamb and garlic and season with salt and pepper. Cook over moderately high heat, breaking up the meat with a wooden spoon, until the lamb is no longer pink, 3 minutes. Add the sun-dried tomatoes, red pepper paste and cumin and cook, stirring, for 1 minute. Remove from the heat and season with salt and pepper.

3. Preheat the oven to 450°. Arrange oven racks in the top and bottom thirds of the oven. Preheat a large rimmed baking sheet in the oven for about 5 minutes.

4. On a lightly floured work surface, punch down the dough and cut into 4 pieces. Roll each piece into a 6-inch round. Arrange the dough rounds on the preheated baking sheet, about 1 inch apart. Bake on the bottom shelf of the oven for 2 minutes. Spread the lamb topping over the dough, leaving a ½-inch border around the edges; brush the borders with olive oil. Crack an egg in the center of each pizza (if using) and bake on the top shelf of the oven for about 6 minutes, until the crust is crisp on the bottom, the egg white is firm and the yolk is runny. Scatter the parsley over the pizzas and serve hot.
—*Semsa Denizsel*

NOTE Turkish red pepper paste, also known as *biber salcasi,* is available at Middle Eastern markets and specialty stores.

WINE Spicy, raspberry-scented Rhône red: 2009 Domaine Monpertuis Vignoble de la Ramière Côtes du Rhône.

Pizza with Garlic Cream and Nettles

📷 PAGE 281
⏱ TOTAL: 45 MIN
MAKES TWO 12-INCH PIZZAS ● ●

Nettles grow wild all year in northern California, and chefs Tyler Rodde and Curtis Di Fede use them as many ways as possible at Oenotri, their restaurant in Napa. Because raw nettles can make you itch, it's best to handle them with kitchen gloves or tongs. Once cooked, the nettles lose their sting and have a deep, earthy flavor that's delicious with the buffalo mozzarella and cream infused with green garlic.

- 2 tablespoons unsalted butter
- 1 or 2 green garlic bulbs (see Note), depending on size, or 3 scallions, white and tender green parts only, thinly sliced
- 1 tablespoon dry white wine
- ¼ cup heavy cream

Semolina, for dusting
Two 8-ounce balls pizza dough

- 6 ounces buffalo mozzarella, sliced

Salt and freshly ground pepper

- 4 ounces nettles or baby arugula
- 2 tablespoons extra-virgin olive oil

Shaved Parmigiano-Reggiano cheese, for serving

1. Place a pizza stone on the bottom rack of the oven and preheat the oven to 500° for 30 minutes.

2. Meanwhile, in a small saucepan, combine the butter with 1 tablespoon of water and bring to a simmer. Add the green garlic and cook over moderate heat until softened, about 5 minutes. Add the white wine and cook for 2 minutes. Add the heavy cream and simmer over low heat until reduced by half, about 5 minutes.

3. On a semolina-dusted work surface, roll or stretch one of the pieces of dough to a 12-inch round; transfer to a semolina-dusted pizza peel. Spread half of the garlic cream on the dough, leaving a 1-inch border all around. Top with half of the mozzarella and season with salt and pepper. In a medium bowl, use tongs to toss the nettles with the olive oil and season with salt and pepper. Mound half of the nettles on the pizza. Turn on the broiler.

4. Slide the pizza onto the stone and broil for about 5 minutes, until golden brown and bubbling. Transfer the pizza to a cutting board and garnish with shaved Parmigiano. Repeat to make the second pizza.
—*Curtis Di Fede and Tyler Rodde*

NOTE Green garlic, also known as spring garlic, is young garlic that hasn't yet formed a large bulb.

WINE Bright, full-bodied white from northern Italy: 2010 Tiefenbrunner Feldmarschall Müller-Thurgau.

● HEALTHY ● MAKE AHEAD ● VEGETARIAN ● STAFF FAVORITE

turkish ground-lamb pizza

Fennel and Sweet Onion Pizzas with Green Olives

ACTIVE: 1 HR; TOTAL: 3 HR
MAKES FOUR 10-INCH PIZZAS

At Harry's Pizzeria in Miami, chef Michael Schwartz uses brown ale, honey and whole wheat flour to flavor his chewy crust. Toppings can range from potato and house-cured bacon to this pie, which is made with Pernod-braised fennel, caramelized onions and Trugole, a semisoft Italian cheese that melts beautifully.

DOUGH

- 1 package active dry yeast (¼ ounce)
- 1 teaspoon honey
- 2½ cups all-purpose flour, plus more for dusting
- ½ cup whole wheat flour
- ½ cup brown ale
- 1 tablespoon extra-virgin olive oil
- 1 teaspoon kosher salt

TOPPINGS

- 2 tablespoons extra-virgin olive oil, plus more for brushing
- 1 fennel bulb, cut into 8 wedges
- ¼ cup dry white wine
- ¼ cup Pernod
- 1 cup chicken stock

Salt and freshly ground pepper

- 1 very large sweet onion, thinly sliced
- 1 pound shredded Trugole or fresh Asiago cheese
- 8 large pitted green Sicilian olives, coarsely chopped

Basil leaves, for garnish

1. MAKE THE DOUGH In the bowl of a standing mixer fitted with the dough hook, combine the yeast, honey and ¼ cup of warm water. Let stand until foaming, about 4 minutes. Add the 2½ cups of all-purpose flour and the whole wheat flour, ale, olive oil, salt and ½ cup of water and mix at medium speed until a smooth dough forms, about 5 minutes. Transfer the dough to a work surface and knead for 2 minutes. Lightly oil the bowl, return the dough to it and cover with plastic wrap. Let the dough rise in a warm place until very billowy, about 1 hour.

2. MEANWHILE, MAKE THE TOPPINGS In a medium skillet, heat 1 tablespoon of the olive oil. Add the fennel wedges and cook over moderate heat, turning once, until lightly browned, about 5 minutes. Remove from the heat and add the wine and Pernod. Return the pan to moderate heat and cook until the liquid has evaporated, about 2 minutes. Add the chicken stock to the skillet. Cover and simmer over moderately low heat, turning the fennel once, until the fennel is very tender and the liquid has nearly evaporated, about 20 minutes. Season with salt and pepper. Transfer the braised fennel to a cutting board and coarsely chop it.

3. Meanwhile, in another skillet, heat the remaining 1 tablespoon of olive oil. Add the onion, cover and cook over moderate heat, stirring once or twice, until softened, about 3 minutes. Uncover the skillet and cook until the onion is caramelized, about 20 minutes. Add a few tablespoons of water to the skillet to prevent scorching.

4. Preheat the oven to 500°. Preheat a pizza stone as close to the oven bottom as possible for 20 minutes.

5. Punch down the pizza dough and divide it into 4 balls. Set the dough balls on an oiled baking sheet and cover with oiled plastic wrap. Let stand for 15 minutes.

6. On a floured work surface, roll or stretch 1 dough ball to a 10-inch round. Set the round on a floured pizza peel, shaking it gently so it doesn't stick. Brush the edge of the dough with oil. Add one-fourth of the cheese, followed by one-fourth each of the braised fennel, caramelized onion and olives. Slide the pizza onto the stone and bake until bubbling on top and the crust is deeply golden, 8 to 10 minutes. Transfer the pizza to a cutting board, sprinkle with basil leaves and cut into wedges. Repeat with the remaining dough and toppings to make 3 more pizzas.
—*Michael Schwartz*

MAKE AHEAD The dough can be refrigerated for up to 2 days or frozen for up to 1 month. The cooked fennel and onions can be refrigerated separately overnight

WINE Juicy, minerally Italian white: 2010 Beni di Batasiolo Gavi.

Hummus and Grilled-Zucchini Pizzas

ACTIVE: 30 MIN; TOTAL: 1 HR
MAKES TWO 12-INCH PIZZAS ● ●

Prepared hummus that comes with a scoop of chopped garlic on top (like the kind sold by Sabra) is the secret ingredient here: The garlic gets mixed with olive oil to marinate the zucchini, while the remaining garlic and hummus flavor the whole pizza.

One 7-ounce container roasted-garlic hummus
¾ cup extra-virgin olive oil, plus more for greasing

Kosher salt and freshly ground black pepper

- 3 medium zucchini (1½ pounds), sliced on the diagonal ¼ inch thick

Two 8-ounce balls pizza dough

1. Place a pizza stone in the oven and preheat the oven to 500° for 30 minutes. Light a grill or preheat a grill pan. Scoop the garlic from the top of the hummus into a small bowl and stir in the ¾ cup of olive oil. Season the garlic oil with salt and pepper. Transfer 3 tablespoons of the garlic oil to a large bowl, add the zucchini and toss to coat. Whisk the hummus into the remaining garlic oil and season with salt and pepper.

2. Working in 2 batches, grill the zucchini slices over high heat until they are lightly charred, about 5 minutes. Brush the zucchini lightly with some of the hummus and grill for 1 minute longer, turning once.

3. Lightly rub 2 sheets of parchment paper with olive oil. Roll or stretch each ball of pizza dough into a 12-inch round on each sheet. Brush each round with one-fourth of the hummus and top with the grilled zucchini. Slide 1 parchment sheet onto the hot stone and bake the pizza for about 8 minutes, until the crust is browned. Transfer the pizza to a work surface and drizzle with some of the remaining hummus. Cut into slices and serve. Repeat with the remaining pizza.
—*Grace Parisi*

WINE Rich, fruit-forward Rhône white: 2010 Michel & Stéphane Ogier Viognier de Rosine.

● HEALTHY   ● MAKE AHEAD   ● VEGETARIAN   ● STAFF FAVORITE

hummus and grilled-zucchini pizza

Melty Feta and Roasted Red Pepper Sandwiches

TOTAL: 20 MIN • 4 SANDWICHES ●

8 large slices of focaccia (½ inch thick)
½ cup *ajvar* (red pepper relish) or other roasted red pepper relish
½ pound creamy feta, such as French, very coarsely crumbled (2 cups)
¼ cup chopped dill

Preheat the oven to 500°. Arrange the focaccia on a large baking sheet and spread each slice with 1 tablespoon of the *ajvar*. Scatter the feta on top. Bake in the upper third of the oven for about 7 minutes, until the focaccia is crisp and the cheese is soft. Sprinkle the dill over the cheese and close the sandwiches. Cut in half and serve. —*Tia Keenan*
WINE Floral, lemony Greek white: 2011 Argyros Atlantis.

SUPER-EASY PICKLES

pickled onions *These magenta-pink onions from Mile End Delicatessen in Brooklyn, New York, have the perfect balance of sugar and tang. A delicious condiment on any sandwich, the jarred pickled onions also make a lovely gift.*

In a medium nonreactive saucepan, combine 2 cups distilled white vinegar, 1 cup sugar, 4 whole cloves, 4 allspice berries, 2 bay leaves, 1 teaspoon whole black peppercorns and ½ teaspoon yellow mustard seeds. Bring to a boil and cook over moderate heat, stirring, until the sugar dissolves, about 5 minutes. Remove from the heat and let cool completely, about 30 minutes. Slice 2 medium red onions into thin rings and layer them in a 2-cup jar. Strain the brine into the jar and let stand at room temperature for 1 hour. Drain the onions and serve. Makes 1½ cups. —*Noah and Rae Bernamoff*

Prosciutto-Mozzarella Piadine

ACTIVE: 35 MIN; TOTAL: 4 HR 15 MIN
4 SERVINGS ●

Piadina is an Italian pan-grilled sandwich made with a quick baking-powder flatbread. (If you're in a rush, you could use a flour tortilla instead.) This recipe is from Casa Olivi, a villa in the Le Marche region of Italy.

2 cups all-purpose flour, plus more for dusting
½ teaspoon baking powder
Kosher salt
¼ cup milk, warmed
4 tablespoons butter, softened
Vegetable oil
4 cups baby arugula (about 3 ounces)
1 tablespoon extra-virgin olive oil
Freshly ground pepper
16 thin slices of prosciutto (12 ounces)
8 slices of fresh mozzarella (½ pound)

1. In the bowl of a standing mixer fitted with the dough hook, mix the 2 cups of flour with the baking powder and 1½ teaspoons of salt. Add ⅓ cup of warm water, the milk and butter and beat at low speed for 10 minutes. Form the dough into a ball and transfer to an oiled bowl. Cover and let stand for 3 hours.
2. On a floured work surface, form the dough into 4 balls and set them on a floured baking sheet. Cover the dough balls and let stand for about 30 minutes.
3. Preheat the oven to 350°. Heat a large cast-iron skillet. Roll out 1 ball of dough to a 10-inch round and prick it with a fork. Oil the skillet. Add the dough round and cook over moderately high heat until it browns on the bottom and bubbles on top. Flip the round and cook until it's browned on the bottom; transfer to a baking sheet. Repeat with the remaining dough.
4. In a bowl, toss the arugula and olive oil; season with salt and pepper. Divide the prosciutto, mozzarella and arugula among the flatbreads and fold over. Bake until the mozzarella is softened, cut into wedges and serve. —*Sophie Heaulme*
WINE Lively Italian white: 2011 Colle Stefano Verdicchio di Matelica.

Israeli Roast Eggplant, Hummus and Pickle Sandwiches

TOTAL: 1 HR • 4 SANDWICHES ● ●

1 large baking potato
Salt
1 medium eggplant, sliced ½ inch thick
3 tablespoons extra-virgin olive oil, plus more for brushing
1 cucumber—peeled, halved, seeded and cut into ½-inch dice
1 large tomato, cut into ½-inch dice
1 large jalapeño, minced
2 garlic cloves, minced
3 tablespoons chopped cilantro
2 tablespoons chopped parsley
2 tablespoons fresh lemon juice
Freshly ground pepper
4 thick, sturdy pita breads, warmed
1 cup hummus
¼ cup tahini, at room temperature
4 large hard-cooked eggs, sliced
4 small dill pickles, thinly sliced

1. Preheat the oven to 425°. In a small saucepan, cover the potato with 2 inches of water and bring to a boil. Cook over moderate heat until the potato is just tender, about 20 minutes. Drain and let cool, then peel the potato and cut it into ¼-inch-thick slices. Season the potato slices with salt.
2. Meanwhile, arrange the eggplant slices on a rimmed baking sheet; brush both sides with olive oil. Season with salt and bake for about 10 minutes, until browned and tender.
3. In a large bowl, add the cucumber, tomato, jalapeño, garlic, cilantro and parsley. Toss with the lemon juice and 3 tablespoons of olive oil and season with salt and pepper.
4. Cut off 2 inches from the side of the warm pitas, then gently open the pitas. Spread the hummus on the bottoms and 1 tablespoon of tahini over it. Layer the potato slices, eggplant, egg and cucumber-tomato salad in the pitas along with some of the salad juices. Top with the pickle slices and serve. —*Michael Shemtov and Stuart Tracy*
WINE Dry, raspberry-scented rosé: 2011 Bernard Baudry Chinon.

● HEALTHY ● MAKE AHEAD ● VEGETARIAN ● STAFF FAVORITE

israeli roast eggplant, hummus and pickle sandwich

Fried Shrimp Flatbreads with Spicy Cardamom Sauce

⏱ **TOTAL: 45 MIN • 4 SANDWICHES** ●

SAUCES

½ cup crème fraîche
2 tablespoons buttermilk
2 tablespoons chopped mint
2 tablespoons minced chives
Finely grated zest of 1 lemon
7 garlic cloves, minced
Salt and freshly ground black pepper
4 Thai chiles, minced
1 teaspoon ground cardamom
½ teaspoon ground cumin
2 tablespoons freshly squeezed lemon juice

FRIED SHRIMP

1 large egg beaten with 1 tablespoon of water
1 cup panko (Japanese bread crumbs)
16 large shrimp (about 1 pound), shelled and deveined
Vegetable oil, for frying
Salt
4 thin 10-inch flatbreads, such as naan, or thick flour tortillas, warmed
1 Hass avocado, sliced lengthwise ¼ inch thick
¼ cup sliced pickled red onions (from a jar of pickled beets and onions)

1. PREPARE THE SAUCES In a bowl, whisk the crème fraîche with the buttermilk, mint, chives, lemon zest and 1 minced garlic clove; season the *crema* with salt and pepper.
2. In a blender, combine the remaining garlic with the chiles, cardamom, cumin and lemon juice. Puree until smooth. Season the cardamom sauce with salt and pepper.
3. PREPARE THE SHRIMP Put the beaten egg and panko in separate shallow bowls. Dip the shrimp in the egg, then dredge in the panko; transfer to a baking sheet. Refrigerate for 10 minutes.
4. Preheat the oven to 350°. In a saucepan, heat 1 inch of vegetable oil to 350°. Fry 4 shrimp at a time, turning once, until they are browned and crisp, about 2 minutes. Transfer the shrimp to a rack set over a rimmed baking sheet to drain and season them with salt. When all of the shrimp have been fried, transfer them to the oven and bake until they are heated through, about 2 minutes.
5. Spread the flatbreads with the cardamom sauce. Arrange the avocado and shrimp on top. Scatter the pickled onion on top, drizzle with the *crema* and serve. —*Josef Centeno*
WINE Rich, spiced white blend: 2008 Henri Milan Le Grand Blanc.

Mushroom and Goat Cheese Tortas

ACTIVE: 30 MIN; TOTAL: 1 HR 30 MIN
6 SERVINGS ●

2 large heads of garlic, cloves peeled and lightly smashed
½ cup extra-virgin olive oil
¼ cup fresh lime juice
Salt
½ pound cremini mushrooms, thinly sliced
½ pound shiitake mushrooms, stems discarded and caps thinly sliced
½ pound oyster mushrooms, stems discarded and caps thinly sliced
3 tablespoons chopped cilantro
6 *bolillo* rolls or other crusty rolls, split
3 cups packed arugula leaves
1 cup prepared tomato salsa
½ pound soft goat cheese

1. Preheat the oven to 325°. Put the garlic in a small, deep baking dish and toss with the olive oil, lime juice and 1 teaspoon of salt. Cover and bake for about 30 minutes, until the garlic is soft and golden.
2. Increase the oven temperature to 400°. Combine all of the mushrooms in a 9-by-13-inch baking dish; toss with the roasted garlic and 1 teaspoon of salt. Cover with foil; bake for 10 minutes. Uncover and bake until the mushrooms are tender and golden, about 35 minutes longer. Stir in the cilantro.
3. Scrape some of the bread out of the center of the rolls and set the rolls on a large baking sheet, cut side up. Spread the mushrooms over the rolls and bake for about 5 minutes to crisp the rolls. Spread the arugula and salsa on one half of the rolls and the goat cheese on the other half. Close the *tortas* (sandwiches) and bake for about 5 minutes, until they are hot and crisp. Cut the *tortas* in half and serve. —*Rick Bayless*
MAKE AHEAD The cooked mushrooms can be refrigerated overnight. Reheat gently.

Grilled-Asparagus Subs with Smoky French Dressing

⏱ **TOTAL: 25 MIN • 4 SANDWICHES** ● ●

¼ cup ketchup
¼ cup mayonnaise
2 tablespoons sherry vinegar
2 tablespoons Dijon mustard
1 garlic clove, chopped
1 chipotle chile in adobo sauce
Salt, preferably smoked salt
2 pounds medium asparagus, peeled and trimmed
Olive oil, for drizzling
Four 7-inch sub or hoagie rolls, split and lightly toasted
¼ cup raisins
4 scallions, thinly sliced
¼ cup crumbled feta cheese

1. In a blender, combine the ketchup, mayonnaise, vinegar, mustard, garlic and chipotle. Puree until smooth; season with salt.
2. In a large pot of salted boiling water, cook the asparagus until bright green, about 2 minutes. Drain the asparagus and spread them out on a large baking sheet to cool.
3. Preheat a large grill pan. Drizzle the asparagus with olive oil and season with salt. Grill over moderately high heat, turning, until tender and lightly charred, about 3 minutes.
4. Spread the cut sides of each roll with 3 tablespoons of the smoky French dressing. Arrange the grilled asparagus on the subs and top with the raisins, scallions and crumbled feta. Close the sandwiches and serve. —*Tyler Kord*
MAKE AHEAD The smoky French dressing can be refrigerated for up to 3 days.
WINE Vibrant, grassy New Zealand Sauvignon Blanc: 2011 Dashwood.

grilled-asparagus sub with smoky french dressing

Mexico City Sandwiches

⏱ TOTAL: 20 MIN • 4 SANDWICHES ●

4 tablespoons unsalted butter, softened
2 chipotles in adobo, minced, plus 1 teaspoon adobo sauce from the can
Salt and freshly ground pepper
4 soft demi baguettes, split
1 medium tomato, sliced ⅛ inch thick
2 tablespoons extra-virgin olive oil
8 large eggs
8 thin slices of Gruyère (½ pound)
1 small Hass avocado—peeled, pitted and sliced ⅛ inch thick
8 thin slices of baked ham (6 ounces)

1. In a small bowl, thoroughly blend the butter with the chipotles and adobo sauce and season with salt and pepper. Spread on the baguettes. Arrange the tomato slices on the bottom halves of the baguettes.
2. Heat a griddle or a very large nonstick skillet. Add the olive oil; when it's hot, crack in the eggs. Cook over-easy over moderate heat, turning once halfway through cooking, about 1½ minutes. Season the eggs with salt and pepper and top each one with a slice of the cheese. Set 2 eggs on the tomatoes on each baguette bottom and top with the sliced avocado and ham. Close the sandwiches and serve right away. —*Ali Bagheri*

Pear, Parsnip and Fourme d'Ambert Tartines

ACTIVE: 25 MIN; TOTAL: 50 MIN
4 SANDWICHES ●

2 medium parsnips, thinly shaved lengthwise on a mandoline or with a vegetable peeler
1 tablespoon extra-virgin olive oil
Salt and freshly ground pepper
Four ¾-inch-thick slices of sourdough bread
¼ cup crème fraîche
1 Bosc pear—halved, cored and thinly sliced lengthwise
4 ounces Fourme d'Ambert, rind removed and cheese thinly sliced

1. Preheat the oven to 350°. On a rimmed baking sheet, toss the shaved parsnips with the extra-virgin olive oil and season with salt and pepper. Roast for about 20 minutes, tossing once, until the parsnips are tender and starting to crisp around the edges. Let the parsnips cool slightly.
2. Preheat the broiler. Arrange the slices of sourdough bread on a medium baking sheet. Spread equal amounts of the crème fraîche on each bread slice, then top with the pear slices, roasted parsnips and cheese. Season the *tartines* with salt and pepper. Broil the *tartines* 8 inches from the heat for about 3 minutes, until the cheese is melted. Serve the *tartines* hot. —*Julianne Murat*
WINE Sparkling rosé: NV Lucien Albrecht Crémant d'Alsace Brut.

Chicken and Two Cheese Tortas

⏱ TOTAL: 30 MIN • 4 SANDWICHES
Fresh mozzarella and aged Cotija cheeses are melted over shredded chicken in this excellent Mexican-inspired sandwich.

1 Hass avocado, chopped
2 tablespoons plain yogurt
1 tablespoon fresh lime juice
½ small red onion, minced
1 small jalapeño, minced
½ teaspoon ground cumin
3 tablespoons extra-virgin olive oil
Salt and freshly ground pepper
3 cups thickly shredded rotisserie chicken (¾ pound)
1½ cups shredded fresh mozzarella
2 tablespoons grated Cotija or pecorino cheese
4 Portuguese or Kaiser rolls, toasted
¼ cup sliced pickled jalapeños
½ cup jarred tomatillo salsa
2 cups shredded iceberg lettuce

1. In a bowl, mash the avocado with a fork. Stir in the yogurt, lime juice, onion, jalapeño, cumin and 1 tablespoon of olive oil and season with salt and pepper.
2. In a large nonstick skillet, heat the remaining 2 tablespoons of olive oil. Add the chicken in an even layer and cook over moderately high heat until crisp on the bottom, about 3 minutes. Scatter the mozzarella and Cotija cheeses over the chicken, cover the skillet and remove from the heat. Let stand until the mozzarella is melted.
3. Split the rolls and spread the mashed avocado on the bottom halves. Top with the chicken mixture, then add the pickled jalapeños, tomatillo salsa and lettuce. Close the *tortas* and serve right away.
—*David Morgan and Brandon Baptiste*
BEER Crisp pilsner: Left Hand Polestar.

Double-Grilled Antipasto Sandwiches

⏱ TOTAL: 30 MIN • 4 SERVINGS

½ pound thinly sliced prosciutto (overlapping on 4 sheets of deli paper)
½ pound soft provolone, sliced ¾ inch thick and cut into 3-inch sticks
Extra-virgin olive oil, for brushing
1 large baguette, split and cut into 4 pieces
1 large garlic clove, halved
½ pound marinated artichokes, drained and thickly sliced
2 roasted red bell peppers, cut into strips

1. On a work surface, lay out the prosciutto on its paper. Lay 3 of the provolone sticks across the bottom of each "sheet" of prosciutto. Roll the prosciutto tightly around the cheese; cut each roll into 3 pieces (you should have about 12 total). Thread the rolls onto 2 pairs of skewers and brush with oil.
2. Light a grill or preheat a grill pan. Brush the cut sides of the baguette with oil. Grill the bread over moderately high heat, turning once or twice, until toasted, about 5 minutes. Rub the cut side of the garlic on the inside of the bread and top with the artichokes and roasted peppers. Grill the prosciutto and cheese skewers, turning, until the cheese is melted, 5 to 6 minutes. Remove the rolls from the skewers and arrange them on the bread. Close the sandwiches and serve.
—*Grace Parisi*

● HEALTHY ● MAKE AHEAD ● VEGETARIAN ● STAFF FAVORITE

double-grilled antipasto sandwiches

Lobster-Roll-Style Salmon Sandwiches

⌛ **TOTAL: 15 MIN • 8 SANDWICHES** ●

In this lighter take on the summertime classic, roast salmon replaces lobster and Greek yogurt stands in for mayonnaise.

½ cup plain 2 percent Greek yogurt
2 inner celery ribs with leaves, finely chopped
2 tablespoons chopped chives
2 tablespoons chopped flat-leaf parsley
1 tablespoon fresh lemon juice
Salt and freshly ground pepper
1½ pounds roast salmon, flaked (4 loose cups; see Note)
8 hot dog buns
Melted unsalted butter, for brushing
Potato chips, for serving

1. In a bowl, combine the yogurt with the celery, chives, parsley and lemon juice. Season with salt and pepper. Fold in the salmon.
2. Heat a griddle. Brush the cut sides of the buns with butter and griddle until toasted. Fill the buns with the salmon salad, top with potato chips and serve. —*Grace Parisi*
NOTE You can use leftover salmon from Grace's Spice-Rubbed Salmon (page 102) or store-bought roast salmon.
MAKE AHEAD The roast salmon salad can be refrigerated overnight.

Beef, Broccoli Rabe and Provolone Panini

⌛ **TOTAL: 30 MIN • 6 SERVINGS**

1 pound broccoli rabe, trimmed and chopped
¼ cup extra-virgin olive oil, plus more for brushing
2 garlic cloves, minced
1 teaspoon anchovy paste
½ teaspoon crushed red pepper
24 thin slices of provolone cheese
6 soft hoagie, hero or *torta* rolls, split
1½ pounds sliced leftover beef tenderloin or deli roast beef
¼ cup chopped Peppadew peppers

1. Preheat a panini press or griddle. In a large pot of boiling water, cook the broccoli rabe until bright green, 3 minutes. Drain well.
2. In a large skillet, heat the ¼ cup of oil. Add the garlic, anchovy paste and crushed red pepper and cook over moderately high heat for 10 seconds. Add the broccoli rabe and season with salt. Cover and cook over moderately high heat, stirring occasionally, until the broccoli rabe is tender, 5 minutes.
3. Layer 2 slices of provolone on the bottom of each roll. Top with the broccoli rabe, roast beef, Peppadews and the remaining provolone. Close the rolls and brush lightly with oil. Grill the sandwiches until toasted and the cheese is melted, about 7 minutes. Serve hot. —*Grace Parisi*
WINE Bold Tempranillo from Spain's Rioja region: 2009 Cune Crianza.

Grilled-Pork Banh Mi

TOTAL: 30 MIN PLUS 2 HR MARINATING
6 SERVINGS ● ●

After marinating in a sweet-spicy marinade, thin slices of pork tenderloin are grilled and then served warm in a baguette Vietnamese-style, with cucumber and cilantro sprigs.

¼ cup Asian fish sauce
1 tablespoon honey
2 tablespoons sugar
1 teaspoon freshly ground pepper
6 scallions, white and tender green parts only, thinly sliced
2 garlic cloves, thinly sliced
1½ pounds pork tenderloin, thinly sliced
Six 8-inch-long rolls or 2 baguettes, cut into 8-inch lengths and split
Hoisin sauce and Sriracha
Vegetable oil, for grilling
½ seedless cucumber, cut into 2-by-½-inch matchsticks
1½ cups loosely packed cilantro sprigs

1. In a blender, puree the fish sauce with the honey, sugar, pepper, scallions and garlic. Transfer the marinade to a bowl, add the pork and toss. Refrigerate for 2 to 4 hours. Thread the pork through the top and bottom of each slice onto 12 bamboo skewers.
2. Spread the rolls with hoisin and Sriracha. Light a grill and oil the grates. Brush the pork with oil and grill over high heat, turning, until just cooked, 4 minutes. Place 2 skewers in each roll, close and pull out the skewers. Top with the cucumber and cilantro and serve. —*Luke Nguyen*
BEER Hoppy IPA from California's Central Coast: Firestone Walker Union Jack.

Open-Face Sardine Sandwiches with Tangy Aioli

⌛ **TOTAL: 25 MIN • 4 SERVINGS** ● ●

Two 4-ounce cans brisling sardines in oil, drained
2 tablespoons finely chopped red onion
1 tablespoon chopped pickled hot chiles
1 large radish, cut into fine matchsticks (¼ cup)
1 tablespoon freshly squeezed lemon juice
1 tablespoon chopped flat-leaf parsley
1 small garlic clove, smashed
Kosher salt
¼ cup mayonnaise
1½ teaspoons Dijon mustard
1 tablespoon extra-virgin olive oil, plus more for brushing
Four large ¾-inch-thick slices of peasant bread

1. In a medium bowl, gently combine the sardines with the red onion, pickled chiles, radish, lemon juice and parsley.
2. In a small bowl, using the back of a spoon, mash the garlic clove to a paste with a pinch of salt. Whisk in the mayonnaise, Dijon mustard and the 1 tablespoon of olive oil and season the aioli with salt.
3. Preheat the broiler. Brush the bread on both sides with oil and broil, turning once, until lightly toasted. Transfer the toasts to a work surface; spread with the aioli. Mound the sardine mixture on top, cut each toast in half and serve right away. —*Grace Parisi*
WINE Light-bodied, citrusy Spanish white: 2010 Martín Códax Albariño.

● HEALTHY   ● MAKE AHEAD   ● VEGETARIAN   ● STAFF FAVORITE

Brothers Mark (left) and Brian Canlis, co-owners of Seattle's Canlis restaurant, go camping in Scotland; they build a campfire to make omelets with bacon cooked in whisky and brown sugar, OPPOSITE; recipe, page 304.

BREAKFAST

& BRUNCH

Eggs Benedict with Bacon and Arugula

⏱ TOTAL: 40 MIN • 4 SERVINGS

For her variation on eggs Benedict, Tara Lazar of Cheeky's in Palm Springs, California, uses crisp applewood-smoked bacon in place of the classic Canadian bacon.

- 8 large whole eggs, plus
  4 large egg yolks
- 2 tablespoons dry white wine
Salt
- 1 stick unsalted butter, melted
- 1½ tablespoons fresh lemon juice
- ¼ teaspoon Tabasco
- 8 slices of applewood-smoked bacon, halved crosswise
- 5 ounces baby arugula
- 2 tablespoons distilled white vinegar
- 4 English muffins, split and toasted

1. In a heatproof bowl set over a pot of barely simmering water, whisk the 4 egg yolks with the wine and a pinch of salt until doubled in volume and slightly thickened, about 2 minutes. Gradually add the melted butter, whisking constantly, until a thick, creamy sauce forms, about 5 minutes. Whisk in the lemon juice and Tabasco and season the hollandaise with salt. Keep the hollandaise sauce warm, whisking occasionally.

2. In a skillet, cook the bacon over moderate heat, turning once, until crisp, 6 minutes. Transfer to a paper towel–lined plate. Pour off all but 1 tablespoon of the fat in the skillet. Add the arugula, toss quickly in the hot oil and transfer to a plate; season with salt.

3. Bring a large, deep skillet of water to a simmer over moderate heat; add the vinegar. One at a time, break the eggs into a small bowl and pour them into the simmering water, leaving plenty of space between them. Poach the eggs until the whites are set and the yolks are still runny, about 4 minutes. Using a slotted spoon, carefully transfer the eggs to a paper towel–lined plate.

4. Arrange the toasted English muffin halves on plates and top with the bacon, poached eggs, arugula and hollandaise sauce. Serve immediately. —Tara Lazar

Three-Egg Omelets with Whisky Bacon

📷 PAGE 303

⏱ TOTAL: 25 MIN • MAKES 4 OMELETS

"I've been making a version of our 'hangover breakfast' since before I was old enough to drink," says Mark Canlis, co-owner of Canlis restaurant in Seattle. He adds a little bit of whisky and brown sugar to "rashers" of ham-like Canadian bacon, then serves them with cheddar-cheese omelets.

WHISKY BACON

- 3 tablespoons unsalted butter
- 1 pound thinly sliced Canadian bacon
- 1½ tablespoons Scotch whisky
- 2 teaspoons light brown sugar
Freshly ground pepper

OMELETS

- 1 dozen large eggs
Salt and freshly ground pepper
- 4 tablespoons unsalted butter
- 1⅓ cups shredded extra-sharp cheddar cheese (about 4 ounces)
- 12 cherry tomatoes, quartered
16 to 20 basil leaves

1. PREPARE THE WHISKY BACON In a very large skillet, melt the butter. Add the Canadian bacon and cook over moderately high heat until browned on the bottom, about 2 minutes. Turn the bacon and add the whisky and brown sugar. Cook over high heat, stirring a few times, until the whisky is slightly reduced, about 30 seconds. Season with freshly ground pepper and remove the skillet from the heat.

2. MAKE THE OMELETS In a bowl, beat the eggs with a pinch each of salt and freshly ground pepper. Heat an 8-inch nonstick skillet. Add 1 tablespoon of butter to the skillet and pour in one-fourth of the eggs. Cook over moderately high heat, stirring, until almost set, about 20 seconds. Remove the skillet from the heat and spread the eggs in an even layer. Scatter ⅓ cup of the cheddar cheese on half of the omelet and arrange 3 quartered cherry tomatoes on top. Cook the eggs over low heat until the cheese starts to melt, about 30 seconds.

3. Remove the skillet from the heat and top the eggs with one-fourth of the basil. Fold the omelet in half over the filling and slide onto a plate. Repeat to make the 3 remaining omelets. Serve hot, with the whisky bacon. —Mark Canlis

Baked Huevos Rancheros

⏱ TOTAL: 45 MIN • 4 SERVINGS ● ●

Traditional huevos rancheros are fried eggs served over tortillas and smothered in sauce and cheese. Here, F&W's Grace Parisi bakes eggs, tortilla chips and cheese in a seasoned tomato sauce in individual gratin dishes. To add a spicy kick, swap in pepper Jack cheese for the Monterey Jack.

- ¼ cup extra-virgin olive oil
- 1 small onion, finely chopped
- ½ small green bell pepper, finely diced
- 1 jalapeño, seeded and minced
- 1 garlic clove, minced
- ½ teaspoon dried oregano, crumbled
Salt and freshly ground pepper
One 15-ounce can tomato sauce
- 3 cups tortilla chips
- 8 large eggs
- ¾ cup shredded Monterey Jack
Chopped cilantro, for garnish

1. Preheat the oven to 400°. In a saucepan, heat the olive oil. Add the onion, bell pepper, jalapeño, garlic and oregano. Season with salt and freshly ground pepper and cook over high heat, stirring, until the vegetables are lightly browned, about 5 minutes. Add the tomato sauce and ¼ cup of water and simmer for another 5 minutes, until the sauce is slightly thickened.

2. Spoon the seasoned tomato sauce into 4 individual shallow baking dishes and arrange the tortilla chips around the sides. Crack 2 eggs into each dish and sprinkle with the shredded cheese. Set the dishes on a baking sheet and bake for 15 to 20 minutes, until the egg whites are set and the yolks are still runny. Sprinkle the chopped cilantro over the tops and serve right away. —Grace Parisi

● HEALTHY ● MAKE AHEAD ● VEGETARIAN ● STAFF FAVORITE

baked huevos rancheros

Smoked-Salmon Scramble with Dill Griddle Biscuits

⏱ TOTAL: 40 MIN • 4 SERVINGS ●

Quick Biscuit Mix (recipe follows)
1½ teaspoons dried dill
Freshly ground black pepper
2 tablespoons canola oil, plus more for the griddle
2 large shallots, thinly sliced
6 large eggs, lightly beaten
4 ounces smoked salmon, coarsely chopped
Hot sauce, for serving

1. In a bowl, combine the Quick Biscuit Mix with the dill and ½ teaspoon of pepper. Stir in ½ cup of water to form a thick batter.
2. Preheat a flameproof rimmed griddle and brush lightly with canola oil. Scoop the biscuit batter into eight 3-tablespoon-size mounds and spread each one to 3 inches. Cook over very low heat until lightly browned on the bottom, about 2 minutes. Brush the biscuits lightly with oil and turn them over. Cover the griddle and cook until the biscuits are puffed and golden, about 2 minutes longer. Transfer the biscuits to a sheet of aluminum foil, cover and keep warm.
3. Heat the 2 tablespoons of oil on the griddle. Add the shallots and cook until lightly browned, 4 to 5 minutes. In a bowl, beat the eggs with the salmon and season with pepper. Scramble the eggs on the griddle, stirring until large curds form, 4 minutes. Serve the eggs with the biscuits and hot sauce.
—*Grace Parisi*

QUICK BISCUIT MIX

⏱ TOTAL: 5 MIN • MAKES 8 BISCUITS ● ●

1 cup self-rising flour
3 tablespoons whole-milk powder
1½ teaspoons sugar
2 tablespoons canola oil

In a bowl, whisk the flour, milk powder and sugar. Using your fingers, work in the oil until incorporated. Use at once or store in an airtight container for up to 2 weeks. —*GP*

Poached Scrambled Eggs with Goat Cheese Sauce

⏱ TOTAL: 30 MIN • 4 SERVINGS ● ●
Chef Daniel Patterson of Coi in San Francisco conceived of this unconventional method for making eggs: He beats the eggs, cooks them quickly in a vortex of boiling water, then immediately drains them in a strainer. The result is super-creamy, perfectly scrambled eggs; topped with goat cheese sauce, the dish becomes a kind of reverse omelet. If you're scrambling just one egg, the cooking time is 20 seconds. For four eggs, the time increases to 40 seconds.

4 ounces soft fresh goat cheese
2 ounces aged hard goat cheese, such as Etude or goat Gouda, shredded (¼ cup packed)
1 tablespoon freshly grated Parmigiano-Reggiano cheese
Salt and freshly ground pepper
4 large eggs
Extra-virgin olive oil, for drizzling
1 teaspoon chopped rosemary, preferably flowering rosemary

1. In a small bowl, whisk the fresh goat cheese with ¼ cup of warm water until smooth. In a small saucepan, bring ¾ cup of water to a simmer. Stir in the aged goat cheese and Parmigiano-Reggiano until melted and smooth. Whisk in the fresh goat cheese sauce and season with salt and freshly ground pepper.
2. In a medium bowl, beat the eggs for 20 seconds. Bring a large saucepan of water to a simmer. Using a wooden spoon, stir the water vigorously in a circular motion to create a whirlpool in the center. Reduce the heat and stop stirring. Immediately pour the scrambled eggs into the center. Cover the pot and cook for exactly 40 seconds. Using a slotted spoon to hold the eggs back, tilt the saucepan and pour off the water. Transfer the scrambled eggs in one piece to a strainer and let drain for 10 seconds. Season well with salt and freshly ground pepper. Spoon the eggs into 4 bowls and spoon the goat cheese sauce all around.

3. Drizzle the eggs with olive oil and season with salt and freshly ground pepper. Garnish with rosemary and serve at once.
—*Daniel Patterson*

WINE Lively sparkling wine: NV Drusian Valdobbiadene Prosecco Extra Dry.

Egg Sandwiches with Mustard Greens and Avocado

⏱ TOTAL: 20 MIN • 4 SERVINGS ● ●
"I usually make these sandwiches on days when there isn't enough time to sit down for a proper breakfast," says Los Angeles chef Sera Pelle, who wraps them in parchment paper for her kids to eat on the go. The sandwich, filled with sautéed mustard greens, fried egg and mashed avocado, is also good for lunch or a late-night snack.

2 tablespoons safflower oil
1 pound mustard greens, thick stems discarded and leaves coarsely chopped
Sea salt
1 large Hass avocado, chopped
1 tablespoon fresh lemon juice
4 large eggs
8 slices of whole-grain bread, toasted and buttered
Hot sauce

1. In a large nonstick skillet, heat 1 tablespoon of the oil until shimmering. Add the mustard greens and cook over moderately high heat, stirring, until tender, about 1½ minutes; season with salt. Transfer the mustard greens to a bowl and keep warm.
2. In a small bowl, mash the avocado. Stir in the lemon juice and season with salt.
3. Add the remaining 1 tablespoon of oil to the skillet. Crack the eggs into the pan and season with salt. Cook over moderate heat until the whites are crisp, about 1 minute. Flip the eggs and cook until the whites are firm and the yolks are runny, 2 minutes longer.
4. Spread the mashed avocado on 4 of the toast slices. Top with the greens and fried eggs and sprinkle with the hot sauce. Close the sandwiches, cut in half and serve right away. —*Sera Pelle*

● HEALTHY ● MAKE AHEAD ● VEGETARIAN ● STAFF FAVORITE

egg sandwich with mustard greens and avocado

Shakshuka with Fennel and Feta

TOTAL: 50 MIN • 6 SERVINGS ● ● ●

"When I was 18 years old, I worked on a beautiful kibbutz in Israel," F&W's Gail Simmons recalls. "I made eggs every morning for hundreds of fellow workers. I developed an affection for humble egg dishes like *shakshuka*, eggs poached in a seasoned tomato sauce. It's a popular dish throughout the Middle East and perfect for any meal of the day."

- 2 tablespoons extra-virgin olive oil
- 1 small onion, cut into ½-inch dice
- 1 small fennel bulb, cored and thinly sliced
- 2 serrano chiles, seeded and chopped
- 1 jalapeño, seeded and finely chopped
- 1 green bell pepper, diced

Kosher salt

- 2 garlic cloves, minced
- 1 tablespoon harissa
- 1 teaspoon sweet Spanish smoked paprika

One 28-ounce can whole tomatoes, chopped, with their liquid
- 6 large eggs
- 2 tablespoons chopped parsley
- ½ cup crumbled feta cheese

1. In a large skillet, heat the oil. Add the onion and fennel and cook over moderately high heat, stirring, until softened, about 3 minutes. Add both chiles and the bell pepper and season with salt. Cook over moderate heat, stirring, until the vegetables are softened, about 8 minutes. Add the minced garlic, harissa and paprika and cook, stirring, until fragrant, 1 minute. Add the tomatoes and ½ cup of water and simmer over low heat until the sauce is thickened, 10 minutes.
2. Crack the eggs into the sauce. Cover and cook over moderately low heat until the whites are firm and the yolks are runny, 5 minutes. Spoon the sauce and eggs into bowls and sprinkle with the parsley and crumbled feta. Serve right away.
—*Gail Simmons*

SERVE WITH Warm pita.

WINE Bright, strawberry-scented Beaujolais: 2010 Château Thivin Côtes de Brouilly.

Mexican Eggs in Purgatory

⏲ **TOTAL: 30 MIN • 8 SERVINGS** ● ●

For the Italian breakfast dish Eggs in Purgatory, eggs are baked in a spicy tomato sauce. In this Mexican-inspired take, F&W's Grace Parisi substitutes a fresh green sauce made with tomatillos, cilantro and scallions.

- 1 pound tomatillos, husked
- 1 poblano or jalapeño, stemmed and seeded (see Note)
- 1½ cups chopped cilantro leaves and stems
- 3 scallions, coarsely chopped, plus sliced scallions for garnish
- ¾ cup low-sodium chicken broth
- 3 ounces thick-cut bacon, cut into ½-inch pieces
- 2 tablespoons extra-virgin olive oil
- 1 garlic clove, minced
- 8 large eggs
- 2 tablespoons grated Cotija cheese or crumbled feta, plus more for garnish

Warm corn tortillas, for serving

1. Preheat the broiler and position a rack about 8 inches from the heat source. In a blender or food processor, combine the tomatillos with the poblano, chopped cilantro, chopped scallions and chicken broth and puree until smooth.
2. In a large, shallow flameproof casserole or skillet, cook the bacon in the olive oil over high heat until the bacon is browned, about 4 minutes. Add the minced garlic and cook for 30 seconds, until fragrant. Add the tomatillo puree and cook over moderate heat until the sauce is thickened and dull green in color, about 15 minutes.
3. Using the back of a spoon, make 8 depressions in the tomatillo sauce. Remove the casserole from the heat and carefully crack the eggs into the depressions. Sprinkle the eggs and tomatillo sauce with the 2 tablespoons of Cotija cheese. Broil the dish until the egg whites are set but the egg yolks are still runny, about 4 minutes. Garnish with more Cotija cheese and the sliced scallions and serve right away, with warm corn tortillas.
—*Grace Parisi*

NOTE For an extra-spicy dish, leave the seeds in the chile peppers.

MAKE AHEAD The green tomatillo sauce can be refrigerated for up to 2 days.

Monte Cristo Strata

ACTIVE: 10 MIN; TOTAL: 1 HR
8 SERVINGS ● ●

Softened butter, for greasing
One 1¼-pound loaf bakery white bread—crusts removed, bread sliced (about 18 slices)
- ¼ cup grainy mustard
- 1 pound thinly sliced Virginia ham
- 2 tablespoons chopped tarragon, plus more for garnish
- ¾ pound Gruyère cheese, coarsely shredded (3 cups)
- 3 cups milk
- 4 large eggs

Freshly ground black pepper

1. Preheat the oven to 375° and butter a 9-by-13-inch glass or ceramic baking dish. Arrange one-third of the bread in the bottom of the dish and spread with half of the mustard. Top with half of the sliced ham, 1 tablespoon of the tarragon and one-third of the shredded Gruyère cheese. Repeat the layering, ending with bread and leaving off the last layer of cheese.
2. In a medium bowl, whisk the milk with the eggs and season generously with black pepper. Pour the custard evenly over the dish, pressing the bread to absorb the liquid. Pat the remaining cheese on top and cover with a sheet of buttered parchment paper.
3. Bake the strata in the center of the oven for 30 to 35 minutes, until bubbling and browned around the edge. Remove the parchment and turn on the broiler. Broil for about 3 minutes, just until the top is golden and bubbling. Let rest for 10 minutes, then cut the strata into squares, garnish with tarragon and serve. —*Grace Parisi*

MAKE AHEAD The unbaked strata can be refrigerated overnight.

WINE Fruity sparkling wine: NV Col Mesian Nove Cento Dieci Spumante Extra Dry.

● HEALTHY ● MAKE AHEAD ● VEGETARIAN ● STAFF FAVORITE

shakshuka with fennel and feta

Ham and Potato Chip Tortilla

⏱ **TOTAL: 7 MIN • 6 SERVINGS** ●

  1 dozen large eggs
One 5-ounce bag jalapeño potato chips,
      lightly crushed
  ¼ cup extra-virgin olive oil
One ½-pound ham steak, cut into
      ½-inch dice
  3 large scallions, sliced

1. Preheat the broiler and position a rack 8 inches from the heat. In a large bowl, beat the eggs. Add the potato chips and mash to break them up.

2. In a large ovenproof nonstick skillet, heat the olive oil. Add the ham and scallions and cook over high heat for 1 minute. Add the eggs and cook until set on the bottom and side, about 3 minutes. Broil the tortilla until the top is lightly browned and the eggs are set, about 2 minutes, . Slide the tortilla onto a plate, cut into wedges and serve.
—*Grace Parisi*

Broccoli Frittata

⏱ **TOTAL: 25 MIN • 4 TO 6 SERVINGS** ● ◐
Chef Marc Murphy of New York City's Landmarc restaurant calls this frittata a "breakfast pizza" when he serves it to his kids. A little garlicky and simple to prepare, it's also satisfying enough for brunch or a light lunch.

  1 garlic clove, thinly sliced
  2 tablespoons olive oil
3½ cups broccoli florets
  ¼ teaspoon crushed red pepper
Salt and freshly ground black pepper
  8 large eggs
  ½ cup grated Parmigiano-Reggiano

1. Preheat the oven to 350°. In a 10-inch ovenproof nonstick skillet, cook the garlic in 1 tablespoon of the oil over moderately high heat for 30 seconds. Add the broccoli and red pepper and cook for 1 minute. Stir in 2 tablespoons of water, season with salt and black pepper and cover. Cook over moderate heat until the broccoli is crisp-tender, 2 minutes; let cool.

2. In a bowl, whisk the eggs with ¼ teaspoon each of salt and black pepper. Stir in the broccoli. Return the skillet to the stovetop and heat the remaining 1 tablespoon of oil. Pour in the eggs and cook over moderately low heat until set around the edge, 3 minutes. Sprinkle with the cheese. Transfer the skillet to the oven and bake until the center is just set, 12 minutes. Serve warm. —*Marc Murphy*

Watercress-Fontina Souffléed Omelet

⏱ **TOTAL: 25 MIN • 4 SERVINGS** ◐ ◐
The trick to this wonderfully puffy souffléed omelet is to beat the egg whites until they form soft peaks, then fold them into the yolks.

  ¼ cup mild-flavored extra-virgin
      olive oil
  5 ounces watercress, chopped (5 cups)
Salt and freshly ground black pepper
  6 large eggs, separated
  4 ounces imported Fontina cheese,
      shredded (1 cup)

1. Preheat the broiler and position a rack 6 inches from the heat source. In a large nonstick ovenproof skillet, heat 2 tablespoons of the olive oil. Add the chopped watercress, season with salt and black pepper and cook over high heat until wilted, 3 minutes. Drain the watercress well, then transfer to a bowl and let cool. Stir in the egg yolks and ¼ cup of the cheese. Wipe out the skillet.

2. In a bowl, beat the egg whites with a pinch of salt until soft peaks form. Fold the whites into the egg yolks until no streaks remain.

3. Heat the remaining 2 tablespoons of olive oil in the skillet. Add the egg mixture, spreading it evenly. Cook over moderately high heat until the omelet is golden on the bottom, about 3 minutes. Sprinkle the remaining ¾ cup of cheese on top and broil the omelet for 4 minutes, until the cheese is melted and the omelet is set on the top. Slide the omelet onto a platter, folding it in half. Cut the omelet into wedges and serve immediately.
—*Grace Parisi*

WINE Brisk, light white: 2010 Louis Métaireau Grand Mouton Muscadet.

Cheddar-Chive Corn Muffins

⏱ **ACTIVE: 10 MIN; TOTAL: 30 MIN**
MAKES 12 MUFFINS ● ◐

1½ cups all-purpose flour
  ¾ cup stone-ground cornmeal
  1 tablespoon baking powder
  1 tablespoon sugar
  1 teaspoon kosher salt
  4 ounces extra-sharp cheddar
      cheese, shredded (1¼ cups)
  ¼ cup chopped chives
  1 cup milk
  1 large egg, lightly beaten
  ¼ cup canola oil,
      plus more for brushing
  2 jalapeños
  8 ounces cream cheese, softened
  ¼ cup hot pepper jelly

1. Preheat the oven to 400° and spray a 12-cup muffin tin with baking spray. In a medium bowl, whisk the flour and cornmeal with the baking powder, sugar and salt. Lightly stir in 1 cup of the cheddar cheese and the chives.

2. In a small bowl, whisk the milk with the egg and the ¼ cup of canola oil. Fold the liquid ingredients into the dry ingredients just until evenly moistened. Spoon the batter into the muffin cups. Sprinkle the tops with the remaining ¼ cup of cheddar cheese. Bake for 22 to 25 minutes, until the muffins are springy and golden. Let the muffins cool for 5 minutes, then turn them out onto a rack to cool.

3. Meanwhile, brush the jalapeños lightly with oil and roast directly over a gas flame or under the broiler, turning, until lightly charred, about 5 minutes. Transfer the chiles to a bowl, cover with plastic wrap and refrigerate to cool slightly, about 5 minutes.

4. Peel, seed and finely chop the jalapeños. Mix them with the cream cheese and pepper jelly. Serve the muffins with the pepper jelly cream cheese. —*Grace Parisi*

MAKE AHEAD The pepper jelly cream cheese can be refrigerated for up to 4 days. The muffins can be stored in an airtight container overnight. Rewarm before serving.

● HEALTHY ● MAKE AHEAD ◐ VEGETARIAN ◐ STAFF FAVORITE

ham and potato chip tortilla

Cornmeal Pancakes with Lemon-Sage Brown Butter

TOTAL: 1 HR • MAKES ABOUT 24 PANCAKES ● ●

Star chefs Daniel Patterson and René Redzepi serve these ultra-light pancakes with maple syrup and brown butter brightened with bits of fresh lemon and sage.

½ cup stone-ground cornmeal
1¼ cups buttermilk
1 large egg, separated, plus 1 large egg white
1½ cups all-purpose flour
½ cup rice flour
⅓ cup sugar
1 teaspoon baking powder
¾ teaspoon baking soda
1 teaspoon salt
Unsalted butter, for the griddle
Lemon-Sage Brown Butter (recipe follows), for serving
Warm pure maple syrup, for serving

1. In a medium saucepan, whisk the cornmeal into 1½ cups of cold water and bring to a boil, whisking. Simmer over moderate heat until thickened to a porridge, 4 to 5 minutes. Transfer to a large bowl and whisk in the buttermilk and the egg yolk.
2. In another bowl, whisk the all-purpose flour with the rice flour, sugar, baking powder and baking soda. Whisk the dry ingredients into the cornmeal mixture. In a large bowl, using a handheld mixer, beat the 2 egg whites with the salt at high speed until firm peaks form. Gently fold the beaten egg whites into the batter.
3. Heat a large griddle. Brush the hot griddle with butter and ladle a scant ¼ cup of batter onto the surface for each pancake, allowing a little space between them. Cook the pancakes over moderate heat until bubbles appear on the surface, about 2 minutes. Flip the pancakes and cook until risen and browned on the bottom, about 2 minutes longer. Serve the pancakes immediately, with the Lemon-Sage Brown Butter and maple syrup. Repeat with the remaining batter. —*Daniel Patterson and René Redzepi*

LEMON-SAGE BROWN BUTTER
TOTAL: 15 MIN • MAKES ½ CUP ● ●

1 stick unsalted butter
Pinch of salt
1 tablespoon chopped lemon (see Note)
1 teaspoon finely chopped sage
½ teaspoon finely grated lemon zest

In a small saucepan, cook the butter with the salt over moderately low heat until nutty brown, about 5 minutes. Scrape the butter into a bowl and chill in another bowl of ice water, stirring frequently, just until it begins to harden around the edges, about 5 minutes. Remove the bowl from the ice water and gently beat with a wooden spoon until the butter is slightly pale and creamy. Fold in the lemon, sage and lemon zest. —*RR*
NOTE To make the chopped lemon, cut the skin and bitter white pith from a lemon. Cut between the membranes to release the sections, then chop.

Flax-Coconut Pancakes

TOTAL: 30 MIN • MAKES ABOUT TWELVE 4-INCH PANCAKES ● ●

Elisabeth Prueitt of Tartine Bakery in San Francisco always mixes ground flax into her pancake batter. "I've never felt great about the low nutritional value of pancakes—it's like eating cake for breakfast—but the flax adds fiber, omega-3s and minerals."

⅓ cup brown rice flour (see Note)
⅓ cup white rice flour (see Note)
¼ cup sugar
3 tablespoons potato starch (see Note)
3 tablespoons tapioca starch (see Note)
3 tablespoons coconut flour (see Note)
2 tablespoons flaxseed meal
2 teaspoons baking powder
¼ teaspoon salt
2 large eggs
1¼ cups milk, at room temperature
¼ cup coconut oil, melted, plus more for the griddle
Fresh fruit and maple syrup, for serving

1. In a large bowl, whisk the brown and white rice flours with the sugar, potato starch, tapioca starch, coconut flour, flaxseed meal, baking powder and salt. In another bowl, whisk the eggs and milk with the ¼ cup of coconut oil; whisk the wet ingredients into the dry ingredients just until the batter is moistened. Add a tablespoon of milk if the batter is very thick.
2. Preheat a griddle and brush lightly with coconut oil. For each pancake, scoop 3 tablespoons of batter onto the griddle, allowing it to spread on its own. Cook over moderate heat until bubbles appear on the surface, about 3 minutes. Flip and cook the pancakes until they have risen and are golden brown on the second side, about 2 minutes longer. Transfer the pancakes to plates and serve with fruit and maple syrup.
—*Elisabeth Prueitt*

NOTE For gluten-free bakers, a combination of brown rice flour, white rice flour, potato starch and tapioca starch makes an excellent substitution for all-purpose flour. These ingredients are available at many specialty and natural food markets and online at *kingarthurflour.com*. Coconut flour is also a healthy, gluten-free alternative to wheat and other grain flours. It is very high in fiber and a good source of protein. It's available at *bobsredmill.com*.

Apple Sandwiches

TOTAL: 10 MIN • 1 SERVING ● ●

These little apple "sandwiches" are layered with creamy almond butter and crunchy granola. They make a super-quick, healthy and satisfying breakfast.

1 firm, tart apple, such as Granny Smith, Honeycrisp or Pink Lady, thinly sliced horizontally
2 tablespoons almond butter
2 tablespoons granola

1. Spread all of the apple slices with the almond butter and sprinkle half of them with the granola.
2. Close the sandwiches and eat right away.
—*Grace Parisi*

flax-coconut pancakes

Light and Fluffy Baked Apple Pancake

⏱ TOTAL: 45 MIN • 6 SERVINGS ●○○

Golden Delicious apples hold their shape after they're caramelized with sugar and maple syrup, making them a perfect choice for this giant one-pan pancake.

- 2 tablespoons unsalted butter
- 2 Golden Delicious apples—halved, peeled, cored and sliced ½ inch thick
- 3 tablespoons sugar
- 1 tablespoon fresh lemon juice
- ¼ cup pure maple syrup, plus warmed syrup for serving
- 1 cup all-purpose flour
- 1 teaspoon baking powder

Pinch of salt

- 4 large eggs, separated
- 1 cup milk

1. Preheat the oven to 375°. In a 10½-inch nonstick ovenproof skillet, melt the butter. Add the apples, 1 tablespoon of the sugar and the lemon juice and cook over moderately high heat, stirring occasionally, until the apples are golden, about 6 minutes. Add the ¼ cup of maple syrup and simmer over low heat until thickened, about 1 minute. Spread the apples in an even layer and remove the pan from the heat.

2. In a medium bowl, whisk the flour with the baking powder and salt. In a measuring cup, whisk the egg yolks with the milk and the remaining 2 tablespoons of sugar. Whisk the liquid into the dry ingredients.

3. In a medium bowl, using a handheld electric mixer, beat the egg whites at medium speed until firm peaks form, about 2 minutes. Fold the beaten whites into the batter and scrape it over the apples; spread the batter to the edge.

4. Bake the pancake in the upper third of the oven for 20 minutes, until golden, puffed and set. Let cool for 5 minutes. Run a knife around the edge to loosen the pancake, then invert it onto a plate. Replace any apples that may have stuck to the pan. Cut the pancake into wedges and serve at once, with warmed maple syrup. —*Grace Parisi*

Chia-Seed Pudding

TOTAL: 15 MIN PLUS 4 HR CHILLING
4 SERVINGS ●●○○

- 2½ cups almond milk
- 3 tablespoons agave nectar
- ½ cup chia seeds (3 ounces)
- ½ teaspoon finely grated lemon zest

In a 1-quart jar, combine the almond milk with the agave nectar. Close the jar and shake to combine. Add the chia seeds and lemon zest, then close the jar and shake well. Refrigerate until the mixture is very thick and pudding-like, at least 4 hours or overnight, shaking or stirring occasionally. Serve the pudding in bowls. —*Grace Parisi*

SERVE WITH Diced mango, almonds, citrus sections and extra agave nectar.

Concord Grape Jelly

TOTAL: 1 HR • MAKES ABOUT 2½ PINTS ●○

- 4 pounds ripe Concord grapes, stemmed (10 cups)
- 1 Granny Smith apple, chopped, with seeds
- 2¼ cups sugar

1. Put the grapes and apple in a large pot and add ½ cup of water. Bring to a boil, cover and simmer over low heat until very juicy, about 10 minutes. Strain the juice through a fine sieve set over a large bowl.

2. Strain the juice again through several layers of dampened cheesecloth, without pressing or squeezing; you should have 3 cups.

3. In a very large saucepan, boil the grape juice and sugar over moderate heat, stirring, until the jelly falls off a cool spoon in sheets and registers 220° on an instant-read thermometer, about 18 minutes.

4. Pour the jelly into hot, sterilized canning jars to within ¼ inch of the rims (for instructions on sterilizing, see next recipe). Seal. Submerge the jars in a pot of water and boil for 5 minutes. Carefully remove the jars and let cool. Check the jar lids to make sure they've fully sealed; refrigerate any jars with imperfect seals. —*Grace Parisi*

Triple-Ginger Nectarine Jam

ACTIVE: 30 MIN; TOTAL: 1 HR 45 MIN
MAKES THREE ½-PINT JARS ●●○

Three ½-pint canning jars with lids and rings
- 2½ pounds firm-but-ripe nectarines
- 1½ cups sugar
- 2 tablespoons fresh lemon juice
- 2 tablespoons minced candied ginger
- 1 tablespoon finely grated fresh ginger
- 2 teaspoons ground ginger

1. Fill a large pot with water, cover and bring to a boil. Add the canning jars, lids and rings along with a set of tongs and a ladle and simmer over low heat for about 10 minutes to sterilize. Cover the pot and turn off the heat.

2. Set a metal rack in another large pot. Fill the pot with water and bring to a boil. Add the nectarines and boil until the skins loosen, about 30 seconds; using a slotted spoon, transfer them to a rimmed baking sheet and let cool. Peel, halve and pit the nectarines and cut them into ½-inch dice.

3. In a large, wide saucepan, combine the nectarines with the sugar, lemon juice and the candied, fresh and ground gingers. Bring to a boil over moderately high heat, stirring to dissolve the sugar and skimming the surface as necessary. Reduce the heat to moderate and simmer the jam, stirring once or twice, until it reaches 220° on a candy thermometer, about 40 minutes longer.

4. Using the sterilized tongs, remove the jars from the hot water and transfer to a large rimmed baking sheet. Ladle the jam into jars, leaving ½ inch at the top. Using the tongs, place the lids on the jars followed by the rings. Screw on the lids securely but not too tightly.

5. Using canning tongs, lower the jars into the boiling water of the pot with the rack at the bottom, making sure they are covered by at least 1 inch of water. Boil over high heat for 10 minutes. Using the canning tongs, transfer the jars to a rack to cool until the lids seal (they will look concave); refrigerate any jars that do not seal. Store the sealed jars in a cool, dark place for up to 6 months.
—*Ernest Miller*

● HEALTHY ● MAKE AHEAD ● VEGETARIAN ● STAFF FAVORITE

DIY YOGURT

Yogurt is one of the healthiest things a home cook can make. Here, two methods plus toppings from **Ron Marks**, founder of AtlantaFresh Artisan Creamery.

Greek-Style Yogurt

TOTAL: 1 HR PLUS CULTURING AND CHILLING

MAKES ABOUT 2 QUARTS ● ● ○ ○

This recipe adds live, active bacteria to milk by using either store-bought yogurt or, for the best result, powdered yogurt culture.

- 1 gallon skim or 2 percent milk, preferably not ultra-pasteurized
- 2 cups nonfat or 2 percent Greek-style plain yogurt with active cultures, at room temperature, or ¼ teaspoon powdered yogurt culture (see Note)

1. In a large saucepan, bring 1½ inches of water to a boil. Set a large stainless steel bowl over the saucepan and add the milk; do not let the bowl touch the water. Turn the heat to low and gradually heat the milk, whisking occasionally, until it registers 180° on a candy thermometer. Keep the milk at 180° for 30 minutes, adjusting the heat as necessary.

2. Remove the bowl from the saucepan and let the milk cool down to 106°, stirring often. Meanwhile, preheat the oven to 110°.

IF USING YOGURT, whisk it with 2 cups of the warm milk in a bowl until smooth, then add it back into the warm milk.

IF USING POWDERED YOGURT CULTURE, sprinkle the powder all over the warm milk.

3. Whisk the cultured warm milk for 3 minutes. Using a funnel, fill several clean jars to 1 inch below the rim with the cultured milk. Cap the jars and place in the warmed oven (or a yogurt maker or other gently heated spot); the cultured milk should stay between 105° and 110° during the entire process.

4. Begin checking the yogurt after 4½ hours; it's ready when it is thick, tangy and surrounded by a small amount of clear whey. If using a pH meter, the yogurt is ready when it registers 4.5. Depending on how active the cultures are, it can take up to 18 hours for the yogurt to set and develop its characteristic tang. Refrigerate until thoroughly chilled or overnight.

5. Line a large mesh colander or strainer with a moistened cotton cloth or several layers of cheesecloth and set it over a large bowl. Scoop the yogurt into the colander. Cover with plastic wrap; refrigerate for about 6 hours, or until it reaches the desired thickness.

NOTE Powdered yogurt culture can be ordered online at *cultures forhealth.com*.

MAKE AHEAD The strained yogurt can be refrigerated in an airtight container for up to 3 weeks.

FOUR GREAT GREEK YOGURT FLAVORINGS

1) honey In a bowl, stir together 1 cup **YOGURT** with 4 tablespoons warmed **WILDFLOWER HONEY.**

2) ginger-peach conserve In a saucepan, combine ¾ cup plus 2 tablespoons **SUGAR,** 2 cups sliced peeled **PEACHES,** ¼ cup **ORANGE JUICE,** 6 tablespoons **DARK BROWN SUGAR** and a pinch of **SALT;** simmer for 5 minutes, stirring. Add 2 tablespoons finely grated **GINGER** and ⅛ teaspoon **CINNAMON;** simmer for 2 minutes. Add ½ teaspoon **CORNSTARCH** dissolved in ½ teaspoon water and simmer until slightly thickened. Using an immersion blender, gently pulse until a chunky sauce forms. Serve chilled.

3) mixed-berry conserve In a medium saucepan, combine 6 ounces **RASPBERRIES,** ¼ cup **ORANGE JUICE,** 2 ounces **BLUEBERRIES,** ¾ cup plus 2 tablespoons **SUGAR** and a pinch of **SALT;** simmer over moderate heat for about 5 minutes, stirring occasionally. Stir in ½ teaspoon **CORNSTARCH** dissolved in ½ teaspoon water and simmer until the liquid is slightly thickened, about 30 seconds. Using an immersion blender, gently blend until a thick sauce forms. Serve chilled.

4) cucumber-dill (tzatziki) In a bowl, stir together 1 cup **GREEK-STYLE YOGURT;** ½ large **CUCUMBER** that has been peeled, halved lengthwise, seeded and cut into ½-inch dice; 2 tablespoons chopped **DILL;** 1 tablespoon freshly squeezed **LEMON JUICE;** and ½ minced **GARLIC CLOVE.** Season the tzatziki with **SALT** and freshly ground **BLACK PEPPER.**

1
2
3
4

Chef and writer Tamar Adler with her brother, John, also a chef; they prepare dessert for a winter party in New York City: oranges with rosemary-infused honey, OPPOSITE; *recipe, page 336.*

TARTS, PIES & FRUIT DESSERTS

Double-Crust Apple-Apricot Pie

ACTIVE: 1 HR 30 MIN;
TOTAL: 3 HR PLUS 2 HR CHILLING
MAKES ONE 9-INCH PIE ● ● ●

- 1 tablespoon all-purpose flour, plus more for rolling
- Perfectly Flaky Yogurt-Butter Pie Dough (double the recipe on page 320)
- 1 egg white, beaten
- 5 large apples (2½ pounds), such as Granny Smith—peeled, cored, quartered and thickly sliced
- ½ cup sugar, plus more for sprinkling
- ½ cup diced dried apricots (2½ ounces)
- 1 teaspoon finely grated orange zest
- 1 teaspoon cinnamon
- 1 tablespoon cold unsalted butter, cut into small dice
- 2 tablespoons milk

1. On a floured work surface, roll out the larger disk of dough to a 13-inch round. Fold the round in quarters and transfer to a 9-inch glass pie dish; unfold the pastry and gently press it into the pie plate. Lightly brush the bottom of the dough with some of the egg white. Roll out the smaller disk of pie dough to a 12-inch round. Fold the round in quarters, transfer it to a wax paper–lined baking sheet and unfold. Freeze the pie shell and the 12-inch round of dough for 15 minutes.

2. Preheat the oven to 400° and position a rack in the lower third. In a bowl, toss the apples with the ½ cup of sugar and the apricots, zest, cinnamon and 1 tablespoon of flour.

3. Scrape the fruit into the pie shell and dot with the butter. Brush the edge with some of the egg white and top with the second round of dough. Press the edges together and, using scissors, trim the overhang to ½ inch. Fold the edge under itself and crimp decoratively. Brush the pie with the milk and sprinkle with sugar. Cut slashes in the top of the pie to vent steam.

4. Bake the pie for 1 hour, until the crust is deep golden and the filling is bubbling through the vents; tent with foil during the last 20 minutes of baking. Let cool completely before serving. —Alice Medrich

Lee's Apple Pie

ACTIVE: 1 HR; TOTAL: 6 HR
MAKES ONE 9-INCH PIE ● ●

PIE DOUGH
- 2½ cups all-purpose flour
- ¾ teaspoon salt
- 2½ sticks cold unsalted butter, cut into ¼-inch dice
- 1 large egg beaten with 2 tablespoons of ice water

FILLING
- ½ cup sugar
- 3 tablespoons all-purpose flour
- ½ teaspoon finely grated orange zest
- ¼ teaspoon cinnamon
- ⅛ teaspoon ground cardamom
- Pinch of freshly grated nutmeg
- Pinch of ground cloves
- 3 pounds assorted apples, such as Mutsu, Golden Delicious, Winesap or Gravenstein—peeled, cored and sliced ¼ inch thick
- 1 tablespoon brandy
- 2 teaspoons heavy cream
- 1 large egg yolk
- Vanilla ice cream, for serving

1. MAKE THE DOUGH In a bowl, whisk the flour with the salt. Using a pastry blender or 2 knives, cut in half of the butter until the mixture resembles cornmeal. Add the remaining butter, sprinkle in the egg-water mixture and, using a fork, quickly toss the dough until evenly moistened. Gently knead the dough until it just comes together. Gather the dough into a ball and cut it in half. Press each half into a disk and cover with plastic wrap. Refrigerate the dough for at least 2 hours or preferably overnight.

2. On a lightly floured work surface, roll out 1 disk to a 14-inch round. Fold the dough in half and transfer it to a 9-inch pie plate. Unfold the dough and gently press it into the pie plate without stretching. Trim the dough flush with the rim of the pie plate. Refrigerate the pie shell. Lightly dust a large baking sheet with flour. Roll out the remaining disk to a 14-inch round; transfer it to the prepared baking sheet and refrigerate.

3. MAKE THE FILLING Preheat the oven to 400°. In a small bowl, combine the sugar with the flour, orange zest, cinnamon, cardamom, nutmeg and cloves. In a large bowl, sprinkle the apples with the brandy. Add the spice mixture and toss well.

4. Fill the pie shell with the apples, arranging the slices so there are no gaps. Drape the dough round over the apples and gently press it, without stretching, to cover the apples. Trim the top dough overhang to ½ inch and fold it under the pie crust bottom. Crimp the edge decoratively to seal. In a small bowl, beat the cream with the egg yolk. Brush this glaze over the top of the pie. Using a small, sharp knife, cut four or five ½-inch vents in the top.

5. Bake the pie in the bottom third of the oven for 45 minutes, until the top is golden brown and crisp and the filling just starts to bubble. Transfer the pie to a rack to cool to room temperature, at least 2 hours, then cut into wedges and serve with vanilla ice cream. —David Tanis

Caramel-Apple Ice Cream

TOTAL: 20 MIN PLUS 4 HR FREEZING
4 TO 5 SERVINGS ● ●

- 2 tablespoons unsalted butter
- 2 Granny Smith apples—peeled, cored, quartered and very thinly sliced
- 1 tablespoon sugar
- ⅛ teaspoon cinnamon
- ¼ cup dulce de leche
- 2 pints vanilla ice cream

1. Melt the butter in a medium skillet. Add the apples and cook over moderate heat, stirring, until softened and lightly browned, about 5 minutes. Add the sugar, cinnamon and ¼ cup of water and cook for 2 minutes. Stir in the dulce de leche until melted. Scrape the mixture into a bowl and refrigerate until chilled.

2. Fold the apple mixture into softened vanilla ice cream and freeze until firm, about 4 hours. Scoop into bowls and serve. —Grace Parisi

● HEALTHY ● MAKE AHEAD ● VEGETARIAN ● STAFF FAVORITE

double-crust apple-apricot pie

DIY PIE CRUST

Star baker **Alice Medrich** shares crucial lessons (like using bleached flour and adding yogurt to tenderize the dough) along with her recipe for making the flakiest pie crust.

Perfectly Flaky Yogurt-Butter Pie Dough

TOTAL: 30 MIN PLUS 2 HR CHILLING
MAKES ONE 9-INCH CRUST ● ○ ●

Use this recipe to make Medrich's Pecan Pie (page 324); double it (make one disk slightly larger than the other) for her Double-Crust Apple-Apricot Pie (page 318).

- 6 ounces all-purpose flour (1¼ cups)
- 1 stick cold unsalted butter—
  5 tablespoons cut into ¼-inch dice
- ¼ cup cold plain whole yogurt
  (not Greek-style)
- ½ teaspoon salt

1. Measure the flour into a glass or ceramic bowl; freeze for 15 minutes along with the 3-tablespoon-size chunk of butter. Put the diced butter on a plate; refrigerate for 15 minutes. In a glass measuring cup, combine the yogurt and salt with 1 tablespoon of cold water and refrigerate for 15 minutes.
2. Using a pastry blender or 2 butter knives, cut the diced butter into the flour until the mixture resembles coarse meal, then rub the mixture between your hands until the fat is evenly distributed and the mixture resembles fine oat flakes. Using a sharp knife or a cheese plane, very thinly slice the remaining butter; freeze for 5 minutes.
3. Add the butter slices to the bowl. Toss gently to separate the slices and cut once or twice to combine them with the flour; the slices should remain cold and intact. Drizzle the cold yogurt into the bowl, using a rubber spatula to stir and toss as you drizzle. Continue tossing the dough, scraping any off the spatula and the side of the bowl, until it is crumbly and evenly moistened. Press the dough into a 6-inch disk and wrap in plastic. Refrigerate the dough for at least 2 hours or overnight, or freeze for 1 month.

TWO WAYS TO CRIMP THE CRUST

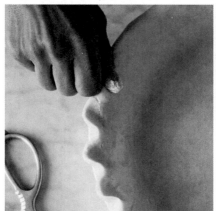

the thumb crimp For an angled, wave-like edge, work on the bias, pinching the dough between your thumb and bent forefinger at even intervals.

traditional fluting For a triangular crimp, form a V with your thumb and forefinger; press the edge of the dough into the V with your other forefinger.

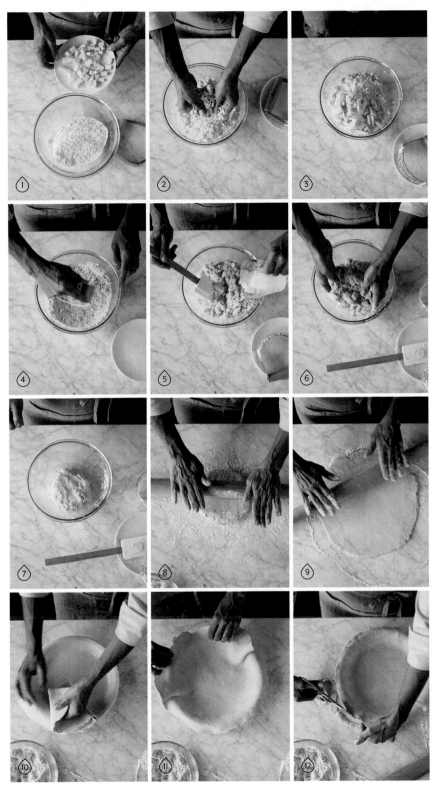

STEP-BY-STEP GUIDE TO PERFECTLY FLAKY YOGURT-BUTTER PIE DOUGH

1. CHILL INGREDIENTS To make sure all of the ingredients are sufficiently chilled, freeze or refrigerate them for about 15 minutes.

2. RUB BUTTER Using your hands, rub the cold diced butter into the flour until it's completely incorporated. (There is no risk here of overworking the dough.)

3. SLICE BUTTER Cut the remaining butter into very thin slices and add them to the flour mixture; now work quickly to keep the butter slices cold.

4. MIX GENTLY Separate the butter slices, cutting once or twice to coat with flour. The slices should remain as intact as possible to ensure a flaky crust.

5. ADD LIQUID Drizzle the cold yogurt-water mixture into the bowl of flour, gently combining the mixture with a rubber spatula.

6. TOSS TOGETHER Continue tossing, scraping any dough off the spatula and the side of the bowl, until the dough feels crumbly and evenly moistened.

7. FORM DISK Press the dough into a 6-inch disk. Wrap it in plastic and refrigerate for at least 2 hours or overnight, to allow the flour to fully hydrate.

8. ROLL OUT On a floured work surface, begin rolling out the dough; it sometimes helps to start by gently pounding the disk with the rolling pin.

9. FORM ROUND Continue to roll out the dough, dusting with flour on top and underneath as needed, to form a 13-inch round. Patch any cracks.

10. CAREFULLY TRANSFER Fold the round of dough into quarters and carefully transfer it to a 9-inch glass or ceramic pie dish.

11. LINE DISH Carefully unfold the round of dough, then gently press it into the pie dish without stretching; patch any cracks that may form.

12. TRIM EDGE Using kitchen scissors, trim the overhanging pie dough to ½ inch. Tuck the edge of the dough under itself and crimp decoratively, using either the thumb crimp or traditional fluting technique (at left).

Brown Sugar–Cranberry Tart

ACTIVE: 35 MIN; TOTAL: 3 HR

MAKES ONE 9-INCH TART ● ●

This stunning dessert features fresh cranberries and creamy custard baked in a buttery tart shell. The sweet-and-tart berries pop when you take a bite.

TART SHELL

- 1 stick unsalted butter, softened
- ⅓ cup granulated sugar
- 1 large egg yolk
- ¼ teaspoon pure vanilla extract
- ¼ teaspoon salt
- 1¼ cups all-purpose flour

FILLING AND TOPPING

- 1½ cups granulated sugar
- 2 cups cranberries (10 ounces)
- 2 large eggs
- ½ cup light brown sugar
- 1½ teaspoons all-purpose flour
- ¼ cup plus 2 tablespoons half-and-half
- ⅛ teaspoon pure almond extract

Confectioners' sugar, for dusting

Lightly sweetened whipped cream, for serving

1. MAKE THE TART SHELL In a standing mixer fitted with the paddle attachment, beat the butter with the granulated sugar at medium speed until light and fluffy, about 3 minutes. Add the egg yolk, vanilla and salt, scrape down the side of the bowl and beat at low speed until smooth. Gradually add the flour, beating until the dough just forms a ball. Pat the dough into a disk and cover with plastic wrap. Refrigerate the dough for at least 1 hour or overnight.

2. Roll out the dough between 2 sheets of parchment paper into a 12-inch round. Carefully peel off the top layer of parchment paper and invert the dough onto a 9-inch fluted tart pan with a removable bottom. Peel off the parchment paper and gently press the dough into the pan. Trim the dough flush with the rim of the tart pan. Patch any cracks with the dough trimmings. Lightly prick the bottom with a fork. Refrigerate the tart shell until firm, about 30 minutes, or freeze it for about 10 minutes.

3. Preheat the oven to 350°. Line the tart shell with aluminum foil and fill with pie weights or dried beans. Bake the tart shell for about 30 minutes, until the rim is lightly golden. Remove the foil and pie weights and bake the tart shell for about 5 minutes longer, until it is lightly golden all over. Set the tart pan on a baking sheet. Increase the oven temperature to 375°.

4. MEANWHILE, MAKE THE FILLING In a medium saucepan, combine the granulated sugar with ¼ cup of water and cook over moderately high heat, stirring, until the sugar dissolves. Add the cranberries, cover and cook over moderate heat for 3 minutes, stirring once or twice. Remove the pan from the heat and let the cranberries cool to room temperature. Drain the cranberries well and reserve the cranberry syrup.

5. In a medium bowl, beat the eggs with the brown sugar and flour. Whisk in the half-and-half and the almond extract. Spread the cranberries in the tart shell. Drizzle 1 tablespoon of the reserved cranberry syrup over the cranberries and then pour in the almond custard topping.

6. Bake the tart in the lower third of the oven until a skewer inserted in the center comes out clean, 16 to 18 minutes. Transfer the tart in the pan to a rack to cool completely, at least 2 hours. Dust the tart with confectioners' sugar, cut into wedges and serve with whipped cream. —*David Tanis*

Puff Pastry Pear Tartlets

⏱ **TOTAL: 45 MIN • 6 SERVINGS** ● ●

To make these elegant tartlets, F&W's Grace Parisi tops puff pastry rounds with crème fraîche, caramelized pears and almonds.

- 14 ounces all-butter puff pastry, chilled
- ¾ cup sugar
- 2½ tablespoons unsalted butter
- 4 large Bartlett pears—peeled, cored and cut into ½-inch wedges
- ¼ cup pear brandy
- ¼ cup plus 2 tablespoons sliced almonds

Salt

- 6 tablespoons crème fraîche

1. Preheat the oven to 425°. On a work surface, sprinkle the top of the puff pastry with ¼ cup of the sugar and, using a rolling pin, roll the sugar lightly into the dough. Flip the puff pastry and sprinkle with another ¼ cup of the sugar. Roll out the puff pastry to a 12-by-16-inch rectangle. Using a 4-inch round plate as a template, cut out six rounds of pastry.

2. Transfer the pastry rounds to a parchment paper–lined baking sheet and poke them all over with a fork. Top with another sheet of parchment paper and a baking sheet and bake for 20 to 25 minutes, until the pastry is lightly browned. Remove the top baking sheet and parchment paper and bake the rounds for 10 minutes longer, until caramelized. Slide the paper and pastry rounds onto a rack and let cool.

3. Meanwhile, in a very large skillet, melt 2 tablespoons of the butter. Add the pear wedges and cook over high heat, tossing gently, until the pears are barely softened, about 2 minutes. Add the remaining ¼ cup of sugar and cook over high heat, stirring occasionally, until lightly caramelized, about 5 minutes longer.

4. Remove the skillet from the heat and add the pear brandy. Return the skillet to the heat and cook until the liquid is nearly evaporated, about 2 minutes.

5. In a small skillet, melt the remaining ½ tablespoon of butter. Add the sliced almonds and cook over high heat, stirring, until the almonds are golden, about 3 minutes. Transfer the toasted almonds to a plate and sprinkle them with salt.

6. Dollop the crème fraîche on the puff pastry rounds and top them with the caramelized pears and toasted almonds. Serve the pear tartlets right away.

—*Grace Parisi*

MAKE AHEAD The baked pastry rounds can be stored in an airtight container at room temperature overnight. The caramelized pears can be covered and refrigerated overnight. Rewarm the pears gently before proceeding with Step 4.

WINE Juicy, lightly sweet sparkling wine: 2010 Saracco Moscato d'Asti.

brown sugar–cranberry tart

Pecan Pie with Candied Ginger and Rum

ACTIVE: 1 HR; TOTAL: 2 HR 30 MIN PLUS 2 HR CHILLING • MAKES ONE 9-INCH PIE ● ●

2 cups pecan halves (7 ounces)
Perfectly Flaky Yogurt-Butter Pie Dough (page 320)
1 cup lightly packed light brown sugar
¼ cup light corn syrup
1 tablespoon unsalted butter
½ teaspoon salt
3 large eggs
2 tablespoons rum
¼ cup minced crystallized ginger

1. Preheat the oven to 350°. Spread the pecans in a pie plate and toast for about 8 minutes, until fragrant. Let cool.
2. Increase the oven temperature to 400°. On a floured work surface, roll out the dough to a 13-inch round; patch any cracks. Fold the round in quarters and transfer to a 9-inch glass pie dish; unfold the pastry and gently press it into the pie plate. Using scissors, trim the overhanging dough to ½ inch. Tuck the edge of the dough under itself and crimp decoratively. Line the dough with foil, shiny side down; prick all over with a fork, piercing the foil and pie dough. Freeze for 15 minutes.
3. Fill the pie with pie weights or dried beans and bake in the lower third of the oven for 30 minutes. Remove the foil and pie weights. Return the crust to the oven and bake until lightly browned, about 12 minutes.
4. Meanwhile, in a heatproof bowl, combine the brown sugar, corn syrup, butter and salt. Set the bowl over a saucepan filled with 1 inch of simmering water and whisk in the eggs 1 at a time. Cook, whisking gently, until the filling is warm to the touch. Remove from the heat and whisk in the rum.
5. Arrange the pecans in the pie shell and scatter the ginger on top. Pour the filling over the pecans. Bake until the filling is jiggly but not cracked, 25 minutes; cover the edge of the crust with strips of foil halfway through baking to prevent overbrowning. Let the pie cool on a wire rack. Cut into wedges and serve. —Alice Medrich

Pumpkin Pie Bread Pudding with Bourbon-Pecan Hard Sauce

ACTIVE: 40 MIN; TOTAL: 1 HR 45 MIN MAKES 2 "PIES" OR 16 SERVINGS ● ●

1 stick plus 3 tablespoons unsalted butter, softened, plus melted butter for brushing
1 pound challah bread, cut into 1-inch cubes
One 3-pound butternut squash
1¼ cups granulated sugar, plus more for sprinkling
4 large eggs
3 cups whole milk
One 14-ounce can pure pumpkin puree
1½ teaspoons cinnamon
½ teaspoon freshly grated nutmeg
¼ teaspoon ground cloves
½ teaspoon kosher salt
2 cups confectioners' sugar
2 tablespoons bourbon
½ cup chopped toasted pecans

1. Preheat the oven to 375°. Butter two 9-inch deep-dish glass or ceramic pie plates. Spread the challah on a large baking sheet and toast for 5 minutes, until lightly golden.
2. Cut the neck from the butternut squash. Peel it and cut it lengthwise into two ¾-inch-thick slabs. Very thinly slice the slabs into long, thin strips on a mandoline. Peel, seed and cut all of the remaining butternut squash into ½-inch dice.
3. In a very large nonstick skillet, melt 3 tablespoons of the butter. Add the diced squash and cook over high heat until lightly browned in spots, about 3 minutes. Add ¼ cup of the granulated sugar and cook, stirring occasionally, until just tender and glossy, about 3 minutes longer. Let cool.
4. In a large bowl, whisk the remaining 1 cup of granulated sugar with the eggs, milk, pumpkin, cinnamon, nutmeg, cloves and salt. Add the sautéed squash and the challah and gently toss to combine. Spoon the mixture into the buttered pie plates and top each with a loose lattice pattern of the squash strips. Brush the strips with butter and sprinkle with sugar. Cover with parchment paper and bake for 30 minutes. Uncover and bake for 30 minutes longer, until the tops are golden and the puddings are set. Let the puddings rest for 15 minutes.
5. In a bowl, whisk the remaining stick of butter with the confectioners' sugar, bourbon and pecans. Serve the pudding with the sauce. —Grace Parisi

Glazed Butternut Squash Tart

ACTIVE: 45 MIN; TOTAL: 2 HR 8 SERVINGS ● ●

One 1-pound neck of butternut squash—peeled, halved lengthwise and sliced crosswise ¼ inch thick
2 tablespoons unsalted butter, melted
2 tablespoons sugar
8 ounces all-butter puff pastry, chilled
4 ounces cream cheese, softened
⅛ teaspoon cinnamon
2 tablespoons apricot preserves, melted
2 tablespoons chopped toasted pecans

1. Preheat the oven to 375°. Line a baking sheet with parchment paper and butter the paper. Brush the squash with the melted butter and sprinkle with 1½ tablespoons of the sugar. Roast for about 45 minutes, flipping the squash slices halfway through, or until softened. Let cool.
2. Meanwhile, roll out the pastry to a 14-by-6-inch rectangle and transfer it to a parchment paper–lined baking sheet. Prick the pastry all over with a fork and refrigerate until firm, about 5 minutes. Top with another sheet of parchment paper and a flat cookie sheet and bake for about 30 minutes, until the pastry is lightly golden on the bottom but not set. Remove the top cookie sheet and parchment and bake for 10 minutes longer, until the pastry is golden and crisp. Let cool.
3. Blend the cream cheese with the cinnamon and the remaining ½ tablespoon of sugar and spread it on the pastry. Arrange the squash slices on top. Brush with the apricot preserves and sprinkle with pecans. Cut the tart into slices and serve.
—Grace Parisi

● HEALTHY   ● MAKE AHEAD   ● VEGETARIAN   ● STAFF FAVORITE

Fried Semolina Dumplings with Apricots and Apricot Preserves

TOTAL: 1 HR PLUS 2 HR CHILLING
8 SERVINGS ● ●

1½ tablespoons margarine,
plus more for greasing
1 quart soy milk
½ cup granulated sugar, plus more
for sprinkling
1 plump vanilla bean, split and
seeds scraped
Pinch of salt
4 ounces dried apricots, finely chopped
1 cup fine semolina (see Note)
2 large egg whites
Confectioners' sugar, for dusting
Warmed apricot preserves and
fresh raspberries and blackberries,
for serving

1. Grease a 9-by-13-inch baking dish with margarine. In a large saucepan, combine the soy milk with the ½ cup of granulated sugar, the vanilla bean and seeds and salt and bring to a simmer. Stir in the dried apricots. Whisking constantly, add the semolina and whisk over moderate heat until thick, about 2 minutes. Let the semolina stand until slightly cooled, about 10 minutes. Remove and discard the vanilla bean.

2. In a medium bowl, using a handheld electric mixer, beat the egg whites just until foamy. While beating the semolina mixture at medium speed, add the egg whites in a steady stream until thoroughly incorporated. Scrape the semolina batter into the prepared baking dish and place a sheet of margarine-greased wax paper on top, pressing to even the surface. Refrigerate the semolina batter until it is set, at least 2 hours or overnight.

3. Turn the semolina out onto a work surface and cut into 24 rectangles (you can also cut them into other shapes, like squares or circles). Melt ½ tablespoon of the margarine in a large nonstick skillet. Add 8 of the semolina rectangles and sprinkle them with granulated sugar. Cook over moderate heat until golden on the bottom, about 2 minutes. Carefully flip the semolina rectangles and cook until the sugar is melted and golden brown, about 2 minutes longer. Transfer the semolina rectangles to a platter and keep warm. Wipe out the skillet and repeat in 2 more batches with the remaining margarine, semolina and sugar, wiping out the skillet between batches.

4. Dust the fried semolina with confectioners' sugar and serve with warmed apricot preserves and berries. —*Roman Albrecht*
NOTE Fine semolina flour, also called extra-fancy durum flour, is available at Italian markets and online at *kingarthurflour.com*.
MAKE AHEAD The recipe can be prepared through Step 2 up to 2 days in advance.
WINE Lively, rich, off-dry German Riesling: 2010 St. Urbans-Hof.

Apricots and Plums Poached in Rosé Wine

⏱ ACTIVE: 15 MIN; TOTAL: 45 MIN
6 SERVINGS ● ●

1 cup sugar
2½ cups dry rosé wine
½ vanilla bean, split
One 3-inch strip of lemon zest
½ teaspoon salt
6 large firm, ripe plums—pitted and
halved, pits reserved
6 large firm, ripe apricots—pitted
and halved, pits reserved
Sweetened crème fraîche and butter
cookies, for serving

1. In a large skillet, combine the sugar, rosé, vanilla bean, zest, salt and fruit pits. Bring to a boil to dissolve the sugar. Cover, remove from the heat and let stand for 15 minutes.
2. Discard the pits. Bring the liquid to a simmer and add the plums and apricots. Poach the fruit over moderate heat, turning a few times, until just tender, 5 to 8 minutes. Let the fruit cool in the liquid to room temperature, then refrigerate until chilled. Serve the fruit in bowls with some of its poaching liquid, along with crème fraîche and cookies. —*Alex Raij*
MAKE AHEAD The poached fruit can be refrigerated for up to 3 days.

Peaches and Plums with Sesame Crumble

⏱ ACTIVE: 20 MIN; TOTAL: 45 MIN
6 SERVINGS ● ● ● ●

To create a crisp topping for this fruit crumble, F&W's Grace Parisi uses tahini (sesame paste). She makes extra sesame crumble to snack on and to top ice cream.

½ cup all-purpose flour
3 packed tablespoons light
brown sugar
¼ teaspoon kosher salt
4 tablespoons unsalted butter,
cut into tablespoons
1 tablespoon tahini
1½ teaspoons black sesame seeds
1 pound purple plums (about 3),
thinly sliced
1½ pounds peaches (about 3),
peeled with a vegetable peeler
and thinly sliced
½ cup granulated sugar
1 tablespoon freshly squeezed
lemon juice

1. Preheat the oven to 350° and line a baking sheet with parchment paper. In a food processor, pulse the flour with the light brown sugar and salt. Add the butter and tahini and pulse until moist crumbs form. Add the black sesame seeds and pulse to combine. Scatter the tahini crumbs on the baking sheet and bake them for about 20 minutes, until they are golden and crisp. Let cool, then break up any big clumps.

2. Meanwhile, in a large skillet, combine the plums and peaches with the granulated sugar and lemon juice and cook over moderate heat, stirring occasionally, until the fruit is just softened and the juices are thickened, about 10 minutes.

3. Scrape the fruit into a shallow gratin dish or glass pie plate; sprinkle with the crumbs. Bake in the center of the oven until the fruit is bubbling, about 10 minutes. Let cool for 5 minutes, then serve. —*Grace Parisi*
MAKE AHEAD The crumble and fruit can be refrigerated separately overnight. Bring to room temperature before proceeding.

● HEALTHY ● MAKE AHEAD ○ VEGETARIAN ● STAFF FAVORITE

Summer Plum Crostata

ACTIVE: 35 MIN; TOTAL: 2 HR 30 MIN

6 SERVINGS ● ◐

This rustic tart is from Colorado chef Kelly Liken, a *Top Chef* Season 7 finalist and the chef-owner of Restaurant Kelly Liken in Vail. Liken uses Colorado plums, which she loves for their "beautiful tartness." Even when ripe, the plums are somewhat tangy, thanks to Colorado's cool nighttime temperatures. Any firm-but-ripe plums will work perfectly here.

1¼ cups all-purpose flour, plus
    more for dusting
½ cup sugar, plus more for sprinkling
¼ teaspoon salt
 1 stick cold unsalted butter,
    cubed and chilled
¼ cup ice water
 1 tablespoon cornstarch
¼ teaspoon cinnamon
¼ teaspoon finely grated
    orange zest
 1 pound firm-but-ripe plums, pitted
    and cut into eighths
 1 large egg yolk mixed with
    1 tablespoon of water

1. In a food processor, add the 1¼ cups of flour, 2 tablespoons of sugar and the salt and pulse to combine. Add the butter and pulse until the mixture resembles coarse meal. Sprinkle on the ice water and pulse until the dough just barely comes together. Gather the dough and pat it into a disk. Wrap the dough in plastic and refrigerate until chilled, about 30 minutes.

2. Preheat the oven to 425° and position a rack in the lower third. Line a baking sheet with parchment paper. Working on a lightly floured surface, roll out the disk of dough to a 12-inch round, then transfer it to the baking sheet. Chill the dough until firm, about 15 minutes.

3. Meanwhile, in a bowl, combine the remaining ¼ cup plus 2 tablespoons of sugar with the cornstarch, cinnamon and orange zest. Add the plums and toss well. Let stand, stirring occasionally, until the sugar is mostly dissolved, about 15 minutes.

4. Arrange the fruit in the center of the dough, leaving a 1½-inch border all around. Fold the edge of the dough up and over the plums. Brush the rim with the egg wash and sprinkle with sugar.

5. Bake the plum *crostata* for about 50 minutes, until the crust is golden and the fruit is tender and bubbling. Let the *crostata* cool on the baking sheet for 30 minutes, then cut into wedges and serve.
—*Kelly Liken*

MAKE AHEAD The pastry disk can be refrigerated for up to 3 days.

Stone Fruit Pie with Almond Streusel

ACTIVE: 45 MIN; TOTAL: 3 HR 15 MIN

MAKES ONE 9-INCH PIE ● ◐ ◐

For anyone who comes home from the farmers' market with an overabundance of stone fruits, this pie from San Francisco pastry chef Lori Baker is the answer. You can fill it with any combination of apricots, peaches, plums, cherries or nectarines.

DOUGH
1½ cups all-purpose flour
1½ teaspoons granulated sugar
½ teaspoon salt
¼ teaspoon baking powder
 1 stick plus 2 tablespoons cold
    unsalted butter, cut into small pieces
 5 tablespoons ice water
STREUSEL
½ cup light brown sugar
 6 tablespoons all-purpose flour
 6 tablespoons slivered almonds
 6 tablespoons rolled oats
 1 teaspoon cinnamon
 1 teaspoon salt
 6 tablespoons cold unsalted butter,
    cut into small pieces
FILLING
2¼ pounds assorted stone fruits, such
    as cherries, apricots, peaches and
    plums, pitted and sliced ⅓ inch thick
    (peaches and plums peeled first)
⅓ cup granulated sugar
 1 tablespoon fresh lemon juice
¼ cup cornstarch

1. MAKE THE DOUGH In a food processor, combine the all-purpose flour with the granulated sugar, salt and baking powder and pulse to blend. Add the small pieces of cold butter and pulse until the mixture resembles coarse meal. Sprinkle the ice water over the mixture and pulse a few times, just until a dough starts to form. Scrape the dough out onto a lightly floured work surface and gently knead it a few times. Gather the dough, pat it into a disk, wrap in plastic and refrigerate until it is chilled and firm, at least 2 hours or overnight.

2. MEANWHILE, MAKE THE STREUSEL In a large bowl, combine the light brown sugar with the flour, almonds, rolled oats, cinnamon and salt. Add the butter and, with a pastry cutter or your hands, cut or rub the cold butter pieces into the mixture evenly. Refrigerate the streusel.

3. Preheat the oven to 350°. On a lightly floured work surface, roll out the dough to a 14-inch round, about ⅛ inch thick. Fold the dough in half and transfer it to a 9-inch glass pie plate. Unfold the dough and gently press it into the plate. Trim the overhanging dough to ½ inch and fold it under itself; crimp the dough decoratively. Freeze the pie shell for 10 minutes.

4. MAKE THE FILLING In a large bowl, toss the sliced fruit with the granulated sugar and lemon juice and let stand for about 5 minutes to let the sugar dissolve. Stir in the cornstarch. Scrape the fruit into the pie shell in an even layer, then scatter the streusel evenly on top of the fruit.

5. Bake the fruit pie in the lower third of the oven for about 1 hour and 15 minutes, until the fruit starts to bubble around the side. Transfer the pie to a wire rack and let it cool to room temperature, then cut the pie into wedges and serve.
—*Lori Baker*

SERVE WITH Vanilla ice cream.

MAKE AHEAD The pastry disk, wrapped in plastic, can be refrigerated for up to 3 days. The baked pie is best served the same day that it's made, but it can be refrigerated overnight. Bring the pie to room temperature before serving.

● HEALTHY ● MAKE AHEAD ◐ VEGETARIAN ● STAFF FAVORITE

summer plum crostata

Fallen Toasted-Almond Soufflés with Poached Pears and Prunes

ACTIVE: 30 MIN; TOTAL: 1 HR
4 SERVINGS ● ●

FRUIT

1½ cups dry rosé wine
2 tablespoons granulated sugar
¼ vanilla bean, split lengthwise
8 pitted prunes, quartered lengthwise
3 Bartlett pears—peeled, halved, cored and sliced lengthwise ⅓ inch thick
1 tablespoon fresh lemon juice

SOUFFLÉS

1⅓ cups whole blanched almonds
Unsalted butter, for brushing
¼ cup plus 2 tablespoons granulated sugar, plus more for sprinkling
5 large egg yolks
⅛ teaspoon pure almond extract
4 large egg whites
Pinch of salt
Confectioners' sugar, for dusting

1. PREPARE THE FRUIT In a medium skillet, combine the wine, granulated sugar and vanilla bean; bring to a simmer over moderately high heat, stirring, until the sugar dissolves. Add the prunes, cover and cook over low heat until softened, about 10 minutes.

2. In a medium bowl, toss the pears with the lemon juice. Add the pears to the skillet, cover and cook, stirring occasionally, until they are tender, about 5 minutes. Remove the vanilla bean. Transfer one-third of the poached pears and 1 tablespoon of the rosé syrup to a mini food processor or blender; puree until smooth. Transfer the pear puree to a small bowl and press a sheet of plastic wrap onto the surface to prevent browning.

3. PREPARE THE SOUFFLÉS Preheat the oven to 350°. Spread the almonds on a large rimmed baking sheet and toast for about 10 minutes, until golden brown. Transfer the toasted almonds to a plate and let cool completely, then coarsely chop them. Transfer the almonds to a food processor and pulse until finely ground and still fluffy.

4. Increase the oven temperature to 400°. Brush four 1-cup ramekins with butter. Sprinkle the ramekins with granulated sugar and turn to coat evenly all over. Tap the excess sugar out of the ramekins.

5. In a large bowl, whisk the egg yolks with 3 tablespoons of the granulated sugar and the almond extract until pale, then stir in the ground almonds and pear puree.

6. In a large stainless steel bowl, beat the egg whites with the pinch of salt until soft peaks form. Add the remaining 3 tablespoons of granulated sugar and beat until the egg whites are firm and glossy. Stir one-fourth of the egg whites into the almond mixture to lighten it, then gently fold in the remaining egg whites.

7. Scrape the soufflé mixture into the ramekins. Smooth the tops and run your thumb around the inside of the rims. Transfer to a baking sheet and bake for about 17 minutes, until the soufflés are risen and browned. Let cool slightly, then carefully loosen the soufflés from the ramekins with a knife.

8. Invert the soufflés onto plates and spoon the prunes, pears and rosé syrup around them. Dust the soufflés with confectioners' sugar and serve. —*Marcia Kiesel*

MAKE AHEAD The poached prunes and pears in rosé syrup can be refrigerated overnight. Rewarm gently before proceeding. The baked almond soufflés can stand in their ramekins at room temperature for up to 2 hours before unmolding.

WINE Sweet, honeyed white Bordeaux from Barsac: 2009 Château Coutet.

Prune Upside-Down Cakes

ACTIVE: 45 MIN; TOTAL: 2 HR 15 MIN
MAKES 8 CAKES ● ●

TOPPING

1 cup granulated sugar
1½ cups dry white wine
1 vanilla bean
1 cinnamon stick
Three 1-inch-thick strips of orange zest
32 large pitted prunes (about ¾ pound)
¾ cup light brown sugar
1 teaspoon unsalted butter

CAKES

¼ cup fresh orange juice
¼ cup low-fat buttermilk
3 large eggs
⅔ cup extra-virgin olive oil
1 cup granulated sugar
¾ cup plain nonfat Greek yogurt
1¾ cups all-purpose flour
1½ teaspoons baking powder
¼ teaspoon baking soda
1 teaspoon salt

1. MAKE THE TOPPING Preheat the oven to 350°. In a medium saucepan, combine the granulated sugar, white wine, vanilla bean, cinnamon stick, orange zest and 3 cups of water and bring to a boil. Simmer over moderate heat for 10 minutes. Add the prunes and simmer over moderately low heat until plumped and tender but not falling apart, about 25 minutes. Using a slotted spoon, transfer the prunes to a plate to cool.

2. Coat eight 1-cup ramekins with vegetable oil spray and set them on a sturdy rimmed baking sheet.

3. In a small saucepan, combine the brown sugar and butter with ¼ cup of water and bring to a boil, stirring to dissolve the sugar. Let cool slightly. Divide the caramel and poached prunes among the ramekins.

4. MAKE THE CAKES In a medium bowl, whisk the orange juice with the buttermilk, eggs, oil, granulated sugar and ¼ cup of the yogurt. In a large bowl, whisk the flour with the baking powder, baking soda and salt. Whisk the egg mixture into the dry ingredients until smooth. Divide the batter among the prepared ramekins, filling them a little more than half full. Spray a sheet of parchment paper with vegetable oil spray and invert it over the ramekins. Set another baking sheet on the parchment paper.

5. Bake the cakes for about 1 hour and 10 minutes, until a tester inserted in the centers comes out clean. Let the cakes cool for 10 minutes, then run a thin knife around the edges and invert them onto plates, allowing any caramel in the ramekins to drip over the cakes. Dollop the remaining yogurt on top of each cake and serve. —*Naomi Pomeroy*

Black Mission Fig Clafoutis

ACTIVE: 40 MIN; TOTAL: 1 HR

6 SERVINGS ●

Cherries are traditional in clafoutis, a classic French dessert. Here it's baked with juicy fresh figs, then topped with port-infused whipped cream and port syrup.

PORT CREAM

- ½ cup ruby or tawny port
- 2 tablespoons granulated sugar
- One 3-by-1-inch strip of orange zest
- ½ cup heavy cream

CLAFOUTIS

- 1 cup half-and-half
- ½ cup granulated sugar,
   plus more for the pan
- 2 large eggs
- 2 teaspoons pure vanilla extract
- ½ teaspoon finely grated orange zest
- ¼ teaspoon salt
- 6 tablespoons all-purpose flour
- Melted butter, for the pan
- ¾ pound fresh Black Mission figs,
   halved lengthwise
- Confectioners' sugar, for dusting

1. MAKE THE PORT CREAM In a small saucepan, combine the port with the sugar and orange zest strip and bring to a boil. Simmer over moderate heat until reduced by half, about 5 minutes. Pour the syrup into a heatproof bowl and let cool. Discard the orange zest and refrigerate the syrup until chilled.

2. In a medium bowl, whip the cream to soft peaks. Add 1½ tablespoons of the port syrup; whip the cream until firm. Refrigerate the cream and remaining syrup separately.

3. MAKE THE CLAFOUTIS In a blender, combine the half-and-half with the ½ cup of granulated sugar and the eggs, vanilla extract, orange zest and salt. Add the flour in 3 batches, pulsing for 10 seconds between additions. Let the clafoutis batter stand at room temperature for 30 minutes.

4. Preheat the oven to 425°. Brush a 9-inch baking dish or cast-iron skillet with melted butter and dust with granulated sugar. Pulse the batter once more and pour it in the dish. Set the figs halved side up in the dish.

5. Bake the clafoutis for 15 minutes. Reduce the oven temperature to 375°. Bake for 20 to 25 more minutes, until the top is lightly golden and the custard is just set. Let the clafoutis cool for 5 minutes. Dust with confectioners' sugar and serve warm, passing the port cream and the remaining port syrup at the table. —*Matthew Accarrino*

MAKE AHEAD The port syrup can be refrigerated for up to 1 week.

WINE Rich, toffee-scented Madeira: 10-Year Broadbent.

Vanilla Semifreddo and Orange Sorbet Terrine

ACTIVE: 1 HR; TOTAL: 2 HR

PLUS OVERNIGHT FREEZING

6 TO 8 SERVINGS ● ○ ○

This creamy, tangy terrine is reminiscent of a Creamsicle. For a shortcut, use store-bought orange sorbet.

SEMIFREDDO

- 6 large egg yolks
- 1½ teaspoons honey
- ½ cup sugar
- 2 cups heavy cream
- 1 vanilla bean, split, seeds scraped

SORBET

- ⅓ cup sugar
- ½ cup light corn syrup
- 2 cups chilled fresh orange juice
- 2 tablespoons chilled fresh lemon juice
- Orange slices, for serving

1. MAKE THE SEMIFREDDO Line a 9-by-5-inch loaf pan with plastic wrap, leaving a few inches of overhang all around. In the bowl of a stand mixer fitted with the whisk, beat the egg yolks at medium speed until they begin to lighten in color, about 2 minutes. In a small microwave-safe bowl, stir the honey into 1½ teaspoons of water until dissolved. Microwave at high power until very hot, about 45 seconds. With the mixer at low speed, slowly pour the hot honey into the yolks; increase the speed to high and whip until pale yellow and fluffy, about 8 minutes.

2. In a small saucepan, combine the sugar with ⅓ cup of water and bring to a simmer, stirring until the sugar dissolves. Brush down the side of the pan with a wet pastry brush. Simmer over moderately high heat, undisturbed, until the syrup reaches 240° on a candy thermometer (soft-ball stage), about 10 minutes; tilt the pan if necessary to get an accurate reading.

3. With the mixer at medium speed, carefully pour the hot sugar syrup down the side of the bowl into the yolks; avoid the whisk. Beat at high speed until the mixture is very pale and thick and the bowl of the mixer is no longer warm to the touch, about 5 minutes. Transfer the semifreddo base to a large bowl and wipe out the mixing bowl.

4. In the mixing bowl, whip the heavy cream with the vanilla seeds until medium-soft peaks form. In three batches, gently fold the whipped cream into the semifreddo base until fully combined. Fill one-third of the loaf pan with the semifreddo and smooth the surface. Freeze for 1 hour, or until partially set. Refrigerate the remaining semifreddo.

5. MEANWHILE, MAKE THE SORBET Fill a large bowl with ice water. In a small saucepan, whisk the sugar with ⅓ cup of water and the corn syrup and bring to a boil, stirring to dissolve the sugar. Pour into a heatproof bowl and set it over the ice water, whisking until cool. Whisk in the orange and lemon juices and stir until cold. Pour the sorbet mixture into an ice cream maker and process according to the manufacturers' instructions, until frozen but still spreadable.

6. Gently spread the sorbet over the frozen semifreddo and smooth the surface. Freeze for 15 minutes. Top with a final layer of semifreddo, filling the loaf pan. (You may have some semifreddo left over; freeze in a separate mold.) Lay a sheet of plastic wrap directly over the surface and freeze until firm, at least 12 hours or overnight.

7. Carefully unmold the terrine onto a platter and discard the plastic wrap. Using a hot knife, cut the terrine into slices. Garnish with orange slices and serve. —*Devin McDavid*

MAKE AHEAD The terrine can be frozen for up to 5 days.

WINE Lightly sweet, frothy Moscato d'Asti: 2010 Beni di Batasiolo Bosc dla Rei.

Lemon, Poppy and Chèvre Cheesecakes with Rhubarb

ACTIVE: 45 MIN; TOTAL: 2 HR PLUS 4 HR COOLING • 8 SERVINGS ● ● ○

CHEESECAKES

¼ cup plus 2 tablespoons sugar, plus more for coating the ramekins

8 ounces cream cheese, at room temperature

6 ounces soft fresh goat cheese, at room temperature

2 teaspoons finely grated lemon zest

1 teaspoon fresh lemon juice

½ teaspoon vanilla bean paste or 1 teaspoon pure vanilla extract

¼ teaspoon salt

1 cup sour cream

3 large eggs, at room temperature

1 tablespoon poppy seeds

COMPOTE

1 pound rhubarb, cut into ½-inch dice

½ cup sugar

½ vanilla bean, split

Pinch of salt

1 teaspoon finely grated orange zest

1 teaspoon finely grated fresh ginger

1 tablespoon St-Germain liqueur or elderflower cordial

1 pint raspberries

STREUSEL

5 tablespoons unsalted butter, at room temperature

¼ cup plus 2 tablespoons sugar

½ teaspoon fresh lemon juice

1 cup graham cracker crumbs (from 1 sleeve)

1 teaspoon all-purpose flour

½ teaspoon salt

¼ teaspoon cinnamon

1. MAKE THE CHEESECAKES Preheat the oven to 325°. Spray eight 4- to 6-ounce ramekins with vegetable oil spray; dust with sugar, tap out the excess, then set in a large roasting pan. In a large bowl, using an electric mixer, beat the cream cheese with the goat cheese and the ¼ cup plus 2 tablespoons of sugar until smooth. Beat in the zest, lemon juice, vanilla and salt. Beat in the sour cream.

Add the eggs, one at a time, beating well between additions. Beat in the poppy seeds.
2. Divide the mixture between the ramekins and set the pan in the oven. Carefully add enough hot water to the pan to reach halfway up the sides of the ramekins. Bake for 20 to 25 minutes, until the cheesecakes are just set. Remove from the oven and let cool in the water bath for 1 hour. Refrigerate the cheesecakes until cooled completely, 3 hours.
3. MEANWHILE, MAKE THE COMPOTE In a medium saucepan, let the rhubarb, sugar, vanilla bean and salt stand until slightly juicy, 20 minutes. Add the zest and ginger and cook over moderate heat, stirring occasionally, until the rhubarb is tender, about 15 minutes. Add the St-Germain and raspberries and cook until slightly thickened, about 5 minutes. Transfer the compote to a bowl and let cool. Discard the vanilla bean.
4. MAKE THE STREUSEL Preheat the oven to 350°. Line a baking sheet with parchment paper. In a bowl, using an electric mixer, beat the butter, sugar and lemon juice until fluffy. Beat in the graham cracker crumbs, flour, salt and cinnamon. Scatter the streusel onto the baking sheet and freeze for 10 minutes.
5. Bake the streusel until fragrant, golden and firm, about 20 minutes. Let cool completely, then crumble the streusel.
6. Run a thin knife around the cheesecakes and invert them onto plates. Spoon the compote on top and garnish with the streusel crumbs. Serve right away. —*Laura Sawicki*

Cocoa Nib Pavlova with Raspberries

ACTIVE: 20 MIN; TOTAL: 2 HR 8 SERVINGS ● ● ● ○

3 large egg whites, at room temperature

Pinch of salt

¼ teaspoon cream of tartar

¾ cup sugar

1 teaspoon pure vanilla extract

1 teaspoon bourbon

3 tablespoons cocoa nibs

1 ounce bittersweet chocolate, melted

2 cups raspberries

1. Preheat the oven to 300° and position a rack in the center of the oven. Draw an 8-inch circle on a sheet of parchment paper and invert it on a baking sheet.
2. In the bowl of a standing mixer fitted with the whisk, beat the egg whites, salt and cream of tartar at medium-high speed until soft peaks form. Gradually beat in the sugar at high speed until the whites are stiff and glossy, 3 minutes. Beat in the vanilla and bourbon. Add the cocoa nibs and beat until just incorporated. Spread the meringue on the paper in an 8-inch round.
3. Bake for 1 hour and 10 minutes, until the surface is dry and lightly browned and the center is still a bit soft. Let cool completely on the baking sheet, 30 minutes.
4. Transfer the Pavlova to a board. Drizzle with the chocolate and top with the raspberries. Cut into 8 wedges and serve.
—*Joy Wilson*

Summer Berry Tarts

⏱ **TOTAL: 45 MIN • 4 SERVINGS** ● ○

7 ounces frozen all-butter puff pastry from one 14-ounce package, thawed in the refrigerator

¼ cup sugar

1 pound blackberries and raspberries (about 4 cups)

1. Preheat the oven to 375° and line a baking sheet with parchment paper. Unfold the puff pastry on the baking sheet and cut it into two 5-by-6-inch rectangles. Cut each rectangle on the diagonal to form 2 triangles. Refrigerate until the pastry is chilled, about 10 minutes.
2. Separate the triangles so they're evenly spaced. Bake the pastry for 25 minutes, or until nicely browned and crisp.
3. Meanwhile, in a saucepan, bring the sugar and ¼ cup of water to a simmer over moderate heat. Add the blackberries and cook, stirring, for 1 minute. Add the raspberries and cook for 10 seconds. Stir a few times; transfer to a bowl.
4. Place the pastry on plates, top with the berries and serve. —*Marcia Kiesel*

● HEALTHY ● MAKE AHEAD ○ VEGETARIAN ● STAFF FAVORITE

lemon, poppy and chèvre cheesecake with rhubarb

Key Lime Pie with Chocolate-Almond Crust

ACTIVE: 30 MIN; TOTAL: 1 HR PLUS 6 HR
CHILLING • MAKES ONE 10-INCH PIE ● ● ●

CRUST

- 6 tablespoons unsalted butter, melted, plus more for greasing
- 1 cup chocolate graham cracker crumbs (from 9 whole crackers)
- ½ cup finely ground almonds
- ⅓ cup sugar

FILLING

- 1¼ cups fresh lime juice, preferably key lime juice (from 25 key limes)
- 1 teaspoon finely grated lime zest
- Two 14-ounce cans sweetened condensed milk
- 2 large eggs at room temperature, lightly beaten

WHIPPED CREAM

- ½ cup cold heavy cream
- ½ cup cold sour cream
- 2 teaspoons sugar
- Key lime slices, for garnish (optional)

1. MAKE THE CRUST Preheat the oven to 375° and butter a 10-inch glass pie plate. In a food processor, pulse the graham cracker crumbs with the almonds and sugar until thoroughly blended. Add the melted butter and pulse until the crumbs are moistened. Press the crumbs evenly over the bottom and up the side of the pie plate. Bake for 20 minutes, just until the almonds are lightly browned. Let cool to room temperature.

2. MAKE THE FILLING In a bowl, whisk the lime juice, lime zest, condensed milk and eggs until smooth. Pour into the cooled crust and bake for 20 minutes, until set around the edge and slightly jiggly in the center. Let cool to room temperature, then refrigerate until very firm, at least 6 hours or overnight.

3. MAKE THE WHIPPED CREAM In a bowl, using a handheld mixer, beat the heavy cream and sour cream until soft peaks form, 2 minutes. Beat in the sugar until stiff peaks form, 1 minute. Mound the whipped cream on the pie. Garnish with the key lime slices and serve.
—*Elissa Bernstein*

Caramel-Pear-Cheesecake Trifle

TOTAL: 45 MIN PLUS OVERNIGHT CHILLING
10 TO 12 SERVINGS ●

- 4 tablespoons unsalted butter
- 5 large, slightly underripe Bartlett pears—peeled, cored and diced
- 1 cup Vanilla Bean and Fleur de Sel Caramel Sauce (recipe follows)
- 1 teaspoon unflavored powdered gelatin
- 16 ounces cream cheese, at room temperature
- 3 cups cold heavy cream
- 8 ounces gingersnap cookies, plus crushed cookies for garnish

1. In a large skillet, melt the butter. Add the pears, cover and cook over moderate heat, stirring occasionally, until just softened, about 8 minutes. Add ½ cup of the caramel sauce, cover and cook over moderately low heat, stirring occasionally, until the pears are tender, 5 minutes. Scrape the pears onto a plate and refrigerate until cool.

2. Meanwhile, in a small microwave-safe bowl, sprinkle the gelatin over 2 tablespoons of water. Let stand until softened, about 5 minutes. Microwave at high power for 5 seconds, just until the gelatin is melted. Transfer the gelatin mixture to a large bowl and add the cream cheese and the remaining ½ cup of caramel sauce. Using an electric mixer, beat at medium-high speed until smooth, about 2 minutes.

3. In another bowl, whip 1½ cups of the heavy cream until firm peaks form. Fold the whipped cream into the cream cheese mixture.

4. Spoon one-fourth of the mousse into a medium trifle bowl. Top with one-fourth of the gingersnaps and one-fourth of the pears. Repeat the layering, ending with a layer of pears. Cover and refrigerate overnight.

5. In a bowl, using an electric mixer, beat the remaining 1½ cups of cream until soft peaks form. Dollop the cream over the trifle and garnish with crushed gingersnaps.
—*Grace Parisi*

WINE Nutty, caramelly tawny port: Quinta do Noval 10 Year Old.

VANILLA BEAN AND FLEUR DE SEL CARAMEL SAUCE

TOTAL: 15 MIN • MAKES 2 CUPS ● ● ●

- 2 cups sugar
- 1 vanilla bean, split, seeds scraped
- 1 cup heavy cream
- ½ teaspoon fleur de sel

1. Put the sugar in a large saucepan and pour ½ cup of water all around. Add the vanilla bean and seeds and cook over moderately high heat, stirring, until the sugar is dissolved. Using a wet pastry brush, wash down any crystals from the side of the pan. Cook without stirring until a deep-amber caramel forms, about 5 minutes. Gently swirl the pan to color the caramel evenly.

2. Remove the pan from the heat and add the cream. When the bubbling subsides, bring the sauce to a boil and cook over moderate heat, stirring, until the hardened caramel is dissolved. Discard the vanilla bean. Stir in the fleur de sel and let cool. —*GP*

Honey-Lime Strawberries with Whipped Cream

TOTAL: 35 MIN • 6 SERVINGS ●

- 2 pounds strawberries, thinly sliced
- 7 tablespoons mild honey
- 2 tablespoons fresh lime juice
- ½ teaspoon finely grated lime zest, plus more for garnish
- Scant ¼ teaspoon ground cardamom
- 1 cup heavy cream
- 2 pints lemon sorbet

1. Put the strawberries in a heatproof bowl. In a saucepan, combine 6 tablespoons of the honey with the lime juice; bring to a boil. Stir in the ½ teaspoon of zest and the cardamom. Pour the syrup over the strawberries, stirring. Let stand, stirring once or twice, until the berries are slightly softened, 25 minutes.

2. In a bowl, whip the cream with the remaining honey until soft peaks form. Scoop the sorbet into glasses; top with the berries, their juices and the whipped cream. Garnish with lime zest and serve right away. —*Grace Parisi*

● HEALTHY   ● MAKE AHEAD   ● VEGETARIAN   ● STAFF FAVORITE

key lime pie with chocolate-almond crust

Lemon Puddings with Candied Lemon Zest

ACTIVE: 30 MIN; TOTAL: 1 HR PLUS 5 HR CHILLING • 6 SERVINGS ● ●

    4 lemons, preferably organic
2¼ cups sugar
3½ cups heavy cream
Pinch of salt

1. Peel the zest in strips from the lemons. Cut the strips into 1-by-⅛-inch julienne. Transfer the zest to a large saucepan and cover with water. Bring to a boil and simmer for 10 minutes. Drain and return the zest to the saucepan. Add 1¼ cups of the sugar and 1¼ cups of water and bring to a boil. Simmer over moderate heat until the syrup is reduced to ⅔ cup and the zest strips are translucent, about 10 minutes. Using a slotted spoon, transfer the strips to a bowl and toss with the remaining 1 cup of sugar. Let cool.

2. Add 3 cups of the heavy cream to the lemon syrup in the saucepan and simmer until reduced to 3½ cups, about 15 minutes.

3. Halve and juice the lemons; you should have ¾ cup of juice. Add the lemon juice and salt to the saucepan and let cool slightly. Pour the pudding into 6 glasses and chill until set; at least 5 hours or preferably overnight.

4. Beat the remaining ½ cup of cream until soft peaks form; dollop on the puddings. Garnish with the zest and serve. —*Grace Parisi*
MAKE AHEAD The lemon custard and candied zest can be made up to 2 days ahead.

Guava–Cream Cheese Pastries

ACTIVE: 15 MIN; TOTAL: 1 HR 30 MIN 6 SERVINGS ● ● ●

    1 large egg yolk
    1 tablespoon milk
All-purpose flour, for dusting
One 14-ounce package all-butter
        puff pastry, thawed
    6 ounces guava paste, mashed
        (see Note)
    6 ounces cream cheese,
        cut into 6 pieces and chilled
Sugar, for sprinkling

1. Preheat the oven to 375°. In a small bowl, whisk the egg yolk with the milk.

2. On a lightly floured work surface, unfold the puff pastry and cut it into 6 squares. Transfer the squares to a parchment paper–lined baking sheet. Cut the guava paste into 6 equal portions and spoon onto half of each pastry square. Top with the cream cheese. Brush the pastry edges with some of the egg wash. Fold the pastry over the filling to form rectangles and crimp the edges with a fork. Refrigerate for 15 minutes, until firm.

3. Brush the pastries with the remaining egg wash and sprinkle with sugar. Bake in the center of the oven for 30 minutes, rotating the pan from front to back halfway through, until the pastries are golden. Let cool for at least 30 minutes before serving.
—*David Guas*
NOTE Guava paste can be found in supermarkets and Latin American food stores.

Oranges with Rosemary-Infused Honey

📷 PAGE 317

⏱ **TOTAL: 35 MIN • 20 SERVINGS** ● ● ● ●

    3 rosemary sprigs, needles
        stripped and stems discarded
1¼ cups honey
  20 mixed oranges, such as navel,
        blood and Cara Cara
Salt

1. Using a pestle or cocktail muddler, lightly bruise the rosemary needles. In a small saucepan, combine the rosemary with the honey and ½ cup of water and warm over moderately low heat for 5 minutes. Remove from the heat and let stand for 30 minutes. Transfer the rosemary-infused honey to a serving bowl or small pitcher.

2. Meanwhile, using a sharp knife, peel the oranges, removing all of the bitter white pith. Cut the oranges crosswise into ¼-inch-thick slices and arrange them on platters. Season the oranges lightly with salt and drizzle with some of the infused honey. Serve the oranges with additional honey alongside.
—*Tamar Adler*

Coconut Baked Alaska with Pineapple Meringue

ACTIVE: 30 MIN; TOTAL: 1 HR 8 SERVINGS ●

To keep the meringue in her baked Alaska stable, pastry chef Waylynn Lucas of Fonuts in Los Angeles uses xanthan gum, an industrial powder beloved by molecular chefs.

    8 ounces fresh pineapple,
        coarsely chopped
One 16-ounce homemade or store-
        bought pound cake, cut into eight
        ½-inch-thick slices
    2 pints coconut ice cream
    ½ cup Simple Syrup (page 372)
    5 tablespoons egg white powder
        (see Note)
    1 gram (¼ teaspoon) xanthan gum
        (see Note)
Lime zest and mint leaves, for garnish

1. In a blender, puree the chopped fresh pineapple until smooth; you should have 1 cup of pineapple puree.

2. Using a 2½-inch biscuit cutter, stamp out 8 rounds from the slices of pound cake and transfer the rounds to a baking sheet. Scoop the coconut ice cream into 8 balls, flatten the bottoms and place them on the pound cake rounds. Freeze until very firm, at least 30 minutes.

3. In a standing mixer fitted with the whisk, combine the pineapple puree with the Simple Syrup, egg white powder and xanthan gum and beat at high speed until stiff peaks form, about 5 minutes.

4. Preheat the broiler and position a rack 6 inches from the heat. Transfer the pineapple meringue to a piping bag and, working quickly, pipe it all over the ice cream and pound cake, covering them completely. Broil the Alaskas until golden, about 1 minute, turning the baking sheet as needed. Transfer the baked Alaskas to plates and serve right away, garnished with lime zest and mint leaves. —*Waylynn Lucas*
NOTE Egg white powder is available at health-food stores and most supermarkets. Xanthan gum is available at many grocery stores.

● HEALTHY ● MAKE AHEAD ● VEGETARIAN ● STAFF FAVORITE

lemon puddings with candied lemon zest

Chef Nico Monday and his wife and co-chef, Amelia O'Reilly, host a party at their Market Restaurant in Gloucester, Massachusetts; for dessert they serve a blackberry-studded buttermilk cake, OPPOSITE; recipe, page 344.

CAKES, COOKIES & MORE

Almond Cake with Lemon and Crème Fraîche Glaze

ACTIVE: 45 MIN; TOTAL: 2 HR 30 MIN
MAKES ONE 10-INCH CAKE ● ●

CAKE

- 1 stick unsalted butter, melted and cooled, plus more for the pan
- 1 cup unsalted raw almonds
- 1⅓ cups all-purpose flour
- ½ cup instant polenta
- 1 tablespoon baking powder
- 1 teaspoon minced rosemary
- Finely grated zest of 1 lemon
- ½ teaspoon salt
- 4 large eggs, at room temperature
- ½ cup granulated sugar
- ¾ cup crème fraîche

SYRUP

- ½ cup granulated sugar
- 1 tablespoon fresh lemon juice

GLAZE

- ½ cup confectioners' sugar
- 3 tablespoons crème fraîche
- 1 tablespoon freshly squeezed lemon juice

1. MAKE THE CAKE Preheat the oven to 350°. Butter a 10-inch springform pan.

2. Spread the almonds on a rimmed baking sheet and bake for about 4 minutes, until they are slightly fragrant. Let the almonds cool completely, then coarsely chop them. In a food processor, pulse the almonds until they are finely ground but not pasty.

3. In a large bowl, whisk together the ground almonds, flour, polenta, baking powder, rosemary, lemon zest and salt. In the bowl of a standing electric mixer fitted with the whisk attachment, combine the eggs and sugar and beat at medium-high speed until tripled in volume, 10 minutes. With the mixer at low speed, add the crème fraîche, then drizzle in the melted butter just until incorporated. Using a rubber spatula, gently fold the egg mixture into the dry ingredients in 3 batches. Scrape the batter into the prepared pan and bake for about 30 minutes, until a paring knife inserted in the center of the cake comes out clean.

4. MEANWHILE, MAKE THE SYRUP In a saucepan, combine the sugar, lemon juice and ½ cup of water and boil for 3 minutes. Let the syrup cool.

5. Place the hot cake on a rimmed baking sheet and pour the syrup evenly over it. Let the cake cool completely. Remove the side and bottom of the pan and transfer the almond cake to a platter.

6. MAKE THE GLAZE In a medium bowl, whisk together the confectioners' sugar, crème fraîche and lemon juice until smooth. Spread the glaze all over the top of the cake. Let stand until the glaze sets slightly, then cut into wedges and serve. —*Jessica Hicks*

Lemon Bundt Cake

ACTIVE: 40 MIN; TOTAL: 2 HR
PLUS COOLING • MAKES ONE 10-INCH
BUNDT CAKE ● ● ●

CAKE

- Nonstick cooking spray
- 1½ cups all-purpose flour, plus more for dusting
- 1½ cups cake flour
- 1 tablespoon baking powder
- 1 teaspoon salt
- 2¾ cups granulated sugar
- ⅓ cup lightly packed finely grated lemon zest (from 10 lemons)
- ½ cup canola oil
- 2 sticks unsalted butter, melted and cooled
- 3 large eggs
- 3 large egg yolks
- 3 tablespoons dark rum
- 2 tablespoons pure lemon extract (see Note)
- ¾ cup heavy cream

LEMON SYRUP

- ¼ cup granulated sugar
- ¼ cup fresh lemon juice
- 1 tablespoon dark rum

GLAZE AND TOPPING

- 1 cup confectioners' sugar
- 2 tablespoons fresh lemon juice
- 1 teaspoon almond extract
- ¼ cup slivered almonds, toasted (optional)

1. MAKE THE CAKE Preheat the oven to 350°. Generously coat a 10-inch Bundt pan with nonstick cooking spray and dust the pan with all-purpose flour. Sift the 1½ cups each of all-purpose flour and cake flour into a medium bowl, along with the baking powder and salt.

2. In the bowl of a standing mixer fitted with the paddle, use your fingers to rub the granulated sugar with the lemon zest until the sugar resembles pale yellow wet sand. Add the canola oil and cooled butter and beat at medium speed until blended, about 1 minute. Beat in the whole eggs, egg yolks, rum and lemon extract until just incorporated, about 1 minute. Reduce the speed to low and beat in the heavy cream and the dry ingredients in 3 alternating batches, starting and ending with the dry ingredients; be sure not to overbeat. Scrape down the side of the bowl and fold the batter until it is blended.

3. Scrape the batter into the prepared pan and use a spatula to smooth the surface. Bake in the middle of the oven for about 1 hour, rotating the pan halfway through, until a toothpick inserted in the center of the cake comes out clean. Let the cake cool on a rack for 30 minutes.

4. MEANWHILE, MAKE THE LEMON SYRUP In a small saucepan, combine the granulated sugar with the lemon juice and rum and bring to a boil. Simmer over moderate heat, stirring, until the sugar dissolves, about 3 minutes. Let the lemon syrup cool slightly.

5. Invert the cake onto a wire rack set over a baking sheet. Using a wooden skewer, poke holes evenly all over the cake and brush with the lemon syrup. Let the cake cool completely.

6. MAKE THE GLAZE AND TOPPING In a medium bowl, whisk the confectioners' sugar with the lemon juice and almond extract until smooth. Pour the glaze over the top of the cake, letting it drip down the sides. Sprinkle the almonds on top and let the glaze set, about 20 minutes. Cut the cake into wedges and serve. —*Matt Lewis*

NOTE Lemon extract is available at specialty food stores or online at *igourmet.com*.

WINE Floral, citrusy sparkling Moscato d'Asti: 2011 Saracco.

● HEALTHY ● MAKE AHEAD ○ VEGETARIAN ● STAFF FAVORITE

DIY LAYER CAKES

At Seattle's Dahlia Bakery, chef **Tom Douglas** offers an ingenious mix-and-match menu of cakes, frostings and fillings. Here, his recipes and tips for re-creating them at home.

MAKE THE CAKE

Brown-Butter Layer Cake
ACTIVE: 50 MIN; TOTAL: 2 HR 10 MIN
MAKES TWO 9-INCH LAYERS ● ○

 3 sticks (12 ounces) unsalted butter,
    plus more for greasing the pans
2¼ cups all-purpose flour,
    plus more for dusting
2¼ teaspoons baking powder
 1 teaspoon salt
1⅔ cups sugar
 1 vanilla bean, split and seeds scraped
 3 large egg yolks
 2 large eggs
1¼ cups milk, at room temperature
Mousse filling and buttercream frosting
    (recipes opposite)

1. Preheat the oven to 325°. Butter two 9-inch cake pans and line the bottoms with parchment paper. Butter the paper and dust the pans with flour, tapping out the excess.
2. In a medium saucepan, melt the 3 sticks of butter. Cook over low heat, stirring occasionally, until foamy, about 5 minutes. Continue to cook, stirring frequently, until the milk solids turn brown and the butter smells nutty, about 4 minutes longer. Scrape the melted butter and browned bits into a large heatproof bowl. Set the bowl in an ice-water bath until the butter begins to set around the edge, about 8 minutes.
3. Meanwhile, in a medium bowl, whisk the 2¼ cups of all-purpose flour with the baking powder and salt.
4. Remove the bowl from the ice water and scrape up the hardened butter. Transfer the butter to the bowl of a standing electric mixer fitted with the paddle and beat until creamy. Add the sugar and vanilla seeds and beat at medium-high speed for about 3 minutes, until

Douglas's cakes can go with any of his frostings and fillings. Here, his brown-butter cake is layered with dark chocolate mousse filling and frosted with rich chocolate buttercream.

fluffy. Beat in the egg yolks, then the whole eggs. Beat in the dry ingredients and milk in 3 alternating additions, scraping down the side and bottom of the bowl as necessary.
5. Pour the batter into the prepared pans; bake in the center of the oven for about 40 minutes, rotating the pans halfway through baking, until the cakes are golden and a toothpick inserted in the centers comes out clean. Cool in the pans for 20 minutes, then invert onto a rack to let the cakes cool completely. Peel off the paper to layer the cake.

LAYER THE CAKE

Set one cake layer on a platter. Spread the mousse filling on top and cover with the second cake layer. Frost the cake all over with a thin layer of buttercream and refrigerate until set, about 5 minutes. Frost the cake with the remaining buttercream. Refrigerate the cake until the frosting is firm, at least 15 minutes, before serving.
For Douglas's Double-Chocolate Layer Cake, see the recipe on page 350.

CHOOSE A FILLING

Dark Chocolate Mousse Filling

TOTAL: 30 MIN PLUS 4 HR CHILLING
MAKES 1½ CUPS, ENOUGH FOR ONE
9-INCH 2-LAYER CAKE ●

"Using a filling that's different from the frosting means less buttercream in the cake," Douglas says. "Otherwise, there's just too much of it." To switch up the fillings, try one of Douglas's variations below: creamy milk chocolate mousse or white chocolate mousse spiked with orange liqueur.

- ½ teaspoon unflavored gelatin
- ½ cup chilled heavy cream
- 2 tablespoons coffee liqueur
- 2 large egg yolks
- 2 tablespoons sugar

Pinch of salt

- 4 ounces bittersweet chocolate, melted and cooled

1. In a small bowl, sprinkle the gelatin over ½ tablespoon of water and let stand until softened.

2. Meanwhile, in a medium bowl, using a handheld electric mixer, beat the cream until it is softly whipped. Refrigerate until chilled, about 10 minutes.

3. In a small, microwave-safe bowl, heat the coffee liqueur at high power until hot, about 45 seconds. Stir in the softened gelatin until dissolved.

4. In another medium bowl, beat the egg yolks with the sugar and salt at high speed until pale and thickened, about 5 minutes. While beating the yolks, beat in the coffee-gelatin liquid; scrape the side and bottom of the bowl. Beat in the melted chocolate. Using a rubber spatula, fold in the whipped cream in 2 additions. Scrape the mousse into a bowl, cover with plastic wrap and refrigerate until firm, at least 4 hours or overnight.

MILK CHOCOLATE MOUSSE Substitute milk chocolate for the bittersweet chocolate.

WHITE CHOCOLATE MOUSSE Substitute white chocolate for the bittersweet chocolate, and substitute orange liqueur for the coffee liqueur.

CHOOSE A FROSTING

Rich Chocolate Buttercream

⏱ TOTAL: 30 MIN
MAKES 3 CUPS, ENOUGH FOR ONE
9-INCH 2-LAYER CAKE ● ●

These classic buttercream frostings are rich and luxurious. Douglas sometimes folds in whipped cream for a lighter touch.

- 1 cup sugar
- 3 large egg whites
- ¼ teaspoon salt
- ½ teaspoon pure vanilla extract
- 2 sticks plus 2 tablespoons (9 ounces) unsalted butter, cut into tablespoons, at room temperature
- 4 ounces extra-bittersweet chocolate, melted and cooled

1. In a blender or food processor, pulse the sugar until powdery. Transfer the sugar to a medium heatproof bowl and whisk in the egg whites and salt. Set the bowl over (not in) a saucepan of simmering water and whisk gently until the sugar is completely dissolved, about 5 minutes.

2. Transfer the warm egg-white mixture to the bowl of a standing electric mixer fitted with the whisk. Add the vanilla and beat at medium-high speed until stiff and glossy, about 8 minutes. Beat in the butter a few pieces at a time, making sure it is fully incorporated before adding more. The buttercream should be light and fluffy; if it appears runny at any time, transfer the bowl to the freezer for 5 to 10 minutes, then return it to the mixer and continue.

3. Beat in the melted chocolate until fully incorporated, scraping down the side and bottom of the bowl. Remove the bowl from the mixer and beat with a wooden spoon to remove any air bubbles.

HAZELNUT BUTTERCREAM Substitute 2 tablespoons hazelnut-praline paste (available online at *kingarthurflour.com*) for the extra-bittersweet chocolate.

WHITE CHOCOLATE BUTTERCREAM Substitute 4 ounces white chocolate for the extra-bittersweet chocolate.

dark chocolate mousse

milk chocolate mousse

white chocolate mousse

rich chocolate buttercream

hazelnut buttercream

white chocolate buttercream

Cornmeal-Almond Cake with Strawberries and Mascarpone

ACTIVE: 30 MIN; TOTAL: 1 HR 45 MIN
MAKES ONE 9-INCH CAKE ● ●

CAKE

- 3 cups sliced blanched almonds
- ⅓ cup all-purpose flour
- 1 teaspoon baking powder
- ½ teaspoon salt
- 1 stick plus 2 tablespoons unsalted butter, softened
- 1 cup granulated sugar
- 1 teaspoon pure vanilla extract
- 3 large eggs, at room temperature
- Finely grated zest of 2 lemons
- 1 tablespoon fresh lemon juice
- 1 cup fine yellow cornmeal

TOPPING

- ¾ cup heavy cream
- ½ cup fresh mascarpone cheese
- 3 tablespoons confectioners' sugar
- 1 quart strawberries, thinly sliced

1. MAKE THE CAKE Preheat the oven to 350°. Butter and flour a 9-inch round cake pan. Spread the almonds on a large rimmed baking sheet and bake for 5 minutes, stirring once, until golden. Let cool completely, then transfer the almonds to a food processor and process until finely ground but not pasty.

2. In a medium bowl, sift together the flour, baking powder and salt. In a large bowl, using an electric mixer at medium speed, beat the butter with the granulated sugar and vanilla, scraping down the bowl, until light and fluffy, 2 minutes. Beat in the eggs 1 at a time, beating well between additions. Scrape down the bowl and beat until fluffy, 1 minute. Beat in the lemon zest and juice. With a rubber spatula, fold the flour mixture into the batter, then the cornmeal and the ground almonds.

3. Scrape the batter into the prepared pan and bake for 45 minutes, until a cake tester inserted in the center comes out with a few moist crumbs attached. Transfer to a wire rack. Let cool to room temperature.

4. MAKE THE TOPPING In a large stainless steel bowl, using an electric mixer, whip the cream to soft peaks. Add the mascarpone

cheese and confectioners' sugar and whip until barely firm peaks form.

5. Run a thin knife around the side of the cake pan and invert the cake onto the wire rack. Place a plate on top of the cake and turn the cake right side up. Cut the cake into wedges and serve with the mascarpone and strawberries. —*Mike Lata*

Orange-Scented Buttermilk Cake Loaves

ACTIVE: 20 MIN; TOTAL: 2 HR
MAKES THREE 8-BY-4-INCH LOAVES ● ●

- 3¼ cups cake flour, sifted
- 1 tablespoon baking powder
- ½ teaspoon baking soda
- 1 teaspoon salt
- ½ teaspoon cinnamon
- 2 sticks unsalted butter, softened
- 2 cups granulated sugar
- 1½ teaspoons finely grated orange zest
- 4 large eggs, at room temperature
- ½ cup sour cream, at room temperature
- 1½ teaspoons pure vanilla extract
- 1¼ cups buttermilk, at room temperature
- Confectioners' sugar, for dusting

1. Preheat the oven to 350°. Spray three 8-by-4-inch loaf pans with cooking spray, dust with flour and set on a baking sheet.

2. In a medium bowl, whisk the flour, baking powder, baking soda, salt and cinnamon. In a stand mixer fitted with the paddle, beat the butter, granulated sugar and orange zest at medium-high speed until fluffy, 4 minutes. Add the eggs 1 at a time, beating well between additions and scraping down the bowl. Beat in the sour cream and vanilla. At low speed, beat in the dry ingredients in 3 additions, alternating with the buttermilk and beginning and ending with the dry ingredients; gently fold just until blended.

3. Scrape the batter into the pans; smooth the tops. Gently tap once to release any air. Bake for 45 minutes; rotate the baking sheet halfway through, until a cake tester comes out with a few moist crumbs attached.

4. Transfer the loaves to a rack for 20 minutes, then turn them out onto the rack and set them right side up to cool. Dust with confectioners' sugar, slice and serve.
—*John Adler*

Buttermilk Cake with Blackberries

📷 **PAGE 339**
ACTIVE: 20 MIN; TOTAL: 1 HR 15 MIN
MAKES ONE 9-INCH CAKE ● ● ●

- 1 cup all-purpose flour
- ½ teaspoon baking powder
- ½ teaspoon baking soda
- ¼ teaspoon salt
- 4 tablespoons unsalted butter, softened
- ⅔ cup plus 1½ tablespoons sugar
- 1 large egg, at room temperature
- 1 teaspoon pure vanilla extract
- ½ cup buttermilk, at room temperature
- 1¼ cups blackberries, plus more for serving
- Sweetened whipped cream, for serving

1. Preheat the oven to 400°. Butter a 9-inch round cake pan and line the bottom with parchment paper. Butter the paper.

2. In a small bowl, whisk the flour, baking powder, baking soda and salt. In a large bowl, using a mixer, beat the butter with ⅔ cup of the sugar at medium-high speed until fluffy, 3 minutes. Beat in the egg and vanilla. At low speed, beat in the buttermilk and dry ingredients in 3 alternating batches, ending with the dry ingredients; do not overbeat. Gently fold the batter just until blended, then scrape into the pan and smooth the top.

3. Scatter the 1¼ cups of blackberries over the batter; lightly press them in. Sprinkle the remaining 1½ tablespoons of sugar over the cake. Bake for 30 minutes, until a cake tester inserted in the center comes out clean.

4. Transfer the cake to a rack to cool for 10 minutes. Turn out the cake and remove the paper. Turn the cake right side up and let cool completely. Serve with whipped cream and more blackberries.
—*Nico Monday and Amelia O'Reilly*

● HEALTHY ● MAKE AHEAD ○ VEGETARIAN ● STAFF FAVORITE

cornmeal-almond cake with strawberries and mascarpone

Reverse Marble Bundt Cake

TOTAL: 1 HR 45 MIN PLUS COOLING
MAKES ONE 10-INCH BUNDT CAKE ● ●

Not-too-sweet and pleasantly dense, this is a great cake for any time of day, whether for dessert or breakfast.

Nonstick cooking spray
2 teaspoons unsweetened Dutch-process cocoa powder, plus more for dusting
10 ounces dark chocolate (60 to 70 percent cacao), chopped
3¼ cups all-purpose flour
1½ teaspoons baking soda
1½ teaspoons baking powder
¾ teaspoon salt
2 sticks unsalted butter, slightly cool (not cold) and cut into chunks
1¾ cups granulated sugar
1 cup light brown sugar
4 large eggs
16 ounces full-fat Greek yogurt
1 teaspoon pure vanilla extract
¾ cup nutty granola without fruit
Confectioners' sugar, for dusting

1. Preheat the oven to 350°. Generously coat a 10-inch Bundt pan with nonstick cooking spray and dust it with cocoa powder.
2. In a large heatproof bowl set over a saucepan of simmering water, melt the chopped chocolate. Remove from the heat and whisk in the 2 teaspoons of cocoa powder.
3. Sift the flour, baking soda, baking powder and salt into a medium bowl. In the bowl of a standing electric mixer fitted with the paddle, beat the butter at medium speed until very smooth. Add both sugars and beat until fluffy, 2 minutes. Scrape down the bowl and beat for 10 seconds longer. Beat in the eggs, 1 at a time, then beat in the yogurt and vanilla. At low speed, beat in the dry ingredients in 3 batches, until just incorporated.
4. Scrape two-thirds of the batter into the chocolate and fold until no streaks remain (the batter will be very thick). Scrape half of the chocolate batter into the pan; smooth the surface. Dollop the vanilla batter into the pan and swirl with a knife. Scrape the remaining

chocolate batter into the pan and swirl a few more times. Sprinkle the granola on top and lightly press it onto the batter.
5. Bake the cake in the center of the oven for 55 to 60 minutes, until a toothpick inserted in the center comes out clean. Let cool on a wire rack for at least 45 minutes. Invert the cake onto a plate and let cool. Dust with confectioners' sugar and serve.
—*Matt Lewis*

Red-Velvet Cake Balls with White Chocolate

ACTIVE: 1 HR 30 MIN; TOTAL: 2 HR 30 MIN
MAKES 40 CAKE BALLS ● ○

Dipped in white chocolate, these red-velvet cake balls are perfect for turning into eyeballs on Halloween. With a steady hand and food coloring, L.A. chef David Burtka paints detailed irises and pupils on each one; for the less artistically inclined, an M&M pressed into the white chocolate before it sets makes for a quick-and-easy creepy alternative.

CAKE
4 tablespoons unsalted butter, melted, plus more for the pan
1¼ cups all-purpose flour, plus more for the pan
¾ cup granulated sugar
1 tablespoon unsweetened cocoa powder
½ teaspoon baking soda
¼ teaspoon salt
1 large egg
¼ cup vegetable oil
½ teaspoon cider vinegar
¼ cup buttermilk
¼ cup sour cream
½ teaspoon pure vanilla extract
1 tablespoon liquid red food coloring
BINDING AND COATING
4½ tablespoons unsalted butter, softened
1½ cups confectioners' sugar
2 teaspoons milk
¾ teaspoon pure vanilla extract
9 ounces white chocolate
Assorted liquid food coloring or M&M's, for decorating

1. MAKE THE CAKE Preheat the oven to 350° and butter and flour a 9-inch round cake pan. In a large bowl, whisk the 1¼ cups of flour with the granulated sugar, cocoa powder, baking soda and salt. In another bowl, whisk the egg with the 4 tablespoons of melted butter and the vegetable oil, cider vinegar, buttermilk, sour cream, vanilla and red food coloring. Stir the wet ingredients into the dry ingredients until moistened.
2. Scrape the batter into the prepared cake pan and bake in the center of the oven for about 35 minutes, until a toothpick inserted in the center of the cake comes out clean. Let the cake cool in the pan for about 10 minutes, then invert it onto a rack and let cool completely.
3. MAKE THE BINDING AND COATING Line a baking sheet with wax paper. In a large bowl, using a handheld electric mixer, beat the softened butter with the confectioners' sugar, milk and vanilla until smooth. Finely crumble the cooled cake into the bowl and stir until combined.
4. Using your hands, briefly knead the mixture. Using a 1-tablespoon ice cream scoop, scoop 40 mounds onto the prepared baking sheet. Using your hands, press and roll the mounds into tight balls. Refrigerate the cake balls until they are firm.
5. In a large microwave-safe bowl, heat the white chocolate at high power in 30-second intervals until nearly melted; stir until smooth. Line another baking sheet with wax paper. Dip the cake balls into the melted white chocolate, allowing the excess to drip back into the bowl, and transfer the coated cake balls to the prepared baking sheet. Let cool until the coating has set. Using a clean, fine-tipped paintbrush, decorate the cake balls with food coloring to look like eyeballs, or press an M&M onto each cake ball before the coating has set. Serve.
—*David Burtka*

VARIATION To make red-velvet cake pops, insert lollipop sticks into the finished cake balls for easy eating.

MAKE AHEAD The finished cake balls can be refrigerated in an airtight container for up to 3 days.

Tunnel of Fudge Cake with Hazelnuts

ACTIVE: 40 MIN; TOTAL: 2 HR PLUS
2 HR COOLING • MAKES ONE 10-INCH
BUNDT CAKE ● ○

Matt Lewis, a Bundt cake–obsessed baker and co-owner of Baked in Brooklyn, New York, elevates this classic American cake (which gets its name from its gooey chocolate center) by adding toasted hazelnuts to the batter and using a high-quality cocoa like Valrhona or Callebaut.

Nonstick cooking spray
¾ cup unsweetened high-quality Dutch-process cocoa powder, plus more for dusting
2 cups hazelnuts (9½ ounces)
2 cups all-purpose flour
1 teaspoon salt
2 cups confectioners' sugar, plus more for dusting
2½ sticks unsalted butter, cut into ½-inch dice and softened
1 cup granulated sugar
¾ cup packed dark brown sugar
3 large eggs
3 large egg yolks
¼ cup vegetable oil
1 tablespoon pure vanilla extract

1. Preheat the oven to 350°. Generously coat a 10-inch Bundt pan with nonstick cooking spray and dust it with cocoa powder.
2. Spread the hazelnuts on a rimmed baking sheet and toast for about 10 minutes, until golden and fragrant. Transfer the hazelnuts to a kitchen towel and let cool slightly, then rub off the skins. Let cool completely. In the bowl of a food processor, pulse the hazelnuts until they are very finely chopped and slightly powdery, then transfer to a medium bowl and whisk in the flour and salt.
3. Sift the 2 cups of confectioners' sugar into another medium bowl with the ¾ cup of cocoa powder. In a standing mixer fitted with the paddle, beat the butter with the granulated sugar and brown sugar at medium speed until fluffy, about 2 minutes. Scrape down the side of the bowl. Reduce the speed to low and beat in the whole eggs and egg yolks, 1 at a time, until just incorporated. Add the vegetable oil and vanilla extract and beat until the batter is uniform in color, about 1 minute. Add the cocoa mixture and beat until incorporated. Using a spatula, gently fold in the hazelnut mixture until no streaks remain.
4. Scrape the batter into the prepared pan, smoothing the top. Bake the cake in the middle of the oven for 40 to 45 minutes, until it starts to pull away from the side of the pan and the top just springs back when you touch it; the center should still be soft. Let the cake cool on a rack for at least 2 hours; it might crack and sink slightly. Invert the cake onto a plate and dust with confectioners' sugar. Cut the cake into wedges and serve.
—Matt Lewis

Vegan Chocolate Cupcakes with Chocolate Frosting

TOTAL: 1 HR 15 MIN PLUS 2 HR CHILLING
MAKES 16 CUPCAKES ● ○

Pureed avocado and coconut oil are the secrets to making these deep-chocolate vegan cupcakes so moist and rich.

FROSTING
2 tablespoons kuzu root starch (see Note)
¾ cup organic coconut milk
1 tablespoon agar powder (see Note)
¾ cup filtered water
1½ cups Grade B pure maple syrup
¾ cup unsweetened cocoa powder
¼ teaspoon fine sea salt
One 10-ounce bag vegan chocolate chips
3 tablespoons coconut oil
2 teaspoons pure vanilla extract
CUPCAKES
1½ cups white spelt flour (see Note)
1 teaspoon baking powder
¾ teaspoon baking soda
¾ teaspoon fine sea salt
1 cup ½-inch diced ripe Hass avocado
¾ cup unsweetened cocoa powder
¾ cup organic coconut milk
1 cup Grade B pure maple syrup
⅓ cup coconut oil
2 teaspoons pure vanilla extract

1. MAKE THE FROSTING In a small bowl, stir the kuzu root starch into the coconut milk until dissolved. In a medium saucepan, whisk the agar into the filtered water and bring to a boil. Simmer over moderately low heat, whisking occasionally, until very thick, 4 minutes. Whisk in the maple syrup, cocoa powder and salt until fully combined. Return to a boil, whisking constantly. Add the kuzu–coconut milk mixture and whisk until smooth. Simmer over moderately low heat, stirring constantly, until very thick and pudding-like, about 5 minutes. Remove the saucepan from the heat and whisk in the chocolate chips, coconut oil and vanilla until the frosting is smooth and glossy. Pour into a glass bowl and let cool to room temperature. Cover with plastic wrap and refrigerate until firm, at least 2 hours or overnight.
2. MEANWHILE, MAKE THE CUPCAKES Preheat the oven to 350° and line 16 muffin cups with paper liners. In a large bowl, sift the spelt flour with the baking powder, baking soda and salt.
3. In a food processor, puree the avocado until smooth. In a medium saucepan, whisk the cocoa powder into the coconut milk and cook over moderate heat, whisking constantly, until just beginning to bubble, about 2 minutes. Immediately add the cocoa mixture to the food processor along with the maple syrup, coconut oil and vanilla. Puree until smooth, scraping down the side of the bowl once or twice.
4. Scrape the chocolate mixture into the dry ingredients in the large bowl and whisk just until combined. Scoop the batter into the lined muffin cups, filling them about two-thirds full. Bake in the center of the oven for about 25 minutes, until a toothpick inserted in the center comes out clean. Let the cupcakes cool in the pans for 15 minutes, then transfer them to a rack to cool completely.
5. Scrape the frosting into a food processor and process until smooth and spreadable. Frost the cupcakes and serve.
—Sera Pelle

NOTE Kuzu root starch, agar powder and white spelt flour are available at well-stocked health-food stores and online at amazon.com.

Seven-Layer Dobos Torte

ACTIVE: 2 HR; TOTAL: 4 HR 30 MIN
12 SERVINGS ● ●

CAKE

Vegetable oil spray
8 large eggs, separated, plus 3 large egg yolks
1 pound confectioners' sugar (4 cups), plus more for dusting
1 vanilla bean, split and seeds scraped
½ teaspoon salt
1 cup all-purpose flour
2 tablespoons milk

BUTTERCREAM

5 ounces bittersweet chocolate, chopped
3 large egg yolks
¼ cup granulated sugar
Pinch of salt
1 cup half-and-half
2 tablespoons unsweetened cocoa powder
5 sticks (1¼ pounds) unsalted butter, cut into tablespoons, softened

MERINGUE

1 cup granulated sugar
3 large egg whites
Pinch of salt

1. **MAKE THE CAKE** Preheat the oven to 350° and position racks in the lower and middle thirds. Spray two 12-by-17-inch baking pans with vegetable oil spray and line the bottoms with parchment paper. Spray the parchment.

2. Put the 8 egg whites in the bowl of a standing electric mixer fitted with the whisk attachment. Add 2 cups of the confectioners' sugar along with the vanilla seeds and salt and beat at medium-high speed until the whites are stiff and glossy, 5 minutes. Scrape the meringue into a medium bowl.

3. Clean the mixing bowl and add the 11 egg yolks along with the remaining 2 cups of confectioners' sugar, the flour and the milk. Beat at medium speed until smooth, about 3 minutes. Beat in one-fourth of the beaten eggs whites to lighten the batter. Using a rubber spatula, fold in the remaining egg whites until no streaks remain.

4. Spread the batter evenly in the prepared baking pans (about 5 cups for each). Bake the cakes for 12 to 15 minutes, until they are golden and set; shift the pans from top to bottom and front to back halfway through baking. Transfer to racks to cool.

5. **MAKE THE BUTTERCREAM** Put the chopped chocolate in a medium bowl. In another medium bowl, whisk the 3 egg yolks with the granulated sugar and salt until pale, 2 minutes. In a medium saucepan, heat the half-and-half with the cocoa powder until hot. Whisk the hot liquid into the yolks, then scrape the mixture back into the saucepan. Cook the mixture over moderate heat, whisking constantly, until it is slightly thickened and an instant read thermometer registers 160°, 4 minutes. Strain over the chopped chocolate and let stand until melted. Whisk until smooth, then let cool completely.

6. In a mixing bowl fitted with the whisk, beat the butter until creamy. Scrape the chocolate mixture into the butter and beat until smooth and creamy.

7. Lightly dust the cakes with confectioners' sugar and top with a sheet of wax paper. Invert the cakes onto a work surface and carefully peel off the parchment paper. Cut each layer crosswise into four 12-by-4¼-inch strips. Spread 6 layers with ½ cup of buttercream each and stack them on a rectangular cake cardboard or cake plate. Top with a seventh layer (save the eighth layer for a snack). Frost the top and sides with the remaining buttercream and refrigerate the cake until it is well chilled, at least 2 hours or preferably overnight.

8. **MAKE THE MERINGUE** In a small saucepan, combine the granulated sugar with ½ cup of water; bring to a boil, washing down the side of the pan with a moistened pastry brush. Boil the syrup until it registers 240° on an instant-read thermometer. Meanwhile, in a clean standing mixer bowl, beat the egg whites with the salt until soft peaks form. Beating at medium speed, slowly drizzle in the hot syrup and beat until incorporated, then beat at high speed until the meringue is stiff and glossy and the side of the bowl is no longer warm, about 7 minutes.

9. Spread a thin layer of the meringue all over the cake, then use the remaining meringue to form decorative swirls on the cake. Using a brulée torch, brown the meringue all over. Refrigerate the cake for at least 1 hour before serving. —*Matt Danko*

MAKE AHEAD The torte can be prepared through Step 7 and refrigerated for 3 days.

Mini Cassata Cakes

🕐 **TOTAL: 30 MIN • 6 SERVINGS** ●

1 cup fresh ricotta
2 tablespoons confectioners' sugar
1 tablespoon amaretto liqueur
2 ounces bittersweet chocolate, finely chopped
2 tablespoons finely chopped candied orange peel (see Note)
3 tablespoons granulated sugar
One 16-ounce pound cake, sliced ½ inch thick and cut into twelve 2½-inch rounds with a cookie cutter
1 tablespoon unsalted butter
Finely grated orange zest, for garnish

1. In a mini food processor, combine the ricotta with the confectioners' sugar and amaretto and puree until very smooth. Add half of the chocolate and candied orange peel and pulse just to combine.

2. Spread the granulated sugar on a small plate. Lightly press both sides of each pound cake round into the sugar to coat, tapping off the excess sugar. In a large nonstick skillet, melt half of the butter. Add the sugared pound cake rounds in 2 batches, using the remaining butter, and cook them over moderate heat, turning once, until the rounds are golden and the sugar is caramelized, about 1 minute per side. Transfer the rounds to a rack to cool slightly.

3. Place 6 rounds on plates and top with half of the ricotta mixture. Top with the remaining rounds and ricotta mixture. Sprinkle the remaining chocolate and candied orange peel on top and garnish with orange zest. —*Grace Parisi*

NOTE Candied orange peel is available at candy shops and specialty food stores.

● HEALTHY ● MAKE AHEAD ○ VEGETARIAN ● STAFF FAVORITE

Sacher Torte

ACTIVE: 1 HR; TOTAL: 2 HR PLUS COOLING
10 TO 12 SERVINGS ● ○ ○

CAKE

- 6 large eggs, separated
- 1 cup all-purpose flour
- ½ cup almond flour or 2 ounces blanched almonds (⅓ cup), ground
- ¼ teaspoon salt
- 1½ sticks unsalted butter, softened
- 1 cup sugar
- 5 ounces bittersweet chocolate, melted and cooled slightly

FILLING AND GLAZE

- 1¾ cups apricot preserves
- ⅔ cup light corn syrup
- 2 tablespoons rum
- 10 ounces bittersweet chocolate, chopped

Unsweetened whipped cream, for serving (optional)

1. MAKE THE CAKE Preheat the oven to 375°. Butter a 9-inch springform pan. Line the bottom of the pan with parchment paper, and butter the paper. Dust the pan with flour, tapping out the excess.

2. In a large bowl, using a handheld electric mixer, whip the egg whites at high speed until soft peaks form.

3. In a small bowl, whisk the all-purpose flour with the almond flour and salt. In another large bowl, beat the butter and sugar until fluffy. Add the egg yolks 1 at a time, and beat until fluffy. Beat in the melted chocolate, then beat in one-fourth of the whipped egg whites. Using a spatula, fold in the rest of the whites until no streaks remain.

4. Scrape the batter into the prepared pan and smooth the top. Bake the cake in the center of the oven for 35 to 40 minutes, until a toothpick inserted in the center comes out with a few moist crumbs attached. Let the cake cool on a wire rack for 30 minutes, then remove the ring and let the cake cool completely. Invert the cake onto a plate and peel off the parchment. Turn the cake right side up. Using a long serrated knife, cut the cake horizontally into 3 even layers.

5. MAKE THE FILLING AND GLAZE In a small microwave-safe bowl, whisk ¼ cup plus 2 tablespoons of the apricot preserves with ¼ cup of water and microwave until melted.

6. Set the bottom of the springform pan on a wire rack and then set the rack on a baking sheet. Arrange the top cake layer, cut side up, on the springform pan. Brush the cake with one-third of the melted apricot preserves. Spread ½ cup of the unmelted apricot preserves on top and cover with the middle cake layer. Brush the surface with another third of the melted preserves and spread another ½ cup of the unmelted preserves on top. Brush the cut side of the final layer with the remaining melted preserves and set it cut side down on the cake. Using a serrated knife, trim the cake edges if necessary to even them out.

7. In the microwave-safe bowl, microwave the remaining ¼ cup plus 2 tablespoons of the apricot preserves until melted, about 30 seconds. Press the preserves through a strainer to remove the solids. Brush the preserves all over the cake until completely coated. Refrigerate for 20 minutes, until set.

8. Meanwhile, in a medium saucepan, whisk the corn syrup with the rum and 2 tablespoons of water and bring to a boil. Cook until slightly thickened, about 1 minute. Put the chopped chocolate into a heatproof bowl and pour the hot mixture on top. Let stand until melted, then whisk until smooth. If the chocolate glaze is too thick to pour, whisk in another tablespoon of hot water. Let the glaze cool to warm.

9. Using an offset spatula, scrape off any excess preserves from the cake so that it is lightly coated. Slowly pour half of the warm chocolate glaze in the center of the cake, allowing it to gently coat the top and spread down the side. Spread the glaze to evenly coat the torte. Microwave the remaining glaze for a few seconds and repeat pouring and spreading. Scrape up any excess glaze. Refrigerate for at least 10 minutes to set the glaze, then cut the torte into wedges and serve with whipped cream. —*Lidia Bastianich*

MAKE AHEAD The torte can be covered and refrigerated for up to 2 days.

Double-Chocolate Layer Cake

ACTIVE: 40 MIN; TOTAL: 1 HR 45 MIN
MAKES TWO 9-INCH LAYERS ● ○ ○

- 2 cups plus 2 tablespoons all-purpose flour
- ¼ cup plus 2 tablespoons unsweetened cocoa powder

Unsalted butter, for greasing the pans

- 1 cup plus 1 tablespoon granulated sugar
- ½ teaspoon baking powder
- ½ teaspoon baking soda
- ½ teaspoon salt
- 2 large eggs, at room temperature
- ⅓ cup dark brown sugar
- 1 cup canola oil
- 2½ ounces bittersweet chocolate, melted
- 1 cup buttermilk
- 2 teaspoons pure vanilla extract

Mousse filling and buttercream frosting (page 343)

1. Preheat the oven to 350°. In a small bowl, whisk together 2 tablespoons each of the flour and cocoa powder. Butter two 9-inch round cake pans and line the bottoms with parchment paper. Butter the paper and dust the pans with the cocoa-flour mixture, tapping out the excess.

2. In a medium bowl, whisk the 2 cups of flour and ¼ cup of cocoa powder with ½ cup of the granulated sugar and the baking powder, baking soda and salt.

3. In the bowl of a standing electric mixer fitted with the whisk, beat the eggs with the brown sugar and the remaining ½ cup plus 1 tablespoon of granulated sugar at medium-high speed until thickened, about 5 minutes. At medium speed, gradually add ½ cup of the oil and beat for 3 minutes. Beat in the melted chocolate, then add the remaining oil in a thin stream until thoroughly blended, scraping the side and bottom of the bowl. At low speed, beat in the buttermilk and vanilla. Remove the bowl from the mixer and gently mix in the dry ingredients by hand.

4. Pour the cake batter into the prepared pans and bake in the center of the oven for about 25 minutes, until a toothpick inserted in the centers of the cakes comes out with a few moist crumbs attached. Cool the cakes in the pans for 20 minutes, then invert them onto a rack to cool completely. Peel off the parchment paper, then fill and frost the cake. —*Tom Douglas*

Icebox Chocolate Cheesecake

TOTAL: 30 MIN PLUS OVERNIGHT CHILLING • 8 TO 10 SERVINGS ● ● ●

This insanely easy recipe—a delicious and brilliant shortcut to chocolate cheesecake—uses only three ingredients.

70 Nabisco Famous Chocolate Wafers (from 2 packages)
Three 8-ounce packages cream cheese, at room temperature
 1 cup chocolate syrup, such as Hershey's

1. Put 20 of the chocolate cookies (reserving 50 whole cookies) into a zippered plastic bag and, using a rolling pin, crush them to fine crumbs. Line an 8-inch round cake pan with enough plastic wrap to extend by 4 inches all around.
2. In a large bowl, using an electric mixer, beat the cream cheese at high speed until fluffy, about 3 minutes. Beat in the chocolate syrup and ¼ cup of water and beat the chocolate cream for 2 minutes.
3. Arrange 9 cookies in an overlapping ring on the bottom of the prepared cake pan and place 1 cookie in the center. Spoon one-fourth of the chocolate cream (about 1¼ cups) over the cookies, being careful not to disturb them. Repeat with the remaining cookies and chocolate cream, ending with a layer of 10 cookies on top. Fold the plastic wrap over the top of the cake. Lightly tap the pan once or twice on a work surface. Refrigerate the cake for at least 8 hours and preferably overnight.
4. Peel back the plastic wrap and invert the cake onto a serving plate. Carefully peel off the plastic wrap. Press the cookie crumbs onto the side of the cake to coat evenly. Cut the cake into wedges and serve.
—*Grace Parisi*

Milk Chocolate and Earl Grey Budino

ACTIVE: 20 MIN; TOTAL: 1 HR 30 MIN
6 SERVINGS ● ● ●

Budino is the Italian word for "pudding." The luxe version here calls for creamy milk chocolate and whipped cream infused with bergamot-scented Earl Grey tea.

 3 ounces milk chocolate, coarsely chopped, plus more for garnish
 1 tablespoon unsalted butter
 3 tablespoons cornstarch
 1 tablespoon unsweetened cocoa powder
⅓ cup granulated sugar
 2 teaspoons Earl Grey tea leaves
 2 cups whole milk
¾ cup heavy cream
 2 teaspoons confectioners' sugar
Chopped candied orange peel (optional) and coarse sea salt, for garnish

1. In a medium heatproof bowl, combine the 3 ounces of chopped milk chocolate with the butter. Sift the cornstarch and cocoa powder into a medium saucepan, then whisk in the granulated sugar and 1½ teaspoons of the tea leaves. Whisk in the milk. Bring to a boil over moderate heat and cook, whisking constantly, for about 2 minutes, until very thick. Strain through a fine-mesh sieve over the chocolate. Let stand for 30 seconds, then whisk until smooth. Spoon the pudding mixture into six 1-cup ramekins. Press plastic wrap directly on the surface of the puddings. Let the puddings cool, then refrigerate until chilled, at least 1 hour.
2. In a mortar or spice grinder, pulverize the remaining ½ teaspoon of tea. In a bowl, whip the cream with the confectioners' sugar to soft peaks. Sift in the powdered tea and whip the cream until firm. Top the puddings with the whipped cream. Garnish with chopped chocolate, candied orange peel and a small pinch of sea salt and serve.
—*Matthew Accarrino*

MAKE AHEAD The milk chocolate *budinos* can be covered with plastic wrap and refrigerated for up to 2 days.

Warm Chocolate Budino

ACTIVE: 20 MIN; TOTAL: 1 HR 30 MIN
8 SERVINGS ● ● ●

Lighter than a flourless chocolate cake, this steamed bittersweet chocolate pudding is still decadent and intensely chocolaty.

½ cup all-purpose flour
½ teaspoon kosher salt
¼ teaspoon baking powder
 9 ounces bittersweet chocolate
1½ sticks (6 ounces) unsalted butter
 2 tablespoons extra-virgin olive oil, plus more for drizzling
⅓ cup sugar
 4 large eggs, lightly beaten
Hot water
Salted roasted almonds and vanilla ice cream, for serving

1. Preheat the oven to 350° and butter and flour an 8-inch round cake pan. Line the bottom with parchment paper and then butter and flour the paper.
2. In a small bowl, whisk the flour with the salt and baking powder. Chop the chocolate and, in a large microwave-safe bowl, heat it with the butter at high power in 30-second intervals until the chocolate is melted. Whisk in the 2 tablespoons of olive oil and the sugar. Add the lightly beaten eggs and whisk until smooth. Whisk in the dry ingredients until evenly combined. Pour the batter into the prepared cake pan.
3. Set the cake pan in a small roasting pan. Transfer the roasting pan to the center of the oven. Carefully pour enough hot water into the roasting pan to reach one-third of the way up the side of the cake pan. Bake for about 40 minutes, until the *budino* is firm to the touch and a toothpick inserted in the center comes out with a few moist crumbs attached. Transfer the cake pan to a rack and let cool for 30 minutes.
4. Run a knife around the *budino* and invert it onto a plate. Peel off the parchment paper and invert the *budino* again. Cut into wedges and serve with roasted almonds and vanilla ice cream drizzled with olive oil.
—*Jennifer Archer*

Beet Cake with Bourbon Sauce

ACTIVE: 30 MIN; TOTAL: 1 HR 30 MIN

6 SERVINGS ● ●

CAKE

   3 medium beets, boiled

1¼ cups all-purpose flour

   1 teaspoon baking powder

  ½ teaspoon baking soda

  ½ teaspoon salt

   3 large eggs, at room temperature

  ¾ cup sugar

  ½ cup vegetable oil

Finely grated zest of 1 lemon

CUSTARD

   3 large egg yolks

  ½ cup sugar

  ¾ cup milk, warmed

  ¾ cup heavy cream, warmed

   3 tablespoons bourbon or whiskey

Sweetened whipped cream, for serving

1. MAKE THE CAKE Peel and chop 2 of the beets, then puree them in a mini food processor. Peel and shred the remaining beet.
2. Preheat the oven to 350°. Butter a 10-by-15-inch jelly roll pan and line it with parchment paper. In a small bowl, whisk the flour, baking powder, baking soda and salt. In a large mixing bowl, beat the eggs with the sugar at high speed until tripled in volume, about 5 minutes. Beat in the vegetable oil and lemon zest. Fold in the pureed and shredded beets, then gradually fold in the dry ingredients. Spread the batter in the prepared pan, smoothing the top. Bake the cake for about 20 minutes, until a toothpick inserted in the center comes out clean.
3. MAKE THE CUSTARD Bring 1 inch of water to a boil in a saucepan. In a stainless steel bowl, whisk the egg yolks with the sugar until thickened. Whisk in the warm milk and cream. Set the bowl over (not in) the simmering water and whisk over moderate heat until the custard is very thick, about 8 minutes. Chill the custard in an ice bath, then stir in the bourbon.
4. Cut the cake into squares and layer with the custard. Top with whipped cream; serve.
—*Michel Nischan*

Brown Butter–Chocolate Chip Cookies

ACTIVE: 30 MIN; TOTAL: 1 HR 30 MIN

PLUS OVERNIGHT CHILLING

MAKES 18 LARGE COOKIES ● ●

Lori Baker, the pastry chef at San Francisco's Baker & Banker, gives classic chocolate chip cookies a delightful tweak by browning the butter for the dough to add a hint of nuttiness. The dough will need to sit overnight in the refrigerator, so plan accordingly.

   2 sticks unsalted butter

2¼ cups all-purpose flour

   1 teaspoon kosher salt

   1 teaspoon baking soda

  ½ cup granulated sugar

   1 cup light brown sugar

   1 large egg, lightly beaten

   1 large egg yolk

   2 tablespoons milk

1½ teaspoons pure vanilla extract

   2 cups semisweet or bittersweet chocolate, coarsely chopped

1. In a medium saucepan, cook the butter over moderate heat until it is browned and nutty-smelling, about 5 minutes. Transfer the browned butter to a small bowl and let it cool to room temperature.
2. In a medium bowl, whisk together the flour, salt and baking soda. In the bowl of a standing mixer fitted with the paddle attachment, beat the cooled browned butter with the granulated and light brown sugars at medium speed until light and fluffy, scraping down the bowl halfway through, about 7 minutes. Beat in the whole egg, egg yolk, milk and vanilla extract. At low speed, beat in the dry ingredients, scraping down the bowl as needed. Mix in the chopped chocolate. Cover the bowl with plastic wrap and refrigerate the cookie dough overnight.
3. Preheat the oven to 375°. Line 3 large baking sheets with parchment paper. Scoop ¼-cup mounds of cookie dough onto each baking sheet. There should be 6 cookies per sheet. Bake one sheet at a time for about 18 minutes, until the cookies are just firm and golden brown on the bottom. Transfer the

sheet to a rack to cool. Repeat to bake the remaining cookies. Serve the cookies warm or at room temperature. —*Lori Baker*
MAKE AHEAD The cookies can be stored in an airtight container for up to 2 days or frozen for up to 1 month.

Chocolate Peanut Butter– Granola Cookies

ACTIVE: 15 MIN; TOTAL: 1 HR

MAKES 1 DOZEN 3-INCH COOKIES ● ●

For these crumbly cookies, F&W's Grace Parisi grinds granola to use in place of flour, then adds whole pieces of granola to the dough for crunch.

   2 cups granola with nuts and dried fruit (see Note)

   1 cup chocolate peanut butter (see Note)

   1 large egg

Pinch of salt

1. Preheat the oven to 350° and line 2 baking sheets with parchment paper. Pick out the dried fruit from 1 cup of the granola and add the fruit to the remaining granola. Transfer the fruit-free granola to a food processor and pulse until finely ground; transfer to a medium bowl. Add the peanut butter, egg and salt. Using an electric mixer, beat the mixture at low speed until smooth, then add the remaining fruit-filled granola. Beat the cookie dough just until combined.
2. Form the cookie dough into 12 balls and arrange them on the prepared baking sheets. Flatten the balls with the tines of a fork to 3-inch rounds. Bake one sheet at a time in the center of the oven for about 15 minutes, until the cookies are lightly browned around the edges. Let the cookies cool completely on the baking sheets before serving.
—*Grace Parisi*
NOTE Look for nut-and-fruit-loaded granola, like those from Viktoria's Gourmet Foods (*vikisgourmet.com*), and either white or dark chocolate peanut butter from Peanut Butter & Co. (*ilovepeanutbutter.com*).
MAKE AHEAD The cookies can be stored in an airtight container for up to 3 days.

chocolate peanut butter–granola cookies

Lebkuchen (Spice Cookies)

TOTAL: 1 HR PLUS 4 HR FREEZING
MAKES ABOUT 3 DOZEN COOKIES ● ●

COOKIES

1½ cups blanched whole almonds
 2 cups all-purpose flour, sifted
1¾ teaspoons baking powder
 2 teaspoons cinnamon
1½ teaspoons ground ginger
 1 teaspoon ground cloves
 1 teaspoon ground allspice
 1 teaspoon fine salt
Pinch of freshly grated nutmeg
1½ cups light brown sugar
 ½ cup sweet orange marmalade
 ¼ cup finely chopped candied ginger
     (1 ounce)
 ¼ cup unsulfured molasses
 5 large eggs

ICING

 3 cups plus 2 tablespoons
     confectioners' sugar
 ¼ cup whole milk
 3 tablespoons unsalted butter,
     softened

1. MAKE THE COOKIES Preheat the oven to 350°. Spread the almonds on a rimmed baking sheet and toast for about 10 minutes, until fragrant and lightly golden. Let cool completely. In a medium bowl, whisk the flour with the baking powder, cinnamon, ginger, cloves, allspice, salt and nutmeg.
2. Transfer the cooled toasted almonds to a food processor and pulse until coarsely chopped. Add the brown sugar and pulse until incorporated. Add the marmalade, candied ginger and molasses and pulse until the mixture is well blended and the nuts are finely chopped. Add the eggs all at once and pulse until just incorporated. Add the dry ingredients and pulse until incorporated and the batter is uniform in color. Scrape the soft batter into a bowl, cover and freeze until very firm, at least 4 hours.
3. Preheat the oven to 350° and line 2 large baking sheets with parchment paper. Using a 2-tablespoon ice cream scoop, scoop 8 level mounds onto each baking sheet, about

3 inches apart. Freeze the remaining batter between batches. Bake the cookies in the upper and lower thirds of the oven for about 20 minutes, until risen and slightly firm; shift the pans from top to bottom and front to back halfway through. Transfer the sheets to racks and let the cookies and pans cool completely. Repeat with the remaining batter.
4. MAKE THE ICING In a bowl, whisk the confectioners' sugar with the milk and butter. Spread the cookies with icing and let dry completely before serving.
—*Justin Chapple*

Chocolate Brownie Cookies

ACTIVE: 30 MIN; TOTAL: 2 HR 30 MIN
PLUS COOLING • MAKES ABOUT 3 DOZEN
COOKIES ● ● ●

 1 pound semisweet chocolate,
     chopped
 4 tablespoons unsalted butter
 4 large eggs, at room temperature
1½ cups sugar
 1 teaspoon pure vanilla extract
 ¼ teaspoon salt
 ½ cup all-purpose flour, sifted
 ½ teaspoon baking powder
One 12-ounce bag semisweet
     chocolate chips

1. In a large bowl set over a saucepan of simmering water, melt the chopped chocolate with the butter, stirring a few times, until smooth, about 7 minutes.
2. In another large bowl, using a handheld electric mixer, beat the eggs with the sugar at medium speed until thick and pale, about 5 minutes. Beat in the vanilla and salt. Using a rubber spatula, fold in the melted chocolate, then fold in the flour and baking powder. Stir in the chocolate chips. Scrape the batter into a shallow baking dish, cover and freeze until well chilled and firm, about 1 hour.
3. Preheat the oven to 350° and line 2 baking sheets with parchment paper. Working in batches, scoop 2-tablespoon-size mounds of dough onto the prepared baking sheets, about 2 inches apart. Bake for about 10 minutes, until the cookies are dry around the

edges and cracked on top. Let the cookies cool on the baking sheets for 10 minutes, then transfer them to a rack to cool completely before serving. —*Belinda Leong*

Walnut Snowball Cookies

ACTIVE: 30 MIN; TOTAL: 1 HR
MAKES ABOUT 3½ DOZEN COOKIES ● ●

1½ cups walnuts (6 ounces)
 2 sticks unsalted butter, at room
     temperature
 ½ vanilla bean, split and seeds scraped
 2 cups confectioners' sugar
 ¼ teaspoon salt
 2 cups all-purpose flour

1. Preheat the oven to 350° and line 2 large cookie sheets with parchment paper. Spread the walnuts on a rimmed baking sheet and bake for about 8 minutes, until golden brown. Let cool, then coarsely chop. Reduce the oven temperature to 325°.
2. In a standing mixer fitted with the paddle, beat the butter with the vanilla bean seeds at high speed until pale, about 2 minutes. Add 1 cup of the confectioners' sugar and beat at medium-high speed until light and fluffy, about 5 minutes, scraping down the side of the bowl with a rubber spatula halfway through. At low speed, mix in the salt, then gradually add the flour and walnuts and beat just until the cookie dough comes together, scraping down the side of the bowl halfway through.
3. Roll level tablespoons of the dough into balls and arrange them on the prepared cookie sheets. Bake the cookies in the upper and lower thirds of the oven for about 17 minutes, until they are lightly browned on the bottom; switch the sheets from top to bottom and front to back halfway through baking. Let the cookies firm up on the sheets for about 5 minutes, then transfer them to a rack to cool slightly.
4. Put the remaining 1 cup of confectioners' sugar in a small bowl. Roll the warm cookies in the sugar to coat and return to the rack to cool completely. Roll again in the sugar and serve. —*Yotam Ottolenghi*

● HEALTHY ● MAKE AHEAD ● VEGETARIAN ● STAFF FAVORITE

lebkuchen (spice cookies)

Chocolate-Mint Cookies

ACTIVE: 1 HR; TOTAL: 3 HR
MAKES 24 SANDWICH COOKIES ● ● ●

Marshmallow crème doctored with peppermint extract and confectioners' sugar makes a speedy filling for these cookies.

COOKIES

1¾ cups all-purpose flour
¼ cup black cocoa (see Note) or unsweetened cocoa powder
1 teaspoon baking soda
½ teaspoon baking powder
½ teaspoon salt
1½ sticks unsalted butter, softened
1 cup granulated sugar
2 ounces unsweetened chocolate, melted and cooled
1 large egg, lightly beaten
1 teaspoon pure vanilla extract

FILLING AND GLAZE

1 stick unsalted butter, softened
1 cup marshmallow crème
2½ cups confectioners' sugar
1 teaspoon pure peppermint extract
5 ounces bittersweet chocolate, chopped
5 ounces white chocolate, chopped
½ teaspoon canola oil

1. MAKE THE COOKIES Sift the flour into a medium bowl with the cocoa, baking soda, baking powder and salt. In a large bowl, using an electric mixer, beat the softened butter with the granulated sugar until creamy. Add the melted chocolate, egg and vanilla extract and beat until smooth. Beat in the dry ingredients until incorporated. Pat the dough into 4 disks, wrap in plastic and chill until firm, at least 20 minutes.

2. Preheat the oven to 375° and line 4 baking sheets with parchment paper. On a sheet of lightly floured parchment, roll out one disk of dough ¼ inch thick. Using a 2½- to 3-inch cookie cutter, stamp out as many cookies as possible; transfer to a baking sheet. Gather the scraps and roll out more cookies; if the dough gets too soft, refrigerate briefly. Chill the cut cookies for 5 minutes. Repeat with the remaining 3 disks of dough.

3. Working in batches, bake the cookies in the middle and lower thirds of the oven until puffed, 12 minutes; shift the pans halfway through baking. Transfer to racks to cool.

4. MAKE THE FILLING AND GLAZE In a large bowl, using a handheld electric mixer, beat the softened butter with the marshmallow crème and confectioners' sugar until fluffy. Beat in the peppermint extract.

5. Pipe or spread the peppermint filling onto the underside of half of the cookies. Top with the remaining cookies, pressing to spread the filling to the edges. Refrigerate the cookies for 20 minutes, or until the filling is set.

6. Put the bittersweet and white chocolates in 2 separate microwave-safe bowls. Microwave at high power in 30-second bursts until melted. Stir ¼ teaspoon of the oil into each.

7. Drizzle the melted chocolate over the cookies or dip them in the bittersweet chocolate or white chocolate (or both); return the cookies to a sheet of parchment paper and refrigerate until set, about 20 minutes, then serve. —*Grace Parisi*

NOTE Black cocoa, a very dark Dutch-process cocoa, is available at *kingarthurflour.com*.

Chocolate-Toffee-Dipped Shortbread Bars

⏱ **TOTAL: 20 MIN • 8 SERVINGS** ● ●

Dessert doesn't get much easier than store-bought shortbread cookie bars dipped in melted bittersweet chocolate and topped with chopped almonds and toffee. The key to success: using high-quality ingredients.

4 ounces bittersweet chocolate, finely chopped
8 shortbread fingers (about 4 inches long)
¼ cup chopped English toffee or Heath bars
¼ cup chopped salted almonds

1. Line a baking sheet with wax paper. In a microwave-safe bowl, heat the chocolate at high power in 45-second bursts until nearly melted; stir until completely melted. Dip two-thirds of each shortbread finger in the chocolate and transfer to the baking sheet.

2. In a small bowl, mix the English toffee and almonds. Sprinkle the mixture over the chocolate. Refrigerate the shortbread bars just until set, about 10 minutes. —*Grace Parisi*

Cocoa-Pepper Waffle Cookies

TOTAL: 1 HR • MAKES ABOUT 20 COOKIES
● ● ●

"I love making cookies without an oven," says blogger and cookbook author Joy Wilson. Because these are not too sweet, she calls them "breakfast meets cookies."

1 stick unsalted butter, softened
¾ cup lightly packed light brown sugar
1 large egg
1 large egg white
2 teaspoons pure vanilla extract
1 cup all-purpose flour
6 tablespoons unsweetened Dutch-process cocoa powder
¼ teaspoon baking soda
¼ teaspoon coarsely ground pepper
2 tablespoons buttermilk
Vegetable oil spray
Confectioners' sugar, for dusting

1. In a large bowl, using a handheld electric mixer, beat the butter with the brown sugar at medium-high speed until fluffy, 4 minutes. Beat in the egg, egg white and vanilla until combined. Sift the flour with the cocoa and baking soda to remove the cocoa lumps. Add the mixture to the bowl along with the pepper and beat at medium-low speed until the batter is moistened. Beat in the buttermilk; the batter will be stiff.

2. Preheat a waffle iron and spray with vegetable oil. For each cookie, spoon 2 tablespoons of batter into a quadrant of the waffle iron; if the iron is large enough, there may be room to make more than one cookie at a time. Close the waffle iron and cook just until fragrant, about 2 minutes, depending on your machine. Carefully lift the cookie and transfer it to a wire rack. Dust the cookie with confectioners' sugar and repeat with the remaining batter, spraying the waffle iron as needed. Serve the cookies warm or at room temperature. —*Joy Wilson*

SHORTBREAD BARS

F&W's **Grace Parisi** creates three fabulous fillings for bar cookies using one crisp, buttery shortbread crust for the base.

MAKE THE SHORTBREAD DOUGH

In a bowl, using an electric mixer, beat 1 stick plus 2 tablespoons of **UNSALTED BUTTER** with ½ cup of **SUGAR** and 1 large **EGG YOLK** until smooth. Add 1½ cups of **ALL-PURPOSE FLOUR**, ½ teaspoon of **BAKING POWDER** and ½ teaspoon of **KOSHER SALT** and beat at low speed until evenly moistened, about 2 minutes. Using your hands, knead once or twice to bring the dough together. The dough can be refrigerated for 2 days or frozen for up to 1 month.

CHOOSE A FILLING

Shaker-Style Lemon Bars

ACTIVE: 30 MIN; TOTAL: 2 HR
PLUS OVERNIGHT MACERATING
MAKES 18 BARS ● ●

- 1 large, firm lemon, scrubbed and halved lengthwise
- 1 tablespoon fresh lemon juice
- ¾ cup sugar

Shortbread Dough (recipe above)
- 2 tablespoons all-purpose flour
- 2 tablespoons unsalted butter, melted
- 2 large eggs

1. Using a mandoline or very sharp knife, slice the lemon halves as thinly as possible and transfer to a medium bowl; pick out the seeds. Stir in the lemon juice and sugar. Cover with plastic wrap and refrigerate overnight.
2. Butter a 9-inch square metal baking pan. Pat three-fourths of the Shortbread Dough into the baking pan in an even layer. Roll the remaining dough into eight 9-inch-long ropes. Transfer to a plate. Refrigerate the crust and ropes until firm, about 10 minutes.
3. Beat the flour with the butter and eggs until smooth. Fold in the lemon-sugar mixture.

4. Preheat the oven to 350°. Spread the filling over the dough and arrange the ropes of dough on top in a crisscross pattern. Bake in the lower third of the oven for 40 to 45 minutes, or until the ropes are golden. Let cool.
5. Run the tip of a knife around the edge of the baking pan. Cut the lemon square into 18 bars and serve.

Fudgy Pecan Streusel Bars

ACTIVE: 25 MIN; TOTAL: 2 HR
MAKES 18 BARS ● ○

Shortbread Dough (recipe above left)
- ½ cup toasted pecans, chopped
- 10 ounces bittersweet chocolate, chopped
One 14-ounce can sweetened condensed milk
- ¼ teaspoon coarse sea salt

1. Preheat the oven to 350°. Butter a 9-inch square metal baking pan. Pat three-fourths of the Shortbread Dough into the baking pan in an even layer. In a bowl, beat the pecans into the remaining dough. Crumble the pecan streusel on a plate. Refrigerate the crust and streusel for 10 minutes.
2. In a medium saucepan, combine the chocolate and condensed milk and stir over low heat until melted and very thick, about 3 minutes. Scrape into a bowl. Press a sheet of plastic wrap directly onto the surface and let cool slightly.
3. Spread the fudgy filling evenly on the shortbread dough in the pan and sprinkle with the coarse salt. Scatter the pecan streusel on top. Bake in the lower third of the oven for 40 to 45 minutes, or until the top is golden. Let cool completely.
4. Run the tip of a knife around the edge of the baking pan. Cut the fudgy pecan square into 18 bars and serve.

Mixed-Berry Snack Bars

ACTIVE: 30 MIN; TOTAL: 2 HR
MAKES 18 BARS ● ○

Shortbread Dough (recipe above left)
Sugar, for rolling
- 1 cup dried cranberries
- 1 cup seedless raspberry preserves
- ½ teaspoon finely grated lemon zest

1. Butter a 9-inch square metal baking pan. Pat three-fourths of the Shortbread Dough into the pan in an even layer. Roll the remaining dough into 36 small balls. Roll the balls in sugar, transfer to a wax paper–lined baking sheet and press the balls to ¼-inch-thick rounds with the bottom of a glass. Refrigerate the crust and rounds for 10 minutes. Preheat the oven to 350°.
2. In a microwave-safe bowl, cover the cranberries with water and microwave at high power for 1 minute, just until plump. Drain, pressing out the water; let cool slightly. Return the cranberries to the bowl and stir in the preserves and lemon zest.
3. Spread the berry filling over the dough; arrange the rounds on top. Bake in the lower third of the oven for 40 to 45 minutes, or until the top is golden. Let cool completely.
4. Run the tip of a knife around the edge of the pan. Cut the square into 18 bars; serve.

Citrus-and-Spice Churros with Mocha Sauce

TOTAL: 1 HR • MAKES 24 CHURROS ● ●

"Churros are such a crowd pleaser," says *Top Chef: Just Desserts* Season 2 winner Chris Hanmer about these Spanish-style ridged doughnuts. "Adults say, 'I can't have any more.' And then they have two more. And the kids will always say, 'Wow!'"

MOCHA SAUCE

1 **cup milk**
½ **cup espresso beans**
½ **pound milk chocolate, chopped**

CHURROS

1 **teaspoon sugar plus 1 cup**
   for coating
2 **tablespoons unsalted butter**
Pinch of salt
1 **cup all-purpose flour**
3 **large eggs**
½ **teaspoon pure vanilla extract**
1 **teaspoon finely grated orange zest**
1 **teaspoon finely grated lemon zest**
½ **teaspoon cinnamon**
¼ **teaspoon ground cardamom**
Vegetable oil, for frying

1. MAKE THE MOCHA SAUCE In a small saucepan, bring the milk just to a boil with the espresso beans. Remove from the heat, cover and let stand for 15 minutes. Strain the milk into a measuring cup; you should have about 5 ounces.

2. Wipe out the saucepan, return the milk to it and bring just to a simmer. Off the heat, stir in the chopped chocolate until melted. Whisk the sauce until smooth and transfer to a bowl. Keep warm.

3. MAKE THE CHURROS In a medium saucepan, combine the 1 teaspoon of sugar with the butter, salt and 1 cup of water and bring to a boil. Off the heat, add the flour all at once and stir until incorporated. Scrape the mixture into a large bowl. Using a handheld electric mixer at medium speed, beat in the eggs one at a time until smooth. Add the vanilla and the orange and lemon zests. Scrape the churro batter into a pastry bag fitted with a ½-inch star tip.

4. In a medium bowl, combine the remaining 1 cup of sugar with the cinnamon and ground cardamom. In a large saucepan, heat 2 inches of vegetable oil to 350°. Working carefully and quickly, pipe about eight 3-inch lengths of churro batter into the hot oil; use a knife to cut between the pieces. Fry over moderate heat, turning once, until the churros are golden and cooked through, 5 to 6 minutes. Using a slotted spoon, lift out the churros and let them drain for about 10 seconds, then transfer them to the spiced sugar and toss to coat. Transfer the churros to a platter and keep warm. Repeat with the remaining batter and spiced sugar. Serve the churros with the warm mocha sauce.
—*Chris Hanmer*

MAKE AHEAD The mocha sauce can be refrigerated for up to 1 week. Rewarm gently over low heat before serving.

Chocolate-Hazelnut Squares

ACTIVE: 45 MIN; TOTAL: 4 HR
MAKES 25 SMALL SQUARES ● ○ ○

Barb Finley, a professional baker and private events caterer in Sebastopol, California, usually serves this French chocolate dessert as one big cake. "But when you have little kiddos around, she says, something bite-size is more practical."

CAKE

Vegetable oil spray
½ **cup hazelnuts**
3 **tablespoons all-purpose flour**
Pinch of salt
5 **ounces semisweet chocolate,**
   finely chopped
1 **stick plus 1 tablespoon unsalted**
   butter, softened
½ **cup plus 1 tablespoon sugar**
3 **large eggs, separated**
1 **teaspoon pure vanilla extract**
GANACHE
½ **cup heavy cream**
1 **tablespoon unsalted butter**
½ **teaspoon instant espresso powder**
5 **ounces semisweet chocolate,**
   finely chopped
Chopped toasted hazelnuts, for garnish

1. MAKE THE CAKE Preheat the oven to 375°. Spray an 8-inch square baking pan with vegetable oil spray. Line the bottom and 2 sides with parchment paper, allowing the paper to extend 1 inch beyond the pan. Spray the paper with vegetable oil spray.

2. In a pie plate, toast the hazelnuts in the oven for about 12 minutes, until the skins blister. Spread the hazelnuts on a clean kitchen towel and let them cool completely. Rub the hazelnuts together to rub off the skins, then transfer them to a food processor. Add the flour and salt and pulse until the hazelnuts are finely ground.

3. In a microwave-safe glass bowl, heat the chocolate at 20-second intervals, stirring a few times, until melted. Let cool to warm. In a bowl, beat the butter with the sugar at medium-high speed until fluffy, 2 minutes. Add the chocolate, egg yolks and vanilla and beat until combined. Beat in the dry ingredients just until incorporated.

4. In another bowl, using clean beaters, whip the egg whites at high speed until soft peaks form. Fold the whites into the batter until no streaks remain. Scrape the batter into the prepared pan and smooth the surface. Bake in the center of the oven for 30 minutes, until a skewer inserted in the center comes out with a few moist crumbs attached. Let the cake cool in the pan for 30 minutes, then freeze until chilled, 1 hour.

5. Line a baking sheet with parchment paper. Invert the cake onto a cutting board and remove the paper. Cut the cake into 5 equal strips, then cut each strip crosswise into 5 squares, wiping the knife between cuts. Transfer the cake squares to the prepared baking sheet.

6. MAKE THE GANACHE In a microwave, heat the heavy cream and butter until very hot. Whisk in the espresso powder. Add the chocolate and let stand until melted, then whisk until smooth.

7. Using a small offset spatula, spread the ganache on the top and sides of each square. Sprinkle the squares with chopped hazelnuts and refrigerate them until the ganache is firm, about 30 minutes, then serve.
—*Barb Finley*

● HEALTHY   ● MAKE AHEAD   ○ VEGETARIAN   ● STAFF FAVORITE

citrus-and-spice churros with mocha sauce

Hazelnut–Brown Butter Brownies

ACTIVE: 30 MIN; TOTAL: 1 HR 30 MIN PLUS COOLING

MAKES 20 LARGE BROWNIES ● ● ●

- 7 ounces hazelnuts
- 1 cup plus 2 tablespoons unsweetened cocoa powder
- 1 teaspoon salt
- 3 cups sugar
- 1 pound (4 sticks) unsalted butter
- 12 ounces bittersweet chocolate (70 percent), chopped
- 6 large eggs
- 1 tablespoon instant coffee dissolved in 1 tablespoon of hot water

1. Preheat the oven to 325°. Line a 9-by-13-inch baking pan with foil, pressing it into the corners and leaving overhang on the 2 short sides.

2. Spread the hazelnuts in a pie plate and toast for 15 minutes, until fragrant and the skins blister; transfer to a kitchen towel to cool slightly, then rub off the skins. Let cool completely. Transfer the nuts to a food processor. Add the cocoa, salt and ½ cup of the sugar and pulse until finely ground.

3. In a large saucepan, cook the butter over moderate heat, shaking the pan occasionally, until nutty-smelling and golden and the foam subsides, about 5 minutes. Remove from the heat and add the chopped chocolate; let stand until melted, about 2 minutes. Whisk the butter and chocolate until smooth, scraping up any browned butter solids from the bottom of the pan. Let cool slightly.

4. In a large bowl, using an electric mixer, beat the eggs with the remaining 2½ cups of sugar and the coffee until tripled in volume, about 5 minutes. Beat in the chocolate-butter mixture, then add the cocoa-hazelnut mixture; beat to combine, scraping down the bowl. Scrape the batter into the prepared pan and bake for about 50 minutes, until the top is glossy and a toothpick inserted in the center comes out with a few moist crumbs attached. Let the brownie cool completely on a rack, then refrigerate until chilled.

5. Lift the brownie out of the pan and peel off the foil. Cut into 20 pieces and serve. —*Stella Parks*

SERVE WITH Ice cream.

Chocolate-Chunk Bread Pudding

ACTIVE: 25 MIN; TOTAL: 3 HR PLUS COOLING • 12 SERVINGS ● ●

- 5 large eggs
- ¾ cup granulated sugar
- ¾ cup light brown sugar
- ½ teaspoon kosher salt
- 1 tablespoon pure vanilla extract
- 5 cups whole milk, at room temperature
- 1 pound white sandwich bread, torn
- 12 ounces bittersweet chocolate, cut into ½-inch pieces (2 cups)

Softened unsalted butter, for greasing

Hot fudge sauce and chocolate shavings, for serving

1. Preheat the oven to 350° and position a rack in the center of the oven. In a large bowl, whisk the eggs with the granulated sugar and light brown sugar until smooth. Add the salt, vanilla and milk and whisk until the sugars are dissolved.

2. Spread the bread pieces in a 9-by-13-inch glass baking dish and pour the custard on top. Press the bread pieces into the custard and let stand, stirring occasionally, until the bread is evenly moistened, about 15 minutes. Fold in the chocolate chunks and smooth the top of the pudding.

3. Cover the dish with buttered foil and set it in a large roasting pan. Transfer the roasting pan to the oven and pour enough hot water into the pan to reach halfway up the sides of the baking dish. Bake the pudding for about 2 hours, until the center is completely set. Remove the baking dish from the water bath and let cool.

4. Serve the bread pudding warm with hot fudge sauce and chocolate shavings, or refrigerate until very firm, at least 4 hours or overnight, and serve in scoops.
—*Sarah Schulz*

Milk Chocolate Crémeux with Sesame Crème Anglaise

ACTIVE: 30 MIN; TOTAL: 1 HR PLUS CHILLING • 8 SERVINGS ● ● ●

This silky, pudding-like milk chocolate dessert is laced with bourbon, then topped with a simple sesame-custard sauce.

CRÉMEUX

- 1½ cups heavy cream
- 12 ounces best-quality milk chocolate, chopped
- 1 ounce unsweetened chocolate, chopped
- 1½ tablespoons bourbon

SESAME CRÈME ANGLAISE

- ⅔ cup white sesame seeds
- 1¾ cups whole milk
- 4 large egg yolks
- ¼ cup sugar

Toasted black sesame seeds, finely grated lime zest and fleur de sel, for garnish

1. MAKE THE CRÉMEUX In a medium saucepan, bring the cream to a simmer. Remove from the heat. Add both chocolates and let stand until melted, about 2 minutes. Whisk vigorously until smooth, then stir in the bourbon. Pour the *crémeux* into 8 glasses. Refrigerate until chilled, at least 1 hour.

2. MAKE THE SESAME CRÈME ANGLAISE In a medium saucepan, toast the white sesame seeds over moderate heat, shaking the pan, until golden, 1 to 2 minutes. Remove from the heat and let cool slightly. Add the milk, cover and let steep for 30 minutes.

3. Set a heatproof bowl in a bowl of ice water. Transfer the sesame milk to a blender and pulse several times, until the sesame seeds are chopped but not ground. Rinse out the saucepan and strain the milk into it, pressing hard on the solids to extract as much milk as possible. Return the milk to a simmer.

4. In a medium bowl, whisk the egg yolks with the sugar until pale. Whisk in ½ cup of the hot milk, then whisk the mixture into the saucepan. Cook over moderate heat, whisking, until thickened, 5 minutes. Pour the crème anglaise into the bowl set over ice water; let cool completely, stirring occasionally.

● HEALTHY ● MAKE AHEAD ● VEGETARIAN ● STAFF FAVORITE

5. To serve, gently pour the chilled crème anglaise over the *crémeux*. Sprinkle with toasted black sesame seeds, grated lime zest and fleur de sel and serve right away.
—*Shawn Gawle*

MAKE AHEAD The crème anglaise and the *crémeux* can be refrigerated separately for up to 3 days.

Maple-Bourbon Custards with Almond-Orange Streusel
TOTAL: 45 MIN PLUS OVERNIGHT CHILLING • 8 SERVINGS ● ●

At his Baltimore restaurant Wit & Wisdom, Michael Mina serves these custards with orange toffee and a bourbon-and-smoked-vanilla gelée. This simplified version is perfect for entertaining at home, since everything can be made days in advance.

CUSTARD
1½ teaspoons unflavored powdered gelatin
3 cups heavy cream
4 large egg yolks
Pinch of salt
1 cup plus 2 tablespoons pure maple syrup
3 tablespoons bourbon
STREUSEL
⅓ cup whole blanched almonds, chopped
2 tablespoons all-purpose flour
2 tablespoons sugar
Pinch of salt
2 tablespoons unsalted butter, melted
¼ teaspoon finely grated orange zest

1. **MAKE THE CUSTARDS** In a small bowl, sprinkle the powdered gelatin evenly over 3 tablespoons of cold water and let stand until softened, about 5 minutes.

2. In a medium saucepan, bring the cream to a simmer over moderate heat. Meanwhile, in a small heatproof bowl, gently whisk the egg yolks. Slowly whisk in ½ cup of the hot cream, then scrape the yolk mixture into the remaining hot cream. Add the salt and cook over moderate heat, whisking constantly, until slightly thickened, 3 minutes; don't let the custard boil. Remove from the heat and whisk in the dissolved gelatin, then whisk in the maple syrup and bourbon.

3. Pour the maple-bourbon custard into eight 6-ounce ramekins or glasses, cover and refrigerate them overnight.

4. **MAKE THE STREUSEL** Preheat the oven to 275°. In a mini food processor, pulse the almonds until coarsely ground. Add the flour, sugar and salt and pulse a few times to blend. Add the melted butter and pulse to combine. Transfer the mixture to a rimmed baking sheet and crumble with your fingers to form clumps. Spread the clumps in an even layer and bake for about 12 minutes, until starting to dry out. Using 2 forks, toss the mixture once, then bake for 5 minutes longer, until lightly golden.

5. Increase the oven temperature to 350°. Break up the streusel into crumbs. Bake the crumbs for about 3 minutes longer, until they are golden brown and crisp. Stir in the orange zest and let cool completely.

6. Top the maple-bourbon custards with the almond-orange streusel and serve.
—*Michael Mina*

Frozen Crème Caramels
ACTIVE: 30 MIN; TOTAL: 13 HR WITH CHILLING AND FREEZING
6 SERVINGS ● ●

The staff at Nebo Lodge on Maine's tiny North Haven island is obsessed with egg-based desserts like this crème caramel, which gets a refreshing twist by being served partially frozen, almost like an extra-custardy semifreddo.

CUSTARD
1⅔ cups heavy cream
¾ cup milk
½ vanilla bean, split and seeds scraped
3 large egg yolks
1 large egg
½ cup sugar
Pinch of salt
CARAMEL
⅔ cup sugar
Whipped cream, for serving (optional)

1. **MAKE THE CUSTARD** In a small saucepan, combine the heavy cream with the milk and vanilla bean and seeds. Bring to a simmer over moderate heat, then cover and remove the saucepan from the heat. Let the cream mixture stand for 10 minutes, then remove the vanilla bean.

2. Preheat the oven to 300°. Fill a large bowl with ice water. In a medium bowl, whisk the egg yolks with the whole egg, sugar and salt, then slowly whisk in the cream mixture. Set the bowl in the ice water bath and let stand, stirring the custard occasionally, until chilled, about 20 minutes.

3. **MEANWHILE, MAKE THE CARAMEL** Arrange six 4-ounce ramekins in a large baking dish. In a medium saucepan, combine the sugar and ¼ cup of water and bring to a simmer. Cook the mixture over moderate heat, washing down the side of the pan with a wet pastry brush, until a light amber caramel forms, about 15 minutes. Carefully stir in another 3 tablespoons of water and simmer until the caramel is dissolved. Pour the caramel into the ramekins, swirling to coat the bottoms evenly. Let the caramel cool for about 15 minutes.

4. Fill the ramekins with the chilled custard. Carefully pour enough hot water into the baking dish to reach halfway up the sides of the ramekins. Cover the baking dish with aluminum foil and bake for 45 minutes, until the custards are almost set but still slightly jiggly in the center. Remove the foil and let the custards cool to room temperature in the water in the baking dish, 30 minutes. Wrap the ramekins in plastic and refrigerate until the custards are thoroughly chilled, at least 6 hours or overnight.

5. Freeze the chilled crème caramels for at least 4 hours or overnight.

6. Thirty minutes before serving, take the crème caramels out and let them stand at room temperature until just slightly frozen in the center. Run a thin knife around the crème caramels and invert them onto plates. Serve with whipped cream.
—*Amanda Hallowell*

MAKE AHEAD The crème caramels can be frozen for up to 1 week.

DIY ICE CREAM

Here, recipes and tips for making two types of ice cream—simple American and lush, custardy French-style—from **Molly Moon's Homemade Ice Cream** shop in Seattle.

American-Style Ice Cream

ACTIVE: 15 MIN; TOTAL: 5 HR

MAKES ABOUT 1 QUART ● ● ●

Molly Neitzel, the owner of Molly Moon's ice cream shops in Seattle, recommends using the best-quality local milk and cream. "You can really taste the difference when making American-style ice creams," she says.

- 2 cups heavy cream
- 1 cup whole milk
- ¾ cup sugar
- Pinch of salt

1. Set a medium bowl in a large bowl of ice water. In a small saucepan, combine the heavy cream with the milk, sugar and salt and bring to a simmer, stirring to dissolve the sugar completely. Pour the ice cream base into the medium bowl and let cool completely, stirring occasionally. Refrigerate the ice cream base until it's very cold, at least 1 hour or overnight.

2. Pour the base into an ice cream maker with flavorings, if using (see page 364), and freeze according to the manufacturer's instructions. Transfer the ice cream to a plastic container, cover and freeze until firm, at least 3 hours.

French-Style Ice Cream

ACTIVE: 25 MIN; TOTAL: 5 HR

MAKES ABOUT 1 QUART ● ●

Molly Moon's head chef, Christina Spittler, says that egg yolks in the custard base help make a denser ice cream.

- 6 large egg yolks
- ¾ cup sugar
- 1¾ cups heavy cream
- 1¼ cups whole milk
- Pinch of salt

1. Set a medium bowl in a large bowl of ice water. In another medium bowl, whisk the egg yolks with ½ cup of the sugar until pale, about 3 minutes.

2. In a medium saucepan, combine the heavy cream, milk, salt and remaining ¼ cup of sugar and bring to a simmer, whisking until the sugar is completely dissolved. Whisk the hot cream mixture into the beaten egg yolks in a thin stream.

3. Transfer the cream-and-egg mixture to the medium saucepan and cook over moderately low heat, stirring constantly with a wooden spoon, until the custard is thick enough to lightly coat the back of the spoon, about 4 minutes; don't let it boil. Pour the custard through a fine-mesh strainer into the medium bowl in the ice water. Let the custard cool completely, stirring frequently. Refrigerate the custard until it is very cold, at least 1 hour.

4. Pour the custard into an ice cream maker with flavorings, if using (see page 364), and freeze according to the manufacturer's instructions. Transfer the frozen custard to a plastic container, cover and freeze until firm, at least 3 hours.

THREE CUSTARD TIPS FOR FRENCH-STYLE ICE CREAM

temper the eggs Gradually whisk the hot cream mixture into the beaten egg yolks to heat them gently and prevent them from scrambling.

spoon test The custard is ready when it lightly coats the back of a wooden spoon and when a finger drawn across it leaves a path.

strain it A well-made custard won't have bits of cooked egg yolk in it; pouring it through a fine-mesh strainer eliminates the possibility.

french-style (top) and american-style ice cream

Cuban Custard with Cinnamon

TOTAL: 20 MIN PLUS 4 HR CHILLING
6 SERVINGS ● ●

6 large egg yolks
¼ cup cornstarch
Pinch of salt
1 quart whole milk
1 cup sugar
2 teaspoons pure vanilla extract
Cinnamon, for dusting

1. In a medium bowl, whisk the egg yolks with the cornstarch and salt. Whisk in ½ cup of the milk until smooth.
2. Set a fine-mesh strainer over a large bowl. In a large saucepan, heat the remaining 3½ cups of whole milk with the sugar until small bubbles appear around the side of the saucepan. Whisk in the egg-yolk mixture in a slow, steady stream and cook over low heat, stirring with a rubber spatula, until the custard is thickened and gently simmering, about 5 minutes. Immediately strain the custard into the bowl and stir in the vanilla extract. Press a sheet of plastic wrap directly onto the surface of the custard and refrigerate until chilled, about 4 hours. Spoon the custard into bowls, sprinkle with cinnamon and serve. —*David Guas*

ICE CREAM ADD-INS

Add these flavorings to either of the ice creams on page 362 at the beginning of the freezing cycle.

chocolate-toffee 1 cup broken chocolate-and-toffee-covered saltines or pretzels.

blackberry-sage ¾ cup blackberry preserves mixed with 1 tablespoon minced fresh sage.

salted caramel ¾ cup pourable salted-caramel sauce.

strawberry-jalapeño 1 cup strawberries macerated in 3 tablespoons sugar with 1 teaspoon minced jalapeño.

German Chocolate Cake Sundaes

⏱ **TOTAL: 30 MIN • 6 SERVINGS** ● ●

In this play on German chocolate cake, rich caramel mixed with toasted pecans and coconut is poured over coconut ice cream and topped with crispy chocolate crumbs.

1 cup unsweetened wide-flake coconut chips (2 ounces)
¾ cup pecan halves (2 ounces)
1 cup sugar
2 tablespoons light corn syrup
¾ cup heavy cream
1 teaspoon pure vanilla extract
Pinch of sea salt
2 pints coconut ice cream
1 cup coarsely crumbled chocolate wafer cookies

1. Preheat the oven to 350°. Spread the coconut chips and pecan halves in 2 separate pie plates. Toast the coconut chips for 5 minutes and the pecan halves for 10 minutes, until the edges of the coconut chips start to brown and the pecans are fragrant. Let the toasted coconut and pecans cool, then coarsely chop the pecans.
2. Meanwhile, in a large saucepan, combine the sugar with the light corn syrup and 2 tablespoons of water and bring to a boil, stirring to dissolve the sugar. Wash down the side of the pan with a wet pastry brush. Cook the syrup over moderately high heat without stirring until a deep amber caramel forms, about 5 minutes. Remove from the heat and carefully add the cream. When the bubbles subside, stir to combine. Add the vanilla and salt and let the caramel cool slightly. Stir in the toasted pecans and all but ¼ cup of the toasted coconut chips.
3. Scoop the coconut ice cream into glasses and sprinkle with half of the chocolate cookie crumbs. Top with the warm caramel sauce and the remaining cookie crumbs and coconut and serve right away.
—*Grace Parisi*

MAKE AHEAD The caramel sauce can be refrigerated overnight. Reheat in the microwave, then stir in the pecans and coconut.

Butter Pecan Cookie and Peach Ice Cream Sandwiches

ACTIVE: 20 MIN; TOTAL: 2 HR
8 SERVINGS ● ● ●

"Ice cream sandwiches are universally popular, and everyone loves peach ice cream," says Atlanta chef Linton Hopkins. "To make this recipe really Southern, we use pecans in the cookie dough."

1 cup pecans
½ cup all-purpose flour
¼ teaspoon baking powder
Pinch of baking soda
¼ teaspoon salt
2 sticks unsalted butter, softened
½ cup light brown sugar
1 large egg
½ teaspoon pure vanilla extract
2 pints peach ice cream, softened slightly

1. Preheat the oven to 375° and line a 10-by-15-inch jelly roll pan with parchment paper. Spread the pecans in a pie plate and toast for about 8 minutes, until fragrant. Let cool, then coarsely chop the pecans.
2. In a small bowl, whisk the flour with the baking powder, baking soda and salt. In a medium bowl, using an electric mixer, beat the butter with the brown sugar at medium-high speed until smooth. Beat in the egg and vanilla extract. At low speed, beat in the dry ingredients. Spread the dough onto the entire jelly roll pan in an even layer and sprinkle the chopped pecans on top. Freeze for 5 minutes, just until firm.
3. Bake the bar in the center of the oven for about 12 minutes, until golden. Let cool completely, then invert the bar onto a work surface. Peel off the parchment paper and cut the bar into 2 equal pieces. Spread the softened ice cream on one half and top with the other half, nut side up. Return the bar to the freezer and freeze until firm, at least 1 hour. Cut into 8 bars and serve right away.
—*Linton Hopkins*

MAKE AHEAD The uncut ice cream sandwiches can be frozen in an airtight container for up to 1 week.

● HEALTHY ● MAKE AHEAD ● VEGETARIAN ● STAFF FAVORITE

Chocolate Frozen Yogurt with Caramelized Bananas

ACTIVE: 30 MIN; TOTAL: 3 HR 15 MIN
MAKES ABOUT 1 QUART ● ● ○

For this healthy dessert, bananas are caramelized in brown sugar, then folded into a homemade low-fat chocolate frozen yogurt.

>   2 tablespoons unsalted butter
>   2 large ripe bananas,
>   cut into 1-inch rounds
>   2 tablespoons light brown sugar
>   1 tablespoon dark rum
>   ½ cup plus 3 tablespoons
>   2 percent milk
> 2½ tablespoons unsweetened
>   Dutch-process cocoa powder
>   ⅔ cup granulated sugar
> Pinch of salt
>   1 teaspoon pure vanilla extract
> 1¼ cups plain nonfat Greek yogurt
>   1 ounce bittersweet chocolate,
>   finely chopped

1. In a nonstick skillet, melt the butter. Add the bananas in a single layer and sprinkle with the brown sugar. Cook over moderate heat, turning once, until the bananas are caramelized, about 8 minutes. Off the heat, add the rum and swirl the pan to dissolve the sugar. Scrape three-quarters of the bananas into a food processor and add 3 tablespoons of the milk. Puree until smooth. Transfer the puree to a small bowl and freeze until chilled, 15 minutes. Chop the remaining bananas and freeze until chilled.

2. In another bowl, whisk the cocoa with the granulated sugar, salt, vanilla and the remaining ½ cup of milk. Whisk in the yogurt until smooth, then the banana puree.

3. Transfer the yogurt mixture to an ice cream maker and freeze according to the manufacturer's instructions until nearly frozen. Mix in the chilled chopped bananas and the chopped chocolate. Scrape the frozen yogurt into an airtight container, cover and freeze until firm, at least 2 hours.
—Joy Wilson

MAKE AHEAD The frozen yogurt can be frozen in an airtight container for up to 1 week.

Toasted Sesame Cookies

☺ **ACTIVE: 20 MIN; TOTAL: 45 MIN**
MAKES 32 COOKIES ● ●

After baking at health-food stores, Sarah Kelby Lewis created Sustenance, her line of sweets that use alternative sugars like the Sucanat in these cookies.

>   ½ cup whole wheat pastry flour
>   ½ cup all-purpose flour
>   ¼ teaspoon baking soda
>   ¼ teaspoon salt
>   4 tablespoons unsalted butter,
>   softened
>   ½ cup evaporated cane sugar
>   ½ cup Sucanat sugar (see Note)
>   1 large egg
>   1 teaspoon pure vanilla extract
>   1 cup toasted sesame seeds
>   (4 ounces)

1. Preheat the oven to 350°. Line 2 baking sheets with parchment. In a small bowl, whisk the flours, baking soda and salt. In a large bowl, beat the butter until creamy. Beat in the sugars, then the egg and vanilla. Beat in the sesame seeds and dry ingredients.

2. Scoop tablespoons of the dough onto the baking sheets and roll into balls; press into 2-inch rounds. Bake the cookies for 10 to 12 minutes, until golden. Let cool for 10 minutes, then transfer to racks to cool completely.
—Sarah Kelby Lewis

NOTE Sucanat, a whole cane sugar, is available at health-food stores.

Peanut Butter Rice Krispie Treats

ACTIVE: 15 MIN; TOTAL: 1 HR 30 MIN
MAKES 24 SQUARES ●

Rice Krispies Gluten Free cereal, made with brown rice instead of white, is the secret to these crisp and chewy sweets.

>   3 tablespoons coconut oil, plus
>   more for greasing
> One 10-ounce bag marshmallows
>   ¾ cup creamy peanut butter
>   7 ounces Rice Krispies Gluten Free
>   with Brown Rice (6 cups)

Lightly grease a 9-by-13-inch baking pan with coconut oil. In a large pot, melt the 3 tablespoons of coconut oil. Add the marshmallows and cook thoroughly over low heat, stirring constantly, until they are melted, about 5 minutes. Add the creamy peanut butter and stir until incorporated. Remove the pot from the heat and immediately add the Rice Krispies. Using a wooden spoon or firm spatula, stir to coat them completely. Scrape the mixture into the prepared baking pan and, using a sheet of wax paper, press evenly on the mixture to compact it. Let the Rice Krispie treats cool completely, then cut them into squares and serve.
—Elisabeth Prueitt

Campfire Biscuit S'mores

☺ **TOTAL: 30 MIN • 4 SERVINGS**

This hearty twist on classic s'mores is made with chocolate-studded biscuits.

> Quick Biscuit Mix (page 306)
>   2 tablespoons sugar
>   ½ cup mini chocolate chips
> Extra-virgin olive oil, for brushing
>   ¼ cup seedless raspberry jam
>   8 marshmallows (or 4 jumbo)
>   4 large sturdy rosemary branches,
>   bottom three-fourths of the leaves
>   stripped off

1. In a bowl, combine the Quick Biscuit Mix with the sugar. Stir in ½ cup of water to form a thick batter, then stir in the chocolate chips.

2. Preheat a flameproof rimmed griddle and brush lightly with oil. Scoop the batter into eight ¼-cup mounds and spread each one to 3 inches. Cook over very low heat until lightly browned on the bottom, about 2 minutes. Brush the tops lightly with oil and flip. Spread the jam over the biscuits, cover the griddle and cook until the biscuits are puffed and golden, about 2 minutes longer.

3. Meanwhile, thread the marshmallows on the rosemary branches and toast until golden and melted. Sandwich the marshmallows between the biscuits, jam side in, and pull to remove the skewers. Serve the s'mores right away. *—Grace Parisi*

Spiced Cashew Brittle and Chocolate Crunch Bark

TOTAL: 1 HR 15 MIN PLUS COOLING
MAKES ABOUT 2 POUNDS ● ○

BRITTLE
1½ cups whole raw cashews
1 cup sugar
½ cup light corn syrup
1 stick unsalted butter, cut into tablespoons
½ teaspoon baking soda
¼ teaspoon cayenne pepper
BARK
8 ounces bittersweet chocolate, finely chopped
1½ cups Rice Krispies or *feuilletine*

1. MAKE THE BRITTLE Preheat the oven to 325°. Spread the cashews on a small baking sheet and toast for 10 minutes, stirring once. Keep the cashews warm.
2. Line a rimmed baking sheet with buttered parchment paper. In a saucepan, bring the sugar, corn syrup, butter and ¼ cup of water to a boil. Cook over moderately high heat, stirring frequently, until a deep amber toffee forms, about 10 minutes. Remove the saucepan from the heat. Whisk in the baking soda and cayenne; it will bubble up. Using a wooden spoon, stir in the warm cashews.
3. Pour the hot candy onto the prepared baking sheet and spread it out as thinly as possible. Let the brittle cool completely, then break it into large shards.
4. MAKE THE BARK Line a baking sheet with parchment paper. In a heatproof bowl set over (not in) a saucepan of simmering water, melt two-thirds of the chocolate. Stir until the chocolate reaches 130°. Remove the bowl from the heat and stir in the remaining chocolate until melted and the temperature drops to 85°. Return the bowl to the saucepan and warm the chocolate to 90°, stirring. Remove from the heat. Fold in the Rice Krispies. Spread the mixture on the parchment paper in a ¼-inch-thick layer. Let the bark harden completely, then break into large shards. Serve the bark with the brittle.
—*Bryce Caron*

MILK CHOCOLATE BARK Use milk chocolate instead of dark. Follow the same method: Melt two-thirds of the chocolate to 113°. Add the remaining chocolate and stir until 80°. Warm the chocolate to 85° and then fold in the Rice Krispies.

Soft Apple-Cider Caramels

ACTIVE: 1 HR 45 MIN; TOTAL: 2 HR 45 MIN PLUS OVERNIGHT CHILLING
MAKES 150 CARAMELS ● ○

2 quarts apple cider
3 cups heavy cream
½ cup sweetened condensed milk
4 cups sugar
¾ cup light corn syrup
1½ teaspoons kosher salt
1 stick cold unsalted butter, diced
½ teaspoon cinnamon
Pinch of ground allspice
Pinch of ground cloves
Neutral oil, such as canola or grapeseed, for brushing

1. In a large saucepan, simmer the apple cider over moderate heat, stirring occasionally, until reduced to 1 cup, about 1 hour. Pour the reduced cider into a bowl.
2. Line a 9-by-13-inch rimmed pan with foil and coat the foil with nonstick cooking spray. In a medium saucepan, combine the heavy cream and condensed milk and bring to a simmer over moderate heat; keep the mixture warm over low heat.
3. In another large saucepan, combine the sugar with the reduced apple cider, corn syrup, salt and ¼ cup of water and bring to a boil. Simmer over moderate heat until the sugar dissolves, about 5 minutes. Carefully whisk in the butter until melted. Gradually whisk in the warm cream mixture until incorporated. Cook over moderately low heat, stirring frequently, until a golden caramel forms and the temperature reaches 245° on a candy thermometer, about 45 minutes. Stir in the cinnamon, allspice and cloves and scrape the caramel into the prepared pan. Let cool completely, then refrigerate the caramel overnight.

4. Lightly brush a sheet of parchment paper with oil. Invert the caramel onto the parchment and peel off the foil. Using a sharp knife, cut the caramel into 1-inch-wide strips, then cut the block crosswise into ½-inch rectangles. Wrap each caramel in a square of parchment paper or a candy wrapper and twist the ends to seal. Serve or pack the caramels into boxes. —*Justin Chapple*
MAKE AHEAD The wrapped caramels can be stored in a cool spot or refrigerated for up to 2 weeks. The uncut caramel can be tightly wrapped in plastic and refrigerated for up to 2 weeks; cut just before serving.

Brazilian Truffles

TOTAL: 50 MIN • MAKES 30 TRUFFLES ● ○
Known as *brigadeiros* in Portuguese, these candies look like French-style truffles but taste more like chewy chocolate caramels.

One 14-ounce can sweetened condensed milk
1 ounce bittersweet chocolate, chopped
1 teaspoon salted butter, plus more for rubbing
Chocolate sprinkles, for rolling

1. In a nonstick saucepan, combine the condensed milk with the chocolate and the 1 teaspoon of butter. Cook over moderately low heat, stirring constantly, until shiny and very thick, 15 to 18 minutes. Spread the mixture in a shallow dish and let cool for 15 minutes, then refrigerate until chilled.
2. Arrange 30 paper candy cups on a baking sheet. Pour the sprinkles into a shallow bowl. Rub your hands with butter. Scoop up rounded teaspoons of the candy mixture and roll them into balls. Roll the candy in the sprinkles and set them in a paper cup. Repeat to form the remaining candies. Serve slightly chilled or at room temperature.
—*My Sweet Brigadeiro*
PECAN-CINNAMON VARIATION Replace the bittersweet chocolate with white chocolate. In place of the sprinkles, blend 1 cup chopped toasted pecans with 1 teaspoon cinnamon and use to coat the candies.

● HEALTHY ● MAKE AHEAD ○ VEGETARIAN ● STAFF FAVORITE

spiced cashew brittle and chocolate crunch bark

At a holiday party hosted by New York City event planner Bronson van Wyck, a self-serve bar allows guests to customize their own Bloody Marys, OPPOSITE; *recipe, page 370.*

DRINKS

Hellfire Club Bloody Mary

📷 PAGE 369

TOTAL: 20 MIN PLUS 2 HR CHILLING
MAKES 8 DRINKS

For this spicy Bloody Mary, named after a group of the X-Men's arch enemies, guests can customize their drinks with red and/or green flavored ice cubes (recipe follows).

3½ cups tomato juice
1¼ cups vodka
½ cup olive juice
⅓ cup red wine vinegar
½ teaspoon finely grated lemon zest
2 tablespoons fresh lemon juice
1 tablespoon Worcestershire sauce
1 tablespoon freshly ground black pepper, plus more for garnish
1 tablespoon Tabasco
2 serrano chiles, seeded and minced
2 teaspoons minced dill
1 Peppadew pepper, minced
1 large garlic clove, minced
½ teaspoon celery salt
½ teaspoon kosher salt
Ice cubes
Celery ribs and green olives, for garnish

In a pitcher, combine all of the ingredients except the ice cubes and garnishes and stir well. Cover and refrigerate until chilled, at least 2 hours. Serve the cocktails in ice-filled Collins glasses, garnished with celery ribs, green olives and black pepper. —*Bronson van Wyck*

CUCUMBER-BASIL AND TOMATO-CHILE ICE CUBES

TOTAL: 30 MIN PLUS 3 HR FREEZING
MAKES ABOUT 5 DOZEN ICE CUBES ●

2½ cups chopped Persian cucumber
¾ cup lightly packed basil leaves, torn
1 serrano chile, seeded and chopped
1 teaspoon light brown sugar
Kosher salt
3 cups tomato juice
1 jalapeño, seeded and chopped
¼ cup lightly packed dill
½ teaspoon Tabasco

In a blender, puree the cucumber, basil, serrano chile, brown sugar and ¾ teaspoon of salt with 3 cups of water. Strain through a fine sieve into 2 ice cube trays and freeze for at least 3 hours. Clean out the blender. Add the tomato juice, jalapeño, dill and Tabasco and puree. Season the puree with salt and pour into 2 ice cube trays. Freeze for at least 3 hours. —*BVW*

Gin-Campari Old-Fashioned

⏱ **TOTAL: 5 MIN • MAKES 1 DRINK** ●

One 2-inch-long strip of lemon zest
1 teaspoon Demerara simple syrup (see Note)
1 teaspoon Campari
3 dashes of grapefruit bitters
Scant pinch of fine sea salt
2 ounces gin, preferably Knickerbocker or Beefeater 24
Ice

In a rocks glass, muddle the lemon zest with the simple syrup, Campari, grapefruit bitters and sea salt. Add the gin and a few ice cubes and stir until well chilled. Top with more ice and serve right away. —*Dave Kwiatkowski*
NOTE To make Demerara simple syrup, in a small saucepan, dissolve ¼ cup Demerara sugar (a coarse, raw cane sugar) in ¼ cup water over moderate heat.

Rosalind Russell

⏱ **TOTAL: 5 MIN • MAKES 1 DRINK** ●

Matt Piacentini, owner of The Beagle in New York City, named this drink for the Hollywood star and aquavit fan.

Ice
2 ounces aquavit
1 ounce sweet vermouth
2 dashes of Angostura bitters
1 lemon twist, for garnish

Fill a pint glass with ice. Add the aquavit, sweet vermouth and Angostura bitters and stir well. Strain into a chilled coupe. Garnish the cocktail with the lemon twist.
—*Matt Piacentini*

Punch Parker

TOTAL: 5 MIN PLUS 4 HR CHILLING
MAKES 12 TO 15 DRINKS ● ●

Allen Katz, mixologist at The Shanty and a partner in New York Distilling in Brooklyn, New York, uses his own Dorothy Parker gin to make this fruity punch.

2 oranges, 2 lemons and 1 lime, thinly sliced (halved or quartered if large)
½ pint fresh raspberries
1 cup cubed fresh pineapple
One 750-milliliter bottle Dorothy Parker gin
1¾ cups fresh lemon juice (about 12)
1¼ cups Simple Syrup (page 372)
½ cup orgeat (almond-flavored syrup)
1 cup framboise liqueur
One 750-milliliter bottle Prosecco, chilled
1 large ice block

In a large punch bowl, combine all of the ingredients except for the Prosecco and ice. Refrigerate for 4 to 5 hours. Just before serving, add the Prosecco and ice block.
—*Allen Katz*

Pepino's Revenge

⏱ **TOTAL: 5 MIN • MAKES 1 DRINK** ●

This tequila, cucumber and basil drink is served at the bar at London's 45 Park Lane.

Four ½-inch-thick slices of Japanese cucumber, plus thin cucumber slices for garnish
2 large basil leaves, plus small basil leaves for garnish
1½ ounces silver tequila, such as Patrón
½ ounce fresh lime juice
½ ounce Simple Syrup (page 372)
Ice

In a cocktail shaker, combine the thick slices of cucumber with the large basil leaves and muddle well with a wooden spoon. Add the tequila, lime juice, Simple Syrup and ice and shake well. Strain into an ice-filled glass. Garnish with a few small basil leaves and thin cucumber slices. —*Lee Hefter*

● HEALTHY ● MAKE AHEAD ● VEGETARIAN ● STAFF FAVORITE

Creole Old-Fashioned

⏱ **TOTAL: 5 MIN • MAKES 1 DRINK** ● ●

Ice
1 ounce Cognac
1 ounce Demerara rum (a dark rum made in Guyana)
1 teaspoon Xanthan Simple Syrup (recipe follows)
Dash of Angostura bitters
Dash of orange bitters
1 orange twist, for garnish

Fill a rocks glass with ice. In a cocktail shaker, stir the Cognac, rum, Xanthan Simple Syrup and both bitters. Pour into the rocks glass and garnish with the twist. —*Kevin Denton*

XANTHAN SIMPLE SYRUP

TOTAL: 30 MIN PLUS 4 HR RESTING
MAKES 2¼ CUPS ● ●
This simple syrup, thickened slightly with xanthan gum, gives drinks a silky texture.

1½ cups sugar
0.5 gram (⅛ teaspoon) xanthan gum

In a medium saucepan, combine the sugar with 1½ cups of water and bring to a boil. Let the syrup cool completely, then transfer to a blender. With the blender on, add the xanthan gum and blend until the syrup is slightly thickened, about 15 seconds. Transfer the syrup to a jar, cover and refrigerate until clear, at least 4 hours or overnight. —*KD*

SIMPLE SYRUP

A quick combination of sugar and water, this clear syrup is used to sweeten countless cocktails.

Simmer ½ cup sugar with ½ cup water in a saucepan over moderate heat, stirring, until the sugar dissolves. Let the syrup cool completely, then refrigerate for up to 1 month.

Pomegranate-and-Tequila Cocktail

⏱ **TOTAL: 15 MIN • MAKES 8 DRINKS** ●

Black lava salt (see Note) or kosher salt
Lime wedges
Ice
1½ cups silver tequila
1½ cups fresh lime juice
1 cup pomegranate syrup (see Note)
24 dashes of orange bitters

1. Spread salt in a shallow dish. Run a lime wedge around the rims of chilled cocktail glasses, then dip the rims in the salt to coat.
2. In an ice-filled pitcher, combine the tequila, lime juice, pomegranate syrup and bitters. Stir well. Strain into the cocktail glasses. —*David Burtka*

NOTE Black lava salt is available at *amazon. com.* To make pomegranate syrup, whisk together ¾ cup unsweetened pomegranate juice with ¾ cup sugar until the sugar is dissolved; you should have 1½ cups.

Classic Daiquiri

⏱ **TOTAL: 5 MIN • MAKES 1 DRINK** ●

2½ ounces white rum
1½ ounces fresh lime juice
4 teaspoons superfine sugar
Ice
1 lime wheel, for garnish

In a cocktail shaker, stir the rum, lime juice and sugar until the sugar is dissolved. Add the ice and shake until chilled. Strain into a chilled cocktail glass, garnish with the lime wheel and serve. —*David Guas*

Blackberry-Mint Julep

⏱ **TOTAL: 5 MIN • MAKES 1 DRINK** ● ●

Small ice cubes
¼ cup blackberries, plus 1 blackberry for garnish
2 tablespoons mint leaves, plus 1 mint sprig for garnish
1 tablespoon sugar
1½ ounces bourbon

Fill a rocks glass halfway with ice. In a shaker, combine the blackberries, mint leaves, sugar, bourbon and ⅓ cup of ice cubes and shake well. Strain into the glass through a coarse sieve, pressing on the solids. Garnish with the blackberry and mint sprig. —*Jeff Banker*

Kentucky Special

⏱ **ACTIVE: 10 MIN; TOTAL: 45 MIN**
MAKES 1 DRINK ●

1 Lapsang souchong tea bag
6 ounces Heering cherry liqueur
Ice
1½ ounces bourbon
1 dash of Angostura bitters
2 brandied cherries skewered on a pick, flaky sea salt and 1 lemon twist, for garnish

In a glass, steep the tea bag in the Heering for 30 minutes. Press excess liquid from the tea bag and discard. Fill a pint glass with ice. Add the bourbon, bitters and ½ ounce of the infused Heering; stir well. Strain into an ice-filled rocks glass. Dust the skewered cherries with salt. Garnish the drink with the cherries and lemon twist. —*Evan Zimmerman*

Summer Breeze

⏱ **TOTAL: 10 MIN • MAKES 6 DRINKS** ●

1½ cups raspberries, plus 6 berries for garnish
1 tablespoon sugar
6 ounces Scotch whisky
6 ounces guava nectar or juice
1½ ounces framboise (raspberry eau-de-vie)
Ice
Chilled club soda
6 small mint leaves, for garnish

In a large shaker, muddle the 1½ cups of raspberries with the sugar. Add the whisky, guava nectar and framboise. Fill the shaker with ice; shake well. Finely strain the cocktail into a pitcher. Pour into rocks glasses. Top each drink with a little club soda; garnish with raspberries and mint. —*Martine Nouet*

● HEALTHY ● MAKE AHEAD ▾ VEGETARIAN ● STAFF FAVORITE

DIY BARREL-AGED COCKTAILS

Aging cocktails in wood barrels can soften harsh edges and add layers of flavor. Mixologist **Jeffrey Morgenthaler** of Clyde Common in Portland, Oregon, shares his techniques.

SIX GREAT BARREL-AGED COCKTAILS

When aging cocktails, remember that smaller, newer barrels work faster than larger, used ones. The trick is to taste every week until you get the gently oaked flavor you want. The recipes below are meant to be aged in a 1-liter oak barrel (see Note). For larger barrels, multiply each recipe proportionately. Follow the directions for mixing, aging and serving, below.

AGED CHRYSANTHEMUM

ACTIVE: 20 MIN; TOTAL: ABOUT 1 MONTH
MAKES ABOUT 1 LITER ● ● ●

One 1-liter oak barrel (see Note)
10½ ounces Bénédictine
21 ounces dry vermouth
1¾ ounces absinthe
Ice
Orange twists, for serving

AGED MARTINI

ACTIVE: 20 MIN; TOTAL: ABOUT 3 WEEKS
MAKES ABOUT 1 LITER ● ●

One 1-liter oak barrel (see Note)
22 ounces gin
11 ounces dry vermouth
Ice
Lemon twists, for serving

AGED NEGRONI

ACTIVE: 20 MIN; TOTAL: ABOUT 1 MONTH
MAKES ABOUT 1 LITER ● ● ●

One 1-liter oak barrel (see Note)
11 ounces gin
11 ounces sweet vermouth
11 ounces Campari
Ice
Orange twists, for serving

AGED WHITE MANHATTAN

ACTIVE: 20 MIN; TOTAL: ABOUT 1 MONTH
MAKES ABOUT 1 LITER ● ●

One 1-liter oak barrel (see Note)
16 ounces unaged white whiskey, such as Trybox Series New Make
16 ounces white vermouth, such as Dolin Blanc
½ ounce orange bitters
Ice
Lemon twists, for serving

AGED EL PRESIDENTE

ACTIVE: 20 MIN; TOTAL: ABOUT 1 MONTH
MAKES ABOUT 1 LITER ● ●

One 1-liter oak barrel (see Note)
18½ ounces gold rum, such as Flor de Caña
9 ounces dry vermouth
3 ounces Grand Marnier
2 ounces grenadine, such as Small Hand Foods from *caskstore.com*
Ice
Orange twists, for serving

AGED BAMBOO

ACTIVE: 20 MIN; TOTAL: ABOUT 1 MONTH
MAKES ABOUT 1 LITER ● ●

One 1-liter oak barrel (see Note)
16 ounces amontillado sherry
16 ounces dry vermouth
½ ounce orange bitters
1 teaspoon Angostura bitters
Ice
Lemon twists, for serving

1. If the barrel is new and dry inside, fill it with water and let stand until watertight, about 24 hours. Drain.
2. Using a funnel, fill the barrel with all the liquid ingredients. Let the cocktail age, tasting a sample once a week, until a rounded but not overly oaky flavor develops, about 1 month (3 weeks for the Martini).
3. Strain the cocktail through a coffee filter–lined funnel into a glass container and store indefinitely.

TO SERVE For the Negroni, pour 3 ounces of the cocktail into an ice-filled rocks glass and stir well, then garnish the drink with a twist. For each of the other five cocktails, pour 3 ounces into an ice-filled cocktail shaker and stir until chilled. Strain the drink into a chilled cocktail glass and garnish with a twist.
NOTE 1-, 2-, 3- and 5-liter oak barrels are available online at *tuthill town.com* ($60 to $96).

Hard Cider Sangria

⟳ TOTAL: 15 MIN • 4 SERVINGS ● ● ●

1 cup quartered and thinly
   sliced unpeeled green, yellow
   and red apples
1 navel orange, quartered
   and thinly sliced crosswise
1 cup apple juice, chilled
2 tablespoons fresh lemon juice
¼ cup apple brandy
One 22-ounce bottle hard apple cider,
   chilled
Ice

In a pitcher, combine the apple and orange slices with the apple juice, lemon juice and brandy. Just before serving, add the cider. Serve in tall glasses over ice. —*Grace Parisi*

Melon Sparkler with Tapioca Pearls

ACTIVE: 30 MIN; TOTAL: 1 HR
MAKES 6 DRINKS ● ●

½ cup black tapioca pearls (see Note)
One 3½-pound honeydew melon,
   halved and seeded
One 750-milliliter bottle Moscato d'Asti,
   chilled

1. In a medium saucepan, cover the tapioca with 5 cups of water and bring to a boil. Cover the saucepan and cook over moderate heat until the tapioca is chewy and plump, 5 to 6 minutes. Drain and cool under running water. Transfer the tapioca to a medium bowl. Rinse out the saucepan.
2. Using melon ballers of different sizes, scoop out 2 cups of melon balls. Chop the remaining melon and transfer to a blender. Puree until smooth. Strain the puree, without pressing on the solids, to extract clear green juice. Add 2 tablespoons of the juice to the tapioca. Refrigerate the remaining juice.
3. In the same saucepan, bring ½ cup of the Moscato to a boil. Simmer until reduced to 2 tablespoons, about 10 minutes. Pour the syrup over the tapioca and refrigerate until chilled, about 15 minutes.

4. Spoon the tapioca and melon balls into Champagne flutes and top with the chilled melon juice and Moscato. —*Grace Parisi*
NOTE Nicely chewy black tapioca pearls are available at *bobateadirect.com* and *amazon. com*. Serve the drinks with spoons and boba straws (jumbo, extra-wide straws, also available at *amazon.com*).

Cucumber-Lemonade Mocktail

⟳ TOTAL: 10 MIN • MAKES 1 DRINK ● ●

1 paper-thin, lengthwise slice of
   European cucumber, for garnish
Ice
¼ teaspoon finely chopped dill,
   plus 1 dill sprig for garnish
1 tablespoon agave nectar
1 tablespoon fresh lemon juice
1 tablespoon fresh lime juice
¼ cup fresh cucumber juice (see Note)
¼ cup chilled club soda

Press the cucumber slice against the inside of a chilled highball glass and add ice. In a cocktail shaker, muddle the chopped dill with the agave nectar, lemon and lime juices and 1 tablespoon of water until the nectar dissolves. Add ice, then add the cucumber juice and shake well. Strain into the prepared glass and stir in the club soda. Garnish with the dill sprig. —*Pascaline Lepeltier*
NOTE To make cucumber juice, puree peeled cucumber chunks in a blender; strain the puree through a fine sieve. One large cucumber yields about ¾ cup of strained juice.

Emerald Palmers

⏲ TOTAL: 30 MIN • MAKES ABOUT 2½ QUARTS ● ●
Brisk and refreshing, this green-tea mocktail is also delicious with gin.

8 Persian cucumbers, chopped
2 cups mint leaves
1½ cups fresh lemon juice
½ cup agave nectar
1 tablespoon matcha green tea powder
Kosher salt
Ice

1. In a bowl, toss the cucumbers with the mint leaves. Transfer half of the mixture to a blender and puree until chunky.
2. In a large pitcher, stir the lemon juice, agave and matcha with 5 cups of ice water. With the blender on, add half of the lemon mixture to the puree; blend until very smooth. Transfer to a punch bowl. Blend the remaining cucumbers, mint and lemon mixture until very smooth; transfer to the punch bowl. Season the drink lightly with salt and serve in ice-filled glasses. —*Susan Feniger*

A Clockwork Orange

⟳ TOTAL: 15 MIN • MAKES ABOUT 2 CUPS ● ●

One 2-inch piece ginger (about 1 ounce)
1 small golden beet (about 4 ounces),
   scrubbed and cut into wedges
5 medium carrots (about 12 ounces),
   cut into 3-inch pieces
½ medium cantaloupe
   (about 1 pound)—seeded, peeled
   and cut into 3-inch pieces
Cayenne pepper, for garnish

In an electric juicer, juice all of the ingredients except the garnish. Sprinkle lightly with cayenne and serve. —*Brandi Kowalski*

The Radiant Glow

⟳ TOTAL: 15 MIN • MAKES ABOUT 2½ CUPS ● ●

One 1-inch piece of fresh ginger
   (about ½ ounce)
1 lemon (about 4 ounces)—peeled,
   pith removed and halved
5 Tuscan kale leaves (about 4 ounces)
1 Gala apple (about 8 ounces)—
   halved, cored and cut into wedges
1 small red beet (about 8 ounces),
   scrubbed and cut into wedges
1 large cucumber (about 12 ounces),
   cut into 3-inch pieces

In an electric juicer, juice all of the ingredients and serve right away.
—*Leslie Needleman*

● HEALTHY ● MAKE AHEAD ○ VEGETARIAN ● STAFF FAVORITE

emerald palmer

Cilantro-Celery Juice Punch

◌ TOTAL: 15 MIN • MAKES ABOUT 2 CUPS
● ○

One 1-inch piece of fresh ginger
    (about ½ ounce)
1 large bunch of cilantro
    (about 4 ounces)
1 Granny Smith apple (about
    8 ounces)—halved, cored and
    cut into wedges
8 celery ribs (about 12 ounces)
2 teaspoons fresh lemon juice

In an electric juicer, juice the ginger, cilantro, apple and celery. Stir in the lemon juice and serve right away. —Amanda Chantal Bacon

Mulling Spices

ACTIVE: 30 MIN; TOTAL: 7 HR
MAKES 8 SPICE PACKETS ● ○
Store-bought mulling spices can often taste muted. In this vibrant version, oranges and fresh ginger are dehydrated and blended with cinnamon sticks, allspice berries and other whole spices. Each spice packet is designed to flavor one bottle of apple cider or a soft, fruity red wine, such as Zinfandel (mulling instructions follow the recipe).

4 oranges, sliced into
    ⅛-inch rounds (about 40 slices),
    ends discarded
One 8-ounce piece of fresh ginger
8 cinnamon sticks
40 black peppercorns
24 allspice berries
24 star anise pods
16 cloves

1. Preheat the oven to 175° and set large wire racks on each of 3 large rimmed baking sheets. Arrange the orange slices in a single layer on 2 of the racks. Dry the oranges in the upper and lower thirds of the oven for about 4 hours, until the flesh is slightly tacky and the peel is crisp; flip the orange slices and shift the pans from top to bottom and front to back halfway through drying. Let the slices cool completely on the racks.

2. Meanwhile, trim the ginger as necessary to fit the width of a mandoline. Slice the ginger into lengthwise strips ⅛ inch thick; discard the end pieces. Arrange the ginger in a single layer on the remaining rack. Dry the ginger in the oven for about 3 hours, until dry to the touch; flip the ginger over and shift the pans from front to back halfway through drying. Let the ginger cool.

3. Divide the dried oranges, ginger and whole spices among 8 bags and secure with twine. —Justin Chapple

MULLING INSTRUCTIONS In a saucepan, combine the contents of 1 spice packet with one 750-milliliter bottle of wine or apple cider. Bring to a simmer and cook over low heat for 1 minute. Remove the saucepan from the heat, cover and let steep until well flavored, 10 to 15 minutes.

MAKE AHEAD The spice packets can be kept in a cool place for 6 months.

Ruby-Red Cranberry Syrup

TOTAL: 30 MIN PLUS 1 HR CHILLING
MAKES 3 CUPS ● ● ●
This pretty, sweet-tart syrup can be stirred into a cocktail or poured over cheesecake, pancakes or ice cream.

2 pounds fresh or frozen cranberries
    (8 cups), chopped
2¾ cups sugar
Pinch of salt
1 tablespoon fresh lemon juice

1. In a large saucepan, combine the cranberries, sugar and salt with 2½ cups of water and bring to a boil. Simmer over moderately low heat, stirring, until the sugar dissolves and the mixture is bright red, 8 to 10 minutes.
2. Strain the cranberry syrup through a fine-mesh sieve set over a heatproof bowl, without pressing; reserve the solids for another use. Stir in the lemon juice. Let the syrup cool completely, then funnel it into glass bottles and refrigerate until chilled, about 1 hour. Shake the syrup well before serving.
—Justin Chapple

MAKE AHEAD The syrup can be refrigerated for up to 1 month.

Salty-Sweet Spiced Pickled Plums

ACTIVE: 40 MIN; TOTAL: 1 HR
MAKES FOUR 1-PINT JARS ● ● ●
Serve these plums in a refreshing soda made by mixing them with their pickling liquid and sparkling water; garnish with Thai basil.

Four 1-pint canning jars with lids
    and rings
2 cups unseasoned rice vinegar
1 cup distilled white vinegar
2 cups packed dark brown sugar
½ cup kosher salt
2½ pounds ripe but firm plums, pitted
    and cut into 8 wedges each
8 cloves
4 star anise pods
One 2-inch cinnamon stick, broken
    into 4 pieces
2 teaspoons pink peppercorns
1 teaspoon fennel seeds

1. Fill a large pot with water, cover and bring to a boil. Add the canning jars, lids and rings along with a set of tongs and a ladle and simmer over low heat for about 10 minutes to sterilize. Cover the pot and turn off the heat.
2. Set a metal rack in another large pot. Fill the pot with water, cover and bring to a boil.
3. Meanwhile, in a saucepan, combine both vinegars with the brown sugar and salt and bring to a boil to dissolve. Using the sterilized tongs, remove the jars from the hot water and transfer them to a rimmed baking sheet.
4. Pack the plums, cloves, star anise, cinnamon, peppercorns and fennel seeds into the jars, leaving ½ inch at the top. Ladle the hot brine over the plums, stopping ½ inch from the top. Using the tongs, screw the lids and rings on the jars securely but not too tightly.
5. Using canning tongs, lower the jars onto the rack in the boiling water, making sure they are covered by 1 inch of water. Boil over high heat for 20 minutes. Using the canning tongs, transfer the jars to a rack to cool until the lids seal (they will be concave); refrigerate any jars that do not seal. Store the sealed jars in a cool, dark place for up to 6 months.
—Minh Phan

● HEALTHY   ● MAKE AHEAD   ● VEGETARIAN   ● STAFF FAVORITE

MAKEOVER OF A CLASSIC SIDECAR

Mixologist **Jonny Raglin** of San Francisco's Comstock Saloon interprets the iconic cocktail, including a classic version as well as three modern updates.

THE CLASSIC

Sidecar

⏱ **TOTAL: 5 MIN**
MAKES 1 DRINK

Ice
1¾ ounces VSOP Cognac
¾ ounce Grand Marnier
¾ ounce fresh lemon juice
¼ ounce Simple Syrup
(recipe below)
Dash of orange bitters
1 orange twist, for garnish

Fill a cocktail shaker with ice. Add the remaining ingredients except the garnish and shake well. Strain into a chilled coupe and garnish with the orange twist.

SIMPLE SYRUP In a small saucepan, simmer ½ cup water with ½ cup sugar over moderate heat for about 3 minutes, stirring to dissolve the sugar; let cool. Makes about 6 ounces.

THE TWIST

Cherry Slidecar

⏱ **TOTAL: 5 MIN**
MAKES 1 DRINK
Cherry bitters, cherry liqueur and a brandied cherry flavor Raglin's favorite sidecar variation.

Ice
1¼ ounces brandy
1 ounce Heering cherry liqueur
¾ ounce fresh lemon juice
2 dashes of Fee Brothers cherry bitters
1 brandied cherry, for garnish

Fill a cocktail shaker with ice. Add the remaining ingredients except the garnish and shake well. Strain into a chilled coupe and garnish with the brandied cherry.

THE REINVENTION

Bondage

⏱ **TOTAL: 5 MIN**
MAKES 1 DRINK
This intensified sidecar contains two aged, 100-proof spirits, plus a shot of ginger liqueur.

Ice
¾ ounce bonded rye whiskey, preferably Rittenhouse Rye 100 Proof
¾ ounce bonded apple brandy
½ ounce ginger liqueur
½ ounce pear liqueur
¾ ounce fresh lemon juice
Dash of orange bitters
1 lemon twist, for garnish

Fill a cocktail shaker with ice. Add the remaining ingredients except the garnish and shake well. Strain into a chilled coupe and garnish with the lemon twist.

THE MOCKTAIL

Steve McQueen

⏱ **TOTAL: 5 MIN**
MAKES 1 DRINK

1 orange wedge
Sugar
Ice
3 ounces apple cider
1½ ounces fresh orange juice
1 ounce Ginger Gastrique (recipe below)
3 dashes of Fee Brothers Old Fashion aromatic bitters (optional)

Moisten the rim of a coupe with the orange and coat with sugar. Fill a cocktail shaker with ice. Add the remaining ingredients and shake well. Strain into the coupe.

GINGER GASTRIQUE In a small saucepan, bring ½ cup minced fresh ginger, 4 ounces apple cider vinegar, 2 ounces sherry vinegar and 2 ounces water to a boil. Stir in 1 cup sugar and simmer for 20 minutes. Fine-strain the gastrique into a heatproof jar and let cool. Refrigerate for up to 2 weeks. Makes about 8 ounces.

the reinvention

the twist

the mocktail

bucatini all'amatriciana, PAGE 84

RECIPE INDEX

A

B

PAGE NUMBERS IN **BOLD** INDICATE PHOTOGRAPHS

D

E

F

G

H

O

P

S

PAGE NUMBERS IN **BOLD** INDICATE PHOTOGRAPHS

PAGE NUMBERS IN **BOLD** INDICATE PHOTOGRAPHS

V

W

X

Y

Z

PAGE NUMBERS IN **BOLD** INDICATE PHOTOGRAPHS

CONTRIBUTORS

FOOD & WINE ANNUAL 2013

RECIPES

matthew accarrino is the chef at SPQR in San Francisco and a co-author of *SPQR: Modern Italian Food and Wine.*

grant achatz, an F&W Best New Chef 2002, is the chef and co-owner of Alinea and Next and co-owner of The Aviary bar, all in Chicago. His most recent publication is an e-book series dedicated to Next's changing menus.

john adler is a chef de cuisine at Franny's in Brooklyn, New York.

tamar adler is a cook and writer based in Brooklyn, New York, and the author of *An Everlasting Meal: Cooking with Economy and Grace.*

bruce aidells is the founder of Aidells Sausage Company in San Leandro, California. He is also the author of *The Great Meat Cookbook.*

roman albrecht is the chef at the Kosher Classroom in Berlin.

erik anderson, an F&W Best New Chef 2012, is a co-chef at the Catbird Seat in Nashville.

josé andrés is the chef and owner of numerous restaurants in Las Vegas, Washington, DC, Beverly Hills and South Beach, Florida. He has authored several cookbooks, including *Tapas: A Taste of Spain in America* and *Made in Spain: Spanish Dishes for the American Kitchen,* a companion cookbook to his PBS series of the same name. He is also the founder of World Central Kitchen, a nonprofit organization.

jennifer archer is the pastry chef at Oenotri in Napa, California.

amanda chantal bacon is the owner of Moon Juice in Venice, California.

ali bagheri is the chef and owner of Sundevich in Washington, DC.

lori baker is the pastry chef and co-owner of Baker & Banker in San Francisco.

nicolaus balla is the chef at Bar Tartine restaurant in San Francisco.

jeff banker is the chef and co-owner of Baker & Banker in San Francisco.

jimmy bannos, jr., is the chef and co-owner of the Purple Pig in Chicago.

brandon baptiste is the sous-chef at Fundamental in Los Angeles.

silvana baranzoni is the chef at Opera 02 winery and resort in Levizzano, Italy.

dan barber, an F&W Best New Chef 2002, is the chef and co-owner of Blue Hill in New York City and Blue Hill at Stone Barns in Pocantico Hills, New York.

lidia bastianich is a chef and co-owner of six restaurants in New York City, Pittsburgh and Kansas City, Missouri, among them Manhattan's Felidia, Esca and Del Posto, and a co-owner of Eataly, a market and restaurant complex in New York and Chicago. She is also the host of the PBS cooking show *Lidia's Italy in America* and a cookbook author. Her most recent book is *Lidia's Favorite Recipes: 100 Foolproof Italian Dishes, from Basic Sauces to Irresistible Entrees.*

mario batali is the chef and co-owner of over a dozen restaurants in New York, Las Vegas, L.A. and Singapore and a co-owner of Eataly, a market and restaurant complex in New York and Chicago. He stars in ABC's *The Chew* and recently published *Molto Batali: Simple Family Meals From My Home to Yours.*

rick bayless, an F&W Best New Chef 1988, is the chef and owner of Frontera Grill and Topolobampo and owner of XOCO and Tortas Frontera, all in Chicago. Winner of *Top Chef Masters* Season 1, he also hosts the PBS series *Mexico—One Plate at a Time* and has written several cookbooks, most recently *Frontera: Margaritas, Guacamoles, and Snacks.*

paul berglund is the chef at the Bachelor Farmer in Minneapolis.

noah bernamoff and his wife, **rae bernamoff,** own Mile End in Brooklyn, New York, as well as Mile End Sandwich in Manhattan; they also co-authored *The Mile End Cookbook.*

elissa bernstein is the blogger behind 17 and Baking.

chris bianco is the chef and owner of Pizzeria Bianco, Pane Bianco, Bar Bianco and Italian Restaurant, all in Phoenix, and a co-owner of Union Jacks in London.

jamie bissonnette, an F&W People's Best New Chef 2011, is a co-chef and co-owner of Toro and Coppa, both in Boston.

richard blais, winner of *Top Chef All-Stars,* is the chef and restaurateur behind HD1 and The Spence, both in Atlanta, as well as Flip in Atlanta and Birmingham, Alabama.

anthony bourdain is a chef, writer, host of the forthcoming CNN travel show *Parts Unknown* and former host of *No Reservations* and *The Layover,* both on the Travel Channel. He has written cookbooks and memoirs; his latest publication is the graphic novel *Get Jiro!*

ron boyd is the chef at Plum restaurant in Oakland, California.

sylvan mishima brackett is the chef and owner of Peko-Peko, a catering company in Oakland, California, and a co-author of *The Slow Food Guide to San Francisco and the Bay Area.*

steven brown is the chef and co-owner of Tilia restaurant in Minneapolis.

paola budel is the chef at Venissa Ristorante Ostello on the island of Mazzorbo in Venice.

david burtka is a co-chef and co-owner of Gourmet M.D., a catering company in L.A. He is also an actor and *E! News* correspondent.

mark canlis is a co-owner of Canlis in Seattle.

mario carbone, an F&W Best New Chef 2012, is a co-chef and co-owner of Torrisi Italian Specialties, Parm, Carbone and the Lobster Club sandwich shop, all in New York City.

bryce caron, an F&W Best New Pastry Chef 2012, was the pastry chef at Graham Elliot restaurant in Chicago.

cesare casella is the chef and owner of Salumeria Rosi Parmacotto in New York City. He is also the dean of Italian Studies at the International Culinary Center and the author of several cookbooks. His latest cookbook is *Introduction to Italian Cuisine.*

josef centeno is the chef and owner of Baco Mercat and the forthcoming Bar Ama, both in Los Angeles.

justin chapple is F&W's Test Kitchen associate editor.

CONTRIBUTORS

leah chase is the chef and owner of Dooky Chase in New Orleans and the author of several cookbooks, including *And I Still Cook* and *The Dooky Chase Cookbook*.

cecilia chiang was the chef and owner of The Mandarin in San Francisco. She chronicled her life in recipes in *The Seventh Daughter: My Culinary Journey from Beijing to San Francisco*.

roy choi, an F&W Best New Chef 2010, is the chef and co-owner of Kogi BBQ food trucks, Chego and A-Frame, all in Los Angeles, and Sunny Spot in Venice, California.

scott conant, an F&W Best New Chef 2004, is the chef and owner of Scarpetta restaurants in Beverly Hills, Las Vegas, Miami, New York City and Toronto and D.O.C.G. at The Cosmopolitan of Las Vegas. He is also a judge on Food Network's *Chopped* and the author of *New Italian Cooking* and *Bold Italian*.

cat cora is an Iron Chef on the Food Network, a cooking instructor, a cookbook author and the chef and owner of Kouzzina by Cat Cora in Orlando, Florida, CCQ in Costa Mesa, California, and Cat Cora's Kitchen and Markets at airports across the country. Her most recent cookbook is *Cat Cora's Classics with a Twist*.

chris cosentino, winner of *Top Chef Masters* Season 4, is the chef at Incanto and owner of Boccalone salumeria, both in San Francisco. He is also the author of *Beginnings: My Way to Start a Meal*.

tim cushman, an F&W Best New Chef 2008, is the chef and owner of O Ya in Boston.

matt danko is the pastry chef at the Greenhouse Tavern and Noodlecat, both in Cleveland.

siegfried danler is the chef at Pauly Saal restaurant in Berlin.

iside maria de cesare is a co-chef and co-owner of La Parolina in Trevinano, Italy.

dante de magistris is the chef and co-owner of Il Casale in Belmont, Massachusetts, and Restaurant Dante in Cambridge, Massachusetts.

semsa denizsel is the chef and owner of Kantin restaurant and Kantin Dükkan take-out shop in Istanbul.

kevin denton is the bar manager at WD-50 in New York City.

curtis di fede is a co-chef and co-owner of Oenotri in Napa, California.

tom douglas is the chef and restaurateur behind Lola, Palace Kitchen, Dahlia Lounge, Dahlia Bakery, Etta's, Serious Pie restaurants, Seatown, Brave Horse Tavern, Cuoco, Serious Biscuit and Ting Momo food truck, all in Seattle. He has written several cookbooks, including *Tom Douglas' Seattle Kitchen* and *The Dahlia Bakery Cookbook: Sweetness in Seattle*.

daniel duane is a journalist and writer based in San Francisco; his latest book is *How to Cook Like a Man: A Memoir of Cookbook Obsession*.

wylie dufresne, an F&W Best New Chef 2001, is the chef and owner of WD-50 in New York City.

naomi duguid is a Toronto-based food writer and photographer. Her most recent cookbook is *Burma: Rivers of Flavor*.

hugh fearnley-whittingstall is the founder of River Cottage, a local produce–focused nonprofit organization, restaurant and cooking school in Axminster, England. He is also the host of the *River Cottage* TV show in the UK and author of related cookbooks; the most recent is *The River Cottage Fish Book*.

susan feniger is a chef, restaurateur and co-author of several books, including *Cooking with Too Hot Tamales* and *Susan Feniger's Street Food*. She owns Street restaurant in Los Angeles and co-owns Border Grill in Las Vegas, L.A. and Santa Monica, California.

barb finley is a professional baker in Sebastopol, California.

bobby flay is the chef and owner of many restaurants in the US and Bahamas, among them Mesa Grill and Bar Americain in New York City, and the host of several cooking shows, including *Bobby Flay's Barbecue Addiction* and *Brunch at Bobby's*. He has written 11 cookbooks; his most recent is *Bobby Flay's Bar Americain Cookbook*.

sara forte is the blogger behind Sprouted Kitchen and author of *The Sprouted Kitchen: A Tastier Take on Whole Foods*.

jason fox is the chef and co-owner of Commonwealth in San Francisco.

jose garces is the chef and owner of numerous restaurants in the US, including Amada, Distrito and Tinto in Philadelphia and Mercat in Chicago. His latest cookbook is *The Latin Road Home: Savoring the Foods of Ecuador, Spain, Cuba, Mexico, and Peru*.

shawn gawle, an F&W Best New Pastry Chef 2012, is the pastry chef at Saison in San Francisco.

hiyaw gebreyohannes is the founder of Taste of Ethiopia, a line of fresh, organic and vegan prepared foods produced in New York City.

spike gjerde is the chef and co-owner of Woodberry Kitchen, Artisan coffee shop and Half Acre, all in Baltimore.

asha gomez is chef and owner of Cardamom Hill restaurant in Atlanta.

romano gordini is a co-chef and co-owner of La Parolina in Trevinano, Italy.

alyssa gorelick is the chef at the vegetarian restaurant Fern in Charlotte, North Carolina.

danny grant, an F&W Best New Chef 2012, was the chef at the now-closed Ria in Chicago.

eden grinshpan is the host of *Eden Eats* on the Cooking Channel.

alex guarnaschelli is the chef at Butter and The Darby, both in New York City; the host of the TV show *Alex's Day Off*; and a judge on *Chopped* and a sous-chef on *Iron Chef America*.

david guas is the chef and owner of Bayou Bakery in Arlington, Virginia. He also co-authored *DamGoodSweet*.

josh habiger, an F&W Best New Chef 2012, is a co-chef at the Catbird Seat in Nashville.

amanda hallowell is the chef at Nebo Lodge on North Haven island in Maine.

chris hanmer, the winner of *Top Chef: Just Desserts* Season 2, founded the School of Pastry Design in Las Vegas.

david hawksworth is the chef at Hawksworth Restaurant in the Rosewood Hotel Georgia in Vancouver.

sophie heaulme is the owner of Casa Olivi in Treia, Italy.

lee hefter, an F&W Best New Chef 1998, is a managing partner and executive corporate chef for the Wolfgang Puck Fine Dining Group and Wolfgang Puck Catering and Events.

maria helm sinskey, an F&W Best New Chef 1996, is the culinary director of Robert Sinskey Vineyards in Napa. Her latest cookbook is *Williams-Sonoma Family Meals*.

jessica hicks is the pastry chef and co-owner of Astro Coffee in Detroit.

peter hoffman is the chef and owner of Back Forty and Back Forty West, both in New York City.

linton hopkins, an F&W Best New Chef 2009, is the chef and owner of Restaurant Eugene and Holeman & Finch Public House, both in Atlanta.

michael hudman is a co-chef and co-owner of Andrew Michael Italian Kitchen and Hog & Hominy, both in Memphis.

mike isabella, a *Top Chef All-Stars* finalist, is the chef and owner of Graffiato and Bandolero, both in Washington, DC. He is also the author of *Mike Isabella's Crazy Good Italian*.

madhur jaffrey is the author of numerous cookbooks; her latest is *Madhur Jaffrey's Curry Nation*.

paul kahan, an F&W Best New Chef 1999, is a co-chef and co-owner of Blackbird, Avec, The Publican and Big Star, all in Chicago.

allen katz is a co-founder of New York Distilling Company and a co-owner and mixologist at The Shanty, both in Brooklyn, New York.

tia keenan is a *fromager* in New York City.

sarah kelby lewis owns Sustenance Rustic Craft Bakery in the Pittsburgh Public Market.

nate keller is the chef and co-owner of Gastronaut catering in San Francisco.

thomas keller, an F&W Best New Chef 1988, is the chef and restaurateur behind the French Laundry and Ad Hoc in Yountville, California, Per Se in New York City and Bouchon Bistro and Bouchon Bakery locations throughout the country. He is also the author of numerous cookbooks; his latest is *Bouchon Bakery.*

marcia kiesel, formerly F&W's Test Kitchen supervisor, co-authored *The Simple Art of Vietnamese Cooking.*

bill kim is the chef and owner of UrbanBelly, Belly Shack and BellyQ, all in Chicago.

jae kim is the chef and owner of Chi'Lantro, a food truck that roams Austin and Houston.

daniel klein is a co-founder of the Perennial Plate, an online video series about sustainable and adventurous cuisine.

dan kluger, an F&W Best New Chef 2012, is the chef at ABC Kitchen in New York City.

tyler kord is the chef and co-owner of No. 7 restaurant and No. 7 Sub sandwich shops in New York City.

brandi kowalski is the head "juiceologist" at the Butcher's Daughter in New York City.

katie kwan is a co-founder of Rice Paper Scissors, a pop-up Vietnamese café, and the creator of KitchenSidecar, a Vietnamese food stand, both in San Francisco.

dave kwiatkowski is the owner of the Sugar House in Detroit.

emeril lagasse is the chef and owner of several restaurants around the country, including Emeril's and NOLA in New Orleans; host of *Emeril's Table;* and author of 17 cookbooks. His latest book is *Emeril's Kicked-Up Sandwiches.*

mike lata is the chef and co-owner of Fig and The Ordinary, both in Charleston, South Carolina.

tara lazar is the chef and owner of Cheeky's, Birba and Jiao in Palm Springs, California.

corey lee, an F&W Best New Chef 2012, is the chef and owner of Benu in San Francisco.

edward lee is the chef and co-owner of 610 Magnolia in Louisville, Kentucky.

belinda leong is the pastry chef and co-owner of B. Patisserie in San Francisco.

pascaline lepeltier is the sommelier at Rouge Tomate in New York City.

brian lewis is the chef and owner of Elm in New Canaan, Connecticut.

matt lewis is a co-owner of Baked in Brooklyn, New York, and a co-author of several cookbooks; his latest book is *Baked Elements: Our 10 Favorite Ingredients.*

kelly liken is the chef and owner of Restaurant Kelly Liken in Vail, Colorado.

anita lo, an F&W Best New Chef 2001, is the chef and owner of Annisa in New York City.

jenn louis, an F&W Best New Chef 2012, is the chef and co-owner of Lincoln and Sunshine Tavern, both in Portland, Oregon.

ryan lowder is the chef and owner of Plum Alley in Salt Lake City.

waylynn lucas is the pastry chef and co-owner of Fonuts in Los Angeles.

valerie luu is a co-founder of Rice Paper Scissors, a pop-up Vietnamese café, and the creator of Little Knock, a Vietnamese food stand, both in San Francisco.

lachlan mackinnon-patterson, an F&W Best New Chef 2005, is the chef and co-owner of Frasca Food and Wine in Boulder, Colorado.

cormac mahoney, an F&W Best New Chef 2012, is the chef and owner of Madison Park Conservatory in Seattle.

ron marks is the founder of AtlantaFresh Artisan Creamery based in Atlanta.

nobu matsuhisa, an F&W Best New Chef 1989, is the chef and owner of dozens of restaurants across America, including Nobu in New York City, Los Angeles and Las Vegas, and abroad in Asia, Africa, Australia and Europe. His latest cookbook is *Nobu's Vegetarian Cookbook.*

devin mcdavid, an F&W Best New Pastry Chef 2012, is the pastry chef at Quince and Cotogna in San Francisco.

jeff mcinnis is the chef and co-owner of Yardbird in Miami.

thomas mcnaughton is the chef and co-owner of Flour + Water, Central Kitchen and Salumeria, all in San Francisco, and the author of the forthcoming *Flour + Water Cookbook: Four Seasons of Pasta from the Dough Room.*

alice medrich is the former pastry chef and owner of Cocolat chocolate shops in California. She has authored several cookbooks, most recently *Sinfully Easy Delicious Desserts.*

ernest miller is the chef at the Farmer's Kitchen in Los Angeles.

michael mina is the chef and restaurateur behind numerous restaurants across the country, including his eponymous restaurant in San Francisco. His latest cookbook is *Michael Mina.*

aida mollenkamp is a chef and host of *FoodCrafters* on the Cooking Channel. She is also the author of *Aida Mollenkamp's Keys to the Kitchen: The Essential Reference for Becoming a More Accomplished, Adventurous Cook.*

nico monday is the co-chef and co-owner of the Market Restaurant on Lobster Cove in Gloucester, Massachusetts.

johnny monis, an F&W Best New Chef 2007, is the chef and co-owner of Komi and Little Serow, both in Washington, DC.

eric monkaba is a co-founder of Qasr Twenty, a cooking school in Cairo, and founder of Backpacker Concierge, an excursion-based travel agency.

david morgan is the chef and co-owner of Fundamental in Los Angeles.

jeffrey morgenthaler is the bar manager at Clyde Common in Portland, Oregon.

seamus mullen is the chef and owner of Tertulia in New York City and author of *Seamus Mullen's Hero Food: How Cooking with Delicious Things Can Make Us Feel Better.*

julianne murat is the pastry chef and co-owner of Vergennes Laundry, a bakery and café in Vergennes, Vermont.

marc murphy is the chef and owner of Benchmarc, Landmarc and Ditch Plains restaurants and Benchmarc events, all in New York City. He is also a judge on the Food Network's *Chopped.*

david myers is the chef and founder of Pizzeria Ortica in Costa Mesa, California, Comme Ça in Los Angeles and Las Vegas and David Myers Café and Sola in Tokyo.

nathan myhrvold, co-founder and CEO of Intellectual Ventures, co-authored *Modernist Cuisine* and *Modernist Cuisine at Home.*

leslie needleman is a co-owner of The Gem, a juice and tea bar in Dallas.

molly neitzel is the owner of Molly Moon's Homemade Ice Cream in Seattle and co-author of a cookbook of the same name.

bryant ng, an F&W Best New Chef 2012, is the chef and owner of the Spice Table in Los Angeles.

luke nguyen is the chef and owner of the Red Lantern in Sydney and host of the TV show *Luke Nguyen's Vietnam* on the Cooking Channel. His most recent cookbook is *My Vietnam: Stories and Recipes.*

karen nicolas, an F&W Best New Chef 2012, is the chef at Equinox in Washington, DC.

adina niemerow is a holistic chef, health coach and author of *Super Cleanse: Detox Your Body for Long-Lasting Health and Beauty.*

CONTRIBUTORS

magnus nilsson is the chef and owner of Fäviken Magasinet in Jämtland, Sweden, and author of *Fäviken* cookbook.

michel nischan is the founding chef and co-owner of Dressing Room in Westport, Connecticut; resident chef on *The Victory Garden* series on PBS; and president of Wholesome Wave, a nonprofit that brings fresh, local food to underserved communities nationwide. He is also the author of *Sustainably Delicious: Making the World a Better Place, One Recipe at a Time.*

ken norris is a co-chef and co-owner of Riffle NW in Portland, Oregon.

martine nouet is a food and spirits writer based in Islay, Scotland; her latest cookbook is *Carnet de recettes de Normandie.*

benny ojeda is the chef and owner of Benny's Seafood in Miami.

amelia o'reilly is a co-chef and co-owner of the Market Restaurant on Lobster Cove in Gloucester, Massachusetts.

yotam ottolenghi is a chef and co-owner of Ottolenghi, a restaurant and chain of prepared-food shops in London. He is also a contributor to the *Guardian,* the author of *Plenty* and co-author of *Ottolenghi: The Cookbook* and *Jerusalem.*

grace parisi is F&W's Test Kitchen senior editor and writes the magazine's Fast column. She is also the author of *Get Saucy.*

stella parks, an F&W Best New Pastry Chef 2012, is the pastry chef at Table 310 restaurant in Lexington, Kentucky.

daniel patterson, an F&W Best New Chef 1997, is the chef and owner of Coi in San Francisco and the owner of Plum and Haven restaurants in Oakland, California.

sera pelle is a consulting chef at Mohawk Bend in Los Angeles.

jacques pépin, an F&W contributing editor, is the dean of special programs at the International Culinary Center in New York City and the host of *Jacques Pépin: More Fast Food My Way* on PBS. He is also the author of over 20 cookbooks; his most recent is *Jacques Pépin: New Complete Techniques.*

brian perrone is the chef and co-owner of Slows Bar BQ in Detroit.

adam perry lang is the chef and owner of Daisy May's BBQ in New York City. He is also the author of numerous barbecuing and grilling cookbooks; his latest is *Charred & Scruffed.*

minh phan is the consulting chef at Beachwood Café in Los Angeles.

matt piacentini is a co-owner of The Beagle in New York City.

michael pirolo is the chef at Macchialina Taverna Rustica in Miami.

naomi pomeroy, an F&W Best New Chef 2009, is the chef and owner of Beast in Portland, Oregon.

elisabeth prueitt is the pastry chef and co-owner of Tartine Bakery and Bar Tartine in San Francisco. She co-authored *Tartine* with her husband and Tartine co-owner, Chad Robertson.

wolfgang puck owns over 25 restaurants all over the world, including his pioneering Spago in Beverly Hills. He is also the author of six cookbooks; his most recent is *Live, Love, Eat! The Best of Wolfgang Puck.*

paul qui, winner of *Top Chef* Season 9, is a consulting chef at Uchiko, a co-owner of East Side King restaurant and food trucks and the chef and owner of the forthcoming Qui, all in Austin.

jennifer quist norris is a co-chef and co-owner of Riffle NW in Portland, Oregon.

jonny raglin is the owner of Comstock Saloon in San Francisco.

alex raij is a co-chef and co-owner of Txikito, El Quinto Pino and La Vara, all in New York City.

rené redzepi is the chef and owner of Noma in Copenhagen and author of *Noma: Time and Place in Nordic Cuisine.*

akasha richmond is the chef and owner of Akasha Restaurant in Culver City, California. She has authored two cookbooks, most recently *Hollywood Dish: More Than 150 Delicious, Healthy Recipes from Hollywood's Chef to the Stars.*

alex roberts is the chef and owner of Restaurant Alma and Brasa, both in Minneapolis.

tyler rodde is a co-chef and co-owner of Oenotri in Napa, California.

silvena rowe is the chef at Quince in the May Fair Hotel in London and author of *Purple Citrus & Sweet Perfume.*

peter rudolph is the chef at Madera restaurant in the Rosewood Sand Hill hotel in Menlo Park, California.

cavit saatci is the chef and owner of Asmali Cavit in Istanbul.

cristina salas-porras collaborates with Hudson Vineyards in Napa, California.

veronica salazar is the chef and owner of El Huarache Loco street vendor and restaurant in San Francisco and Larkspur, California.

marcus samuelsson, winner of *Top Chef Masters* Season 2, is the chef and owner of Red Rooster Harlem, Ginny's Supper Club and American Table Café and Bar, all in New York City. He is also a co-founder of Food Republic, a food- and drink-focused website, and the author of the memoir *Yes, Chef.*

nick sandler is the creative chef for Pret A Manger and a co-author of *The Sausage Book: The Complete Guide to Making, Cooking & Eating Sausages.*

ferit sarper is the chef and owner of Münferit restaurant in Istanbul.

laura sawicki, an F&W Best New Pastry Chef 2012, is the pastry chef at La Condesa in Austin.

jonathon sawyer, an F&W Best New Chef 2010, is the chef and co-owner of the Greenhouse Tavern and Noodlecat, both in Cleveland.

jesse schenker is the chef and owner of Recette in New York City.

sarah schulz is the owner of Schulzies Bread Pudding in San Francisco and Venice Beach, California.

michael schwartz is the chef and owner of Michael's Genuine Food & Drink in Miami and Grand Cayman in the Cayman Islands and Harry's Pizzeria in Miami. He is also the author of *Michael's Genuine Food: Down-to-Earth Cooking for People Who Love to Eat.*

didem senol is the chef at Lokanta Maya and Gram, both in Istanbul.

michael shemtov is the owner of Butcher & Bee in Charleston, South Carolina.

gail simmons is F&W's special projects director and a judge on Bravo's *Top Chef.* She is also the author of *Talking With My Mouth Full: My Life as a Professional Eater.*

sarah simmons is the chef and owner of City Grit, a culinary salon in New York City.

justin smillie is the chef at Il Buco Alimentari e Vineria in New York City.

art smith is the chef and co-owner of Table Fifty-Two in Chicago, Art and Soul in Washington, DC, Southern Art and Bourbon Bar in Atlanta, LYFE Kitchen in Palo Alto, California, and Joanne Trattoria in New York City. He has authored three cookbooks, most recently *Back to the Family: Food Tastes Better Shared with the Ones You Love.*

michael solomonov is the chef and owner of Zahav, Federal Donuts and Percy Street Barbecue and the chef at Citron and Rose, all in Philadelphia.

annie somerville is the chef at Greens Restaurant in San Francisco and the author of two cookbooks, *Everyday Greens* and *Fields of Greens: New Vegetarian Recipes from the Celebrated Greens Restaurant.*

angelo sosa, a finalist on *Top Chef* Season 7, is the chef and owner of Social Eatz and Añejo Tequileria in New York City. He is also the author of the cookbook *Flavor Exposed.*

christina spittler is the pastry chef at Molly Moon's Homemade Ice Cream in Seattle and a co-author of a cookbook of the same name.

jeremy stanton is the chef and owner of the Meat Market butcher shop and Fire Roasted Catering, both in Great Barrington, Massachusetts.

alex stupak is the chef and owner of Empellón Taqueria and Empellón Cocina in New York City.

dale talde, who competed on *Top Chef* Season 4, is the chef and co-owner of Talde, Pork Slope and Thistle Hill Tavern in Brooklyn, New York.

sami tamimi is the head chef and co-owner of Ottolenghi, a restaurant and chain of prepared-food shops in London, and a co-author of *Ottolenghi: The Cookbook* and *Jerusalem*.

david tanis is a chef, cookbook author and the City Kitchen columnist for the *New York Times*. His most recent cookbook is *Heart of the Artichoke and Other Kitchen Journeys*.

bill telepan is the chef and owner of Telepan in New York City and the author of *Inspired by Ingredients: Market Menus and Family Favorites from a Three-Star Chef*.

andy ticer is a co-chef and co-owner of Andrew Michael Italian Kitchen and Hog & Hominy restaurants, both in Memphis.

rich torrisi, an F&W Best New Chef 2012, is a co-chef and co-owner of Torrisi Italian Specialties, Parm, Carbone and the Lobster Club sandwich shop, all in New York City.

stuart tracy is the chef at Butcher & Bee in Charleston, South Carolina.

bronson van wyck is the founder of Van Wyck & Van Wyck, an event production and marketing company in New York City.

sara vaughn co-owns, with her husband, winemaker Matt Duffy, Vaughn Duffy in Sonoma County, California.

josh vogel is the owner of Blackcreek Mercantile & Trading, Co., a handcrafted-kitchenware company in Kingston, New York.

sameh wadi is the chef and owner of Saffron Restaurant and Lounge and the World Street Kitchen food truck in Minneapolis.

alice waters is the chef and owner of Chez Panisse in Berkeley, California, and the author of 10 books; her latest is *40 Years of Chez Panisse: The Power of Gathering*. She is also the founder of the Edible Schoolyard Project, a nonprofit program that aims to get an "edible education" into public schools through hands-on experience in school kitchens, gardens and lunchrooms.

jonathan waxman is the chef and owner of Barbuto in New York City and the author of *Italian, My Way*.

garrett weber-gale, an Olympic swimmer with two gold medals, founded Athletic Foodie, a health and fitness blog.

blaine wetzel, an F&W Best New Chef 2012, is the chef and co-owner of the Willows Inn on Lummi Island, Washington.

joy wilson is the founder of Joy the Baker blog and author of *Joy the Baker Cookbook*.

katie workman is the founding editor in chief of the website Cookstr and author of *The Mom 100 Cookbook*.

martin yan is a cooking-show host, culinary instructor and the author of over 30 cookbooks; his latest is *Martin Yan's China,* a companion cookbook to his PBS series of the same name. He is also the chef and owner of M.Y. China in San Francisco and Yan Can restaurants in San Diego, Santa Clara and Pleasant Hill, California.

kris yenbamroong is the chef and owner of Night + Market and Talesai, both in Los Angeles.

salih yildiz is the chef at Karaköy Lokantasi in Istanbul.

anna zepaltas owns A Special Delivery, a meal courier service for new parents in Santa Rosa, California.

evan zimmerman is the spirits and beverage director at the Woodsman Tavern and Ava Gene's, both in Portland, Oregon.

andrew zimmern, an F&W contributing editor, writes the weekly Kitchen Adventures column on foodandwine.com. He is also the host and creator of *Bizarre Foods with Andrew Zimmern* and the chef behind AZ Canteen food truck. His most recent cookbook is *Andrew Zimmern's Field Guide to Weird, Wild, and Wonderful Foods*.

PHOTOGRAPHS

antonis achilleos 13, 47, 199, 371

lucas allen 115, 129, 147, 193, 373, 377

cedric angeles 338, 339

quentin bacon 309

paul costello 41, 57, 71, 105, 229, 307, 345, back cover (cake)

chris court 15, 21, 67, 83, 103, 180, 181, 301, 311

christina holmes front cover, 43, 63, 95, 155, 185, 239, 289, 325, 357

richard jung 263 (from *Burma: Rivers of Flavor* by Naomi Duguid, Artisan Books. Copyright 2012.)

john kernick 23, 29, 37, 75, 79, 91, 97, 109, 113, 117, 120, 121, 131, 133, 145, 159, 175, 183, 187, 200, 201, 209, 245, 247, 261, 279, 302, 303, 315, 319, 320, 321, 335, 349, 355, 362, 363, 368, 369, back cover (ham)

ken kochey 34, 35, 329

dave lauridsen 31, 76, 77, 197, 375

ryan liebe 48, 51, 327

lisa linder 17

kate mathis 107, 111, 135, 359

martin morrell 192

marcus nilsson 81, 166, 167, 207, 341, 378

peden + munk 39, 87, 100, 101

pernille pedersen 69, 269, 305, 342, 343

con poulos 6, 45, 49, 53, 55, 89, 99, 119, 123, 139, 143, 149, 165, 177, 179, 191, 195, 211, 227, 231, 233, 265, 267, 285, 293, 313, 337, 353, back cover (beans)

tina rupp 141, 255, 271, 299

lucy schaeffer 127, 217, 221

seth smoot 125, 173

fredrika stjärne 4, 8, 9, 65, 163, 203, 224, 225, 251, 280, 281, 323

michael turek 60, 61, 153, 169, 256, 257, 291, 316, 317

jonny valiant 11, 27, 73, 213, 259, 295, 297, 333, 367

eric wolfinger 136, 137, 236, 237, 241, 275, 287

product images amazon.com (52), Crate & Barrel (68), Edlund (74), Rao's Specialty Foods (94), Island Creek Oysters (128), Rancho Gordo (278)

MEASUREMENT GUIDE

BASIC MEASUREMENTS

gallon	quart	pint	cup	ounce	tbsp	tsp	drops
1 gal	4 qt	8 pt	16 c	128 fl oz			
½ gal	2 qt	4 pt	8 c	64 fl oz			
¼ gal	1 qt	2 pt	4 c	32 fl oz			
	½ qt	1 pt	2 c	16 fl oz			
	¼ qt	½ pt	1 c	8 fl oz	16 tbsp		
			⅞ c	7 fl oz	14 tbsp		
			¾ c	6 fl oz	12 tbsp		
			⅔ c	5⅓ fl oz	10⅔ tbsp		
			⅝ c	5 fl oz	10 tbsp		
			½ c	4 fl oz	8 tbsp		
			⅜ c	3 fl oz	6 tbsp		
			⅓ c	2⅔ fl oz	5⅓ tbsp	16 tsp	
			¼ c	2 fl oz	4 tbsp	12 tsp	
			⅛ c	1 fl oz	2 tbsp	6 tsp	
				½ fl oz	1 tbsp	3 tsp	
					½ tbsp	1½ tsp	
						1 tsp	60 drops
						½ tsp	30 drops

US TO METRIC CONVERSIONS

THE CONVERSIONS SHOWN HERE ARE APPROXIMATIONS. FOR MORE PRECISE CONVERSIONS, USE THE FORMULAS TO THE RIGHT.

volume			weight			temperature			conversion formulas
1 tsp	=	5 mL	1 oz	=	28 g	475°F	=	246°C	tsp × 4.929 = mL
1 tbsp	=	15 mL	¼ lb (4 oz)	=	113 g	450°F	=	232°C	tbsp × 14.787 = mL
1 fl oz	=	30 mL	½ lb (8 oz)	=	227 g	425°F	=	218°C	fl oz × 29.574 = mL
¼ c	=	59 mL	¾ lb (12 oz)	=	340 g	400°F	=	204°C	c × 236.588 = mL
½ c	=	118 mL	1 lb (16 oz)	=	½ kg	375°F	=	191°C	pt × 0.473 = L
¾ c	=	177 mL				350°F	=	177°C	qt × 0.946 = L
1 c	=	237 mL	**length**			325°F	=	163°C	oz × 28.35 = g
1 pt	=	½ L	1 in	=	2.5 cm	300°F	=	149°C	lb × 0.453 = kg
1 qt	=	1 L	5 in	=	12.7 cm	275°F	=	135°C	in × 2.54 = cm
1 gal	=	4.4 L	9 in	=	23 cm	250°F	=	121°C	(°F − 32) × 0.556 = °C